W9-ADA-443

Dear Chris,

Thank you for your contribution to this casebook. The Genzyme case greatly enhances the quality of this text and we appreciate your letting us use it.

John Gourville

Dear Chris,

With much thanks and appreciation.

Karl Rayan

Chris, Much appreciate your contribution

John Quelch

Problems and Cases in Health Care Marketing

John T. Gourville
Harvard Business School

John A. Quelch
Harvard Business School

V. Kasturi Rangan
Harvard Business School

Boston   Burr Ridge, IL   Dubuque, IA   Madison, WI   New York   San Francisco   St. Louis
Bangkok   Bogotá   Caracas   Kuala Lumpur   Lisbon   London   Madrid   Mexico City
Milan   Montreal   New Delhi   Santiago   Seoul   Singapore   Sydney   Taipei   Toronto

The McGraw·Hill Companies

McGraw-Hill
Irwin

PROBLEMS AND CASES IN HEALTH CARE MARKETING

Published by McGraw-Hill/Irwin, a business unit of The McGraw-Hill Companies, Inc., 1221 Avenue of the Americas, New York, NY, 10020. Copyright © 2005 by The McGraw-Hill Companies, Inc. All rights reserved. No part of this publication may be reproduced or distributed in any form or by any means, or stored in a database or retrieval system, without the prior written consent of The McGraw-Hill Companies, Inc., including, but not limited to, in any network or other electronic storage or transmission, or broadcast for distance learning.

Some ancillaries, including electronic and print components, may not be available to customers outside the United States.

This book is printed on acid-free paper.

1 2 3 4 5 6 7 8 9 0 CCW/CCW 0 9 8 7 6 5 4 3

ISBN 0-07-288776-1

Vice president and editor-in-chief: *Robin J. Zwettler*
Editorial director: *John E. Biernat*
Associate sponsoring editor: *Barrett Koger*
Editorial assistant: *Jill M. O'Malley*
Marketing manager: *Kim Kanakes*
Media producer: *Craig Atkins*
Project manager: *Harvey Yep*
Production supervisor: *Gina Hangos*
Design coordinator: *Kami Carter*
Photo research coordinator: *Kathy Shive*
Supplement producer: *Joyce J. Chappetto*
Senior digital content specialist: *Brian Nacik*
Cover design: *Krista Lehmkuhl*
Cover image: © *Comstock Inc.*
Typeface: *10/12 Times New Roman*
Compositor: *Lachina Publishing Services*
Printer: *Courier Westford*

Library of Congress Cataloging-in-Publication Data
Problems and cases in health care marketing / [edited by] John T. Gourville, John A. Quelch, V. Kasturi Rangan.
    p. cm.
    Includes index.
    ISBN 0-07-288776-1 (alk. paper)
    1. Medical care—Marketing. I. Gourville, John T. (John Timothy) II. Quelch, John A. III. Rangan, V. Kasturi.
RA410.56.P756 2005
362.1'068'8—dc22

2003060254

www.mhhe.com

About the Authors

John T. Gourville

John T. Gourville is an Associate Professor of Marketing at the Harvard Business School. He holds a PhD in Marketing from the University of Chicago and an MBA and an engineering degree from Cornell. His research focuses on consumer decision making, where he is an expert on the role of pricing and the consumer buying process. His research has appeared in the *Journal of Consumer Research, Journal of Marketing Research, Journal of Retailing, Marketing Letters,* and *Harvard Business Review.* In addition, he has written numerous HBS cases focusing on issues of pricing, product adoption, and the marketing of innovative technologies, especially in the biotech and pharmaceutical industries. Prior to academia, he held positions at New York Telephone, Mobil Oil, and Booz, Allen & Hamilton.

John A. Quelch

John A. Quelch is Senior Associate Dean and Lincoln Filene Professor of Business Administration at Harvard Business School. Between 1998 and 2001 he was Dean of London Business School. Prior to 1998, he was the Sebastian S. Kresge Professor of Marketing and Co-Chair of the Marketing Area at Harvard Business School. Professor Quelch is the author or co-author of 16 books including *Global Marketing Management* (4th edition, 1999), *Cases in Advertising and Promotion Management* (4th edition, 1996), and *Ethics in Marketing* (1992). He has published over 50 articles in leading journals such as *Harvard Business Review, McKinsey Quarterly,* and *Sloan Management Review.* He holds an MS from the Harvard School of Public Health and serves on the boards of Inverness Medical Innovations and PharmaNor. He is often quoted in business publications such as *Business Week, The Economist, Financial Times,* and *The Wall Street Journal.*

V. Kasturi Rangan

Kash Rangan is the Malcolm P. McNair Professor of Business Administration at the Harvard Business School and was recently the chairman of its Marketing Department. He has authored books on *Business Marketing Strategy* and *Channels of Distribution* and his work has broadly appeared in academic and management journals. His most recent research explores how channels of distribution evolve and adapt in the information age, with a view to understanding what firms and channel managers should do in order build and maintain channel stewardship. In addition to his interest in business marketing, he actively studies the role of marketing in nonprofit organizations and, specifically, how it influences the adoption of social products and ideas. He has written numerous case studies and articles on the topic; he serves as one of the founding co-chairs of the Social Enterprise Initiative at Harvard; and he is currently developing a strategic framework for nonprofit organizations. He holds a Bachelor of Technology from IIT in Madras, an MBA from IIM in Ahmedabad, and a PhD in Marketing from Northwestern University.

Preface

By almost any measure, health care is big business. In 2001, spending on health care in the United States totaled $1.4 trillion—almost 15 percent of the nation's gross domestic product. Within a decade, experts estimate that this spending will grow to $3 trillion, or 20 percent of the nation's GDP. Worldwide, these numbers are even more staggering as Latin America, Africa, the Middle East, and Southeast Asia deal with the health ravages of AIDS, malnutrition, and internal conflict.

In the United States, the health care system is at a delicate juncture. Life expectancy, overall quality of care, and likelihood of recovery from disease are all at historic highs. The average American is now expected to live to the age of 76.9 years, up from 62.9 years in 1940. Infant mortality rates have decreased by 75 percent over that same period. And the likelihood of surviving a heart attack has increased by one-third since the 1950s.

Yet, these improvements have come at an ever-increasing cost. Across the board, current health care costs are rising at three to four times the rate of inflation. Annual corporate health insurance premiums now regularly exceed $5,000 per employee, forcing employers and health care providers to shift more of the insurance burden on those being insured. Prescription drug costs exceed $150 billion and are growing at more than 15 percent per year. And the United States General Accounting Office estimates that by 2050 two-thirds of the federal budget will be spent on health care.

Underlying these figures are a host of sometimes conflicting trends. These include an aging U.S. population. In 2000, the 35 million people age 65 or over accounted for 13 percent of the American population and 33 percent of all health care spending. By 2020, this figure is expected to increase to 55 million, or 20 percent of the American population. Another trend is the declining state of health care research productivity. In 2001, U.S. pharmaceutical firms spent in excess of $30 billion on new drug development, more than in any previous year. Yet that same year, the FDA approved only 66 new drugs for sale, the smallest number of drugs approved since 1994. As a consequence, in 2002, the cost of bringing a new drug to market was estimated to be $500 million and 10 years. Finally, this lack of productivity is compounded by the industry's increasing reliance on "blockbuster drugs," leaving it vulnerable to the threat of generics. Between 2002 and 2006, over 40 major drugs with combined sales in excess of $40 billion will come off patent, opening the way for the sale of generic alternatives at a fraction of the branded price. And all of this is happening under unprecedented price pressure from the government, insurers, employers, and consumers.

Worldwide, the trends are no less dramatic, as pharmaceutical firms and health care providers struggle with the added stress of a two-tiered marketplace. Nowhere is this more evident than in the industry's response to the AIDS crisis, where developing countries cannot afford to spend even a small fraction of what more developed countries can for treatment of the disease. This has led, temporarily at least, to a global marketplace in which the very same AIDS drugs are being sold in South Africa, India, and Brazil for a fraction of the price that they are being sold in the United States and Western Europe. But even at these reduced prices, most victims of AIDS in developing countries go untreated, still unable to afford even the cheapest of care. The result? The precedents being set in the pricing of AIDS drugs around the world are being watched closely by governments, drug companies, insurance companies, health care providers, and the general public.

All of these factors place enormous pressures on the wide range of players in the health care industry. The dozen largest and hundreds of smaller pharmaceutical and biotechnology firms, the 6,000 or more for-profit and nonprofit hospitals, the tens of thousands of device manufacturers, the over 500,000 physicians, and the myriad of distributors, service providers, insurance firms, and other players all face a complex, rapidly changing landscape. Yet, the application of sound business practice to the health care sector only recently has become a focus for management research. The cases collected for this book are an attempt to add to this effort—to shed light on the unique management and marketing challenges faced by firms in the provisioning of health care goods and services in the United States and abroad.

Part 1 of this book, "**Developing a Marketing Strategy**," takes a look at the development and defense of a corporate strategy when investments are large, development of new products is lengthy, and the cost of errors are potentially fatal (both for the firm doing the developing and the end users doing the consuming). As the cases chosen for this chapter make clear, these characteristics create both challenges and opportunities. For the firms that manage them well, cost, time to market, and quality of product can be the means to establish and defend one's firm in an unforgiving playing field. For the firms that manage them poorly, they can prove to be one's downfall.

In **Part 2,** "**Developing New Products**," we take a closer look at the challenges inherent in developing new goods and services for the health care industry. For instance, how should a drug firm think about new product development when 1 in 5,000 new drug candidates reaches market? How should a firm trade off "risk" versus "reward" in an industry where the success of a single product is often measured in the billions of dollars and where failure can lead to bankruptcy? And how should firms think about product development in an industry where customers also can be development partners?

In **Part 3,** we tackle "**Launching New Products**" and highlight the complexities of selling into the typical health care setting. As the cases outline, launching new products in the health care industry requires selling into a multilayered, buying organization—one in which doctors, pharmacists, and administrators, among others, all need to be sold on a new drug, medical device, or procedure based on widely different sets of criteria. In such a setting, how do you change entrenched behavior, as typified by that doctor or that hospital that has been treating a disease or using a particular drug for decades? How do you promote the replacement of a $5 solution with a superior $300 solution? And, if you are a start-up, how do you do all of this with very limited resources?

Part 4 brings us to the challenges of "**Managing Distribution**," where we explore the dual pressures of minimizing cost, but fostering strong channel partners. For instance, what roles do channel partners have in the distribution of medical products and what incentives are provided for them to play these roles? How should firms think about forward and backward integration in markets where price and quality are increasingly critical to a firm's success? And how does modern technology, such as the Internet, change the way firms think about satisfying demand for medical goods and services? Across the board, as cost pressures increase, as new markets are being opened up and as distribution technology advances, the channel structure for firms in the health care industry are being redefined. How should firms leverage these changes?

In **Part 5,** we address the increasingly complex question of "**Managing Communications.**" With the advent of direct-to-consumer advertising in the pharmaceutical market and the increased visibility of everything from hospitals to device manufacturers, a growing focus on marketing communications is clearly evident. Whether it involves the promotion of new drugs, the transition of a prescription drug to an OTC drug, the position of a community hospital among other treatment facilities, or the adoption of new forms of birth control, the goals are often the same—to effectively and efficiently reach the critical decision makers. How best to do this are explored in the cases selected for this part of the text.

Part 6, "**Managing the Brand,**" investigates the concept of branding in the health care domain. Long a favorite topic in the marketing of consumer packaged goods, consumer durables, and the service industry, the concept of "managing the brand" is no less important for drug companies, device manufacturers, health care providers, and hospitals. Here we take a look at the challenges of developing and managing a brand in the health care arena. For instance, what types of consumers is a firm looking to attract and not attract? What image is the firm looking to convey to those consumers? How does a firm differentiate itself when it is first to market? What if it is later to market? These and other questions go a long way toward determining the salience of the brand in the minds of consumers, a critical factor in a market where a 5 percent shift in share can translate into several hundred million dollars in revenue.

Finally, in **Part 7,** we take a look at the challenges of "**International Marketing,**" where we compare and contrast the provisioning of health care in the United States and Western Europe with that of the developing world. In particular, what roles and responsibilities does the health care industry have in places like South Africa and India? And how can the industry balance the basic needs of developing nations with the increasingly customized demands of the well-to-do? Few industries possess the moral dilemmas inherent in the rationing of health care services between those who can pay and those who cannot.

As is the nature of case writing, asking and answering these questions has proven to be a collaborative effort. First, we are deeply indebted to all of the companies and executives who provided us access to their practices, insights, and efforts. Without them, these cases would never exist. Second, we are grateful to our many colleagues who have given their permission for the use of their cases in this text. These include Ernst Berndt, Frank Cespedes, John Deighton, Robert Dolan, Charles King, Lisa Klein, Melvyn Menezes, Michael Roberts, Al Silk, Debora Spar, and Stefan Thomke. Next, we recognize the invaluable contributions of our research assistants, without whom these cases would be much the poorer. Finally, we thank the support of our employer, the Harvard Business School, which has allowed us the freedom and resources to pursue the type of research that motivates us greatly.

John T. Gourville

John A. Quelch

V. Kasturi Rangan

Contents

Preface   iv

PART ONE
Developing a Marketing Strategy   1

1   Millennium Pharmaceuticals, Inc.   3
     Stefan Thomke and Ashok Nimgade

2   Hikma Pharmaceuticals   27
     John A. Quelch and Robin Root

3   The Aravid Eye Hospital, Madurai,
     India: In Service for Sight   39
     V. Kasturi Rangan

PART TWO
Developing New Products   63

4   Abgenix and the XenoMouse   65
     Robert Dolan

5   CardioThoracic Systems   79
     *Michael J. Roberts and Diana S.
     Gardner*

6   Innovation at 3M Corporation (A)   99
     Stefan Thomke and Ashok Nimgade

PART THREE
Launching New Products   119

7   The Medicines Company   121
     John T. Gourville

8   Biopure Corporation   139
     John T. Gourville

9   Synthes   157
     John T. Gourville

PART FOUR
Managing Distribution   175

10   Merck-Medco: Vertical Integration in
     the Pharmaceutical Industry   177
     V. Kasturi Rangan and Marie Bell

11   Becton Dickinson & Company:
     VACUTAINER Systems Division   209
     *V. Kasturi Rangan and Frank V.
     Cespedes*

12   CVS: The Web Strategy   229
     John Deighton and Anjali Shah

PART FIVE
Managing Communications   245

13   Pepcid AC (A): Racing to the OTC
     Market   247
     *Charles King III, Alvin J. Silk, Lisa R.
     Klein, and Ernst R. Berndt*

14   LifeSpan, Inc.: Abbott Northwestern
     Hospital   263
     Melvin A. J. Menezes

15   Population Services International   283
     V. Kasturi Rangan

PART SIX
Managing the Brand   301

16   The Dana-Farber Cancer Institute:
     Development Strategy   303
     V. Kasturi Rangan and Marie Bell

17   Bayer AG (A)   327
     John A. Quelch and Robin Root

18 Warner-Lambert Ireland: Niconil   345
John A. Quelch and Susan P. Smith

PART SEVEN
International Marketing   361

19 Life, Death, and Property Rights: The Pharmaceutical Industry Faces AIDS in Africa   363
Debora Spar and Nicholas Bartlett

20 Phase Two: The Pharmaceutical Industry Responds to AIDS   385
Debora Spar and Nicholas Bartlett

21 Ciba-Geigy Pharmaceuticals: Pharma International   397
N. Craig Smith and John A. Quelch

22 Genzyme's Gaucher Initiative: Global Risk and Responsibility   411
Christopher A. Bartlett and Andrew N. McLean

Part 1

Developing a Marketing Strategy

1. Millennium Pharmaceuticals, Inc. (A)

2. Hikma Pharmaceuticals

3. The Aravind Eye Hospital, Madurai, India:
   In Service for Sight

Chapter 1

Millennium Pharmaceuticals, Inc. (A)

Stefan Thomke and Ashok Nimgade

"Great meeting" were the words echoing in the halls of Millennium's new headquarters in Cambridge, Massachusetts, as a dozen people in business suits swarmed out of the meeting room, shaking hands and slapping backs. Their dark suits contrasted sharply with the daily informal wear at the fast-moving biotechnology firm where even the CEO often appeared in loud Hawaiian shirts. Six of the meeting participants representing the European agribusiness conglomerate Lundberg had flown in by private plane. Their eagerness to access Millennium's genetic technology for agricultural applications showed throughout the meeting. The proposed alliance enjoyed support from the very highest levels at Lundberg; in fact, C. Marie Lundberg, heiress to the closely held family business and a senior vice president herself, had attended this August 1999 meeting.

The real question, however, that CEO Mark Levin pondered was the amount of middle-level support from Lundberg for the deal. Although no specific amount of money had been discussed, both sides remained aware that since 1993, Millennium had graduated to multi-hundred-million-dollar technology and drug discovery deals. The firm was currently involved with a half-dozen technology and pharmaceutical deals worth over a billion dollars. In fact, even without a single drug even close to clinical development, just on the basis of its technology and drug discovery deals alone, Millennium had broken into the ranks of the top biotechnology firms. Just one year ago, it had created history by signing a half-billion-dollar alliance with the German multinational company Bayer AG—the largest deal ever between a biotechnology and a pharmaceutical firm.

Professor Stefan Thomke and Research Associate Ashok Nimgade prepared this case. HBS cases are developed solely as the basis for class discussion. Cases are not intended to serve as endorsements, sources of primary data, or illustrations of effective or ineffective management.

Copyright © 1999 President and Fellows of Harvard College. To order copies or request permission to reproduce materials, call 1-800-545-7685, write Harvard Business School Publishing, Boston, MA 02163, or go to http://www.hbsp.harvard.edu. No part of this publication may be reproduced, stored in a retrieval system, used in a spreadsheet, or transmitted in any form or by any means—electronic, mechanical, photocopying, recording, or otherwise—without the permission of Harvard Business School.

Over the past year, Millennium's stock had skyrocketed, creating unexpected fortunes for its staff, which received part of its compensation as stock options. But continued performance on Wall Street meant pleasing both investors and analysts who wanted to see the company continue its highly successful alliance stream (see Exhibit 1.1 for financials). Already many biotech firms were starving for money and a clear sense of strategic direction.

Although the firm attracted some of the world's leading human genetics experts, it viewed itself as operating in a much larger context; in the words of its CEO and founder Mark Levin, "I never thought of Millennium as just a technology company." Millennium, in fact, sought to break into the ranks of the giant pharmaceutical firms. And it planned to do so by revolutionizing drug development—a process as notoriously lengthy as it was unpredictable. As Chief Technology Officer Michael Pavia, Ph.D., outlined his vision, "Developing drugs ought to be managed like any other complex development process; some day, we will make it as predictable as developing and making automobiles." To accomplish this vision would require time and a lot of cash.

The Biotechnology Revolution(s)

In the mid-1970s, stunning biological breakthroughs set the stage for the modern biotechnology industry. Scientists could now cut and paste snippets of deoxyribonucleic acid (DNA), the blueprint of life and the longest known molecule in the universe. In fact, if all the DNA in any given human cell were laid end to end, it would span over a meter across. Since there are trillions of cells in the human body, all of the DNA in a given adult would easily stretch from earth to the sun and back, *several times over.* This provides just one index of the complexity of the human body. Each second in the body, millions of basic compounds are being synthesized and thousands of interrelated biochemical reactions occur. These all rely ultimately on the accuracy with which DNA in each cell is being deciphered to create proteins, vital building blocks of the body. A small misstep virtually anywhere in these processes can potentially result in morbidity and mortality.

By gaining the power to revise DNA and create new protein products, biologists in the laboratory could more precisely manipulate the primary biological molecules of life. In the 1970s and 1980s, commercial possibilities for the new technologies were seen well in advance of the ability to deliver on them. In these decades, Wall Street and individual speculators poured millions of dollars into new biotech firms, often even without the faintest idea of what differentiated a gene from its homonym.

Part of the excitement stemmed from the fact that the traditional way of finding cures for diseases was extremely effort-intensive and expensive. Large pharmaceutical companies spent up to 15–20 percent of sales in R&D. In the United States, as part of an extensive, highly regulated safety approval process, each drug had to pass three phases of clinical trials under the scrutiny of the U.S. Food and Drug Administration (FDA): Phase I, which tested clinical safety; Phase II, which assessed drug efficacy; and Phase III, which tested adverse effects from long-term use. For each successful product the sponsoring drug firm typically spent more than $230 million, with the average time to market being 14.8 years—over twice as long as it took the U.S. space program to get a man on the moon. (See Exhibit 1.2 for a description of drug development.)

Metaphorically, drugs were molecular-sized "keys" that had to fit "locks" or targets; chemists were the locksmiths. Indeed, they were effectively semi-blind locksmiths, for they had to make up thousands of different keys to find the one that matched. Newly synthesized molecular keys were then tested by biologists, typically using animals that served as models for a disease (for example, a mouse with a neurological problem similar to Parkinsonism). Most compounds would show no activity or be too toxic for further evaluation. A few, however, might show promise, and chemists would modify these "lead compounds" until a good clinical candidate emerged. Typically, for each successful drug that made it to market, a firm began with roughly 10,000 starting compounds. Of these, only 1,000 would make it to more extensive *in vitro* trials (i.e., outside living organisms in settings such as a test tube), of which 20 would be tested even more extensively *in vivo* (i.e., in the body of a living organism such as a mouse) before ten compounds made it to human clinical trials. The entire process represented a long and costly commitment, with the human trials closely monitored by the U.S. government.

Biotechnology, by promising a shortcut through the cumbersome and risky drug development process, promised investors wealth. It attracted entrepreneurs and maverick scientists. The hub of biotech activity was near academic centers like San Francisco and Cambridge (some observers even transformed the old Boston-Cambridge moniker "beantown" into "genetown"). In the 1980s the guiding principle behind quicker drug discovery was "rational drug design." By finding out about the disease-causing receptor in the body on which a potential drug compound acts, scientists hoped to make better compounds. The analogy would be to find out about key features of a lock before designing a properly fitting key rather than a brute force strategy of making keys at random with the hope that one might eventually fit.

But rational drug design often turned out difficult to implement because of the subtle complexities of biological systems and the difficulties of finding the right receptors. In fact, the biotech industry generally disappointed investors in the 1980s partly because of the hype, and partly because biotechnology firms were not large enough to absorb the high rate of failures in drug development. A crushing blow to a biotech firm might be absorbed like a gnat's sting by a pharmaceutical firm. The crushing blows, unfortunately, came usually late in the drug development process during human clinical trials, after considerable investments of time and money had been made. Following announcements of negative human clinical trial outcomes, stock prices for biotech firms dipped by an average of a third—quite often they remained depressed for the following half-year.[1] Thus, even with the newest technologies up their sleeves, small biotech firms often played David to the pharmaceutical Goliaths, with a few exceptions such as the California firm Amgen.

Here, however, biblical parallels end, for most biotech upstarts wanted nothing more than to become fully integrated pharmaceutical giants themselves. But after more than a decade of inflated promises made by biotech firms, investors became increasingly wary. Biotech firms established primarily for product discovery often disappointed investors. As a result, many biotech firms were forced to form partnerships with pharmaceutical firms or even merged with one another.

In the 1990s, the nascent fields of "combinatorial chemistry" and "high throughput screening" breathed new life into the industry by allowing scientists to create and screen prodigious numbers of novel compounds. Returning to the lock-and-key metaphor, scientists could now churn out keys by the thousands and test them almost equally rapidly. Drug companies, however, would still need to muster as many biochemical tricks as they could to identify worthwhile pharmaceutical "targets" (the industry parlance for the "locks" in the lock-and-key metaphor).

While technologies evolved, so did industry dynamics. Biotech firms in the late 1990s wove more intricate alliances with their pharmaceutical partners, often leveraging these

[1] G. S. Burrill, *Biotech 98: Tools, Techniques, and Transition* (San Francisco: Burrill & Co., 1998).

relationships to gain access to Wall Street money and gaining downstream synergies for manufacturing and marketing infrastructures. The giant firms, in return, gained access to emerging technologies that could often be protected; furthermore, they could add to their product pipelines. For a pharmaceutical giant with $10 billion annual revenues to continue growing at 10 percent a year would require three to four new products a year (a typical product generating $300–$400 million annually). Even more would be needed to cover drugs going off patent. With internal pipelines producing less than one significant product a year, big firms increasingly needed to partner with smaller firms.

Many newer generation biotech firms began emphasizing sales of drug development technologies more than pharmaceutical products. These firms, sometimes termed "tool companies," hoped to generate revenue faster by providing services to drug discovery companies, thus avoiding the high cash "burn-rates" involved in searching for drugs. Many of these firms developed multiple relationships with different drug firms, thus blurring the line between sales and strategic partnerships. By the late 1990s, two decades into the biotech revolution, about 300 biotech-based drugs were on the market, and nearly 450 were in clinical trials.[2] These seemingly impressive numbers paled in comparison to the over 1,300 biotech firms actually in existence. The year 1997 saw 228 new biotech-pharmaceutical collaborations, valued at $4.5 billion.[3] Those biotech firms unable to create products or merge with other companies often foundered, leaving their investors holding worthless stock. In such an environment, pharmaceutical firms could often "cherry-pick" drug candidates from financially troubled smaller companies. Only a half-dozen U.S. biotech firms had marketed major drugs without selling majority stakes to pharmaceutical firms. Of these, only Amgen, a California firm with a market valuation of over $30 billion, had emerged as a major drug company with very successful drugs. Onto this sea of broken dreams and treacherous regulatory currents Millennium set sail in 1993.

Birth of a New Millennium

When Mark Levin interviewed early in his career at the pharmaceutical giant Eli Lilly without socks, his staid recruiters thought him "a little weird." Even as CEO, he continued raising eyebrows, taking family outings to the local horse racetrack, and appearing annually at Millennium Halloween parties in drag—in a recent year he appeared, wife and daughter in tow, dressed as a French maid in a low-cut dress. Photographs of Levin in any of his large collection of colorful shoes, including zebra-patterned, adorned investor publications.

A one-time Midwestern shoe salesman and former donut shop owner, Levin leveraged his training in chemical engineering to climb his way out of small-town obscurity. After helping start up a beer-brewing plant and getting exposure to the pharmaceutical world through Lilly (he did get the job), Levin quickly found his niche in the emerging biotech industry of the early 1980s. While working for Genentech, the pioneering California-based biotech firm, Levin's brilliance in managing complex projects won him a job at Mayfield Fund, a San Francisco venture capital firm. Here Levin founded some 10 biotech firms—serving as interim CEO of five. His crown jewel, however, proved to be Millennium Pharmaceuticals (see Exhibit 1.3 for historical milestones).

[2] D. Stipp, "Hatching a DNA Giant," *Fortune,* May 24, 1999.
[3] Burrill, *Biotech 98.*

Levin's concept for Millennium proved so new and strange that an extensive executive search concluded that only Levin could head up the proposed company. According to Grant Heidrich, general partner at Mayfield, Levin "has tremendous vision for what is looming out there. For most people, there are those elements that are hidden in the fog bank. But Mark finds these disconnected pieces and just pulls them together."[4] The plan was to build a drug development company around findings emerging from the Human Genome Project, an ambitious international effort to identify and map every bit of human DNA (which in its entirety is termed the "genome").

Genes causing disease could prove potential targets for drug development. These targets could then be used to develop families of new drugs the world has never seen before. Mapping the human genome "may be the most important step we've taken in science," according to Nobel laureate James Watson, co-discoverer of the DNA structure.[5] Since every disease has a genetic component, deciphering the "Book of Life," as some scientists refer to the genome, promised to revolutionize medical research over decades to come. Even if only 5–10 percent of all estimated 30,000 to 100,000 human genes would yield viable drug targets, it could still open up a rich lode of pharmaceutical drug leads. For the past 100 years, after all, the painstaking efforts involved in drug research had limited medicines developed to less than 500 targets. Even several decades after Watson and Crick discovered the structure of DNA, scientists of the 1980s took years to find and sequence just a single gene or a stretch of DNA of particular interest. For drug companies in 1999, the new revolution could not have been better timed because patents on some 30 major drugs were to expire in the next three years, placing pressure to add to the product pipeline.

With this vision in mind, starting in 1993 with $8.5 million in venture capital funding, Levin set up the company in Cambridge, Massachusetts, in order to court the nation's leading genome scientists. Even without a written business plan or formal organizational charts, Levin sold his vision for a new Millennium well. "The reason spectacular scientists want to come to Millennium is that spectacular scientists work at Millennium," according to Professor Eric Lander, a scientific founder of Millennium and himself one of the leading genome experts in the world, "Mark saw that from the beginning."[6] Levin and his team leveraged off the star scientist reputations to raise large amounts of funding with which to create far better research facilities than even the finest universities.

The firm's roster of brilliant technologists included its Chief Technology Officer, Michael Pavia, a pioneer in the combinatorial chemistry revolution. Pavia wanted to leverage the lessons he learned as former head of research at Sphinx Pharmaceuticals, another Cambridge-based biotech firm that was acquired by Eli Lilly, and also wanted to take part in the next revolution: that of transforming the drug development process itself. Millennium also recruited top businesspeople and legal counsel, some of whom were high-performing mavericks in larger pharmaceutical firms and many of whom had nontraditional backgrounds. The company's Chief Business Officer, Steven Holtzman, for instance, is an Oxford-trained Rhodes Scholar whose philosophy training in making fine distinctions helped craft partnership deals that left Millennium with sizable shares of finely cut pies.

Senior management strategically highlighted technology development from the very start. Levin and Holtzman wanted to avoid the mistakes of other biotech firms,

---

[4] K. Blanton, "Millennium's Chief Found His Calling Starting up New Biotechnology Firms," *Boston Business Journal,* December 5–11, 1997.

[5] A. Zitner, A. Saltus, and R. Saltus, *The Boston Globe,* September 26, 1999, p. 1+.

[6] Blanton, "Millennium's Chief Found His Calling."

which often found themselves stranded in the vise of big pharmaceutical firms because of not having resources to market drug compounds or not having a broad enough technology platform to avoid becoming research boutiques. If risk diversification for a biotech firm proved difficult on the basis of different products, then at least it should occur on the basis of leading-edge technologies.

The initial vision of Millennium was to marry molecular biology with automation and informatics. This would allow for discovering and processing huge amounts of information about genes, making thousands of new targets possible. A dramatic increase in targets would also require quicker screening technologies in order to test many more compounds. Proprietary lab technology included software for analyzing gene function, and machines that decode DNA sequences. Harking on Levin's background as a chemical engineer with work experience in process control, the *Economist* noted:

> Whereas biologists tend to see biotech as the search for a compound, Mr. Levin thinks of it as a complex production process. While they concentrate on the bio, he also thinks hard about the technology. Mr. Levin focuses on trying to make each link in the discovery chain as efficient as possible. . . . He has assembled an impressive array of technologies—including robotics and information systems as well as molecular biology. He then enhances them and links them together in novel ways to create what the engineer in him likes to call "technology platforms," [which] should help drug searchers to travel rapidly on their long and tortuous journey from gene to treatment. And Mr. Levin is prepared—keen, even—to use or buy other people's technology to help in the struggle to keep up to date. One observer has called him the "Mao Zedong" of biotech, a believer in continuous revolution in both technology and organization.[7]

By creating a technology platform considered the finest available, the firm generated capital for updating the platform to keep ahead of the competition. Biotechnology promised a shortcut for finding cures for human genetic diseases. It allowed for skirting the traditional time-consuming study of family trees of diseased individuals in order to track down the responsible genes. Since these genes could be anywhere along the vast expanse of human DNA, some firms tried to take advantage of rulings that allowed for filing patents on naturally occurring gene sequences as fast as they could find them. "The important thing is to get California instead of Appalachia" in this pharmaceutical land grab, according to Millennium executive John Maraganore.[8] To find these prime pieces of genetic real estate, researchers analyzed hundreds of gene sequences simultaneously using miniature "DNA probes" that could ferret out promising stretches of DNA. These probes were derived through research on DNA samples from people suffering from diseases of particular interest.

Not only could a gene sequence be patented, but also the specific protein produced by that gene as well as the engineered drug produced by splicing the gene into a microbe for production could be. In addition, patents could be filed for the use of the gene in diagnostics tests as well as in drugs targeted at the gene. By 1999, although every large drug company had incorporated combinatorial chemistry into its R&D arsenal, such was not the case with genomics. In April 1999, several large drug companies including the two giant firms Glaxo Wellcome and Bayer AG started a collaboration to locate tens of thousands of areas on the genome that may be implicated with disease and put these in the public domain.[9] Skeptics view this as an effort of the Goliaths to thwart growth of the biotech Davids.

---

[7] "Millennium's Bugs," *Economist,* September 26, 1998, p. 70.

[8] Stipp, "Hatching a DNA Giant."

[9] I. Amato, "Industrializing the Search for New Drugs," *Fortune,* May 10, 1999.

Millennium's genomics-based approach reversed the traditional process by first identifying and understanding the role of genes implicated in causing a disease. This should allow for selecting drug candidates based on their ability to intervene in disease initiation and progression—thus targeting the root genetic basis of illness. The firm's strategy relied on using many advanced biotech technologies as well as other computer and robotics technology advances based on the Human Genome Project (see Exhibit 1.4 for some of the technology).

Some experts warned that the new interest in genomics might turn out to be another disappointment just as rational drug design of the 1980s had. According to genomics entrepreneur Craig Venter, himself involved with co-founding of the leading-edge genomics firm Celera, "genomics has been oversold, although it does mark a 'new starting point.'"[10]

Managing Growth

Millennium's vision is to focus on activities that allow us to take the highest downstream share of a drug's profit—wherever these profits may occur. How much you participate in downstream activities and what you have to do has changed and will continue to change in this industry.

Steven Holtzman, Chief Business Officer

From its genesis in 1993 with only 20 individuals, Millennium grew rapidly, drawing upon its founders' willingness to experiment and try new strategies, and systematically learn from failures of other firms. Itself a small company, its rapid growth stemmed from research collaborations with dozens of other biotech firms and university scientists. Although the company prided itself on avoiding the trappings of hierarchy—no formal organizational charts existed—several divisions and subsidiaries evolved over time. By the late 1990s, Millennium saw itself as a family of the different groups working toward a common end of developing expertise in genomics as well as revolutionizing drug development (see Exhibit 1.5).

Central to its success and growth, however, was its ability to attract good employees based on scientific merit and interpersonal skills. "You get interviewed about twelve times before they hire you," stated Kenneth Conway, who was recruited to head the predictive medicine subsidiary in 1997. "First they want to know if you have the drive and intelligence to do the job. Then they reinterview you six times to find out if you'll fit in personally."[11] According to Vincent Miles, vice president of business and technology management, "In spite of a tight labor market, we have managed to get to 800 excellent employees without major politics. At a small biotech firm I worked at previously, there were always two camps of seven individuals each, and the CEO would have to act as tie-breaker. Here, people will cover for each other."

Many workers attributed the relative lack of internal politics to top management's low-key approach in running the company. At meetings, Levin often remained in the background, speaking primarily to keep the discussion from going off-track. His office, a modest affair with wall-mounted shelves, underlined the flat structure of the organization. Levin, Holtzman, and Pavia also set the pace for the hard-working

---

[10] Ibid.

[11] Stipp, "Hatching a DNA Giant."

environment, usually arriving every morning to their spartan offices before five or six A.M. Employees arriving early enough were often treated to the sight of their CEO working with headphones to the beat of rock music. All employees received stock options, which had resulted in very significant capital gains after Millennium's stock started to skyrocket in mid-1998.

Through its half-dozen years in existence, senior management realized it needed to chart its own destiny despite its need for large partners. According to Miles, "we did not want to be managed by remote control by committees of larger firms." Indeed, biotech managers often complained of the manner in which large companies dragged their feet. A life-or-death decision for a biotech firm, after all, could represent an hour's revenues for a pharmaceutical giant. Scientists at biotech companies were often demoralized by these delays, since it frequently meant delaying their valued scientific publications because of patent considerations.

To achieve its goals of independence, senior management adopted several strategies. First, it intended to eschew the traditional full-time equivalent (FTE) model of funding favored by many biotech firms. In the FTE system, biotech firms would charge their partners for the time spent on alliance-specific activities—similar to the way a consulting firm would bill its client for time spent on a project. Although this FTE system tied funding for individual researchers to specific partnership deals and generated predictable cash flow, it often led to a "clock puncher" attitude, with researchers focused on meeting goals of individual partnership projects rather than on the growth and mission of the company itself. Second, Millennium sought partnerships that would fund the type of R&D that would bring it closer to becoming a major drug development firm. Third, as much as possible, it signed only those partnership deals that would enhance, rather than stymie, its ambitious goals for future growth. (See Exhibit 1.6 for its revenue structure.)

Management's negotiating strategy for strategic alliances reflected the company's long-term goals by carefully carving out enough choice cuts for the firm itself. Because countless other biotech firms had been frustrated by the slow pace of their larger partners, Millennium crafted agreements that held the feet of its larger partners to the fire, making them answerable for unmet scheduled milestones. For instance, in a recent Millennium alliance, once it found a potential drug target, the partner would need to screen it within a given time; otherwise the rights to the target would revert back to Millennium.

Millennium also sought to retain rights to unforeseen discoveries in the course of a partnership. "We grant select rights of high value to our partners," according to Miles, "while retaining new knowledge and the remaining rights to ourselves." Focusing on such select rights actually worked well with pharmaceutical partners, largely because the big company executives tended to think along divisional lines and focused on rights that fell within their strategic focus. This allowed Millennium to reserve some rights for its own future drug development, such as selected geographic markets or particular therapeutic applications, that were not of immediate interest to its alliance partners. Millennium's contracts were long and explicit, drawing upon some of the most talented lawyers in biotechnology as well as upon Holtzman's attention to both big picture issues and small but crucial details. For instance, in the field of cancer, senior management carved out separate arrangements with three different firms in a manner that eventually boosted its revenues by tens of millions of dollars. At the same time, few of its partners complained. In the words of Paul Pospisil, associate director of business development and strategy, "Large companies salivate over parts of our state-of-the-art technology platform, and our negotiating team is smart enough not to discuss money prematurely."

Millennium underwent one merger when, in 1997, it bought neighboring biotech firm ChemGenics for $90 million. At that time, it had five alliances with drug firms for finding specific gene targets (the "locks"). Through these alliances, Millennium began to realize that it lacked expertise in going from drug targets to actual lead compounds (the "keys")—a major weakness if the firm itself wanted to develop its own drugs someday or simply validate the feasibility of targets that it supplied to its larger partners. Buying ChemGenics with its expertise in lead discovery was a step toward addressing this weakness and would also allow Millennium to negotiate with big firms from a position of greater strength. There was also a feeling among senior executives that general drug targets were becoming increasingly commoditized. Validated targets, on the other hand, where evidence for downstream drug development potential could be demonstrated early were still rare.

Thus, when Millennium realized that ChemGenics was planning an initial public offering, it essentially bought out ChemGenics. A bonus was ChemGenic's expertise in the area of infectious disease—an attractive area for drug development with more predictable and shorter clinical trials than newer therapeutic areas such as central nervous diseases. Culturally, too, the companies appeared compatible. Both, having been launched next to the Cambridge Brewery, were imbued with the very same spirit—the hard-working, hard-playing, high-tech ethos.

By drawing on world-class personnel, and through tough negotiating strategies that led to key mergers, acquisitions, and value-adding relationships with universities and other firms, Millennium had vaulted into the front rank of biotech firms. Unlike most other biotech firms, it posted profits early. For three of its first six years—not counting a one-time charge for the ChemGenics acquisition—Millennium had posted profits.

Being a pioneer in a new field, Millennium got surprisingly little heat from direct competition. Somewhere between two and three dozen genomics biotech firms existed, with a market value of the leading 14 firms of $4.7 billion. Only two of these biotech firms, however, could be considered the firm's peers: Human Genome Sciences (HGS) in Rockville, Maryland, and Incyte Pharmaceuticals in Palo Alto, California.

In the late 1990s, HGS rode high after finding more disease related gene targets for its pharmaceutical partner SmithKline Beecham (under their original 1993 $125 million agreement) than even one multinational drug company could use. HGS had also negotiated to retain several targets for itself, and by spring 1999 one HGS compound was already undergoing human trials with 25 other candidates to follow suit. HGS also claimed to have applied for patents on 3,000 genes.[12] Incyte, on the other hand, used an entirely different strategy to become a leading genomics firm. It sold drug companies' information in user-friendly databases about the genome. Despite licensing out this information nonexclusively, it reaped subscription fees well over $100 million in 1998 alone.

Part of what shielded Millennium from direct competition with other biotech firms was its own success in attracting large partners to create record-breaking alliances, which generally had either a pharmaceutical or technology focus or sometimes a combination of both (see Exhibit 1.7 for a list of alliances).

Technology Alliances: The Monsanto Deal

For thousands of years, farmers have crossbred crops and herders have crossbred livestock. Agriculturists, unencumbered by human genetic ethics or the long life span of humans, could experiment with crops in ways not possible with humans. Darwin, in

[12] Ibid.

fact, drew upon the accumulated centuries of knowledge gleaned from agriculture in explaining the theory of evolution through natural selection. Thus, agriculture should have drawn upon biotechnology earlier than pharmaceutical companies. Surprisingly, however, agricultural firms were slow to do so despite the fact that in the late 1990s the 1.5 percent world population growth rate outstripped the rate of growth of agricultural productivity (<1 percent) in a global setting of decreased availability of fresh water and arable land.[13] The slowness of agribiotech to bloom, however, stemmed partly from tremendous technical challenges facing agricultural biotechnologists: unlike human researchers, agriculturalists diffused their research efforts across dozens of different species, some of which possessed genomes even larger than human genomes.

One of the first of the giant multinational giants to realize the potential of biotechnology, however, was the Midwestern U.S. firm Monsanto. In 1997, Monsanto approached Millennium to gain access to state-of-the-art genomics technologies. The acquisition of ChemGenics had made it even more attractive to Monsanto. (ChemGenics had already been talking with agricultural firms in a preliminary fashion.) Millennium, in turn, was looking to leverage the integrated platform for agriculture and create near-term value.

The challenge to senior management, however, was to avoid being distracted from its focus on human therapeutics, particularly at a time when the staff was already extended. Millennium contemplated several structures for its partnership including a typical biotech-pharmaceutical partnership, a joint venture, and a technology transfer. To avoid being distracted from its focus on human health, Millennium sought the last option. By agreement with Monsanto, it agreed to replicate or "clone" its technology platform in an agricultural milieu through creating Cereon Genomics, a Monsanto subsidiary. Even the local character was preserved by basing Cereon in Cambridge.

Millennium would receive up to $218 million ($118 million in an up-front fee, and the remainder in yearly $20 million increments based on achieving milestones over the next five years). The milestones were set to be "80 percent achievable." This was to avoid the game of the biotech firm being conservative and the pharmaceutical firm being aggressive. Examples of milestones included number of DNA lanes sequenced over a given time period; total sequencing capabilities of Cereon by certain time intervals; and software to be set up.

Millennium involved 100 of its scientific staff to help deliver the technology to Monsanto. Nonetheless, the firm learned quickly that the venture would require hiring new staff largely in order to help Cereon *receive* the technology. Technology transfer, after all, always takes place at both ends of the transfer mechanism. Monsanto, however, had generally underestimated the size, infrastructure, and training of its technological staff that were necessary to make full use of genomics technology. The middle-ranking scientists and technologists generally found the technology transfer relationship symbiotic; the transfer process, for instance, forced Millennium to document its protocols and software more formally—steps that would help its own new staff members. In the course of working out glitches, useful new information also flowed back to Millennium. Socially, strong bonds were formed through weekend activities such as a joint softball team that consisted of Millennium and Cereon employees.

Over the course of the Monsanto alliance and other deals, Millennium grew from 400 to 700 employees, with 30 new applicants arriving each Monday for five interviews each, and eventually added over $20 per share to its stock. It achieved all the milestones agreed with Monsanto, thus obtaining the maximum fees outlined in its contract. According to Miles, "This was our first value-based deal. We thought we

[13] Burrill, *Biotech 98.*

could replicate this model over and over again. We were blown away by our success at replicating our technology platform." But only a string of success stories could keep the stock price continuing upward.

Pharmaceutical Alliances: The Bayer Deal

With the ink still drying on the Monsanto-Cereon deal, Millennium underwent a period of soul-searching. It realized that its staff was increasingly stretched across a variety of medical areas in terms of upstream drug target development. Although the Monsanto-Cereon deal indicated that Millennium could go on creating new technology deals, the company still lacked the capabilities to take drugs all the way to market and a robust pipeline of drug development opportunities to pursue on its own behalf. It would have to look for strategic alliances with drug firms to make up for these weaknesses.

At the same time, across the Atlantic, Bayer AG, a large German research firm with 145,000 employees worldwide—best known for introducing Aspirin—was also undergoing a soul-searching exercise termed internally the "Vision 2000" initiative. In 1997, pharmaceuticals accounted for a third of Bayer's $30 billion business, but senior management realized that it lagged behind in terms of target discovery and biotechnology. To address this, the company surveyed hundreds of biotech companies for acquisition or partnership deals. With a large war chest it could easily broker deals with a dozen or more biotech firms.

In late October 1997, Bayer invited 55 senior managers from leading biotech companies to what industry insiders termed a "biotech beauty pageant." Millennium, a leading contender, had a prime place on the roster. This came as no surprise, since as early as June of 1996, a Bayer manager had put out "feelers" (i.e., tentative approaches) to a Millennium executive in Paris. A few days later, Bayer invited the firm to partner with it in several areas. With Millennium, Vision 2000 had recognized a natural partnership—one that extended far beyond the similarity of names—and which would allow for "one-stop-shopping" for both sides.

The two companies signed an agreement under which Millennium would find 225 new drug targets for Bayer—an impressive number considering that over the past century, all of the world's drug discoverers combined had found around 500 drug targets. In effect, Millennium would take responsibility for finding half of all targets going into Bayer's drug development pipeline. Areas to be covered included cancer, cardiovascular diseases, pain, osteoporosis, viral infections, and blood disorders. Consistent with its strategy, Millennium would also retain rights to several targets found in the course of the collaboration.

In return for up to $465 million over five years, Bayer would also obtain a 14 percent equity stake in Millennium. The Bayer deal ended up becoming the largest alliance ever between a biotech firm and a pharmaceutical firm. Again, Millennium's stock jumped, creating remarkable capital gains for its stockholders inside and outside the firm.

A New Drug Development Paradigm

"When Mark hired me, he told me that I had five years to revolutionize drug development. I have about four and a half years left."

Michael Pavia, Ph.D., Chief Technology Officer, July 1999

Fundamental to Millennium's strategy was its ability to revolutionize drug development, which, in the late 1990s, was still long, costly, and very risky. In 1997, CEO Mark Levin hired Michael Pavia as Chief Technology Officer with the charter to help make the drug development process "twice as fast and half as expensive" within five years, with the countdown starting in the beginning of 1999. As Pavia translated his charter for industrializing the drug discovery process, "the only way to achieve such an aggressive goal is to question everything and to hire people that challenge assumptions held by the industry for decades."

Millennium was by no means the only company thinking along these bold lines. Most large pharmaceutical firms had initiatives under way to shorten the development cycle significantly and make drug development more predictable. Current practice seemed unsustainable. Pharmaceutical firms would bring several successful drugs to market each year and bear the cost of failure in the very long and expensive clinical phase where only 1 out of 10 drug candidates would make it to the market. Eli Lilly, for instance, had announced its internal goal of "2000 days by the year 2000," implying an aggressive compression of the traditional 12- to 14-year drug development cycle into less than seven years.

Nonetheless, recruits were often attracted to Millennium because of their frustration with the slow progress of large firms. The revolutionary technology platform they saw mirrored the very different training and mind-set of the firm's founders. Millennium, being new and unencumbered by corporate inertia—let alone formalized plans—could learn from the mistakes of prior firms and aggressively challenge conventional wisdom. For instance, could traditional drug makers drive costly drug failures to the early phases of development when failure was relatively inexpensive? After all, drug discovery would always involve trial and error. But errors discovered in late development were very costly and could only be absorbed by large firms.

Many lessons in drug development were brought in through recruits from larger companies. It was an experienced job candidate interviewee, for instance, who pointed out that the Food and Drug Administration (FDA) nowhere mandates that pre-clinical trials must be done in defined sequential phases in lock-step. (Perhaps, therefore, attempts to "frontload" problems—one of Millennium's development strategies—might lead it to reshuffle the order in which drugs would be tested.)

To revolutionize drug development, Pavia's group aggressively approached its task using the following three strategies: (1) speed up individual steps of the development process, including rapid feedback on critical tests such as toxicology; (2) carry out serial steps in parallel wherever possible; and (3) "front-load" drug failure modes through the use of new technologies. More will be said about each of these strategies below:

1. *Speed up individual steps of the process:* For the early research phase of drug discovery, scientists and engineers sought to speed up the various steps involved in isolating, characterizing, and understanding DNA. By drawing on automation experts and engineers with manufacturing experience, Millennium sought to automate truly complex process steps and create an industrial "R&D factory" (see Exhibit 1.4), using robots and other equipment often used in advanced production of other products. To achieve this, engineers opportunistically outsourced and modified emerging technologies, often creating machines envied even by leading universities. Like other firms, Millennium also planned to use combinatorial chemistry and high-throughput screening to reduce the time required in the laborious, traditional random search process for drug candidates. Interestingly, no matter how much each step was sped up, however, a crucial bottleneck in the entire R&D process remained: the ability of scientists to assimi-

late and make sense of the staggering amount of information made available. To address this, Pavia felt that an increased focus on the rapidly growing field of bioinformatics was essential for Millennium.

2. *Carry out serial steps in parallel wherever possible:* In early 1999, Pavia established a group that reviewed the entire drug development process, using basic principles of operations management, for ways to compress the drug development timeline by allowing more steps to be conducted in parallel. This shift in thinking could save considerable time during drug discovery as well as human clinical trials when drug developers evaluated each candidate compound for *target validity, organ-specificity* (i.e., was the target specific to the organ of interest), *bioavailability* (i.e., would the compound be absorbed appropriately by the body), and *toxicity*. Rather than addressing each of these issues one by one in the traditional sequential fashion, Millennium decided it would seek to do a series of several "quick and dirty" tests on minute quantities of each candidate compound in a fairly simultaneous fashion to see if a candidate was even in the "right ballpark." This was analogous to prescreening job candidates over the telephone in parallel so that only a smaller batch of higher-yield candidates would be invited in for in-depth interviews.

3. *Find new technologies that could "front-load" critical problems, thus eliminating less promising drug candidates early:* In the 1990s, only 1 out of 10 drug candidates typically made it through clinical development—by far the costliest phase of drug development. Pavia wanted to improve these odds by at least half. His staff sought to diminish this wastage by trying to find the potential failure modes through, for instance, prescreening drug candidates as discussed above. Gaining information about, say, the toxicological profile of a drug early on could significantly improve the predictability of its likely success. Pavia's group also decided that it would systematically seek to use other failed drug candidates to see if new technologies could indeed pick up these "failures" earlier (for an example of such a new technology, see Exhibit 1.8). Pavia charged Paul Pospisil, a chemist trained at Harvard who also had strategic responsibilities, to scour conventions and trade fairs for cutting-edge technologies that would provide earlier feedback on candidate drugs. The point was not necessarily to avoid failure, but to shift failures to earlier phases in the process.

Thus, in terms of reducing the product development cycle, much potential for technological improvement existed alongside the uncertainties inherent in all drug development projects. Like most of the major pharmaceutical firms aiming to shorten the drug development cycle, Millennium realized it would have to focus on many, if not all, links in the drug development process. Focusing on just early drug development through combinatorial chemistry and high-throughput screening, for instance, could save only an estimated half-year to one year. Thus, downstream phases would also need to be shortened. These downstream changes could be achieved through administrative as well as technological changes. For instance, reviewing toxicology data as it was generated might compress the traditional nine-month cycle for a toxicology review into as little as a month.

Taking Stock

At Millennium we believe that nothing is impossible.

Millennium Corporate Value Statement

With the Bayer deal, Millennium entered the realm of very large pharmaceutical alliances and now basked in the glow of Wall Street's approval. Unlike other biotech firms, however, it resisted the temptation to sell stock after going public, preferring instead to live off its deals. It did not want to get locked into the traditional pattern of seeking up-front funding in return for royalties—the type of arrangement that pleased investors but did not necessarily build up a biotech firm's long-term capabilities. With Millennium's stock price now at unprecedented heights—having doubled to $60 per share from spring through the summer of 1999—*Fortune* magazine observed, "No drug company wannabe has mustered as much value with as little red ink."[14]

By 1999, the company had grown to about 800 scientists. Millennium remained aware that the current tight job market did not apply to it. In fact, a recent newspaper ad for jobs for mid-level research personnel led to a line well over a block long just for the privilege of dropping off resumes. Many had come from other local biotech firms. Nonetheless, senior management now planned for its growth, at least for the foreseeable future, to plateau at 1,000 scientists.

But even at that size the company dynamics would have to change, despite the best of efforts to retain its small company roots. CEO Levin exclaimed in a 1999 press interview, "It was a lot easier to walk out the bathroom with my [Halloween] costume on when there were 30 people in the company and I knew them all well. Now I walk out into this crowd of 800 wondering if most of them are thinking, 'Who is this idiot?' But it's fun."[15]

But signs of strain in the organization were showing throughout all levels. According to Pavia, "Growing the organization from 100 to 200 was relatively easy; doubling from there to 400 was a bit harder but manageable; but to think of growing beyond 800 would place all sorts of new strains and would need re-thinking on how we do things." With growth, high-ranking scientists had to supervise more people while contending with having their skills marketed to more outside partners. Indications of increased stress at lower levels came from the Human Relations department's latest semi-annual survey from March 1999. It showed that despite general high employee satisfaction, the areas that scored the lowest were in terms of workload, expectations, and manageability of stress. These areas scored a hairline lower than a half-year ago.

"I absolutely love what I am doing," one worker commented on the questionnaire, "but the workload sometimes is unmanageable. . . . Sometimes you don't know whether you are swimming or sinking." Another worker added, "I think my workload and the expectations are higher than in the other industrial settings where I've worked—I've worked for three other companies." Yet another worker quantified this frustration: "I am currently committed to do two scientists' worth of work. Consequently I feel that I have to make a choice between trying to do it all in a mediocre way, or I can only do part of it well and leave the rest undone—if I take the latter route, there is no good decision mechanism to tell me what is the most important: I'm told 'Everything is important!'"

To manage stress within the firm, the company's human relations department under Peter McLaughlin wanted to avoid stopgap measures such as occasional stress-reduction seminars. Instead, in early 1999, it sought to make all managers responsible for having regular one-to-one sessions with subordinates to discuss such issues. How this change in approach would work had yet to be seen. In any case, the company was more aware that money alone could not buy its way out of the stress dilemma. According to Miles, VP of business and technology management:

---

[14] Amato, "Industrializing the Search for New Drugs."
[15] Stipp, "Hatching a DNA Giant."

In the past we were driven by financing. We made commitments without detailed planning. For example, the Bayer deal was so huge that we would do whatever they wanted. Now we are pickier. Our strategy just two years ago was not as clearly defined as now. But we realized that technology alliances could be either financing vehicles or distractions. Every time we thought about a new deal we worried about several tensions: were we biting off more than we could chew? After all, we were already quite extended. Were we in danger of losing our focus? Several other prominent biotech firms have a hard time stating exactly what they do.

Without a formal plan, Millennium had found its path to its present prosperity. Its vision had encompassed becoming a genomics firm and helping revolutionize the drug development process. Already, with these two visions not even fully implemented, its managers and scientists were talking about what could only be whispered at most other biotech firms: the prospect of growing into a fully integrated pharmaceutical firm.

Big Deal

In June 1999, after a presentation at an industry conference, a Millennium senior executive was quietly approached by an executive from Lundberg, a multinational agribusiness concern and one of the largest privately held companies in Europe. Despite not being a household name, Lundberg impacted the daily lives of most Europeans through its dealings in livestock and agricultural produce. It was ironic, therefore, that a company that made fortunes in the futures market from one-cent price swings of commodities sold by the ton now approached a firm that operated on the scale of milligrams.

Through Millennium, Lundberg sought access to genomics technology, much in the manner of the Millennium-Monsanto deal. Lundberg specifically sought access to technology that would help identify plant genes as well as for high throughput screening capabilities. For Lundberg, the applications were limitless. It would, for instance, allow for facile manipulation of the fat content of livestock or the carbohydrate content of grain. For Millennium's senior management, three issues loomed large in their minds as they thought about a potential deal with Lundberg: strategic fit, impact on its R&D productivity, and potential conflict with its prior relationship with Monsanto.

If the Lundberg deal did not fit strategically with Millennium's own goals, the company decided it would consider the deal a distraction. Strategic fit would have to be analyzed by considering impact on the entire company. For instance, although at first glance informatics did not appear to be directly involved, the firm would have to help create software for the new venture. This was no small venture, because the Millennium software platform was orders of magnitude larger than commercial office software and would require frequent upgrades. On the other hand, through a partnership with Lundberg, it could pay for some of the work it needed to do for itself anyway. For instance, software documentation for Lundberg would also help Millennium internally.

In terms of the impact of the Lundberg deal on Millennium's own productivity, many variables remained unclear. If a deal with Lundberg were to hamper productivity, it could stifle growth several years later. For instance, it was clear that Lundberg did not possess an infrastructure for receiving any transferred genomics technology, and therefore Millennium would have to set up a system that would allow Lundberg to receive the technology. This implied using Millennium's senior staff to interview and hire new personnel on Lundberg's behalf. On the other hand, once the interviewing was done, Millennium's top-level staff would be minimally distracted by the Lundberg deal. Furthermore, Millennium's staff generally appeared confident it could repeat its first agribiotechnology technology transfer even quicker the second time, building on experience and expertise that was built as a result of the Monsanto alliance.

Potential conflict with the Monsanto deal turned out not to be an important consideration. The Monsanto agreement allowed for considerable areas of collaboration between Millennium and any other agricultural concern. For instance, while Millennium could not help manipulate the fat content for plant foods because of its relationship with Monsanto, it could do so for livestock.

While Millennium grappled with the issues discussed above, eight senior Lundberg executives created time on their busy calendars to come to Cambridge. No figures were quoted by either party, although Millennium's senior management hinted from the outset that the alliance would have to be at least as large as the Monsanto deal. As these issues were discussed in the meeting, Levin and Holtzman were surprised to learn that Lundberg, for its part, had done little due diligence; it had not even examined the SEC filings for the Monsanto-Millennium collaboration. It was also unclear how the company expected to receive the technology platform as its middle management had not been involved in any of the discussions. On the other hand, Lundberg's senior management, led by a family member that held a majority position in the privately held firm, showed strong consensus and were ready to make a major financial commitment right away.

The business development team that had prepared the meeting for Levin felt very good—the discussions showed little conflict or disagreement between the two senior executive teams. Announcement of the deal would please Wall Street analysts and probably add a quarter billion dollars or more of cash to Millennium's financial coffer. After the meeting, Levin sat down in his office and reflected on his company's future. In a few minutes, several key executives, including Holtzman and Pavia, would come to his office to discuss the final decision on whether to pursue the Lundberg alliance. Counting the chairs in his modest office, he wondered whether there would be enough room for the small group.

Glossary

Analog: A structural variation of a parent molecule. Useful analog compounds may exhibit fewer adverse effects or might be therapeutic in smaller doses.

Assay: A test to determine properties of a chemical entity such as strength or purity or activity in a biological system.

Chemical Library: A collection of differing compounds (analogous to a library of books), usually maintained for further study. Drug firms often maintain libraries of all compounds synthesized in the past by their scientists.

Combinatorial Chemistry: A branch of synthetic chemistry developed that allows for systematically generating large numbers of chemically diverse but related compounds. Combinatorial chemistry thus potentially allows drug makers to rapidly generate and explore thousands of compounds in just weeks in order to find promising compounds.

Compound: A distinct chemical entity formed by the union of two or more ingredients in a distinctive proportion. Drug compounds are formed from a distinctive proportion of differing chemical elements.

Molecular Diversity: The importance of molecular diversity—analogous to diversity found within the human race—stems from the fact that even minor changes in molecular structure can tremendously alter function. As a result, drug makers seek to adequately explore molecular diversity of a promising drug's analogues in order to field the best possible drug (just as a good company recruits from an adequate diversity of candidates).

Rational Drug Design: An approach that uses very advanced scientific methods such as X-ray crystallography and/or nuclear-magnetic resonance (NMR) spectroscopy to determine the three-dimensional shape and structure of a target that they wish to influence with a drug. With the aid of computer simulation, scientists would then be able to design drug molecules that bind to the target receptor.

Receptor: A specialized protein located on or within cells in the body capable of detecting specific environmental changes. Receptors in the nervous system, once activated by neurotransmitters, will often trigger specific responses within the body.

Screening: A process of systematically examining a collection of compounds to find those with the most promise for a given purpose (such as drug development). "High throughput screening" refers to the ability to screen a large number of compounds in a short time period—a capability needed to successfully apply combinatorial chemistry.

Synthetic Chemistry: The branch of chemistry dealing with the creation of compounds in the laboratory.

Target: A receptor, enzyme, or molecule associated with a particular disease. The goal of drug discovery is to find or create compounds that will bind to a particular target with a required degree of tenacity (binding affinity) and, at the same time, not bind to other targets that may be structurally similar but have different functions.

EXHIBIT 1.1
Selected Financials for Millennium Pharmaceuticals
Selected financial data (dollars in millions, except per-share data)

Source: Financial reports.

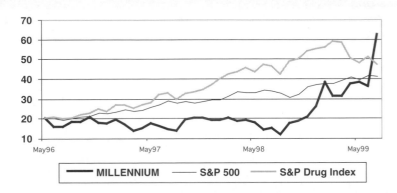

Millennium Pharmaceuticals Stock Price

	1995	1996	1997	1998
Sales	22.9	31.8	89.9	133.7
Cost of goods sold	19.4	38.9	81.6	125.0
Gross profit	**3.5**	**−7.1**	**8.4**	**8.7**
Operating income before depreciation	3.5	−7.1	8.4	8.7
Depreciation, depletion, and amortization	1.7	3.9	12.2	16.3
Operating Profit	**1.7**	**−11.0**	**−3.8**	**−7.6**
Net income	**1.2**	**−8.8**	**−81.2**[a]	**10.3**
Other Data:				
EPS (primary)	0.07	−0.39	−2.87	0.34
Dividends per share	0	0	0	0
ROA (%)	5.1%	−10%	−56%	4%
ROE (%)	9.8%	−13%	−88%	5%
Market value ($ Mil.)		415.5	554.2	903.6

[a]Includes acquisition of ChemGenics.

EXHIBIT 1.2
Summary of Drug Development in the United States

Sources: J. A. DiMasi, "New Drug Development: Cost, Risk, and Complexity," *Drug Information Journal*, May 1995; FDA, "From Test Tube to Patient: New Drug Development in the United States," *FDA Consumer*, Special Issue, January 1995; Kenneth I. Kaitin and Hub Houben, "Worthwhile Persistence: The Process of New Drug Development," *Odyssey, The Glaxo-Wellcome Journal of Innovation in Healthcare*, June 1995.

New drug development is a costly affair with high failure rates. For each therapeutic drug entering the market, pharmaceutical firms invest more than $230 million (estimates go up to $359 million) and 14.8 years (up from 14.3 years in the 1970s). Estimated costs include out-of-pocket expenses, costs of failed projects, and opportunity costs. A brief outline of the drug development process follows:

Basic Research (About 2 years)   This phase typically starts through the initial screening of plants, microorganisms, and other naturally occurring substances to find a "hit" or "lead" compound. In a painstaking iterative process, organic chemists would then make analogues or modifications of existing leads. Although this stage typically cost a firm $30–50 million, it represented a point of great leverage for speeding up a firm's drug development process. Only 40 out of an initial 10,000 compounds might make it to the next stage of pre-clinical testing.

Pre-Clinical (Biological) Screening (About 3 years)   Pre-clinical trials, which often overlapped the basic research phase, involved animal testing to assess drug safety and to gather data on biological effects (e.g., absorption, metabolism, and excretion). Only one in four drugs typically made it through this phase to enter human clinical testing as "Investigational New Drugs" (INDs).

Human Clinical Trials (About 6 years)   Investigational New Drugs faced the FDA's regulatory hurdles, the most stringent and time-consuming approval process for therapeutic drugs in the world. Total costs for conducting clinical trials topped $200 million, but with increasing proportions of this cost occurring with each of the three successive phases described below.

    Phase I Safety Trials (1 year):   In Phase I trials, researchers determined highest tolerated doses, toxicities, and safe ranges in one or two dozen healthy volunteers. This phase also yielded invaluable information on absorption, metabolism, and excretion of the drug in humans.

    Phase II Efficacy Trials (2 years):   Phase II tested efficacy of drug candidates in up to several hundred volunteer patients based at test sites composed of participating hospitals. To ensure statistically relevant data, from this point onward, a portion of the volunteers received the drug while the others received placebos. Roughly one-third of all drug candidates survived Phases I and II.

    Phase III Long-Term Efficacy Trials (3 years):   In the longest and most expensive phase of drug testing, researchers monitored drug use in thousands of volunteer patients for long-term safety, optimum dosage levels, and subtler adverse effects. Only about a fourth of all drug candidates survived Phases I, II, and III, and moved on to the FDA review stage.

FDA Review (About 2–3 years)   Despite a trend toward computer-assisted applications, the hundreds of thousands of pages submitted in the New Drug Application (NDA) to the FDA represented a tribute to the pharmaceutical industry's data-generating capacity. The NDA included data on each patient, as well as on the company's plans for producing and stocking the drug. The FDA committee took up to three years to review the NDA. Even after approval, however, post-marketing surveillance by the FDA continued. Only one-tenth of all drug candidates entering clinical trials ultimately reached the market.

EXHIBIT 1.3
Important Milestones
for Millennium

1865   Austrian monk Gregor Mendel's plant-breeding experiments find evidence for hereditary transmission of traits. He postulates building blocks of heredity that later scientists would term "genes." Mendel's findings collect dust for decades.

1869   Swiss scientist Miescher discovers an abundant and seemingly useless material in the cell nucleus that he terms "nuclein." Later known as DNA, nuclein's role in transmitting genetic information would not be appreciated until later.

1953   Structure of deoxyribonucleic acid (DNA) elucidated by Watson and Crick, who would later receive a Nobel prize for their work.

Early 1970s   Biotech industry starts, primarily in California and Massachusetts, based on discoveries that allow scientists to excise and recombine bits of DNA.

1990   Human Genome Project launched by U.S. government with the mission of identifying every bit of human DNA including all 100,000 or so human genes. Technological advances accelerate anticipated project completion date (by three years to 2002) in a manner worth emulating by other government initiatives.

1993   Millennium founded with Mark Levin as CEO in Cambridge, Massachusetts, and with $8.5 million in venture capital funding.

March 1994   Millennium signs its first major pharmaceutical deal with Hoffmann-La Roche. The deal centers around finding new drug targets in obesity and diabetes.

October 1995   Millennium signs equity funding and research deal with Eli Lilly & Co.—the first of several deals with Millennium CEO Mark Levin's old employer.

February 1997   Millennium acquires neighboring biotech firm ChemGenics for $90 million. This expands Millennium's downstream capabilities for developing drug targets into leads and boosts Millennium's bargaining power with big firms.

October 1997   Millennium signs agreement with Monsanto and creates Cambridge-based Cereon to transfer the genome technology platform for agricultural purposes.

September 1998   Millennium announces the biggest biotech-pharma alliance ever: the nearly half-billion-dollar deal with Bayer AG. The agreement covers drug target identification in several medical fields.

August 1999   Case setting: Current offer from Lundberg for a technology deal paralleling the Monsanto alliance.

EXHIBIT 1.4
Millennium's R&D Factories: Automated DNA Sequencing

Source: Millennium Pharmaceuticals.

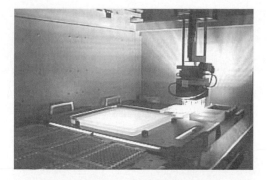

(a) **Colony Picking:** "Libraries" of DNA corresponding to healthy and diseased individuals are grown in bacteria and picked up by robot arm for DNA sequencing.

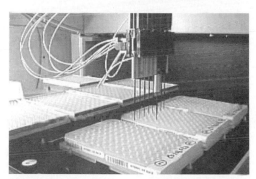

(b) **DNA Preparation:** The DNA molecules are isolated from the rest of the bacterial materials.

(c) **Reaction Assembly:** Pure DNA materials are dispensed for automatic sequencing.

(d) **DNA Sequencing:** The identity of DNA molecules is "read" by an automated sequencing process.

EXHIBIT 1.5
Millennium's
Corporate Structure

Millennium saw itself as a family of the following groups working toward a common end of developing expertise in genomics as well as gearing toward ultimate drug development:

- *Pharmaceutical Division:* This division worked on providing pharmaceutical companies with high-value drug targets and drug leads. Scientists here generally focused on small therapeutic molecules. Customers included multinationals such as Hoffmann-La Roche, Lilly, Astra, Wyeth-Ayerst, and Pfizer. The 1997 acquisition of ChemGenics (see below) greatly extended the downstream drug development capabilities.

- *Millennium BioTherapeutics, Inc. (MBio):* Millennium's first subsidiary, launched in 1997, used biotech and genomics technologies to discover and develop larger therapeutic molecules such as proteins and gene products for drug companies. From the very beginning, Lilly invested $20 million in MBio for an 18 percent ownership interest. Millennium retained rights to half the drug candidates identified by the research collaborations with Lilly.

- *Technology Division:* This division provided to other branches of Millennium as well as third-party clients, high-value R&D technologies pertaining to genomics and related fields such as high-throughput screening and combinatorial chemistry. Despite a preference for technologies based on internal efforts, the division actively scanned the industry for external acquisition of technologies useful for enhancing the company's technology platform. Many of this division's customers overlapped with those of MPharma.

- *Millennium Predictive Medicine, Inc. (MPMx):* This subsidiary, launched in 1997, focused on genomics-based products and technologies for improving the diagnosis and prediction of disease. By elaborating the relationship between genes and patients' reactions to drugs, this group would hopefully help physicians with deciding with tailoring therapeutics toward individual patients.

- *Cereon Genomics:* This wholly owned subsidiary of Monsanto marked Millennium's foray into agriculture. This allowed for making the company's technology platform available to a partner in an area far removed from Millennium's general province of human healthcare: plant agriculture.

EXHIBIT 1.6
Millennium's Revenue
Structure

Source: Millennium
Pharmaceuticals.

Consolidated revenue (dollars in 000s; December 31, 1994, through June 30, 1999)						
	1994	1995	1996	1997	1998	June 30, 1999
Contract (FTE)	5,963	11,250	23,171	44,569	51,983	25,226
License fees (one-time)	2,000	11,130	6,250	43,438	20,000	15,000
Milestones	—	500	1,400	1,100	23,350	3,625
Bayer alliance	—	—	—	—	33,400	42,500
Reimbursed collaborations/ support	—	—	944	827	4,949	1,913
Total	7,963	22,880	31,764	89,933	133,682	88,264

EXHIBIT 1.7 **Lists of Millennium's Alliances (by Company, Year, Therapeutic Area, Dollar Amount)**

Source: S. Matthews and M. Watkins, "Strategic Deal-Making at Millennium Pharmaceuticals," Harvard Business School Case No. 899-242 (1999).

Date	Alliances	Terms	Focus
March 1994	Hoffmann-La Roche Inc.	Equity: $6 M; full-time equivalent (FTE) funding: $10 M/year over 5 years; milestone fees and royalties	Obesity, Type II diabetes
October 1995 and March 1996	Eli Lilly and Company	Equity: $8 M; up-front licensing fee: $4 M; FTE funding: $10 M/year over 5 years; milestone fees and royalties	Atherosclerosis and oncology
December 1995	Astra AB	Up-front licensing fee: $10 M; FTE funding: $8 M/year over 5–7 years; milestone fees and royalties	Inflammatory respiratory diseases
June 1996	American Home Products (Wyeth-Ayerst)	Up-front licensing fee: $10 M; FTE funding: $10 M/year over 5–7 years; milestone fees and royalties	Central nervous system disorders
February 1997	ChemGenics Pharmaceuticals, Inc.	4,783,680 shares of common stock	Antibacterial small molecule drug targets
May 1997	MBio	Joint funding with Eli Lilly; share rights to discoveries (see below)	(See below)
May 1997	Eli Lilly	Research funding: $8–$10 M/year over 3 years (option to renew for 2 years); $20 M MBio stock; 18 percent equity interest in MBio; licensing and milestone fees and royalties	Therapeutic proteins
October 1997	Monsanto Company	Up-front licensing fee: $38 M; technology fees: $180 M over 5 years; royalties; exclusive rights to plant agritechnology; nonexclusive rights to nonagritechnology	Agritechnology (via Cereon)
September 1998	Bayer AG	Up-front licensing fee: $33.4 M; ongoing licensing fee and research funding: $219 M; performance target delivery: up to $116 M; $96.6 M (4.96M shares) Millennium common stock	Cardiovascular disease; oncology (separate, from Eli Lilly targets); osteoporosis; liver fibrosis; hematology; viral infections. 225 targets over five-year period

EXHIBIT 1.8
Genomics Technology
in Drug Discovery:
Front-Loading
Toxicology Assess-
ment through
Transcriptional
Profiling

Extreme diseases demand severe cures.

Hippocrates

Hippocrates notwithstanding, in a world where most drugs have undesired side effects, modern drug makers continually sought kinder, gentler drugs. To achieve this goal, drug makers screened compound candidates for those with a high margin of safety between doses producing the desired, therapeutic effects and doses producing toxic doses. Sometimes, as in the case of anti-cancer chemotherapies, for lack of better alternatives, physicians were forced to use rather toxic drugs.

To understand and assess the potential damage wrought by drug compounds in the body, we must examine the liver, since most of the body's detoxification occurs here. Liver cells, often described as the body's factory, use a variety of mechanisms to rid the body of toxins. All detoxi-fication steps in the specific mechanism are ultimately controlled by specific genes. Toxins that cannot be removed may ultimately damage the liver itself over time, leading, for example, to the liver cirrhosis of excessive alcohol drinkers.

The classic approach to examining the liver's actions against a drug involved studying drug metabolism in lab animals at the pre-clinical stage. This proved a long and expensive process, since weeks or months would pass before the effects on the animal livers could be assessed. Newer methods, however, allow for exposing liver tissue slices to the test chemicals to assess for drastic effects such as cell death on liver tissue. In the late 1990s, this was routinely done. Through increasing biochemical finesse, however, researchers sought to discover which of the many important detoxification mechanisms in the liver were being used in order to create strate-gies for modifying the chemical compound to less toxic forms.

A powerful genomics technology for assessing toxicology is "transcriptional profiling." Tran-scriptional profiling is a technology that allows for assessing what genes are active (i.e., being "transcribed" by the cell's genetic machinery into genetic messages that would serve as architec-tural blueprints for making proteins, the building blocks of the body). The DNA in each human cell contains the same set—or genome—of about 100,000 genes, of which about 15,000 differ-ent genes will be active during a cell's lifetime. Different combinations of genes would be active in different cell types, with the highly active liver cells likelier to activate a large number of genes.

To identify the set of genes in liver cells associated with detoxifying a specific class of drugs, genomics researchers compare the "transcriptional profile" of a dormant liver cell with liver cells actively metabolizing the drugs in question. Any discrepancies likely reflect the use of genes specifically activated for ridding the body of the specific toxins. (To ferret out these discrepan-cies, copies of all known genes are placed in a systematic array on a surface. The cellular genetic "messages" churned out by the activated liver cells would then combine in a "like-seeks-like" fashion with the genes on these arrays most like their parent genes.) By thus identifying the genes most relevant for detoxifying a given compound, drug makers could now quickly under-stand how difficult a drug might prove to be to detoxify.

Transcriptional profiling, thus, can potentially provide a quick way to "front-load" failure modes early in the drug development process and thus steer a company away from a likely unfruitful avenue of research at a stage when it was still inexpensive and quick to switch course.

Chapter 2

Hikma Pharmaceuticals

John A. Quelch and Robin Root

On May 19, 1996, Mr. Samih Darwazah, chairman of Hikma Investment, the holding company for Hikma Pharmaceuticals, proudly announced that the Jordanian company had begun exports of approved drugs to the United States:

> The shipment is of $100,000 worth of prescription drugs to four U.S. distributors. Hikma is the first Arab-owned drug company from the Middle East to obtain Food and Drug Administration (FDA) approval to sell to the U.S. market, following inspection of our plants in Jordan by an FDA team. This is a vote of confidence which will not only enable us to sell in the U.S. but also boost our sales in Jordan and the Arab world. It's the latest in a long series of marketing challenges that we've overcome.

Hikma was already selling drugs in the U.S. manufactured by its West-ward subsidiary, acquired in 1991 and run by Said, Mr. Darwazah's son. Hikma's top management team was keenly debating the appropriate strategy for the company's U.S. operations, how they should fit with Hikma's other operations in Jordan and Portugal, and how important a role they should play in the company's overall growth.

Company Background

Mr. Samih Darwazah, Hikma's founder, was born in Palestine. He came to the United States in the late 1960s on a scholarship to the St. Louis College of Pharmacology, earned a master's degree in industrial pharmacy, and joined Eli Lilly on graduation. After fourteen years in a variety of international marketing positions in Europe and the Middle East, Mr. Darwazah decided in 1977 to settle in Amman, Jordan. His

Research Associate Robin Root and Professor John A. Quelch prepared this case as the basis for class discussion rather than to illustrate either effective or ineffective handling of an administrative situation. Confidential data have been disguised.

Copyright © 1997 by the President and Fellows of Harvard College. To order copies or request permission to reproduce materials, call 1-800-545-7685 or write Harvard Business School Publishing, Boston, MA 02163. No part of this publication may be reproduced, stored in a retrieval system, used in a spreadsheet, or transmitted in any form or by any means—electronic, mechanical, photocopying, recording, or otherwise—without the permission of Harvard Business School.

objective, with the assistance of his two sons, was to create a pharmaceutical company to serve the Arab world. Mr. Darwazah explained:

> Jordan is a small country—only 4.3 million people. And a relatively poor country—with per capita income of only $1,650. Yet the multinational pharmaceutical companies were already selling here, so we had to think internationally from the outset.

First, Mr. Darwazah established a joint venture in Amman with an Italian firm. The joint venture negotiated a license from Fujisawa Pharmaceutical Corp. of Japan to manufacture in Jordan and market in the Middle East cefazolin,[1] one of the world's top-selling injectable (rather than oral) cephalosporins (cephs).[2] In addition, the company manufactured and marketed its own formulation of another common, but less technically advanced, class of penicillin-based antibiotics called amoxicillin. However, because the Jordanian market was already well-served by multinational pharmaceutical firms, Mr. Darwazah knew he had to differentiate his new firm if he was to succeed. He built credibility among local physicians, who were skeptical of the quality of locally manufactured products, by emphasizing the company's commitment to research and new product development, by inviting them on plant tours, and by stressing added-value customer services delivered by highly trained salespeople, most of whom were former pharmacists. He identified three keys to the company's success: procure additional manufacturing licenses to expand the firm's product line; develop cutting-edge generics that were more than just "me-too" products; and market these product lines in ways that would make his firm an indispensable source to physicians in the Arab world.

Production began in 1978. Over time, manufacturing licenses were obtained from Fujisawa, Chugai, and Dainippon of Japan for a range of additional drugs including anti-rheumatics, cardiovascular drugs, tranquilizers, anti-diabetics, anti-spasmodics, anti-ulcer medications, and hormones. The factory was expanded in 1984 to include a sterile area for the production of injectables. To comply with best practices and avoid cross-contamination, a separate plant was set up in 1988 for production of cephalosporins and penicillins.

During the 1980s, Hikma supplemented the production of licensed products with branded generics to leverage further its sales and distribution organization.[3] Hikma became the first Arab drug company to perform bioequivalency studies. The company expanded the dosage forms for amoxicillin. First, Hikma developed a more convenient twice-a-day (as opposed to three times a day) dosage form of amoxicillin, which resulted in higher patient compliance. Hikma also developed a chewable version of amoxicillin, previously unavailable even in the United States. As a result, Hikma enhanced its reputation as a quality company with a growing research and development capability.

Hikma gradually increased its focus on cephs. In 1985, the firm secured a second license from Fujisawa to manufacture Cefizox, another injectable ceph. Shortly thereafter, the company signed a manufacturing agreement with Smith, Kline and French Laboratories for a third injectable ceph (which needed to be administered to a patient only once a day). In return, Hikma furnished these multinationals with royalty payments on its sales.

---

[1] Lederle held the license from Fujisawa to market cefazolin in Europe.

[2] See pages 33–34 for a full description of cephalosporins.

[3] In the United States, generic imitations of off-patent drugs did not usually carry brand names. In Europe and the Middle East, they often did and were, as a result, called branded generics.

As the focus on cephs increased, Mr. Darwazah decided that Hikma should backward integrate into the production of raw materials. Although supplies of the necessary raw materials were plentiful, he wanted to tighten quality control by backward integrating and to ensure Hikma's independence from outside sources. In 1990, a sterile plant was established with an initial annual production capacity of 24 tons of bulk cephs but with expansion potential to 48 tons. Only a few plants in India could produce bulk cephs at lower cost.

By 1995, Hikma was making 40 drug products in Jordan. The top five sellers accounted for 50 percent of sales. Oral cephalosporins accounted for 30 percent of sales, drugs manufactured under license for 30 percent, and branded generics for 50 percent.[4]

International Expansion

By 1994, Hikma Investments included wholly owned manufacturing operations in Portugal and the United States as well as four plants in Jordan. Exhibit 2.1 details Hikma's sources of revenues between 1990 and 1996, while Exhibit 2.2 breaks down Hikma Jordan's sales by drug class in 1990 and 1996. In 1996, the proportion of total company profits generated by Hikma Jordan was 45 percent and its capacity utilization rate was 70 percent. The corresponding figures for Hikma Portugal were 10 percent and 30 percent, and for West-ward (the United States operation) were 30 percent and 95 percent.

Hikma employed around 500 persons in Jordan, 70 percent of them college graduates; many managerial positions were held by women. Hikma also owned Arab Medical Containers, a health care–related plastics manufacturing company which supplied Hikma and other companies with containers, tamper-resistant bottles, and other drug packaging. A manufacturing joint venture had been established in Tunisia in 1992 to produce cephs and penicillins under the Hikma name for supply to the French-speaking countries of North and West Africa. Through a second joint venture, Hikma provided technical support for the manufacture and marketing of products in Egypt, the largest pharmaceutical market in the Middle East. A third joint venture had been signed to build a $35 million plant in Saudi Arabia, completion of which was expected at the end of 1997. Hikma had marketing offices in 20 countries, including Russia, Slovakia, and China.

The pharmaceutical industry was the second most important exporter in Jordan. Hikma, as the largest pharmaceutical company in Jordan, was, therefore, one of the country's most significant exporters. In 1995, the Jordanian pharmaceutical industry produced $225 million worth of drugs, of which $120 million worth were exported. Hikma exports in 1995 accounted for $50 million of the company's $60 million in sales. In contrast to exports, Hikma sales in Jordan were only $10 million in 1995. Despite Hikma's efforts, locally made drugs accounted for only 30 percent of Jordan's consumption. In 1996, Hikma was trying to persuade the Jordanian government to approve increases in local drug prices. Margins were so low that Hikma's ability to invest in research and development was limited. Hikma was contemplating curtailing the production of certain drugs, which would leave only the more expensive imported substitutes available to the Jordanian consumer.

---

[4] Percentages do not total 100 because some of Hikma's oral cephs were made under license.

The Arab World

Mr. Darwazah's initial vision was to develop "an Arab company that serves the Arab world." In the early 1980s, he found markets for his joint venture's generic products in the Middle East and North Africa, winning government procurement contracts in Iraq, Syria, and Tunisia. The firm's growth was restricted, however, as Saudi Arabia, a key market in the region, allowed only originator manufacturers to sell their drugs in the market. Hikma was the first company to secure permission from Saudi Arabia to market generic drugs, but then faced the further obstacle that Saudi Arabia provided tax exemptions only to 100 percent Arab-owned firms. To achieve this exemption, Mr. Darwazah bought out his Italian partner in 1984, and then obtained permission from his licensors to expand distribution into Saudi Arabia, Syria, and Iraq. In 1986, Hikma, an Arabic word denoting wisdom and reason, was selected as the company's new name.

Over time, Mr. Darwazah concluded that his initial vision for Hikma was too limiting and that the company should diversify further its sales base. He commented:

> Increasingly Saudi Arabia, Syria, and other countries in the region decided to promote their own pharmaceutical industries and protect them against imports, even from an Arab neighbor. Spimaco, a $100 million Saudi pharmaceutical manufacturer, has, for example, pressured the Saudi government to protect the large domestic market for its benefit. In addition, the disruption to regional trade caused by the Gulf War in 1991 convinced us that we had to diversify further afield—though we cemented our relationships with Iraq's doctors by keeping supply lines open to them during the crisis.

In selecting countries for international expansion beyond the Middle East, Hikma's initial impulse was to explore opportunities in other Muslim markets, such as Malaysia and Indonesia, in order to gain experience that would equip the company to take on the more competitive European and U.S. markets. Senior managers soon discovered, however, that the health services in these developing countries were not yet set up to accept imported generic drugs. Moreover, the predominantly European and North American (as opposed to Asian) experience of most of Hikma's senior managers justified an earlier-than-expected shift in the company's market focus toward Europe and the United States. Nevertheless, in 1996, 90 percent of Hikma exports from Jordan were still to the Middle East and North Africa.

Expansion into Europe

Mr. Darwazah realized that the pharmaceutical industry was increasingly global, that there were no obvious reasons why generic drug manufacturers should not, like the research-based companies, sell internationally, and that Hikma could not survive merely as a regional player. The Jordanian market was becoming cluttered as Hikma's success prompted half a dozen new pharmaceutical manufacturing companies to be established by 1987. Meanwhile, discussion of European economic integration attracted Mr. Darwazah's attention. For a small pharmaceutical firm, the prospect of a single new drug registration filing in Brussels to secure access to the 330 million consumers of the European Union was especially appealing. Finally, Mr. Darwazah had been able to recruit high-caliber scientists and managers into Hikma's Jordanian operations, many of whom had European education and/or experience; their continued motivation depended in part on sustained corporate growth.

Mr. Darwazah therefore began to explore the possibilities of establishing a manufacturing plant in Europe. He focused on Ireland and Portugal, both members of the European Union with access to some 330 million consumers. The national governments of both countries along with the European Union in Brussels offered attractive investment and tax incentives to foreign companies interested in establishing high-technology manufacturing plants. Mr. Darwazah explained why Hikma settled on Portugal:

> There were three reasons. First, most of the major multinational pharmaceutical companies already had operations in Ireland. In Portugal, the pharmaceutical industry was less developed so we could offer something special by coming in. At the same time, our manufacturing processes were not that complicated so we didn't need a big pool of talented people to recruit from.
>
> Second, the population of Portugal was 12 million versus 3 million in Ireland. Sales in the domestic market could justify the plant even if we didn't export that much.
>
> Third, the multinational pharmaceutical companies were consolidating their Portuguese and Spanish operations in anticipation of the 1992 European Union market integration. This often resulted in the closure or downsizing of their Portuguese plants. As a result, there were many pharmaceutical managers and workers in the job market.

Jordanian banks that had already invested in Hikma's Jordanian operations were reluctant to loan Mr. Darwazah capital. However, the International Finance Corporation of the World Bank provided a $7 million loan commitment in 1988, and also purchased a 6 percent equity stake in Hikma Investment, which owned 100 percent of Hikma Portugal.

The plant took three years to be completed. The fully automated 4,800-square-meter plant outside Lisbon was designed to incorporate two separate operations that both met Food and Drug Administration standards:

- A filling plant for injectable cephalosporins with an annual capacity of 30 million vials.
- A liquid filling plant for other chemical entities with an annual capacity of 42 million vials and ampoules.

By 1996, Hikma Farmaceutica, the Portuguese subsidiary, was generating sales of $10 million. All but 5 percent of these sales were of cephalosporins; 80 percent of the ceph sales were of injectables, 20 percent were of oral drugs. Sixty percent of ceph production was of cephs still under patent, manufacturing of which was licensed from Fujisawa, while 40 percent was of generic cephs. Certain of the raw materials for ceph production were imported from Jordan. The non-ceph 5 percent of revenues came from sales of branded drugs including oral antibiotics and tranquilizers that Hikma manufactured under license in Jordan and for which the company was able to obtain Portuguese marketing licenses. Marketing of these drugs occupied the firm's 25 salespeople and provided cash flow while production of injectable cephs was coming on line and the relevant manufacturing approvals were being obtained from the Portuguese health authorities.

Seventy percent of Hikma Portugal's sales were exported. Of the exports, 20 percent were of generic cephs shipped to Germany, 10 percent were sent to China, and 70 percent were exported to the Middle East and North Africa. In effect, the role of the Portuguese operation was to produce injectable cephs for Hikma's worldwide marketing network.

Mr. Darwazah was concerned about Hikma Farmaceutica's marketing efforts in Europe. While contracts with private hospital chains had been obtained, it was proving difficult to sell into the government agencies that dominated drug procurement for the national health care systems of many European countries. In particular,

French manufacturers of injectable cephs defended their market shares vigorously. Another difficulty in Europe was that Brussels regulations (unlike U.S. regulations) precluded generic manufacturers from working on formulations of patented drugs until they actually came off patent. As a result, Mr. Darwazah was keenly waiting for FDA inspectors to visit the Portuguese plant in 1997 as part of the approval process that would permit Hikma to sell its generic injectable cephs in the United States. Mr. Darwazah believed U.S. demand could prompt a doubling of injectable ceph output within a year.

Entry into the United States

In the late 1980s, Mr. Darwazah conceived a three-pronged geographical production strategy in the United States as well as in Europe and the Middle East. Mr. Darwazah explained:

> There were at least four reasons why I wanted to secure a foothold in the United States. First, the United States is the largest and most competitive pharmaceutical market in the world. If you can make it there, you can make it anywhere. Second, the prospects for generic drugs gaining a larger share of prescriptions were excellent as keeping health care costs under control became an ever more pressing political issue. Third, the U.S. is a well-organized and open market; the large Asian markets are not so straightforward. Fourth, I felt our manufacturing quality was up to U.S. standards. Finally I have to admit that cracking the U.S. market was an entrepreneurial challenge and, having studied in the States, I wanted the satisfaction of succeeding in the American market.

Hikma began, in 1989, to look for an acquisition candidate in the United States. The pharmaceutical manufacturing sector in the United States was consolidating; the pressure to control health costs put many small companies under margin pressure. Cost concerns were also increasing the penetration of generics and many managed care health providers were mandating substitution of generics for their patients. Moreover, numerous drugs were scheduled to come off patent and thereby become available to generic competition. Hikma identified the West-ward company of New Jersey as one of several possible acquisition candidates and, after negotiations and due diligence, a deal was struck in June 1991.

West-ward's founders were manufacturing entrepreneurs with high quality standards. In the late 1980s, West-ward had been an approved vendor to many large hospital chains. However, the West-ward manufacturing operation had been acquired by a large drug wholesaler in 1988, and within two years, the firm's quality control standards were challenged by the FDA. West-ward's 1990 sales of $12 million were primarily of off-patent drugs sold on contract. Convinced that Hikma technicians could bring West-ward's production facilities back into compliance with FDA standards, Mr. Darwazah decided to make an offer for the company. Following the acquisition, a team of managers and technicians from Jordan worked at the West-ward plant to secure FDA recertification.

As of 1996, West-ward had 83 tablet and capsule products in its line. Forty of these were based on Abbreviated New Drug Applications (ANDAs)[5] approved by the FDA, 35 of which had been approved since the Hikma acquisition. Forty percent of West-ward sales were private label products sold to several health maintenance organizations; 40 percent were tablets and caplets sold under the West-ward branded

---

[5] Once the FDA approved an ANDA, the new drug could, de facto, be sold almost anywhere in the world except Canada, Japan, and Western Europe, which had their own approval procedures.

generic label to drug wholesalers; and 20 percent were products manufactured to the specifications of several major drug companies. Sales of $15 million in 1996 resulted in an $800,000 pretax profit. According to Said Darwazah, the West-ward operation had recovered to 80 percent of its peak performance in the 1980s.

Hikma's Strategic Focus

By 1996, it was clear that Hikma's growth had stemmed from two key judgments Mr. Darwazah had made a decade earlier: the decision to focus on cephalosporins and the decision to focus on the manufacture of added-value generics. Mr. Darwazah believed that continuation of these two strategies would enable Hikma to expand significantly its business in the United States. The proportions of Hikma sales that were cephs and generics in 1996 are shown in Table 2.A.

TABLE 2.A Hikma Sales of Cephs and Generics: 1996E

	% Cephs[a]	% Generics
Jordan (domestic)	25	50
Jordan (export)	20	50
Portugal (domestic)	50	30
Portugal (export)	100	60
United States	0	100

[a]Around 50 percent of ceph sales were of generics

Cephalosporins

Cephalosporins were a class of anti-infective drugs with similar uses to penicillins. They were deployed against a broad array of bacteria-induced infections, especially those that occurred during or as a result of surgery. Most were used in hospitals rather than for out-patient treatment. In 1995, the value of all drugs sold worldwide at the dose form level was $270 billion. Of this, anti-infectives accounted for $23 billion, of which cephs, often described as "workhorse" antibiotics, accounted for 45 percent (or $10.2 billion), penicillins for 15 percent, and quinolones for 11 percent. Cephs were the eighth most frequently prescribed category of drugs in the United States (60 million prescriptions in 1995).

Oral cephs accounted for around 70 percent of total doses taken but for only 50 percent of sales value. The best-known oral cephs were Eli Lilly's Ceclor and Ceflex with around 43 percent of the oral ceph market. Ceclor went off-patent in December 1994. Injectable cephs, accounting for 25 percent of total doses, were more effective than oral cephs and were used more heavily in hospitals to treat acutely sick patients.

By 1995, there were several generations of cephs on the market. The first- and second-generation cephs were largely off-patent, and therefore subject to competition from generics, while newer, third- and fourth-generation cephs had been developed, either to combat more virulent infections or to address more finely targeted indications. As shown in Exhibit 2.3, these cephs commanded higher margins than earlier generations. There were around 50 ceph products on the market; the cephalosporin molecule lent itself more readily than penicillin to line extensions because there were three places at which new chains could be attached. The frequency with which new versions of cephs were introduced led some physicians to refer semi-facetiously to the latest ceph discovery as the "ceph du jour."

The market share leaders in cephs were Eli Lilly (16 percent of doses worldwide in 1995), Glaxo Wellcome (15 percent), and Fujisawa (10 percent). Bristol Myers Squibb and Upjohn were developing and launching fourth-generation cephs. Fujisawa had already licensed marketing of its fourth-generation injectable ceph to Johnson & Johnson. Around one-third of cephs were sold in North America, one-third in Europe, and one-third in Asia, principally Japan.

Bulk cephs, from which doses of cephs were made, were produced and marketed by a variety of companies, including companies in India and Taiwan. In 1995, 4,700 metric tons of bulk cephs were sold at prices ranging from $400 to $6,000 per kilo.

Generic Versions of Patented Products

Mr. Darwazah recognized in the 1980s that demand for generic drugs was increasing and was likely to continue. Generic drugs, called by their basic chemical names, had the same active ingredients, strength, dosage form, and medical effects as their brand name counterparts. As patents on brand name drugs expired, there was an opportunity for lower-priced generic manufacturers to capture market share.

In most Middle Eastern countries, drug patents were recognized for 10 years (as opposed to 20 years in the United States) and slight variations in manufacturing processes permitted generic equivalents to be registered under new names. While generic versions of patented products could not be marketed in countries where the patents on the brand name drug were still in force, they could be sold in many developing countries where patent enforcement was not as tight. Hikma increasingly focused on the manufacture of generic cephs. Given the extra lead time and the opportunity to manufacture patented drugs under license, the company could perfect their production before they came off patent in the United States. Comparative cost and price structures for generic and branded injectable cephs are shown in Exhibit 2.4.

In the United States, where health care costs accounted for 15 percent of the gross national product, there was significant political pressure on the drug companies, even though pharmaceuticals represented only 7 percent of the total health care burden. Between 1985 and 1995, generics more than doubled their volume share of U.S. prescription drug sales to 43 percent, but their share of the $50 billion U.S. prescription market was only 12 percent in value terms. Sales of generics were boosted in 1991 by the so-called drug product selection law, which permitted pharmacists to substitute cheaper generics in place of brand name drugs when filling prescriptions and required that health care providers charge the government-run Medicaid and Medicare the lowest possible drug prices.[6]

Price-sensitive consumers paying health care insurance through managed care companies and health maintenance organizations fueled demand for lower-priced generics. The FDA set up a special office to handle ANDAs from generic drug manufacturers; these applications, of which 250 were approved in 1995 alone, could be filed before a brand name drug's patent expired, required bioequivalency studies, and took, on average, eighteen months to process.

Adding further to the potential for generic drug sales to increase in the United States was the fact that, between 1995 and 2005, 60 major brand name drugs, representing $40 billion in annual sales, would come off patent. Between 1995 and 2000, five major cephs were due to come off patent; as a result, Hikma was especially keen to file ANDAs for its generic equivalents, and obtain approval for them as soon as possible.

---

[6] Although generic purchases by pharmacies represented 12 percent of total prescription dollars, the same generics accounted for 30 percent of pharmacy dispensing revenues, indicating higher markups than on brand name drugs.

The large, research-based drug companies reacted to the advent of generic competition in several ways. In some cases, successful generic manufacturers were acquired. In other cases, the research-based drug companies fought generic competition, claiming that the generic differed in some key way (for example, a binding or dispersing ingredient or chemical delivery variation). A third approach was to offer special long-term pricing contracts to the large managed care organizations while a drug was still covered by patent to insulate against share erosion when it expired. A fourth approach was to sign an agreement with a generic drug manufacturer ahead of patent expiration to try to influence the pricing of both the generic and the brand name versions. Eli Lilly signed such an agreement with Mylan Pharmaceuticals on Ceclor, its leading ceph, a year before the U.S. patent expired in 1994. By 1995, Ceclor's market share had, nevertheless, dropped from 36 percent to 14 percent.

Cephalexin was, in 1995, the tenth most frequently prescribed generic drug in the United States, accounting for 2.8 percent of generic prescriptions. Amoxicillin, which Hikma also produced in a generic version, accounted for 17 percent of generic prescriptions.

Because of the size of the ceph market, there were not so many generic competitors as in some of the more heavily prescribed drug categories. However, Hikma was far from being the only small pharmaceutical company interested in producing and marketing generic cephs. Marsam of the United States and Rambaxy of India were well-known in the field. Another competitor, Lupin Laboratories of India, signed an agreement with Merck Generics in 1995 to manufacture and market a line of injectable cephs.

U.S. Growth Options

Having established a U.S. foothold by purchasing West-ward, Said Darwazah was keen to grow Hikma's sales in the United States. His ambition was to achieve $30 million in sales of West-ward manufactured drugs by 2000 with another $70 million coming from sales of cutting-edge injectable cephs made in Portugal. These drugs would not be subject to import tariffs, and transportation costs would be minimal. Hikma Portugal was not finding it easy to make sales in other European countries so capacity to supply the U.S. market was likely to be available. West-ward would continue to manufacture tablets and capsules; the plant could not be upgraded to produce injectable cephs. However, sales and distribution of these highly technical drugs from Portugal would add to West-ward's reputation and help boost sales of its branded generics.

Two large firms had approached Hikma offering quantity purchase deals on the firm's injectable cephs. The first option was to sell injectable cephs to Northaid,[7] which was the fifth largest manufacturer of ethical pharmaceuticals in the United States in 1995 and a division of a giant consumer goods company. West-ward had manufactured orally administered drugs for Northaid for several years through a joint venture in which both parties shared the profits equally. Northaid purchases accounted for 10 percent of West-ward's sales in 1995. Said Darwazah commented on Northaid's proposal:

> They have indicated an interest in buying $60 million worth of injectable cephs from us by 2000 plus $30 million worth of generic drugs manufactured by West-ward. Northaid wants a U.S. exclusive on our injectable cephs.

[7] Disguised name.

A second option was to supply Sanitas,[8] a large managed care organization that had distribution contracts to supply drugs to over 1,000 hospitals throughout the United States. Sanitas sales represented about 20 percent of 1995 hospital purchases of drugs through managed care organizations. Darwazah commented on the Sanitas opportunity:

> Sanitas have told us they can take all the injectable cephs we can supply. They say they'll need to procure $200 million worth of injectable cephs by 2000. We would have to double the capacity of our plant in Portugal to supply them at this level. Of course, they want rock-bottom prices, guaranteed delivery dates, and an exclusive on sales of our injectable cephs in the U.S. They would put the Sanitas name on the product label; West-ward would not be mentioned.
>
> Sanitas would not normally be talking to a company of our size, but we have the range and quality of injectable cephs they need. They gave West-ward a one-year contract to supply them with some generic drugs to check out our quality control and customer service. That worked well but, unlike Northaid, they really don't want West-ward's branded generics. But, like Northaid, they want to sign a deal with a supplier soon, and we're not the only game in town.

Said Darwazah was attracted by the high-volume purchase commitments these companies were prepared to make. Agreeing to one of these deals would, however, reduce Hikma's independence and practically turn it into a captive OEM supplier. Said wondered if he could develop a strong enough sales and distribution system in the United States with the necessary breadth and depth of hospital contacts to go it alone and promote the West-ward brand. Alternatively, a two- or three-year agreement with Northaid or Sanitas would give Hikma time and cash to establish its reputation in the U.S. market and then sell direct with branded generics.

---

[8] Disguised name.

EXHIBIT 2.1
Sources of Hikma
Sales ($000)[a]

	1990	1991	1992	1993	1994	1995	1996E
Jordan (domestic)	2.8	5.2	6.5	10.6	3.3	7.8	8.2
Jordan (exports)	21.9	19.5	30.8	41.2	34.2	30.9	27.9
Portugal (domestic)	—	—	0.6[b]	2.6[b]	4.9[b]	1.6	2.6
Portugal (exports)						4.6	4.1
USA (domestic)	N/A	3.5[c]	5.9	9.6	11.9	12.7	14.4

[a]Internal transfer sales have been excluded.
[b]Portugal domestic and export sales combined.
[c]United States 1991 reflects six months of sales only.

EXHIBIT 2.2
Sources of Hikma
Jordan Sales by Drug
Class: 1990 and
1996E

	Hikma Jordan	
	1990	1996E
Oral cephs	2.7	5.7
Injectable cephs	0.8	4.4[a]
Amoxicillins	4.0	1.2
Anti-inflammatories & anti-rheumatics	3.4	4.7
Cardiovasculars	2.0	1.0
Anti-diabetics	1.9	0.6
Anti-spasmodics	1.6	0.4
Anti-ulcer	1.1	0.5
Tranquilizers	0.1	0.4

[a]Around 30 percent of Hikma Jordan's injectable cephs were
exported.

EXHIBIT 2.3
Index of
Cephalosporin
Prices: 1996

Generation of Cephs	Middle East	Europe	USA
Generic:			
First	100	160	90
Second	200	250	N/A
Branded:			
First	150	200	120
Second	300	400	400
Third	500	500	600

EXHIBIT 2.4
Comparative Cost and
Price Structures for
Hikma Injectable
Cephs: 1996[a]

	Generic	Branded
Raw material cost ($ per gram)[b]	$0.50	$2.00
Vial and label	0.50	0.50
Quality control	0.20	0.20
Variable manufacturing cost	1.20	2.20
Clinical trials	—	0.20
Sales and marketing	0.10	1.00
Total cost	$1.30	$3.40
Average manufacturer selling price	1.90	5.00
Profit margin	0.60 (32%)	1.60 (32%)

[a]Prices of injectable cephs (including those produced by Hikma) varied widely depending on the sophistication of the drug. Some third-generation cephs sold for $36 or more per gram.
[b]A gram was a typical patient dosage.

3

The Aravind Eye Hospital, Madurai, India: In Service for Sight

V. Kasturi Rangan

I (the casewriter) arrived early at 7:00 A.M. at the outpatient department of the Aravind Eye Hospital at Madurai, India. My sponsor, Thulasi (R. D. Thulasiraj, hospital administrator), was expecting me at 8:00, but I came early to observe the patient flow. More than 100 people formed two lines. Two young women, assisted by a third, were briskly registering the patients at the reception counter. They asked a few key questions: "Which village do you come from?" "Where do you live?" "What's your age?" and a few more, but it all took less than two minutes per patient. The women seemed very comfortable with the computer and its data-entry procedures.

Their supervisor, a somewhat elderly man with grey hair, was hunched over, gently nudging and helping them along with the registration process. He looked up and spotted me. I was the only man in that crowd who wore western-style trousers and shoes. The rest wore the traditional South Indian garment ("dhoti" or "veshti"), and many were barefooted because they could not afford "slippers." The old man hobbled from the registration desk and made his way toward me. The 50-foot distance must have taken him 10 minutes to make because he paused every now and then to answer a question here or help a patient there. I took a step forward, introduced myself, and asked to be guided to Thulasi's office. "Yes, we were expecting you," he said with an impish smile and walked me to the right wing of the hospital where all the administrative offices were. He ushered me into his office and pointed me to the couch across

Professor V. Kasturi Rangan prepared this case as the basis for class discussion rather than to illustrate either effective or ineffective handling of an administrative situation.

Copyright © 1993 by the President and Fellows of Harvard College. To order copies or request permission to reproduce materials, call 1-800-545-7685, write Harvard Business School Publishing, Boston, MA 02163, or go to http://www.hbsp.harvard.edu. No part of this publication may be reproduced, stored in a retrieval system, used in a spreadsheet, or transmitted in any form or by any means—electronic, mechanical, photocopying, recording, or otherwise—without the permission of Harvard Business School.

from his desk. It was only when I noticed his crippled fingers that I realized this grand old man was Dr. Venkataswamy himself, the 74-year-old ophthalmic surgeon who had founded the Aravind Eye Hospital and built it from 20 beds in 1976 to one of the biggest hospitals of its kind in the world in 1992, with 1,224 beds.

Dr. V. spoke slowly and with a childlike sense of curiosity and excitement:

Tell me, can cataract surgery be marketed like hamburgers? Don't you call it social marketing or something? See, in America, McDonald's and Dunkin' Donuts and Pizza Hut have all mastered the art of mass marketing. We have to do something like that to clear the backlog of 20 million blind eyes in India. We perform only one million cataract surgeries a year. At this rate we cannot catch up. Modern communication through satellites is reaching every nook and corner of the globe. Even an old man like me from a small village in India knows of Michael Jackson and Magic Johnson. [At this point, Dr. V. knew that he had surprised me. He suppressed a smile and proceeded.]

Why can't we bring eyesight to the masses of poor people in India, Asia, Africa, and all over the world? I would like to do that in my lifetime. How do you think we should do it?

"I'm not sure," I responded, completely swept away and exhausted by the grand vision of this giant human being. But I don't think he wanted an answer that did not match his immense enthusiasm. He wanted a way to further his goal, not a real debate on whether the goal was feasible.

The Blindness Problem

As of 1992, there were 30 million blind people in the world—6 million in Africa, 20 million in Asia, 2 million in Latin America, and the rest in Europe, the former Soviet Union, Oceania, and North America.[1] The prevalence of blindness in most industrialized countries of Europe and North America varied between 0.15 percent and 0.25 percent, compared with blindness rates of nearly 1.5 percent for the developing countries in Africa, Asia, and Latin America. While age-related macular degeneration, diabetic retinopathy, and glaucoma were the dominant causes in developed countries, cataract was the major cause of blindness in the developing countries, accounting for nearly 75 percent of all cases in Asia. Of the several types of cataracts, more than 80 percent were age-related, generally occurring in people over 45 years (and increasing dramatically in the over-65 age group).

Cataract

As illustrated in Figure 3.1, the natural lens of the eye, which is normally clear, helps to focus light on the retina. The lens becomes clouded in a cataract eye and light is not easily transmitted to the retina. The clouding process takes 3 to 10 years to reach maturity and surgical removal of the clouded lens is the only proven treatment. Ophthalmic surgeons in some developing countries usually preferred to remove cataracts only when they were mature (i.e., when they significantly diminished sight).

Cataract removal was considered a fairly routine operation, usually performed under local anesthesia, with a higher than 95 percent chance of improved vision. Two

---

[1] A distance of 20 feet (or 6 meters) is used as a minimum standard in measuring the eye's ability to recognize certain sizes/profiles/shapes of objects. A less-than-normal eye would be able to recognize objects only at this minimum distance, which a normal eye could distinguish at a further distance (e.g., 40 feet or 12 meters). Such a vision, 20/40 or 6/12, would then have to be corrected with glasses. According to the World Health Organization, sight worse than 20/400 or 3/60 (even after correction with glasses) is considered blind.

FIGURE 3.1

Cross Section of a normal eye

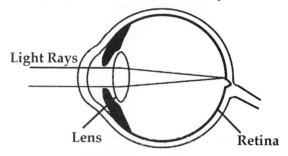

The lens focuses light on the retina.

Cross Section of a cataract eye

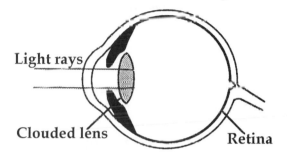

As a cataract forms, the lens becomes opaque and
light cannot easily be transmitted to the retina.

principal surgical techniques were used: intracapsular surgery without intraocular
lens (ICCE) and extracapsular surgery with intraocular lens (ECCE). ICCE remained
the most widely used procedure in the developing countries. The surgery, almost
always performed without an operating microscope, used fairly simple instruments
and could be completed in under 20 minutes. Some three to five weeks after surgery,
after the eyeball returned to its original shape, the patient was fitted with aphakic
spectacles (rather thick lenses that improved vision to an acceptable level). In contrast, the ECCE technique was always performed under an operating microscope.
This surgery often required close to 30 minutes, because the surgeon left the posterior
capsule intact when removing the natural lens, and then inserted a tiny transparent
plastic intraocular lens (IOL) in the posterior chamber. Patients often therefore did
not require corrective spectacles to restore vision. Moreover, the quality of the
restored sight was near-natural and free of distortion or magnification. Unlike ICCE
patients, ECCE patients usually experienced significant improvement in sight within
days of the operation. ICCE patients, on the other hand, usually experienced gradual
improvement over a three- to five-week period.

India

India's population of 850 million in 1991 was the second-highest in the world, after
China. Although there were nearly 20 million blind eyes in India, with another two
million being added annually, only 12 million people were classified as blind because
the rest had better than 20/200 or 6/60 vision in one eye. Cataract was the main cause

in 75 to 80 percent of the cases. The annual per-capita income of an Indian citizen was Rs. 6,800 ($275), with over 70 percent below the Rs. 2,500 ($100) poverty line; the incidence of cataract blindness, however, was fairly uniformly distributed across the various socioeconomic groups. Although India's 8,000 ophthalmologists[2] (eye doctors) performed nearly 1.2 million cataract operations a year, the medical infrastructure to clear the backlog of cataract cases was woefully inadequate in making maximal use of existing resources. The United States, for instance, had twice as many ophthalmologists for a population of only about 250 million. India had about 42,000 eye hospital beds,[3] and the medical resources and infrastructure were two-thirds skewed to the urban areas where less than one-third of the nation's population lived. The government, through its Ministry of Health and Family Welfare, took an active role in blindness prevention programs. Its 425 district hospitals (about one for every two million people) offered free eye care and cataract surgery to people who could not afford private treatment. About 30 percent of all cataract surgeries in India were performed in the government sector (both central and state), free of cost to the patients. Another 40 percent were performed in the private sector for a fee, and the remaining 30 percent were performed free of cost by volunteer groups and NGOs (nongovernment organizations). The government currently allocated about Rs. 60 million ($2 million) annually for blindness prevention programs. A recent report to the World Bank estimated that nearly $200 million (Rs. 6,000 million) would be required immediately to build the infrastructure for training personnel, purchasing equipment, and building facilities to overcome the country's blindness problem.

Dr. V. and the Aravind Eye Hospital

The eldest son of a well-to-do farmer, Dr. Govindappa Venkataswamy was born in 1918 in a small village near Madurai in South India. After his education in local schools and colleges, Dr. V. graduated with a bachelor's degree in medicine from Madras University in 1944. During his university years, and immediately thereafter, he was deeply influenced by Mahatma (meaning "great man") Gandhi, who united the country in a nonviolent movement to seek independence from British rule. Dr. V. reasoned that the best way to serve his country in the struggle for freedom would be in the capacity he was best trained for—as a doctor. So he joined the Indian Army Medical Corps in 1945, but was discharged in 1948 because of severe rheumatoid arthritis. Dr. V. recalled,

> I developed severe rheumatoid arthritis and almost all the joints were severely swollen and painful. I was bedridden in a Madras hospital for over a year. The arthritis crippled me badly and for years I could not walk long distances, which I was accustomed to doing as a village boy. In the acute stage, for several months I could not stand on my feet and I was confined to bed for over a year. I still remember the day I was able to stand on my feet. A relative of mine had come to see me in the hospital ward and I struggled hard to keep my feet on the ground and stand close to the bed without holding it. When I did, it felt as though I was on top of the Himalayas. Then, for several years, I used to struggle to walk a few yards or squat down on the floor. Even now in villages we normally squat on the

---

[2] Ophthalmologists are trained eye doctors with medical degrees. They examined patients and prescribed treatment; if the treatment involved corrective glasses, the patients could get them from an optician. Unlike in the United States, there were very few optometrists (professionals who measured eyesight and prescribed glasses) in the Indian medical system.

[3] These were located in government hospitals, medical college hospitals, mobile hospitals, eye hospitals, and private nursing homes.

floor when we eat, and I find it difficult. I could not hold a pen with my fingers to write in the acute stage of arthritis. We normally eat food with our fingers. I found it difficult to handle the food with my swollen fingers. Later I trained slowly to hold the surgeon's scalpel and cut the eye for cataract operations. After some years, I could stand for a whole day and perform 50 operations or more at a stretch. Then I learned to use the operating microscope and do good, high-quality cataract and other eye surgeries.

By the time of his retirement in 1976, Dr. V. had risen to head the Department of Ophthalmology at the Government Madurai Medical College and also to head the Department of Eye Surgery at the Government Erskine Hospital, Madurai. After retirement, in order to fulfill a long-cherished dream– the creation of a private, non-profit eye hospital that would provide quality eye care—Dr. V. founded the Aravind Eye Hospital, named after an Indian philosopher and saint, Sri Aurobindo. Dr. V. noted:

> What I learnt from Mahatma Gandhi and Swami [saint] Aurobindo was that all of us through dedication in our professional lives can serve humanity and God. Achieving a sense of spirituality or higher consciousness is a slow, gradual process. It is wrong to think that unless you are a mendicant or a martyr you can't be a spiritual person. When I go to the meditation room at the hospital every morning, I ask God that I be a better tool, a receptacle for the divine force. We can all serve humanity in our normal professional lives by being more generous and less selfish in what we do. You don't have to be a "religious" person to serve God. You serve God by serving humanity.

History

The 20-bed Aravind Eye Hospital opened in 1976 and performed all types of eye surgery, its goal was to offer quality eye care at reasonable cost. The first three surgeons were Dr. V.; his sister, Dr. G. Natchiar; and her husband, Dr. P. Namperumalswamy (Dr. Nam). A 30-bed annex was opened in 1977 to accommodate patients convalescing after surgery. It was not until 1978 that a 70-bed free hospital was opened to provide the poor with free eye care. It had a four-table operating theater with rooms for scrubbing, changing, and sterilization of instruments.

A main hospital (for paying patients), commenced in 1977 and completed in 1981, had 250 beds with 80,000 square feet of space in five floors, four major operating theaters (two tables per theater), and a minor one for septic care. There were specialty clinics in the areas of retina and vitreous diseases, cornea, glaucoma, and squint corrections, diabetic retinopathy, and pediatric ophthalmology; the heads of all but one of these clinics were family members of Dr. V., and all had received training in the United States. The Main Hospital was well-equipped with modern, often imported, equipment to provide the best possible eye care for its patients. (In 1992, there were about 240 people on the hospital's staff, including about 30 doctors, 120 nurses, 60 administrative personnel, and 30 housekeeping and maintenance workers.)

In 1984 a new 350-bed free hospital was opened. A "bed" here was equivalent to a $3' \times 6'$ mattress spread out on the floor. This five-story hospital had nearly 36,000 square feet of space and its top story accommodated the nurses' quarters for the entire Aravind group of hospitals. The hospital had two major operating theaters and a minor theater for septic cases. On the ground floor were facilities for treating outpatients; in-patients were housed in large wards on the upper floors. The Free Hospital was largely staffed with medical personnel from the Main Hospital. Doctors and nurses were posted in rotation so that they served both facilities, thereby ensuring that nonpaying and paying patients all received the same quality of eye care.

Until 1989, all the patients in the Free Hospital were attracted from eye camps. In 1990, Aravind opened its Free Hospital to walk-in patients. Every Saturday and Sunday, teams of doctors and support staff with diagnostic equipment fanned out to several rural sites to screen the local population. Eye camps were sponsored events, where a local businessman or a social service organization mobilized resources to inform the local public within about a 25- to 50-mile radius of the forthcoming screening camp. Camps were usually held in towns that served as the commercial hub for a number of neighboring villages. Local schools, colleges, or marriage halls often served as campsites. Patients from surrounding villages who traveled by bus to the central (downtown) bus stand were transported to the campsite by the sponsors. Several patients from the local area came directly to the campsite. The Aravind team screened patients at the camp, and those selected for surgery were transported the same afternoon by bus to the Free Hospital at Madurai. They were returned three days later, after surgery and recuperation, back to the campsite, where their family members picked them up. Patients who came from nearby villages were taken to the central bus stand and provided return tickets to their appropriate destinations. A clinical team from Aravind went back to the campsite after three months for a follow-up evaluation of the discharged patients. Patients were informed of the dates for the follow-up camps well in advance—in many cases, at the time of the initial discharge after surgery. Aravind provided the services of its clinical staff and free treatment for the patients selected for surgery; the camp sponsors bore all other administrative, logistical, and food costs associated with the camp. (Exhibit 3.1 shows the location of the various Aravind hospitals; Exhibits 3.2 and 3.3 show the inpatient ward at the Aravind Main Hospital and Free Hospital and some typical eye camp activities.)

As the Aravind Eye Hospital grew from a 20-bed to a 600-bed hospital, many members of Dr. V.'s family joined in support of his ideals. His brother, G. Srinivasan, a civil engineering contractor, constructed all the hospital buildings at cost and later became the hospital's finance manager. A nephew, R. D. Thulasiraj (Thulasi), gave up a management job in the private sector to join as the hospital's administrator. Thulasi, at Dr. V.'s insistence, trained at the University of Michigan in public health management before assuming administrative duties at Aravind. Thirteen ophthalmologists on the hospital's staff were related to Dr. V. In order to provide continuous training to its ophthalmic personnel, Aravind had research and training collaborations with St. Vincent's Hospital in New York City and the University of Illinois's Eye and Ear Infirmary in Chicago; both institutions also regularly sent their own ophthalmologists for residency training to Aravind. Aravind was also actively involved in training ophthalmic personnel in charge of administering blindness prevention projects in other parts of Asia and Africa. Explaining the unfailing support of his family members, Dr. V. recalled:

> We have always been a joint family through thick and thin. I was 32 when my father died. I was the eldest in the family, and in a family system like ours, I was responsible for educating my two younger brothers and two younger sisters, for organizing and fixing their marriages—that is the usual custom we have—for finding suitable partners for them. I was the head of the family and looked after all of them. But that was not a problem. I was not married, because of my arthritis trouble. Now it has become a boon. My brother takes care of me, and I stay with him all the time. His children are as much attached to me as they are to him.

Dr. Natchiar, Dr. V.'s sister and now the hospital's senior medical officer, elaborated:

> When Brother retired from government service, he seemed awfully impatient to serve society in a big way. He asked me and my husband [Dr. Nam] if we would give up our government jobs to join him. Usually in India, when one leaves government service to enter private practice, incomes go up threefold. In this case, we were told that our salaries would be about Rs. 24,000 a year (approximately $1,500 in 1980). And worse still, Brother

always believed in pushing the mind and body to its highest effort levels. So we would have to work twice as hard for half the salary. My husband and I talked it over and said yes. We did not have the heart to say no. But what we lost in earnings was made up by the tremendous professional support that Brother gave us. We were encouraged to attend conferences, publish papers, buy books, and do anything to advance our professional standing in the field. It is only in the last five years that our senior surgeons' salaries are reasonably consistent with their reputation in the field.

On his insistence that the hospital staff be totally committed and dedicated to the mission of the Aravind Hospital, Dr. V. expressed his philosophy:

> We have a lot of very capable and intelligent people, all very well trained in theoretical knowledge. But knowledge by itself is not going to save the world. Look at Christ: you cannot call him a scholar; he was a spiritual man. What we need is dedication and devotion to the practice. When doctors join us for residencies, we gradually condition them physically for long hours of concentrated work. Most believe they need work only for a few hours and that, too, for four days a week. In government hospitals, rarely do surgeons work for more than 30 hours a week; we normally expect our doctors to go 60 hours. Moreover, in the government hospitals there is a lot of bureaucracy and corruption. Patients feel obliged to tip the support staff to get even routine things done. Worse still, poor villagers feel totally intimidated. We want to make all sorts of people feel at ease, and this can only come if the clinical staff and their support staff view the entire exercise as a spiritual experience.

Aravind Eye Hospital: 1992

By 1988, in addition to the 600 beds at Madurai, a 400-bed hospital at Tirunelveli, a bustling rural town 75 miles south of Madurai, and a 100-bed hospital at Theni, a small town 50 miles west of Madurai, were also started (see Exhibit 3.1). There were plans afoot to set up a 400-bed (Rs. 10 million) hospital at Coimbatore, a city 125 miles north of Madurai. Coimbatore, like Madurai, was the hub of its district and was bigger than Madurai in population and commerce. Dr. Ravindran, a family member who currently headed the Tirunelveli Hospital, was slated to run the Coimbatore Hospital. Succession plans for the Tirunelveli Hospital would then have to be worked out. Managing the Theni Hospital, which was located in Dr. Nam's home town, was not a big problem: first, because the facility was small, and second, because of the informal supervision it received whenever Dr. Nam visited his home town. In fact, Dr. Nam had been instrumental in setting up this facility to serve his community.

In Madurai, by adding a block of 50,000 square feet to the Main Hospital and some reorganization in the Free Hospital, another 124 beds were added in 1991–94 in the Main Hospital and 50 in the Free Hospital, respectively.

By 1992, the Aravind group of hospitals had screened 3.65 million patients and performed some 335,000 cataract operations—nearly 70 percent of them free of cost for the poorest of India's blind population. (See Exhibit 3.4 for a performance summary since the hospital's inception in 1976, Exhibit 3.5 for details of its 1991 performance.) All this was achieved with very little outside aid or donations. According to Dr. V.:

> When we first started in 1976, we went around asking for donations, but we didn't have the credibility. A few friends promised to help us, but even they preferred to avoid monetary assistance. It was simple: we had to get started. So I mortgaged my house and raised enough money to start. Then one thing led to another and suddenly we were able to plan the ground floor of the Main Hospital. From the revenue generated from operations there, we built the next floor, and so on until we had a nice five-story facility. And then with the money generated there, we built the Free Hospital. Almost 90 percent of our annual budget is self-generated. The other 10 percent comes from sources around the world, such as the Royal Commonwealth Society for the Blind [U.K.] and the SEVA

Foundation [USA]. We expend all our surplus on modernizing and updating our equipment and facilities. We have enough credibility now to raise a lot of money, but we don't plan to. We have always accepted the generosity of the local business community, but, by and large, our spiritual approach has sustained us.

(See Exhibit 3.6 for a 1991–1992 statement of income and expenses and Exhibit 3.7 for a historical financial summary.)

Having grown from strength to strength, Aravind in 1991 made a bold move to set up a facility for manufacturing intraocular lenses (IOLs).

IOL Factory

IOLs, which were an integral part of ECCE surgery, cost about $30 (Rs. 800) apiece to import from the United States. At a cost of Rs. 8 million, in 1991, Aravind had therefore set up a modern IOL manufacturing facility. Called the Auro Lab, it could produce up to 60,000 IOLs a year. Currently, Auro Lab production yielded about 50 percent defect-free lenses, quality rated on par with imported lenses. Mr. Balakrishnan, a family member with extensive engineering experience and doctoral education in the United States, had returned to manage Auro Lab. Dr. V. reasoned that within a year or two, when the factory yield improved, it would be possible to bring down the manufacturing costs from approximately Rs. 200 per lens to approximately Rs. 100:

> People come for cataract surgery very late in life, because the quality of regained vision after intra-cap surgery is so-so, but not excellent. With extra-cap surgery and IOL implants, the situation is dramatically different. People would opt for surgery earlier, because they can go back to their professions and be productive right away. My aim is to offer 100 percent IOL surgeries for all our patients, paying and free. That is the better-quality solution, and we should provide it to all our patients.

Thulasi, Aravind's hospital's administrator, explained the challenges ahead (see Exhibit 3.8 for occupancy statistics):

> Yes, our expansion projects are all very exciting, but we cannot take our eye off the ball. We have to concentrate on the things that made us good in the first place. For instance, my biggest concern is the occupancy rate in the free hospital. On Monday, Tuesday, and Wednesday we are choked and overflowing with patients. Our systems have all got to work at peak efficiency to get by. But on Thursday and Friday, we suddenly have a slack. We need some continuity to keep our staff motivated and systems tuned.

Dr. Ravindran, head of the Tirunelveli hospital, concurred:

> We have some fundamental management problems to sort out. While our cash flows and margins look all right at Tirunelveli, I am unable to repay the cost-of-capital. Thank God, Madurai buys all the equipment on our behalf. We started the Tirunelveli hospital with a lot of hope and experience. Even the physical design was an improvement over our Madurai facility. We have integrated the paying and free hospitals for economies of scale. The wards and patient examination rooms in the free section are far more spacious than at Madurai. Moreover, in order to better utilize operating room capacity, we have a central surgical facility which the free and paying sections of the hospital jointly utilize. Yet, after four years, we are not yet financially self-sufficient at Tirunelveli.

Thulasi mentioned another issue:

> When we expand so fast, we have to keep in mind that we need to attract quality people. Fortunately our salary scales are now reasonable in comparison with the private sector, but we are still not there. For example, an ophthalmologist at Aravind would today, on an average, make Rs. 80,000 annually. Not bad, compared to government sector salaries of about Rs. 60,000. Of course, in private practice, some ophthalmologists can make

Rs. 300,000. But not everyone has the up-front capital to get top-notch equipment to facilitate such practice. Our nurses are paid Rs. 12,000 a year on average, which is not bad at all given that our staff is recruited and trained from scratch by us. They don't come from nursing school; we provide the training for them. It is like getting a prestigious degree and job training all in one.

A Visit to the Aravind Eye Hospital

The Main Hospital

Located one block from the Free Hospital, the Main Hospital functioned very much independently. Complicated cases from the Free Hospital were brought in when necessary for diagnosis and treatment, but by and large all patients at this hospital paid for the hospital's services. Patients came to this hospital from all over Madurai district (i.e., towns and villages surrounding the city). The cost of a normal cataract surgery (ICCE), inclusive of three to four days' post-operative recovery, was about Rs. 500 to Rs. 1,000. If the patient required an IOL implant (ECCE), the total cost of the surgery was Rs. 1,500 to Rs. 2,500. The hospital provided A, B, and C class rooms, each with somewhat different levels of privacy and facilities and appropriately different price levels.

The morning rush was usually very heavy, and by early afternoon, most people divided into two groups for a sequential series of evaluations. First, ophthalmic assistants recorded each person's vision. The patient then moved to the next room for a preliminary eye examination by an eye doctor. There were several eye doctors on duty, and ophthalmic assistants noted the preliminary diagnosis on the patient's medical record. Ophthalmic assistants then tested patients for ocular tension and tear duct function, followed by refraction tests. The final examination was always conducted by a senior medical officer. Not all patients passed through every step; for example, those referred to specialty clinics (such as retina and vitreous diseases) would directly move to the specialty section of the hospital on the first floor. Similarly, patients diagnosed as needing only corrective lenses would move to the optometry room for measurement and prescription of glasses. Those diagnosed as requiring cataract surgery would be advised in-patient admission, usually within three days. Most such patients followed up on the advice.

On the day of the surgery, the patient was usually awakened early, and after a light breakfast, was readied for surgery. On a visit to the operating theater, I noticed about 20 patients seated in the hallway, all appropriately prepared by the medical staff to enter into surgery, and another 20 in the adjacent room in the process of being readied by the nursing staff. The procedure involved cleaning and sterilizing the eye and injecting a local anesthetic. The operating theater had two active operating tables and a third bed for the patient to be prepared prior to surgery.

I (the casewriter) watched several operations performed by Dr. Natchiar. She and her assistants took no more than 15 minutes for each ECCE cataract surgery. She generously offered me the east port of the operating microscope to observe the surgical procedure. She operated from the north port, directly behind the patient's head. A resident in training from the University of Illinois occupied the west port. I had never seen a cataract surgery before, but was amazed at the dexterity of her fingers as she made the incision and gently removed the clouded lens, leaving the posterior chamber in place. Then she inserted the IOL [intraocular lens], and carefully sutured the incision. Even while she was operating, she explained to me in a methodical step-by-step fashion the seven critical things she had to do to ensure a successful operation and recovery. When she was done, she simply moved on to the adjacent operating table, where the next patient and a second supporting team were all ready to go. Meanwhile, the previous surgical team helped the patient off the operating table to walk to the recovery room and prepared the next patient, who was already waiting in the third bed for the next surgery. Dr. Natchiar had started that day at about 7:30 A.M., and when I left at about 10:30 A.M. was still going strong in a smooth, steady, uninterrupted fashion. The whole team carried on about their tasks in a well-paced, routine way. There was none of the drama I had expected to encounter in an operating theater.

In contrast, Dr. Nam was performing a retina detachment repair in the adjoining operating theater. Without looking up from his task, Dr. Nam told me that he was in the midst of a particularly difficult procedure and it would probably be another hour before he could comfortably converse. His surgical team bent over the operating table in deep concentration, reflecting the nonroutine nature of their task.

The Free Hospital

The outpatient facilities at the Free Hospital were not as organized as the Main Hospital's. There was a temporary shelter at the Free Hospital's entrance where patients waited to register. Those who came for a return visit were directed to a different line from those who came for the first time. The patient flow inside also seemed somewhat crowded. The sequence, however, remained the same: registration; vision recording; preliminary examination; testing of tension and tear duct function; refraction test; and final examination.

The people in the hallways and waiting rooms appeared significantly poorer than those I had seen at the Main Hospital. A handful of administrative assistants in blue uniforms moved around in the crowd, helping patients and guiding them along in the sequential flow. As I walked up to the operating theaters on the next floor, patients from the previous day's "eye camp" were awaiting their turn to be prepared for surgery. Some older patients, clearly tired, had spread themselves out on the floor and against the walls. There was a lot more commotion here than at the Main Hospital.

Almost all the surgeries at the Free Hospital were of the intracapsular (ICCE) type. An extracapsular (ECCE) procedure with IOL was performed only when medical reasons dictated against an intracapsular surgery.

The operating theaters also appeared more crowded and cramped. The uniforms of the supporting staff here were green, whereas they were blue at the Main Hospital, and only one of the other operating tables was equipped with an operating microscope. The patient preparation for surgery and flow was similar to that at the Main Hospital. Two surgeons operated in the same theater, and each had two operating tables and one staging bed to organize the workflow. Historically, at Aravind, a team of five surgeons and 15 nurses could operate on about 150 cases in about five hours.

Dr. Narendran, who was in the midst of a cataract operation, invited me to the operating table. The critical steps in surgery here were essentially the same as I had seen in the Main Hospital except that the intact clouded lens, along with its supporting membrane capsule, was removed here with a cryogenic device and the incision was sutured. An IOL was not inserted. These patients would be fitted with aphakic glasses three days later. Dr. Narendran had the following conversation with his patient:

Doctor: Old man, what do you do for a living?
Patient: I don't do anything. I just sit at home.
Doctor: Does your wife provide you with food?
Patient: No, my wife died long ago. My daughter-in-law takes care of me.
Doctor: Does she take good care of you?

Patient: No, but she does the best she can. Once a day she gives me "kanji" [boiled rice and salt]. That, with some water, takes care of my needs.

Doctor: What will you do after you regain your eyesight?

Patient: I will go back to tending a herd of sheep. I used to know the owner [rancher]. He used to pay me a small fee.

Doctor: What will you do with that money?

Patient: Oh, I can then buy some meat once in a while. And I can also take my granddaughter to the temple fair next year.

Unlike the Main Hospital, patients in the Free Hospital did not have "beds" in which to recuperate and recover, but rather were taken to big rooms on the upper floors and each was provided with a 3′ × 6′ bamboo/coir mat, which was spread out on the floor as a bed, and a small-sized pillow. There were several such rooms, each accommodating 20 to 30 patients. Each room had self-contained bathroom facilities. People from the same or nearby villages were usually accommodated in the same room. They moved together as a cohort, both before and after surgery. The post-operative recovery period was usually three days, when the bandage was removed, patients' eyes checked and, if all was well, aphakic glasses fitted. Patients were advised to come back in three months for follow-up evaluation.

At the Free Hospital, detailed records were kept of all post-operative complications (see Exhibit 3.9) Some complications, such as iritis, were considered minor and easily treatable, while others required extra care and additional hospital stay. Such complications were directly traced to the operating team, even to the level of the individual surgeon. Senior medical officers reviewed the data with the individuals concerned and offered coaching and advice to rectify operating techniques, if necessary.

At the records room in the Free Hospital, I pulled out six patient records at random to get a sense of the improvement in sight after surgery. A summary is provided below.

	Preoperative Sight Recording	Post-Operative Sight Recording
Patient 1	No vision; can register hand movements	6/12 [20/40]
Patient 2	No vision; can register hand movements	6/12 [20/40]
Patient 3	No vision; cannot register hand movements; can perceive light	6/36 [20/120]
Patient 4	No vision; can register hand movements	6/06 [20/20]
Patient 5	No vision; can register hand movements	6/18 [20/60]
Patient 6	6/60 [20/200]	6/12 [20/40]

The Eye Camp

I visited a typical eye camp, at Dindigul, a semi-urban town about 100 miles east of Madurai. These screening camps were almost always conducted with the help of local community support, with either a local business enterprise or a social service organization taking the lead role in organizing them.

The local sponsors provided information regarding the eye camp to all the neighboring communities (about a 25-mile radius). Public announcements in marketplaces, newspaper advertisements, information pamphlets, and other publicity material were prepared and distributed one to three weeks in advance of the camp. The camp was usually promoted under the sponsor's name, with the Aravind service playing only a supporting role. The sponsor not only paid all the publicity costs but also the direct costs associated with organizing the camp—patient transportation, food, and aphakic glasses. In addition, the sponsors also paid for the costs of transporting, feeding, and bringing back the patients selected for surgery. This portion was estimated at Rs. 200 per patient. Aravind bore the costs of surgery and medicines.

The camp at Dindigul was sponsored by a local textile mill owner. There were three other Aravind-associated camps in other parts of the Tamil-Nadu state that day. One was sponsored by a religious charity (Sathya Sai Baba Devotee's Association), one by a popular movie actor fan club (Rajni Kanth Appreciation Club), and the third by the Lions Club. According to Dr. V.:

> The concept of eye camp is not new. As the head of the government hospital, I used to go out with a team of doctors and support staff several times a year to screen patients in their own villages. Many of my colleagues in other parts of India also use this idea as part of their outreach programs. We were somewhat fortunate in the sense that we invested in the infrastructure, such as the vans and the equipment, and committed doctors to support the demand we got from philanthropic individuals and organizations.

In the formative years of Aravind, patients attending the screening camps were examined and those needing surgery were appropriately advised. Even though surgery was free, the patients had to come to Aravind at their own expense. The response rate was less than 15 percent. Concerned by the low turnout, a research team from Aravind conducted in-depth home interviews with a randomly selected group of 65 patients for whom surgery was recommended but who didn't respond for over six months. The study revealed the following constraints:

- Still have vision, however diminished   26%
- Cannot afford food and transportation   25
- Cannot leave family   13
- Fear of surgery   11
- No one to accompany   10
- Family opposition   5
- Others   10

As a consequence, Aravind requested and the camp sponsors readily agreed to bear the costs of food, transportation, and, in many cases, the cost of aphakic glasses to be worn by the patient after surgery. In order to reduce the fear of surgery, as well as to encourage a support group, patients were transported to Madurai as a group by buses. Patients were asked to bring a small travel bag in case it was necessary to go to Madurai. The sequence of screening steps matched those at the base hospitals:

1. Registration
2. Vision recording
3. Preliminary examination
4. Testing of tension and tear duct function
5. Refraction
6. Final examination by a senior medical officer
7. Optical shop (for those that needed it)

In addition, those selected for surgery had to undergo tests for blood pressure and urine sugar and, if qualified, their surgery papers were prepared on the campsite. In addition, Aravind camp organizers, as well as local community elders, explained and reassured the patients regarding the importance of the surgery and the other logistics involved. Bus trips were so organized that individuals from the same or nearby villages were always clustered in the same bus trip, which reduced the need for anyone to accompany the patients. They were all returned together after three or four days. This established a support group during their recovery phase. A team from Aravind returned for follow-up after three months.

The Dindigul camp was very well run. Soundararaja Mills (the sponsors) had organized bus shuttles from the central town bus stand to transport passengers to the campsite. About 1,000 people came from villages within a 25-mile radius of the town. The mill owner had sought the cooperation of a local college, of which he was a trustee and a significant donor, for providing the physical facilities. At the campsite, the college principal was actively supervising the arrangements. He brought me a chart of the historical performance of the Soundararaja camp for the last five years. Many volunteer students were helping the Aravind staff organize the patient flow. The mill owner's son, also its finance manager, walked around the camp constantly inquiring about the arrangements. There was a sense of festivity in the air, as recorded "nadaswaram"[4] music was being played over the public address system. A packed lunch was provided for those selected for surgery, and refreshments and a sit-in lunch for all the doctors and support staff participating in the camp. One of the school-teachers who had organized the marketing of the camp explained:

> My students simply worked flat out in the last one week. Soundararaja Mills provided us transportation to cover over 1,000 driving miles. Our "propaganda" was effected through handbills, wall posters, and traveling megaphone announcements. Last Thursday night, they were mounting publicity posters on every public bus. We could not do it earlier because buses in this town are all scrubbed and cleaned every Wednesday night.

The camp had commenced on a Sunday morning at 8:00 A.M., and when I left at about 2:00 P.M., about 800 people had been screened and nearly 150 selected for surgery. The first group of patients were ready to leave for Madurai. Dr. Nam and his team were working away at a steady pace. He explained to me that nearly two-thirds of the work was done, but the turnout was a little lower than expected, because just two months prior to this camp, another organization had conducted an eye camp in the same area. (Exhibit 3.10 provides a history of Aravind's "eye camp" performance. Exhibit 3.11 provides further detail by type of sponsor for the 1991 eye camps.)

In the past, Aravind had also conducted several surgical camps. That is, patients identified as needing surgery would be provided the requisite treatment on-site. Recently, however, there was a conscious effort to move away from surgery camps because of the higher cost as well as lower quality of service they provided. For example, the makeshift operating theaters were not air-conditioned, cleanliness and hygiene were often not up to hospital standards, patient amenities were inferior, and post-operative complications were difficult to monitor.

The Aravind organization included a 10-person team of camp organizers. These individuals reported to Meenakshisunadaram (Sundar), the camp manager. Camp organizers were responsible for working closely with the camp sponsors, helping and guiding them with directions for mounting publicity, organizing the logistics, and arranging physical facilities for the eye camp. In addition to working closely with the sponsors who needed help, camp organizers also guided new sponsors who approached Aravind for their expertise and help in bringing eye-care to certain targeted communities. Camp organizers were aligned by district as shown in the territory map (Exhibit 3.12) and traveled extensively within their assigned territories. They all met at Aravind's headquarters at Madurai once a week under the chairmanship of

---

[4] Nadaswaram, a wind instrument much like a clarinet, was often played at auspicious occasions such as weddings in South India.

Dr. V. At one such meeting which I attended, Dr. V. went around the table from person to person asking for territory plans and every once in a while urged a camp organizer, "Why was the camp yield so poor in your territory? We could get only 14 surgery cases from a catchment population of nearly 100,000! Something is not right. Brother, find out what is going on! Work with the sponsor to improve propaganda." (See Exhibit 3.13 for districtwide camp particulars.)

According to Sundar, the camp manager:

> We really don't have to sell the idea of an eye camp to anyone. There are far more individuals, businesses, and social organizations that need our services than what we can effectively offer. The prestige and goodwill that our sponsors earn, in their communities, far outweighs the financial burden. What they really need help on is how to organize the camp, how to create propaganda, and how to organize the logistics. That is where we are trying to put together a consistent set of procedures and a common set of principles.

Conclusion

I asked Dr. V. what his biggest challenge for the next three years was. His reply:

> My goal is to spread the Aravind model to every nook and corner of India, Asia, Africa; wherever there is blindness, we want to offer hope. Tell me, what is this concept of franchising? Can't we do what McDonald's and Burger King have done in the United States?

EXHIBIT 3.1
Aravind Eye Hospital
Locations

The four Aravind locations are shown in italics.

EXHIBIT 3.2 **The Aravind Hospitals**

(a) A private room in the main hospital.

(b) In-patient ward at the Free Hospital.

EXHIBIT 3.3 **Eye Camp Activities**
From top, clockwise: (a) Patients arriving by bus to the campsite. (b) Patients registering at the campsite. (c) Testing and preparing patients selected for surgery.

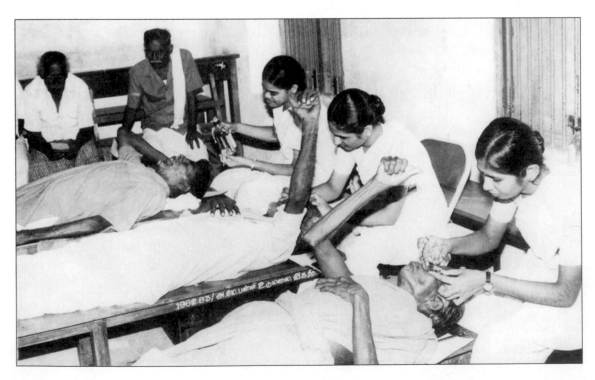

EXHIBIT 3.4
Historical Patient Statistics (Consolidated)

Source: Aravind Eye Hospital.

	Paying		Free and Camp[a]	
Year	**Outpatient Visits**	**Surgery**	**Outpatient Visits**	**Surgery**
1976	—	248	—	—
1977	15,381	980	2,366	—
1978	15,781	1,320	18,251	1,045
1979	19,687	1,612	47,351	2,430
1980	31,334	2,511	65,344	5,427
1981	39,470	3,139	75,727	8,172
1982	46,435	4,216	79,367	8,747
1983	56,540	4,889	101,469	11,220
1984	69,419	5,796	103,177	11,954
1985	89,441	7,194	153,037	17,586
1986	111,546	8,202	164,977	19,623
1987	121,828	9,971	180,181	21,562
1988	182,274	12,702	232,838	23,635
1989	203,907	15,103	290,859	25,867
1990	227,243	17,896	338,407	31,162
1991	241,643	19,511	327,692	31,979
Total	1,471,929	115,290	2,184,043	220,409

[a]The 1990 and 1991 outpatient visits data include camp patients as well as walk-in patients. See Exhibit 3.11 for camp details.

EXHIBIT 3.5
Patient Statistics: 1991

Source: Aravind Eye Hospital.

		Madurai	Tirunelveli	Theni	Total
Outpatient visits	— Paying	167,884	50,802	22,957	241,643
	— Free	212,809	91,482	23,401	327,692
Surgery	— Paying	16,447	2,572	492	19,511
	— Free	23,110	7,339	1,530	31,979
Hospital outpatient visits		263,518	84,360	30,457	378,335
Eye camp outpatient visits		117,175	57,924	15,901	191,000
Total outpatient visits		380,693	142,284	46,358	569,335
Screening camps		331	293	83	707
Surgery Details:					
Cataract and other lens removal procedures (without IOL)		23,321	6,618	1,535	31,474
Intraocular lens (IOL)		7,846	1,466	227	9,539
Trabeculectomy		359	80	13	452
Retinal detachment		401	1	—	402
Vitreous surgery		331	—	—	331
Membranectomy		61	2	—	63
Squint correction		262	—	—	262
Keratoplasty and therapeutic grafting		65	—	—	65
Ptosis		27	—	—	27
DCR, DCT, and other septic operations		1,347	669	158	2,174
Pterygium		297	181	14	492
Laser and xenon photocoagulation		1,467	—	—	1,467
Nd Yag iridotomy		787	133	—	920
Nd Yag capsulotomy		806	201	—	1,007
Argon laser trabeculoplasty		43	—	—	43
Other surgical procedures		2,137	560	75	2,772
Total surgery		39,557	9,911	2,022	51,490

EXHIBIT 3.6
Income and Expenditures for 1991–1992 (Rupees)

Source: Aravind Eye Hospital.

	Cumulative Total	Percentage
Revenue:		
1. Medical services	3,380,985.00	9.57%
2. Operation charges	23,235,389.00	65.77
3. Treatment charges	2,225,609.25	6.30
4. Consulting fees	3,424,728.35	9.69
5. Laboratory charges	857,265.49	2.43
6. X-ray charges	206,890.00	0.59
7. Donations	771,474.80	2.18
8. Interest	1,062,889.50	3.01
9. Miscellaneous, course and others	129,666.65	0.37
10. Sale of ophthalmology books	33,835.00	0.10
Total revenue	35,328,733.04	100.00%
Operating Expenses:		
1. Medicine and cotton	1,307,968.00	3.70%
2. Hospital linen	148,848.30	0.42
3. Library and subscription	66,519.40	0.19
4. Building maintenance	1,117,550.04	3.16
5. Electricity charges	1,667,964.01	4.72
6. Installation and equipment maintenance	774,129.46	2.19
7. Electric items and bulbs	196,195.55	0.56
8. Printing and stationery	564,841.48	1.60
9. Postage and telephone charges	447,750.30	1.27
10. Building rent	7,980.00	0.02
11. Cleaning and sanitation	356,515.70	1.01
12. Stipends and staff salaries	4,285,017.70	12.13
13. Employer's PF contribution	190,208.50	0.54
14. Bank commission	9,748.08	0.03
15. Traveling expenses	758,876.91	2.15
16. Miscellaneous expenses	236,508.18	0.67
17. Photography	181,316.90	0.51
18. Resident doctors' hostel expenses	54,338.10	0.15
19. Camp expenses	1,347,457.90	3.81
20. Vehicle maintenance	459,361.43	1.30
21. IOL	2,926,520.00	8.28
Expenditure total	17,105,615.94	48.41%
Costs Offset by:		
1. W.H.O., Ford Foundation, and Jain Hospital	96,246.00	
Actual expenditure total	17,009,369.94	
Percentage		48.41%
Net Surplus	18,319,363.10	51.59%

EXHIBIT 3.7
Historical Financial Summary (Rupees)

Source: Aravind Eye Hospital.

Year	Income	Expenditure	Percentage of Expenditure Over Income
1979–1980	933,306.62	131,641.80	14.10
1980–1981	979,991.18	242,968.70	24.80
1981–1982	2,936,440.45	1,385,642.50	47.20
1982–1983	3,546,240.27	2,142,939.20	60.36
1983–1984	4,334,257.49	2,688,550.23	62.03
1984–1985	5,971,711.49	3,526,423.49	59.05
1985–1986	6,614,342.74	5,018,583.94	75.87
1986–1987	9,325,540.79	5,349,419.00	57.36
1987–1988	12,694,531.22	9,268,150.96	73.00
1988–1989	17,840,116.84	10,987,700.44	61.58
1989 1990	21,054,621.30	12,669,999.79	60.18
1990–1991	29,320,202.61	15,837,644.93	54.02

Note. One U.S. dollar was convertible to Rs. 12–Rs. 15 during 1979 to 1984; Rs. 18 Rs. 20 during 1985 to 1989; and Rs. 25–Rs. 28 during 1990 and 1991.

EXHIBIT 3.8
January–July 1992 Performance Summary

| | Paying | | | | Free | | | | | | | | | Grand |
| | Madurai | Tirunelveli | Theni | Total | Madurai | | Tirunelveli | | Theni | | Total | | Total |
					Direct	Camp	Direct	Camp	Direct	Camp	Direct	Camp	
Outpatients:													
New cases	50,498	14,710	5,669	70,877	30,662	65,669	8,900	30,863	3,662	7,312	43,224	103,844	217,945
Review cases	57,428	16,831	4,196	78,455	28,912	0	11,215	0	2,797	0	42,924	0	121,379
Total patients	107,926	31,541	9,865	149,332	59,574	65,669	20,115	30,863	6,459	7,312	86,148	103,844	339,324
Cataract operations	7,382	1,211	228	8,821	5,192	8,290	1,195	2,739	402	551	6,726	11,580	27,127
Other major surgery	905	55	1	961	278	15	23	9	0	0	301	24	1,286
Other minor surgery	3,171	761	75	4,007	1,236	319	378	318	83	30	1,697	667	6,371
Total surgery	11,458	2,027	304	13,789	6,706	8,624	1,596	3,066	485	581	8,724	12,271	34,784
Bed capacity	324	200	40	564	400		200		60		660		1,224
Beds occupied per day (six-month average)	265	51	10	326	167	229	62	92	14	14	243	335	903

Source: Aravind Eye Hospital.

EXHIBIT 3.9
Free Section Compli-
cation Details for the
Patients Operated on
in the Month of
October 1992

Source: Aravind Eye
Hospital.

Complications	Preoperative		Post-Operative		Total	
	Number	Percent	Number	Percent	Number	Percent
A/C shallow	0	0.0	39	2.7	39	2.7
Accidental extra	2	0.1	0	0.0	2	0.1
Blood clot	1	0.0	113	7.8	114	7.9
Cornea edema	0	0.0	55	3.8	55	3.8
Cortex	2	0.1	36	2.4	38	2.6
Endophthalmitis	0	0.0	1	0.0	1	0.0
Exudate in pupil area	0	0.0	8	0.5	8	0.5
Flap turn	0	0.0	6	0.4	6	0.4
Hyphema	2	0.1	34	2.3	36	2.4
Hypopyon	0	0.0	10	0.6	10	0.6
Hypotony	0	0.0	1	0.0	1	0.0
Iridodialysis	1	0.0	1	0.0	2	0.1
Iris prolapse	0	0.0	1	0.0	1	0.0
Iritis	0	0.0	226	15.6	226	15.6
P.A.S.	1	0.0	0	0.0	1	0.0
Posterior synechiae	1	0.0	0	0.0	1	0.0
Pupillary block (air in PC)	0	0.0	2	0.1	2	0.1
S.K. (straight keratitis)	0	0.0	55	3.8	55	3.8
Vitreous bulge	0	0.0	1	0.0	1	0.0
Vitreous disturbance	5	0.3	0	0.0	5	0.3
Vitreous loss	2	0.1	0	0.0	2	0.1
Wound leak	0	0.0	1	0.0	1	0.0

EXHIBIT 3.10
Eye Camp
Performance

Year	Screening Camps	Operating Camps	Outpatients Seen	Operations
1978	118	—	18,251	1,045
1979	215	—	47,351	2,430
1980	198	10	65,344	5,427
1981	140	13	75,727	8,172
1982	205	9	79,367	8,747
1983	204	9	101,469	10,975
1984	247	21	103,177	11,796
1985	475	18	153,037	17,586
1986	516	13	164,977	19,623
1987	506	12	180,181	21,562
1988	536	9	232,838	23,635
1989	818	2	290,859	25,867
1990	884	3	203,805	20,852
1991	707	3	191,000	20,818
	5,769	122	1,907,383	198,535

EXHIBIT 3.11
1991 Eye Camps[a]

Source: Aravind Eye
Hospital.

Name or Organization	Number of Camps	Total Outpatients	Surgery		
			Cataract	Others	Total
Lions Clubs	105	42,439	5,071	139	5,210
Rotary Clubs	42	17,629	1,941	69	2,010
Vivekananda Kendra	190	30,899	2,657	240	2,897
Bhagavan Sri Sathya Sai Seva Organization	20	7,114	1,472	47	1,519
Jaycees	18	3,823	309	10	319
Banks	27	4,854	371	18	389
Mills and factories	28	10,543	966	53	1,019
ASSEFA	6	900	104	5	109
Schools and colleges	50	8,577	475	17	492
Hospitals	12	4,291	974	57	1,031
Trusts	16	6,329	1,224	34	1,258
Youth and fan associations	37	6,291	365	27	392
Other religious organizations	41	12,696	1,315	47	1,362
Other voluntary service organizations	75	23,356	1,913	68	1,981
Others	40	11,259	791	39	830
Total	707	191,000	19,948	870	20,818

[a]These statistics include the work of all three hospitals. For example, in 1991, the breakdown by hospital was as follows:

	Total Camps	Outpatients	Operations
Madurai	331	117,175	14,951
Tirunelveli	293	57,924	4,922
Theni	83	15,901	945
Total	707	191,000	20,818

EXHIBIT 3.12
Camp Organizer
Territories

Source: Aravind Eye
Hospital.

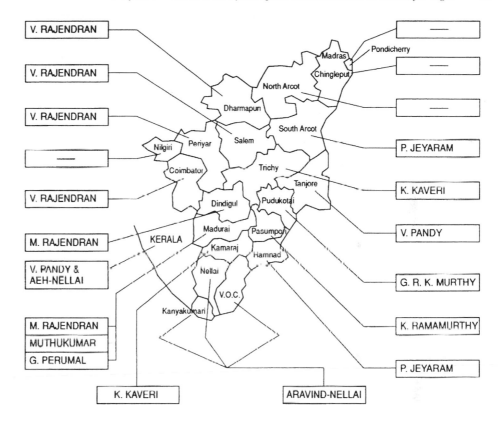

EXHIBIT 3.13
Districtwise Camp
Particulars—1991

Source: Aravind Eye
Hospital.

District	Population (millions)	Number of Camps	Number of Cases Screened	Number Advised Surgery	Number Accepting Surgery
1. Madras City	3.795	—	—	—	—
2. Chingleput	4.621	—	—	—	—
3. North Arcot	3.000	—	—	—	—
4. South Arcot	4.871	4	4,491	1,058	1,009
5. Dharmapuri	2.396	5	4,495	657	609
6. Salem	3.914	17	14,026	3,333	3,179
7. Periyar	2.323	21	12,760	2,145	2,064
8. Nilgiris	0.705	2	465	22	19
9. Coimbatore	3.531	19	11,836	2,114	2,002
10. Trichy	4.114	12	7,029	654	592
11. Tanjore	4.527	23	9,264	1,208	1,095
12. Pudukottai	1.322	12	2,432	231	201
13. Madurai	3.448	119	19,992	1,693	1,184
14. Dindigul	1.769	45	9,399	991	828
15. Pasumpon	1.075	32	5,514	583	427
16. Kamaraj	1.554	44	8,800	1,185	1,004
17. Ramnad	1.136	46	6,402	769	647
18. Nellai	2.493	123	18,031	2,680	1,795
19. Kanyakumari	1.591	60	8,994	796	529
20. VOC	1.156	75	11,066	1,678	1,174
21. Pondicherry	0.500	4	2,893	288	258
22. Kerala state[a]	12.000	44	33,111	2,912	2,202
Total		707	191,000	24,997	20,818

[a]The first 21 districts listed in the above exhibit are part of the Tamil-Nadu state. Kerala is a neighboring state. Statistics for Kerala have been aggregated for its 10 districts.

Developing New Products

Part

2

4. Abgenix and the XenoMouse

5. CardioThoracic Systems

6. Innovation at 3M Corporation (A)

Chapter 4

Abgenix and the XenoMouse

Robert Dolan

Meet XenoMouse

"Meet XenoMouse™" headlined the piece from the Abgenix information kit. (See Exhibit 4.1.) If ever there was a mouse worth meeting, XenoMouse was probably it. While Lee Majors played bionic man Steve Austin in the popular *Six Million Dollar Man* television series in the 1970s, XenoMouse could well be termed the "Three Billion Dollar Mouse." XenoMouse lived at Abgenix in Fremont, California, just across the Dunbarton Bridge from Silicon Valley's famed Highway 101. While no product based on the genetically engineered XenoMouse had yet reached the market, he was the source of the company's near $3 billion market capitalization of March 31, 2000.

The product of a seven-year, $40 million research and development effort, XenoMouse was a unique strain of transgenic mice capable of producing antibodies potentially useful in the treatment of human disorders including cancer, transplant rejection, and inflammation. The idea of using mice to produce antibodies for treating human diseases dated back to the 1970s; but only recently had therapies based on this approach passed the rigorous safety and efficacy tests necessary for regulatory approval. Many industry observers were now predicting an "antibody wave" as genomics research identified thousands more possible disease targets for antibody therapy. And the new generation of technologies for generating antibodies from mice, including XenoMouse, was capable of producing therapies which were believed to be

Professor Robert Dolan prepared this case as the basis for class discussion rather than to illustrate either effective or ineffective handling of an administrative situation. Certain data have been disguised.

Copyright © 2001 by the President and Fellows of Harvard College. To order copies or request permission to reproduce materials, call 1-800-545-7685, write Harvard Business School Publishing, Boston, MA 02163, or go to http://www.hbsp.harvard.edu. No part of this publication may be reproduced, stored in a retrieval system, used in a spreadsheet, or transmitted in any form or by any means—electronic, mechanical, photocopying, recording, or otherwise—without the permission of Harvard Business School.

more effective and well tolerated by humans. Major pharmaceutical and biotech companies had licensed access to XenoMouse.

In April 2000, R. Scott Greer, President and Chief Executive Officer of Abgenix, described the company as "well positioned to ride the antibody wave" due to a strong financial position from a recently completed series of private placements and follow-on public offerings of stock, raising over $600 million. (See Exhibit 4.2 for a balance sheet as of March 31, 2000, and income statements for years 1998 and 1999.)

Abgenix generated revenues in two ways. First, it licensed XenoMouse technology to numerous corporate collaborators including leading pharmaceutical and biotechnology companies. (See Exhibit 4.1 for list.) A collaborating company typically identified a specific disease target it was trying to "hit" with an antibody. Abgenix then sold exclusive access rights to using XenoMouse to develop antibodies for that specific target only. A collaborator paid an upfront fee and agreed to payments as the drug development program reached certain milestones and a royalty on sales should the drug be commercialized. A typical arrangement had total fees before commercialization ranging from $7 to $10 million. Royalty rates ran from 4 to 6 percent.

The Food and Drug Administration (FDA) prescribed and oversaw the drug testing and development process. Before testing in humans was permitted, "Preclinical Trials" had to show sufficient evidence of safety and desired biological activity to gain FDA approval of an "Investigational New Drug Application" (IND). Testing then proceeded through three phases with humans. Phase I focused on safety, Phase II on effectiveness against designated diseases, and Phase III was large-scale testing with the doses to be prescribed when the product was sold commercially. Drug development was a risky business. The vast majority of drugs initially tested fail to gain FDA approval.

The second way Abgenix hoped to generate revenues was by pursuing the early stages of XenoMouse-based drug development, meeting with some success, and then selling off the rights to develop and market the drug. As shown in Figure 4.1, Abgenix had four XenoMouse-generated drugs in various stages of the FDA process on March 31, 2000. ABX-CBL was in Phase III clinicals and ABX-IL8, targeted at inflammatory disorders such as psoriasis and arthritis, was in initial human effectiveness studies. ABX-EGF, targeted at various cancers, had shown outstanding effectiveness in preclinical studies on mice and was in initial small-scale safety testing with humans. ABX-RB2, for organ transplant rejection, was not yet tested with humans. In each case, as the figure from an investor presentation shows, Abgenix described the program as "worldwide rights available."

By selling the rights to a firm with a marketing capability in place, Abgenix avoided the many costs of bringing a drug to market—not the least of which was developing a field sales force. Abgenix would participate in the upside potential by keeping with industry practice of structuring a deal involving its receiving royalty payments as a percentage of sales. While substantive discussions were in process with a number of firms on the developmental programs, no "sales" of programs had yet been made. The "sales cycle" for such a "product" was typically long as the buying company had to understand fully the test results so far and assess future prospects—all in an environment characterized by Ray Withy, Abgenix Chief Business Officer, as having "some element of unresolvable uncertainty." From its side, Abgenix had to scrutinize the "buyer" since the buyer's degree of success would ultimately determine Abgenix's financial returns given the significance of the royalty rate on the sales price of any deal.

Seventeen partners' programs moving ahead, many new technology licensing collaborations in the negotiation phase, and four promising proprietary development programs had made XenoMouse "The $3 Billion Mouse" in the eyes of the stock market. Greer faced key challenges: (i) pick the right partners for collaboration, (ii) continue

FIGURE 4.1 **Development Programs**

Source: Company records.

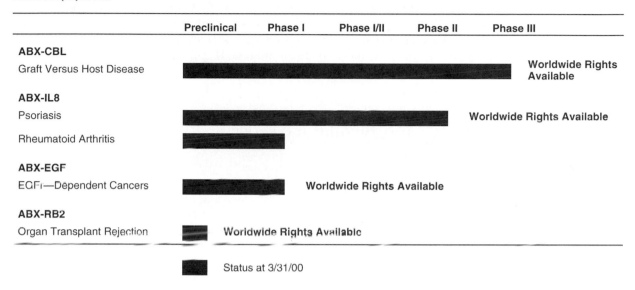

	Preclinical	Phase I	Phase I/II	Phase II	Phase III

ABX-CBL
Graft Versus Host Disease — Worldwide Rights Available

ABX-IL8
Psoriasis — Worldwide Rights Available

Rheumatoid Arthritis

ABX-EGF
EGFr—Dependent Cancers — Worldwide Rights Available

ABX-RB2
Organ Transplant Rejection — Worldwide Rights Available

Status at 3/31/00

to develop Abgenix skills and capabilities for the long term, and (iii) properly balance risk and potential reward in negotiated deals. This was made all the more challenging given the "unresolvable uncertainty" inherent in the biotechnology business— as both his knowledge of industry history and his chief business officer often reminded him.

ABX-EGF Decisions

While two programs were further along in human testing, the ABX-EGF program, targeting various cancers, was perhaps the biggest decision management faced in April 2000. In preclinical trials, ABX-EGF had eradicated preformed human cancer tumors injected into and growing in *all* test mice. As such, the "worldwide rights available" designation on the program had attracted a number of potential partners willing to negotiate an up-front fee plus milestone payments triggered by events along the development path, followed by a percentage royalty on sales. In particular, Pharmacol, a large pharmaceutical company with whom Abgenix had no current relationship, seemed a good potential partner. It had the skills Abgenix deemed necessary for guiding the product through human trials, managing the regulatory process, and effectively bringing the product to market. It was also clear that Pharmacol understood the extraordinary opportunity and market potential for ABX-EGF if all worked out in the development process. Pharmacol's understanding of the potential upside meant that it would agree to a royalty rate that was "high" by industry standards.

Biopart, a biotechnology firm with a focus on oncology, was a different opportunity. In spirit, this would be a 50/50 partnership. Instead of handing off to Biopart for a fee-plus-royalty, Abgenix and Biopart would run hand-in-hand sharing costs and profits incurred over time. Biopart was willing to make some payments initially to Abgenix in light of what it and XenoMouse would bring to the partnership.

Conceptually, a third option was to "go it alone," developing the in-house skill to carry the product through FDA approval and marketing. Greer, however, did not think this a viable proposition for Abgenix, especially in light of his statements to the investment community about not incurring these costs and thus becoming profitable quickly.

Greer would have to choose between doing a Pharmacol "hand-off" deal or Biopart "hand-in" deal now or he could simply wait a while. ABX-EGF had just recently even started Phase I trials, so it was early, by industry standards, to sell off the rights. Abgenix could continue on to Phase II and see how that went before making a deal.

Biotechnology Industry and Regulatory Process

The two leading biotechnology companies in 1999 were Genentech and Amgen. Biotechnology was distinguished from conventional pharmaceutical approaches by focus on producing therapeutics based on molecules present in the human body. In 1982, Genentech's work with a process known as "recombinant DNA technology" produced human insulin. It licensed the marketing rights to Eli Lilly. Three years later, Genentech became the first "FIBCO" (fully integrated biotechnology company) not only developing but also marketing and selling Protropin, a growth hormone for children. Amgen used recombinant DNA technology to develop two blockbuster drugs stimulating blood cell growth. Epogen and Neupogen generated $3 billion in sales for Amgen in 1999 and funded the year's $823 million R&D spending.

While both Genentech and Amgen were FIBCOs, capable of bringing their own products to market, each also had an extensive set of collaborations. Amgen described its model as "creation through collaboration," explaining: "From the beginning, corporate collaborations have been viewed as the path to accelerate transformation of Amgen into an independent commercial enterprise by accessing research and markets in areas where Amgen alone could not invest sufficient resources." (Amgen website: www.amgen.com) The collaborations were driven by the high cost and low likelihood of success for drug development programs. The "odds" were often described as follows: Of every 1,000 compounds tested in the lab, only one made it to human testing. Only 20 percent of those tested in humans received FDA approval. Thus, it took 5,000 lab-tested therapies to yield one marketed product.

The process was also very costly. When testing was complete, all the scientific data related to the drug including lab tests, animal testing, human testing, and manufacturing process specification were collected and filed in a "New Drug Application" to the FDA. These data were also pivotal in gaining international acceptance. A typical New Drug Application is a volume of over 1,000 pages.

Once a product has been approved and marketed, the company still files reports with the FDA documenting side-effect incidence. In several notable cases, the FDA forced withdrawal of a previously approved drug from the market.

Antibodies

Antibody production was the second major technology besides recombinant DNA in the biotechnology field. An antibody is a protein developed by the immune system. When a foreign substance (an antigen) enters the body, the immune system produces an antibody to fight that antigen. The antibody binds to the antigen, neutralizing it and preventing it from reacting with normal cells. The antibody production capability of a human is limited, however. First, even when "normal," it cannot generate antibodies to its own tissues that are multiplying out of control—as is the case with cancer. Second, an individual's immune system may become deficient.

In either case, an antibody produced in a different species, such as a mouse or monkey, could prove useful. The antibody was produced and administered to the human in need. To work effectively, the administered antibody needed

1. "High specificity"—meaning it binds to only the one particular kind of antigen it is targeted against.
2. "High affinity"—it binds tightly so it can neutralize the antigen.

Antibodies generated in mice were found to have these two properties in many situations. Technology was developed to fuse together the antibody-producing cells of the mouse and an immortal myeloma cell which created a cell line capable of producing the same antibody indefinitely. In this way, the antibody-producing cells continued to secrete antibodies. These antibodies could then be gathered and administered to humans in therapeutic doses. Before development of XenoMouse, two problems plagued these efforts.

1. When the potentially therapeutic antibody was entered into the human body, the mouse protein in the antibody caused it to be recognized as foreign and the body immediately began to try to reject it. Consequently, the antibody would have to be readministered frequently to have therapeutic effect.
2. With repeated dosing, the body began to develop its own antibodies to the administered, hopefully therapeutic antibody. This was known as the Human Anti-Mouse Antibody or HAMA response. In many cases, the HAMA response prevented the mouse antibody from having the desired effect and induced allergic reactions.

The first, partial, solution to this was development of processes to treat antibodies to make them appear more "human-like." These approaches greatly reduced the mouse protein content, sometimes to as little as 5–10 percent of the antibody.

The 1980s had hailed antibodies as "magic bullets," in reference to their ability to find and bind only target antigens. Useful products, however, were slow to develop. It was not until November 1997 that Rituxan (from IDEC and Genentech) became the first antibody-based cancer treatment (non-Hodgkin's lymphoma) to receive FDA approval. By September 1999, eight antibody products had reached the market including Genentech's Herceptin, a humanized antibody for metastatic breast cancer. For 1999, Genentech reported sales of $279 million for Rituxan and $188 million for Herceptin. Each antibody product on the market in early 2000 was "humanized," containing some mouse protein. The "humanization" of antibodies was both time consuming and expensive. This plus the therapeutic limitations of humanized antibodies spurred development efforts in a second direction, i.e., the humanization of the source of the antibodies rather than after-the-fact partial humanization of the antibodies. Competing "humanized" mice were developed by Abgenix and GenPharm International (later acquired by Medarex): XenoMouse and "HuMAb-Mouse," respectively. To settle an intellectual property dispute, the two firms cross-licensed their technologies. In this way, each pursued its own method but without fear of a suit from the other. Abgenix believed it had a superior mouse as XenoMouse contained more human antibody genes than "HuMAb-Mouse." Medarex had 1999 revenues of $10 million and partnerships with noted firms such as Amgen, Bristol-Myers Squibb, Merck, and Novartis. Compared to conventional mouse approaches, both XenoMouse and HuMAb-Mouse promised

1. Longer-lasting therapeutic effects as the body did not attempt to eliminate the drug.

2. Fewer unwanted side effects.

3. Faster product development time as no time was needed to "humanize" the antibody produced.

Abgenix Business Model

Abgenix conceptualized the antibody product development value chain to have eight steps as shown in Figure 4.2.

Steps 1 and 2: Target discovery and validation. An antigen target is identified and its link to a disease verified. This was work many academic scientists carried out. Small biotechnology firms could also do this as the investment was not overwhelming. As an example, a number of published scientific papers identified Epidermal Growth Factor (EGF) as a possible target. Research has shown that the EGF receptor was "overexpressed" on many kinds of cancer tumors. For example, over 80 percent of prostate cancers "overexpressed" the EGF receptor. Having too many EGF receptors on a cell meant the cell was overly sensitive to normal EGF's signaling to grow and perhaps divide.

Step 3: Antibody creation. Having a verified target, the next step is to generate an antibody that can bind the target in a specific way, i.e., without bothering healthy cells. XenoMouse is one source of such antibodies.

Steps 4 and 5: Preclinical and clinical development. This is carrying through the FDA-prescribed process described above.

Step 6: Process development. Design the processes to manufacture quality-assured product in an economic fashion.

Steps 7 and 8: Manufacturing and marketing. Make it and sell it.

In terms of this value chain model, Abgenix's two businesses could be described as

1. Technology licensing of XenoMouse—do Step 3 only.

2. Proprietary product development programs—do Step 3, Step 4, and some but not all of Step 5.

FIGURE 4.2   Product Development Value Chain

Source: Company records.

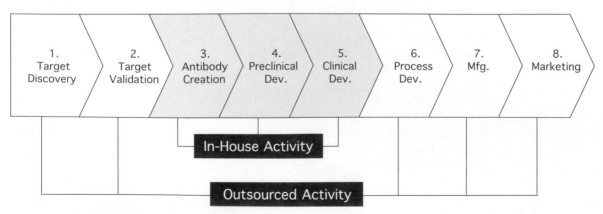

Ray Withy, Chief Business Officer, described the strategy as follows:

> Our source of comparative advantage has been XenoMouse. It's a product-generating platform. We started as an antibody-creating company—doing only Step 3. Collaborators brought us their targets and we generated an antibody for them or gave them XenoMouse and they could do it themselves. Then we went to a dual commercialization strategy, doing lots of signups to do Stage 3 for people, but we also saw there were some important validated targets in the literature. People were doing Steps 1 and 2 for us for free, so we took that and went ahead and did Step 3 for ourselves and then pushed forward into pre-clinicals of Step 4. How much of this we do and how far we take it is a critical decision for us. We need to not only generate some profits but also build our capabilities so we'll be a viable node in the network of biotechnology and pharmaceutical companies getting set up out there. How do we get the right connections in the network?

Abgenix's four development programs had proceeded to different stages although Abgenix had not yet even neared the point of filing a New Drug Application with the FDA for any of them. ABX-CBL had been tested in a Phase III study with 140 people but much more Phase III testing was needed. ABX IL8 had just moved into a Phase II clinical trial for one indication last month; ABX-EGF was in Phase I trial with 33 people, and ABX-RB2 was still in the preclinical stage. Withy described the thinking on the criticality of Phase II success, being the first test of drug effectiveness with rigorous statistical analysis, in terms of the perceived value of program rights by sketching out a value-by-stage diagram (Figure 4.3).

He noted:

> We start with what we get for XenoMouse over on the left—that's just access to the technology—with no risk or incremental spending on our part. Now, here's how it *typically*

FIGURE 4.3

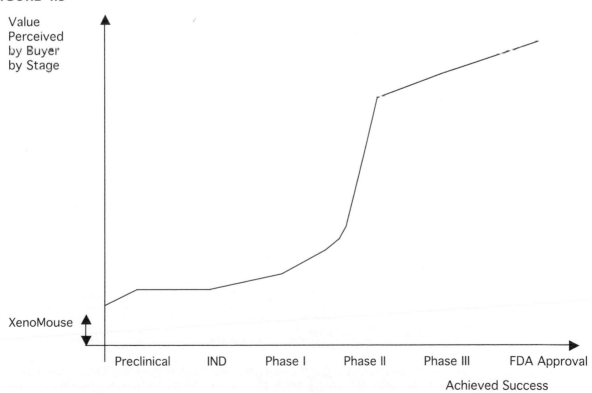

Value Perceived by Buyer by Stage

XenoMouse

Preclinical   IND   Phase I   Phase II   Phase III   FDA Approval

Achieved Success in This Phase

works—if there is such a thing as typical in this business. If we are doing development ourselves and have success in preclinicals, that bumps the value some over just access to the technology. INDs (Investigational New Drug applications filed with the FDA to get approval for human testing) and Phase I trials are not that big a deal for antibody therapies like ours because the theory so strongly indicates we won't have safety problems. The experiments, while necessary, and giving us dosing information, don't add a lot in terms of new information about likely eventual success. Phase II is the inflection point where you get the big bump in value. In Phase II, you have shown it effective to a statistically significant degree. Sure, there are things to still work out in Phase III and with the FDA. But that's been our thinking, if you can get it to Phase II, you can hand it off there and capture a lot of the value. Now, with EGF, maybe we have to think about this differently. Are the preclinical results so compelling that we have already created lots of perceived value? Or, on the other hand, is there so much potentially on the table that we should not be thinking about handing it off at all?

Geoff Davis, Chief Technical Officer, concurred:

We have always had a strategy of being out by the end of Phase II. That's where the inflexion point on the value curve is. We don't even have anyone in the company who has been all the way through the end of a Phase III. We have to be sure we recognize our emotional attachment to EGF. We are pretty proud of the preclinical results—justifiably so—but we can't let our ego get in the way of figuring out where best to go from here.

EGF Market[1]

As described above, Epidermal Growth Factor and, in particular, the EGF receptor, had been identified as a target and verified to be associated with cancer. These results were well-known throughout the industry, and many firms were developing therapies with EGF as the disease target. An internal Abgenix report summarized the market potential for an EGF direct therapy as follows:

Market Potential
- Cancer is the second-leading cause of death in the United States.
- Over one million cases of cancer are diagnosed each year and half receive chemotherapy.
- The direct cost of cancer in the United States, including patient care, was estimated in 1990 to be $35 billion, or 6 percent of the total cost of health care.

	Number of Cases	Number of Deaths	Percent Overexpressing EGF Receptor
Prostate	180,400	31,900	80–90%
Breast	184,200	41,200	20–30
Lung (NSCLC)	136,200	130,200	60–80
Colon and rectum	130,200	56,300	80–90
Urinary tract	86,700	24,600	50–70
Oral cavity and pharynx	30,200	7,800	50–90
Renal	31,200	11,900	70–90
Ovary	23,100	14,000	30–50

Note: The U.S. estimated new cases (2000), deaths, and percent overexpression of EGF receptor for cancer.
Source: American Cancer Society, "Cancer Statistics 2000," *Cancer Journal for Clinicians* (2000).

[1] Lehman Brothers report on "EGF Receptor Antagonists: An Important New Class of Anticancer Agents" by M. Wood, A. R. Leheny, and B. M. Bizoza was helpful background information for this section.

Using the midpoint of the "percent overexpressing EGF receptor" range given, the number of new cancer cases with overexpression of EGF in the United States in 2000 can be estimated to be 512,760. Herceptin, Genentech's antibody product for breast cancer, priced out at over $1,000 per week of therapy, and an average therapy costs over $20,000.[2]

Two different approaches to EGF receptor therapies were undertaken in the industry. Small molecule drugs, capable of crossing the cell membrane, sought to block signaling of an activated EGF receptor. These drugs could be taken orally. Antibodies, which had to be administered intravenously, blocked the EGF receptor.

Small Molecule Competitors

The two leading players in small molecule drugs based on organic chemistry appeared to be AstraZeneca with IRESSA and OSI Pharmaceutical with OSI-774. AstraZeneca was one of the five largest pharmaceutical companies in the world with health care sales over $15 billion. In 1999, it spent $280 million on the discovery and development of new treatments for cancer. It had four major cancer drugs on the market and over 300 sales representatives focusing on this market. In March 2000, it reported results of Phase I trials with 64 patients. IRESSA was "well tolerated . . . and showed encouraging antitumor activity . . ." It planned to be in Phase III clinicals for lung cancer treatment by the end of 2000.[3]

OSI was in Phase II clinicals. OSI described itself as "dedicated to being a leading pharmaceutical research and development organization." Also, "our business strategy and limited resources require us to enter into collaborative arrangement with various research partners." It had collaborations in place with Aventis, Novartis, and Pfizer, among others. It was conducting Phase II studies of OSI-774 both as a complement to chemotherapy and administered alone.[4] Small molecule drugs had shown some side effects: rash and gastrointestinal system upset.

Antibody Competitors

The major competitor producing an antibody therapy was ImClone with C225. It had begun human testing of the C225 antibody in 1994. C225 was a "humanized" antibody, not fully devoid of mouse protein. In one early test, it showed complete response when used in combination with radiation in 13 of 15 treated head and neck cancer patients. The other two patients had more than 50 percent tumor regression. It had two Phase III clinicals in place—one as a complement to chemotherapy and one as a complement to radiation therapy. In late 1998, it granted exclusive C225 rights outside the United States to Merck KgaA of Darmstadt, Germany. In 1999, it spent $30 million on R&D and had revenues of $2.1 million. It was believed to be building an in-house sales force and had stated in a company press release that its strategy was "to become a fully integrated biopharmaceutical company, taking its development programs from the research stage to the market."

Status of ABX-EGF

ABX-EGF performance in preclinical trials with animals was outstanding. Mice as the treatment subjects were injected with human epidermal cancer cells. No treatment was administered initially and the cancer tumors began to grow. After about two weeks, the test mice were injected with ABX-EGF twice a week for three weeks. Mice

---

[2] Ibid., pp. 10, 19.

[3] AstraZeneca website.

[4] OSI Pharmaceutical website.

received no other cancer treatment, i.e., this was a test of ABX-EGF as a "monotherapy" rather than as a complement to chemotherapy or radiation. The result was that ABX-EGF completely cleared the preformed tumors in the mice. No relapse of the tumor was observed after discontinuation of the treatment.

In November 1999, Abgenix began Phase I trials. These trials involved escalating doses up to seven levels on 33 patients with five different cancer types. Testing to date had proceeded through the first several levels and no toxicity/safety problems had been noted.

Comparative tests versus ImClone's antibody product, C225, in mice showed ABX-EGF to generate superior results. In addition, ABX-EGF would have the benefit of being a fully human antibody while C225 was one-third mouse and two-thirds human.

Moving Forward

Both Ray Withy, Chief Business Officer, and Geoff Davis, Chief Scientific Officer, had been "on the road" a great deal presenting the clinical data telling the ABX-EGF story to prospective partners. As Withy put it, "we targeted everyone who could be a player and went out to see them." Not unexpectedly, ABX-EGF generated lots of interest. Selling the ABX-EGF development program involved not only selling the program but the company as well; a potential buyer typically presented a complex decision-making unit to Abgenix with people from the scientific side to process the preclinical data, development and clinical people to assess where the program would go next and likely results, and manufacturing representation to assess how the product could be made in sufficient quantities and at what cost.

Abgenix had to develop its own sense of how good each collaborator would be because its financial return depended upon the collaborator's success in gaining FDA approval and marketing the drug. With this in mind, Pharmacol seemed the best option. Pharmacol was a pharmaceutical company with $12 billion in sales in 1999, drugs in many areas including cancer, and a sales force that compared to AstraZeneca's in size and skills. Ray Withy commented: "With Pharmacol, we saw a potential sales revenue of $700 million per year when the market was fully developed in 10 years' time."

Through a long series of discussions, the likely structure of a deal with Pharmacol took shape. Pharmacol's payments to Abgenix before marketing of the drug would be

Upon signing of deal:	$ 5 million
Beginning of Phase II trials:	$ 5 million
If/when Pharmacol begins Phase III:	$ 8 million
If/when FDA approval received:	$10 million

Abgenix would receive a 10 percent royalty on sales in perpetuity. Since this was a "hand-off" to Pharmacol, Abgenix would incur no costs once the deal was signed. Withy anticipated that it would take five years to get ABX-EGF to market with Pharmacol even if things went according to plan. Exhibit 4.3 shows the annual sales levels projected for the first 10 years after launch.

Biopart presented a different opportunity to Abgenix. Instead of a "hand-off," Abgenix would keep a "hand-in" a joint venture relationship. A biotechnology firm that had "gone public" in the first wave with Amgen and Genentech in the early 1980s, Biopart had focused on recombinant DNA technology. Its 1999 revenues were $510 million and had a good reputation for innovation and managing the regulatory process. The general parameters of a deal with Biopart would be

1. Biopart would pay $5 million on signing of the deal and $5 million when Phase II clinicals began.

2. All costs and revenues would be shared equally by Biopart and Abgenix.

3. Abgenix and Biopart would jointly design and conduct Phase II tests. Biopart would take the lead on Phase III testing with some involvement from Abgenix.

4. Biopart would take the lead in marketing given its existing sales force for cancer therapies. Abgenix could, if it wished, develop its own sales force to work alongside Biopart reps. (Costs for this would be shared by the partnership per item #2).

As with the Pharmacol case, Withy estimated that it would take five years to get to market. He estimated product development costs over this period as follows:

	Total Development Cost for Abgenix/Biopart Partnership (in millions)
Year 1	$10
Year 2	20
Year 3	25
Year 4	35
Year 5	35

If the product were to be commercialized, an additional $15 million would be needed for premarketing launch activities in the launch year. Ongoing cost of goods sold would be approximately 10 percent of sales and S,G,&A would be 25 percent of sales.

In assessing the relative merits of the Pharmacol and Biopart alternatives, one factor Abgenix management had to consider was the likelihood of attaining FDA approval and how much of the market would be tapped. The major difference between the Pharmacol approach and the Abgenix/Biopart partnership was the scale of the marketing effort Pharmacol could bring to bear. Thus, Abgenix projected that an Abgenix/Biopart partnership would generate 20 percent less sales than Pharmacol's estimates in Exhibit 4.3. However, given Biopart's clinical skills and the predominant role of the drug itself in testing, management thought the two routes represented the same time-to-market (five years) and a likelihood of ultimate FDA approval and market introduction (40 percent). Management felt it was highly likely that the development program would at least enter Phase III under either scenario. The $35 million in year 5 development costs for the Abgenix/Biopart partnership would be incurred only if FDA approval was achieved.

Abgenix Decisions

"Hand-Off," "Hand-In," or "Do Phase II's and Then Decide"—these were the three options Greer had to decide among. He would then have to support his chosen alternatives to his board of directors. Should he do a "hand-off" to Pharmacol—most likely what was expected by the board, the investment community, and others given Abgenix's declared strategy? Or was ABX-EGF special enough to warrant a "hand-in" joint venture agreement—which, while not new to the industry, would be new to Abgenix? Or, should he wait to go to Phase II clinicals on a solo basis? This would mean the $30 million in year 1 and 2 development costs shown above would fall to

Abgenix alone. Success at that stage though would greatly boost Abgenix's bargaining power for either a "hand-off" or "hand-in" negotiation. Greer felt sure he wanted a partner in this ABX-EGF effort at some point—but which type and when was a critical decision to make and manage. If he decided Pharmacol—what did he say to Biopart? If he decided Biopart—what did he say to Pharmacol? If he decided to do Phase II's himself, what did he say to each—you both stay here at the altar and I may show up to marry you in a couple of years? These were weighty decisions for the custodian of "The $3 Billion Mouse."

EXHIBIT 4.1

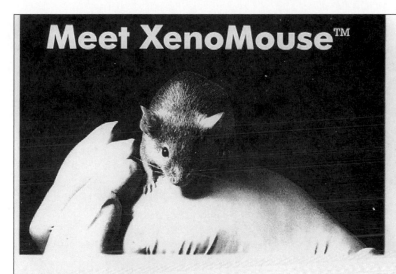

Meet XenoMouse™

We have humanized a mouse so you don't have to humanize antibodies.

Corporate Collaborators

Biotech	Pharma
Amgen	Abbott
AVI BioPharma	BASF
Cell Genesys	Elan
Chiron	J&J/Centocor
Corixa	Pfizer
Genentech	Schering-Plough
Genzyme Transgenics	SmithKline Beecham
Gliatech	**Genomics**
Other	Curagen
RCT	HGS
US Army	Millennium

XenoMouse-Derived MAbs

- Fully human
- High affinity ($K_D = 10^{-9} - 10^{-11}$ M)
- Antigen-binding specificity
- Choice of IgG isotypes (IgG_1, IgG_2, IgG_4)

Technology Advantages

→ Faster Product Development
→ Lower Product Commercialization Costs

- One-step process to create MAbs
- Creates MAbs to human antigens and non-human antigens
- No need for molecular engineering
- MAbs can be produced in hybridoma cell lines
- MAbs can be produced in other cell lines utilizing proprietary technology

Abgenix

7601 Dumbarton Circle ■ Fremont, CA 94555
(510)608-6500 ■ Fax (510)608-6511
www.abgenix.com

EXHIBIT 4.2

Statement of Operations (in thousands except per share data)

	Year Ended December 31,	
	1999	**1998**
Revenue	$ 12,285	$ 3,842
Operating expenses:		
General and administrative	5,164	3,405
Research and development	21,106	17,588
Equity in (income) losses in XenoTech joint venture		
Termination fee	8,667	—
Total operating expenses	$ 34,391	$ 21,100
Interest (income) expense, net	$ (2,067)	$ (431)
Foreign income tax	1,000	—
Net loss	$ (20,499)	$ (16,827)
Net loss per share	$ (1.41)	$ (3.00)
Shares used in computing net loss per share	14,537	5,603

Balance Sheet (in thousands)

	March 31, 2000 (unaudited)	December 31, 1999
Cash, cash equivalents, and marketable securities	$568,003	$ 58,012
Property and equipment, net	5,253	5,300
Long-term investment	39,176	29,225
Intangible assets, net	45,814	46,591
Other assets	4,825	9,413
Total assets	$663,071	$148,541
Deferred revenue	13,367	3,767
Other current liabilities	6,286	7,143
Long-term debt and other	296	571
Stockholders' equity	643,122	137,060
Total liabilities and stockholders' equity	$663,071	$148,541

EXHIBIT 4.3
Projected Sales by Year by Pharmacol with Product Introduction in "Year 1" (for Years 1 to 10)

Year	Dollar Sales (in millions)
1	$ 20
2	70
3	135
4	250
5	330
6	450
7	540
8	620
9	700
10	700

5

CardioThoracic Systems

Diana S. Gardner
Michael J. Roberts

Richard Ferrari, Jeff Gold, and Geoffrey Dillon were gathered around the table discussing CardioThoracic Systems's (CTS) sales and marketing efforts. It was April of 1998, and the three were CEO, COO, and VP of sales and marketing, respectively, of CTS. The young Silicon Valley company had developed a technique for performing a coronary artery bypass graft (CABG) procedure on a *beating* heart. The CABG was a widely used "open-heart" surgical procedure in which healthy blood vessels from the leg or chest were transplanted and used to replace (bypass) a blocked artery that fed the heart (see Exhibit 5.1 for illustration). During this procedure, the heart was almost always stopped, so that the surgeon could operate on motionless tissue. In order to accomplish this, the patient was placed on a heart-lung machine, which oxygenated the blood and pumped it through the patient's body.

CTS sold a disposable $1,000 kit that permitted cardiac surgeons to perform the operation *without* having to stop the heart—and thus without the need for a heart-lung machine. This was an important advance because stopping the patient's heart was the source of both significant cost and patient trauma. The use of the heart-lung machine during heart surgery was associated with longer hospitalization and recovery periods. In addition, stopping and restarting the heart could easily introduce "debris" in the bloodstream, which could in turn cause clots to form, and ultimately lead to brain or other organ damage. Neurological problems such as coma, stroke, or even death

Entrepreneurial Studies Fellow Diana S. Gardner prepared this case at the HBS California Research Center under the supervision of Senior Lecturer Michael J. Roberts as the basis for class discussion rather than to illustrate either effective or ineffective handling of an administrative situation.

Copyright © 1999 by the President and Fellows of Harvard College. To order copies or request permission to reproduce materials, call 1-800-545-7685, write Harvard Business School Publishing, Boston, MA 02163, or go to http://www.hbsp.harvard.edu. No part of this publication may be reproduced, stored in a retrieval system, used in a spreadsheet, or transmitted in any form or by any means—electronic, mechanical, photocopying, recording, or otherwise—without the permission of Harvard Business School.

occurred in approximately 6 percent of post-CABG surgery cases.[1] Moreover, subtle neurological complications had been reported in up to 30 percent of these patients.[2]

The team around the table had learned considerably from the past 15 months of trying to sell the CTS system. Unfortunately, however, the company's sales trajectory had failed to live up to the expectations that had been set at the time of the company's IPO in April 1996. The company had trouble selling its first-generation system because it required surgeons to perform a technically difficult procedure through a very small opening in the side of the chest. In response, the company developed a second-generation system that relied on a larger—and more classic—incision through the breastbone. Unfortunately, however, many surgeons had resisted CTS's second-generation system as well. Both the first- and second-generation systems were limited because surgeons could only access the two vessels on the front of the heart. There were several vessels underneath the heart that surgeons often desired to replace during the CABG, but that had remained inaccessible using the existing CTS system.

The CTS team believed their newest system addressed this issue. They had developed a technique that permitted surgeons to tilt the heart up, which in turn provided access to the vessels beneath the heart. Nevertheless, the team knew that the sales process was difficult and complex. Before they launched this newest system, they wanted to reassess their overall sales and marketing strategy and make sure that they had leveraged their experiences of the past 15 months. Gold, the company's COO, explained:

> We have learned a lot and have made several changes to our product, pricing, sales, and marketing efforts. It has been frustrating, but we have made progress. Of the approximately 16,000 beating heart procedures that were performed in 1997, 8,000 were performed with our technology, which gives us an approximately 50 percent share of the "beating heart" business. But there were 330,000 CABG procedures done with the traditional heart-lung machine, so we still have a relatively low penetration of the entire CABG market. Penetration is the key issue.

Geoff Dillon, VP Sales and Marketing, offered his perspective:

> We have pioneered a lot of the advances in this field, but you cannot patent a "technique." Many of the features in our devices are easily copied. This is a tremendously competitive field. So we need to move beyond the point of just selling a product. We have to deliver an entire experience that makes the physicians want to do business with us.

CEO Richard Ferrari continued:

> We have hit the classic "early adopters," and have identified some physicians who use our technique and equipment in 80 percent of their cases. But the average surgeon who has been trained in our technique uses the device in four or fewer procedures a month—less than 10 percent. And we have only trained approximately 400 of the 3,000 cardiac surgeons that are out there. Therefore, *we* really need to drive adoption. Of course, there is a classic S-curve adoption cycle, but we want to shorten this phase we are in. We need to use every lever at our disposal to get more surgeons exposed to our device, and to get those that have been trained to use the device in a greater percentage of their procedures. We will have succeeded when the surgeons ask themselves why *not* do this procedure in this fashion.

---

[1] "Adverse Cerebral Outcomes after Coronary Bypass Surgery," *New England Journal of Medicine,* December 19, 1996.

[2] "Off-Pump Multivessel Coronary Bypass via Sternotomy Is Safe and Effective," *Annals of Thoracic Surgery* 66 (1998), pp. 1068–72.

Background

Cardiovascular Disease

The cardiovascular system consists of arteries—which transport oxygenated blood away from the heart—and veins—which carry deoxygenated blood to the heart. The coronary arteries supply blood from the heart to the heart muscle itself, and serve to feed the surrounding tissue. There were four primary coronary arteries—two on the "front" of the heart and two on the "back." Of these four, the single most important artery was the LAD (left anterior descending), which was located on the front of the heart. Coronary artery disease resulted from the build-up of plaque (caused by cholesterol or other fatty materials) in the arterial walls. The accumulation of plaque constricted the size of the opening in the artery, which in turn obstructed normal blood flow. Reduced blood flow in the coronary arteries, in turn, restricted oxygenation of the muscle tissue of the heart. This narrowing of the coronary arteries was termed atherosclerosis; it caused deterioration of heart muscle, chest pain (angina), and, ultimately, led to a heart attack. Coronary artery disease affected approximately 1.5 million adults per year[3] and was the leading cause of death in the United States.

CABG

In response to this problem, many sophisticated medical procedures and devices had been developed to increase blood flow to the heart. One of the oldest of these was the coronary artery bypass graft—or CABG (pronounced "cabbage")—procedure, in which veins from the leg were harvested and transplanted to the heart, thereby "bypassing" the narrowed vessels of the diseased arteries. In order to bypass a diseased vessel, the surgeon sewed one end of the transplanted vessel to the portion of the heart muscle that was receiving insufficient bloodflow; the other end was inserted into an incision in a healthy vessel, and sewn into place. (See Exhibit 5.1 for illustration of a CABG.) The heart had several major blood vessels that fed its muscle tissue. By injecting radiopaque dyes into the blood vessels, and using special x-ray techniques, doctors could accurately "map" the blood vessels and determine, prior to surgery, which arteries needed replacement.

The standard CABG procedure included two particularly invasive components.

First, in order to expose the heart, the surgeon had to make a 12-inch (30-centimeter) incision down the middle of the patient's chest (a sternotomy), and then spread the rib cage approximately 6 inches (15 centimeters) apart. The incision caused a great deal of patient trauma and post-operative pain. In the United States, a standard CABG procedure involved a surgery of 3 to 5 hours and a total cost of approximately $36,000. The total in-hospital recovery period, including 1 to 3 days of intensive care, was approximately 7 days, and the average recuperation period post–hospital discharge ranged anywhere from 4–10 weeks.[4] Patients were also subject to the risk of severe complications associated with the sternotomy. Specifically, there was a 1.1 percent risk of post-operative infection in the chest area. For a patient with such wound complications, the average length of in-hospital stay was 43 days, and the in-hospital costs were three times higher than for patients with no such complications.[5]

Second, in order to operate on the heart, the surgeon needed to stop the heart from beating. This required the use of a heart-lung machine, which served to temporarily oxygenate and circulate the patient's blood—as the lungs and heart normally do—while

---

[3] D. A. Gruber and A. C. Smith, "Interventional Vascular Management in the Millennium," Piper Jaffray Industry Research Report, October 1998, p. 6.

[4] Massachusetts General Hospital: CABG Surgery (A), HBS Case No. 696-015.

[5] CardioThoracic Systems IPO Prospectus, April 19, 1996, p. 27.

the patient's own heart was being operated upon. Of the several major complications associated with the CABG procedure, the majority were related to the use of the heart-lung machine. During this procedure, the main vessel that carried blood out of the heart—the aorta—was clamped. As a result, certain blood vessels had no blood flow. In addition, the manipulation of the aorta required for this procedure could loosen plaque that lined the blood vessel's walls. When the heart was taken off the heart-lung machine and "restarted," this material could find its way to the brain, where it impaired blood flow and subsequently caused paralysis and/or reduction of mental faculties (stroke). Short- and long-term neurological damage to the brain (including coma, seizures, memory deficit, or deterioration in intellectual function) was a known risk of "open heart" surgery. It was estimated that major adverse complications (death, coma, stroke) occurred in approximately 6 percent of all CABG procedures, with even higher rates in older patients.[6] Moreover, up to 50 percent of the patients who underwent this type of surgery reported some form of subtle neurological and cognitive deficit.[7]

According to one study, there was also a direct correlation between the use of a heart-lung machine and increased hospital costs and post-operative length of stay. In this study, which compared clinical outcomes of patients who underwent coronary artery bypass with ("on pump") and without ("off pump") a heart-lung machine, the "off-pump" patients had 50 percent shorter hospital stays and 30 percent lower hospital costs.[8]

Given the traumatic nature of CABG surgery, physicians typically replaced *all* of the diseased vessels, regardless of the severity of the blockage, rather than risk additional surgery in subsequent years. Thus, nearly 80 percent of all CABGs involved the replacement of three or more vessels (triple, quadruple, or quintuple bypass).

Although a highly invasive and traumatic "open-heart" procedure, CABG surgery was considered to be the most effective and longest-lasting treatment for severe coronary artery disease. Approximately 330,000 U.S. patients underwent conventional CABG surgery in 1996 (600,000 worldwide).[9] (See Exhibit 5.2 for data on worldwide CABG procedures.)

Balloon Angioplasty and Stenting

In response to the trauma, cost, and side effects associated with the traditional CABG procedure, cardiologists developed a less-invasive technique for treating coronary artery disease—balloon angioplasty. In this technique, which was developed in the late 1970s, an approximately five-foot (150-centimeter)-long guide wire was inserted into a blood vessel in the thigh, and guided through that vessel to the narrowed portion (the "stenosis" or "lesion") in the coronary artery. A balloon-tipped catheter was then guided over the wire and inflated to break apart the plaque and restore blood flow to the heart. Most of this plaque was contained within a layer of cells that formed the lining of the blood vessel, and therefore, cracking the deposits did not induce a significant stream of debris into the blood. Frequently, successively larger balloons were inflated at the diseased site, which required the use of multiple catheters/balloons. An interventional cardiologist, not a surgeon, performed this procedure in a catheterization lab ("cath lab"), while the patient was sedated but conscious.

Balloon angioplasty—which did not require a heart-lung bypass machine or an incision in the chest—was an attractive, less-invasive alternative to CABG. However,

[6] "Adverse Cerebral Outcomes."

[7] "Off-Pump Multivessel Coronary Bypass," p. 1068.

[8] Ibid., p. 1070.

[9] "How to Mend a Broken Heart," PaineWebber Cardiovascular Industry Research Report, June 23, 1997, p. 41.

in approximately 40 percent of the cases, patients developed a restenosis—a severe renarrowing of the artery at the original site of treatment—within approximately 6 months post-procedure.

One of the explanations for restenosis was that the interior wall of the blood vessel—which was ruptured during the angioplasty procedure—was attempting to heal itself by forming a type of scar tissue. This healing process, in turn, formed the same kind of plaque that had created the blockage in the first place. In response, physicians developed the stent—an expandable metal frame (like a short, mesh, drinking straw) that was positioned in the coronary artery at the site of the balloon inflation. The expanded stent was used to scaffold the vessel and keep it open. Although stents had not eliminated restenosis, studies showed that stents dramatically reduced the rate of restenosis following angioplasty, from 40 percent to approximately 20 percent in most cases.

The first stent on the U.S. market was Johnson & Johnson's Palmaz Schatz stent, which received FDA approval in August 1994. By the end of 1997, the worldwide stent market was approximately $1.5 billion and estimated to grow at a 13 percent CAGR over the next four years. (See Exhibit 5.3 for information on the coronary stent market.) In 1997, an estimated 638,000 angioplasty procedures were performed in the United States, with 49 percent involving stents. The average cost for a balloon angioplasty procedure was approximately $10,000 to $15,000,[10] and the additional cost of an elective stenting procedure (balloon angioplasty with stent), assuming approximately 1.5 stents per procedure, was $2,200.[11]

Existing Treatment Patterns

Gold estimated that, at any point in time, approximately three million Americans had sufficiently severe atherosclerosis to be under a doctor's care for this condition. Of these three million Americans, approximately two million received an x-ray diagnostic (angiogram) which revealed a precise determination of the number and position of the blockages. Of these two million, approximately one million received one or more of the two dominant treatments: CABG or balloon angioplasty. Gold estimated that this one million population had the following distribution of disease:

Number of Vessels Blocked	Percent of Patients Diagnosed
1	35%
2	30
3	15
4	10
5	10

Of the one million patients treated, Gold estimated that 350,000 received a CABG, and the remainder an angioplasty (often with a stent). However, the use of the two treatments varied widely as a function of the distribution of the disease: It was relatively rare for a patient with more than two vessel blockages to receive an angioplasty. Likewise, it was uncommon for a patient with two or fewer vessel blockages to receive a CABG. Gold explained the complex diagnosis, decision, and referral process that influenced these patterns:

---

[10] Morgan Stanley Dean Witter Industry Research Report, *Investors Guide to Interventional Cardiology,* May 29, 1998, p. 4.

[11] "Ballooning Stents," Hambrecht & Quist Industry Research Report, January 28, 1998, p. 20.

Most people don't just show up in the emergency room with a heart attack and go under the knife. If you have heart problems, your first visit is with a medical cardiologist. The average patient is initially treated with some form of drug therapy to lower cholesterol or to minimize angina. However, as the problem gets more severe, the medical cardiologist refers the patient to an interventional cardiologist. The interventional cardiologist then performs a stress test and takes an angiogram. [Similar to an x-ray, an angiogram involved injecting a radiopaque dye into the patient's circulatory system and then viewing a "shadow-gram" of the arterial vessels via an imaging system.] Based on the results of the tests, the interventional cardiologist then decides whether an angioplasty or CABG is the best course of treatment. If the patient has disease in only one or two vessels, the interventional cardiologists are inclined to try to handle the problem by themselves. If there are three or more blocked vessels, however, the cardiologist will tend to pass the patient along to the cardiac surgeon, figuring that "starting fresh" with grafted vessels from the leg will give the patient a better chance over the long term.

Minimally Invasive Cardiac Surgery (MICS)

In 1996, a new technique for treating coronary artery disease was introduced—Minimally Invasive Cardiac Surgery (MICS). The goal of this approach was to combine the clinical benefits of CABG surgery with the lower cost and faster recovery advantages of a less-invasive procedure. In this procedure, surgeons accessed the heart through small (approximately three inches) incisions ("ports") in the chest, and used highly specialized tools to perform the surgery. Although this procedure was performed on a stopped heart, and thus still required the use of a heart-lung bypass machine, it did not require a sternotomy and thus caused significantly less patient trauma and required a much shorter hospital stay (on average 2.5 days versus 6.8 days for conventional CABG surgery).

In 1996, very few operations had actually been performed using the minimally invasive techniques. A front-page article in *The Wall Street Journal* discussed this issue:[12]

> For all the excitement, only about 2,000 patients have had the new operations so far—compared with 10 million open-heart operations worldwide in the past 25 years. The old-fashioned way (CABG) has an impressive track record: its mortality rate is 4 percent or less at most of the 900 U.S. medical centers. And recent studies show the repairs can last 15 years or more in 90 percent of patients.

Nevertheless, there was a tremendous amount of excitement surrounding this technology, generated, in part, by the companies that were pursuing MICS: Heartport and CTS.

Heartport

Heartport was founded in 1991 by two surgeons at Stanford Medical School. Its founders, Drs. Sterman and Stevens, believed it was possible to perform heart surgery without cracking open the chest. In their "closed-chest" technique, a surgeon made a small incision in the groin and inserted a set of catheters into the patient's circulatory system. These catheters were used to stop the heart and place the patient on a heart-bypass machine. In order to access the heart, the surgeon then inserted Heartport's specially designed instruments through a number of small tubes, or "ports," which were placed between the patient's ribs. As the heart wasn't visible to the naked eye

---

[12] "Slice of Life: Hope and Hype Follow Heart Surgery Method That's Easy on Patients," *The Wall Street Journal,* April 22, 1997, p. A1.

during the procedure, surgeons relied on a video camera to monitor the surgery. After a lengthy FDA process Heartport finally received approval for its minimally invasive Port-Access™ system in October 1996, six months after its successful IPO.[13]

The company's Port-Access™ technology and disposable cardiac catheters were considered to be revolutionary because they allowed a patient to undergo conventional heart bypass surgery—and be on a heart-lung machine—without the need for a large incision in the chest (sternotomy). The implied benefits for both the patient and the health care system were numerous and included reduced trauma, fewer complications, faster recovery period, shorter hospital stays, and lower overall costs. Heartport's surgical kit cost $5,000, but the company hoped this would be more than offset by the reduced cost of post-operative care.[14]

CTS Background

Chuck Taylor founded CardioThoracic Systems in November 1993. A former engineer at Heartport, Taylor was looking to start and run his own company. He left Heartport to explore opportunities in the medical device field and soon realized that there was a business opportunity if he could develop a procedure for operating on a beating heart. The only emerging minimally invasive technology, at that point, was Heartport's Port-Access™ system. However, Heartport had defined "minimally invasive" in terms of the size of the incision required to *access* the heart. Heartport's system still required the use of a heart lung machine, thus, the numerous neurological side effects that were associated with being "on-pump" still remained.

Operating on a beating heart was not a new idea. For many years, beating heart operations had been standard practice in poor countries that couldn't afford the cost of a $150,000 heart-lung machine. In those cases, however, doctors stitched the beating heart as it pulsed. This resulted in grafts that weren't as secure or enduring as those that had been stitched on an immobile surface.[15] Taylor tracked down a surgeon, Dr. Federico Benetti, who had mastered this beating heart procedure. Benetti, who had developed this technique in Argentina, agreed to collaborate with Taylor. At approximately the same time, Taylor solicited Rich Ferrari, an experienced and well-respected manager within the medical venture community, to help him write his business plan. Ferrari explained his willingness to help Taylor:

> When Taylor first approached me about CTS, I was CEO of Cardiovascular Imaging Systems, a public company which developed intravenous ultrasound imaging equipment. In February 1995, it was sold to Boston Scientific for $100 million. When I met with Taylor I was impressed with his approach, so I agreed to help him develop his business plan. At this point, I had formed a business model in my own mind: the strategy was to develop a set of disposable tools that would enable surgeons to operate on a beating heart, without the heart-lung machine.

In June 1995, Dr. Benetti flew to San Francisco to demonstrate this surgical technique on a pig. Ferrari was impressed, as were the several venture capitalists he had invited to observe the operation. Phil Young of U.S. Venture Partners (USVP), a Silicon Valley VC firm, offered his reaction to this surgical technique:

[13] Heartport, Inc., Stanford Business School Case S-SB-169A, by Joseph M. Welsh.

[14] PR Newswire, June 6, 1996.

[15] "The New Vein in Heart Surgery," *San Jose Mercury News,* November 8, 1998, p. 1D.

Of course I was incredibly impressed, but I still had a few unanswered questions. Our concerns were not *if* CTS had created a viable procedure, but *how* they planned to convince doctors to adopt a new technique that required extensive training. The situation was complicated by the fact that the person who screens the patient for either open heart surgery or angioplasty is the invasive cardiologist—the doctor who does the angioplasty. And the advent of the stent has cut restenosis rates from 40 percent to 20 percent. This data unnerved me. It gave cardiologists an even stronger reason to hold on to patients.

My other concern was related to the potential market size. The procedure is performed on a beating heart so surgeons could only operate on the one or two vessels that were located immediately below the chest portal—on the "front" side of the heart. This fact significantly limited the company's customer base, given that single- and double-vessel surgeries represented only 23 percent of the worldwide cardiac surgery market.[16]

Nevertheless, we really wanted to move forward with the investment, so we used these questions to ask ourselves "how do we best help them to make this happen?"

CTS and Heartport Financing

Overall, Heartport had raised approximately $25 million in venture funding over three rounds of financing, which occurred in 1992, 1994, and 1995, respectively. Backed by some of the most prominent West Coast venture firms including Sierra Ventures and Kleiner, Perkins, Caufield & Byers, Heartport went public on April 26, 1996. The company raised $105 million at an approximately $500 million post-money valuation.

In September 1995, CTS received its first and only round of outside funding from a group of top-tier West Coast venture capital companies. USVP and Vertical Fund Associates led the investment, and four other venture capital companies participated: New Enterprise Associates, Morgenthaler, Venrock, and Weiss, Peck & Greer. These firms had also invested, along with USVP, in Ferrari's former company, Cardiovascular Imaging Systems. CTS needed the money in order to fund its Phase I product development, to commence the 510(k) regulatory approval process, and to begin developing its marketing strategy. CTS raised a total of $5.0 million from the venture capitalists, at a $7.8 million post-money valuation.

CTS announced its intention to go public in early 1996. The company's decision to go public in the spring of 1996 was twofold. First, the company needed a significant infusion of capital in anticipation of its product launch at the end of the year. Second, favorable market conditions had resulted in an unusually attractive financing environment. 1995 and 1996 witnessed a dramatic increase in the number of cardiovascular device IPOs. (See Exhibit 5.4 for cardiovascular IPO activity.) More specifically, there was a tremendous amount of interest in minimally invasive surgery. This was largely a result of the huge publicity campaign that Heartport launched in anticipation of its IPO—which occurred April 26, 1996. In an effort to generate awareness and enthusiasm among the local media, Heartport had circulated press kits and video news releases to local hospitals. Heartport's marketing campaign was largely focused on consumers (patients), but it also included some targeted comments against CTS and its beating heart procedure, which were circulated throughout the medical community.

Fundamentally, the debate surrounded the definition of "minimally invasive." Heartport argued that the incision, which patients don't like because it is a visible reminder of their operation, is what makes heart surgery so invasive. CTS believed that the heart-lung machine was the primary source of patient trauma.

---

[16] "Heartport, Inc.—From Concept to Reality," Goldman Sachs Research Report, December 8, 1997, p. 10.

At the time of its IPO, CTS was still in the early stages of product development and its instruments had been tested on humans only on a limited basis. CTS had no patents and no strategic partner. Nevertheless, the investor interest was overwhelming. Gold related:

> Investors couldn't get enough of us. There had been so much hype surrounding Heartport, and its pending IPO—that everyone believed minimally invasive surgery was the wave of the future—that it would almost immediately replace the existing open-heart surgery procedure. Everyone wanted in.

CTS went public on April 18, 1996. The company's 3.75-million-share offering was priced at $18, at the high end of the original filing range of $16–$18. The offering raised $80.1 million for the company at a $221 million post-money valuation. CTS rose 20 percent on its first day of trading and closed at $25 per share, approximately a $300 million market capitalization.

Just eight days later, Heartport completed its IPO. A Wall Street "darling," Heartport had originally filed at a price range of $14–$16, before its underwriters –led by Morgan Stanley—revised the filing range upward to $17–$19. The company completed its five-million-share offering on April 26, 1996, at $21 per share. The day that HPRT's stock opened, it reached a high of $37.75 before closing at $35, a 67 percent gain from its offering price. It was the seventh most actively traded stock on the Nasdaq that day. At the time of Heartport's IPO, only 14 surgeries had been completed using Heartport's technology versus 100 with the CTS system.

Nevertheless, in late April 1996, just weeks after their respective IPOs, Heartport had a valuation of $850 million, significantly greater than CTS's valuation of $300 million. The subsequent stock price performance of the two companies, both relative and absolute, was extremely volatile. By June of 1996, the majority of the hype in the MICS sector had settled down, which caused both companies' respective stock prices to drop significantly. Both companies introduced their systems in January of 1997. CTS's stock price increased, relative to Heartport, because surgeons initially found Heartport's system to be too technically challenging. Throughout 1997, however, the stock prices of both companies steadily declined as the adoption rates of their respective systems continued to perform under expectations. In late 1997, the two stocks—which had been tracking each other closely– diverged sharply. CTS "missed" its third quarter, due largely to issues related to international sales. (See Exhibits 5.5 through 5.9 for the financing histories and stock performance of Heartport and CTS.)

Product Evolution

Upon closing of this financing, CTS's founders focused on perfecting the design of their surgical tools and developing the company's manufacturing capability. The Food and Drug Administration (FDA) did not apply regulatory standards to surgical *procedures*. However, any *interventional device*—intended to be inserted inside the body—required a form of clearance from the FDA known as a 510(k) approval. (See Exhibit 5.10 for an overview of the FDA review process for medical devices.)

First Generation—MIDCAB I

CTS's early product development was driven by two key goals: (1) the desire to perform the CABG through a small incision in the ribs (without a sternotomy) *and* (2) the ability to perform the surgery on a beating heart (without having to place the patient on a heart-lung machine). Given these characteristics, the company believed its system would both reduce patient trauma and result in lower overall costs to the health care system.

CTS's first device was available on the market in January 1997. Using this first-generation system, the "MIDCAB" (for Minimally Invasive Direct Coronary Artery Bypass), the heart was accessed through a small incision in the ribs. The surgeon then inserted CTS's *Access Platform,* which allowed the surgeon to maximize access to the chest cavity. The *Access Platform* was subsequently expanded, which spread the ribs and surrounding tissue, in order to create optimal exposure of the heart. CTS's disposable device kit also included the *Stabilizer.* The *Stabilizer* was a small metal plate with two prongs that sat against the portion of the heart on which the surgeon was stitching and served to stabilize that area of the heart. (See Exhibit 5.11 for a picture of the CTS Access Platform and Stabilizer.)

This system, or kit, was initially priced at $2,500 and distributed through the company's own direct sales force. The company began with four salespeople, and that number grew to eight over the course of several months. Gold explained the company's roll-out strategy:

> We had four or five top surgeons with whom we worked, who learned the procedure and who began to use it pretty steadily. These were the classic "early adopters"—guys who are known for being "leading edge," who value that characteristic as part of their reputation, and who make the necessary investment, in terms of time and energy, to learn these techniques.

Initial sales of the MIDCAB system were very disappointing. Surgeons complained that the system was "hard to use." Gold amplified:

> Our first-generation device asked the surgeon to make several radical changes at once: to operate through an extremely small incision with little space to maneuver; to operate from the "side" of the heart (because the incision was through the ribs rather than the sternum); *and* to work on a heart that was still beating. The truth is that doctors wanted a "safety valve." In the event that something went wrong in the operating room, they wanted to be able to fall back to their "classic" and more familiar technique. With traditional open-heart surgery, surgeons could see if something went wrong because everything was exposed—the heart was right in front of them. With the chest "closed," they couldn't do this.
>
> Another problem with this system was that surgeons couldn't touch the blood vessels with their hands. Surgeons liked to feel the vessels that they were working on. When they touched a vessel, they could better determine the location and significance of the lesions. This helped them identify exactly where to insert the graft.
>
> All of these factors caused us to rework our first-generation system. We redesigned our technique into an open-chest procedure. This was just easier for the surgeons because they could see what they were doing.

Second Generation—Access MV

In September 1997, CTS released its second-generation system: The Access MV was similar to the first system, and used similar tools, except that the procedure involved a bigger incision down the center of the chest—through the breastbone (a sternotomy). This approach provided the surgeon with full access to, and direct vision of, the heart, and thus addressed many of the objections of CTS's first-generation system. Nevertheless, the MIDCAB II was met with other sources of resistance. Jeff Gold, who had joined CTS in March 1997 as EVP and who had become Chief Operating Officer, explained:

> We knew from the beginning that being limited to the two vessels on the front of the heart was a problem. But we had several reasons for going ahead. First, when you look at the base of 1 million patients who are treated for coronary artery disease, the majority are

treated by interventional cardiologists for one or two vessels. We thought that our system was a way for surgeons to win back the one- and two-vessel patients from the cardiologists.

Mary Kay Baggs, CTS's director of marketing, offered her view of some of the particular challenges:

Our first- and second-generation devices were targeted toward patients with only one or two diseased vessels—we weren't able to do more than that. We believe that our technique eliminated the most serious side effects of a CABG, and that it was preferable to an angioplasty for some patients with one or two diseased vessels. But this is a very delicate message to sell to our surgeons. Since the surgeons get all their patients through the cardiologist, they don't want to get out and be seen as *competing with* cardiologists for these one- and two-vessel patients.

Gold continued:

We also thought that since the LAD (left anterior descending) vessel—on the front of the heart—is by far the most significant vessel, access to multiple vessels wouldn't be a significant issue. Many studies suggest that if a doctor just fixes the LAD, sufficient blood flow is restored to the heart and the patient is able to live a normal life. But as it turned out, the surgeons' "complete revascularization" philosophy—their desire to fix multiple vessels during the same procedure—was hard to overcome.

Ferrari offered his thoughts behind CTS's strategy:

One of the approaches that I had advocated from the beginning was "hybrid revascularization"—the idea that you would fix the front vessels with our MIDCAB approach and the back vessels with angioplasty. If we could convince surgeons to perform CTS's off-pump procedure on the two front vessels and then have invasive cardiologists perform the standard angioplasty procedure on those vessels beneath the heart, then CTS would have a solution for multivessel disease. From the patient's point of view this would be the ideal scenario because they'd get all of their vessels taken care of, but without an on-pump procedure.

But it was unrealistic to think that a surgeon would give up his patient to an interventional cardiologist when only half of the procedure was done. Not to mention the fact that the combined procedure would be quite expensive—the health care system just wouldn't pay for it.

In response to competitive pressures, particularly from other companies that had introduced nondisposable imitations of the company's product, the company reduced the price of the Access MV device to $1,000 per system. Dillon explained some of the marketing challenges:

In the early phase of the technology's adoption curve, some of the benefits are still hard for the physicians to quantify—the reduced neurological problems, the faster recovery time. And the economics of the health care system don't always drive things in the right direction. The vast majority of the CABG procedures are reimbursed under a flat fee of approximately $30,000 that includes the surgeon's fees, the operating room, the post-op recovery, the whole hospital stay. And most hospitals don't have the systems to track these other benefits. So, here when we introduced a device that adds $1,000–$1,500 to the basic cost of the procedure, some hospital purchasing agent feels like their margin just dropped by the same amount.

In the fourth quarter of 1997, approximately 1,400 procedures were performed utilizing the Access MV system. (See Exhibit 5.12 for quarterly sales revenues and financial data.)

Sales and Marketing Strategy

Throughout 1997 and into the first quarter of 1998, CTS's sales and marketing approach had several components.

First, the company had hired a skilled sales force of individuals familiar with cardiovascular surgery. Having begun with four salespeople, the company had a team of 16 salespeople and 9 clinical surgical specialists by early 1999. These clinical specialists visited surgeons after they had been through training to provide additional training as required.

Michael Moore, a sales rep at this time, described a typical sales approach:

> Basically, you want to find a surgeon that is receptive to new techniques. You may know physicians personally or by reputation. If not, you ask the doctors you do know, or the hospital administrators or the nurses, who would be a good candidate to learn this technique. If you ask the right questions, people will point you in the right direction. Also, the company is sending out brochures with cards for people to mail back if they are interested, and there are always leads from meetings—we have a booth at all the major heart surgery conferences and conventions, and we collect leads that way.
>
> The basic pitch we made was the reduction in neurological complications. All the doctors think of themselves as scientists, so once we had some data, the story got easier to tell.

CTS had begun collecting data on its MIDCAB patients as soon as the product was on the market, and in September 1997 published data on the first 2,000 patients, indicating that the grafts were just as successful (i.e., restored blood flow to the heart), and that the rate of stroke was just 0.1 percent, versus approximately 6 percent for on-pump CABG.

Jeff Gold described some of the challenges of selling to the surgeons who were CTS's target customers:

> When you tell them that our approach reduces these complications, they say "well, a 6 percent stroke rate is the *average* for the *average* doctor; my numbers are better." Well, in reality, they don't know what their numbers are. No one tracks them, and often a surgeon won't even find out what happens to a typical patient. The cardiologist sees the follow-up and they just stop referring to the surgeons who do a poor job.

The company estimated that it had trained 400 surgeons in its procedure, out of approximately 3,000 cardiac surgeons nationwide. With 8,000 CTS procedures performed in 1997, this translated into an average of 20 procedures per physician. But as Mary Kay Baggs explained, the averages were misleading:

> An "average" surgeon may perform 120 CABGs per year, but this is misleading. Twenty percent of the surgeons are really busy, and perform 200 to 250 procedures per year. These are the top people, and they account for almost half of the procedures done nationwide. They are our target market segment.

Once the company had identified its leads, it invited them to a two-day course, where the technique was explained. Gold described the training:

> Our early approach was to get 75 or so doctors and invite them to a two-day session. The bulk of the session consisted of talks by experts and videos. On the second day, they could watch a live procedure performed by a surgeon. Then, near the end of the session, the surgeons could practice the procedure on a pig.

But this approach did not yield the adoption and sales levels that the company had hoped. Geoff Dillon explained:

We would give a live demonstration to a group of 75 or so surgeons. By the end of the day, though, when it came time for them to test our system, most of them were eating cookies or looking at their watches. Out of the 75 or so surgeons who attended, only 10 percent of them showed interest and only one or two of those actually stayed to try it out. So the question was, "why did the majority of the surgeons leave?" We thought they came to these training sessions to learn *how* to do the procedure, but in reality, they came just to see what it was all about.

Gold described the sense he had of the efficacy of training as of the first quarter of 1998:

We weren't happy with the early results, so we shrunk the course to 20 surgeons or so, shortened it, and got to the hands-on component more quickly. Still, we find that only 10–20 percent of the surgeons we train actually attempt a procedure. Partly, I think the case is that they come to our training to get exposed and learn *about* the procedure, not really learn *how* to do it. At a cost of $50,000 or so—for a 20-physician program—this is quite expensive for us.

Of the surgeons that do attempt a procedure, we find they do get relatively comfortable with it, but that it is tough for them to break out of the situation where they are only using our approach for 10–20 percent of their surgeries.

I think we all agree that we need to support OPCAB with a stronger program.

Introducing the Third-Generation System—OPCAB

In response to this feedback from surgeons, CTS focused on developing a system that would allow surgeons to access to all of the major vessels of the heart. By April of 1998, this system was ready. Gold explained how the third-generation system worked:

We went back to the drawing board and designed *another* system that would enable access to multiple vessels of the beating heart—the OPCAB procedure (Off Pump Coronary Artery Bypass). The OPCAB procedure offered the same off-pump benefits of the Access MV system except that it allowed surgeons to access all the vessels of a beating heart. You can't just lift the heart out and twist it while it is beating—if you do, you will restrict blood flow. So we developed a technique that allows the surgeon to tilt the heart back using our specialized equipment. This will permit treating three, four, or five vessels. We prepared to launch this system in April 1998.

Competitive Landscape—1998

Overall, growth in the MICS industry had been slower than initially expected by analysts, due largely to difficulties surgeons experienced in learning to use these systems, as well as skepticism regarding the long-term safety and efficacy of these procedures.

Like CTS, Heartport also experienced adoption issues. Many patients had heard of MICS as a result of the Heartport publicity, and they were asking their doctors for it. But doctors were reluctant to provide it. The Heartport system was not only more expensive (at $5,000 per kit) than the existing on-pump technique, but it was more complex and very demanding on the surgeon. On average it took physicians four to six hours to perform a procedure using the Heartport system versus three to five hours using the traditional approach. And it required that the surgeon perform many procedures to become even this proficient.[17]

[17] Heartport, Inc., Research Report, Goldman Sachs, October 1998.

Moreover, although there was evidence that patients recovered more quickly with Heartport surgery than with standard CABG, resulting in shorter hospital stays and faster "time back to work," the overall cost-effectiveness of the Heartport system was still unproven: the Heartport system could actually increase costs due to the cost of equipment and additional time in the operating room.

In addition to Heartport, CTS faced emerging competition from some of the bigger medical device companies. Medtronic, U.S. Surgical, Baxter, and Genzyme Surgical Products ("Genzyme") had all entered the race to develop a beating heart kit.

Medtronic sold a disposable stabilizing device, the Octopus, that used tentacles, lined with a series of suckers, to grip the heart muscle and form a vacuum seal. A leader in conventional cardiac surgery disposables, Medtronic had significant technological expertise in the minimally invasive market, in addition to its sales and marketing leverage.

U.S. Surgical's product was a Mini-CABG instrumentation system, which included an extensive set of disposable tools for minimally invasive beating heart surgery. The company's products included a Site-Light for illuminating the site of operation, a Site-Blower, for maintaining a clean operating field, and a Stabilizer, which allowed the surgeon to control the heart throughout the operation.

Genzyme's device—the Cohn Stabilizer—looked like a soup ladle that had a flattened platform at the soup end of the ladle. This partially reusable device consisted of a long metal rod attached to a plastic, rectangular platform. Doctors used the long handle to press the flattened end of the soup ladle against the diseased artery, and subsequently operated through a cutout window in the plastic platform.

Baxter sold numerous products to facilitate MICS, for both on- and off-pump applications. Baxter's tools included both a surgical site visualization device and a heart positioner.

At the time of the case, CTS had an approximately 50 percent share of the beating heart market, and the aforementioned players, combined, shared the other 50 percent of the market. Gold estimated that Medtronic, U.S. Surgical, Genzyme, and Baxter held a 25 percent, 10 percent, 10 percent, and 5 percent market share, respectively.

What to Do?

Although the marketing team felt that the company was making progress, Ferrari, Gold, and Dillon still felt they needed to drive adoption of the CTS beating heart procedure, and increase utilization of their tools and techniques. Gold explained:

> The success of our company revolves around penetration and changing behavior patterns. Balloon angioplasty wasn't an ordinary event until 1988. People forget that interventional cardiology had a 10-year adoption curve from 1978 to 1988. With MICS, we are looking at a procedure that had its first demonstration to surgeons in 1995. We are only in the third year of this cycle. That being said, we still need to proactively drive the market. We can't just wait for the market to catch up to our technology.

EXHIBIT 5.1

Illustration of a CABG

Source: "Massachusetts General Hospital; CABG Surgery (A)," HBS Case No. 696-015.

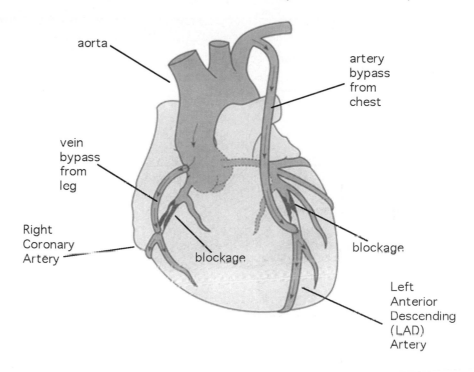

aorta

artery bypass from chest

vein bypass from leg

Right Coronary Artery

blockage

blockage

Left Anterior Descending (LAD) Artery

EXHIBIT 5.2   **Worldwide CABG Procedures**

Source: PaineWebber Industry Research Report, "How to Mend a Broken Heart," July 23, 1997, p. 41.

	1990	1995	1996	1997E	1998E	1999E	2000E	2001E	1990–1995	1996–2001
CABG										
United States										
Single vessel	26,000	32,000	33,280	34,611	35,996	37,435	38,933	40,490	4.2%	4.0%
Multiple vessel	234,000	288,000	299,520	311,501	323,961	336,919	350,396	364,412	4.2	4.0
Total	260,000	320,000	332,800	346,112	359,956	374,355	389,329	404,902	4.2	4.0
Rest of World										
Single vessel	15,400	20,650	21,579	22,550	23,565	24,626	25,734	26,892	6.0	4.5
Multiple vessel	204,600	274,350	286,696	299,597	313,079	327,167	341,890	357,275	6.0	4.5
Total	220,000	295,000	308,275	322,147	336,644	351,793	367,624	384,167	6.0	4.5
Worldwide										
Single vessel	41,400	52,650	54,859	57,162	59,561	62,061	64,667	67,382	4.9	4.2
Multiple vessel	438,600	562,350	586,216	611,098	637,040	664,087	692,286	721,687	5.1	4.2
Total	480,000	615,000	641,075	668,259	696,600	726,148	756,953	789,069	5.1	4.2

EXHIBIT 5.3
U.S. Coronary Stent Market, 1996–2000E (in $millions)

Source: Goldman Sachs Medical Device Industry Research Report, "Cardiology Market Update," March 11, 1999, p. 3.

	1996	1997	1998E	1999E	2000E
U.S. Market					
Angioplasty procedures	592,480	639,878	728,602	797,833	877,616
Stent penetration	40.0%	52.0%	68.0%	78.0%	90.0%
Stent procedures	236,992	332,737	495,449	622,310	789,855
Stents per procedure	1.60	1.62	1.70	1.75	1.80
Stents used	379,187	539,034	839,786	1,089,043	1,421,739
Price per stent	$1,500	$1,450	$1,543	$1,378	$1,150
Stent revenues per procedure	$2,400	$2,349	$2,616	$2,412	$2,070
Total stent revenues	**$568.8**	**$781.6**	**$1,295.9**	**$1,500.7**	**$1,635.0**

EXHIBIT 5.4
Cardiovascular IPO Activity 1991–1997

Source: "How to Mend a Broken Heart," Piper Jaffray Industry Research Report, June 23, 1997, p. 76; "Interventional Vascular Management in the Millenium," Piper Jaffrey Industry Research Report, October 1998, p. 35.

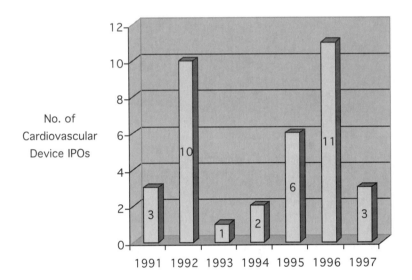

EXHIBIT 5.5
Heartport's Financing History

Source: www.venturesource.com, January 29, 1999.

Round	Amount Raised	Date of Closing	Post-Money Valuation	Company Stage
First	$ 3.3 million	09/92	$ 7.1 million	Product development
Second	$ 6.0 million	04/94	$ 47.3 million	Product development
Third	$ 16.0 million	06/95	$114.5 million	Product in clinical trials
IPO	$105.0 million	04/96	$492.3 million	Product in clinical trials

EXHIBIT 5.6
CTS's Financing History

Source: www.venturesource.com, January 29, 1999.

Round	Amount Raised	Date of Closing	Post-Money Valuation	Company Stage
First	$ 5.0 million	09/95	$ 7.8 million	Product development
IPO	$80.1 million	04/96	$221.0 million	Product development

EXHIBIT 5.7
Heartport's Price Performance: IPO to January 29, 1999

Source: Yahoo! Finance, http://quote-yahoo.com/ q?s=HRPT&d=t, January 29, 1999.

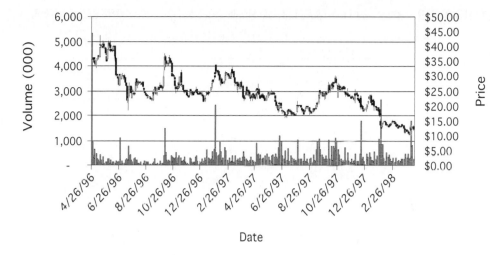

EXHIBIT 5.8
CTS's Price Performance: IPO to January 29, 1999

Source: Yahoo! Finance, http://quote-yahoo.com/ q?s=CTSI&d=t, January 29, 1999.

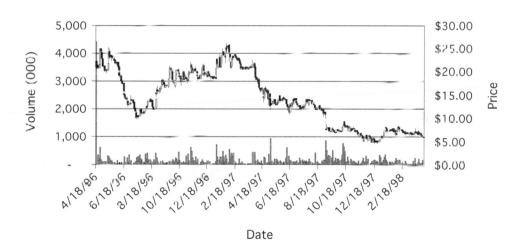

EXHIBIT 5.9   **CTS and Heartport Indexed Stock Price Performance: IPO to April 1998**

Source: Yahoo! Finance, http://quote-yahoo.com/q?s=CTSI and HRPT&d=t, January 29, 1999.

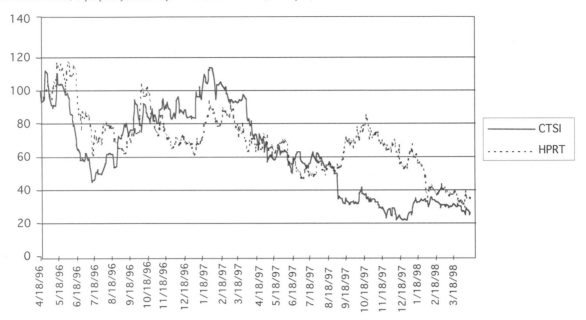

EXHIBIT 5.10
FDA Review Process for Medical Devices

Source: Company prospectus and "Note on the FDA Review Process for Medical Devices," HBS No. 796-063, by Research Associate James Leonard under the supervision of Professor Elizabeth Olmstead Teisberg.

Devices requiring Food and Drug Administration (FDA) approval fell into two broad categories.

Class II: less stringent control and lower requirements for review and approval (than Class III). Devices were characterized as Class II if they were "substantially equivalent" to existing devices and were not "life-sustaining" or "life-supporting" devices. A catheter, for instance, would be a Class II device, while a stent would require more stringent testing and control because it is implantable. A pacemaker would also be a Class III device. (See below.) A Class II device demonstrates "substantial equivalence" by showing that it has the same use and technological characteristics as an existing approved device. The applicant seeking approval files a 510(k) premarket notification asking the FDA to certify the device as Class II, and this typically takes three to six months.

Class III: these devices require higher levels of examination and scrutiny, because their failure could cause death or serious injury. The applicant files an "Investigational Device Exemption" (IDE) application in which they seek clearance to perform limited human trials. If this experience is favorable, the company goes back to the FDA to seek permission for human clinical studies. These can easily take two years or so, at the end of which the company returns to the FDA and files a Pre-market Approval Application (PMA), seeking permission to market the device broadly.

EXHIBIT 5.11
Picture of the CTS System

Source: Company.

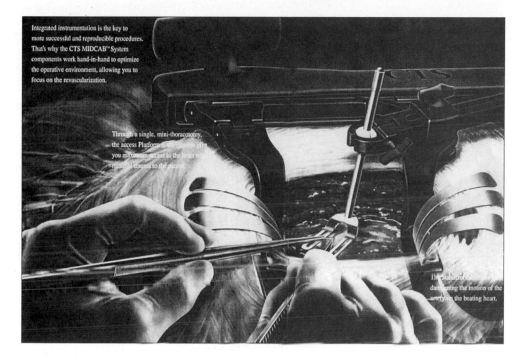

EXHIBIT 5.12 **Quarterly Sales Revenues and Financial Data (in thousands)**

Source: Company.

	2Q96	3Q96	4Q96	1996 Total	1Q97	2Q97	3Q97	4Q97	1997 Total	1Q98
Net sales	0	0	141	141	2,112	2,836	1,629	2,802	9,379	2,962
Cost of sales	0	213	629	842	1,472	1,744	1,115	1,631	5,962	1,603
Gross profit	0	(213)	(488)	(701)	640	1,092	514	1,171	3,417	1,359
Operating expenses	4,025	5,202	9,225	18,452	6,360	6,893	7,331	8,842	29,426	7,807
Loss from operations	(4,025)	(5,415)	(6,638)	(16,078)	(5,720)	(5,801)	(6,817)	(4,026)	(22,364)	(6,448)

Chapter 6

Innovation at 3M Corporation (A)

Stefan Thomke and Ashok Nimgade

On the evening of October 23, 1997, Rita Shor, senior product specialist at 3M, looked across the conference room at her team from the Medical-Surgical Markets Division. She wondered when to draw to a close the intense ongoing debate on the nature of the team's recommendations to the Health Care Unit's senior management. A hand-picked group of talented individuals, the team had embarked on a new method for understanding customer needs called "Lead User Research." But this initiative to introduce leading-edge market research methods into 3M's legendary innovation process had now grown into a revolutionary series of recommendations that threatened to rip apart the division.

While senior management wanted the "Lead User" team to execute a manageable project involving surgical draping material to protect surgery patients from infections, the team now wanted to rewrite the entire business unit's strategy statement to also include more proactive products or services that would permit the *upstream containment* of infectious agents such as germs. This went against the incrementalist approach that for so long had pervaded 3M. After all, as Mary Sonnack, division scientist and an internal 3M consultant on the new Lead User methodology, noted, "3M gets so much revenue from incremental products . . . like a blue Post-it note instead of just a yellow one."

Outside the window, the late autumn breeze rippled through the tall Minnesota grass—a seasonal reminder that it had been a year since the group first embarked on the Lead User process (see Exhibit 6.1). The method, including training, had called for less than six months dedicated to the entire process. But the lengthy commitment from participants as well as 3M senior management might just pay off if it took the

Professor Stefan Thomke and Research Associate Ashok Nimgade, M.D., prepared this case as the basis for class discussion rather than to illustrate either effective or ineffective handling of an administrative situation. Some names and company-confidential data have been disguised.

Copyright © 1998 by the President and Fellows of Harvard College. To order copies or request permission to reproduce materials, call 1-800-545-7685, write Harvard Business School Publishing, Boston, MA 02163, or go to http://www.hbsp.harvard.edu. No part of this publication may be reproduced, stored in a retrieval system, used in a spreadsheet, or transmitted in any form or by any means—electronic, mechanical, photocopying, recording, or otherwise—without the permission of Harvard Business School.

Medical-Surgical Markets division from a stagnating business to a reinvigorated enterprise. Clearly, however, unless the team came up with successful product ideas and effective positioning, the new methodology for product innovation would die with the winter frost. And so might the entire business unit.

History of 3M Corporation[1]

In 1902, on the banks of Lake Superior, five investors got together to excavate what they thought was high-quality corundum, a mineral almost as hard as diamond that manufacturers used for producing abrasives. What they dug up under the banner of the Minnesota Mining and Manufacturing Company, however, turned out low-grade and worthless. After filling one $20 order, the venture folded up its mining operations and turned instead to the sandpaper business. Here, disaster struck again: the abrasives they had imported from Spain refused to stick to the sandpaper.

Research and development (R&D) then at 3M, as the company became known, took place in a primitive laboratory so small the sole technician had to back out to let the boss in. The young technician figured out the problem after plunging some sandpaper into water and noting an oil slick. Follow-up investigations revealed that during shipment from Spain, an ocean storm had caused olive oil to leak into the abrasive material. This insight allowed for fixing the sandpaper problem while also establishing the emphasis on technology and innovativeness at 3M.

By 1916, survival assured, the company started paying stock dividends. The firm, now headquartered in St. Paul, Minnesota, initially stayed close to abrasives, developing the world's first waterproof sandpaper in the early 1920s. 3M technicians began bypassing purchasing agents in order to better understand product needs. Often, they walked into factories and workplaces and talked directly to workers, an unheard-of practice that yielded unexpected dividends.

While visiting an auto-body shop in the 1920s, for instance, Richard Drew, a young lab assistant, heard a torrent of screams and curses. Workers had apparently just ruined a two-tone paint job when paint peeled away as they removed glued newspaper strips used as masking materials. Back in the lab, while working with a new and crinkly backing material for sandpaper, Drew came up with the idea that would provide the world with masking tape. To spend the long hours needed to perfect the new tape, however, he had ignored a direct order from the company head to put all his efforts into improving a preexisting product. Drew's success helped spawn the legend of the subversive 3M inventor and the 3M aphorism: "It's better to seek forgiveness than to ask for permission." It also helped inspire a "get-out-of-the-way" attitude on the part of management toward product developers. At the same time, Drew had opened up another "core technology" for 3M. A few years later, in fact, Drew went on to also invent Scotch® brand cellophane tape, which would help the company prosper through the Great Depression.

Over the decades, 3M enjoyed national and global growth as well as a reputation for remaining a "hothouse" of innovation. "We'll make any damn thing we can make money on," stated a past 3M president, Richard Carlton.[2] According to the *International Directory of Company Histories:*[3]

[1] Much of the information on 3M history comes from G. C. Nicholson, "Keeping Innovation Alive," *Research-Technology Management* 41, no. 3 (May/June 1998), pp. 34–40; and 3M Annual Report, 1998.

[2] *International Directory of Company Histories* (Chicago/London: St. James Press, 1988), vol. 1, pp. 488–501.

[3] Ibid.

Observers and outsiders frequently describe 3M in terms approaching awe. 3M earns such respect because of its improbable, almost defiantly non-corporate nature. The company is gigantic, yet it is as innovative and as full of growth potential as though it were a small venture.

3M inventors did not share directly in product royalties; rather, the firm hoped that individual love for discovery would drive innovation. 3M sought to encourage innovation through a variety of means including awards for innovation as well as in-house grants for innovative projects. The company also allowed all staff to spend 15 percent of their time to explore new ideas outside of assigned responsibilities. Post-it® notes were developed on the 15 percent time scheme by 3M inventor Art Fry, who first used a weak adhesive to produce convenient hymnal markers for his music recitals.

3M also employed a "dual ladder" approach that allowed senior, technically inclined individuals with attractive career opportunities to advance, without having to switch to management. In addition, the company held internal showcases for products and ideas to help encourage interdepartmental cross-pollination or "bootlegging" of discoveries. As a result of these steps, 3M employees tended not to move to other companies.

The 3M model of expansion involved splintering off decentralized units based on new key product areas that were sufficiently different from prior key technologies. The first core technology from the 1920s had been adhesives and sandpaper. By the late 1990s, however, over 30 key technologies existed at 3M. Much market growth for 3M also came from finding new twists to existing product platforms; for instance, digital "Post-It Software Notes," or the use of 3M's Thinsulate®, first introduced in 1978 for apparel, in reducing sound in automobiles.

In the 1990s, 3M operated with four objectives: producing 30 percent of sales from products that did not exist four years earlier—an attempt to accelerate away from the incrementalism that had served as an engine for growth in the past few decades; greater than 10 percent annual growth in earnings per share; greater than 27 percent return on capital employed; and 20–25 percent return on equity. It also sought to change the mix of new products to emphasize products truly new to the world, instead of line extensions, which typically had provided two out of three new-product sales dollars. By 1997, completely new products produced two out of three sales dollars.

To achieve high rates of innovation, 3M placed a heavy emphasis on R&D. In 1997, it employed 4,500 scientists, engineers, and technicians in the United States, and another 2,000 overseas. On average, 3M spent 6.5–7.0 cents of every sales dollar on laboratory-based R&D, which amounted to just over $1 billion in 1997—not including process engineering and quality control expenses. In 1997, 3M companies operated in more than 60 countries, and overseas businesses generated half of the firm's $15.07 billion in revenue and half of its $2.7 billion in operating income. 3M employed 75,000 workers, of whom 36,000 were outside the United States. (See Exhibits 6.2 and 6.3.)

The Medical Products Division, the first 3M division dedicated solely to health care, was founded in 1961. A decade later, the Health Care Group at 3M provided an umbrella for all health-related product divisions including the Medical-Surgical Markets Division. By 1997, 3M could claim over 10,000 health-related products ranging from surgical drapes to dental fillings to respirators to software. By 1994, Health Care sales topped $2 billion.[4]

[4] 3M brochure entitled "3M Health Care," 1996.

Innovation at 3M in the 1990s

Product teams at 3M typically involved "skunkworks" teams primarily comprising technical individuals; teams also involved process engineers to help ensure that the particular product under development could be efficiently made. These engineers also provided teams with feedback about 3M's manufacturing capabilities. The entire team faced no risk if an idea flopped—indeed, there might even be a celebration. In case of failures, members of disbanded teams could go on to other projects. Although failures were often celebrated, each technical person's output over one or two years would be evaluated as a whole. The 3M mythology allowed for technical employees to take matters in their own hands—as exemplified by the Post-it notes story.

Marketing input traditionally came from current customers and sales representatives. Product developers focused on finding new angles or twists on early trends. At the same time, few market researchers worked at 3M; only one market researcher served 900 engineers. Instead, the firm hired out for market research reports from smaller market research firms. To identify market needs and trends, 3M product developers in the Health Care unit, for instance, utilized several tools:

- Data from sales representatives with daily contact with physicians or registered nurses.
- Focus groups: for example, one business unit within the Medical-Surgical Division would gather some 30 nurses biannually from across the nation in a room to obtain reactions to proposed products.
- Customer evaluations of currently marketed products.
- Site visits by 3M scientists and technologists to observe physicians and nurses at work, with the intent to identify unforeseen needs.
- Data on risk factors for diseases.

Several disadvantages to these methods had become apparent over the years. A major disadvantage was that the information obtained was not necessarily proprietary. Anyone, for example, could open up a medical textbook to find key risk factors for diseases. Attempts to seek more proprietary information through, say, focus groups provided virtually no clue about market needs some 5 to 10 years down the road. While visiting customers provided an opportunity for Thomas Edison–type "innovations by serendipity," customers were somewhat blind about their own needs, and thus could not provide clues about developing revolutionary products.

Even these customer visits, although traditionally a part of 3M, had often become deemphasized during the past few decades of successful growth through incremental innovation. This often led to situations where, as Mary Sonnack pointed out, "Typically, one or two product developers or even marketers think of a product, then they throw it over the wall to the commercializers." As a result, thousands of 3M product concepts and inventions awaited markets and languished on drawing boards and R&D labs.

The Medical-Surgical Markets Division

Over the past century, a few medical pioneers, including Benjamin Lister and Florence Nightingale, had demonstrated that the cleanliness of health care providers and the hospital environment could reduce the rate of new infections in patients. Previously, patients died on account of the hospital nearly as much as because of what put them there in the first place. It took several decades, however, for the pendulum to swing from the medical establishment to ridiculing such a stress on sanitation to mandating high standards of hygiene among health professionals. As a result, surgeons and attending staff now scrubbed with an almost ritualistic devotion using antiseptic detergents and donned sterile clothing and foot covers before entering operating rooms.

What was being operated upon was also antiseptically prepared or "prepped" for surgery. Thus, operating teams carefully established "sterile fields" on the skin around the pertinent area, freeing it from microbial contamination. A key part of this process involved use of surgical drapes, which served to isolate the "field of surgery" from all other potential sources of infection including the rest of the patient's body, the operating table, the anesthesiologist's equipment, and all members of the surgical team. But the diversity of the microbial world constantly challenged this artificial fortress. As a result, medical personnel had to remain vigilant about catheters and tubes along which agents of infections could migrate into the patient.

From mid-century on, surgical operating rooms became a product developer's dream-come-true. Product categories dedicated to preserving sterility included razors and clippers for shaving hair, presurgical soaps for scrubbing hands, sterile surgical gloves and masks, drapes, handwashes, antibiotics, lavages for washing away excess blood in a sterile fashion, sponges with or without handles, antiseptic solutions, and dressings.

The surgical drapes business unit within the Medical-Surgical Division focused largely on reducing infections from the skin through surgical drapes and surgical prepping. For 3M, the drape business represented one extension of Richard Drew's attempts to meet the needs of auto-body workshops. By the mid-1990s, 3M was highly penetrated in one niche of surgical drapes that brought the company over $100 million in yearly sales. But sales in the United States had limited growth remaining in these market niches. Overseas markets were limited by the high cost of 3M products, when converted into local currencies.

Most surgical drape products were developed using the equivalent of one full-time product developer and generated about $1 million in sales each. Occasionally, a $1–$20 million product would come along, but these big products were becoming fewer and fewer. Typically, it would take about two years to get a surgical drape product out from initial product conception to market. In the best case, this could be shortened to a year; in worse cases, it could take up to four years.

The surgical drapes section of the Medical-Surgical Markets Division had discovered the hard way that technological excellence by itself meant little. In the early 1990s, for instance, the division had spent three years developing a virus-proof gown that would let water vapor but not viruses pass through the fabric through microscopic pinholes. This manufacturing feat, however, came in just as managed care was taking hold. Although customers loved the fabric, the 10–15 percent price premium banished the product into a tiny niche in the European market.

By 1996, the business unit had gone almost a decade with only one successful product. Senior management charged Rita Shor with the mandate of developing a breakthrough product within the existing business strategy. She was assigned to the task not only because of her seniority, having been at the division 11 years, but also because she was thought of as being creative and a consensus builder.

Lead User Research at 3M's Medical-Surgical Markets Division

Shor realized, at the outset, that 3M's traditional methods for understanding customer and market needs would not suffice. Market research reports provided an abundance of data but contained little useful information for conceptualizing a breakthrough product. She recalled, however, an in-house lecture given a few weeks before by Mary Sonnack, a 3M division scientist and consultant who had become increasingly involved with new product development using a new methodology termed "Lead User Research" that she had studied at the Massachusetts Institute of Technology (MIT). Shor wondered if this might provide the key to a breakthrough product.

The premise of this novel methodology was that certain consumers experienced needs ahead of other consumers and that some of the former would seek to innovate on their own. By tapping the expertise of these so-called lead users, manufacturers could find invaluable sources of innovation. Lead users had often already created innovations to solve their own leading-edge needs—familiar examples were white-out ("liquid paper"), invented by a secretary for correcting typographical mistakes, and the sports drink Gatorade, developed in Florida with invaluable input from athletes.

3M's experience with traditional market research had been disappointing; it had not led to the kinds of innovations senior management wanted for the marketplace. As Chuck Harstad, former vice president of the Commercial and Office Supply Division and now vice president of Corporate Marketing, recalled:

> At the end of the day, we didn't learn anything from our market research department. 3M had to find new ways to identify leading-edge customer needs and develop concepts for breakthrough products and services. Traditional market research methods couldn't deliver the goods. And product developers would not assume ownership for understanding customer needs because they considered that to be the responsibility of market researchers. So we ended up eliminating the market research department to learn about customer needs!

Sonnack, under mandate from Harstad to seek out newer and better customer-focused product development processes, thought that Lead User research fit well with 3M's customer-focused philosophy (see Exhibit 6.4). In 1994, she began an unusual year-long stay at MIT to study with Professor Eric von Hippel, who had pioneered Lead User research. For von Hippel, the collaboration represented a way to develop a step-by-step methodology for practitioners and seek further validation of Lead User concepts. Since he had not charted out a "how-to" manual, he started this process with the help of Sonnack and Minnesota organizational psychologist Joan Churchill.

One of Sonnack's and Churchill's goals was to disseminate the Lead User process throughout 3M. Support for the new methodology existed at high levels within the company. William Coyne, 3M's Head of Research and Development, for instance, was fairly critical of the strategic planning process because he felt that "traditional strategic planning does not leave enough room for innovation. And innovation cannot be planned ahead of time." This view did not go unchallenged within 3M's senior management and represented a radical departure from the incrementalist approach to innovation. "Strategic planning looks in the rearview mirror and cannot keep up with the rate of change in today's markets," added Coyne. "We need to understand leading-edge customer needs to change the basis of competition." Widespread adoption of the Lead User process could help get 3M back to its roots of working more closely with customers and understanding such market needs.

Through one of Sonnack's in-house lectures, Shor first heard about the new methodology. In June of 1996, she telephoned Sonnack to say:

> Our business unit has been going nowhere. While we are number one in the surgical drapes market niche, and pull in over a hundred million in yearly sales, we are stagnating. We need to find new customer needs we haven't thought of before. If we don't bring in radically new ways of looking for products, upper management may have little choice but to sell off the business.

At the time, Sonnack's and Churchill's in-house consulting schedule was crowded. But Shor's degree of commitment appeared to match Sonnack's enthusiasm for the new methodology, and the two women agreed to meet. Were the Medical-Surgical Markets Division to focus product development based on the Lead User method, it would become one of the first divisions at 3M to do so. During their preliminary meeting, Sonnack warned Shor about the need for high-level commitment from both team members and their management.

Selling the new approach to senior management would use much of Shor's time and efforts. At first, senior management had balked at such a large commitment. But Shor pointed out that an adequate human resources commitment to the new methodology might prove more cost-effective than having 10–15 people working disjointedly. She tactfully reminded management that far more human resources were often redeployed for attacking technical problems that developed later in the product development process: "3M can pour a hundred thousand dollars at the drop of a hat for a production problem late in the product development process, but it is not used to doing so for such an early stage." Finally, however, Shor obtained support from her senior management to assemble a product innovation team on the basis of creativity and enthusiasm from the Medical-Surgical Markets Division. In a few weeks she was able to assemble an impressive interdisciplinary team.[5]

All team members were to commit half their time to the project. But as it turned out, several team members found that their managers still expected them to perform most of their traditional duties. As a result, much of the teamwork took place on Saturdays or outside the office at restaurants. The team sought in a disciplined manner to follow a project schedule with four stages prescribed by the Lead User research methodology (see Exhibit 6.4).

Stage I: Project Planning (~1.5 Months at 3M)

Stage I goals: In this "homework" or scouting stage of the study, which typically lasted four to six weeks, teams identified the types of markets and new products of interest, and the desired level of innovation.

In September of 1996, as the first stage started, Sonnack and Churchill sat in on Shor's early Lead User team meetings to focus the process. The two co-leaders probed the team with questions like "what do you know about this market . . . what don't you know?" "How about reimbursement policies?" "How important is the skin itself as a source of infection?" The team met for four hours each week in a conference room lined with some 20 flip charts so that ideas could be jotted down quickly. Between meetings, team members would search the Internet, literature, and their people network for information on relevant topics. Through this process, the team built up an invaluable database of information. For instance, it learned that 30 percent of infections occurred from the patient's own skin—a figure that highlighted the need for good surgical drapes.

Stage II: Trends/Needs Identification (~1.5 Months at 3M)

Stage II goals: The ultimate goal of this stage, which typically lasted five to six weeks, was to select a specific need-related trend(s) to focus upon for the remainder of the study. Typically a four-day team workshop kicked off this stage.

[5] The Medical-Surgical Markets Division (MSMD) team included Rita Shor, senior product specialist; Susan Hiestand, business manager with a marketing background; John Pournoor, polymer chemist; Matt Scholz, senior research specialist; Maurice Kuypers, market development supervisor; and Mark Johnson, process development specialist, Medical Products Resource Division.

The 3M team started Stage II with a five-day workshop intended to make sense of all the information gathered in Stage I. Through the workshop, which marked the culmination of all weekly meetings thus far, the team developed the following parameters for a breakthrough product: It should conform to the body, prove more effective than current products, and be easy to apply and remove.

The team, by now, had reached a stage where secondary literature could no longer add much of value. The second half of the workshop provided a turning point for the next phase of research: identifying appropriate expertise residing in experts at the leading edge of practice. The team undertook intensive group brainstorming about identifying appropriate experts to contact for more ideas and information from analogous areas of product development. Toward this end, workshop leaders encouraged participants to "step outside the box" because the most logical person might not prove the most appropriate expert. Through the rest of this stage, team members collected information from these identified experts.

Team members started talking over the telephone to a wide range of experts ranging from veterinary sciences to medics from the U.S. Mobile Army Surgical Hospital (MASH) unit in Bosnia. The MASH unit, discovered by team co-leader John Pournoor, had been considered a potential lead user because of its needs for portable, inexpensive, and flexible products. Product flexibility would ideally allow for low inventory, a prime consideration for a mobile medical unit. Hospitals, in contrast, could stock dozens of different product sizes and types. Interestingly, the MASH physicians did not fully realize their own need for manageable inventories since they focused on problems of communications, computerization, and telemedicine in the field; thus, they were not the lead users the team was looking for.

Although the MASH physicians would not be able to collaborate more intimately with the 3M Medical-Surgical Markets Division, this stage turned up other experts—from the theater make-up business to veterinary sciences to oceanographers—who would contribute to later stages.

Stage III at 3M: Preliminary Concept Generation (~6 Months)

Stage III goals: In this stage, which typically lasted five to six weeks, Lead User groups acquired a more precise understanding of market needs in the selected areas of focus. The teams began to generate preliminary concepts involving ideal attributes and features that would best meet customer needs.

By casting a wide net for product concepts, the division's business unit rapidly realized it knew precious little about the needs of customers outside the developed world. While sanitary conditions in the developed world had long since moved infectious disease down the roster of major killers (below causes such as cardiovascular and cancer), in the developing world infectious diseases were still major killers. If 3M hoped to find a breakthrough infection control product here, however, the team quickly realized it should visit several emerging market sites. The majority of new growth opportunities might lie here, even though disposable products were not popular or affordable.

Through December 1996 and January 1997, the team broke up into groups of two and traveled to hospitals in South America and Asia. Shor and Pournoor visited Malaysia, Korea, Indonesia, and India. This was the first time the Medical-Surgical Markets Division had sent product developers, rather than marketers, to visit potential customers. It allowed the 3M team members to see how operating room personnel coped with infection challenges of extreme environments. According to Shor:

> While we saw some excellent, world-class hospitals in India, we also observed hospitals in which surgeons operated barefoot and even we visitors had to take off our shoes. For sur-

gical field preparation, these teams used cloth (often with holes) that provided no resistance to fluids migrating to the wound itself! Sometimes, surgeons would use pieces of raincoat to cover over the patient's groin and other dirtier areas to keep microbes from migrating. Some surgeons used antibiotics wholesale, since these seemed cheaper to them than disposable drapes. . . . Often, only in side conversations would surgeons reveal that surgical infection was a problem. We also quickly realized that many other nations did not care about labor savings from our products. Labor was inexpensive and unlikely to be replaced or reduced. As a result, we realized we should not over-engineer our products for these markets.

The international fact-finding trips lengthened the expected duration of Stage III almost fourfold. While they yielded invaluable information about extreme environments and international market needs, they turned up no experts on lead use in terms of product efficacy.

With an eye toward bringing the project to a useful culmination, individual team members, under Sonnack's and Churchill's guidance, continued searching for appropriate lead users that might actually help develop product concepts. Team members continued talking with customers, academics, and industry experts, as well as searching through refereed journals and the Internet. The team found no single lead user with the exact set of specifications that the proposed 3M breakthrough product or products would need. Instead, a variety of lead users were found with expertise about different relevant attributes.

Commenting on the often painstaking search for an appropriate expert, Pournoor felt, "It is like finding a partner for marriage." Some experts came from traditional backgrounds—for instance, an expert on infection control that consulted with the U.S. Centers for Disease Control. Sometimes experts were found in the least likely places. During the premiere of the *Lion King* show in Minneapolis, for instance, a team member ended up chatting backstage with one of the make-up artists. As it turned out, the artist's husband, himself a make-up artist, had consulted with an orthopedic products firm. This make-up artist possessed specialized knowledge about the application of materials to the skin, which the team eventually felt would prove useful for developing breakthrough products.

How to pool together the combined knowledge and talent of this diverse array of knowledge to develop product concepts would prove the challenge of the final project stage.

Stage IV at 3M: Final Concept Generation (~3 Months)

Stage IV goals: In this stage, which typically lasts five to six weeks, Lead User teams take preliminary concepts developed in Stage III toward completion and also seek to ensure that all possible solutions have been explored. This stage centers around a workshop with invited lead users.

In the summer of 1997, bad luck struck the team in the form of a change in senior management. Thus far, the team had kept upper management apprised of the team's progress because "that way, when you make recommendations and submit proposals, there are no surprises."[6] The new business unit manager, Sam Dunlop, was one of the rare managers to come with a traditional market research background. His vision was aligned with the old 3M strategy of incremental growth in high-margin products. Dunlop had accepted the new post against his will, with the mandate to "stop the hemorrhage of profits and reconsolidate the division." He was close to retirement, and over the past few years none of the units he headed had thrived.

[6] "Teamwork with a Twist Helps 3M'ers Think Differently," *3M Stemwinder*, April 15, 1998.

In an initial meeting with team leaders, Dunlop stated more than once, "We must not tax the current operating income!" Although he recognized the need for departing from traditional product development, the focus on finding "wild-eyed" lead users made him uncomfortable. His marketing training had stressed logic and quantifiable data, which could be collected and analyzed in a predictable, linear fashion. The Lead User methodology, in contrast, collected qualitative data from people, with new questions leading to new concepts, which in turn started up a new cycle of questions that begged further answers. Where the process would ultimately lead was never known with full certainty at the project's start. As a temporary compromise, Dunlop reduced the Lead User team by one member and made his opposition to the project quite clear.

Shor and her team had to sell the program starting from scratch, reminding the new managers about how inefficient the old ways of developing products had been. One tactic was to invite some of the business managers to join several team brainstorming sessions. This, according to Pournoor, "got them out of the box," and made them more receptive. Nonetheless, team members remained uncomfortably aware of the watchdogs of corporate profitability nipping at their ankles.

* * *

Even with the project's green light blinking anemically, the team finally decided to center the Stage IV workshop around the bold question, "Is there a revolutionary approach to infection control?" In deference to management's concern with the near-term bottom line, however, the team decided to focus specifically on product efficacy and cost. Rita Shor expressed the workshop goals to 11 3M personnel (see Exhibit 6.5) and 11 outside experts (see Exhibit 6.6) that had gathered on August 8 at a St. Paul hotel:

> By the end of the workshop, we want at least three product concepts that could dramatically improve microbial control in the surgical setting of today and tomorrow, with significant cost savings for surgeons in the United States and in the rest of the world. We seek breakthrough innovations that range from being so big as to render obsolete the current system, or, alternatively, so simple that they would use our existing technologies in new ways.

All assembled experts signed intellectual property rights to 3M, but received modest financial remuneration in the form of an honorarium. The workshop lasted two and a half days, a period, described by Lead User team co-leader John Pournoor, a veteran of many product development focus groups, as "not too long and not too short." This length of time allowed for two to three iterations of concepts.

In the introductory session, group members introduced themselves and discussed how their backgrounds might pertain to the task on hand. The group of experts, varying in age from 35 to 79, came from disciplines ranging from dermatology to make-up artistry to veterinarian sciences (see Exhibit 6.6). The workshop was divided into exercise sessions lasting several hours each. For each session, participants divided up into smaller groups of three to five individuals. Although groups constantly changed, "An element of competition among groups developed," according to Pournoor. "This reminded me of my old work at Boeing, where we'd have two different teams working in parallel on the same project."

Group members and facilitators faced at least four major challenges. The first arose from the lack of structure found in many corporate meetings. As a result, some groups tended to "flounder" during much of the exercise sessions. In a surprisingly large number of sessions, however, teams adhered to a strict schedule, which served to shepherd them toward solutions in the last few minutes.

A second challenge came from introverted and extroverted participants. Initially, for instance, the make-up artist, according to Pournoor, "felt intimidated by all the big words being thrown around, and I think he began to wonder what he was doing there. As time went on, however, his expertise and our needs converged. He contributed more and more." By contrast, the surgeon tended to squash all new ideas that arose early in the session. During a break, however, the veterinarian took him aside, saying, "Do you remember how during your training you were under someone's thumb? Well, that's what you're doing to us." After reflecting upon these words, the surgeon actually stayed up much of that night searching the Internet for new information, and thereafter went on to encourage other team members' contributions.

A third challenge came from finding ways to marry very creative ideas with technical feasibility. A rare nexus of lead user need and technological reality occurred following a period when the veterinarian stopped to reflect on his view of the ideal operating room:

> I—and probably most surgeons—want to focus on only one area on the operating table. I don't want to see anything except what I'm focused on, especially when I'm tired or under stress. With this in mind, could we create a material that we could quickly pull out of the wall or a box and place directly over the patient to create an infection barrier? Such a material should ideally draw the surgeon's attention to only the area being operated upon. This would prove valuable because time is of the essence, and surgery is a waltz that must be performed correctly every single time.

Subsequent brainstorming identified a preexisting material found in 3M's current line of products as possibly capable of bringing the veterinarian's needs to product reality. This exchange of ideas ended up forming the basis of one of the workshop's key product concept recommendations.

The fourth challenge lay in navigating a sea of facts. Here, an intricate interplay of questions and answers between experts from a diverse range of interrelated disciplines helped keep the entire product development process afloat. For example, one participant asked, "How do we make all these antimicrobial materials stick to the patient's body?" The make-up artist, heretofore in the background, pulled open his large binder of dozens of pre-fabricated/pre-made concoctions of skin-adhesive materials that 3M would have otherwise missed. By the end of the ensuing discussion, he ended up sketching a product concept for layering on materials onto surfaces with smooth contours that could be shown to the other participants.

In the course of several sessions, the invitees successfully rose to the challenges facing them and generated numerous product concepts. In the final session, the group met as a whole to rate and prioritize all concepts on the basis of commercial appeal and technical feasibility. Finally, team members agreed upon the next steps for refining the leading candidates (see Exhibit 6.7). The external experts ended up rating the workshops highly, from an A− to A+ largely because, in Shor's words, "They'd been in brainstorming sessions where everybody tossed out ideas, but this time, they got to turn the ideas into concrete concepts. . . ."[7] (See Exhibit 6.8.)

* * *

After the lead users and other invitees had left town, the product development team from the Medical-Surgical Markets Division met to decide upon its final recommendations to senior management. The team felt the following "metrics" should

---

[7] "Lead User Research Picks up the Pace of 3M Innovation," *3M Stemwinder,* September 24, 1997.

be used for ranking the product development concepts that had arisen from the recent workshop:

- Customer preference for the new products.
- Creation of new growth for the division, with the goal of double-digit annual growth. Creation of new businesses and industries that could change the basis of competition for the business unit.
- Boosted global presence of the division.
- Higher growth for the rest of 3M through, as much as possible, incorporation of proprietary 3M technology with patent protection.

The team ended up with three product recommendations that involved an "economy" line with a strong focus on cost, a "Skin Doctor" line, and an antimicrobial "armor" line (see Exhibit 6.7). The first two recommendations represented straightforward linear extensions of existing 3M product lines. The last, the team thought, represented a departure from past activities, and might thus open the door to new business opportunities. The team felt solidly confident in presenting these three recommendations to senior management, especially given the scope for synergy with 3M's existing activities and business unit strategy. For instance, all these proposed product lines could potentially boost sales from preexisting 3M products that helped reduce microbial contamination. As another example, the first proposal could also draw from a preexisting line of 3M drapes.

It was the fourth recommendation, however, that divided the team and formed the basis for a long, heated discussion among the team members.

The Fourth Recommendation: Evolution or Revolution?

Over the past few months, the product development team had become increasingly aware of a gaping hole in medical knowledge involving infection containment. Discussions with lead users and associated experts indicated that the medical community still groped for ways to prevent infections and was easily swayed by any report that appeared credible. No health care company had yet stepped in to take leadership in the area of early intervention in the disease process. Thus a vacuum existed in which 3M could find a new growth area.

For the fourth recommendation, therefore, the product development team had begun thinking about rewriting the business unit's strategy statement to include *upstream containment* of infections or, in other words, to keep infections from happening by precautionary upstream measures. Entering the area of upstream containment, however, meant becoming adept at a new set of skills and knowledge. It meant, for example, being able to track early contamination and its possible consequences in a health care facility—not only detecting specific contaminants but also identifying and, depending on their risk level, targeting individuals for interventions.

The new approach thus called for much more sophistication than the traditional industrial viewpoint, which held one patient just as deserving as the next of the latest surgical drape or the newest handwash. With the new approach, for instance, a malnourished patient might be targeted for nutritional interventions in addition to standard interventions, and diabetic patients might be identified for extra antibiotic coverage.

At 3M, such sophistication called for combining technologies from more than one core area or from areas in which 3M lacked depth. In particular, the product development team recognized the need to combine technologies from its Medical-Surgical division with diagnostics. But because the term "diagnostics" held a negative connotation at 3M—following the brief and unhappy acquisition of a small diagnostics company in the 1980s—the team diplomatically substituted the word "detection" in wording its recommendations.

The very need for diplomacy with phrasing of recommendations brought home the ramifications of a shift in direction. "While traditional product development team members at 3M face no immediate consequences for failures," according to Pournoor, the polymer chemist, "we were actually thinking about challenging the entire business strategy. We were crossing boundaries. . . . I think this resulted from using the Lead User methodology, which, in addition to allowing us to gather and use information differently than before, also provided emotional support for change. Team members no longer felt like 'lone-rangers' as they might have under the traditional regime."

In the evening before the final recommendations were to be presented, the team met to resolve a deadlock over the fourth recommendation. Maurice Kuypers, the market development supervisor, sparked the debate by stating, "We don't want the Lead User methodology to be viewed as a means for fomenting revolution. We already have three great product recommendations. If the team proceeds too quickly with the fourth recommendation, senior management may pull the plug on everything: the product recommendations as well as the Lead User method itself."

Mark Johnson, the process development specialist, countered, "When I started with this method, I thought we were just going to develop new products. But now, talking with these lead user experts has shown me that what we were planning was not too effective anyway. We should seriously question our unit's business strategy."

Susan Hiestand, the business manager, chipped in: "Wasn't our mandate to find breakthroughs? We were warned that with the Lead User method we will never be able to predict the final outcome or the path we will end up taking. Well, here we are with our breakthrough: It's not a product you can drop on your foot; it turns out to be a process or a service!"

"I think in the back of his mind," John Pournoor warned, "Dunlop would not mind seeing this process fail. Let's not give him any excuses for scrapping everything we've worked and sacrificed for, with our extra hours of hard work on this process. Let's focus on the first three recommendations, plant a few seeds about infection prevention, and draw the managers into making the intellectual leap themselves. Let them become the revolutionaries . . . or 'corporate visionaries.'"

Rita Shor looked at her watch. In less than an hour she would have to draw the discussion to a close and seek consensus. She recalled how, in the final workshop, the sessions often floundered until very close to the end, when miraculously the group would arrive at consensus. But that—as invaluable to fostering creativity as it had proven—now seemed like playing a board game on a rainy day. Today's decisions would ripple through the very real world of business, with the future of a sizable business unit at stake.

EXHIBIT 6.1
Important Milestones

Source: Case interviews.

1902	Minnesota Mining and Manufacturing founded.
1948	3M Steri-Drape® Surgical Drape introduced.
1961	Medical Products Division, the first 3M division dedicated solely to health care, founded.
1993	
May	MIT Professor Eric von Hippel contacts Mary Sonnack to see if 3M would help test Lead User methodology. Sonnack would spend the entire next year to learn and help formalize the Lead User methodology and initiate the involvement of psychologist Joan Churchill in the later part of the year.
1996	
June	Rita Shor given task of finding breakthrough products for Medical-Surgical Markets Division. Shor approaches Mary Sonnack after hearing Sonnack lecture internally at 3M about Lead User methodology.
September–October	Stage 1 of Medical-Surgical Markets Division Lead User project starts. Shor's product development team meets with Mary Sonnack.
End of October	Stage 2 starts.
December	Stage 3 starts. The product development team decides to search internationally for breakthrough ideas on surgical draping.
1997	
January–March	Medical-Surgical Markets Division team visits South America and Asia for breakthrough ideas on surgical draping.
April	Lead User meetings/workshops result in several concepts. Team starts search for appropriate lead users.
June–July	New management in Medical-Surgical Markets Division seeks justification for Lead User process and wants accelerated outcome. The team convinces new management to maintain support. Stage 4 starts.
August	Large 2.5-day Lead User workshop with 11 outside experts and 11 3M insiders.
October 27	Scheduled date for Medical-Surgical Markets Division team's presentation to management concerning recommendations generated from Lead User process.
November	Medical-Surgical Markets Division management's deadline for resource allocation for product concepts generated from Lead User process.

EXHIBIT 6.2
Selected 3M Financial Data (Dollars in Millions, Except Per-Share Data)

Source: 3M Financial Reports.

	1995	1996	1997
Sales	$13,460	$14,236	$15,070
Cost of goods sold	6,861	7,216	7,710
Gross profit	$ 6,599	$ 7,020	$ 7,360
Selling, general, and administrative expense	3,440	3,646	3,815
Depreciation, depletion, and amortization	859	883	870
Operating profit	$ 2,300	$ 2,491	$ 2,675
Net income (after taxes)	976	1,526	2,121
Other Data:			
EPS (primary)—excluding extra items and discontinued operations	3.11	3.63	5.14
Dividends per share	1.88	1.92	2.12
ROA (%)	9%	11%	16%
ROE (%)	19%	24%	36%
Market value	27,791	34,597	33,212
R&D expenses	883	947	

EXHIBIT 6.3
3M Revenue by Classes of Products/Services ($millions)

Source: R. P. Curran, "Minnesota Mining & Manufacturing Co.—Company Report," *Merrill Lynch Capital Markets,* New York, July 11, 1997.

	1995	1996	1997E	1998E
Tape products	$ 2,042	$ 2,096	$ 2,215	$ 2,370
Abrasive products	1,220	1,270	1,375	1,510
Automotive and chemical products	1,328	1,460	1,620	1,800
Connecting and insulating products	1,470	1,564	1,688	1,850
Consumer and office products	2,272	2,460	2,672	2,925
Health care products	2,221	2,356	2,545	2,775
Safety and personal care products	1,220	1,301	1,385	1,505
All other products	1,687	1,729	1,835	1,980
Total	$13,460	$14,236	$15,335	$16,715

EXHIBIT 6.4
**Lead User Research
Methodology**

Source: This exhibit draws
from E. von Hippel, J.
Churchill, and M. Sonnack,
*Breakthrough Products and
Services with Lead User
Research* (Cambridge, Mass.,
and Minneapolis, Minn.:
Lead User Concepts, Inc.,
1998, forthcoming Oxford
University Press). For a
detailed discussion and
description of Lead User
research, see also S. Thomke
and A. Nimgade, *Note on
Lead User Research,* Harvard
Business School Case No.
699-014.

> If the outer appearance of things matched their inner nature,
> there would be no point to science.
>
> *Galileo*

The Lead User method, pioneered by Professor Eric von Hippel of the Massachusetts Institute of Technology (MIT), provides a means to unearth product development opportunities that are not immediately obvious by traditional methods. It allows for accurately forecasting market opportunities by tapping the expertise and experience base of "lead users," the individuals or firms that experience needs *ahead* of the market segment in which they operate. Lead users may lead in either the *target* or *analogous* markets. Some lead users may be involved with just one or more of the important *attributes* of the problems faced by users in the target market.

Ideally, Lead User methods allow new product development to flow out of a sensitive understanding of product features that matter most to customers several years later. Specific benefits of Lead User methods include richer and more reliable information on the needs of emerging customer needs; better products and service concepts since these come out of better data on quality needs; and acceleration of the product and service development process.

These benefits, however, come only after substantial commitment of resources on the part of the sponsoring firm. Research indicates that three elements remain necessary for success in the Lead User process: *supportive management,* use of a *cross-disciplinary team of highly skilled people,* and a clear *understanding of the principles of Lead User research.*

Success of the study relies heavily on selecting a talented core team. Typically, the team consists of four to six people from marketing and technical departments, with one member serving as project leader. These team members typically spend 12 to 15 hours per week for the entire project on a Lead User project. This high level of immersion fosters creative thought and sustains project momentum.

Lead User projects typically take five or six months, in which time the four to six people involved spend up to a third of their time on the project. In conducting a Lead User study, four stages are involved, as described below, with typical time commitments provided in parentheses:

- *Stage I: Project Planning (4–6 weeks).* In this "homework" or scouting phase of the study, the team identifies the types of markets and new products of interest, and the desired level of innovation. For instance, does the company seek a "breakthrough" product or does it wish to merely extend current product or service lines? At the same time, the team identifies key business constraints. The team typically starts Stage I by informally interviewing industry experts, including customers, suppliers, and internal company managers, to get a feel for current trends and market needs. This lays the groundwork for developing strategies for future data collection and for helping focus on key market trends.

- *Stage II: Trends/Needs Identification (5–6 weeks).* The ultimate goal of this stage is to select a specific need-related trend(s) to focus upon for the remainder of the study. Typically a four-day team workshop kicks off this stage. In this workshop, members digest the information collected during Stage I to get a sense of the "conventional wisdom" relating to trends and market needs. Thereafter, the focus shifts to finding top experts, through querying experts, telephone "networking," scanning literature, and consulting with in-house colleagues. Thereafter, telephone interviews can start. Three or four weeks into Stage II, the team generally develops a good understanding of major trends and is now positioned for the vital task of "framing" the customer need that can be addressed by a new product or service. These initial ideas are reworked and refined throughout this stage.

- *Stage III: Preliminary Concept Generation (5–6 weeks).* In this stage, the group acquires a more precise understanding of the needs it has selected as the area of focus. The team begins to generate preliminary concepts involving ideal attributes and features that will best meet customer needs. The team also seeks to informally assess business potential for the product or service being conceptualized. The team continues interviewing lead user experts for technical knowledge that pertains to concept generation. Toward the end of Stage III, the team meets with key managers involved with implementing concepts after completion of the entire project to confirm that identified needs and initial concepts fit well with important business interests.

- *Stage IV: Final Concept Generation (5–6 weeks).* In this stage, the team takes the preliminary concept developed in Stage III toward completion. Participants in this stage seek to ensure

EXHIBIT 6.4
(continued)

that all possible solutions have been explored. Activity in Stage IV centers around a one- to two-day Lead User workshop with invited lead users to improve and add to the preliminary concepts. Typically, 15 to 18 people attend this workshop, of which a third may come from the project team and from in-house technical or marketing divisions. In these workshops, sub-groups comprised of in-house personnel as well as invited experts discuss independent parts of the problem to generate alternative product concepts. Thereafter, the entire group evaluates the concepts in terms of technical feasibility, market appeal, and management priorities. Finally, the entire group arrives at consensus on the most commercially promising concepts and develops recommendations for further steps to refine them.

After the workshop, the team refines the preliminary concept on the basis of knowledge gained from the workshop. At a meeting with managers, the team presents the proposed products or services, covering design principles. The team comes prepared with solid evidence about why customers would be willing to pay for them. For any concept chosen for commercialization, at least one member of the Lead User team should remain involved in further steps needed to take the concept to market. This helps fully leverage that vast body of knowledge captured through the Lead User method.

While Lead User methodology stresses qualitative probing of the right questions over the traditional focus on quantifiable questions, ongoing studies seek to compare performance of the new method with traditional methods.

EXHIBIT 6.5
3M Staff Participating in the Stage IV Workshop

Source: 3M.

Lead User Team Members:
- Rita Shor, Senior Product Specialist, Medical-Surgical Markets Division (MSMD), and Lead User team co-leader
- Susan Hiestand, Business Manager, MSMD
- John Pournoor, PhD, Research Specialist, MSMD, and Lead User team co-leader
- Matt Scholz, Senior Research Specialist, MSMD
- Maurice Kuypers, Market Development Supervisor, MSMD
- Mark Johnson, Process Development Specialist, MSMD

Lead User Team Consultants
- Joan Churchill, PhD, Clinical Psychologist
- Mary Sonnack, Division Scientist and Internal 3M Consultant

Other 3M Staff Members Involved
- *Microbiologist:* Joanne Bartkus, PhD, Clinical Studies
- *Business Development Manager:* German Chamorro, 3M Latin America
- *Synthetic Chemist:* John Dell, PhD, Senior Research Specialist
- *Organic Chemist:* Roger Olsen, R&D Manager
- *Marketing Manager:* Nicola Stevens
- *Product Designer:* Joy Packard

EXHIBIT 6.6
Outside Experts Participating in the Stage IV Workshop

Expertise on Advanced Methods for Understanding Bacteria
- *General surgeon and chemist (MD, PhD),* possessed considerable experience in minimally invasive surgery with very ill patients as well as epidemiological expertise. *Area of innovation:* understanding surgical contamination.
- *Dermatologist/surgeon (MD),* had worked on laser excision of skin cancer and possessed expertise on skin infection. *Area of innovation:* surgical wound healing.

Expertise on Methods for "Fast Track" to Market
- *Antimicrobial pharmacologist (PhD),* had chaired the Food and Drug Administration's Antimicrobial Committee for pharmaceutical drugs and had worked with skin care and pharmaceutical products for 30 years. He had worked on a similar product focus group that had led "tortuously" to the anti-cold medication Nyquil. *Area of innovation:* antimicrobial agents.

Expertise on Advanced Agents to Kill Bacteria
- *Disease control expert (MS),* a water-purifying expert who had worked for the Centers for Disease Control (appearing here as a private consultant) and had a background in epidemiology and hospital staff–mediated infections. *Area of innovation:* expertise in controlling infections in wet environments as evinced by getting a flood-stricken hospital back in operation with antiseptic systems working within six days.
- *Antimicrobial chemist (PhD),* with training in synthetic organic chemistry, held over 50 patents in better delivery of antiseptic solutions and had also researched synthetic materials used to make artificial skin. *Area of innovation:* delivery of antiseptic solutions.
- *Biologist (PhD),* had started out researching meat industry infection but ended up appreciating the need for preventive medicine through "looking upstream" for the earlier sources of infection involving livestock. *Area of innovation:* study of the relationship between different microorganisms; development of light and reduced fat cheese.
- *Biochemical engineer (PhD),* a university professor who worked in the areas of tissue engineering and sterilization. *Area of innovation:* tissue engineering and sterilization.

Expertise on Ease of Application to Skin
- *Hollywood make-up artist,* had served as a consultant to an orthopedic products firm. *Area of innovation:* application of materials and cosmetics to the skin.
- *Veterinarian surgeon (DVM),* explained his presence on the panel in terms of the extreme challenges infection control in animals poses since, in his words, animals "have hair, do not bathe, and carry no insurance!" Veterinarian input, thus, could help address an extreme end of the spectrum of human infection that was traditionally neglected. *Area of innovation:* surgical techniques and implant design, for which he had won the 1996 veterinarian "Practitioner of the Year" award.
- *"Creative health practitioner" (MD),* a psychiatrist with a BS in microbiology, also had a background in the assessment of performance of paint products. *Area of innovation:* assessment of chemical applications on hard surfaces.
- *Polymer chemist,* who had also studied acupuncture, in addition to polymers. *Area of innovation:* study of acupuncture, polymers, and rheology (the study of the flow of matter).

EXHIBIT 6.7
Excerpt from Memo on Product Recommendations

The abbreviated descriptions below are the Lead User team's recommendations for three product lines for the Medical-Surgical Markets Division (MSMD). (Note that these are the leading contenders from the six concepts that came out of the final product development workshop.)

1. *The "economy" line.* The MSMD should consider a line of surgical drapes using a combination of low-cost materials. Preexisting 3M adhesives and fastening devices may provide a variety of ways for sticking the materials to the body. A one-size-fits-all strategy and time-saving dispensing systems will boost product acceptance in the current cost-containment environment as well as in developing countries. (Impetus for this product line, in fact, came out of the divisional fact-finding trips to the developing world.) Following the veterinarian lead user's advice, these materials should allow focus on only the part of the body being operated upon. Being based on preexisting 3M technologies, this represents an incremental proposal.

2. *The "Skin Doctor" line* (see Exhibit 6.8). The MSMD should consider a line of hand-held devices resembling hand-held vacuums for antimicrobial protection. These devices would layer antimicrobial substances onto surfaces being operated upon. An advanced generation of the Skin Doctor could potentially operate in two modes: a vacuum mode, which could mop up surface liquids, in addition to the original layering mode. Impetus for this came from the Lead User workshop. Being based on preexisting 3M technologies, this also represents an incremental proposal.

3. *Antimicrobial "armor" line.* Currently, 3M focuses on only surface infections and thus ignores other infection control markets that included blood-borne, urinary tract, and respiratory infections. An armor product line would use 3M technologies to "armor" catheters and tubes from unwelcome microscopic visitors. This line would represent a breakthrough product because it is consistent with the current business strategy of reactive infection control but would provide the company entry into a new $2 billion market.

EXHIBIT 6.8
Drawing of the "Skin Doctor" Product Concept Generated during the Lead User Workshop

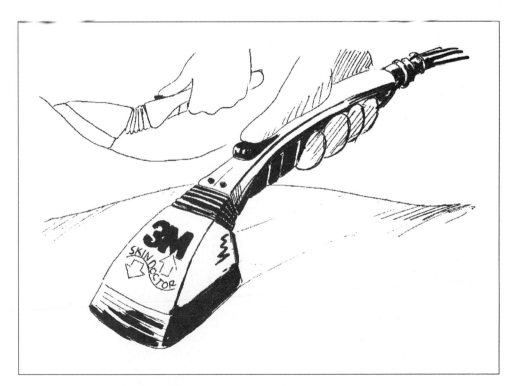

Part 3

Launching
New Products

7. The Medicines Company

8. Biopure Corporation

9. Synthes

Chapter

The Medicines Company

John T. Gourville

"When people first hear our business concept, they think we're crazy," stated Clive Meanwell, the founder, president, and CEO of The Medicines Company. Formed in 1996, The Medicines Company "acquired, developed, and commercialized pharmaceutical products in late stages of development," meaning that it purchased the rights to drugs that other companies had abandoned. As Meanwell explained it:

> We founded our company on the premise that sometimes there is still value in drugs that fail to meet a developer's initial expectations. Companies develop drugs with particular applications, users, price points, and market sizes in mind. When clinical testing calls these expectations into question, companies often halt development. But drugs that seem unprofitable for one application or user group might prove quite profitable for others. Our job is to find such drugs, acquire them at reasonable prices, complete their development, and bring them to market.

By early 2001, this strategy seemed to be working. Four years earlier, the company had acquired the rights to Angiomax, a blood thinning drug or "anticoagulant" that Biogen had abandoned after $150 million and seven years of development. On December 17, 2000, after completing the required clinical trials, The Medicines Company received United States Food and Drug Administration (FDA) approval to sell the drug for use in conjunction with an artery-clearing procedure known as an angioplasty. Exhibit 7.1 provides a newspaper account of this drug approval.

Professor John T. Gourville prepared this case. HBS cases are developed solely as the basis for class discussion. Cases are not intended to serve as endorsements, sources of primary data, or illustrations of effective or ineffective management. Some nonpublic company data have been disguised and some business details have been simplified to aid in classroom discussion.

Copyright © 2001 President and Fellows of Harvard College. To order copies or request permission to reproduce materials, call 1-800-545-7685, write Harvard Business School Publishing, Boston, MA 02163, or go to http://www.hbsp.harvard.edu. No part of this publication may be reproduced, stored in a retrieval system, used in a spreadsheet, or transmitted in any form or by any means—electronic, mechanical, photocopying, recording, or otherwise—without the permission of Harvard Business School.

In spite of this good news, several issues remained for Meanwell and his management team. The first issue involved pricing. Angiomax was positioned as an alternative to "heparin," the most widely used anticoagulant in emergency coronary heart care. The problem was that heparin cost about $2 per dose. While it was clear that The Medicines Company would price Angiomax above heparin, the question was "how much above?"

The second issue involved the need to develop a product portfolio. Meanwell had long argued that the company's success depended on the development of a drug pipeline. However, the company had run into problems with its second acquisition—a migraine headache drug—and had halted its further development. This setback and Angiomax's recent FDA approval had Meanwell wondering whether there truly was the need for a drug pipeline.

Finally, as a public company, The Medicines Company faced the realities of the stock market. In fact, many investors had expected a sharp stock price increase with the approval of Angiomax. Instead, the company's stock (NASDAQ: MDCO) fell over 25 percent in the month following FDA approval (see Exhibit 7.2). This caused some people to question the company's core business strategy.

The Drug Development Industry[1]

By any measure, prescription drugs were big business. At the manufacturer level, prescription sales in 2000 approached $220 billion worldwide, with growth projected at 10 percent per year through 2010. The largest market for these drugs was the United States, accounting for 50 percent of all sales.

The United States also was home to most of the world's major drug companies (see Exhibit 7.3). The largest of these was Pfizer/Warner-Lambert, with annual drug revenues in excess of $25 billion worldwide and $14 billion domestically. As for profitability, the United States drug industry ranked first among all major industries, with net incomes at almost 20 percent of revenues in 1999.[2]

In 2000, several trends were impacting the United States drug market. These included

- An aging population. In 1999, people age 65 or over accounted for 15 percent of the population, but 33 percent of prescription drug sales in the United States. Between 2000 and 2020, this population was expected to grow from 35 million to 55 million.

- Increased price pressure. Prescription drugs accounted for 9 percent of medical expenses in 2000 and were growing at a 20 percent annual rate. As a result, managed care organizations (which paid for 70 percent of all prescription drugs) and the government (which paid for 10 percent) were pressuring drug companies to contain or lower drug prices.

- The growth in generics. As a rule, a generic drug came to market soon after the patent on a branded drug expired, typically at a price 25 percent to 75 percent below the price of the branded drug. Between 2000 and 2010, generic sales were expected to grow from $10 billion to $60 billion as several blockbuster drugs came off patent.

[1] Much of these data were drawn from S&P's industry survey, "Healthcare: Pharmaceuticals," December 21, 2000.

[2] "Health's Price Tag," *The Boston Globe,* March 28, 2001, p. D4.

Drug Development

Historically, new drugs were the lifeblood of the pharmaceutical industry—drugs under development at any point in time representing the potential blockbuster drugs that would drive the industry 5 to 10 years later. The successful development of a new drug was far from easy, however. Beginning in 1938, the United States FDA required drug developers to follow a complex process designed to prove the safety and effectiveness of any proposed new drug. Accordingly, pharmaceutical firms followed a sequential drug development process:

- In *preclinical/animal trials,* a candidate drug was identified, studied for its chemical properties, and tested on animals to assess safety and effectiveness. Most drugs were eliminated at this stage due to unacceptable side effects or failure to work as expected.

- In *Phase I clinical trials,* the drug was given to a small number of healthy people in order to test safety. Initially, small doses were administered, with dosage increased over time to assess safety at higher levels.

- In *Phase II clinical trials,* the drug was given to people suffering from the condition that the drug was intended to treat. This stage usually included a larger number of people and a longer period of time than in Phase I.

- *Phase III clinical trials* were the most critical of the four stages.[3] They were the largest, most complex, and most rigorous of the human trials, designed to test fully the safety, effectiveness, and dosing levels of the drug on actual patients.

- An *FDA submission* typically followed a successful Phase III trial. It came in the form of a new drug application (NDA) seeking FDA approval for the commercial release of the drug. Each year, the FDA approved about half of all the NDAs it received.

This drug development process was remarkable in several respects. First, as outlined in Figure 7.1, for every drug that received FDA approval, approximately 4,000 candidate drugs began the process. Second, the process took an average of 10 years to complete successfully. Third, the process was capital intensive, with U.S. drug companies spending $26 billion on drug development in 2000 (Exhibit 7.4 provides a breakdown of how this money was spent). Finally, a company generally applied for (and received) a 20-year patent for a drug it had under development. After completing development, however, only about 10 to 15 years of patent protection remained (for instance, in the United States, the Angiomax patent was due to expire in 2010).

FIGURE 7.1   **Stages of Drug Development (Average Years in Each Stage in Parentheses)**

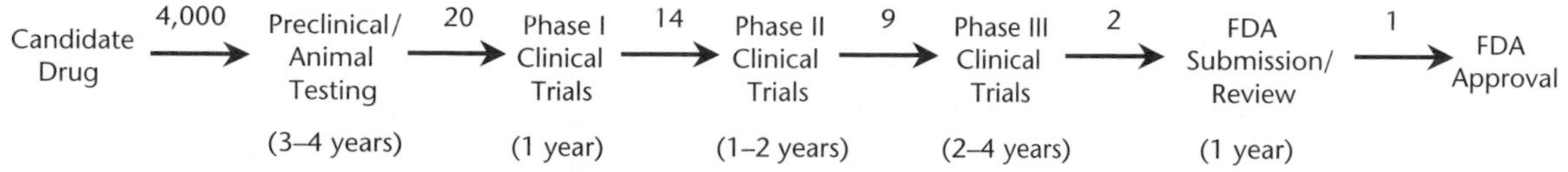

[3] Typically, Phase II and Phase III clinical trials were done across several hospitals, with doctors administering the candidate drug to a random sample of patients seeking treatment for the target disease. Quite often, the process was "double-blind," with neither the doctor nor the patient knowing what drug was administered.

These factors combined to create an industry that relied heavily on "blockbuster drugs"—premium-priced breakthrough drugs that generated in excess of $1 billion in sales per year. In 1999, 19 drugs met this threshold in the United States (see Exhibit 7.5 for the 10 top-selling domestic prescription drugs). Meanwell described this focus on blockbuster drugs in the following fashion:

> In any given year, only about 90 drugs receive FDA approval. Across 40 drug companies, this means that the average drug firm is turning out only one or two new drugs a year— maybe three in a good year. If you are Merck, with over $10 billion in sales and your investors expect 10 percent growth per year, these one or two drugs have to generate a lot of revenue. A drug that brings in $200 million just won't do it for you.

The Medicines Company History

The Medicines Company was founded in July 1996 by Meanwell and a small group of investors on the premise that there was opportunity where other companies saw failure. Their corporate strategy was to acquire drugs that were in the late stages of product development but were "undervalued" by their developing companies. Once such drugs were acquired, The Medicines Company planned to complete product development, navigate the regulatory process, and commercialize the drugs in the United States and abroad.

While some questioned the logic of this business model, 15 years of experience in international drug development had convinced Meanwell that such a strategy made sense. As director of Product Development for Hoffmann-La Roche, one of Europe's largest drug developers, Meanwell had come to believe that drug firms often overreacted to clinical results, sometimes abandoning drugs that still had value. *The Boston Globe* described Meanwell and his company's business strategy as follows:

> You might say Dr. Clive Meanwell is a bit of a scavenger. . . . After all, he founded a company four years ago based on the idea that there was money to be made off drugs other companies cast aside. His Cambridge start-up . . . picks through and rescues products languishing because of lackluster results, shifting corporate priorities, or development problems.[4]

Of course, the first task for Meanwell and his colleagues was deciding what drugs to "rescue." To guide them in their acquisitions, Meanwell and his colleagues looked for drugs that met the following criteria:

- Required less than four years to get to market.
- Required less than $60 million to get to market.
- Had at least a 65 percent chance of getting to market.
- Had the potential to generate at least $100 million per year in sales.

Beginning in late 1996, the team spent six months reviewing potential acquisitions— starting with 3,000 candidates, quickly weeding those down to 20, and then seriously considering 3 or 4. By early 1997, they had settled on Angiomax, an anti–blood clotting drug that Biogen had been developing as a more effective alternative to heparin, the anti-clotting drug most widely used in the acute treatment of coronary heart disease. In 1994, Biogen had halted development of Angiomax after clinical tests suggested that it was no more effective than heparin. Upon reviewing Biogen's clinical test results, however, Meanwell became convinced that a market still existed for the drug.

---

[4] "The Rescuers," *The Boston Globe*, September 13, 2000.

Thus, in March 1997, The Medicines Company acquired all rights to Angiomax and set out to complete the clinical trials that Biogen had started. Finally, in December 2000, The Medicines Company received FDA approval for the use of Angiomax in the prevention of blood clots during a coronary procedure known as an "angioplasty."

Following a similar screening process, in 1998 The Medicines Company acquired the rights to IS-159, a drug designed to treat acute migraine headaches. And in 1999 it acquired the rights to CTV-05, a drug designed to treat gynecological infections in women of childbearing age.

During its four-year effort, The Medicines Company relied upon two sources of funds. From its inception through mid-2000, the company received approximately $100 million in several rounds of funding from several private equity firms. Then, in August 2000, the company raised $101.4 million (after fees) from an initial public offering of 6,900,000 shares at $16 per share.

Through early 2001, these funds were used almost exclusively to acquire and develop the company's three drugs. In fact, through December 2000, the company had yet to report revenues of any kind (see Exhibit 7.6). At the same time, the company had close to $100 million in cash and short-term assets to finance the commercial launch of Angiomax and the continued development of its other products (see Exhibit 7.7).

Angiomax

Without question, Angiomax was The Medicines Company's lead product, representing the company's first attempt at "rescuing" a seemingly failed drug. The specific application for which Angiomax received FDA approval was for the treatment of "high-risk" patients who were undergoing a "balloon angioplasty." A balloon angioplasty was a procedure developed in the 1970s to restore normal blood flow to arteries in the heart that were clogged by a fatty build-up called "plaque." In an angioplasty, a small incision was made in a blood vessel in the groin and a long flexible tube with a deflated balloon was threaded through an artery until it reached the clogged artery in the heart. The balloon was then inflated, compacting the plaque against the artery wall and opening the artery to increased blood flow.[5]

Sometimes, this procedure would lead to the formation of an unwanted blood clot in the area of the angioplasty. This blood clot had the potential to reclog the artery, leading to chest pains and a possible heart attack. Angiomax was designed to reduce the likelihood that such a clot would form.

Coronary Heart Disease

Through the late 20th century, coronary heart disease was the leading cause of death in the United States, accounting for one in every five deaths. It involved the narrowing of the arteries of the heart due to the gradual build-up of plaque on the inside of the artery walls. Over time, this build-up would narrow the artery and reduce the flow of blood and oxygen to the heart muscle, often resulting in chest pains following physical exertion. This type of pain was called "stable angina."

Sometimes, a portion of the built-up plaque would tear or break off, triggering the rapid formation of a blood clot at the site of the tear. This blood clot would further reduce the flow of blood to the heart, causing steadier and more intense chest pains

---

[5] In about 65 percent of cases, in addition to the angioplasty, a small metal mesh tube called a "stent" was threaded through the artery and placed at the site of the blockage. This tube was meant to permanently prop open the artery to restore blood flow.

called "unstable angina." In extreme cases, the blood clot would completely cut off the blood supply to the heart and cause a "heart attack." If the blood supply were cut off for a long enough period of time, the cells of the heart would die, leading to permanent disability or death.

By the late 1990s, an estimated 14 million Americans had some form of coronary heart disease, 7 million of whom suffered from stable angina. Of these, about 1.5 million experienced unstable angina each year, another 1.1 million suffered a full-blown heart attack, and close to 500,000 died.

While patients suffering from stable angina were treated with a regimen of diet, exercise, and a variety of slow-acting drugs, patients with unstable angina or full-blown heart attacks required emergency care. Typically, such patients immediately received a combination of several fast-acting drugs, including TPA, which was meant to break apart the clot that had formed, and an "anticoagulant," which was meant to prevent a new clot from forming.

Shortly after this initial treatment, most emergency care patients underwent either a balloon angioplasty or coronary artery bypass surgery (CABG), which involved surgically replacing the clogged coronary arteries with healthy blood vessels taken from the patient's leg. In 1999, roughly 700,000 angioplasties and 400,000 CABGs were performed in the United States. Both types of operations had the potential to further disrupt arterial plaque, leading to the formation of a new blood clot. Therefore, anticoagulants also were widely administered to prevent blood clots from forming before, during, and after these procedures.

Heparin

By far, the most widely prescribed anticoagulant in acute coronary heart treatment was heparin. Discovered in 1916, heparin was initially used to prevent the coagulation of blood samples drawn from patients. By the 1990s, however, it was the primary drug used to prevent unwanted blood clots from forming as the result of unstable angina, heart attacks, and coronary surgery. Having never been subject to patent protection, heparin was viewed as a commodity drug and sold by many different manufacturers at about $2 per vial. As reflected in Table 7.A, Meanwell estimated that about 3.5 million coronary care patients received heparin each year to prevent unwanted blood clots.

Despite its almost universal use, heparin was not without it shortcomings, however, as Meanwell was quick to point out. These included

- Unpredictability. Both within and across patients, the anti-clotting effect of heparin was unpredictable. Its use required very close monitoring.
- High risk of bleeding. Some patients who received heparin had a high incidence of uncontrolled bleeding.
- Adverse reaction. In 2 percent to 3 percent of patients, heparin caused a sometimes fatal immune reaction called "heparin-induced thrombocytopenia" or HIT.

TABLE 7.A
Heparin Use across Treatments

Source: Medicines Company estimates.

Treatment	Number of Patients per Year Receiving Drug
Unstable angina (i.e., elevated chest pains)	1,300,000
Heart attack	1,000,000
Balloon angioplasty	700,000
Coronary artery bypass surgery	400,000
Other	100,000

These shortcomings led some medical experts to question the ongoing use of heparin. As one cardiologist pointed out:

> Heparin is easy to use, but difficult to use properly. Its effectiveness depends on achieving a certain degree of anticoagulation in the blood. Too much anticoagulation and the patient can suffer from uncontrolled bleeding. Too little anticoagulation and you might not prevent a blood clot. But that window of proper dosing differs across patients and across time. As a result, you need to monitor the patient very closely. Making the problem more complex, it takes several hours for the effects of heparin to kick in and wear off. This means that you might have to wait three or four hours to see if a given dose of heparin has the desired effect.[6]

To assess the prevalence of this viewpoint, The Medicines Company conducted a random survey of 90 leading interventional cardiologists (the doctors who perform angioplasties) that asked them to rate their satisfaction with heparin. Results of this survey are shown in Figure 7.2.

Biogen's Angiomax: A Replacement for Heparin

Angiomax began its life in the mid-1980s in the laboratories of Biogen. Biogen's insight into Angiomax began with the observation that certain animals, such as leeches, drew blood from their victims without triggering the victim's blood clotting process. Armed with this insight, Biogen isolated the chemicals in leech saliva that caused this anti-clotting response. Once isolated, Biogen was able to reproduce it using recombinant technologies.

As initially conceived, Angiomax was to replace heparin for use during angioplasties. According to Meanwell, Biogen expected the typical angioplasty patient to require about four doses of the drug. Longer term, Biogen hoped Angiomax would replace heparin in almost all applications.

Over the next seven years, Biogen spent $150 million bringing Angiomax through to Phase III trials. In 1994, however, Biogen came to two unsettling conclusions. First, its Phase III clinical trial involving "high-risk" angioplasty patients suggested that Angiomax was only slightly better than heparin at preventing blood clots. Second, given the complexity of the drug, Biogen expected that it would cost $100 per dose to produce Angiomax. In an industry where the typical "price" to "cost of goods sold"

FIGURE 7.2 **Overall Satisfaction with Heparin among Interventional Cardiologists**

Source: Company records.

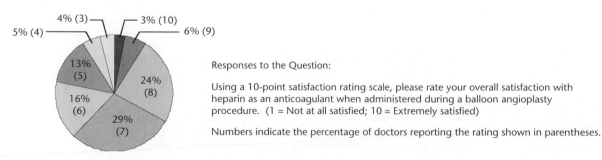

Responses to the Question:

Using a 10-point satisfaction rating scale, please rate your overall satisfaction with heparin as an anticoagulant when administered during a balloon angioplasty procedure. (1 = Not at all satisfied; 10 = Extremely satisfied)

Numbers indicate the percentage of doctors reporting the rating shown in parentheses.

[6] Reflects comments obtained from a cardiologist in interviews conducted by The Medicines Company.

ratio was 10 to 1, this implied a selling price of $1,000 per dose. Reluctantly, Biogen halted development of Angiomax, concluding that its benefits did not justify such a price. Meanwell described Biogen's decision as follows:

> In 1994, Biogen was at a bit of a crossroads. To that point, they had licensed products to other drug companies. But, in the summer of '94, they had two drugs in Phase III trials—their first attempts to bring a product to market. One was Angiomax. The other was Avonex, a drug to treat multiple sclerosis. In July, the Phase III Avonex study showed very promising results. Then, in September, the Phase III Angiomax study showed mixed results. As a result, Biogen decided to pour its resources into Avonex and to shelve Angiomax. In the end, this may have been the right decision. Biogen received FDA approval for Avonex in 1996 and quickly turned it into the world's best-selling multiple sclerosis drug. In 2000, they sold over $750 million worth of Avonex.

The Decision to Acquire Angiomax

Following its decision to shelve Angiomax, Biogen actively "shopped" the drug to other biotech and pharmaceutical firms in the hopes that one would acquire or license the drug. One such firm was Hoffmann-La Roche, where Meanwell was head of drug development. While he decided not to pursue Angiomax, two things struck Meanwell about the drug. First, although the drug was not as effective as Biogen would have liked, it still was more effective than heparin. Second, if the cost to produce the drug could be reduced by half, the economics became attractive.

Several years later, Angiomax once again came across Meanwell's radar screen as The Medicines Company searched for its first acquisition. Remembering his initial impressions of the drug, the team re-analyzed Biogen's Phase III results. These results are shown in Table 7.B. Biogen's study had involved 4,312 "high-risk" angioplasty patients, with half receiving Angiomax and half receiving heparin. For this study, patients were defined as "high-risk" if they had previously had a heart attack or if they were admitted to the hospital because of unstable angina. On average, such "high-risk" patients accounted for about 50 percent of all angioplasty patients.[7]

In addition, The Medicines Company found that for a particular subgroup of "high-risk" patient—those who had experienced a heart attack in the two weeks immediately preceding the angioplasty—the benefits of Angiomax were more pronounced. Table 7.C provides a comparison of heparin and Angiomax for these "very high risk" patients. On average, these patients represented 20 percent of the high-risk patients (or 10 percent of all angioplasty patients).

When asked to account for these results, Meanwell noted that Angiomax did not have many of the drawbacks that heparin had. Specifically, he noted:

TABLE 7.B

Phase III Results for "High-Risk" Patients Undergoing an Angioplasty

Source: The Medicines Company.

Outcome within 7 Days of Treatment (number of patients in condition)	Heparin (2,151)	Angiomax (2,161)
Death	0.2%	0.2%
Heart attack	4.2%	3.3%
Need for a repeat angioplasty	2.8%	2.5%
Experienced major bleeding	9.3%	3.5%

[7] For the remaining 50 percent of angioplasty patients—i.e., "low-risk" patients—Meanwell estimated that the relative benefits of Angiomax over heparin were about half as great as those shown in Table 7.B.

TABLE 7.C
Phase III Results for "Very-High-Risk" Patients

Source: The Medicines Company.

Outcome within 7 Days of Treatment (number of patients in condition)	Heparin (372)	Angiomax (369)
Death	0.5%	0.0%
Heart attack	5.6%	3.0%
Need for a repeat angioplasty	3.5%	2.4%
Experienced major bleeding	11.8%	2.4%

Unlike heparin, the effects of a dose of Angiomax are very exacting and very crisp. Physicians who use Angiomax have been pleasantly surprised by how predictable their results are, which is important in an acute care setting where you are trying to minimize uncertainty. Second, the product works better among patients at risk for bleeding, where heparin often proves problematic. Third, the product works faster than heparin. Instead of taking 2 to 3 hours to take full effect, Angiomax only takes 30 minutes. Finally, there is no immune reaction to Angiomax, so you don't have to worry about unexpected reactions to the drug. These benefits seem to have the greatest impact for the very high-risk patients.

Based on their re-analyses, Meanwell and his colleagues agreed to acquire all rights to the drug's formulation, its manufacturing specifications, and its clinical trial results. These clinical trial results included the Phase III results for angioplasty, but also included Phase II results for studies looking at the impact of Angiomax in the treatment of heart attack, unstable angina, and heparin-induced thrombocytopenia (HIT).

The cost of this acquisition was an upfront fee of $2 million, a commitment to invest another $28 million in the continued development of the product, and a future royalty that started at 6 percent of sales and rose to 20 percent of sales as sales volumes increased.

Bringing Angiomax to Market

Upon acquiring Angiomax in 1997, The Medicines Company set out to address several issues. First, the company conducted a confirmatory clinical study using "high-risk" angioplasty patients, obtaining results similar to those shown in Table 7.B. On the combined strength of Biogen's initial studies and this confirmatory study, The Medicines Company submitted a new drug application (NDA) in early 2000 and on December 17, 2000, obtained FDA approval to market Angiomax for use in "high-risk patients undergoing a balloon angioplasty." Meanwell estimated that The Medicines Company spent a total of $12 million in finishing these clinical trials and gaining FDA approval.

The second thing that the company did was to focus on bringing down the cost of using Angiomax. This was accomplished in two ways. First, rather than four doses of Angiomax, further clinical testing revealed that about 70 percent of angioplasty patients would require a single dose, with the other 30 percent requiring two or three doses. Second, in 1999 The Medicines Company contracted out production of Angiomax to UCB Bioproducts, with the understanding that UCB would attempt to develop a second-generation manufacturing process to bring down the cost of production. The Medicines Company contributed almost $10 million to this development effort. The result was a new production process that reduced the "cost of goods sold" from $100 per dose to about $40 per dose.

The third thing the company did was to push forward on the other Angiomax clinical trials. In particular, it undertook additional studies to confirm the benefits of

Angiomax (1) for patients experiencing heart attacks and unstable angina, (2) for patients at risk for HIT, and (3) for patients undergoing coronary artery bypass surgery. By early 2001, the company had five sets of clinical trials either completed or underway, as reflected in Exhibit 7.8.

The Marketing of Angiomax

Making the Case for Angiomax

As it became apparent that Angiomax would gain FDA approval, the company's next big task was to establish a "going to market" strategy for the drug. As part of this strategy, the company hired Dr. Stephanie Plent as Senior Director of Medical Policy. Part of Plent's job was to communicate the benefits of Angiomax to cardiologists and hospital administrators. She explained these benefits in the following fashion:

> When a hospital performs an angioplasty on a patient covered by insurance, it is reimbursed at a predetermined rate. Currently, that rate is $11,500. In most cases, this more than covers the cost of the procedure—an angioplasty with no complications costs a hospital about $9,500 to perform.
>
> In a small percentage of cases, however, complications do arise. But insurance companies do not reimburse the cost of these complications. Instead, hospitals are forced to absorb these added expenses. On average, a hospital incurs an additional $8,000 to treat a person who has a heart attack, requires a repeat angioplasty, or experiences major bleeding. These added costs are largely due to the fact that the patient's hospital stay is extended by four or five days. Even a death costs the hospital an additional $8,000. Angiomax helps avoid some of these costs.

At the same time, Plent noted that this message had a different impact on the various members of the hospital staff. She pointed out that there were three major groups that influenced the purchase and use of any new drug: (1) the doctor who would use the drug, (2) the hospital pharmacist who would carry the drug, and (3) the hospital administrator who would approve the drug for ongoing use within the hospital. Each of these groups had a different set of incentives, as Plent pointed out:

> Selling a premium-priced new drug to a hospital is a tricky process. First, there are the doctors. You have to convince them that the drug works. They are not concerned with price so much as they are with results. Next, there are the hospital pharmacists. They have an annual budget for all the drugs they dispense and are rewarded for meeting or beating that budget. Replacing a widely used $10 drug with a $100 drug really kills that budget. Unless they can justify the cost of the new drug to the hospital administrators and get the added expense incorporated into their budgets, it is unlikely they will carry it. Finally, there are the hospital administrators. They take the big picture into account—does this drug make economic sense. Unfortunately, drug companies rarely have direct access to these administrators. Rather, we have to work through the doctors and the pharmacists and get them to push for the drug.

Assembling a Sales Force

The task of selling Angiomax into this complex network of hospital personnel fell to Tom Quinn, vice president of Sales and Marketing. It was Quinn's job to assemble a sales force, promote the use of Angiomax, and ramp up sales over time.

According to Quinn's analysis, 1,300 medical centers around the country performed angioplasties, with the typical center staffed by 5 to 20 interventional cardiologists. Across these 1,300 centers, Quinn decided to focus on those 700 centers that were responsible for 92 percent of all angioplasty procedures. These 700 angioplasty centers were divided into five sales regions.

To service each of these five regions, Quinn hired a regional manager and out-sourced to a marketing services firm for 10 to 15 account reps. Quinn explained his thinking behind this approach:

> When we looked at what we needed to do, we realized we needed people with existing relationships within the acute coronary care community. Also, we wanted to ramp up rapidly. The answer was Innovex, a marketing services firm. They provided us with fully dedicated sales people with an average of five years of sales experience and with existing relationships with the doctors and pharmacists we wanted to reach. As for our regional managers, we hired them as Medicines Company employees to retain control and to create stability over time.

Quinn was also responsible for educating the marketplace. This included publication of academic journal articles, presentations at trade shows, and the advertising of Angiomax in medical journals. Beginning in the fall of 2000, for instance, Quinn's marketing department started drawing attention to the shortcomings of heparin. Such an approach was made necessary by FDA regulations that forbade the marketing of a drug that was not yet approved for use. Therefore, at medical trade shows and in medical journals in October, November, and December, the company presented material designed to get doctors to question the safety of heparin. One such bit of material was an academic article on the "deficiencies of heparin" that appeared in the *Journal of Invasive Cardiology*. Once Angiomax was approved, the company followed with trade show presentations, journal articles, and advertisements in medical journals identifying Angiomax as the preferred alternative to heparin. Exhibit 7.9 provides an example of one such ad.

Finally, Quinn sought to create advocates within the medical community. Through early 2001, the company sponsored four weekend getaways for thought leaders (and their families) in the cardiology community. These invitees were handpicked by the sales force and included 400 cardiologists, 75 nurses, and 30 pharmacists. Over the course of two days, they would participate in about eight hours of presentations designed to educate them on the company and the product. Quinn estimated that The Medicines Company spent about $3 million on these efforts.

Other Drugs under Development by The Medicines Company

In addition to Angiomax, The Medicines Company had acquired two other "abandoned" drugs. In July 1998, the company acquired the rights to IS-159, a nasal spray designed to treat acute migraine headaches. And in August 1999, it acquired the rights to CTV-05, a drug designed to treat gynecological infections in women of childbearing age.

IS-159

Acquired from Immunotech S.A. of France, IS-159 was an acute migraine drug in Phase II trials that promised rapid absorption into the bloodstream. Under the acquisition agreement, the company paid an up-front fee of $1 million, was obligated to pay an additional $4.5 million upon reaching certain development milestones, and would pay a 5 percent royalty on sales upon commercialization of the product. At the time of the acquisition, Meanwell noted that the drug had shown promise in its Phase II trials, offering "an impressively rapid onset of action and a convenient form of administration." At that time, Meanwell estimated the migraine drug market to be about $2 billion.

By mid-1999, however, development of IS-159 had been halted by The Medicines Company. After spending an additional $6 million in clinical trials, the company had run into problems with the drug's formulation. Specifically, for the nasal spray to be absorbed into the bloodstream, an additive was needed. The additive being used was "modified coconut oil." However, while modified coconut oil had gained FDA approval as an additive in oral medications, it had not yet gained FDA approval as an additive in nasal medications. As a result, the company faced the daunting task of either finding a new additive or conducting clinical trials to show the safety and effectiveness of coconut oil as a nasal additive. Meanwell estimated that either course of action would cost as much as $30 million and take five years.

CTV-05

With Angiomax looking like it would gain FDA approval, the failure of IS-159 in mid-1999 presented a problem. With plans to go public in the near future, all parties felt that it was critical to have a second drug under development to avoid the appearance that the company was a one-drug enterprise. IS-159 was supposed to have been that other drug. With its failure, the company was forced to "rescue" some other drug that was underappreciated.

That drug turned out to be CTV-05, a drug designed to treat bacterial vaginosis (BV), an infection that was common in women of childbearing age. By one estimate, 10 percent to 15 percent of college-age women suffered from BV, which often resulted in premature termination of pregnancies and in low-birth-weight babies. Under the terms of the acquisition, The Medicines Company obtained worldwide rights to the drug for an up-front fee of $1 million and future royalties of about 5 percent.

Upon reflection, Meanwell noted that the company's acquisition of CTV-05 was quite different from the company's earlier acquisitions. As he pointed out:

> With Angiomax, we knew the drug worked. Even with IS-159, we knew the drug worked—we just hadn't anticipated problems with its formulation. With CTV-05, we were "taking a bit of a flier." We needed another drug under development, but there were no obvious alternatives. We didn't know if CTV-05 worked—it was only in Phase I trials—but we knew we could get it at low cost. So far, we have been happy with the results. We have invested about $4 million and we are currently completing Phase II trials. What started out as a high-risk investment is showing a lot of promise.

Looking Ahead

Moving forward, Meanwell knew that he and his colleagues had several decisions to make. First, they had to decide on the pricing of Angiomax. On the one hand, he felt that the product warranted a vast premium over heparin. On the other hand, he knew that replacing a widely accepted $2 drug with any drug costing many times more would raise a few eyebrows. Second, he had to decide whether the business strategy that brought the company to this point still made sense moving into the future. In particular, while a productive "drug pipeline" would be a nice thing to have, was it essential? Finally, Meanwell wondered how success with Angiomax would change the company and its underlying business model.

For the moment, however, Meanwell and his colleagues enjoyed the feeling of having "rescued" a drug with the potential to make a difference in people's lives.

EXHIBIT 7.1
Excerpt from *The Boston Globe,* December 19, 2000

Source: *The Boston Globe,* December 19, 2000, p. C3.

Medicines Co. Receives FDA Approval for Blood Thinner: Drug up against Cheaper Heparin

by Naomi Aoki,
Globe Staff

Medicines Co. yesterday said it won regulatory approval to market its first product, a blood thinner designed as an alternative to the 85-year-old standard treatment, heparin.

The drug, called Angiomax, was approved by the US Food and Drug Administration for use in an artery-clearing procedure known as angioplasty. The drug was developed to prevent blood clots that can lead to heart attacks.

. . . Angiomax [is expected to be] significantly more expensive than heparin, which sells at about $10 a vial. But the Cambridge company said data from more than 4,300 patients [showed the drug to be a superior alternative to heparin].

"Obviously, this is a very major milestone for Medicines Co.," said Dr. Clive Meanwell, the company's president and chief executive. "We think it is also a major milestone for the field of interventional cardiology. But most of all, we think it should be a significant milestone for patients."

Meanwell also hailed the approval as a confirmation of the young company's business model, based on the idea that there is money to be made off drugs that other companies cast aside.

Since other companies bring the products through the early stages of development, Medicines Co. bears less risk. Still, there is no guarantee that the products—sometimes shelved because of lackluster test results or unresolved developmental problems—will get to market.

In fact, at one time, the deck seemed stacked against Angiomax. The drug was discovered by Biogen Inc., among the nation's oldest and biggest biotechnology companies, but was abandoned after disappointing results from broad-based clinical trials.

Biogen's disappointment became Medicines Co.'s first project. The company licensed the drug from Biogen in 1997. . . .

Jay B. Silverman, a senior biotech analyst with Robertson Stephens Inc. in New York, said he expects Angiomax to perform well against heparin. . . . The challenge will be to persuade doctors and hospitals to change from heparin to Angiomax, he said, efforts that are already underway.

"That is always the challenge with these hospital products," Meanwell said. "Doctors are appropriately demanding of the data. They want to know how this drug will impact practices and costs."

The company has plans to conduct clinical trials at hundreds of hospitals nationwide to allow doctors to gain hands-on experience with the drug, Meanwell said. It anticipates a series of articles to be published in upcoming issues of independent, peer-reviewed scientific journals.

Meanwell said the company has gathered a team of experienced sales and marketing executives to head the 52-person sales force. And the product will be launched officially next month, after a weeklong educational meeting for the sales staff. . . .

"This approval is about the best Christmas present I could get," Meanwell said. "We're very excited, very relieved, and very grateful." . . .

EXHIBIT 7.2   The Medicines Company Stock Performance—August 8, 2000, to January 31, 2001

Source: Adapted from website, http://finance.yahoo.com.

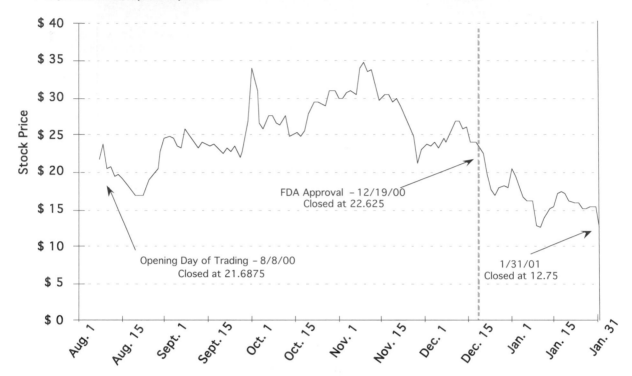

EXHIBIT 7.3
Leading Pharmaceutical Companies, Ranked by United States Sales (in millions)[a]

Source: Standard & Poor's industry survey, "Healthcare: Pharmaceuticals," December 21, 2000.

Company (Headquarters)	U.S. Sales
Pfizer/Warner-Lambert (U.S.)	$14,607
Glaxo Wellcome/SmithKline (U.K.)[b]	12,490
Merck (U.S.)	10,486
Bristol-Myers Squibb (U.S.)	8,778
Astra/Zeneca (U.K.)	8,304
Johnson & Johnson (U.S.)	7,636
Eli Lilly (U.S.)	6,173
Pharmacia (U.S.)	6,055
American Home Products (U.S.)	5,832
Schering Plough (U.S.)	5,716

[a] For 12 months ending September 30, 2000.
[b] Merger pending.

EXHIBIT 7.4
The Allocation of $26 Billion in Research and Development in 2000

Source: "Health's Price Tag," *The Boston Globe*, March 28, 2001, p. D4.

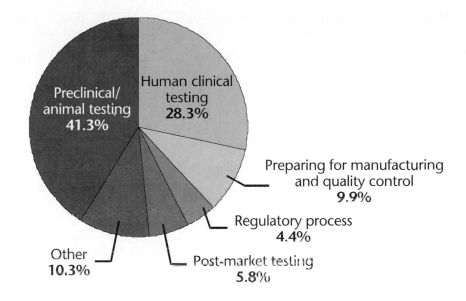

Preclinical/ animal testing
41.3%

Human clinical testing
28.3%

Preparing for manufacturing and quality control
9.9%

Regulatory process
4.4%

Other
10.3%

Post-market testing
5.8%

EXHIBIT 7.5
Best-Selling Prescription Drugs in the United States in 1999

Source: Standard & Poor's industry survey, "Healthcare: Pharmaceuticals," December 21, 2000.

Drug (Company)	Use	Retail Sales (in millions)
Prilosec (Astra/Zeneca)	Anti-ulcer	$4,187
Lipitor (Warner Lambert)	Cholesterol reducer	3,002
Prozac (Eli Lilly)	Antidepressant	2,571
Prevacid (TAP)	Anti-ulcer	2,364
Zocor (Merck)	Cholesterol reducer	2,301
Epogen (Amgen)	Red blood cell stimulant	1,842
Zoloft (Pfizer)	Antidepressant	1,737
Claritin (Schering Plough)	Antihistamine	1,534
Paxil (SmithKline Beecham)	Antidepressant	1,516
Zyprexa (Eli Lilly)	Antipsychotic	1,495

EXHIBIT 7.6   **The Medicines Company Operating Income: 1997 to 2000**

Source: Company records.

	1997	1998	1999	2000
Revenue from operations:	$ 0	$ 0	$ 0	$ 0
Operating expenses:				
Research & development	$16,044,367	$24,004,606	$30,344,892	$39,572,297
Sales, general & administrative	2,420,373	6,248,265	5,008,387	15,033,585
Total operating expenses:	$18,464,740	$30,252,871	$35,353,279	$54,605,882
Loss from operations:	($18,464,740)	($30,252,871)	($35,353,279)	($54,605,882)

EXHIBIT 7.7
The Medicines Company Balance Sheet: 1999 and 2000 (FY Ending December 31)

Source: Company records.

	1999	2000
Assets:		
Cash, cash equivalents, and marketable securities	$ 7,237,765	$80,718.013
Inventory	0	1,963,491
Fixed assets (net)	430,061	965,832
Other assets	323,572	715,794
Total assets:	$ 7,991,398	$84,363,130
Liabilities and stockholders' equity:		
Current liabilities	$11,495,321	$15,124,147
Long-term liabilities	91,053,732	0
Stockholders' equity (deficit)	(94,557,655)	69,238,983
Total liabilities and stockholders' equity:	$ 7,991,398	$84,363,130

EXHIBIT 7.8   **Status of Angiomax Clinical Trials**

Source: The Medicines Company 2000 Annual Report.

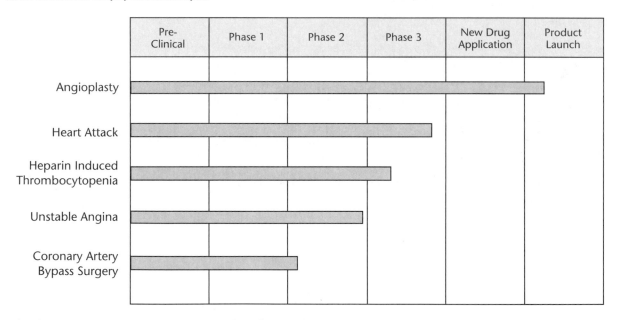

EXHIBIT 7.9   An Example of a Two-Page Angiomax Ad—January 2001

Source: Company documents.

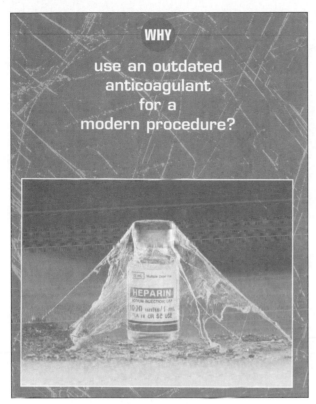

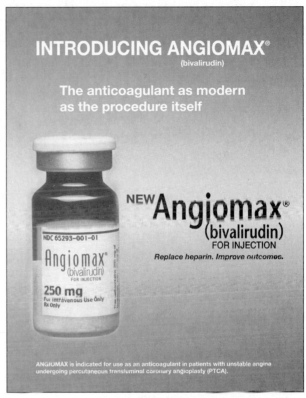

Page 1

Page 2

Chapter 8

Biopure Corporation

John T. Gourville

It was February 5, 1998, as Carl Rausch, president and CEO of Biopure Corporation, opened his *Boston Globe* and read about the U.S. government's final approval of Oxyglobin (see Exhibit 8.1). Oxyglobin was the first of two new "blood substitutes" on which Biopure's future depended—Oxyglobin for the veterinary market and Hemopure for the human market. While Oxyglobin was ready for launch, Hemopure was still two years away from final government approval. This timing was the source of an ongoing debate within Biopure.

Ted Jacobs, vice president for Human Clinical Trials at Biopure, argued that the release of Oxyglobin should be delayed until *after* Hemopure was approved and had established itself in the marketplace (see Exhibit 8.2 for an organizational chart of Biopure). Given that the two products were almost identical in physical properties and appearance, he felt that Oxyglobin would create an unrealistic price expectation for Hemopure if released first. As he made clear in a recent management meeting,

> [T]he veterinary market is small and price sensitive. We'll be lucky to get $150 per unit. The human market, on the other hand, is many times larger and we can realistically achieve price points of $600 to $800 per unit. But as soon as we come out with Oxyglobin at $150, we jeopardize our ability to price Hemopure at $800. Hospitals and insurance firms will be all over us to justify a 500 percent price difference for what they see as the same product. That's a headache we just don't need. We've spent $200 million developing Hemopure—to risk it at this point is crazy. We should just shelve Oxyglobin for now.

At the same time, Andy Wright, vice president for Veterinary Products, had his sales organization in place and was eager to begin selling Oxyglobin. He argued that the benefits of immediately releasing Oxyglobin outweighed the risks,

Professor John Gourville prepared this case as the basis for class discussion rather than to illustrate either effective or ineffective handling of an administrative situation. Some nonpublic data have been disguised and some business details have been simplified to aid in classroom discussion.

Copyright © 1998 by the President and Fellows of Harvard College. To order copies or request permission to reproduce materials, call 1-800-545-7685, write Harvard Business School Publishing, Boston, MA 02163, or go to http://www.hbsp.harvard.edu. No part of this publication may be reproduced, stored in a retrieval system, used in a spreadsheet, or transmitted in any form or by any means—electronic, mechanical, photocopying, recording, or otherwise—without the permission of Harvard Business School.

Oxyglobin would generate our first revenues ever—revenues we could use to launch Hemopure. And while the animal market is smaller than the human market, it is still attractive. Finally, I can't stress enough the value of Oxyglobin in learning how to "go to market." Would you rather make the mistakes now, with Oxyglobin, or in two years, with Hemopure?

While Carl Rausch listened to this debate, he also considered his colleagues' growing desire to take Biopure public in the near future. He wondered whether a proven success with Oxyglobin might not have a greater impact on an IPO than the promise of success with Hemopure.

An Overview of Biopure

Biopure Corporation was founded in 1984 by entrepreneurs Carl Rausch and David Judelson as a privately owned biopharmaceutical firm specializing in the ultrapurification of proteins for human and veterinary use. By 1998, this mission had taken Biopure to the point where it was one of three legitimate contenders in the emerging field of "blood substitutes."[1] Blood substitutes were designed to replicate the oxygen-carrying function of actual blood, while eliminating the shortcomings associated with the transfusion of donated blood. Through the end of 1997, no blood substitute had received approval for use anywhere in the world.

Biopure's entries into this field were Hemopure, for the human market, and Oxyglobin, for the animal market. Both products consisted of the oxygen-carrying protein "hemoglobin" which had been removed from red blood cells, purified to eliminate infectious agents, and chemically modified to increase its safety and effectiveness. What distinguished Hemopure and Oxyglobin from other "hemoglobin-based" blood substitutes under development was the fact that they were "bovine-sourced" as opposed to "human-sourced"—they were derived from the blood of cattle. To date, Biopure had spent over $200 million in the development of Oxyglobin and Hemopure and in the construction of a state-of-the-art manufacturing facility.

Both of Biopure's products fell under the approval process of the United States Food and Drug Administration (FDA), which required that each product be proven safe and effective for medical use (see Exhibit 8.3 for an overview of the FDA approval process). In this regard, Oxyglobin had just received final FDA approval for commercial release as a veterinary blood substitute, while Hemopure would soon enter Phase 3 clinical trials and was optimistically expected to see final FDA approval for release as a human blood substitute sometime in 1999.

This recent FDA approval of Oxyglobin brought to a peak a long-simmering debate within Biopure. With its primary goal being the development of a human blood substitute, Biopure's entry into the animal market had been somewhat opportunistic. During preclinical trials for Hemopure, the benefits of a blood substitute for small animals became apparent. In response, Biopure began a parallel product development process which resulted in Oxyglobin. However, there was little question within Biopure that Oxyglobin was an ancillary product to Hemopure.

As it became apparent that Oxyglobin would gain FDA approval prior to Hemopure, Carl Rausch and his management team discussed how best to manage Oxyglo-

---

[1] While the term *blood substitute* has historically been used to describe this class of product, Biopure and the medical community increasingly have used the term *oxygen therapeutic* to describe the latest generation of product. For simplicity, however, we will continue to use the term *blood substitute* in this case.

bin. As the first "blood substitute" of any type to receive full government approval, Rausch was eager to get the news out. With this in mind, Andy Wright and a small marketing team had been assembled to bring Oxyglobin to market. However, Ted Jacobs and others questioned whether the immediate release of Oxyglobin might not impinge on Biopure's ability to optimally price Hemopure. After months of debate, it was time to decide on the fate of Oxyglobin.

The Human Blood Market

Blood is essential for life. It performs many functions, the most acutely critical of which is the transportation of oxygen to the organs and tissues of the human body. Without oxygen, these organs and tissues will die within minutes.

That portion of blood responsible for oxygen transportation is the red blood cells (RBCs). RBCs capture inhaled oxygen from the lungs, carry that oxygen to the cells of the body, release it for use where needed, capture expended carbon dioxide from those cells, and carry that carbon dioxide back to the lungs, where it is released. The key to this process is "hemoglobin," the iron-containing protein found within each RBC to which oxygen and carbon dioxide molecules bind.

The adult human body contains 5,000 milliliters (ml) or about 10 pints of blood. An individual can naturally compensate for the loss of up to 30 percent of this volume through some combination of increased oxygen intake (i.e., faster breathing), increased flow of the remaining blood (i.e., faster heart rate), and the prioritization of blood delivery to vital organs. In cases of blood loss of greater than 30 percent, however, outside intervention is typically required—generally in the form of a "blood transfusion."

Human Blood Transfusions

A blood transfusion entails the direct injection of blood into a patient's bloodstream. As of 1998, the most common form of blood transfusion was the intravenous transfusion of donated RBCs.[2] Typically, a healthy individual would donate one unit or 500 ml of "whole" blood, which would be tested for various infectious diseases, sorted by blood type, and separated into its usable components (e.g., plasma, platelets, and RBCs). This process would yield one unit or 250 ml of RBCs, which then would be stored until needed by a patient.[3]

While potentially lifesaving, the transfusion of donated RBCs has limitations. These include

• The need for exact blood typing and cross-matching between donor and recipient. The RBCs of each human may contain specific blood sugars, or antigens. The existence or absence of these antigens creates a complex set of allowable transfusions between donor and recipient, as shown in Exhibit 8.4. Transfusions outside of those outlined can be fatal to the recipient.

[2] Historically, whole blood transfusions were the norm. Since the 1970s, however, whole blood increasingly had been separated into RBCs, platelets, and plasma, allowing for (1) several patients to benefit from a single unit of donated blood and (2) a reduced likelihood of negative reaction for any given patient.

[3] In blood medicine, one unit is defined in terms of its therapeutic value. Therefore, "one unit" or 250 ml of RBCs provides the oxygen-carrying capacity of "one unit" or 500 ml of whole blood. Similarly, "one unit" of a blood substitute (i.e., typically 125 ml) provides the same oxygen-carrying capacity of "one unit" of RBCs or whole blood.

- The reduced oxygen-carrying efficiency of stored RBCs. RBCs stored for 10 days or more are only about 50 percent efficient at transporting oxygen in the first 8 to 12 hours after transfusion.
- The limited shelf-life for stored RBCs. RBCs can be safely stored for only about six weeks, after which time they are typically discarded.
- The need for refrigeration. For optimal shelf-life, RBCs must be stored at 4° Celsius (~40° F).
- The risk of disease transmission. While donated blood is tested for infectious agents, there still exists the risk of disease transmission. For example, the risk of AIDS is 1:500,000, the risk of Hepatitis B is 1:200,000, and the risk of Hepatitis C is 1:100,000.

Autologous Transfusions

In an attempt to overcome some of these limitations, the use of "autologous" or self-donated RBCs has become increasingly common. In an autologous RBC transfusion, a medically stable patient who anticipates the need for RBCs would have his or her own blood drawn weeks in advance, separated into its components, and saved until needed. Research has shown this process to significantly reduce a patient's rate of complication and post-operative infection, thereby hastening recovery and shortening his or her stay in the hospital.

Human Blood Supply and Demand

Human Blood Supply

Fourteen million units of RBCs were donated by eight million people in 1995 in the United States. Approximately 12.9 million of these units came from individuals who voluntarily donated to one of over 1,000 nonprofit blood collection organizations. By far, the largest of these organizations was the American Red Cross, which collected half of all the blood donated in the United States in 1995 through a network of 44 regional blood collection centers. Typically, the Red Cross and the other blood collection organizations supported "blood mobiles," which traveled to high schools, colleges, and places of employment to reach potential donors. The remaining 1.1 million units of RBCs were autologous donations made directly to a hospital blood center.

Increasingly, blood collection was a struggle. While 75 percent of all adults qualified as a donor, fewer than 5 percent actually donated in a given year. Historically, reasons for donating included altruism and peer pressure, while reasons for not donating included fear of needles and lack of time. Since the mid-1980s, an additional reason for not donating involved the misconception that donating put one at risk for contracting AIDS. Public education had failed to counteract this misconception.

Given the low rate of donation and the relatively short shelf-life of RBCs, it was not uncommon for medical facilities and blood banks to experience periodic shortages of RBCs. This was especially true during the winter holidays and the summer months, periods which routinely displayed both increased demand and decreased rates of donation.

Human Blood Demand

Of the 14 million units of RBCs donated in 1995, 2.7 million were discarded due to contamination or expiration (i.e., units older than six weeks). Another 3.2 million units were transfused into 1.5 million patients who suffered from chronic anemia, an ongoing deficiency in the oxygen-carrying ability of the blood. The remaining 8.1 million units were transfused into 2.5 million patients who suffered from acute blood loss brought on by elective surgeries, emergency surgeries, or trauma. Exhibit 8.5 offers a breakdown of RBC transfusions in 1995.

In elective and emergency surgeries, RBCs were routinely transfused in situations where blood loss was greater than two units, as was typical in heart bypass and organ transplant surgeries. In surgeries with blood loss of one to two units, however, RBCs typically were not transfused in spite of their potential benefit. In these "borderline" transfusion surgeries, doctors typically avoided transfusions for fear of disease transmission or negative reaction caused by the transfused RBCs. There were approximately one million "borderline transfusion" surgeries in the United States each year.

RBC transfusions were also required in the approximately 500,000 trauma cases which occurred every year in the United States. These cases were characterized by the massive loss of blood due to automobile accidents, gunshot wounds, etc. However, due to the resources required to store, type, and administer RBCs, only 10 percent of trauma victims received RBCs "in the field" or at the site of the accident. Blood transfusions for the remaining 90 percent of victims were delayed until the victim arrived at a hospital emergency room. This delay was often cited as a contributing factor to the 30 percent fatality rate seen in these trauma cases, as evidenced by the 20,000 trauma victims who bled to death each year prior to reaching the hospital. As one doctor put it,

> . . . [T]hose first few minutes after a trauma are known as the "Golden Hour." Life and death often depends on how fast the lost blood is replaced in this period.

Looking forward, while the demand for RBCs to treat chronic anemia was expected to remain stable, the demand for RBCs to treat acute blood loss was expected to rise with the aging U.S. population. Individuals over 65 years of age comprised 15 percent of the adult population in 1995 and received over 40 percent of all "acute blood loss" transfusions. By the year 2030, this over-65 segment was expected to double in absolute numbers and to grow to 25 percent of the adult population.

Human Blood Pricing

Since the AIDS crisis, it has been illegal for an individual to sell his or her blood in the United States. As such, all blood donations are unpaid. In turn, to cover their expense of collection and administration, blood collection organizations sell this donated blood to hospitals and medical centers. Once obtained, hospitals incur additional costs to store, handle, transport, screen, type, cross-match, and document the blood. Estimates for these costs are outlined in Exhibit 8.6. Typically, these costs are passed on to the patient or to the patient's insurance provider.

The Veterinary Blood Market

The role of RBCs for animals is biologically identical to its role for humans: RBCs transport oxygen to an animal's tissues and organs. In practice, however, the availability and transfusion of blood were considerably more constrained in the veterinary market than they were in the human market.

Veterinary Market Structure

There were approximately 15,000 small-animal veterinary practices in the United States in 1995. Of these, about 95 percent were "primary care" practices, which provided preventative care (e.g., shots, checkups), routine treatment of illness (e.g., infections, chronic anemia), and limited emergency care (e.g., simple surgery and trauma).

The remaining 5 percent of practices were "emergency care" or "specialty care" practices. Approximately 75 percent of primary care practices referred some or all of their major surgery and severe trauma cases to these emergency care practices. Across both the primary care and emergency care practices, patient volume was concentrated in dogs (~50 percent of patient volume) and cats (~35 percent of volume). Exhibit 8.7 provides a staffing and patient profile of small-animal veterinary clinics in the United States.

Veterinary Blood Demand

In practice, blood transfusions in the veterinary market were infrequent. In 1995, for example, the average veterinary practice was presented with 800 dogs suffering from acute blood loss. About 30 percent of these dogs would have benefited significantly from a transfusion of blood, but only about 2.5 percent were deemed "critical cases" and received a transfusion.

The incidence of these acute blood loss cases was relatively concentrated, with 15 percent of veterinary practices handling 65 percent of all canine surgeries and 10 percent of practices handling 55 percent of all canine trauma cases. Not surprisingly, these "high incident" practices tended to be the larger primary care practices and the emergency care practices. This concentration was also evident in blood transfusions. In 1995, an average of 17 units of canine blood was transfused by each primary care practice, while an average of 150 units was transfused by each emergency care practice.

Veterinary Blood Supply [4]

Historically, the biggest constraint to veterinary transfusions was the lack of an adequate blood supply. In contrast to the human market, there existed few animal blood banks. As a result, the sole source of blood for most veterinary practices was donor animals, which were housed at the practice for the express purpose of donating blood. When a dog or cat was in need of blood, blood was drawn from a donor dog or cat and then transfused into the animal in need. For primary care practices, donor animals provided 93 percent of all transfused blood, while blood banks provided the remaining 7 percent. In emergency practices, these proportions were 78 percent and 22 percent.

About 15 percent of veterinary practices found the "donor animal" system to be administratively or financially prohibitive and did not offer it as a service. Of the 85 percent of practices that did use a donor system, few had a good sense of its cost. In particular, few practices explicitly tracked the cost of housing the donor animal or the time required to draw the blood. As a proxy for these costs, practices typically looked to the price of a unit of blood from an animal blood bank. In 1995, that cost was $50 to $100. In turn, a typical primary care practice charged a pet owner $80 to $120 per unit and a typical emergency care practice charged a pet owner $130 to $170 per unit.

Finally, most practices that conducted transfusions lacked the time and resources to properly type both the donor and recipient blood. According to one estimate, only one-tenth of practices reported always typing the blood of both the donor and recipient animal. While complications due to incompatible blood types were not nearly as severe for dogs as they are for humans, this lack of blood typing and cross-matching was shown to prolong the recovery of a patient animal.

---

[4] Unlike the human market, transfusions in the animal market still tended to be "whole blood" transfusions.

These factors resulted in many veterinarians viewing the transfusion of animal blood as the treatment of last resort, with 84 percent of veterinary doctors reporting overall dissatisfaction with the blood transfusion alternatives currently available in the marketplace.

Human Blood Substitutes

Originally conceived as a vehicle to treat wounded soldiers in battlefield settings, the potential for a human blood substitute for nonmilitary use became increasingly apparent since the 1950s. This period saw a significant rise in auto accidents, the advent of open heart and organ transplant surgeries, and the AIDS crisis, which called into question the safety of the blood supply.

By 1998, several companies appeared to be on the verge of a viable blood substitute with a class of product called "hemoglobin-based blood substitutes." These products attempted to exploit the natural oxygen carrying capabilities of hemoglobin while eliminating the limitations associated with donated RBCs. Each of these companies was attempting to (1) extract the hemoglobin found within human or animal RBCs, (2) purify that hemoglobin to eliminate infectious agents, and (3) modify the otherwise unstable free hemoglobin molecule to prevent it from breaking down. These purification and modification processes were nontrivial and represented the bulk of blood substitute research conducted over the past 20 years.

Product Benefits
In theory, these hemoglobin-based blood substitutes eliminated many of the limitations associated with donated RBCs. In particular, they

- Were "universal" blood substitutes, eliminating the need for blood typing and cross-matching.
- Were free of infectious agents and contamination.
- Had increased shelf-life. These blood substitutes could be safely stored for up to two years.
- Were immediately 100 percent efficient at transporting oxygen. Unlike whole RBCs, modified hemoglobin did not require a period of time to achieve peak oxygen-carrying efficiency.

In addition to these "anticipated" benefits, hemoglobin-based blood substitutes were displaying several "unanticipated" benefits, which companies were only just beginning to investigate. In particular, given that hemoglobin molecules were significantly smaller than RBCs, they were able to flow to regions of the body that RBCs might not be able to reach. It was believed that this could lead to improved treatments in cases of stroke and heart attack—cases where RBCs often were slowed or restricted from reaching vital organs due to either artery blockages or decreased blood pressure.

Product Shortcomings
At the same time, these "hemoglobin-based" blood substitutes did have some shortcomings, including

- A short half-life. While donated RBCs remained in the body for up to two months after transfusion, these blood substitutes were excreted from the body within two to seven days.

- The potential for higher toxicity. While the human body could tolerate the limitless and continuous replacement of one's blood with donated blood, the safety of these blood substitutes had been demonstrated only up to transfusion levels of 5 to 10 units.

In spite of these shortcomings, Dr. C. Everett Koop, the former Surgeon General of the United States, proclaimed,

> When the history of 20th-century medicine is written, the development of blood substitutes will be listed among the top ten advances in medicine. . . . [B]ecause of its purity, efficacy and convenience, this product class has the potential to revolutionize the practice of medicine, especially in critical-care situations. . . . [T]he next generation will not know how tough it was for those of us in medical practice before this technology became available.[5]

Others were less optimistic. One industry analyst presented a less attractive scenario for hemoglobin-based blood substitutes:

> . . . [W]e feel that there is no urgent need for blood substitutes since donated human blood is, for the most part, safe and effective. The expectation that blood substitutes will command vast markets and high price premiums is based on the assumptions that blood substitutes will prove safer and more effective than donated blood. While only time will tell if this is true, it will be an uphill battle given the widespread acceptance of donated blood.

The FDA Approval Process

Human blood substitutes fell under the strict regulation of the U.S. government's Food and Drug Administration (FDA), which required that a product be proven safe and effective for medical use before being approved for commercial release (refer back to Exhibit 8.3). By early 1998, three companies had products that were in the final stages of this process. These products differed in their source of raw hemoglobin and in the process by which that hemoglobin was purified and modified. The FDA approval process was sensitive to these differences. Short of beginning the FDA approval process anew, each company was limited in its ability to substantially alter either the source of their hemoglobin or the process by which that hemoglobin was purified and modified. In addition, given that most of the companies had patented their purification and modification processes, there was little opportunity for a new entrant to quickly gain FDA approval.

Competitors for a Human Blood Substitute

As of 1998, Baxter International and Northfield Laboratories were the only other companies in late-stage development of a hemoglobin-based blood substitute. All other competitors were either several years behind in their development of a hemoglobin-based product or were pursuing a less promising technology.

In contrast to Biopure's use of cattle as its source of hemoglobin, both Baxter and Northfield relied on human blood as their source of hemoglobin. In particular, both companies had developed a technology to extract raw hemoglobin from "outdated" human RBCs (i.e., RBCs intended for transfusion, but which had been stored for more than six weeks). While their production processes and their pending FDA approval did not preclude them from using fresh RBCs, it was the stated intention of both companies to initially rely on outdated human RBCs. Through 1998, Baxter had an agreement with the American Red Cross to obtain outdated RBCs at a cost of $8 per unit. Until recently, Northfield had a similar $8 per unit agreement with Blood Centers of America, another national blood collection agency. However, in early

---

[5] Biopure company website.

1997, Blood Centers of America raised their price to Northfield to $26 per unit for outdated RBCs.

In addition to their reliance on human blood, the products of Baxter and Northfield also differed from Biopure's in that they needed to be frozen or refrigerated until used. Biopure's Hemopure was shelf-stable at room temperature.

Baxter International

With over $5.4 billion in sales and $670 million in net income in 1996, Baxter was an acknowledged leader in the development, manufacture, and sale of blood-related medical products, ranging from artificial heart valves to blood-collection equipment. In addition, Baxter had a long history of product breakthrough, having developed the first sterile blood collection device in 1939, the first commercially available artificial kidney machine in 1956, and the first Factor VIII blood-clotting factor for the treatment of hemophilia in 1966.

"HemAssist," Baxter's patented blood substitute, was expected to add to this string of breakthroughs. Representing 30 years and $250 million in effort, HemAssist was the first human blood substitute to proceed to Phase 3 clinical trials in June 1996. Initially, these trials were expected to lead to full FDA approval by late 1998. However, in October 1997, Baxter revised its estimate to late 1999 or early 2000—an announcement that was followed by a 10 percent dip in Baxter's stock price.

Despite this delay, Baxter recently constructed a $100 million facility with a production capacity of one million units of HemAssist per year. Aside from its variable cost of source material, Baxter was expected to incur production costs of approximately $50 million per year, independent of production volume. While still just industry speculation, it was anticipated that Baxter would price HemAssist between $600 and $800 per unit.

Northfield Laboratories

Northfield Laboratories of Illinois also had recently entered Phase 3 trials with a hemoglobin-based blood substitute. Northfield's product, "PolyHeme," was very similar to Baxter's HemAssist in its production and usage profile. Based on early positive results from its Phase 3 trials, Northfield anticipated full FDA approval in late 1999.

In contrast to Baxter, Northfield was a small, 45-person firm that was founded in 1985 for the sole purpose of developing a human blood substitute. As such, PolyHeme represented its only product. Analysts expected PolyHeme to be priced comparably to HemAssist upon release.

By early 1998, Northfield had spent $70 million in its development of PolyHeme and in the construction of a pilot production facility with an output capacity of 10,000 units per year. While this facility was sufficient to satisfy demand during clinical trials, Northfield management recognized the need for a full-scale production facility. With this in mind, they hoped to construct a $45 million facility with a capacity of 300,000 units per year. With this factory in place, aside from the cost of raw material, production costs were expected to be about $30 million per year, independent of production volume. By early 1998, selection of a factory site and plant construction had not yet begun.

Animal Blood Substitutes

Through early 1998, Biopure was the only company that was actively engaged in the development of a blood substitute for the small-animal veterinary market. And while there was little to prevent Baxter or Northfield (or anyone else) from attempting to enter the veterinary market, any company wishing to do so would have to initiate an FDA-approval process specific to the veterinary market. By one estimate, assuming a company immediately began such a process, it would take two to five years to bring a product to market.

Biopure and Its Blood Substitutes

Hemopure and Oxyglobin were nearly identical in terms of physical characteristics and production processes. The only difference between the two products was in the size of the hemoglobin "clusters" that were contained in the final products. In the production of Oxyglobin, both large and small clusters of hemoglobin molecules were naturally formed. However, the small clusters tended to cause minor gastrointestinal problems and discoloration of urine. While considered acceptable in the animal market, these side effects were undesirable in the human market. As a result, Hemopure followed the same production process as used to make Oxyglobin, with a final step added to remove the small hemoglobin clusters.

Biopure had a single manufacturing facility, with an output capacity varying by the production mix of Oxyglobin and Hemopure. The same equipment was used to produce either product, but only one product could be produced at a time. This resulted in an annual capacity of 300,000 units of Oxyglobin or 150,000 units of Hemopure or some linear combination in between. The lower output for Hemopure reflected the facts that (1) the added step to remove the small hemoglobin clusters decreased the rate of production and (2) the removal of the small hemoglobin clusters decreased yield.

To support these levels of output, aside from the cost of raw material, Biopure anticipated overall production costs of $15 million per year, independent of volume. For raw material, it anticipated a ready supply of bovine blood priced at $1.50 per unit. Biopure paid this money to cattle slaughterhouses to collect and transport the blood of cattle that were being processed for their meat—blood that otherwise would have been discarded. It was estimated that 10,000 cattle could supply enough raw material to support full production in Biopure's existing manufacturing facility.

Status of Hemopure

As of early 1998, Hemopure was in Phase 3 clinical trials in Europe, with FDA approval for Phase 3 trials in the United States appearing imminent. In anticipation of this approval, Biopure had established sites for Phase 3 trials and was ready to proceed immediately upon approval. While acknowledging the potential pitfalls of any clinical trials, Biopure was confident that the Phase 3 trials would be successful and that the FDA would grant full approval sometime in 1999. Biopure expected to commercially release Hemopure sometime in late 1999 or early 2000.

In line with the anticipated price of Baxter's HemAssist, Biopure planned to price Hemopure at $600 to $800 per unit. However, little systematic testing had been done by Biopure to determine the acceptability of these prices. In particular, little was known of the price sensitivity of medical personnel, insurance providers, or patients when it came to human blood substitutes.

Status of Oxyglobin

In 1997, Biopure established the Veterinary Products Division and hired Andy Wright to oversee the marketing and sale of Oxyglobin. Working under the assumption that Biopure would begin selling Oxyglobin immediately upon approval, Wright faced a host of decisions, including how to price and how to distribute Oxyglobin. Supporting him in these decisions was a team of seven employees—one director of marketing, one technical service representative (to answer technical questions and complaints), two customer service representatives (to support ordering and billing), and three sales representatives (to make sales calls and generate orders).

The Pricing of Oxyglobin

Some members of Wright's sales team argued for Oxyglobin to be priced at $80 to $100 per unit. These team members pointed to the price sensitivity of the vet market, arguing that few pet owners carried health insurance on their animals. They also noted that the average cost of a visit to the vet was only about $60, with few procedures costing more than $100 (see Exhibit 8.8). Finally, they noted that vets tended to use a simple "doubling rule" when pricing a medical product to the pet owners, bringing the end-user price of Oxyglobin to $160 to $200 per unit.

Other members of Andy Wright's sales team felt that Oxyglobin should carry a premium price of up to $200 per unit, reflecting the many advantages of Oxyglobin relative to donated animal blood. These team members pointed out that while the average cost of a visit to a primary care practice might be only $60, the cost of a visit to an emergency care practice could easily run from $200 to over $1,000. They also questioned whether veterinary doctors would just blindly double the price of Oxyglobin without regard for its high dollar contribution. Finally, they noted that at a low price, Biopure could never hope to recoup the massive cost of product development.

To better understand the channel's willingness to pay for an animal blood substitute, Biopure conducted two surveys in 1997—one survey of 285 veterinarians and another of 200 dog owners. Table 8.A offers results of the veterinarian survey and Table 8.B offers results of the owner survey.

In reviewing these surveys, Wright reminded himself that veterinarians often played the role of gatekeeper when it came to potential treatments, recommending less-expensive over more-expensive treatments in an effort to save their clients'

TABLE 8.A
Veterinarians' Reported Willingness to Trial Oxyglobin

Source: Biopure company records.

Price to Veterinarian	Percent of Veterinarians Who Would Trial Product	
	Noncritical Cases	Critical Cases
$50 per unit	95%	100%
$100 per unit	70	95
$150 per unit	25	80
$200 per unit	5	60

TABLE 8.B
Pet Owners' Willingness to Trial Oxyglobin

Source: Biopure company records.

Price to Pet Owner	Percent of Pet Owners Who Would Trial Product	
	Noncritical Cases	Critical Cases
$100 per unit	60%	90%
$200 per unit	40	85
$300 per unit	35	75
$400 per unit	30	65

money. At the same time, 90 percent of pet owners reported that they wanted to be made fully aware of all the alternatives available to treat their pets.

The Distribution of Oxyglobin

Andy Wright also had to decide how best to sell and distribute Oxyglobin and how to educate veterinarians on its use. In approaching this question, he looked to the current distribution practices for medical products in the veterinary market.

In 1997, $1.2 billion worth of product was sold to veterinary practices through a network of 200 independent distributors—each of whom sold and distributed the products of many manufacturers. Two of these independent distributors were national in scope, 18 were regional (e.g., New England), and 180 were local (e.g., metropolitan Boston). Table 8.C provides a sales and staffing profile for these distributors. A manufacturer might contract with one national distributor, several nonoverlapping regional distributors, and many nonoverlapping local distributors. In return for their selling and distribution efforts, a distributor would receive 20 percent of the manufacturer selling price on a more-established product and 30 percent of the selling price on a less-established or new product.

A veterinary practice could expect one 15-minute visit per week from the sales representatives of its primary distributor. These 15-minute visits would entail a focused discussion of current promotions on existing products and a more limited discussion of products new to the market. Typically, a sales rep might introduce 100 new products in a given year. To educate a particular distributor's sales reps on a new product, a manufacturer might set up a series of training sessions. These training sessions would be conducted for groups of about 10 sales representatives each and last anywhere from one to four hours, depending on the complexity of the new product.

Another $300 million worth of products were sold directly to veterinary practices through manufacturer sales forces. Termed "manufacturer direct," this type of distribution often was used by manufacturers with either high-volume, well-established products or products that required a very sophisticated sales pitch. If Biopure chose this route, in addition to the cost of maintaining a sales force, Andy estimated the cost to physically distribute Oxyglobin to be $10 to $15 per unit.

Andy Wright also considered trade publications and trade shows as another means by which to educate veterinarians about the existence and benefits of Oxyglobin. A quick investigation revealed that five journals had almost universal coverage across veterinarians and tended to be well-read. In addition, six large veterinary trade shows held in the United States each year attracted 2,000 to 10,000 veterinarians each. Typically, these trade shows were taken seriously by attendees and were a valued source of information. Andy wondered if either of these avenues made sense for Biopure.

TABLE 8.C
Profile of Independent Distributors of Veterinary Medicines

Source: Biopure company records.

Type of Distributor	Number	Percent of Total Sales	Average Number of Sales Reps
National	2	25%	100
Regional	18	60	40
Local	180	15	1.5

Biopure's Decisions

While Andy dealt with the question of how best to market Oxyglobin, Carl Rausch wrestled with the larger question of whether and when to launch Oxyglobin. Should he listen to Ted Jacobs and postpone the launch of Oxyglobin until *after* Hemopure had established itself in the marketplace? Or should he listen to Andy and immediately launch Oxyglobin and reap the near-term benefits?

Not lost on Carl was the potential impact of Oxyglobin on a possible initial public offering of Biopure stock. To this point, Biopure had remained a privately held firm with very little debt. And while they currently had no revenues, a recent round of capital venture financing had provided them with $50 million—enough money to support operations for another two years. Nevertheless, many stakeholders in Biopure were anxious to take the company public. In this regard, Carl wondered whether a veterinary product with small but steady sales might not prove more attractive to investors than a human product still under development. He was especially sensitive to this issue in light of some recent, high-profile product failures in the Massachusetts biotechnology community (see Exhibit 8.9).

With all of this in mind, as president and CEO of Biopure, Carl Rausch pondered how best to leverage the opportunity offered by Oxyglobin without jeopardizing the potential of Hemopure.

EXHIBIT 8.1
Excerpts from *The Boston Globe* **Article, February 5, 1998**

Source: Reprinted with courtesy of *The Boston Globe*.

Biopure's Blood Substitute for Dogs OK'd

Veterinarians scrambling to find blood for badly injured dogs now have a blood substitute. Biopure Corp. of Cambridge said yesterday it received federal regulatory approval to market oxygen-carrying blood derived from the blood of cows.

Tested in over 250 dogs, the company's blood substitute, called Oxyglobin, is initially aimed at the [canine blood transfusion market], according to Andrew W. Wright, vice president of Biopure's veterinary products.

The U.S. Food and Drug Administration approval makes Oxyglobin the first blood substitutes for dogs, designed for dogs needing blood transfusions because of blood loss from accidents, surgeries, parasite infections, or rare anemia cases.

"This is breakthrough development because it quickly gets oxygen into tissue and organs and buys time for the dog's own regenerative red blood cells to come back," said Dr. Robert Murtaugh, professor of veterinary medicine and section head for emergency and critical care services at the Tufts University School of Veterinary Medicine.

The canine version is designed to largely replace drawing blood from donor dogs some veterinarians use in emergency situations.

Unlike blood that contains red blood cells, Biopure's technology uses a highly purified bovine hemoglobin that does not require blood typing or cross-matching. [Oxyglobin] can be stored in a veterinarian's storage area at room temperature for up to two years. A single bag—equivalent to a pint of whole blood—is sufficient for small to medium-sized dogs; two bags might be needed for larger dogs.

EXHIBIT 8.2 **The Organizational Structure at Biopure Corporation**

Source: Biopure company records.

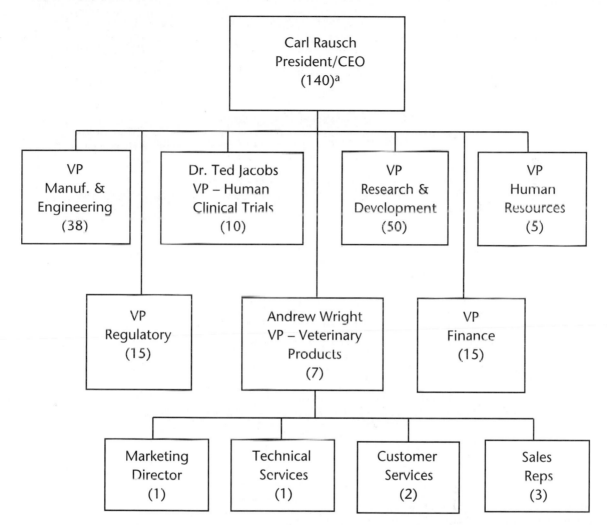

[a] Numbers in parentheses represent the total number of employees that fall under a particular position's span of control. Thus, 140 employees either directly or indirectly report to Carl Rausch.

EXHIBIT 8.3
The United States FDA Approval Process

Source: Biopure company records.

Phase	Goals	Characteristics
Preclinical trials	Safety in animals	—Typical length = 5–10 years —Need to show safety —Hope to show efficacy —Testing animals include mice, rats, dogs, sheep, etc.
Phase 1 clinical trials	Safety in healthy human subjects	—Typical length = 2–3 years —20–100 individuals —Single-site testing location
Phase 2A & 2B clinical trials	2A — Safety in human patients 2B — Safety & efficacy in human patients	—Typical length = 1–2 years —100–200 individuals —Single-site or multisite testing locations
Phase 3 clinical trials	Large-scale safety & efficacy in use	—Typical length = 1–2 years —100–500 individuals —Multisite testing locations —Double-blind testing (i.e., neither patient nor doctor aware of specific product or brand)

EXHIBIT 8.4
Human Blood Typing and Allowable Transfusions[a]

Source: The American Red Cross.

Donor Blood Type	Percent of Population	Acceptable Recipients
AB	4	AB[b]
A	40	A, AB
B	11	B, AB
O[c]	45	O, A, B, AB

[a] In addition to ABO blood typing, RBCs are either Rh+ or Rh−, further complicating allowable transfusions.
[b] AB is often referred to as the "universal recipient."
[c] O is often referred to as the "universal donor."

EXHIBIT 8.5
Red Blood Cell Donations and Transfusions in the United States in 1995

Source: Stover & Associates LLC.

Use of Red Blood Cells	Units (in 000s)
Acute blood loss:	
Elective surgery:	
Anonymous donations	5,800
Autologous donations[a,b]	1,100
Emergency surgery (in hospital)	1,000
Trauma (in field administration)	200
Acute blood loss subtotal	**8,100**
Chronic Anemia	**3,200**
Not Transfused	
Due to rejection	1,200
Due to expiration	1,500
Not transfused subtotal	**2,700**
Total:	**14,000**

[a] Autologous donations are in elective surgery only. All other uses of RBCs represent anonymous donations.
[b] Autologous donations include both those units transfused and those unused units discarded.

EXHIBIT 8.6
Cost to Patient of Donated Human Blood

Source: Stover & Associates LLC.

	Low Estimate (per Unit)	High Estimate (per Unit)
Anonymous donations:		
Hospital acquisition cost	$ 75	$150
Screening/typing/cross-matching	25	40
Transportation/administration	25	35
Final price of anonymous	**$125**	**$225**
Autologous donations:		
Added administration and handling	+150	+200
Final price of autologous	**$275**	**$425**

EXHIBIT 8.7   Profile of the 15,000 Veterinary Practices in the United States (1995)

Source: Biopure company records.

Class of Practice	Average Number of Doctors	Relative Frequency	Average Monthly Case Load			Average Gross Revenues
			Dogs	Cats	Other	
Primary care:						
1 doctor practices	1	25%	200	125	80	$265,000
2 doctor practices	2	30	300	200	120	460,000
3+ doctor practices	4.6	40	450	300	160	800,000
Average primary care	2.7	95	412	265	140	570,000
Emergency care:						
Average emergency care	4.0	5%	400	240	130	$770,000

EXHIBIT 8.8
Small-Animal Veterinary Fees for Typical Procedures in Primary Care Practices in 1995

Source: *Veterinary Economics,* October 1996, p. 45.

Procedure	Average Fee
Average charge per visit	**$ 58**
Office call—average minimum charge	$ 25
Boarding	10
Hospitalization	19
Anesthesia	45
X-rays	40
Blood transfusion	100
Hysterectomy	80
Heartworm treatment	250
Annual vaccinations	27
Rabies vaccination	12
Lab tests—average	23
Dental cleaning	75
Deworming	15

EXHIBIT 8.9
Massachusetts Biopharmaceutical Companies' Proposed Drugs Sidelined in the Second Quarter, 1997

Source: *The Boston Globe.*

Firm/Location	Date	Problem	Status of company
ImmunoGen Norwood, MA	March 18	Oncolysin B cancer drug halted after Phase 3 trial failure	Significantly downsized operations, extensive layoffs, major restructuring, sold biomanufacturing plant, and relocated corporate offices
OraVax Cambridge, MA	March 19	HNK20, a nosedrop designed to reduce hospitalization for lower respiratory infections caused by respiratory virus in infants, failed in a pivotal overseas clinical trial	Layoff of 20 people in April as part of a corporate reorganization
AutoImmune Lexington, MA	April 21	Myloral, an oral multiple sclerosis drug, did no better than placebo in Phase 3 trial	Major restructuring, now employs 20, down from 90 employees
Genzyme Cambridge, MA	May 5	Sepracoat, a surgical antiadhesion coating, was rejected by FDA advisory committee for lack of sufficient evidence of clinical effectiveness	Company selling Sepracoat in Europe; has FDA approval on related Seprafilm product
Cambridge Neuroscience Cambridge, MA	June 24	Cerestat clinical trial is halted over safety concerns by corporate partner, Boehringer Ingelheim	Six-month investigation begins to find reasons for concern

Chapter 9

Synthes

John T. Gourville

It was the morning of January 16, 2001, as Tom Priest watched the HBS field study team wrap up its presentation to Synthes management. Priest, a Synthes product development manager, had been given the job of supervising the HBS team, which was asked to assess the potential for "bioresorbable internal fixation devices."

Synthes was the leading maker and distributor of "internal fixation devices" used by orthopedic trauma surgeons to repair fractured bones. Internal fixation involved the surgical placement of plates, rods, and screws to stabilize the broken bones and allow the body to repair itself over time (see Exhibit 9.1 for examples of these devices). Collectively, these devices were referred to as "implants." With a domestic market share approaching 50 percent, Synthes was the leader in the U.S. orthopedic trauma implant market. In 2000, it sold over $240 million in trauma implants, which were used in over 300,000 patients in the United States.

As of 2001, implants almost exclusively were made of stainless steel or titanium—two metals that were strong and cost effective, but that often needed to be removed after the bones had healed. In the fall of 2000, three HBS second-year students—Kevin Bozic, Shauna Finnie, and Michael Meyer—had been asked to look at the opportunity presented by "bioresorbable" implants. Relatively new to the market, bioresorbable implants "dissolved" over time, eliminating the need for their removal. Made of advanced polymers, bioresorbables were intended to be rigid for many weeks, time enough to repair most fractures, after which they would dissolve, or resorb, into the body. These devices did not always perform as intended, however, and sometimes led to incomplete healing or inflammatory reactions.

Professor John T. Gourville prepared this case with the assistance of Kevin Bozic, MBA '01, Shauna Finnie, MBA '01, and Michael Meyer, MBA '01. HBS cases are developed solely as the basis for class discussion. Cases are not intended to serve as endorsements, sources of primary data, or illustrations of effective or ineffective management. Some names and data contained herein have been disguised or simplified.

Copyright © 2001 President and Fellows of Harvard College. To order copies or request permission to reproduce materials, call 1-800-545-7685, write Harvard Business School Publishing, Boston, MA 02163, or go to http://www.hbsp.harvard.edu. No part of this publication may be reproduced, stored in a retrieval system, used in a spreadsheet, or transmitted in any form or by any means—electronic, mechanical, photocopying, recording, or otherwise—without the permission of Harvard Business School.

As the team finished its presentation—concluding that bioresorbables represented a great opportunity for the company that "got it right"—the Synthes managers started asking questions:

- If such a great opportunity, why was the market for bioresorbables developing so slowly?
- What were the dangers in letting another company take the lead in this new technology?
- What if Synthes entered the market and "got it wrong"?

The HBS team considered these points and knew that it would take more than just a few PowerPoint slides to convince Synthes that bioresorbables made sense. Or did they make sense?

The United States Market for Internal Fixation Devices

The human body contains 206 bones that provide structure, allow for movement, and protect the internal organs of the body. Broken bones, or "fractures," result when the body sustains forces that exceed the strength of the underlying bone, as sometimes occurs in automobile accidents, sporting injuries, and accidental falls. The orthopedic trauma market consists of fractures to the bones of the legs, arms, hands, and feet. In 2000, there were six million such fractures in the United States, 80 percent of which occurred in adults and 20 percent of which occurred in children under age 18.

In 2000, over 85 percent of trauma fractures were relatively simple and could be treated without surgery using plaster casts. In the remaining cases, the fracture was more severe, with the bone completely broken or (even worse) shattered. In these cases, surgery was required to align and stabilize the bone fragments, often with the help of an internal fixation device (Table 9.A identifies the types of fractures for which such devices were required). On average, these surgeries took two to four hours, required the patient to be hospitalized for two days, and cost $5,000 to $10,000.

In 2000, manufacturer sales of internal fixation devices exceeded $540 million, with steady 5 percent annual growth. These devices included (1) plates, which were attached with screws to the surface of the broken bones; (2) rods, which were inserted into the center or medullary canal of broken bones; and (3) screws (used without plates), which helped to realign bone fragments. Exhibit 9.2 provides sales data across types of devices and manufacturers.

The market prices for these devices varied greatly according to type, size, and application, with plates priced from $100 to $600, rods from $500 to $1,500, and screws from $5 to $100. Exhibit 9.3 provides product pricing data across competitors. It was believed that "cost of goods sold" ran at about 50 percent of the list prices shown.

TABLE 9.A
The Use of Internal Fixation Devices across Types of Fractures in 2000

Source: *Orthopedic Network News.*

Type of Fracture	Number of Patients
Femur (upper leg)	285,239
Tibia/fibula (lower leg)	222,431
Radius/ulna (lower arm)	67,716
Humerus (upper arm)	59,823
Other (e.g., hand/foot)	77,044
Total	712,253

The Need for Implant Removal

Historically, implants were made of either stainless steel or titanium. These metals were strong, tended not to be rejected by a patient's body, and were cost effective. However, after the bones had healed, steel and titanium implants needed to be removed in about 20 percent of adults and 40 percent of children. In adults, the most common reasons for removal included (1) lingering pain; (2) the fact that the implant was visible just below the skin of the hand, foot, or forearm; and (3) a fear of having metal within one's body. In children, additional reasons for removal included (4) the potential that the implant would interfere with the further development of the bones and (5) a parent's insistence that the plate be removed. Table 9.B shows the rate of implant removal across types of fractures.

While less complex than the surgery to insert an implant, the surgery to remove an implant lasted from 30 minutes to several hours, required a hospital stay of one or two days, and cost $2,000 to $4,000. As noted by one surgeon, removing implants was a no-win situation:

> You can never look good taking hardware out! Even if everything goes right, you've placed the patient through another round of pain and recovery. And something can always go wrong . . . you might create a new fracture taking a plate or rod out . . . or an infection might set in . . . or you might damage a muscle or a nerve. Removing an implant is a headache none of us looks forward to.[1]

The decision to leave an implant in a patient's body was not without its shortcomings, however. Priest identified several potential problems with leaving an implant in:

- *The implant is palpable.* Perhaps the single biggest drawback to leaving an implant in was that sometimes it could be felt under the surface of the skin. This was especially true for bones of the hands, feet, wrists, and ankles.
- *Reduced blood flow to the bone.* The pressure of a plate against the surface of a bone sometimes disturbed the normal flow of blood to that bone, slowing the growth of new blood vessels and the long-term healing of the bone.
- *Imaging shadow.* In many cases, steel and titanium implants interfered with X-rays and MRIs, obscuring the underlying bone and preventing a clear view of the healing fracture.
- *Gradual loosening of the implant.* In about 5 percent of cases, a metal implant would shift or loosen with the motion of the repaired bone leading to discomfort and, sometimes, a need to remove the implant.
- *"Re-fractures" and joint replacements.* If a healed bone was "re-fractured" later in life, the original implant often had to be removed before that bone could be

TABLE 9.B

The Frequency of Removal of Internal Fixation Devices across Types of Fractures

Source: Field study team estimates.

Type of Fracture	Estimated Rate of Removal	
	Adult Patients	Pediatric Patients
Femur (upper leg)	15%	30%
Tibia/fibula (lower leg)	25	50
Radius/ulna (lower arm)	20	40
Humerus (upper arm)	5	10
Other (e.g., hand/foot)	50	70

[1] From an HBS field study team member's interview with an orthopedic trauma surgeon.

treated. Similarly, the placement of an artificial joint often required the removal of any implants near that joint. As noted by one surgeon, such procedures always proved difficult. "If you think taking out an implant six months after it had been put in is difficult, try taking one out 5, 10, or 20 years after."

An Overview of Synthes

By 2000, Synthes was the recognized leader in trauma implants in the United States and sold its products to almost every major hospital and medical school in the United States. By Priest's estimate, over 80 percent of orthopedic trauma surgeons used a Synthes implant sometime in 2000, with 30 percent using Synthes implants almost exclusively.

The AO: The Roots of Synthes

Synthes traced its roots to a Swiss nonprofit research group called the Association for the Study of Internal Fixation (widely known by its Swiss initials, AO). Formed in 1958, the AO brought together a small group of orthopedic surgeons, metallurgists, and other scientists who hoped to perfect and promote an alternative to the use of plaster casts or traction to treat complex bone fractures. Priest explained the founding of the AO as follows:

> In the 1950s, if you broke your leg skiing or in a car accident, the treatment was to align the bones as best you could and to place the patient in traction or a cast for two to three months. Sometimes it worked and sometimes it didn't. Following traction or casting, the lucky patients suffered through several months of rehabilitation, while the unlucky patients were left with a permanent disability. In fact, at the time the AO was formed, the Swiss government was paying disability compensation to one-third of all patients with tibia fractures and two-thirds of all patients with femur fractures. The AO was founded by four doctors who felt there had to be a better way. They did not invent internal fixation, but they set out to improve and standardize the science behind it.

Over the next 40 years, the AO became known for three things. The first was its *research* into the science of internal fixation. It developed an in-house staff of surgeons and researchers and fostered relationships with the world's leading orthopedic trauma surgeons to constantly improve the materials and techniques used in internal fixation.

Second, the AO sought to *educate*. Almost from the beginning, the AO offered multiday courses to teach and update orthopedic surgeons on the techniques of internal fixation. Over time, these courses became extremely popular and were offered around the world (see Exhibit 9.4 for a sample). By one estimate, 75 percent of the world's leading orthopedic trauma surgeons had been through at least one AO course, with many attending multiple courses over their careers.[2] In addition, the AO literally "wrote the book" on internal fixation, having published the two most influential books in the field—*Techniques of Internal Fixation of Fractures*, in 1963, and the *Manual of Internal Fixation*, in 1969.

---

[2] To highlight the respect these AO courses commanded, one HBS team member noted that the AO charged attending surgeons about $2,000 for one of its five-day basic or advanced courses. In contrast, competing manufacturers charged nothing for courses that they claimed were equivalent. Nevertheless, most surgeons attend the AO courses instead of the competitors'.

Third, the AO *developed* a family of trauma implants based on the AO philosophy for internal fixation. As part of its efforts to advance the techniques of internal fixation, the AO became the leading developer of steel and titanium implants in the world. It was the development of these devices that led to the formation of Synthes in 1974.

The Formation of Synthes in 1974

Recognizing its limitations as a nonprofit research group, in the 1970s the AO worked with several for-profit Swiss companies to distribute its state-of-the-art internal implants. Each of these companies was given exclusive distribution rights to a particular region of the world and paid royalties back to the nonprofit AO. These companies were (1) Synthes, founded in 1974 and given distribution rights to North America; (2) Stratec, with distribution rights to Western Europe and Latin America; and (3) Mathys, with distribution rights to Eastern Europe, Asia, and Africa.

From these beginnings, under the direction of it president, Hansjörg Wyss (HBS '65), Synthes went from a *distributor* to a *manufacturer* of AO devices—which it sold under the Synthes trademark. By 2001, Wyss had purchased controlling interest in Synthes, had taken on the titles of chairman and CEO, and had appointed Scott Hastings as president of the company.

In addition, by 2001, Synthes had grown to become "Synthes North America," which consisted of four operating companies with combined sales of over $500 million and over 2,000 employees. These four companies were

- *Synthes Orthopedics.* The largest of the operating companies, Synthes Orthopedics specialized in trauma devices. It employed 400 people and accounted for half of all Synthes sales. Internal fixation devices made up 85 percent of its sales.
- *Synthes Spine.* With 160 employees, Synthes Spine specialized in metallic implants to fuse sections of the vertebrae together. These devices were used to treat fractures, malformations, and degenerative diseases of the spine.
- *Synthes Maxillofacial.* With 60 employees, Maxillofacial specialized in the sale of plates, screws, and thin, mesh-like devices used to treat fractures of the skull and face.
- *Synthes Canada.* Also with 60 employees, Synthes Canada was responsible for selling all Synthes products throughout Canada.

A fifth unit under Hastings's control was the 1,300-person manufacturing group, which was responsible for two facilities—one in Pennsylvania and one in Colorado. A sixth unit was "Osteobiologics," a newly formed group of about 20 people who were given the task of exploring new materials for use in the company's products.

Synthes Orthopedics

By 2001, Synthes Orthopedics was the recognized leader in trauma implants in the United States with nearly 50 percent market share (refer back to Exhibit 9.2). The HBS team identified three factors that were critical to building this dominant market share.

Education

The first stemmed from Synthes's long-standing and widely recognized relationship with the AO. While technically a separate company, Synthes was viewed by many surgeons as the "AO affiliate" in the United States. This perception extended to the AO's training courses. Kevin Bozic, one of the HBS team members, explained the impact of these courses as follows:

> In our interviews with surgeons, the AO courses came across as a tremendous asset for Synthes. While the name "Synthes" does not appear on any AO course material, almost every surgeon we talked to referred to these courses as the "Synthes courses." With 75 percent of surgeons attending these courses, it's not surprising that the name Synthes has become synonymous with leading-edge orthopedic trauma care.

Product

The second critical factor was Synthes's exclusive access to the AO family of implants. While these implants were branded as "Synthes" products, they were widely regarded as "AO" products. As Bozic explained, several benefits arose from this arrangement:

> It provides Synthes with implants that are recognized as the best in the business—the "gold standard," as they were referred to on several occasions. Also, it provides Synthes with implants that are believed to be well researched and well tested. As one surgeon put it, "If Synthes introduces a new product, I feel safe using it." Finally, with over 10,000 SKUs across 200 product categories, it provides Synthes with the most extensive product line in the business. Many of the surgeons we talked to told us that they never had to go outside the Synthes product line in the course of their work.

To maintain this advantage, Synthes and the AO worked closely with each other and with practicing surgeons to develop new devices. Within the AO, 50 engineers and scientists were responsible for basic research on fracture fixation devices. Within Synthes, another 50 people were responsible for developing products that met the more immediate needs of the marketplace. Finally, there was strong collaboration with the leading orthopedic surgeons to develop products specific to their needs. As Bozic pointed out:

> Once the need for a new implant is identified, Synthes and the AO go to some of the leading surgeons in the world. Listening to and working with these surgeons, they develop a product that meets those surgeons' needs. In the end, the product works because the surgeons helped develop it.

Sales Force

The final critical factor the team identified was Synthes's 300-person direct sales force, believed to be the most experienced in the field. This sales force sold to most of the 5,000 hospitals and clinics and 20,000 orthopedic surgeons in the United States.

One characteristic that distinguished Synthes's sales force from that of its competitors was its close working relationship with orthopedic surgeons. It was not unusual for an orthopedic surgeon and a Synthes sales consultant to be in contact with one another several times per week. This extended to the point where a Synthes sales consultant often discussed difficult trauma cases with an orthopedic surgeon prior to an operation. This close working relationship led many trauma practices to use nothing but Synthes devices. By one estimate, about one-third of orthopedic trauma surgeons in the United States exclusively used Synthes implants. No other device manufacturer came close to this level of exclusivity.

Bozic tried to capture the importance of the Synthes sales force as follows:

> By providing high-quality training and advice, the Synthes sales consultants are a trusted and valuable part of many surgeons' practices. When faced with a difficult procedure that requires the use of a complex or new implant, most surgeons wouldn't think twice about calling a Synthes rep at home at 2 A.M. and asking them to come to the operating room.

And just as important, the sales consultant would not think twice about "not coming." They are available 24 hours a day, 7 days a week, 52 weeks a year.

Marketplace Forces

In spite of these advantages, the market for metallic implants was highly competitive. As pointed out by one industry analyst:

> Service, training, and broad product lines drive [internal] fixation sales. In the bone fixation market, there are few standout product features that allow manufacturers to substantially differentiate themselves. Material differences, such as titanium versus stainless steel . . . are used to position companies. For the most part, however, this segment is focused more on a relationship sell . . . , with service, physician training, and broad product lines all requirements for success. Synthes has used this approach quite successfully to become the market share leader in fixation. We expect this to change as many of the larger orthopedic companies approach this segment more aggressively . . . [3]

While not completely agreeing with this viewpoint, Priest did suggest that it was increasingly difficult to stay ahead of the competition. He noted:

> We are constantly fighting the threat of commoditization. The time it takes competitors to copy our new products has shrunk from a couple of years to about six months. At the same time, hospitals and HMOs are constantly demanding lower prices, with our competitors often willing to meet these demands. But with product enhancements, cutting-edge education, and a top-notch sales force, we have stayed ahead of the competition.

Bioresorbable Fixation Devices

Bioresorbable implants were a 40-year-old dream in orthopedic trauma care, with surgeons long recognizing the value of an implant that did not need to be removed. In the mid-1980s, the first generation of bioresorbable implants had appeared in the marketplace. These products employed "advanced polymers" (a type of plastic) that were slowly broken down by the body's natural chemical processes into nontoxic by-products. These by-products were then excreted from the body via respiration and urination.

In addition to eliminating the need for removal, these bioresorbable implants promised several benefits relative to metallic implants:

- Better blood flow to the bone. As these products broke down, they returned blood flow to the healing bone, hastening healing relative to metallic implants.
- Lack of an imaging shadow. Bioresorbables were transparent in X-rays and MRIs.
- Elimination of the need for removal in the case of a re-fracture or nearby joint replacement.

To realize these benefits, however, a bioresorbable implant needed to pass two critical hurdles. First, the initial strength of the resorbable material had to be sufficient to keep the fractured bone in place. Second, the resorption rate of the polymer had to be slow enough to allow sufficient time for the bone to heal, but fast enough to be eliminated from the body within an acceptable period of time.

---

[3] Excerpt from a Dain Raucher Wessels analyst report, August 1998, p. 73.

The First-Generation Bioresorbables

By 1987, the first generation of bioresorbable implants believed to meet these criteria began to appear on the market, led by Johnson & Johnson's (J&J) Orthosorb™ pins. Composed of polydiosanone (PDS), these pins were designed to repair simple, non-weight-bearing fractures. Other competitors quickly followed suit with bioresorbable screws, pins, and plates of their own, the majority of which were composed of polyglycolic acid (PGA).

While eagerly anticipated in the marketplace, these products soon ran into problems. In particular, both PDS and PGA tended to break down too quickly, losing much of their strength within six to eight weeks—a period insufficient for fractures of the long bones of the legs and arms and for some of the "stubborn" fractures of the hands and feet. By one estimate, the use of these first-generation implants led to incomplete fracture healing in about 10 percent of cases. In addition, PDS and PGA sometimes broke down more quickly than the body could excrete the by-products. This led to a phenomenon known as "sterile abscess" where the body perceived the by-products to be the result of an infection—leading to swelling and discomfort. Treating these symptoms sometimes required surgery. It was believed that PGA-based implants led to a sterile abscess in 10 percent to 20 percent of patients.

Aside from these medical problems, these first-generation implants were 50 percent more expensive, twice as thick, and one-sixth as strong as the metallic implants they were replacing. Given these drawbacks, many surgeons viewed these products with concern and sales never reached more than a few million dollars per year. The HBS team described the legacy of these early devices:

> These first-generation PGA implants left many orthopedic trauma surgeons dissatisfied. Rather than aiding recovery, they sometimes complicated it. Just try telling a parent that their child's fracture did not heal properly because of a new implant that did not work as expected. It takes only a case or two like that to sour a surgeon on the entire concept of bioresorbable implants and on the companies that make them.
>
> At the same time, it's not surprising that these first-generation products failed to meet expectations. They were unproven, there was little published research on their effectiveness, and they had no clinical track record. Also, given their much lower strength profile, they only were appropriate for fractures that were under low stress, such as with the small bones of the hands and feet.

Priest noted that Synthes was not a player in this first round of bioresorbable implants. Instead, Synthes worked to improve its metallic implants. As he summed up the situation:

> By the 1980s, Synthes was becoming the dominant player in the trauma implant market. Not wanting to risk this position, we focused our efforts on new products that were clinically proven. Bioresorbables were just too much of a risk. Instead, we worked on improving the metallic devices that we were known for. As we learned more about the mechanics of internal fixation, we worked on creating metallic implants that provided a better "anatomic fit" with the bones that they were supposed to repair. We also focused on the repair of bones that had become soft or brittle with age. The repair of fractures of these "osteoporotic bones" requires stronger plates and rods and differently designed screws to overcome the weakness that has developed in these bones. These various efforts expanded our product line, further differentiated our products in the marketplace, and helped improve our market share.

The Second-Generation Bioresorbables

Building on the lessons of the first-generation devices, advances in bioresorbable implants were made on several fronts through the 1990s. These advances included

- New polymers, including polylactic acid (PLA) and a PGA/PLA blend.[4] The strength and resorption rates of these polymers are shown in Exhibit 9.5.
- Improved production that increased the "strength-to-size" ratio of the implants, allowing for devices that were either stronger or less bulky.
- Improved production that resulted in bioresorbable implants costing only 10 percent more to produce than comparable metallic implants. At the same time, these devices were expected to command a 20 percent to 30 percent price premium over metallic devices.
- Ongoing clinical studies and published research looking at the benefits and limitations of bioresorbables.
- The growing use of bioresorbables in other fields of orthopedics. Given the lower stresses and the faster recovery times associated with ligament and tendon repair, bioresorbable wires and pins were gaining acceptance in sports medicine, where sales approached $100 million per year. And in the maxillofacial market, mesh-like plates to stabilize fractures of the skull and face were increasingly being made of bioresorbables.
- The continued use of bioresorbables in trauma. While sales remained low, J&J and others continued to develop their product lines. By 2000, bioresorbable trauma sales had grown to $10 million per year and consisted of pins and screws (90 percent of sales) and small plates (10 percent). These devices were used almost exclusively for fractures of the hands and feet.

For many individuals in the medical community, these advances offered signs that bioresorbables were (again) ready to enter mainstream orthopedic trauma care. As one industry insider stated:

> Bioresorbable implants represent a small, but high-growth segment of the fixation market. As the technology improves, resorbables have the potential to replace many of the metal implants used for non-weight bearing bone fixation. . . . Long term, we believe that resorbables could ultimately replace many of the weight-bearing internal fixators.[5]

Other industry insiders were not so sure, as reflected in the following thoughts:

> I just don't see the need for them. There are not many surgeons jumping up and down to use bioresorbables.[6]

> They have failed in the past and I haven't seen anything that leads me to believe that they won't fail in the future. It's a lot simpler to just use a metallic implant.[7]

Competitive Environment

While Synthes was debating whether to enter the bioresorbable market, several competitors had established a growing presence in the field. The HBS team grouped these players into Heavyweights, Specialists, and Potentials. The Heavyweights included Johnson & Johnson (J&J) and Biomet, both of whom were broad suppliers of orthopedic devices and actively marketed a line of bioresorbable implants. The Specialists

---

[4] As a rule, the patents for these polymers were held by the materials suppliers, while the patents on the production techniques used to turn them into trauma implants were held by the implant manufacturers.

[5] Excerpt from a Dain Raucher Wessels analyst report, August 1998, p. 73.

[6] From an HBS field study team member's interview with an implant sales representative.

[7] From an HBS field study team member's interview with an orthopedic surgeon.

included Bionx and Macropore, two firms that produced only bioresorbable devices. And the Potentials included Smith & Nephew, a major player in the metallic implant market, but a dabbler in bioresorbables.

Johnson & Johnson (Heavyweight)

Any discussion of potential competitors had to start with J&J, a $24 billion per year supplier of medical products and one of the most dominant players in the field of orthopedic devices. J&J was the leading maker of artificial hips and knees, with sales of $1 billion per year; it was the number two maker of orthopedic devices for the spine; and it had recently entered the trauma market through its purchase of DePuy, a well-respected maker of metallic plates, rods, and screws. With an orthopedic sales force of over 400, it had access to just about every hospital and orthopedic surgeon in the United States.

Importantly, J&J had pioneered bioresorbable implants with its launch of Orthosorb™ pins in 1987. While never a big revenue producer, the Orthosorb™ product line maintained a 90 percent market share in bioresorbable implants through much of the 1990s and, by 2000, accounted for $2.6 million in revenues. In 2001, J&J was believed to be investing heavily in bioresorbable technology and was in the process of building a corporate research center fully dedicated to bio-materials research.

Biomet (Heavyweight)

While smaller than J&J, Biomet was also a major presence across all segments of the orthopedic device market, with a focus in trauma, maxillofacial, and joint replacement. In 2000, it had close to $1 billion in sales across these markets. Its efforts in bioresorbables came in the form of its recently introduced ReUnite™ line of trauma implants, the most extensive line of bioresorbable small plates and screws yet introduced to the marketplace (see Exhibit 9.6). Designed specifically to treat fractures of the hands and feet, the ReUnite™ line had garnered $1.6 million in its first year of sales. Biomet's efforts in bioresorbable devices were supported by its strong presence in the sports medicine market, where bioresorbables had established a more significant presence.

Bionx and Macropore (Specialists)

In contrast to J&J and Biomet, Bionx and Macropore focused exclusively on the manufacture and sale of bioresorbable devices for the trauma, sports medicine, and maxillofacial markets. Both Bionx (with $2.4 million in trauma device sales) and Macropore (with $1.2 million) offered a moderately extensive line of pins, screws, and plates for use in the repair of hand and foot fractures. Bionx, in particular, had made a name for itself as a young, innovative, and responsive firm. However, with total sales of under $25 million each, some questioned the long-term viability of each of these companies as stand-alone entities.

Smith & Nephew (Potential)

The final firm identified as a potential competitor in bioresorbables was Smith & Nephew, the second-largest player in the orthopedic trauma market and a company with over $1.5 billion in sales across products ranging from implants to plaster-casting systems to burn-care products. The HBS team did not view Smith & Nephew as a current player in bioresorbables, but felt it had the potential to become one at some point in time.

HBS Team Research

To complement its general overview of the trauma implant market, the HBS team conducted some primary research to determine the possible market acceptance of bioresorbable implants and their market potential. In interpreting this research, the HBS team cautioned that orthopedic trauma surgeons were quick to try new products, but equally quick to abandon those products in the face of negative outcomes.

Possible Market Acceptance

To understand the potential acceptance of bioresorbables, the team interviewed 16 prominent U.S. orthopedic trauma surgeons in the fields of pediatrics, hand surgery, foot and ankle surgery, and general trauma surgery. Of these 16, 6 had published research articles on the use of bioresorbable technology in orthopedic surgery. The team noted that this level of experience with bioresorbables was exceptional, given that only about 15 percent of trauma surgeons in general had any significant experience with bioresorbables.

During these interviews, the surgeons were asked to provide their general thoughts on the use of bioresorbables in orthopedic trauma and their specific thoughts on Synthes's possible development of bioresorbables. Exhibit 9.7 provides some responses to these questions. Next, these surgeons were asked whether they would use bioresorbable implants if they were readily available in the marketplace. Results to this question were as follows:

- 7 of the 16 surgeons said they would immediately use bioresorbables if available.
- 6 surgeons said they would use bioresorbables, but only for very specific applications.
- 2 surgeons said they might use them, but only if they were clinically tested first.
- 1 surgeon said that he definitely would not use bioresorbables.

While promising, the team had some doubts about these numbers. In particular, there seemed to be a negative relationship between a surgeon's prior experience with bioresorbables and his or her "willingness to use." Surgeons with the least experience with bioresorbables were the ones most eager to trial them. In contrast, the lone surgeon who reported that he would *not use* bioresorbables was a prominent surgeon with extensive clinical experience with bioresorbables. It was his opinion that the latest generation of bioresorbables did not have the strength to support the proper healing of most broken bones—especially the large bones of the arms and legs.

Further questioning revealed that even surgeons who said that they would likely use bioresorbables had concerns. The most common concern was around the formation of a "sterile abscess," which many feared would delay the healing of the fracture or require a second surgery. Another concern surrounded the strength of the implants relative to more traditional metal implants. Finally, some surgeons worried about the bulk of the bioresorbable implants, especially when used just below the skin of the hands or feet.

When asked how these concerns could be overcome, the surgeons were near unanimous in their responses. First, they wanted to see more clinical data and peer-reviewed academic research that compared metal implants with bioresorbable implants. Second, they wanted to know that the current leaders in the field were using these devices routinely. Finally, they wanted to know that "third-generation" polymers were actively being developed.

Clinical Applications

In addition to asking about their "willingness to use," the HBS team asked these surgeons where they envisioned using bioresorbable implants. Most felt strongly that the current generation of implants should be aimed at non-weight-bearing or low-weight-bearing applications, where 12 weeks of full strength would be sufficient for the healing of complex fractures.

In the near term, these surgeons pointed to hand, foot, wrist, and ankle surgeries—applications for which bioresorbables already existed—as the most promising areas for application. The HBS team estimated that if bioresorbables were widely available and proved effective, they could replace metallic implants in 25 percent of all hand, foot, wrist, and ankle surgeries within five years.

Some surgeons also suggested that bioresorbables might be appropriate in pediatrics, where the weight-bearing stresses on the long bones of the arms and legs were considerably less than in adults. The team noted, however, that bioresorbable plates and rods for pediatric long-bone surgeries were not currently available in the marketplace and that there was little indication they were being actively developed. Nonetheless, if they were available and proved clinically sound, surgeons indicated that they could replace metallic implants in 20 percent of all pediatric surgeries within five years.

Finally, most of the surgeons felt the second-generation polymers lacked the strength to support the healing of the long bones of the arms and legs in adults. It was felt that 12 to 24 weeks of full strength was required for these bones, a performance characteristic that current polymers did not seem to meet. At the same time, these surgeons held out hope that the next (third)-generation polymers would make the widespread use of bioresorbables in adult patients a reality. While some companies were actively researching these third-generation polymers, they were not expected to be ready for commercial application for at least 5 to 10 years.

Synthes Bioresorbable Capabilities

The final piece of the team's analysis was assessing Synthes's existing capabilities when it came to bioresorbables. These capabilities came in the following forms:

- Over the past several years, Synthes Maxillofacial had built a 10-person, $3 million per year business in bioresorbable plates and screws for fractures of the skull and face. While these products did not transfer to orthopedic trauma, the effort provided Synthes with some experience in second-generation polymers and production techniques.

- The Synthes Osteobiologics group, under Peter LaBlanc, had several engineers working on the development of polymers and manufacturing techniques that could be appropriate for trauma devices. Similar efforts were under way within the AO.

- One of Synthes's sister companies, Stratec, had recently begun to manufacture bioresorbable trauma implants. If needed, it might be possible for Synthes to outsource production of some bioresorbable plates and screws.

Given these resources, the HBS team believed that Synthes could match or surpass the quality of bioresorbable devices currently on the market within three to five years. They estimated that such an effort would require a $20 million development effort and a team of 20 to 30 engineers, product managers, and production personnel.

The Decision Facing Synthes

Having sat through the HBS team's presentation, Scott Hastings and his managers were still left with the question: "Should Synthes make bioresorbable implants?" For the past 14 years, manufacturers and industry analysts had touted bioresorbable implants as the next great breakthrough in internal fixation. Over that same period, the bioresorbable market had grown to only $10 million per year—not exactly the revolution that pundits had predicted. But there now seemed to be renewed interest in the field. Manufacturers such as Biomet had recently introduced new product lines, the second-generation devices offered improvements over the first-generation devices, and orthopedic surgeons seemed ready to at least try bioresorbable implants again.

Capturing the situation in which Synthes found itself, Priest noted:

> When it comes to bioresorbables, we are facing a game of "catch-up." Currently, we are probably two or three years behind our competitors in bioresorbables. If we don't do anything and the market for bioresorbables does materialize, we could find ourselves 5 to 10 years behind. But if the market fails to materialize, as it very well might, we'll thank ourselves for not investing time and money in a failed experiment.

As the HBS team looked on, the Synthes managers debated their options:

- Synthes could *ignore* bioresorbables—as they had in the mid-1980s—and focus its efforts on further improving its metallic implants.

- Synthes could take a *wait-and-see* approach to bioresorbables, allowing other manufacturers to test the waters and educate the market. Under this option, Synthes would spend the $20 million needed to develop (but not market) a line of bioresorbable products. In doing so, Synthes would be ready to quickly enter the market should bioresorbables prove clinically sound and gain marketplace acceptance.

- Synthes could make a concerted effort to quickly *develop and market* a line of bioresorbable products using the currently available polymers. Under this option, Synthes would initially develop a line of plates and screws designed specifically for fractures of the hands, feet, wrists, and ankles. Shortly after, Synthes could develop a line of products for pediatric fracture treatment.

- Or Synthes could turn its efforts toward the *research and development* of the next (third) generation of bioresorbable implants. It was predicted that improvements in polymer technology and production processes would further improve the strength and safety of bioresorbable implants. But it was not clear how far into the future or how significant these improvements would be.

Hastings considered these options, wondering what it would take to "get it right."

EXHIBIT 9.1   **Examples of Internal Fixation Devices**

Source: Synthes.

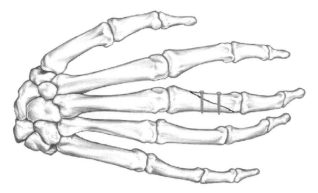

Two screws fixing a fracture of the middle finger

A single screw fixing a fracture of
the wrist (a distal radius fracture)

A plate and screw system designed for fractures
of the wrist (a distal radius fracture)

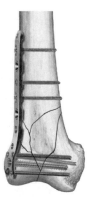

A plate and screw system designed for fractures of
the thigh bone at the knee (a distal femur fracture)

A rod (placed inside the center of the bone)
designed for fractures of the long bones of the
legs and arms. In this case, the rod is placed in
the tibia (shin bone).

EXHIBIT 9.2
Estimated U.S. Sales across Trauma Implant Manufacturers in 2000

Source: Adapted from *Orthopedic Network News,* April 2001.

Company	Total Sales	Plates and Screws	Rods	Hip Fixation[a]	Other[b]
Synthes Orthopedics	$262.5	$153.8	$ 42.0	$ 40.7	$26.0
Smith & Nephew	91.9	9.9	38.2	38.5	5.3
Zimmer	59.8	20.9	12.9	17.7	8.3
Stryker	46.3	0.5	11.8	22.8	11.2
Johnson & Johnson	26.8	9.3	7.6	7.6	2.3
Biomet	22.1	0.5	10.6	8.0	3.0
Other	32.0	16.6	12.3	3.1	0.0
Total	**$541.5**	**$211.5**	**$135.4**	**$138.5**	**$56.1**

[a] "Hip fixation" includes specialized plates and screws used to treat upper femur (i.e., hip) fractures.
[b] "Other" includes pins, wires, and other materials used to hold bone fragments in place.

EXHIBIT 9.3
2001 List Prices for a Representative Sample of Trauma Implants

Source: Adapted from *Orthopedic Network News,* April 2001.

Product		Manufacturer			
	Synthes	Smith & Nephew	Stryker	Johnson & Johnson	Biomet
Plates & screws systems:					
Large fragment plates	$ 159.50	$ 151.62	$221.00	$ 248.00*	—
Small fragment plates	139.90	129.15	142.00	226.00*	—
Mini fragment plates	108.20	70.55	73.00	—	—
Distal radius fragment plates (e.g., wrist)	601.50	—	—	370.00*	—
Pelvic fragment plates	284.00	293.30	264.00	401.00*	—
Rod systems:					
Femoral rods	957.00*	1,089.00	846.00*	882.00*	944.00*
Tibial rods	1,033.00*	1,197.00	938.00*	1,006.00*	1,087.00
Humeral rods	1,306.00*	1,305.00	938.00*	1,139.00*	1,164.00

Note: Figures marked with an asterisk indicate titanium implants. All other figures represent stainless steel implants.

EXHIBIT 9.4
AO Courses Offered to North American Trauma Surgeons in 2000

Source: AO continuing education, 2000 course schedule.

Dates	Course Title	Location
January 20–23	Principles of Fracture Management	East Brunswick, NJ
March 25–27	Hand and Wrist Fracture Course	Colorado Springs, CO
March 25–30	Principles of Fracture Management	Colorado Springs, CO
March 25–30	Advanced Controversies in Fracture Care	Colorado Springs, CO
April 15–18	Pelvic and Acetabulum Fracture Management Course	Toronto, Canada
April 27–29	Principles of Managing Complex Fractures	Key Largo, FL
June 8–11	Podiatric Advance Course	Ft. Lauderdale, FL
July 20–23	Principles of Fracture Management	Chicago, IL
Sept. 14–17	Principles of Fracture Management	Birmingham, AL
Nov. 16–19	Principles of Fracture Management	Toronto, Canada
Nov. 16–19	Advanced Controversies in Fracture Care	Toronto, Canada
December	Basic and Advanced Courses	Davos, Switzerland

EXHIBIT 9.5

The Characteristics of Second-Generation Bioresorbable Materials

Source: Adapted from Medical Data International.

Polymer/Blend	Initial Strength	Resorption Rate	Manufacturers Using
Polyglycolic acid (PGA)	High	No strength at 6 to 8 weeks Totally resorbs in 12 months	Bionx
Polylactic acid (PLA)	Low	No strength at 6 to 12 months Totally resorbs in 4 to 5 years	Bionx
PLA/PGA blend	Medium–high	Long	Biomet
Polydiosanone (PDS)	Medium	No strength at 6 to 8 weeks	Johnson & Johnson
Polyglyconate	No data	No data	Smith & Nephew

EXHIBIT 9.6

A Sample of Biomet's ReUnite™ Resorbable Product Line

Source: Adapted from Biomet website, www.biomet. com/resorbables/reunite.cfm, December 6, 2001.

ReUnite™ 5.0 mm Diameter Screw
- Lengths from 15 mm through 70 mm
- Fully threaded and partially threaded designs available
- Unique "twist-off" hex driver head optimized insertion torque
- Easy screw removal, if necessary
FDA clearance for use in fixation of ankle fractures.

ReUnite™ 3.5 mm Diameter Screw
- Lengths from 10 mm through 40 mm
- Unique "twist-off" hex driver head optimizes insertion torque
- Easy screw removal, if necessary
FDA clearance for use in fixation of metacarpal (hand) and phalangeal (finger) fractures.

ReUnite™ 2.5 mm Diameter Screw
- Lengths from 5 mm through 27 mm
- Can be used alone or with ReUnite™ Orthopedic Plates
- Unique "twist-off" hex driver head optimizes insertion torque
- Easy screw removal, if necessary
FDA clearance for use in fixation of metacarpal (hand) and phalangeal (finger) fractures.

ReUnite™ 2.0 mm Diameter Screw
- Lengths from 5 mm through 17 mm
- Can be used alone or with ReUnite™ Orthopedic Plates
- Unique "twist-off" hex driver head optimizes insertion torque
- Easy screw removal, if necessary
FDA clearance for use in fixation of metacarpal (hand) fractures.

ReUnite™ Orthopedic Plates
- Multiple plate designs maximize surgical options
- Heat adaptability permits easy bending and shaping to fit bone
- Used with 2.0 and 2.5 mm diameter ReUnite™ Orthopedic Screws
FDA clearance for use in fixation of metacarpal (hand) fractures.

EXHIBIT 9.7
**A Sampling of
Surgeon Comments
during the HBS
Team Interviews**

Source: HBS interviews of
orthopedic surgeons.

Question #1: What Comes to Mind When You Think of Bioresorbables?
Representative responses:
- "No implant removals." (mentioned by every surgeon)
- "It's a good idea, but the polymer technology needs to catch up to the potential applications."
- "Only for limited, non-weight-bearing applications, such as wrists."
- "Difficult to justify the additional cost of the implants."
- "At this stage, they are too weak for general applications."
- "I think they are a good idea. One good clinical study in a well-respected journal and most surgeons' concerns will go away."
- "Patients don't like metal in their body."
- "Pediatrics is a natural application for resorbables because of the fast healing times and the lower stresses."
- "You might get young surgeons to try them; they will try anything. But the older surgeons are going to take a wait-and-see approach."

Question #2:   If Synthes Had a Bioresorbable Implant System, Would You Use It?
Representative responses:
- "Yes, but only for specific applications."
- "Yes. As it currently stands, every time I want to use a bioresorbable implant I have to call the Bionx or Biomet sales rep. If it were part of Synthes's portfolio, I could just deal with a single sales rep."
- "Probably, if the data were convincing."
- "Definitely!"
- "Absolutely, but why should they? They would only be competing with themselves. Why play with the little dogs when you are the big dog?"
- "Probably not. Last year I would have said yes, but now I get the resorbable implants I need from Biomet and am happy with the results."

Part 4

Managing Distribution

10. Merck-Medco: Vertical Integration in the Pharmaceutical Industry
11. Becton Dickinson & Company: VACUTAINER Systems Division
12. CVS: The Web Strategy

10

Merck-Medco: Vertical Integration in the Pharmaceutical Industry

V. Kasturi Rangan and Marie Bell

The period between 1993 and 1994 marked a watershed in the U.S. pharmaceutical industry. In a stunning development, three major pharmaceutical manufacturers acquired distribution intermediaries called pharmacy benefit managers (PBMs). Pharmacy benefit managers typically provided a range of services to large self-insured employers, insurance carriers, Blue Cross/Blue Shield plans, managed care organizations, and government health plans that provided prescription drug coverage to their employees, retirees, or members. The market reach of the PBMs was measured by the number of patient lives covered on behalf of these customers.

PBM services included assisting in the design of pharmacy benefit plans; processing prescription drug claims submitted for plan members from retail pharmacies; reviewing prescriptions to prevent drug interactions; implementing programs to encourage the use of lower-cost generic and brand name drugs; and dispensing drugs through mail service pharmacies. These services were based on the ability of the PBMs to link financial and healthcare information between patients, physicians, pharmacists, and the providers of the benefit. By doing so, PBMs were able to manage the cost of drug benefits, improve the appropriate use of prescription drugs, and improve the quality of patient care.

Professor V. Kasturi Rangan and Research Associate Marie Bell prepared this case as the basis for class discussion rather than to illustrate either effective or ineffective handling of an administrative situation.

Copyright © 1998 by the President and Fellows of Harvard College. To order copies or request permission to reproduce materials, call 1-800-545-7685, write Harvard Business School Publishing, Boston, MA 02163, or go to http://www.hbsp.harvard.edu. No part of this publication may be reproduced, stored in a retrieval system, used in a spreadsheet, or transmitted in any form or by any means—electronic, mechanical, photocopying, recording, or otherwise—without the permission of Harvard Business School.

As seen in Table 10.A below, the amount that pharmaceutical manufacturers paid for these PBMs was significant. In at least one case the purchase price represented over 45 times earnings of the acquired PBM.

Subsequently, other pharmaceutical manufacturers sought agreements with other leading PBMs; Pfizer Inc. forged an agreement with Caremark and Value Health, while Bristol-Myers Squibb allied with Caremark. Appendix A provides a brief overview of the various mergers and alliances.

In 1995, soon after its PBM purchase, Eli Lilly stated in its annual report,

> The key to a total quality approach to healthcare is information. Whether it's a scientist searching for a cure, a physician seeking a precise diagnosis, a pharmacist filling a prescription, or a patient wondering about an illness, all depend on the intelligent use of information for successful outcomes. . . . Using its [PCS] electronic pharmaceutical-information databases, we can improve communication among patients, doctors, pharmacists, and payors. We can better administer cost-effective drug treatments; we can better analyze and understand how those treatments are working; and we can better educate payors, providers, physicians, and especially patients.

Yet in June 1997, two and a half years after the initial euphoria, Eli Lilly announced a $2.4 billion write-down of its PCS asset, acknowledging that it had overpaid for its PBM acquisition. According to a business report,

> When Lilly announced its purchase in mid-1994, companies like PCS were all the rage. Many on Wall Street suggested that a big pharmaceutical player like Lilly couldn't survive without one. After all, it was argued, these companies, which administer prescriptions for millions of Americans and negotiate drug prices with thousands of employers, could shift hundreds of millions of dollars in drug sales from one drug company to another. . . . When Eli Lilly paid a stunning $4.1 billion for PCS Health Systems Inc. in 1994, Lilly chief executive Randall L. Tobias promised that PCS would stop diluting the parent company's earnings by late 1996. He termed PCS the "jewel" in the business of processing drug prescriptions.
>
> But instead, PCS looks more like fool's gold. Not only is it far from adding to Lilly's per-share earnings, but analysts say it is losing money for Lilly shareholders after taking into account a whopping $300 million in estimated yearly payouts. What's more, PCS hasn't done much more to sell Lilly drugs—one of the main goals of the acquisition.[1]

There was no public response from SmithKline Beecham. Meanwhile, Merck-Medco announced impressive growth in retail drug spending, prescriptions managed, and covered lives (see Table 10.B for growth from 1993–1996).

Medco managed approximately $3.0 billion in drug spending for its clients at the time of the acquisition. By 1997, it had grown to nearly $12.0 billion, with impressive

TABLE 10.A
PBM Acquisitions

Parent Company	PBM	Purchase Date	Acquired Price (billions)	Patients Covered When Acquired (millions)
Merck	Medco	November 1993	$6.6	38 million (about 19 million mail order)
SmithKline	Diversified Pharmaceutical Services (DPS)	May 1994	$2.3	11 million
Eli Lilly	PCS Health Systems (PCS)	November 1994	$4.1	50 million

[1] *The Wall Street Journal,* June 24, 1997.

TABLE 10.B   Merck-Medco Growth, 1993–1996

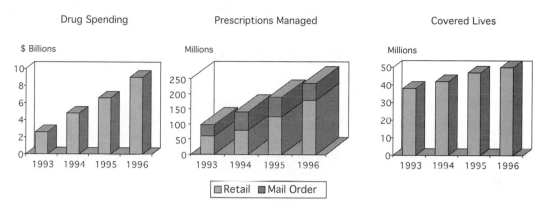

customer gains in almost every segment of the healthcare market. Medco managed pharmacy benefits for a little more than 2,000 clients, double the number at the time of the acquisition. Within Blue Cross/Blue Shield plans, growth in drug spending increased over $2.3 billion with the addition of Blue Cross/Blue Shield of Michigan, Massachusetts, Kansas, as well as other Blue Cross/Blue Shield customers. Drug spending in the employer segment grew $2.5 billion, partially driven by the addition of over 15 major employers including PepsiCo, Du Pont, and Citibank. The addition of new managed care customers such as Maxicare, Preferred Care, and Central Mass. Health Care contributed to an $800 million increase in drug spending in the managed care segment, while new government accounts in the states of Arkansas, South Carolina, and Nevada assisted in that segment's $733 million growth. Per Lofberg, CEO of the Merck-Medco Managed Care division, commented,

> Because Eli Lilly took a write-down, some people may believe that PBM acquisitions are strategic mistakes. As far as we're concerned, the Merck-Medco merger is an unqualified success. Both Merck and Medco have flourished in each other's company. The name of the game in healthcare today is health management. One needs to be able to integrate the functions of R&D, manufacturing, and distribution in order to effectively execute such a strategy. We have all the pieces in place and are excited by the possibilities.

Ray Gilmartin, Merck's new CEO who had taken over from Roy Vagelos in June 1994, provided this perspective:

> Many in the industry considered Medco a distributor, but we saw it differently. With pharmaceutical costs far outstripping inflation in the nation's healthcare expenditures, many believed that we were in for commoditization and price competition. On the contrary, we saw the immense potential for adding value. We were and we will continue to be a premier supplier of breakthrough drugs. We had a great opportunity to enhance patients' well being by linking them to pharmacists and physicians through an information network.

Industry Background

The $65 billion U.S. (1997) pharmaceutical industry was composed of three major product types: brand name drugs, generic versions of off-patent brand drugs, and over-the-counter (OTC) drugs. The first two types of drugs could only be obtained with a doctor's prescription. Prescription drugs accounted for 80 percent of industry sales and profits in the early 1990s, with OTCs accounting for the rest. Drugs were also classified by therapeutic category. Typically a therapeutic area could draw on all three types of drugs. For example, in the gastrointestinal category, one could expect to find patented, brand name drugs such as Pepcid, generics, and OTC drugs such as Mylanta and Pepcid AC, the OTC version of Pepcid.

In the mid-1990s, approximately 25 percent of pharmaceuticals were used in clinical settings (hospitals, nursing homes, and other inpatient facilities), while 75 percent were used in outpatient settings, distributed through wholesalers to hospitals, HMOs, and retail pharmacies. Within the United States there were approximately 80 drug wholesalers that distributed primarily brand name drugs (80 percent) as well as generic products (20 percent) to nearly 60,000 retail outlets. The drug wholesalers distributed their products via 260 distribution centers and earned gross margins of 5 to 8 percent, with the leading wholesalers achieving sales in excess of $2 billion. One of the fastest growing retail segments was the mail service pharmacy, which had grown from less than $2 billion in 1990 to nearly $8 billion by 1997. Some of the larger mail service pharmacies bought directly from the manufacturer, skipping the wholesale level.

Traditionally, success in the pharmaceutical industry was driven by the development of patented brand name ethical drugs. The successful development and FDA approval of a breakthrough, or blockbuster, drug[2] in a leading therapeutic category could mean hundreds of millions of dollars in sales. Conversely, when a patent expired, the drug was exposed to generic competition, which could result in a rapid sales decline. For example, in 1993, when Novartis's arthritis drug Voltaren came off patent, sales fell 23 percent from $357 million to $275 million.[3] The dynamics of the prescription are seen in Exhibits 10.1–3. Exhibit 10.1 outlines the number of blockbuster drugs for major pharmaceutical companies; Exhibit 10.2 indicates the leading drugs by therapeutic category; and Exhibit 10.3 indicates the estimated value of the drugs coming off patent from 1994–2002.

Competition for leadership of key therapeutic categories was intense. For example, Merck battled Bristol-Myers in the cardiovascular area where Merck's Vasotec led Bristol's Capoten in treatment of hypertension using ACE (angiotensin converting enzyme) inhibitors; Merck's cholesterol reducers Zocor and Mevacor dominated Bristol's Pravachol. While Merck was the leading player in cardiovascular drugs, it held a second-place position in other therapeutic categories such as ulcer therapy, where its Pepcid product was a distant second to Glaxo's Zantac. While generally therapeutic efficacy was the key determinant of a blockbuster drug, the manufacturer's reputation and sales and marketing effectiveness were also important factors in sustaining sales volume.

Effective research and development was the lifeblood of drug companies. Pharmaceutical manufacturers spent billions of dollars developing and guiding their products to market. Estimates suggested that pharmaceutical companies invested nearly $300 million over 10 years before a product reached market,[4] with only 1 in 10,000 projects actually reaching the marketplace. In the preliminary stages of development, pharmacologists tested hundreds of compounds to determine those candidates most likely to be successful in fighting a particular disease. The viability of these compounds was then tested in animals to determine the likely efficacy and side effects

[2] The term *blockbuster* was loosely defined to include those drugs with U.S. sales in excess of $500 million.

[3] *MedAd News,* May 1994, p. 5.

[4] This represents a "fully loaded cost" and includes the cost of those projects which failed to reach the market as well as those that did gain FDA approval. *Pharmaceutical R&D: Cost, Risks & Rewards,* Office of Technology Assessment, 1993.

on humans. Based on that success, manufacturers applied to the FDA for an investigational new drug application, informing the agency that they would commence human trials within 30 days unless there was an objection by the FDA.

Prior to being placed in the market, drug companies required FDA approval—a process that required three phases of clinical trials in humans. Estimates by the FDA indicated that only one in 20 drugs successfully passed through all three phases of clinical trial.[5] During Phase I the manufacturer gave the test drug to healthy subjects in increasing dosages in order to determine its safety. If safety requirements were met, then the drug proceeded to Phase II trials in which the drug was administered to patients suffering from the disease the drug was intended to treat. Phase II trials generally included a larger population and a lengthier testing period than Phase I. Drugs that passed Phase II moved into complex and rigorous Phase III trials where the drug was tested on a larger group of patients in order to determine its safety, efficacy, and dosage requirements.

In recent years, increasing pressure had been applied to expedite the drug approval process, which had risen to an average of 12 years. Given that pharmaceutical companies applied for their 17-year patent at the time of compound discovery, many manufacturers had only five years in the market before patent expiration. As the costs of discovery rose, manufacturers were under pressure to increase the yield from their research and development activities. Additionally, to supplement the new product flow, many firms had embarked on joint ventures with other pharmaceutical firms. For example, in the early 1990s, Merck signed a strategic alliance with Swedish manufacturer Astra for the marketing of Astra's compounds in the United States. Astra contributed the clinical product, while Merck provided sales and marketing experience and expertise in guiding the drug through the FDA's clinical trials to obtain timely product approval.

In the early 1990s, the healthcare industry was under attack. Healthcare spending had grown to nearly 12 percent of GNP. Employers were seriously concerned about their healthcare costs and were taking measures to curtail them. The weak U.S. economy of the late 1980s and subsequent downsizing had left an aging, anxious workforce also concerned about healthcare coverage. Soon after his election in 1992, President Clinton formed a task force focused on healthcare costs and coverage. The pharmaceutical industry, traditionally removed from the picture as it represented only about 8 percent of healthcare costs, found itself increasingly in the spotlight over both the rising cost of its products and the margins it earned. "Heightened publicity exposed long term hyperinflation in U.S. pharmaceutical prices and wide discrepancies between drug prices in the U.S. and those in foreign countries. Drug-makers were accused of reaping exorbitant profits at the expense of the sick and the elderly."[6]

The Clinton Plan called for universal coverage under the guidance of a National Health Board that defined a basic benefits package and reviewed pricing. Large employers and regional alliances would contract with healthcare providers through HMOs, fee-for-service, or combination plans, with individual employers contributing 80 percent of the cost of the healthcare premiums and individuals paying the remaining 20 percent.

Even as the Clinton administration pursued its healthcare initiative (which was later shelved for lack of political consensus), there were significant shifts in the industry. The healthcare industry began moving from a traditional fee-for-service environment dominated by individual physicians and specialists referring patients to hospitals, to

---

[5] "Healthcare: Pharmaceuticals, Standard & Poor's Industry Survey," August 29, 1996, p. 17.
[6] Ibid., p. 9.

one that increasingly emphasized managed care organizations (MCOs), such as preferred provider organizations (PPOs) and health maintenance organizations (HMOs). Appendix B provides a description of those alternative healthcare delivery systems. While non–managed care/private-office physicians had accounted for 60 percent of pharmaceutical sales in 1986, by 1992 that percentage had fallen to 43 percent. (See Exhibit 10.4.) Conversely, PPOs' and HMOs' share had risen from a combined share of 7 percent in 1986 to 22 percent in 1992. In 1995, IMS Managed Care Services reported that managed care accounted for 52.5 percent of total pharmaceutical sales and many expected that managed care's share of the market would reach 90 percent by the year 2000. In the early 1990s, it was estimated that about half of PPOs had a prescription benefit program, with over 90 percent of HMOs having some kind of prescription drug plan, either as a basic benefit or as a rider, typically purchased with the basic benefit.

The shift from fee-for-service to managed care had a profound impact on both healthcare and pharmaceutical companies. In the physician-controlled environment, price was rarely an issue as insurance companies paid for the price of prescriptions. In managed care, organizations who depended on cost control for their profitability and survival made sure each link in the value chain was cognizant of cost issues. MCOs attempted to use their purchasing power to secure discounts on drugs, medical products, and physician and hospital services. Some employed therapeutic substitution or interchange[7] in which a lower-priced drug was used instead of a more expensive one if it were of similar efficacy. Indeed, MCOs' preference for generic substitution was the major reason that generic's share of total prescriptions had risen from 22 percent in 1985 to 43 percent in 1995 and was forecasted to reach 66 percent by the year 2000.

The shift in the managed care environment had a significant impact on how pharmaceuticals were sold. One industry observer contrasted a traditional fee-for-service sales call with one in a managed care environment:

> On the first call, the rep sees the doctor between patients and receives about two minutes of face time. Subsequent calls will involve more product literature, office supplies, food, and other gifts; hosting "educational" seminars at fancy spots. Over time, through sheer persistence and call coverage—the fact that historically price was not the primary concern—a rep developed a dialogue with the doctor. And once doctors prescribed a drug, they usually remained loyal to it.
>
> By contrast, calls on MCOs are strictly by appointment with the Director of Purchasing or a Formulary Committee of M.D.s and administrators. Detailed product information about the therapeutic area and alternative medications is necessary. Physician input is important but, given basic levels of safety and efficacy, the group's system economics often drive buying decisions.[8]

Moreover, the increased emphasis on managed care further distanced pharmaceutical reps from physicians. For example, some HMOs, anxious to enforce formulary (i.e., a list of drugs approved by the HMO's committee of experts as to the ones that were therapeutically effective and cost-efficient) recommendations, prohibited sales rep visits to doctors. In other cases, reps with access found that physicians had less time for rep visits as they were increasingly restricted from prescribing nonformulary products.

---

[7] Therapeutic substitution usually referred to change in a prescription without seeking physician counsel. Therapeutic interchange referred to a change in a prescription with the consent of a physician.

[8] Drawn from HBS Case No. 594-045, "Astra/Merck Group" by Frank Cespedes and Marie Bell.

Despite its decline in market share, fee-for-service remained an important market segment. As the market shifted toward managed care, MCOs attracted predominantly the younger, healthier enrollees. As a result, on a per capita basis, managed care organizations utilized fewer drugs in volume and dollars than fee-for-service systems. However, when MCOs did prescribe medication, it was more often filled and taken than was the case for fee-for-service.

In addition to the changes in the traditional pharmaceutical distribution channel, the mail service distribution channel began to grow rapidly. Mail service was not new to the industry, having begun in 1946 when the Veterans Administration (VA) began sending prescription medications to entitled veterans via the postal service. In addition to the VA, the American Association of Retired Persons (AARP) had begun mail service distribution to its members in 1959. Many attributed the rapid growth in mail order, from less than $100 million in 1981 to $8 billion in the mid-1990s, to an increased emphasis on cost containment and a more efficient dispensing process. Mail service firms purchased drugs directly from the manufacturer and typically dispensed a 90-day supply of medication rather than the traditional 30-day supply, reducing annual co-payment costs to the customer. The patient paid only one co-payment for a 90-day supply rather than one for each 30-day supply. But more importantly, the plan sponsor saved substantial drug costs because of the lower mail service price (from 5 percent to 15 percent) compared to retail. As a result, the mail order channel was best suited to chronic conditions that required repeat filling of prescriptions. To compensate for the lack of personal contact, mail service pharmacies offered a range of services including 24-hour access to registered pharmacists, refill reminders, Braille labeling, and communications for the hearing impaired.

Pharmacy Benefit Management

As outlined in Figure 10.1, pharmaceutical manufacturers typically supplied products to wholesalers, chain and independent pharmacy retailers, or mail service retailers who in turn supplied products to consumers. (In the case of wholesalers, the products went through an additional level of retail distribution before reaching consumers.) A bottle of pills sold by the manufacturer to the wholesaler at a price of $100 (with perhaps an additional 2 percent cash discount) would typically be listed at retail for about $125 (called the average wholesale price, AWP). Retail pharmacies typically purchased prescription drugs at an 18 percent to 20 percent discount off the AWP price. The wholesaler margin was usually between 5 percent and 8 percent.

AWP was also used by managed care organizations, pharmacy benefit managers, and insurers as an index for negotiating pharmaceutical product reimbursement rates for retail pharmacies. Before PBMs, health plans and insurers typically reimbursed retail pharmacies for pharmaceutical products at a rate above the AWP price. In addition, pharmacies received dispensing fees of several dollars for each prescription dispensed.

One of the market changes fostered by pharmacy benefit managers on behalf of healthcare payors was to negotiate lower reimbursement rates from retail pharmacies in exchange for inclusion in networks established to serve particular health plans or employer plans. As a result of these negotiations, retail pharmacies were typically reimbursed for pharmaceutical products below the AWP index, contributing to lower healthcare costs. In addition, the competition created among retail pharmacies by PBMs also reduced dispensing fees paid to pharmacies by healthcare payors.

FIGURE 10.1
**Physical Distribution
of Pharmaceuticals**

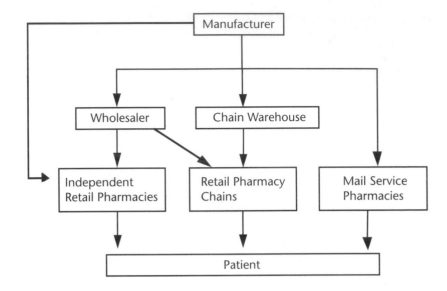

When dispensing a prescription for a patient covered by a PBM drug plan, the pharmacist typically collected a small co-payment from the patient for the prescription, and electronically submitted a claim to the pharmacy benefit manager for the balance due. The PBM then reimbursed the pharmacy according to the agreed-upon dispensing fee and discounted price for the pharmaceutical product that had been negotiated off the AWP index. In turn, the PBM submitted to the plan sponsors invoices for its own reimbursement plus a small administrative fee.

The facilitation from the point of retail to the payor was provided by the PBM's electronic network. PBMs like Merck-Medco and PCS typically had approximately 50,000 retail pharmacies participate in their retail networks. Most pharmacies (other than those which were HMO proprietary) were members of several PBM networks.

Working on behalf of their customers, typically corporations or managed care organizations (such as HMOs), the PBM's goal was to reduce the cost and optimize the use of medications, while maintaining quality. PBM's customers were varied. Estimates indicated that about one-third were self-insured employers, another third were HMOs, and the remaining third were PPOs and indemnity insurers. HMOs frequently contracted with a PBM to manage their enrollees' drug benefits and provide the HMO with drug utilization data, with about 57 percent of HMOs in the United States using a PBM to manage its pharmacy benefit program.

While initially PBMs focused primarily on claims processing, with the rise of managed care PBMs grew in scope and by the mid-1990s had developed mechanisms to control drug costs primarily through negotiated discounts with pharmacy networks, formulary development and management, and rebates from brand name drug manufacturers. A full-service PBM typically was responsible for the design, implementation, and administration of pharmacy benefit programs and had four defining characteristics: claims processing and adjudication, pharmacy network management, formulary development and management for clients, and rebate negotiations with pharmaceutical manufacturers. Some PBMs like Medco had well-developed mail order divisions while others like PCS had set them up only recently. Commenting on their growing role in proactive pharmaceutical management rather than passive distribution, one PBM executive remarked,

With the evolution toward managed care, there has been more interest on the part of payors in finding intermediaries who serve as gatekeepers to monitor how care is delivered, influence practice patterns, and negotiate with doctors and hospitals to improve the quality of care. What we're doing in pharmacy benefits is a microcosm of that.[9]

PBMs had slowly but surely become significant players in the healthcare market, with some estimates indicating that about half the U.S. population received pharmacy benefits through a PBM.[10] The industry was highly concentrated, with the five largest firms responsible for managing the benefits for over 80 percent of the health plan enrollees covered by PBMs.[11] (See Exhibit 10.5 for a list of the largest 12 PBMs including the number of covered lives, prescriptions written per year, and the number of pharmacies under contract.) The largest, PCS, had its origins in claims processing. Merck-Medco, the second-largest PBM, covered about 50 million lives and had its roots in mail service pharmacy. By contrast, Diversified Pharmaceutical Services was a subsidiary of one of the largest HMO managers, United HealthCare. Many large health plans, such as Kaiser Permanente, performed their PBM functions in house rather than contracting with an outside firm. Exhibit 10.6 shows the top five players in mail service pharmacy. Merck-Medco was far and away the dominant player with a 50 percent share.

What Do They Do?

In the mid 1980s, PBMs had provided value through claims processing, but by the mid-1990s, PBMs were increasingly involved in providing additional cost and utilization services to their clients such as formulary design and the emerging area of disease management. Generally, PBMs' services were categorized into the traditional, lower value-added administrative functions and the newer, more innovative drug use control functions. The main administrative functions included

- Developing and maintaining a network of providers. PBMs recruited pharmacies and negotiated prices and payment terms and contracts with pharmacies to ensure the optimal level of coverage.
- Claims processing. Activities included online adjudication of claims, payment to providers, and record keeping and reporting to clients.
- Benefit program design input. While the plan sponsor designed the terms of the benefit program including the covered drugs, exclusions and limits, cost-sharing provisions such as differential co-payments for generic or preferred drugs, and mail order dispensing, the PBMs provided a variety of options and alternatives as input.

While the PBM's administrative functions served to make the existing system run efficiently, its drug use control functions sought to actively manage and drive the drug prescribed by the physician. The major drug use control functions of formulary development and management, drug use review, and disease management are discussed below.

The *use of formularies*[12] was a major tool in drug use control. PBMs used formularies to help control their customers' drug costs by encouraging the use of formulary

---

[9] David Cassak, "From Mail Service to Managed Care," *Invivo*, January 1993.

[10] GAO, "Pharmacy Benefit Managers, Early Results on Ventures with Drug Manufacturers," November 1995.

[11] Ibid.

[12] A formulary is a listing of preferred drugs by therapeutic class often with cost designations.

drugs through compliance programs that informed physicians and enrollees about which drugs were on the formulary; limiting the number of drugs a plan covered; or developing financial incentives that encouraged the use of formulary products. In developing the formulary, PBMs used pharmacy and therapeutic (P&T) committees consisting of pharmacists and physicians to analyze the safety, efficacy, and substitutability of prescription drugs. PBMs took the recommendations of the P&T committee to develop a formulary with a sufficient number of drugs to give the physician a number of treatment options.

There were three types of formularies: open, incentive-based, and closed. Open formularies, used by the overwhelming majority of PBMs, did not penalize enrollees if their physicians prescribed nonformulary drugs; all drugs were covered or reimbursed regardless of formulary status. Under an incentive-based formulary, the health plan still reimbursed the enrollee for nonformulary drugs, but required the enrollee to pay a higher co-payment for the nonformulary drug than would have been required for a drug on the formulary. A closed formulary limited payment to formulary drugs only, unless a physician determined that the nonformulary drug was medically necessary for the patient.

PBMs used *drug utilization reviews (DUR)* to "both enhance the quality of pharmaceutical care and to potentially generate savings." There were two types of DUR—retrospective and concurrent. With retrospective DUR, the PBMs analyzed drug utilization practices to identify any instances where potentially inappropriate drugs were prescribed. When a PBM identified inappropriate patterns of consumption or prescription, the PBM contacted the appropriate physician about better and potentially more cost-effective treatment options. Concurrent DUR occurred when the drug was dispensed. When an enrollee presented a prescription, the pharmacist's computer link with the PBM reviewed the prescription and identified whether there was a generic or formulary alternative to the prescribed drug. The system also analyzed whether the prescription duplicated an existing prescription or whether it adversely interacted with other medication the enrollee was taking. If a nonformulary, duplicate, or potentially harmful drug was identified, the pharmacist was notified on the computer screen.

Over time, PBMs found that physicians were becoming more comfortable with drug use control mechanisms such as formularies and DUR. One PBM executive noted,

> It's no longer a foreign concept when a payor asks them to be more cost-conscious in their prescribing. We're usually dealing with physicians for whom a significant part of their practice comes from the funded plans we represent. When we call them up and say that we're calling on behalf of GE and if one product is as medically appropriate as the other, our client would appreciate their prescribing a less expensive drug. They're not unreceptive to our message if a substantial number of their patients are GE employees.

The third drug use control function of PBMs was *health management* (also called *disease management*), a relatively new activity. Under health management, PBMs sought to control overall healthcare costs and improve care for chronic conditions (e.g., asthma and diabetes) by developing specific programs for the treatment of the conditions. In the treatment of these chronic conditions, a small percentage of patients often incurred a disproportionate share of the cost. PBMs evaluated treatment options from existing medical research and identified a program of treatment that resulted in better therapy management and lower cost. When the management program was developed, the PBM then educated both plan enrollees and their physicians about the more cost-effective treatment program and monitored the rate of compliance.

The treatment of diabetes was a major focus for PBM's disease management programs. For example, research showed that better glycemic control and management could reduce the complications associated with diabetes by as much as 60 percent. Moreover, significantly better glucose control could be achieved simply by improved patient self-management and adherence to the acknowledged standards of care. In a fully functional disease management platform, a PBM, by mining its pharmaceutical claims database, could identify those patients that met specific criteria based on the prescriptions both written and filled. The PBM could then design a two-pronged education campaign targeted at both the patient and the prescriber. The patient was contacted and given a newsletter, an 800 number information hotline, counseling, diabetes education referrals, and a primary assessment report. Similarly, the physician received a newsletter, an information hotline, and a primary assessment report, and worked with patients to better control their disease. (See Exhibit 10.7.)

How Do They Work?

While PBMs had only a modest impact on distribution flow, PBMs did significantly impact the financial and information flows. In the mid-1990s, the PBM had two revenue streams: manufacturer rebates and administrative fees from their customers. Some PBMs, like Medco, that had mail service operations had a third revenue stream from that source.

Manufacturer Rebates

A PBM typically negotiated with the drug manufacturers to obtain rebates for a plan sponsor (an employer, an insurer, or an MCO). The size of the discount given was a function of a number of factors, including the number of lives covered by the PBM, its formulary policy, and the demand for a particular drug. For example, a brand-name drug that was selling well would be discounted only slightly, if at all, unless the PBM could provide an opportunity to significantly shift market share, or unless the PBM was willing to include on its formulary a bundle of the manufacturer's products that included the blockbuster drug as well as less highly demanded products. A significant portion of the manufacturer's rebate, 80 to 100 percent, was passed along to the plan sponsor (employer).

Administrative Fees

PBMs charged their plan sponsor a transaction fee per prescription for processing prescription claims. Although this transaction fee was variable, it ranged from $.40 to $.60 per retail pharmacy transaction. This was considered to be the commodity end of the business with minimal margins to be made.

The PBM also negotiated with retail pharmacies to obtain discounts on prescription drug prices and dispensing fees for health plan enrollees. For each prescription, a PBM typically reimbursed participating pharmacies according to a formula based on a drug's average wholesale price (AWP) less a negotiated discount of 10 to 15 percent, plus a dispensing fee. Pharmacies collected the patient's co-payment and electronically submitted the claim to the PBM for the balance. The PBM reimbursed the pharmacy and billed the plan sponsor for costs plus administrative fee. PBMs encouraged pharmacies to support other cost-reduction programs, such as substituting a generic for a brand name when appropriate.[13]

---

[13] To substitute a generic for a brand name medication, the pharmacist did not require physician approval unless the physician had written the prescription "dispense as written." To substitute a generic for a brand name medication prescribed as "dispense as written," or one brand name for another, the pharmacist must first get doctor approval. Some state laws, however, require that the generic be dispensed when available.

For a pharmacy, a PBM's online computerization for verifying claims and processing payment was very important. Typically, a PBM supplied their customer's enrollee with a magnetically encoded card that the pharmacist used to confirm their health plan membership and access the PBM's screen on the pharmacy's computer terminal. The PBM's screen then produced a message regarding the formulary status of the requested drug, potential drug interactions, and requirements for co-payments, and enabled the pharmacist to electronically submit claims and be reimbursed by the PBMs, a method far superior and more cost-effective than traditional methods that relied on mail-in claims.

A PBM's second major influence was their position as a central repository and distributor of information. As part of its retail claims processing and mail service dispensing, PBMs had available aggregated, non–patient identifiable data over a period of time regarding drug prescribing, utilization, and expenditure. These data were a marked improvement over what was available to pharmaceutical companies, who traditionally had access only to information based on prescriptions, which doctors were writing them, and how frequently the prescription was written. Longitudinal data on prescribing, utilization, and expenditures on large patient populations provided PBMs with an opportunity to improve the appropriate use of prescription drugs to help improve patient health and reduce overall healthcare costs. Additionally, PBMs were able to provide their customers with reports that highlighted compliance. As a result, PBMs were an increasingly central link in the healthcare industry: between pharmacies and patients, between PBMs and physicians with information regarding disease management and therapeutic interchange, and between PBMs and payor customers. Figure 10.2 summarizes these linkages.

As previously noted, the presence of the PBMs did not alter *how* drugs were distributed. Increasingly, however, it was responsible for determining *which* drugs would be prescribed and how they would be used. One PBM executive remarked,

> When we were a passive intermediary, the pharmaceutical industry basically paid us no attention; because the physician wrote the prescription and the pharmacist dispensed it, there was no leverage. . . . With this more proactive role, a major new dimension has opened up. To the extent that we can influence physician prescribing patterns and thus influence the market shares of drugs, we have the ability to negotiate with pharmaceutical manufacturers in ways that weren't possible in the past.[14]

How It Affects Customers

The impact of a PBM on the end-user patient varied. When an employee enrolled in a pharmacy benefit program, he/she received an encoded pharmacy card through which pharmacists connected online to the PBM. When the pharmacist electronically read a patient's card and entered information on an incoming prescription, the PBM's central computer checked that against all the available patient history, such as, for example, other prescriptions filled, regardless of which pharmacy effected that transaction. The online system then delivered eligibility and co-payment data in addition to "edits." Edits were an industry term used to describe a message to the pharmacist from the PBM regarding drug interaction alerts, refill information, preferred products, prior approvals, etc. Edits did not, however, reveal a patient's disease or drug history. That information resided securely in the PBM's central information bank.

Patients' experiences varied considerably depending on a number of factors. Consider the following examples:

[14] Cassak, "From Mail Service to Managed Care."

FIGURE 10.2
PBM's Role in
Pharmaceutical Flows

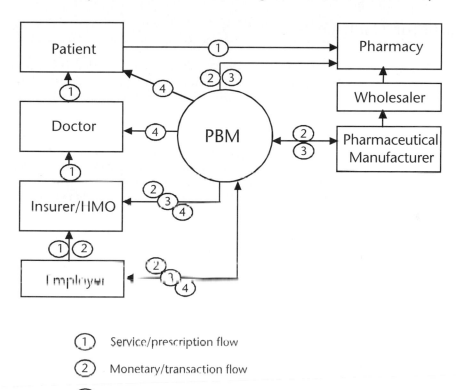

① Service/prescription flow

② Monetary/transaction flow

③ DUR/formulary management

④ Disease management

- John Brown, a generally healthy 20-year-old, has a severe sore throat. A member of a PPO, he goes to the doctor who identifies the condition as a bacterial infection and prescribes a specific brand-name medication. On arrival at a local pharmacy, he presents his pharmacy card and expects to pay his normal $5 co-payment for the drug. However, after swiping John's pharmacy card, the pharmacist informs him that he may have to pay a higher co-payment in order to receive the prescribed drug. Alternatively, he would be able to receive an equivalent generic drug at the $5 co-payment. The pharmacist explains that this is how his employer has structured the pharmacy benefit plan.

- Cynthia Gray is a 60-year-old who suffers from chronic arthritis that requires a continuing dosage of a nonsteroidal anti-inflammatory medication. Her company has pharmacy benefits that offer mail service at advantageous pricing. Cynthia's medication, along with two other equivalent medications, are on the formulary. On reviewing her benefit material, she sees that she can reduce her co-payments by receiving her medication through the mail. After forwarding the prescription in the mail, her doctor's office receives a telephone call from a pharmacist at the mail service pharmacy informing the doctor that another equivalent drug is preferred by the plan and requests the doctor's authorization for this switch. The PBM's pharmacist making the call acknowledges that the PBM is owned by the XYZ pharmaceutical company, and that the preferred drug is indeed an XYZ product. After approval, a letter is sent to both the patient and the physician.

Made for Each Other?

When Merck announced the purchase of Medco Containment Services Inc., a firm that specialized in providing integrated drug benefit plans and pharmacy services to managed care markets, it caught many industry observers by surprise. According to one such observer,

> Historically, no company had better exemplified the drug industry's resistance to managed care than Merck. With its one price policy and a product line against which even the most aggressive managed care organization couldn't substitute, Merck seemed to have had as little use for pharmacy benefit managers as they had for Merck. Over the last few years, Merck had made tentative efforts toward accommodating managed care organizations and the PBMs that served them . . . but the company lagged far behind its competitors.[15]

Despite skepticism Merck believed that the purchase of Medco would create a new paradigm for the pharmaceutical industry. Called "coordinated pharmaceutical care," Merck believed that the marriage of pharmaceutical research and development with a company capable of improving the appropriate use of pharmaceuticals would eliminate key information gaps in the drug delivery system. Merck reinforced its support of coordinated pharmaceutical care in its 1993 annual report, stating,

> Our boldest move was our acquisition of Medco Containment Services, an action that challenges conventional wisdom about what a pharmaceutical company is, who its customers are, and how those customers should be served. Our vision is to create the world's first coordinated pharmaceutical care company that will optimize the discovery, development, selection, delivery, utilization, and value of prescription drugs.

In 1992, Merck had sales of $9.6 billion (Exhibits 10.8 and 10.9 detail dollar sales and sales by therapeutic area). Consistently recognized as one of the world's premier companies, in 1992, Merck was hailed as "America's most admired company" for a record seventh straight time in *Fortune* magazine. Its 2,200 salespeople, 300 sales managers, and national account executives sold pharmaceuticals to hospitals, clinics, physicians, and other groups. In 1993, Merck's sales organization was a repeat winner of *Sales and Marketing Management* magazine's "Best Sales Force in the Industry" award, scoring highest in six of the survey's eight categories including "Recruiting Top Salespeople," "Quality of Training," "Opening New Accounts," "Holding Accounts," and "Reputations Among Customers."

By contrast, in 1992, Medco had sales of $1.8 billion, with an operating income of close to $140 million, and "had been growing at 35 percent a year by riding the very trend that had threatened to capsize Merck."[16] (Exhibit 10.10 outlines Medco's performance from 1988–1992.) Medco was led by Marty Wygod, a former investment banker with no previous medical experience until 1983. After observing corporations struggling with the cost of employees' and retirees' benefits, he saw an opportunity to revolutionize the distribution system through centralized mail service distribution that would save the cost associated with intermediaries' margins. Based on this strategy, Wygod purchased a small mail-order pharmacy in 1983 and soon after acquired PAID, a company that not only processed health claims but also had a network of approximately 50,000 retail pharmacies where participants could have prescriptions filled.[17]

[15] Roger Longman, "Merck-Medco Defining a New Pharmaceutical Company," *Invivo,* Windhover Information Inc.

[16] Brian O'Reilly, "Why Merck Married the Enemy," *Fortune,* September 20, 1993.

[17] Myron Magnet, "Meet the New Revolutionaries," *Fortune,* February 24, 1992.

This strategy fueled the development of five automated pharmacies by 1987. With over $300 million in revenues in 1987, Medco again challenged the industry by offering its clients benefit plans with built-in cost savings (e.g., lower co-payments for prescriptions filled through mail service than for those filled at retail pharmacies), and negotiated discounts from manufacturers.

In the early 1990s, Medco was a full-service PBM that offered its clients "integrated pharmacy services," with the ability to check a patient's prescription drug history no matter where the prescription was dispensed, with a goal of achieving quality care, reporting, and cost containment for its client sponsors. Medco's competitive strength lay in mail service that offered efficient, economical delivery of long-term prescriptions via its 13 pharmacies. (See Exhibit 10.11 for a description of Medco's mail service business.) In addition to its mail service business, Medco continued to offer its retail card program for prescriptions dispensed from participating retail pharmacies (i.e., the PAID network). As Medco delved further into clinically driven programs such as patient profiling and outcomes research, however, it recognized a need for further clinical expertise. As a result, it began looking for joint venture partners among the pharmaceutical manufacturers to provide an additional level of expertise and linkages to research and development.

Motivation

In the summer of 1992, then-CEO Roy Vagelos assigned a team of executives to critically examine Merck's business strategy. The team, code-named Project Paradigm, studied the changing industry environment and concluded that pharmaceutical companies needed to better understand the role of pharmaceuticals in the larger context of healthcare. The team recommended that drug companies redefine their role, not just as purveyors of pills but as providers of healthcare solutions. Based on their analysis, they believed that the choice of therapies would be decided on the efficacy of their outcomes relative to alternate courses of treatment. One Merck executive summarized this view:

> Pharmaceuticals appear to be headed for a commodity status pushed by generics, formularies, and other cost pressures. Regardless of lowering prices, there is an upside for drugs. A pharmaceutical company can get itself out of the commodity/price box by seeing itself as a manager of health. It can draw off some of the 93 percent of non-drug spending to itself and at the same time save money for providers based on the cost efficiencies of pharmaceuticals and the contribution they make to the efficient management of the disease.[18]

With a pharmaceutical company's vested interest in selling drugs, team members of Project Paradigm believed that healthcare decision makers would discount their views on the effectiveness of drug therapy. As a result, the team was increasingly drawn to an alliance with or the acquisition of a PBM who had central relationships with key healthcare players such as physicians, payors, pharmacists, and patients. Indeed, by 1993, many in the industry began to view the PBM as a central link in the management of a total disease outcome. The PBM's electronic access to pharmacies not only managed the cost of pharmaceuticals, but also yielded patient data on utilization habits. Prescribing habits by physicians were also linked to the PBM via tracking of prescriptions by the PBMs. The PBM's relationships with its sponsors, both HMOs and payors, made it a primary interface with those that actually paid not only for pharmaceuticals but also for healthcare.

---

[18] William G. Castagnoli, "Is Disease Management Good Therapy for an Ailing Industry?" *Medical Marketing and Media,* January 1995.

Additionally, Merck believed that the PBM's role as a depository of information could be an important component in directing research and development. It believed that a sophisticated PBM would have aggregated drug utilization data that could be effectively combined with a drug company's medical analysis skills to conduct large-scale, accurate outcomes analysis that would demonstrate how particular drugs or treatment approaches could benefit particular plans and patient populations. With research and development expenses running at 8 percent of sales, any process that lessened development risk could be expected to have an important impact on profits.

By the spring of 1993, Project Paradigm was considering the advantages of acquiring a PBM. Independently another group within Merck was negotiating with Medco on a contract to give Medco clients discounts on Merck products, similar to the ones that Medco had with other pharmaceutical companies like SmithKline Beecham. Merck's move to become part of Medco's formulary was important because it demonstrated Merck's willingness to enter the pharmacy benefit environment.

Additionally, Merck found that Medco's client base was complementary to chronic care drugs. Medco's clients were predominantly Fortune 500 companies; Blue Cross/Blue Shield plans; insurance carriers; federal, state, and local governments; and union plans that covered their enrollees for life. These clients would be more interested in chronic care therapies which, although more expensive in the short term, would likely save cost over the life of the patient.

Just as Merck was becoming increasingly interested in PBMs, and Medco in particular, Bristol-Myers Squibb signed a contract for its cholesterol reduction product Pravachol that gave it a preferred position in several of Medco's formularies. The number three product at that time behind Merck's Zocor and Mevacor, Bristol's Pravachol and its ACE inhibitors Capoten and Monopril competed fiercely with Merck's Zocor, Mevacor, Vasotec, and Prinivil, which in total accounted for more than 50 percent of Merck's U.S. drug sales in the first half of 1993. Beyond its price-based formulary win, rumors were circulating that "Bristol would extend its gains with Medco, acquiring the company and leaving Merck out in the cold." Indeed, while Merck's sales of its cholesterol-reducing medication grew only 2 percent from the first half of 1992 to the first half of 1993, Bristol experienced a 205 percent increase in sales, from $30 million to $105 million.[19] (Indeed, Merck seemed stunned by Pravachol's success. Chief scientist Ed Scolnick remarked, "The degree to which Medco was able to shift market share away from Mevacor was unthinkable," while Robert Hills, the strategic marketing head, commented, "One day it was all quiet on the western front, and the next day it was war. We concluded that we had to change our fundamental business philosophy."[20]

Convinced of the value of PBMs and Medco in particular, Merck purchased Medco within the calendar year. The leader of the Project Paradigm team remarked,

> Now Ed Scolnick [President, Merck Research Labs] has a wonderful way to understand what he needs to do with outcomes studies; a vehicle for communicating results to the marketplace; and a way of seeing the economic return from those outcomes studies.
> In short, he now has a very tight feedback loop to help him justify putting resources into outcomes studies and into the development of particular products for particular indications.

[19] Data in the paragraph are drawn from Longman, "Merck-Medco Defining a New Pharmaceutical Company."

[20] O'Reilly, "Why Merck Bought the Enemy."

Industry Reactions

While industry analysts debated the value of the Medco purchase, retail pharmacists reacted strongly against Merck's association with Medco. The retail pharmacy, especially independent retail pharmacies, struggled for survival in the 1990s. The number of independent pharmacies had shrunk from about 33,000 in the mid-1980s to about 25,000 in the mid-1990s, with independents barely breaking even as they lost business to PBMs and HMOs that dealt primarily with chain pharmacies and other retail outlets such as mass merchandisers and food outlets that had begun to offer pharmacy services. More strikingly, their share of prescription drugs dispensed had dropped from 60 percent in 1990 to about 40 percent in 1995 and was expected to drop below 20 percent by 2000. For their part, chain stores, which relied on pharmacy for 40 percent of their business, faced reduced margins from PBMs and increased competition from mail service pharmacies. But to offset the reduced margins, their share of retail prescription volume had grown from 60 percent in the 1980s to about 70 percent by 1995. The National Association of Retail Druggists issued a press release saying that "it appears that one of the nation's major manufacturers . . . has entered into an unholy alliance with . . . the exemplar of substandard, unregulated mail order pharmacy."[21] Angry retail druggists vowed to substitute $400–500 million of Merck drugs including readily substitutable products such as Moduretic and Clinoril, but also potentially substitutable products like Mevacor, Vasotec, Prinivil, and Pepcid. Despite the vehement response from druggists, many discounted their potential threat to Merck-Medco. One such observer commented,

> Merck has plenty of targets at which angry pharmacists can shoot. The more patients these pharmacists switch from Merck products to competitors because of Merck's new mail order subsidiary, the poorer the financial return from the acquisition. . . . Notwithstanding such opposition, many pharmacists will find themselves with little choice but to cooperate. While organized pharmacy groups may not like Medco, individual pharmacists often can't afford to buck Medco's clout.[22]

As indicated earlier, shortly after the Medco acquisition, two of Merck's key competitors, Eli Lilly and SmithKline Beecham, also purchased PBMs. (See Table 10.A, p. 178.) By the end of 1994, these three pharmaceutical manufacturers had cumulatively spent approximately $13 billion on the purchase of leading pharmaceutical benefit management firms to increase their presence in the rapidly growing managed care sector. The intense activity attracted the attention of the regulators concerned about the merger's potential effects on competition. By the spring of 1995, the FTC began a review of the Lilly/PCS merger and determined that safeguards were necessary to ensure that Lilly and PCS maintained a competitive process for determining which drugs were on PCS's formulary. A subsequent consent agreement between Lilly and the FTC required that PCS maintain an open formulary, that PCS appoint an independent pharmacy and therapeutics committee composed of non-Lilly and non-PCS professionals to oversee the formulary, that Lilly and PCS establish safeguards to ensure each from sharing nonpublic information concerning other drug manufacturers and other PBM bids, proposals, etc., and that PCS accept all discounts or other concessions offered by manufacturers and reflect them when determining the rankings in their open formulary.

---

[21] "Merck on Medco: It's Going to Be Good for Pharmacy," *Drug Topics,* November 22, 1993, pp. 73–77.

[22] Ibid.

These consent agreement guidelines had little impact on the Merck-Medco entity as it was already voluntarily operating under similar terms before the Lilly consent agreement. Per Lofberg, president of Merck-Medco, commented,

> At the time of the acquisition we needed to prove to both our customers and other manufacturers that Medco was going to remain independent from Merck. Our customers wanted reassurance that Medco was going to remain aggressive and keep their costs down. As a result, we instituted procedures that safeguarded payors by having an independent P&T committee. We had a similar situation on the supplier side. No single pharmaceutical company, be it Merck or any other company, has a sufficiently broad product line to fulfill our customers' needs. We needed to demonstrate our independence to retain access to other pharmaceutical companies' products.

Leaving industry considerations aside, Merck and Medco were destined to be independent under new CEO Ray Gilmartin, despite early plans to integrate the two organizations. According to Gilmartin:

> We decided very early on to preserve the best of both cultures rather than integrate and lose the distinctiveness of either organization. We were very strong on the medical, clinical, and science side at Merck. At Medco, we had strong linkages to employers, plan sponsors, and managed care organizations. Therefore, at Merck and Medco we had critical and complementary skills to build our strategy looking forward. We wanted to provide a climate for the two organizations to survive and thrive. Independently, however, we started to address each organization's needs. For example, we brought to Medco several people with clinical expertise from Merck.

In spite of the independent structure, the Merck-Medco operation continued to encounter regulatory challenges. In a complaint, several states alleged that Medco did not adequately explain its relationships with Merck and other manufacturers when conducting formulary management programs for its clients. In November 1995, Merck reached a $1.9 million settlement, with 17 states requiring that Medco pharmacists inform doctors of their Merck connection when calling physicians to suggest alternate prescription behavior. Despite these difficulties, Merck remained pleased with the progress of Medco, with new CEO Ray Gilmartin indicating to analysts that "Merck-Medco is performing according to the internal performance measure set for it."[23]

By 1996, some analysts questioned the value of PBMs to pharmaceutical manufacturers, with one noting "that there is no evidence that they're doing any better right now with the PBMs than they would have done without them."[24] Michael Iafolla, the vice president of Customer Operations for Bristol-Myers Squibb, a leading pharmaceutical firm, who opted not to buy a PBM, remarked,

> Everyone wants to know why Bristol Myers didn't buy a PBM. The answer is that managed care is still evolving, and we believe it's going to look very different in five years. We think that PBMs may always have a place, but that large health plans will consolidate and potentially contract directly with pharmaceutical companies. We also believe that as outcomes data increasingly show the value of pharmaceuticals, there will be a decreasing emphasis in healthcare on curtailing pharmaceutical spending, which is the role that PBMs have played, and more emphasis on controlling the costs of total medical services. So we think it makes sense to work contractually with many different PBMs rather than lock ourselves into outright ownership.[25]

---

[23] *The Wall Street Journal,* December 13, 1995.

[24] "Industry Focus: Value of Some Drug Firms' Acquisitions Is Questioned," *The Wall Street Journal,* November 19, 1996.

[25] Ibid.

Merck-Medco Evolves

By 1997, Merck-Medco believed that it was on its way to achieving its goals. In 1996, the company had increased the number of covered lives by 6 percent and realized an estimated 40 percent increase in drug spending, with a similar increase in the number of prescriptions filled. Merck's share of Medco's $9 billion drug spending had risen to 15 percent (21 percent in mail order and 11 percent in retail), up from approximately 10 percent prior to the merger (13 percent in mail order and 6 percent in retail).

As Per Lofberg reviewed the challenges in front of him, he saw the opportunity for growth provided by the health management offering as the most exciting one. Lofberg described its evolution as follows:

> As of now, the health management piece is only a small portion of our business, less than 5 percent. But it has potential for much larger profit margins than the other two—claims management and mail service—which are almost equal in revenue size. Take claims management, for example. Because of severe competition, that business has evolved into a low-margin transactions-based activity. There is no money in it for anybody. Mail service is fine, but the up-side benefit of health management is tremendous. It could not only give us a good margin, it could reduce our sponsor's healthcare cost tremendously even while increasing quality of life for plan enrollees. It is a win-win for all.

Given Merck's corporate growth target of 15 percent to 20 percent, the health management thrust of Medco was critical to not only sustaining its growth rate, but boosting its profitability as well. Industry analysis had proven that there were a significant number of chronic diseases, with total healthcare spending in excess of $40 billion for each disease, where more appropriate drug therapy could markedly improve patient health and reduce total healthcare cost significantly. (See Exhibit 10.12 for a listing of chronic diseases and pharmaceutical share of total spending.)

Since the acquisition, Merck-Medco had invested substantially in the health management area and had grown Medco's two disease management programs started in 1993 to over 21 programs to be rolled out by 1998. Indeed, one of Merck-Medco's early disease management programs for diabetes demonstrated a $440 total healthcare savings per patient per year, with the savings that accrued from reduced hospital stays more than offsetting the slightly higher pharmaceutical, outpatient, and doctor visit costs. See Exhibit 10.13. Based on the success of this program, Merck-Medco had also developed and rolled out health management programs that addressed health problems such as high cholesterol, hypertension, and arthritis. In total, Merck-Medco's health management programs targeted a potential patient population of about 50 million patients. A Merck-Medco executive remarked on the importance of health management to Merck-Medco:

> At present, the vast majority of our revenues come from services outside of health management. However, because these services are increasingly less value-added to our customers, the margins are becoming thinner and thinner. Health management is where Merck-Medco can add real value and where the margin opportunities exist. These programs are very complex and logistically intense. Our 21 programs encompass over 300,000 doctors, 2,000 benefit plans, and 50 million patients, representing potential savings of approximately $1.6 billion in healthcare costs. The challenge is to develop the program and deliver it with precision, and with zero defects.

Additionally, Merck-Medco had invested heavily in its information systems capabilities. Over the two-year period from 1995–1996, Merck-Medco spent in excess of

$50 million on its customer service systems and $120 million on its information, technology, and management area. Recognizing the importance of data in developing health management and using technology in the delivery of its programs, Merck-Medco had built a stand-alone, state-of-the-art data center with almost five terabytes of storage. The data warehouse stored 27 months of patient history and was composed of over 500 million data rows of prescription claims and over 76 million data rows of patient and member information. Additionally, Merck-Medco had three dedicated call centers and small regional centers that handled in excess of 30 million telephone contacts per year with its patients, physicians, and pharmacists. More importantly, Merck-Medco's data center was integrally linked to its key business activities of health management, formulary management, and customer service. (Exhibit 10.14 outlines the linkages between data information and product/service delivery.)

Merck-Medco believed that it was leading the evolution of the industry to health management based on its ability to provide optimal health outcomes through its integrated PBM capabilities, utilization management, clinical and outcomes expertise, communications and intervention programs and services, and information and technology infrastructure. One Merck-Medco executive commented on the rapidly changing industry:

> Our business environment is constantly changing. In the mid-1980s, we focused on cost reduction by providing administrative services and mail-order services. By 1990, we were managing costs through online retail and mail-order service integration. In the mid-1990s the focus shifted to utilization management, using patient and provider communication to influence drug usage and selection. What's emerging now is health management, using both communication and intervention to improve health outcomes and a reduced total cost. Yesterday, we were merely a distributor of drugs, whereas today we're evolving into a value-added provider with tremendous capabilities. We like to think of ourselves as a channel of customer needs. Even our name reflects the change—we used to be Medco "Containment Services"; now we're Merck-Medco "Managed Care."

Appendix A

Summary of Mergers and Alliances

Merck/Medco

On November 18, 1993, Merck & Co. purchased Medco Containment Services Inc. for $6.6 billion. Immediately following the merger, Medco operated as a subsidiary of Merck under Medco's existing senior management. In January 1994, Merck and Medco formed Merck-Medco U.S. Managed Care Division, which included a unit that marketed Merck products to managed care organizations, as well as Medco, which marketed PBM services to health plan sponsors. The Merck managed care unit was transferred back to Merck's Human Health Division in October 1994. In early 1995, Merck formally adopted a policy under which Medco operated independently of Merck.

SmithKline Beecham/DPS

On May 3, 1994, UK-based SmithKline Beecham announced its purchase of Diversified Pharmaceutical Services (DPS) for $2.3 billion. Founded in 1976, DPS was a subsidiary of United HealthCare Corporation, an operator of HMOs, PPOs, and other healthcare organizations. Following its acquisition, DPS continued to operate as an independent company under its existing senior management. In addition to the acquisition, for a six-year period, SmithKline gained exclusive rights to the medical records of United HealthCare's 1.6 million members. Further, United HealthCare planned to use DPS as its PBM and not compete further in the PBM industry. SmithKline believed that the access to United HealthCare's medical records was a significant competitive advantage in the development of disease management programs.

Lilly/PCS

In November 1994, Eli Lilly and Company purchased PCS Health Systems Inc. (PCS) from McKesson Corporation for $4 billion. Founded in 1968, PCS was a wholly owned subsidiary of McKesson Corporation, the world's largest distributor of pharmaceuticals. Originating as a claims processor, PCS was consistently ranked as the largest PBM. Under the terms of the agreement, McKesson continued to have access to certain PCS capabilities and services such as its information services.

In 1995, PCS acquired Integrated Medical Systems. IMS medical communications networks connect 35,000 physicians and more than 100 medical institutions. Infor-

mation is delivered directly to the doctor's desktop. According to an industry expert, "With these networks, physicians have access to and are able to exchange a wide variety of clinical, administrative, and financial information ranging from laboratory and radiological reports to medical records to prescription and refill authorizations . . . over time PCS will expand IMS technologies to arm physicians and other decision makers with all relevant data with which to make optimal prescribing decisions, while patients are still in the office, before a prescription is filled."

Pfizer/Value Health

On May 3, 1994, Pfizer, Inc., announced a strategic relationship with Value Health, Inc., a provider of specialty managed care benefit programs and healthcare information services. Value Health was composed of six companies including Value Rx, the sixth largest PBM at the time. Key components of the alliance included the participation of Pfizer on Value Rx's formularies in return for rebates; the development of programs such as clinical protocols, educational materials, and outcomes analysis to increase use of Pfizer products; and the contribution of $50 million per partner for the development of disease management programs. As part of the contractual relationship, Value Health remained an independent operating company from Pfizer.

Pfizer, Bristol-Myers Squibb, Eli Lilly, and Rhone-Poulenc Rorer with Caremark

In April 1994, four major pharmaceutical firms developed relationships with Caremark, the fourth largest PBM. As part of Caremark's Drug Alliance Program, for an undisclosed sum each manufacturer had access to both Caremark's formulary and drug utilization statistics of its covered lives. By partnering with the four manufacturers, Caremark received rebates on products in over 85 percent of the therapeutic classes on its formulary.

Sources: Summary drawn from GAO, "Pharmacy Benefit Managers: Early Results on Ventures with Drug Manufacturers," November 1995, and company annual reports.

Major Healthcare Plans

Indemnity Health Insurance Companies

Despite a loss of share, traditional, fee-for-service insurance remained the single most common health insurance product for an individual. In self-funded employer plans, the employer, not the insurer, assumed the risk, although the insurer or a third-party administrator executed the plan. In most plans, the insurer bore the risk. In these plans, subscribers sought healthcare from providers of their choice: physicians, specialists, or hospitals.

The majority of medical policies, whether written for individuals or under group plans, were subject to some form of deductible and co-insurance payments by the insured person. Most indemnity plans paid 80 percent of what is termed "the customary and reasonable" professional fee. The subscriber was responsible for the remaining 20 percent of these fees as well as for an annual deductible. The reasonable fee was determined by the insurer and was often based on the average costs of services in that area. As healthcare costs rose, employers began shifting a greater portion of the healthcare costs back to its employees primarily through deductibles and higher levels of co-insurance payments. Faced with these higher costs, employees often preferred to enroll in a managed care product.

Health Maintenance Organizations (HMOs)

HMOs were insurance and healthcare delivery organizations that received fixed periodic payments to provide comprehensive health services to each member regardless of the extent of service the person requires. In a sense, the HMO bears all the risk. The HMO Act of 1973, passed in response to rising healthcare costs, established a program of financial assistance for the development of HMOs.

HMOs became more attractive as traditional insurers raised their premiums 20–40 percent nationwide in the early 1990s. There were four basic types of HMOs: independent practice associations (IPAs), group models, network models, and staff models. Specifically,

- IPAs were the fast-growing model in which the IPA contracted with individual community physicians who were able to work out of their current facilities.
- Network models were essentially IPA group practices rather than individual physicians.
- Group models contracted for health plan coverage with a group of doctors who worked solely for the HMO and generally did not have outside fee-for-service practices.
- Staff models had a dedicated staff of nurses and physicians on an HMO-owned facility site.

Preferred Provider Organizations (PPOs)

PPOs were networks of physicians who contracted to provide healthcare at discounted rates or who accepted fee schedules below "reasonable and customary" rates. Providers accepted these lower fees in anticipation of a greater volume of patients and agreed to basic managed care principals including utilization review and guidelines for hospital admissions. A PPO typically covered a wider territory than any one HMO, primarily because of the broader network of physicians and clinics. From a patient's perspective, the primary advantage of a PPO relative to an HMO was the retention of their physician of choice.

Point of Service (POS)

POS plans were a hybrid of an HMO and PPO and were sometimes referred to as "open-ended HMOs." This option utilized a network of selected providers. Employees selected a primary care physician who controlled referrals to specialists. If the employee received care from plan providers, he/she did not file a claim and incurred limited or no out-of-pocket charges. Visits to out-of-plan providers entailed higher co-payments and deductibles but no financial penalty. Although it offered the best of both HMO and PPO options, it did so at a higher price.

EXHIBIT 10.1

Number of Block-buster Drugs by Manufacturer

	1992	1993	1994	1995
Merck & Co., Inc.	9	9	8	8
Pfizer Inc.	7	8	8	8
Glaxo Wellcome Inc.	8	7	7	10
Bristol-Myers Squibb Co.	7	6	7	6
Eli Lilly and Co.	6	6	6	6
SmithKline Beecham	5	6	6	6
Ciba[a]	6	5	4	9
Zeneca Pharmaceuticals Group	3	5	5	5
Hoechst-Roussel Pharmaceuticals Inc.	na	4	4	
Hoffmann-La Roche Inc.	4	4	6	5
Schering-Plough Corp.		3	5	5
The Upjohn Co.	3	4		
Wyeth-Ayerst Laboratories[b]	5	4		
Sandoz Pharmaceuticals		2	4	

[a]In 1995 Ciba and Sandoz merged to form Novartis.
[b]In 1994 Wyeth-Ayerst was purchased by American Home Products

EXHIBIT 10.2

Leading Drugs by Therapeutic Category (1995 U.S. Retail Sales, $ millions)

Category: Cardiovascular Drugs			$16,171.4
ACE inhibitors	Vasotec/Renitec	Merck & Co.	$2,395.0
	Capoten	Bristol-Myers Squibb	1,525.0
	Zestril	Zeneca	850.8
	Prinivil	Merck & Co.	375.0
	Accupril	Warner-Lambert	312.0
	Lotensin	Novartis	287.5
Calcium channel	Norvasc	Pfizer	1,265.3
blockers	Adalat line	Bayer	1,259.0
	Procardia line	Pfizer	1,134.0
	Cardizem	Hoechst Marion Roussel	961.0
	Calan line	G.D. Searle & Co.	259.0
Beta blockers	Tenormin	Zeneca	494.1
Alpha blockers	Cardura	Pfizer	413.0
Cholesterol reducers	Zocor	Merck & Co.	1,955.0
	Mevacor	Merck & Co.	1,260.0
	Pravachol	Bristol-Myers Squibb	770.0
Anginal preparations	Transderm-Nitro	Novartis	381.7
Diuretics	Lasix	Hoechst Marion Roussel	274.0
Infection Fighters			**$11,443.0**
Beta-lactamase	Augmentin	SmithKline Beecham	$1,319.3
inhibitors	Primaxin	Merck & Co.	560.0
Quinolones	Cipro/Ciproxin	Bayer	1,259.0
Macrolides	Biaxin/Klacid	Abbott Laboratories	935.0
	Zithromax	Pfizer	399.5
Cephalosporins	Rocephin	Hoffmann-La Roche Inc.	1,190.0
	Ceclor line	Eli Lilly and Co.	722.1
	Ceftin/Zinnat	Glaxo Wellcome	620.9
	Fortaz/Fortum	Glaxo Wellcome	483.5
	Claforan	Hoechst Marion Roussel	370.0
	Duricef	Bristol-Myers Squibb	295.0
Penicillins	Amoxil	SmithKline Beecham	428.2
General antibacterials	Unasyn	Pfizer	331.7
	Cleocin/Dalacin	Phamacia & Upjohn	288.4
	Vancocin	Eli Lilly and Co.	278.5

(continued on next page)

EXHIBIT 10.2
(continued)

Fungal medication	Difulcan	Pfizer	$878.6
	Sporanox	Johnson & Johnson	445.0
	Nizoral	Johnson & Johnson	335.0
	Lamisil	Novartis	303.3
Gastrointestinal Drugs			**$9,856.6**
Histamine H$_2$ receptor	Zantac	Glaxo Wellcome	$3,562.9
antagonists	Pepcid	Merck & Co.	900.0
	Axid	Eli Lilly and Co.	548.3
	Tagamet	SmithKline Beecham	451.9
Proton pump inhibitors	Prilosec/Losec	Astra Merck/Astra AB	3,008.6
Gastroesophageal reflux disease therapies	Propulsid/Prepulsid	Johnson & Johnson	775.0
Antiemetic treatments	Zofran	Glaxo Wellcome	609.9
Central Nervous System Drugs			**$7,416.7**
Antidepressants	Prozac	Eli Lilly and Co.	$2,015.0
	Zoloft	Pfizer	1,039.8
	Paxil/Seroxat	SmithKline Beecham	782.1
Epilepsy therapies	Tegretol	Novartis	392.5
	Klonopin	Hoffmann-La Roche	340.0
	Depakote	Abbott Laboratories	300.0
Antianxiety medicines	Xanax/Alprazolam	Pharmacia & Upjohn	319.8
	BuSpar	Bristol-Myers Squibb	310.0
	Ativan line	American Home Products	288.3
Antipsychotic drugs	Risperdal	Johnson & Johnson	420.0
	Clozaril	Novartis	366.7
Migraine treatments	Imitrex/Imigran	Glaxo Wellcome	578.3
Parkinsonism drugs	Parlodel	Novartis	264.2
Respiratory Therapies			**$4,444.6**
Asthma remedies	Ventolin	Glaxo Wellcome	$831.1
	Beclovent/Becotide	Glaxo Wellcome	627.3
	Serevent	Glaxo Wellcome	428.2
	Proventil	Schering-Plough	422.0
	Vanceril/Vancenase	Schering-Plough	334.0
	Intal	Rhone-Poulenc Rorer	289.0
Allergy relievers	Claritin line	Schering-Plough	$789.0
	Seldane line	Hoechst Marion Roussel	724.0
Anticancer Drugs			**$4,148.2**
Hormones	Lupron line	TAP Pharmaceuticals	$650.0
	Zodalex	Zeneca	344.1
	Eulexin	Schering-Plough	290.0
Antiestrogens	Nolvadex	Zeneca	595.1
Taxoids	Taxol	Bristol-Myers Squibb	580.0
Cytotoxic agents	Paraplatin	Bristol-Myers Squibb	320.0
Biological response modifiers/adjuncts	Neupogen	Amgen	936.0
	Intron A	Schering-Plough	433.0
Anti-inflammatory Products			**$2,713.0**
Nonsteroidal arthritis	Voltaren	Novartis	$1,282.5
treatments	Relafen/Relifex	SmithKline Beecham	410.8
	Feldene	Pfizer	305.3
	Lodine	American Home Products	274.4
Nonsteroidal analgesics	Toradol	Hoffmann-La Roche	440.0

(continued on next page)

EXHIBIT 10.2
(continued)

Hormones			**$2,126.8**
Estrogen-replacement therapies	Premarin line	American Home Products	$912.8
	Provera line	Pharmacia & Upjohn	367.3
	Estraderm	Novartis	346.7
Oral contraceptives	Ortho-Novum line	Johnson & Johnson	500.0
Erythropoiesis Enhancers			**$1,677.6**
	Epogen	Amgen	882.6
	Procrit	Johnson & Johnson	795.0
Antiviral Products			**$1,670.1**
Herpes therapies	Zovirax	Glaxo Wellcome	$1,352.5
AIDS therapies	Retrovir	Glaxo Wellcome	317.6
Immunosuppressive Products			**$1,183.3**
	Sandimmune	Novartis	$1,183.3

EXHIBIT 10.3
Value of Off-Patent Drugs

	Brand	Category	Marketer	1994 Worldwide Sales
1994				
	Cardizem	Antihypertensive	Marion Merrell Dow	$ 933.0
	Tagamet	Antiulcer agent	SmithKline Beecham	740.5
	Seldane	Allergy medication	Marion Merrell Dow	698.0
	Ativan injection	Antianxiety agent	Wyeth Ayerst	323.0
	Clozaril	Antischizophrenic	Sandoz Pharmaceutical	305.8
1995				
	Capoten	Antihypertensive	Bristol-Myers Squibb	1,500.0
1996				
	Sandimmune	Immunosuppressive	Sandoz Pharmaceutical	1038.3
	Lupron	Anticancer	TAP Pharmaceuticals	393.3
	Diprivan	Injectable anesthetic	Zeneca Pharmaceuticals	382.0
	Claforan	Anti-infective	Roechst-Roussel	363.2
1997				
	Zovirax	Antiviral agent	Burroughs Wellcome	1,728.9
	Paxil	Antidepressant	SmithKline Beecham	511.0
	Timoptic	Glaucoma treatment	Merck & Co.	395.0
	Trental	Blood flow enhancer	Hoechst-Roussel	360.8
	Taxol	Anticancer agent	Bristol-Myers Squibb	340.0
1998				
	Claritin	Antihistamine	Schering-Plough Corp	505.0
	Lovenox	Antithrombotic	Rhone-Poulenc Rorer	214.0
1999				
	Pravachol	Cholesterol reducer	Bristol-Myers Squibb	645.0
	Beclovent	Antiasthmatic agent	Glaxo	552.0
	Fortaz	Anti-infective	Glaxo	472.5
	Versed	Anesthetic	Hoffmann-La Roche	380.0
2000				
	Vasotec	Antihypertensive	Merck & Co..	2,185.0
	Augmentin	Anti-infective	SmithKline Beecham	1,126.1
	Rocephin	Anti-infective	Hoffmann-La Roche	930.0
	Pepcid	Antiulcer agent	Merck & Co.	820.0
	Humulin	Antidiabetic medication	Eli Lilly	665.0
2001				
	Prozac	Antidepressant	Eli Lilly	1,664.8
	Mevacor	Cholesterol reducer	Merck & Co.	1,345.0
	Zestril	Antihypertensive	Zeneca Pharmaceutical	765.0
	Prinivil	Antihypertensive	Merck & Co.	340.0
	Eulexin	Anticancer agent	Schering-Plough	231.0
2005				
	Zocor	Cholesterol reducer	Merck & Co.	1,255.0

Source: *MedAd News,* May 1995. Note the data in this exhibit are based on 1994 worldwide sales and therefore do not correspond to the data in Exhibit 10.2, which are based on 1995 U.S. sales.

EXHIBIT 10.4
Pharmaceutical
Industry Sales by
Customer
Segment/Channel

	1986	1992	1996
Non–managed care/private office physicians	60%	43%	
Preferred provider organizations (PPOs)	5	15	
Hospitals	20	11	
Mail order	2	10	
Medicaid	6	9	
Health maintenance organizations	2	7	
Federal government	3	3	
Nursing homes	2	2	

EXHIBIT 10.5 The 12 Largest PBMs

	Covered Lives 1996 (millions)	Covered Lives 1995 (millions)	Rxs per Year (millions)	Pharmacies under Contract 1996 (thousands)	Established
PCS Health Systems Inc.	56	56	320	54	1969
Merck-Medco Managed Care	50	47	235	52	1965
Argus Health System, Inc.	30		150		
Value Rx	27	16	56	42	1985
Diversified Pharmaceutical Services Inc.	26	14	100	43	1976
Caremark Prescriptions Service	15	14		53.8	1985
Pharmacy Gold Inc.	15	18	83	35	1986
TDI Managed Care Services Inc.	11	11.5	30	40	1982
Integrated Pharmaceutical Services	10.5		18		
Alta-Tx First Health	10		80		
First Health Services Corp.	10		76.3		
Wellpoint Pharmacy Management	10		58		

Source: Adapted from *Managed Health Care,* May 1995 and 1996, and *Business Insurance,* April 1995.

EXHIBIT 10.6
The Five Largest
Mail Service Pharma-
cies by Share of $8
Billion Market (1997)

Merck-Medco	55%
Baxter Prescriptions	11
JC Penney	9
Diagnostek	7.5
Walgreens	2

EXHIBIT 10.7   Diabetes Health Management Program

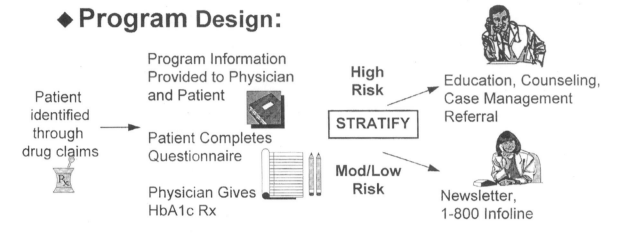

◆ Rationale:

  ◆ Improving patient self-management/provider adherence to standards of care results in better glucose control and can reduce complications by up to 60%

◆ Program Design:

Patient identified through drug claims   →   Program Information Provided to Physician and Patient

Patient Completes Questionnaire

Physician Gives HbA1c Rx

High Risk   →   Education, Counseling, Case Management Referral

STRATIFY

Mod/Low Risk   →   Newsletter, 1-800 Infoline

EXHIBIT 10.8   Merck & Co., Inc., and Subsidiaries ($ in millions except per share amounts)

	1991	1992	1993	1994	1995	1996
Sales	8,602.7	9,662.5	10,498.2	14,969.8	16,681.1	19,282.7
R&D expenses	987.8	1,111.6	1,172.8	1,230.6	1,331.4	1,487.3
Net income	2,121.7	2,446.6	2,166.2	2,997.0	3,335.2	3,881.3
Earnings per common share	$1.83	$2.12	$1.87	$2.38	$2.70	$3.20
Net income as a percent of assets	24.2%	24.1%	14.0%	14.3%	14.6%	16.1%

Note: After 1992, numbers include the impact of Medco from the date of acquisition on November 18, 1993.

EXHIBIT 10.9   Percentage of Merck Sales by Therapeutic Category

	1991	1992	1993	1994	1995	1996
Cardiovasculars	47.5	49.5	45.9	35.8	37.5	38.2
Anti-ulcerants	10.2	11.5	12.6	10.5	6.2	5.7
Antibiotics	11.4	10.4	8.3	5.5	5.0	4.2
Ophthalmologicals	5.3	5.0	4.3	3.2	3.4	3.5
Vaccines/biologicals	4.7	5.4	5.0	3.2	3.2	2.9
Anti-inflammatories/analgesics	6.2	4.7				
Benign prostate hypertrophy			1.8	2.2	2.4	2.3
Osteoporosis						1.4
Other Merck human health[a]			5.7	2.5	1.6	0.4
Other human health[b]	4.8	4.1	2.8	27.4	34.3	36.1
Animal health/crop protection	9.9	9.4	8.7	6.9	6.2	5.3
Specialty chemical			4.9	2.8	0.2	
Total	100.0	100.0	100.0	100.0	100.0	100.0

[a]Other Merck human health includes

For 1995: Fosamax, a treatment for osteoporosis in postmenopausal women, anti-inflammatories/analgesics, psychotherapeutics, and a muscle relaxant. Also included are rebates and discounts on Merck pharmaceutical products

For 1996: Crixivan, an HIV protease inhibitor, cleared for marketing in the United States in March 1996, anti-inflammatory/analgesics, psychotherapeutics, and a muscle relaxant. Also included are rebates and discounts on Merck pharmaceutical products. Note: Fosamax, previously included in this category, is now a separate line item.

[b]Other human health primarily includes Merck-Medco Managed Care sales of non-Merck products and Medco human health services, principally managed prescription drug programs.

EXHIBIT 10.10
Medco Containment Services—Key Statistics (millions)

	1988	1989	1990	1991	1992
Sales	$502.6	$728.2	$1,003.8	$1,342.7	$1,813.2
Operating income	29.6	37.3	53.4	83.9	137.2
Eligible participants	17.0	20	23	25	29

EXHIBIT 10.11
Mail Service Pharmacy Delivery (Illustrative Process at One of Medco's Pharmacies)

About 80 percent of prescriptions came into the pharmacy by mail, with 20 percent received as a result of telephone orders (usually refills). The mail was opened in the mail room, with 55 percent representing new prescriptions and 45 percent refills. Refills were sent directly to data entry while new prescriptions were coded prior to being forwarded to data entry. "Coding" consisted of verifying the dosage, its administration, and any other missing information, including doctors' addresses, telephone numbers, etc. At data entry, the prescription was entered into the Medco system and screened for a series of protocols that highlighted potential concerns: refills received too soon, drug interactions, incomplete data, or nonpreferred products. Prescriptions screened by the protocols were followed up by a pharmacist (if a serious issue) or a technician (for incomplete data). Once complete, the prescriptions were forwarded to filling. The actual process of filling was organized very much in the spirit of an assembly-line operation, as the prescription information and the appropriate labels all coded and generated by the computer traveled together. For example, each order was assigned a unique bar-code identifier. The actual filling of the pills was a thoroughly automatic process with little scope for human error. Nonetheless, in the final stage, each prescription was checked and verified by a licensed pharmacist prior to shipping.

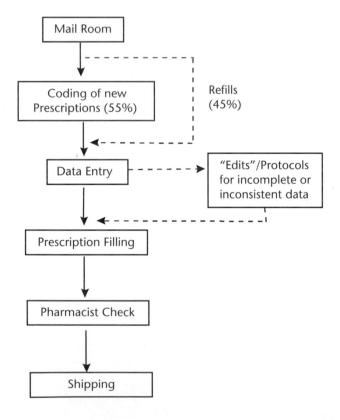

EXHIBIT 10.12
Chronic Disease
Spending and Phar-
maceutical Share

Chronic Disease	Total Cost ($ billions)	Drug Cost ($ billions)	Percent Drug	Potential Drug Impact on Total Cost
Cardiovascular	80	10	13	Significant
Neoplasms	49	1	2	Moderate
Respiratory	38	4	11	Significant
Digestive disorders	36	2	6	Moderate
Muscular/skeletal disorders	28	3	11	Moderate
Mental health	19	1.5	8	Significant

EXHIBIT 10.13
Diabetes Patient
Support Program

Health Care Saving Results

- $440 total health care savings (per member per year)
- Patients who increased insulin use had 2-to-3 fold decrease in medical costs

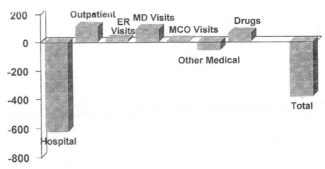

Note: Approximately 1,600 patients, pre- and post-program medical claims.

EXHIBIT 10.14   Merck-Medco's Information Support System

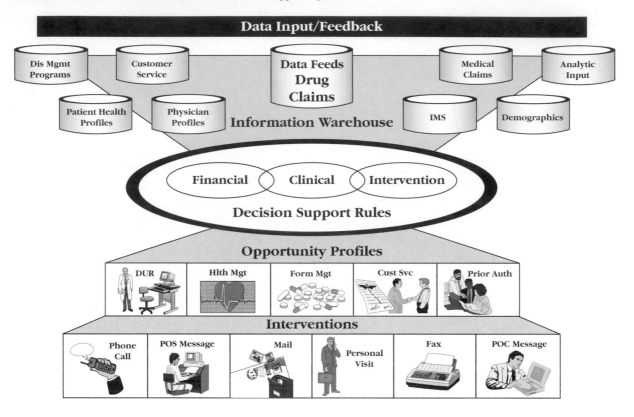

Chapter

11

Becton Dickinson & Company: VACUTAINER Systems Division

V. Kasturi Rangan and Frank V. Cespedes

On Thursday, August 1, 1985, William Kozy, national sales director for Becton Dickinson VACUTAINER® Systems (BDVS), and Hank Smith, BDVS's vice president of marketing and sales, slumped into their seats on the evening flight from Chicago to Newark. They had just completed their fifth round of negotiations in as many months with the materials manager of Affiliated Purchasing Group (APG), a large hospital buying group. Historically, BDVS had supplied most blood collection products bought by individual APG-member hospitals. But in April, APG had announced its intention of initiating group purchasing of one brand of blood collection products for all member hospitals. Since then, Kozy and Smith had represented BDVS in repeated negotiations with APG, while APG had also been negotiating with BDVS's competitors.

The subject of the negotiations was the pricing and delivery terms of a proposed purchasing agreement between APG and BDVS. Traditionally, all of BDVS's products had been sold through its distributors, who also negotiated prices for those (and other) products directly with hospital customers. In recent years, however, BDVS had

Professor Frank V. Cespedes and Professor V. Kasturi Rangan prepared this case as the basis for class discussion rather than to illustrate either effective or ineffective handling of an administrative situation. Certain company data, while useful for discussion purposes, have been disguised.

Copyright © 1986 by the President and Fellows of Harvard College. To order copies or request permission to reproduce materials, call 1-800-545-7685, write Harvard Business School Publishing, Boston, MA 02163, or go to http://www.hbsp.harvard.edu. No part of this publication may be reproduced, stored in a retrieval system, used in a spreadsheet, or transmitted in any form or by any means—electronic, mechanical, photocopying, recording, or otherwise—without the permission of Harvard Business School.

begun a new form of sales agreement, known as a "Z contract," in which BDVS negotiated prices and quantities directly with large accounts but supplied its products through one or more of its authorized distributors. Pricing decisions concerning specific Z contracts were made by a committee composed of Kozy, Smith, and Ed Mehl, contracts administration manager. Alfred Battaglia, president of BDVS, was also involved in establishing the terms of such contracts with some large customers.

The August 1 meeting with APG had been an all-day session, at the end of which both sides agreed that BDVS would submit its final proposal by August 15. At issue were the specific prices and terms for BDVS's two major products. In addition, there were questions raised regarding which distributors would be used to service the contract, and APG negotiators had urged BDVS to consider manufacturing a private label for APG.

"They're bringing out the big guns this time," noted Kozy as the plane began to taxi down the runway. "They certainly are," agreed Smith, "and we'll have to decide what we do about that. Al Battaglia wants to meet with us tomorrow at 1 P.M. about the APG contract. Let's review the situation one more time and make our recommendations."

Company Background

Becton Dickinson (BD) manufactured medical, diagnostic, and industrial safety products for health care professionals, medical research institutions, industry, and the general public. Sales in 1984 were $1.127 billion, with 75 percent coming from U.S. operations (see Exhibit 11.1). The company had three business segments—Laboratory, Industrial Safety, and Medical Products—each a profit center with separate marketing responsibilities.

Medical Products had three divisions: (1) needles, syringes, and diabetic products; (2) pharmaceutical systems; and (3) VACUTAINER blood collection systems, which accounted for a significant portion of Medical Products' operating income. In its 1984 annual report, BD management noted:

> Despite limited sales growth, BD maintained or increased its market share in every major medical product category. We attribute this to three factors: our strong reputation and brand identification, our ability to hold down production costs and thereby prices, and our continuing commitment to quality.

Management also outlined certain "core strategies to guide the company's activities in the marketplace," including "substantial improvements in research and the development of new technologies basic to the company's overall strategy. In a constantly changing industry such as ours, the successful development and introduction of new products are the company's lifeblood over the long run."

Becton Dickinson VACUTAINER® Systems Division (BDVS)[1]

Alfred Battaglia was president of BDVS. He had previously served in various financial positions for BD. Hank Smith was vice president for marketing and sales. Reporting to Smith were three product managers, each responsible for one of the division's product groups, and a sales director, William Kozy, responsible for achieving sales targets through six regional managers who in turn managed 55 sales representatives. (See Exhibit 11.2 for BDVS's organization chart.)

---

[1] Both VACUTAINER® and MICROTAINER® are registered trademarks of Becton Dickinson and Company.

Products

BD introduced blood collection products in the late 1940s. BDVS was formed as a business unit in 1980 with three major product groups having total 1984 sales of $90 million: venous blood collection (about 70 percent of BDVS sales) consisting of VACUTAINER tubes and needles; capillary blood collection consisting of MICRO-TAINER tubes and lancets; and microbiology systems consisting of culture tubes and specimen collectors. Each product group accounted for about 33 percent of BDVS's 1984 operating income.

Venous blood collection systems consisted of a needle and vacuum tube used for collecting blood from a patient's veins. VACUTAINER was the BD brand name for a broad line of tubes and needles designed to meet hundreds of differing needs in hospitals, medical laboratories, and physicians' offices. (See Exhibit 11.3 for sample products.)

In venous blood collection, the tubes were coated with reagents to preserve the integrity of the specimen (the stoppers on the tubes were color coded to indicate the specific reagent inside). The laboratory technician, known as a phlebotomist, collected blood in different tubes depending on the type of test required by the patient's doctor.

Evacuated-tube blood collection was considered superior to the older needle-and-syringe method in providing specimen integrity, convenience, and lower costs. BD was the pioneer in converting the market to evacuated tubes. According to industry sources, BD had an estimated 80 percent market share in the United States, where nearly 100 percent of venous blood collection had been converted to evacuated-tube methods (worldwide, evacuated tube methods accounted for less than 40 percent of blood collection).

Capillary blood collection systems consisted of a lancet for pricking the patient's finger and a tube (MICROTAINER® was the BD brand name) used for blood collection and testing. MICROTAINER tubes used capillary action and gravity for collecting blood samples of smaller volumes than those generally collected by the venous method. MICROTAINER systems could be used for the same blood tests administered through VACUTAINER systems, but the common applications for MICRO-TAINER were in single-tube collections for infants, children, and geriatric patients.

The division marketed VACUTAINER and MICROTAINER systems as complete blood collection systems, but other suppliers' needles and lancets could be used on BD tubes and vice versa. On average, about 2.5 tubes were used per needle, with an estimated 1985 U.S. market, in units, of 80 million tubes and 32 million needles.

Microbiology systems provided a sterile environment for transferring blood specimens from the collection to the testing site. The division's microbiology tubes and collectors were all marketed under the VACUTAINER brand name.

BDVS had the broadest line of blood collection products in the industry. Peter Trow, sales representative for BDVS, noted:

> In this business, quality is not merely a function of needle sharpness or the integrity of the reagents. We also offer the widest range of tubes, and that's crucial. Big hospitals and labs run a multitude of tests, and they require product assortment and color coding schemes to make their jobs easier. That is part of their definition of quality.

Cost-containment pressures resulted in a 1.0 percent compounded annual decline in hospital blood testing between 1983 and 1985. Forecasts indicated hospital blood testing would decline through 1987, but an aging U.S. population should increase testing somewhat in subsequent years. Testing in commercial labs and physicians' offices was expected to be 40 percent of total blood testing by 1990.

Total microcollections were forecast to increase 5 percent annually through 1990 as less expensive, easier-to-use equipment motivated physicians to do more testing in their offices rather than via a hospital or commercial lab. Battaglia also noted that blood collection technology was changing rapidly:

> The clear technological trend is to enable end-users to do more of the diagnostic testing. This means more testing can be done in nonlaboratory settings such as doctors' offices. In turn, that has implications for our distribution network, which tends to be built around lab distributors rather than the medical/surgical distributors who sell to nonlab locations. The technological developments also place more technical selling demands on our sales force.

Industry Background

Blood collection products were used in hospitals, commercial laboratories, and many nonhospital health care centers.

Hospitals

In 1985 approximately 7,000 U.S. hospitals performed 70 percent of all blood tests. Blood collection was generally performed at the patient's bedside and the sample then sent to a hospital laboratory for testing. The 1,800 largest hospitals (200 or more beds each) accounted for 50 percent of the market for medical equipment and supplies.

Within hospitals, the buying process for medical supplies, including blood collection products, was complex and changing. The primary contact of a BDVS salesperson varied depending upon usage requirements and the purchasing process in an individual hospital. Robert Giardino, senior sales representative for BDVS, noted that

> Blood collection tubes are a key product for a hospital lab: if the specimen is not collected properly, the lab has many problems. Hospitals order tubes frequently; most have a standing weekly order with one or more distributors for tubes.
>
> The hospital's chief lab technician is usually the person responsible for testing, ordering supplies, and handling administrative matters. In a large teaching hospital, this person might have an M.D. or a Ph.D.; in other hospitals, it would be someone who came up through the lab ranks. On average, there are six subsidiary lab departments, each headed by a supervisor who reports to the chief lab technician.
>
> Purchasing influences vary, depending on the specific product. In general, the "bench people" (i.e., medical technicians in the lab) have product preferences, and these people tend to be concerned with the best quality and not price. Among the bench people, VACUTAINER is the best-known brand of blood collection tubes. But the department heads and chief lab technicians have budgets to meet. Increasingly, upper levels of hospital administration, and especially the materials managers (who perform a role analogous to that of purchasing agents in industrial concerns) are more influential. These people tend to come from different backgrounds than the lab people do, and they are always price sensitive.

In most hospitals, medical supplies accounted for 10 percent to 15 percent of a hospital's total costs, while the logistical expenses associated with supplies made up another 10 percent to 15 percent. Labor costs usually accounted for at least 70 percent. Blood collection products typically accounted for less than 5 percent of the total supplies purchased. A smaller, 100-bed hospital might purchase 40 cases of tubes (each case contained 1,000 tubes) and 20 cases of needles (each case contained 1,000 needles) annually, while a large 1,100-bed hospital, such as Massachusetts General Hospital, purchased about 1,700 cases of tubes and 800 cases of needles annually.

Commercial Laboratories

In 1985, 700 commercial labs in the United States performed about 25 percent of all blood tests. Larger national labs had 15 to 20 lab locations for which the company purchased blood collection products centrally. In these labs, the purchase process for blood collection products was similar to that in large hospitals. Most commercial labs, however, were smaller, single-location companies where the owner-manager often supervised all purchases personally. In both large and small labs, according to Giardino, "The purchasers are cost conscious, because commercial labs compete with each other primarily on price."

Commercial labs analyzed blood samples sent to them by physicians or small health care centers that had collected the blood but lacked either equipment or expertise to perform tests. Many commercial labs also performed blood tests for hospitals for a fee. A significant percentage of a commercial lab's total revenues came from blood collection and testing.

Nonhospital Health Care Centers

In 1985 these accounted for about 5 percent of blood collection and testing in the United States. But easier-to-use and less expensive technology, as well as changing patterns in health care, indicated that nonhospital centers would account for increased proportions of blood testing in coming years.

In 1985 there were approximately 250,000 physicians in 180,000 offices throughout the United States. A number of physicians—often, 50 to 60 per group—were affiliated with forms of group medical care. These physicians were increasingly performing in their offices many medical activities previously subcontracted to commercial labs or hospitals.

Other nonhospital sites—such as surgicenters, emergency centers, and free-standing diagnostic centers—were also increasing in number. They were expected to perform a higher proportion of medical activities during the coming decade, including blood collection and testing.

Market Trends

> Few industries have gone through such intense trauma in the past two years as the market for health care. New cost containment pressures have forced a wave of cutbacks: hospital use has dropped precipitously, hospitals have shaved their own costs dramatically, and an estimated 100,000 jobs have been lost in a range of health care fields. Out of such chaos a new order seems destined to emerge.[2]

In 1983 a change in how the U.S. government reimbursed hospitals for Medicare patients (40 percent of all hospital patient days) affected the entire health care industry. Previously, hospitals had been reimbursed for all costs incurred in serving those patients. Most observers agreed this cost-plus system did not reward hospitals for efficiency. Federal legislation in April 1983 provided for a change (over a four-year period) to a payment approach based on diagnosis-related groups (DRGs).

Under the new system, the payment to a hospital was based on national and regional costs for each DRG, not on the hospital's costs. Moreover, the national and regional averages were to be updated, so that if hospitals improved their cost performance, they would be subject to stricter DRG-related payment limits.

By 1985 the impact had been dramatic. In 1984, hospital admissions fell 4 percent, the largest drop on record, according to the American Hospital Association; the average

---

[2] *Newsweek*, April 15, 1986, p. 79.

length of a patient's hospital stay fell 5 percent to 6.7 days, also the largest drop ever. For the first time, admission of people over the age of 65 fell. Nonhospital treatment—especially in-home treatment—was expected to account for larger proportions of health care. Conversely, estimates[3] indicated that the number of hospital beds would fall to 650,000 in 1990 from one million in 1983. In their place, it was expected that a variety of smaller, short-term health care facilities would proliferate.

Another important development was increased concern among employers and insurers about the costs of health insurance. Many corporations began to adopt health insurance plans that encouraged patients to shorten their hospital stays and to shun more expensive inpatient treatment in favor of outpatient care.

Thus, changes in health insurance were also expected to spur growth in nonhospital medical care. In 1985, many hospital administrators felt that, for the first time, they faced effective, increasing competition and a need to reduce costs. One response was the acceleration of a trend toward the formation of multihospital chains and multihospital buying groups. Both types of organization were intended to increase the purchasing power of hospitals for equipment and supplies. In 1985, about 45 percent of all U.S. hospitals were affiliated with multihospital chains, and it was predicted that 65 percent would be so affiliated by 1990. Similarly, in 1985 most hospitals were members of buying groups.

Multihospital chains were usually for-profit hospitals that purchased most supplies and equipment through centralized buying organizations. In these chains, individual hospitals submitted purchase requirements and preferences for specific products, but price and delivery terms were negotiated centrally. Buying groups were looser affiliations of not-for-profit hospitals. Like chains, purchases for buying groups were handled centrally, but individual hospitals were often free to accept or reject the terms negotiated on a specific item by the central buying group. Thus, if a given hospital's administration or lab personnel had a strong preference for a given brand, and the buying group had negotiated a volume discount for a different brand, that hospital might purchase its tubes separately while purchasing other items through the centralized buying group. In addition, many hospitals belonged to several buying groups, purchasing different items through different buying groups depending upon the product, specific prices, and other factors. One BD manager noted:

> The chains and buying groups structure negotiations on the premise that they can deliver so many thousands of beds to the manufacturer with the best price. But the actual strength of these groups varies. In some, all of their hospitals purchase through the centralized procedure. In others, a large percentage of the member hospitals do not adhere to the centralized procedure. The result is that the purchasing leverage differs from one group to the next.
>
> In addition, individual hospitals belong to a number of different buying groups, and often switch from one group to the next. The result is that the various buying-group headquarters organizations in effect compete actively with each other to attract and retain hospital clients. Nonetheless, there is no doubt that chains and buying groups have increased the pricing pressures on both manufacturers and distributors of health care products in recent years.

Competition

Competition in the blood collection market was primarily among BD and two other firms. Terumo, a Japanese company, was a global competitor with a 1984 U.S. market share of about 18 percent in evacuated blood collection tubes and nearly 50 per-

[3] Cited in "Hospital Suppliers Strike Back," *New York Times*, March 31, 1985.

cent in blood collection needles. Sherwood Medical Corporation's Monoject division was predominantly a U.S. competitor with a U.S. market share of about 2 percent in tubes and 15 percent in needles.

Over the past seven years, BDVS had maintained about an 80 percent share of the U.S. evacuated blood collection tube market while increasing its average unit price from about 6 cents to 8 cents. During that time, Terumo had increased its share from 10 percent to 20 percent while maintaining its price at about 6.5 cents per unit. In blood collection needles, however, BDVS's share had dropped from 40 percent to 30 percent during this period, while Terumo had doubled its share from 25 percent to 50 percent. In needles, BDVS and Terumo charged approximately 7.5 cents per unit, while Sherwood charged about 10 cents per unit.

A primary objective for BD in both tubes and needles was to maintain a leading market share. Management believed that Terumo was also committed to increasing its share in all segments and would continue to price aggressively. BD planned to combat such competition through accelerated new product developments and annual improvements in product quality, while using its strong market share to become the lowest-cost producer in all product segments.

An important element in BD's marketing strategy was what one executive termed "quality aggression." Since BD had vertically integrated into the production of components such as glass tubes and rubber stoppers, it could keep a tight hold on quality. In addition, BD could process reagents and chemicals in its own plants to especially demanding specifications and pioneer in new tube sterilization techniques that demanded large capital investments in radiation equipment. As one manager noted, "This raises our costs but also forces our competitors to raise their costs even more, since our higher volume allows us to amortize the capital investments over a larger base."

In the past, major companies, including Corning Glass, Abbott Labs, and Johnson & Johnson, had participated in the blood collection market but had then withdrawn. However, BDVS management believed new technologies could provoke renewed competition from these firms as well as from companies that might enter the market from a base in computer equipment, other forms of medical diagnostic equipment, or biotechnology.

BDVS Marketing and Sales Programs

BD's blood collection products were initially sold through the Medical Products group pooled sales force. In 1980, however, separate sales forces were established for VACUTAINER products and a number of other Medical Products divisions. Battaglia explained:

> The basic reason for the reorganization was that the different products were sold to different buyers within hospitals and had different selling requirements. Our division's products require our salespeople to speak with phlebotomists, nurses, physicians, and other technical people as well as the administrators and materials managers at an account. The salespeople must also know a great deal about the people and procedures in the various hospital labs.
>
> In addition, developments in blood collection technology also made our product line wider and required salespeople to learn more about more complex products. Our new product development plans also supported a move toward a separate VACUTAINER sales force.

In 1985 BDVS had 55 sales representatives organized into territories based on the number of hospital beds in a given area. Territories ranged from 10,000 to 20,000 beds. All hospital, commercial lab, and distributor accounts within a territory were the responsibility of that territory rep. Territory reps reported to one of six regional managers, who in turn reported to William Kozy, the national sales director.

Each BDVS sales rep had about 100 accounts and typically made five sales calls daily, four on hospital labs and one on either a distributor or nonhospital lab. A large metropolitan hospital might receive two or three calls monthly, while a small rural hospital might receive one or two calls annually. One rep noted:

> Our sales strategy has traditionally been to sell from the bottom up: we try to work with as many of the bench people as possible—that is, the lab technicians who actually use blood collection products, who care about the quality of what they use, and who will complain to the administrators if they do not get the product they want. BD has a reputation for being more responsive than other firms to end-users.
>
> I think we've maintained our market share because of this philosophy. In recent years, I've seen a number of instances where materials managers wanted to standardize their purchases around a less expensive blood collection product, but the lab people complained and insisted on our product.

During the past year the division had introduced a new needle and had placed major emphasis on converting accounts from competing needle brands. Several sales promotions in 1985 for VACUTAINER needles gave sales reps cash awards for conversions. Results had been very positive, including the conversion of nearly 66,000 beds from competitive needles and a substantial increase in market share for VACUTAINER needles during the last four-month promotion campaign (11/1/84 through 2/28/85).

Distribution

BDVS sold its products through 474 independent distributors who fell into two categories, laboratory products distributors and medical-surgical products distributors. A laboratory products distributor called on hospital and commercial labs and carried a range of items such as glassware, chemicals, spectrometers, lab coats, and thousands of other supply items as well as tubes and needles. According to one BDVS executive, "Lab products distributors feel they must carry blood collection products, which hospitals order regularly, because hospitals often order the more expensive, higher-margin items along with those staple products." Medical-surgical products distributors called on physicians' offices and other nonhospital sites and carried items such as gowns, wheelchairs, examination tables, and other products in addition to tubes and needles.

Battaglia noted that the distribution policies of BDVS and other BD divisions were developed and executed separately:

> We use many of the same distributors other BD divisions do, but the importance of various distributors to different divisions can vary significantly. For example, most of our sales are through lab products distributors, while other divisions sell more of their products through medical-surgical distributors. Those two types of distributors attend different conventions and speak different languages. In addition, we sell nearly all of our products through distributors, but some other BD divisions have a greater percentage of direct sales.

Nationally, there were over 1,000 distributors of hospital/medical supplies, but the 10 largest accounted for nearly 80 percent of hospital supply sales made through distributors. At BDVS, its 6 largest distributors accounted for more than 65 percent of division sales, the 50 largest for 85 percent, and 67 of the division's 474 dealers for nearly 95 percent of division sales.

BDVS's largest distributor was American Scientific Products (ASP), a division of American Hospital Supply Corporation (AHS), which in 1984 had total sales of $3.45 billion.[4] ASP was the largest lab products distributor in the United States, with an estimated 40 percent market share among distributors of products to hospital and commercial laboratories. In 1984, ASP accounted for a similar share of BDVS's sales.

ASP had 21 warehouse locations in the United States. It had installed computer terminals in major hospitals and become an important part of their logistical systems for purchasing supplies. According to ASP, for every dollar a hospital spent on a product, the hospital also spent nearly an additional dollar on acquiring and storing that item. Thus, less costly order entry and delivery could have a significant impact for supply items.

AHS also began in 1978 a Corporate Program for multilocation hospital accounts. Under this program, a hospital chain would agree to purchase from 50 percent to 75 percent of its supplies through ASP, which, in return, would automate the hospital's inventory and materials-handling procedures, promising substantial reductions in overall costs. By 1985, other national distributors of hospital supplies also offered "Prime Vendor" programs analogous to AHS's Corporate Program. But it was estimated that AHS's program encompassed over 13 percent of the hospital beds in the United States, with a total annual dollar volume in excess of $500 million.

ASP paid higher commissions to its salespeople for selling AHS products. One AHS vice president was quoted as saying: "We manufacture 45 percent of what we distribute, but our manufactured products represented 70 percent of our profits last year. Before long, we hope to manufacture 65 percent of what we distribute."[5]

Terumo and Sherwood products were also distributed by ASP. Between 1979 and 1981, according to estimates by industry sources, over 70 percent of Terumo's U.S. sales went through ASP. Beginning in 1981, BDVS managers sought to build its relationship with ASP. BDVS managers held frequent meetings with ASP management, and BDVS salespeople were encouraged to devote more time to sales meetings and product training sessions with ASP branches. In addition, as one BDVS manager noted, "We made clear to ASP our commitment to maintaining our market share and product leadership in blood collection systems and hoped they would support that objective." In 1985, BDVS was ASP's number one supplier of blood collection products. It was estimated that all BD products accounted for about 10 percent of ASP's sales (making BD one of ASP's top suppliers) and that BDVS products accounted for about 25 percent of the BD products sold by ASP.

Other major distributors for BDVS were Curtin-Matheson Scientific (CMS), which had 20 warehouse locations and sold primarily to hospital labs, and Fisher Scientific, which had 20 warehouse locations and sold primarily to medical schools, research centers, and industrial labs.

In total, BDVS sold through six national distributors, with the remainder of its distribution network composed of regional chains and small local distributors. In most market areas, four or five different distributors sold BDVS products. One manager commented:

> Our relatively intensive distribution is a result of several factors. One is a legacy from when we were part of the BD division. Because BD sells syringes to a very fragmented

---

[4] In 1985, American Hospital Supply merged with Baxter-Travenol, Inc., a manufacturer of medical equipment. The merged company was known as Baxter-Travenol and had 1985 sales of approximately $5 billion.

[5] "Hospital Suppliers Strike Back."

physicians' market, intensive distribution is important there, and we retain many distributors that began selling VACUTAINER products when we were not a separate division. Another factor is that established relationships between a small local distributor and a lab have traditionally been important in the blood collection products area. As a result, you sometimes must sell through a certain local distributor to break into an account.

Also, since the DRG regulations, hospitals are more conscious of inventory carrying costs. As they cut stocking levels and order more frequently, some hospitals look more favorably on a supplier whose products are available from a number of different distributors in the area. If there is ever a problem with getting product from one distributor, the hospital knows there is back-up stock available at another in the area.

By contrast, Terumo sold its products primarily through ASP and CMS, the two largest national distributors. Terumo initially entered the U.S. market with needles in 1970 and tubes in 1972, selling through smaller West Coast distributors. In the mid-1970s, however, Terumo established a joint marketing agreement with Kimball Glass, one of ASP's major suppliers of lab products. Smith explained:

> Kimball opened the door for Terumo at ASP, which had been reluctant to take on an unknown line of blood collection products. ASP soon found, however, that Terumo's line provided them with an alternative to VACUTAINER. Terumo developed the relationship by focusing on individual ASP reps in individual branches: they worked closely with those reps to create a champion for their products in the branch.

Changing Buyer Behavior

During the 1980s, the distributor and end-user marketplace was changing significantly. According to a senior executive of one large national distributor of hospital supply products:

> In the past, our customer was the pathologist, chief technologist, or lab manager. This person's responsibility was to produce quality diagnostic tests on specimens brought into the lab and to do it as fast as possible. A key was to ensure that an adequate supply of products was on hand at all times. It was also the element that these people were least prepared to deal with. Most lab managers and chief technologists had risen to their positions on the basis of their clinical skills, not their purchasing skills. In addition, they didn't particularly enjoy the purchasing part of their jobs.
>
> Thus, they tended to do business with a representative they liked and trusted, and who had a product line that encompassed most of their needs. They also wanted a company that would manage most of the purchasing job for them.
>
> Major national distributors flourished in this environment, with the distributor-served portion of the market growing at 10 percent to 17 percent annually throughout the 1970s. Also, distributors generally paid little attention to costs, because customers primarily wanted service and were willing to pay for it. After all, the lab was a true profit center then: hospital reimbursement procedures allowed any increased operating expenses to be passed on to customers.
>
> Those days are gone. First, the customer is different. Buying influence has moved out of the lab in most hospitals. Most decisions on products purchased from distributors are now made by professional purchasing people, who require that traditional levels of service be provided along with lower costs. In addition, the buying influence is in many instances moving beyond the hospital purchasing department to the corporate purchasing department of national multihospital systems. Some distributors probably have over half of their total sales in these national accounts.
>
> Second, the distinction between manufacturers and distributors has become increasingly blurry. Currently, the three largest national distributors have manufacturing capabilities in important market segments such as hematology and therapeutic drug monitoring.
>
> Finally, while most distributors currently serve the hospital and commercial lab markets, little attention has been paid by distributors to the fastest growing customer

segment, the physicians' market, which includes surgicenters, emergency centers, and diagnostic centers as well as the offices of individual doctors. All trends point toward more volume in these locations and less in the hospital.

In this environment, distributors must lower costs. I believe many distributors will carry only two—or even one—vendors' brands in many product categories in exchange for lower prices from those vendors. Moreover, distributors can reduce inventory, transportation, and some administrative costs through consolidation of their product lines.

In the early 1980s, moreover, larger hospitals and buying groups began to favor single-source, high-volume contracts with manufacturers of certain products rather than purchase of these products through distributors. One industry observer noted in early 1985:

> The once popular prime vendor contract, one of the distributor's favorite marketing tools to hospitals, seems to be undergoing an eclipse. Materials managers who eagerly embraced the program's convenience now want to take back much of the ordering and pricing responsibility they feel they have relinquished to the distributor. The new fashion is to use the purchasing power of committed volume to bargain down prices from individual manufacturers. . . . And to get the additional committed-volume business, manufacturers are perfectly willing to accept a portion of the distributor's responsibility, taking some of the cost of the product out of what was formerly the distributor's margin.[6]

Under direct buying contracts, a hospital or buying group negotiated a committed-volume contract directly with the manufacturer. The distributor would still deliver the product to the hospital for a commission from the manufacturer (and often in higher volumes than previously), but that distributor did not negotiate the initial purchase price directly with the hospital.

Further, by standardizing on purchases of certain products, buying groups could negotiate lower prices from the manufacturer and from the distributor: having negotiated a contract with a manufacturer, hospitals often held a second round of negotiations with distributors in order to lower their net purchase price further. The distributor, fearful of losing a big order, often relinquished a significant portion of the commission that the distributor received from the manufacturer. As one distributor manager commented, "With the stroke of a pen, these multihospital systems can swing millions of dollars in revenues from one distributor to another. Having experienced both sides of this double-edged sword, I know what the sports announcers mean when they talk about the 'thrill of victory' and the 'agony of defeat'!"

Exhibit 11.4 indicates the difference in purchasing patterns under prime vendor contracts and the more recent direct purchasing procedures.

BDVS Response

BDVS instituted a Z contract, in which prices and order quantities were negotiated directly with hospitals but still delivered through distributors. Often Z-contract prices with large buying groups were 30 percent to 40 percent lower than list prices. Under a Z contract, as with other BDVS contracts, BDVS's distributors received a set commission from BDVS for stocking, shipping, and billing the hospital.

One BDVS manager explained that "some hospitals negotiate with us and then shop among our distributors for the best price at that level of the chain. They force our distributors to compete away a portion of their commission on Z-contract orders." In response, BDVS offered its distributors periodic promotional cash incentives.

---

[6] "The Devolution of Prime Vendor Contracts," *In Vivo: The Business and Medicine Report,* January–February 1985, p. 20.

With Z-contract customers, a BDVS sales rep called on the buyer 30 to 60 days before the contract expiration date to gather information about the customer's product requirements and any competitive inroads at the account. This information was entered on a Critical Information Questionnaire, which suggested a selling price and which the rep submitted to the regional manager. One sales rep estimated he spent 25 percent of his time on contract negotiations:

> Until recent years, only four or five of my accounts were on Z contracts, but now almost all are. That means more paperwork and legwork. It also means less time spent with the bench people and more time with purchasing people. I've also been spending more time in negotiating seminars, since these contract sessions can be difficult and tense. I've been in the business for nearly 15 years; selling in the health care industry is more complicated, and less fun, than it used to be.

By 1985, most BDVS venous blood collection products and approximately 20 percent of the division's capillary and microbiology products were sold through Z contracts. Many of BDVS's hospital customers were affiliated with several different buying groups, each of which had separate Z contracts with BDVS. While there were approximately one million hospital beds in the United States, Z contracts encompassed nearly 2.8 million hospital beds by 1985.

Affiliated Purchasing Group

Affiliated Purchasing Group (APG) was founded in 1975. A group of independent, not-for-profit hospitals were affiliated as shareholders with a central organization that provided various services for member hospitals, including purchasing programs. APG's motto was "In Unity There Is Strength," and the group sought to use the power of centralized purchasing while maintaining local autonomy among member hospitals.

APG headquarters personnel negotiated national purchasing agreements with suppliers, but member hospitals were free to make individual purchases separately with manufacturers or distributors of the products. APG purchasing staff monitored national and regional costs, and these data became the basis for their contract negotiations with manufacturers and distributors. The aim, according to one APG manager, was to "pay the lowest price available."

From a group of 20 hospitals in 1975, APG included more than 500 hospitals by 1985, accounting for more than 10 percent of all U.S. hospital beds and nearly two million annual admissions. Many large, prestigious hospitals affiliated with medical schools were APG members. In 1985, APG had national purchasing agreements with about 100 medical equipment suppliers, and the number of such agreements had grown consistently in recent years.

In addition to group purchasing, APG offered other services to member hospitals, especially for hospital administrative personnel. APG maintained a database on department administrators at APG-member hospitals, and this database was made available to APG hospitals seeking new managers. The intent was to offer administrators an opportunity to move among APG hospitals while retaining quality administrators within APG-affiliated hospitals. APG maintained a similar database on doctors. The group also coordinated a program that brought together doctors, nurses, and administrators from different APG-affiliated hospitals to discuss cost-reduction opportunities and develop specific action plans. The program allowed member hospitals to compare their costs by product line, therapy type, and department.

APG had been aggressive and innovative in other areas. It had recently established a private-label program in which it sought to have its suppliers use the APG trademark on products sold through APG purchasing agreements. By mid-1985, this private-label program encompassed a dozen product categories and APG expected to add 30 to 40 additional products by 1986. According to James Wilson, APG's vice president for materials management and the person who had initiated many of APG's recent programs, APG eventually hoped to private-label "virtually all" products sold through APG purchasing agreements.

In early 1985, Wilson also announced APG's intention of establishing its own distribution network. Throughout 1985, APG negotiated with a number of smaller, regional medical products distributors to provide warehousing, trucking, and related functions for hospitals that purchased under APG agreements. APG then sought to have its suppliers distribute their products to APG-affiliated distributors who, in return for a larger share of the high-volume APG contracts, distributed products for lower margins than hospital supply distributors had traditionally received.

Wilson announced that the program would eventually involve a national order-entry system linking these distributors with APG affiliated hospitals. He expected that, if the system could achieve sufficient utilization by suppliers and APG member hospitals, it could lower the hospital's costs by 3 percent to 12 percent on most supply items.

By mid-1985, both the private-label and distribution programs were being aggressively promoted by APG materials management. Some manufacturers had agreed to participate in these programs, while others had rejected participation. BDVS's management knew of at least two manufacturers that had not been awarded APG contracts after rejecting participation in these programs. At the same time, distributors not part of the APG distribution network, including the large national distributors of hospital supply products, were reportedly ready to stop supporting (and perhaps sever agreements with) manufacturers that agreed to the program.

Negotiations with APG

In 1982, APG had first sought to standardize its purchase of needles and tubes and had demanded substantial price reductions from BDVS. BDVS had resisted negotiating prices and terms directly with APG headquarters and had continued dealing separately with individual hospitals. Then APG established a national purchasing agreement with Terumo. BDVS's field salespeople were able to retain most sales of BDVS tubes at individual APG-affiliated hospitals, in part by lowering prices when necessary on a hospital-by-hospital basis.

BDVS's success in retaining the business created a number of repercussions. One manager recalled:

> There was some ill will between us and APG for some time afterward. Their purchasing people had naturally worked hard to get the national contract in place and felt our success tended to undermine them with administration at member hospitals. In addition, the experience made the whole issue of compliance by member hospitals with national purchasing agreements more visible and important for them.

APG subsequently established a group of field personnel charged with promoting the importance of compliance with APG-negotiated contracts at member hospitals. In turn, BDVS field salespeople soon reported that their Z relationships with many accounts in the APG system seemed to be suffering. One salesperson noted:

> There was a period in which I couldn't get phone calls returned from people I had done business with for years. This was especially true of certain administrators who had

introduced APG programs in their hospitals. The word on the street was that APG personnel were bad-mouthing us with their numbers. I don't think this appreciably affected my actual volume with individual departments in hospitals, but it certainly made life uncomfortable.

In response, BDVS managers sought to mend fences with certain administrators and with APG headquarters personnel. One manager recalled:

We held meetings with these people in different regions and explained over dinner that our actions had been based on a reasonable business decision intended to retain our presence in those accounts and nothing personal had been intended. There is definitely an emotional dimension to business situations like this, and it's important to establish lines of communications with important individuals.

Following this series of meetings, BDVS field salespeople reported a "better atmosphere" at certain hospitals.

In April 1985, Wilson announced his intention of establishing a new national purchasing agreement for blood collection products. He asserted that the supplier awarded the contract would receive 90 percent of the business in these product lines from APG-affiliated hospitals. Informally, one APG manager also informed BDVS that APG considered the blood collection agreement to be a "showcase program in which a high degree of compliance by member hospitals is important to us: we'll work for that." BDVS management estimated that VACUTAINER products currently represented more than 80 percent of the venous blood collection tubes and 40 percent of the needles purchased by APG hospitals, totaling about $6 million in 1984 purchases from BDVS.

In contrast to 1982, BDVS management in 1985 decided to negotiate directly with APG headquarters. Management felt that the APG system had grown considerably during the past three years, the central purchasing organization had increased its strength with member hospitals, and there was more risk in refusing to negotiate. Kozy recalled:

These meetings with APG in Chicago were tense. At the first meeting, they dramatically announced that 90 percent of their business was available to the vendor with the right price. We then surveyed our sales force and, based on their contacts with users at APG affiliates, concluded that a substantial portion, but not 90 percent, of our business with these hospitals was at risk.

At the next meeting, the APG manager pulled out a thick binder with the price of *every* item purchased by *every* member from *every* supplier. At the third meeting, out came another binder with their estimates of prices in our product category to all other hospital-buying groups in the United States. This is a difference from previous negotiations: they are very well prepared this time around.

At a fourth meeting, they announced they had received bids from our competitors and wanted to know if we would meet their prices, which were considerably lower than our list prices and, because of the volume involved, lower than our prices on other Z-contract accounts.

Traditionally, BDVS products were sold through its authorized distributors to APG-affiliated hospitals as to other BDVS accounts. At the start of the new negotiations with APG, Kozy noted that:

We told our distributors we were negotiating a potential contract with APG and that the negotiations had the potential to be bloody: if we lost the contract, we would be very aggressive in seeking to retain business at end-user accounts and wanted their support, even if the contract went to another supplier whose products they also distributed. Since then, our distributors, who do lots of business with APG-member hospitals, have sought ongoing information about developments.

The Guns of August

At the fifth meeting on August 1, Kozy and Smith proposed a Z contract with prices approximately 20 percent higher than competitors' proposals. The proposal required APG to deliver within 90 days of the initial contract date 95 percent of their member hospitals' purchases of venous blood collection tubes and 90 percent of their purchases of blood collection needles. If these targets were not achieved within 90 days, prices on BDVS products covered by the contract would automatically increase by 5 percent during the remaining 21 months of the proposed two-year contract agreement.

APG negotiators rejected this proposal and gave BDVS until August 15 to submit a new proposal. They also announced that they wanted all blood collection products covered by a national purchasing agreement to be part of the private-label program and thus carry the APG logo. They also wanted all products covered by the agreement to be supplied through distributors affiliated with APG, and they provided a list of these distributors. The list did not include most of BDVS's major distributors. According to the APG negotiators, moreover, BDVS's competitors had maintained their original pricing proposals and had agreed to both the private-label and distribution demands.

EXHIBIT 11.1
Summary of Selected Financial Data (Years ending September 30) (thousands of dollars, except per-share data)

	1984	1983	1982
Operations			
Net sales	$1,126,845	$1,119,520	$1,113,921
Gross profit	498,128	469,077	478,291
Gross profit margin	44.2%	41.9%	42.9%
Interest income	23,824	18,211	15,147
Interest expense	22,757	32,511	32,336
Income before income taxes[a]	92,908	33,652	106,198
Income tax provision (credit)	29,505	(2,278)	29,506
Net income	63,403	35,930	76,692
Financial position			
Current assets	$565,526	$553,281	$557,242
Current liabilities	245,794	190,222	229,523
Current ratio	2.3	2.9	2.4
Pretax income as a percent of sales	8.2%	3.0%	9.5%
Net income as a percent of sales	5.6%	3.2%	6.9%
Return on net operating assets	8.2%	5.8%	10.6%
Return on equity	10.5%	6.1%	13.3%
Additional data			
Capital expenditures	$82,324	$91,031	$130,008
Research and development expense	57,735	55,149	49,308
Number of employees	17,700	19,000	21,200

Summary by Business Segment

	1984	1983	1982
Health care			
Medical product sales	$668,757	$685,275	$685,553
Laboratory product sales	260,828	264,234	266,425
Total health care sales	929,585	949,509	951,978
Segment operating income	108,178	100,069	130,342
Percentage of income to sales	11.6%	10.5%	13.7%
Industrial safety			
Sales	$197,260	$170,011	$161,943
Segment operating income	22,635	4,616	15,839
Percentage of income to sales	11.5%	10.5%	13.7%

[a]1983 income was significantly affected by a one-time nonrecurring charge.

Source: Company annual reports.

EXHIBIT 11.2   **Blood Collection Systems Division**

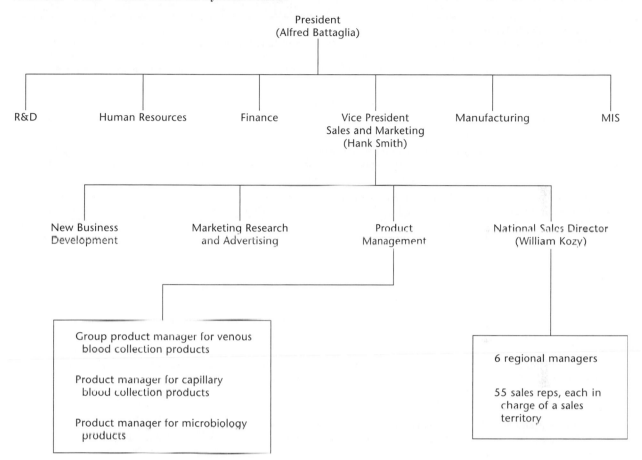

President
(Alfred Battaglia)

R&D   Human Resources   Finance   Vice President
Sales and Marketing
(Hank Smith)   Manufacturing   MIS

New Business
Development   Marketing Research
and Advertising   Product
Management   National Sales Director
(William Kozy)

Group product manager for venous
blood collection products

Product manager for capillary
blood collection products

Product manager for microbiology
products

6 regional managers

55 sales reps, each in
charge of a sales
territory

EXHIBIT 11.3   Sample Products

Sterile VACUTAINER Brand Evacuated Tubes

After 40 years, the goals and achievements of the VACUTAINER Brand Tube line are still unique. VACUTAINER Brand products offer unique benefits for the laboratory valuing the most extensive research and development program . . . an unequaled depth of product line . . . and an unrivaled commitment to specialized service. It's all here, exclusively with VACUTAINER Tubes.

Here is the most comprehensive line of evacuated blood collection tubes available today   All sterile for safety. And featuring the widest array of tube sizes, draw and approved formulations . . . for chemistry, hematology, coagulation studies, special procedures, and blood banking.

Here are the most extensively researched and documented tubes you'll find   They have to be. That's the extra commitment we bring as the people who not only manufacture them, but pioneer their develoopment as well. Every VACUTAINER Tube is backed by in-depth clinical and/or research studies. Data is available on request.

Here are the most significant tube introductions and improvements seen anywhere in recent years   We improved blood collection tubes for trace element studies, therapeutic drug monitoring, and coagulation studies. We've developed new tubes for special procedures like activated clotting time (ACT), LE cell preps and STAT tests. We've expanded our choice of tubes for serum preparation. Starting with our top-of-the-line SST™ (Serum Separator Tube with gel barrier material), we added our new CAT™ (Clot Activator Tube), and then improved our standard red-top tube with a new hemorepellent stopper. For laboratories that prefer their own labeling system, we now offer a new line of VACUTAINER Tubes with SeeThru labeling that provides all the essential information without impeding visibility of the specimen.

Here is the caliber of service support available only through VACUTAINER Systems . . . the company that stands behind every tube you use. Becton Dickinson VACUTAINER Systems is capable of meeting your special needs because we're not just a manufacturer, but researchers and originators ready to anticipate and respond to changes in your diagnostic procedures. Our sales representatives are accessible specialists in the laboratory field. Our nationwide distribution network is always ready to get you the supplies you need, when you need them. Our technical service team is available for immediate consultation (call toll free 800-631-0174). And, to help you train your staff for the best venous blood collection techniques, our educational materials—publications, films, and sound/slide programs—are at your disposal.

The following page contains the latest information on our complete line of Sterile VACUTAINER Tubes and VACUTAINER Needles.

VACUTAINER Brand Needles and Accessories

The VACUTAINER System offers a wide selection of blood collection needles and accessories that meet both demanding technical requirements and patient needs during venipuncture. Sterile needles are available for single sample or multiple sample collection, with standard or thin-wall cannulae, in peel-apart packages or plastic cases, and in lengths and gauges you require.

Improved VACUTAINER Multiple Sample Needles feature the most up-to-date improvements for sharpness and ease of use. A new point configuration, special polishing, and a new lubrication process allow extra smooth vein entry and reduce "drag." Laser inspection of *every needle* detects even microscopic flaws for virtually flawless quality control. All needle hubs and shields are color-coded for quick identification of gauge. New tamper-evident labels protect against inadvertent use of an already opened needle.

There is a VACUTAINER Holder/Needle Combination designed to fit any VACUTAINER Blood Collection Tube or VACUTAINER Culture Tube. Available with choice of single sample or multiple sample needles, with standard or small diameter holder. VACUTAINER Holder/Needle Combinations are sterile, single-use units that assure protection of the sterile pathway from patient to blood collection tube. Preassembled, they offer the additional advantage of eliminating assembly and clean-up time requirements. Also available are VACUTAINER Reusable Holders in three sizes to meet any need. And sterile, single-use Luer Adapters—unique to the VACUTAINER System—that allow the use of a variety of attachments (needle holders, catheters) under a single venipuncture, sparing the patient unnecessary trauma.

EXHIBIT 11.3 Sample Products *(continued)*

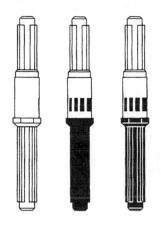

Improved Multiple Sample Needles in Plastic Package with Tamper-Evident Label

Gauge	Length	Cannula Wall	Color Code	Reorder Number
20	1″	regular	Yellow	7214
20	1 1/2″	regular	Yellow	7215
21	1″	thin-wall	Green	7212
21	1 1/2″	thin-wall	Green	7213
22	1″	thin-wall	Black	7210
22	1 1/2″	thin-wall	Black	7211

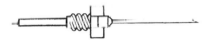

Multiple Sample Needles, Peel-Apart Package

Gauge	Length	Cannula Wall	Color Code	Reorder Number
20	1″	regular	Yellow	7205
20	1 1/2″	regular	Yellow	5749

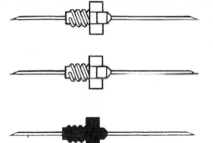

Single Sample Needles, Peel-Apart Package

Gauge	Length	Cannula Wall	Color Code	Reorder Number
18	1″	regular	Pink	5747
20	1″	regular	Yellow	5745
20	1 1/2″	regular	Yellow	5746
21	1″	thin-wall	Green	5743
21	1 1/2″	thin-wall	Green	5744
22	1″	regular	Black	5741
22	1 1/2″	regular	Black	5742

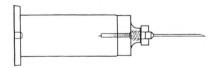

Multiple Sample Holder Needle Combination, Peel-Apart Package

Holder Size	Needle Gauge	Needle Length	Color Code	Reorder Number
Standard	20	1 1/2″	Yellow	7226
Small Diameter	22	1″	Black	7227

EXHIBIT 11.4
Purchasing Patterns

Source: "The Devolution of
Prime Vendor Contracts,"
*In Vivo: The Business and
Medicine Report*, January–
February 1985, pp. 22–23.

PRIME VENDOR CONTRACT 1982   **A**

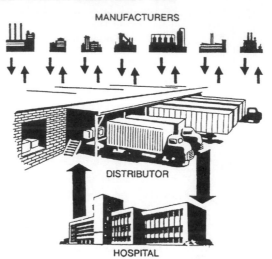

This figure illustrates the forces affecting prime vendor contracts and distributors. Under the older prime vendor contract (A), the distributor dealt more directly with many different suppliers, often negotiating the actual purchasing contracts for hospitals. As the suppliers' major conduit into the hospital, the distributor could drive a harder bargain. But as hospitals begin to cut back on the number of suppliers they deal with (B), standardizing their purchasing to increase buying power for their own direct negotiations with vendors, the distributor's role and power in the purchasing process are shrinking, as are the distributor's margins. The distributor becomes less the product broker and more of a product warehouser.

HOSPITAL PURCHASING TODAY   **B**

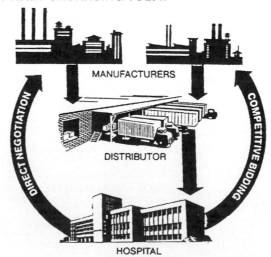

Chapter 12

CVS: The Web Strategy

John Deighton and Anjali Shah

On June 3, 1999, under pressure from Wall Street to respond to Web-based drugstores like Drugstore.com and Planet Rx, the CVS drugstore chain acquired a Web startup, Soma.com, for $30 million in stock. One consequence for Helena Foulkes was a wetter-than-usual summer. As vice president of marketing at CVS, she traveled often from the CVS headquarters in Woonsocket, Rhode Island, to Seattle to work with Soma's founder, Tom Pigott, and others to relaunch Soma as CVS.com before the end of August.

Many tough decisions had been made and many tougher ones had been deferred, but the August deadline had been met. As she flew into Logan Airport on a bright, dry autumn morning, Foulkes looked forward to picking apples with her four children (the youngest barely a year old), and putting behind her for a weekend the problems of building a bicoastal organization.

She reflected on the uncertainties of the online drugstore world. It was not at all clear who would emerge with the upper hand in the pharmaceutical industry's newest distribution channel. Pharmaceutical Benefit Managers (PBMs) had threatened to exercise their muscle and deny reimbursement to online pharmacies. Defiantly, the startup online drugstores were spending heavily to build brand awareness. The strategic question was whether reimbursement muscle or brand awareness would matter more in the formative years of the online channel. The tactical question was how much revenue the channel would generate in the near term.

Foulkes, who had joined CVS as the director of Strategic Planning in 1992, saw this as the most fascinating role she had played to date. The market for drugstore products was four times the combined sales of books and CDs, two sectors that had flourished on the Web. But drugs and CDs had little in common. She pondered, "Now that we have built an online drugstore, how do we make it work?"

Research Associate Anjali Shah (HBS MBA 1999) prepared this case under the supervision of Professor John Deighton as the basis for class discussion rather than to illustrate either effective or ineffective handling of an administrative situation.

Copyright © 1999 by the President and Fellows of Harvard College. To order copies or request permission to reproduce materials, call 1-800-545-7685, write Harvard Business School Publishing, Boston, MA 02163, or go to http://www.hbsp.harvard.edu. No part of this publication may be reproduced, stored in a retrieval system, used in a spreadsheet, or transmitted in any form or by any means—electronic, mechanical, photocopying, recording, or otherwise—without the permission of Harvard Business School.

The Drugstore Industry

Drugstores were among the oldest of U.S. retail institutions. They owed their existence to regulations that prohibited the sale of prescription drugs except under the supervision of a licensed pharmacist, and under this protection they had survived changes in transportation, urbanization, and social custom across the century. Nevertheless they did evolve. They introduced self-service in response to supermarkets in the 1950s, and they lost the drugstore soda fountain business to fast-food restaurants in the 1960s. Independent drugstores gave way to chains during the 1980s and 1990s. By 1999 chains controlled 69 percent of the $115 billion in drugstore revenues. (Exhibit 12.1 lists the top 10 chains.) At first, the larger chains, CVS, Walgreen, Rite Aid, and Eckerd, pursued strategies of regional dominance. CVS's base was in the Northeast, Walgreen's the Midwest, Rite Aid's the East, and Eckerd's the Southeast. When CVS bought Revco in Rite Aid's territory in 1997 and Arbor Drug in Walgreen's territory a year later, it signaled the end of this period of harmony and the beginning of a contest for national presence. Rite Aid responded by buying chains in the South.

The typical chain drugstore in 1999 was a retail unit of about 9,000 square feet, less than a quarter the size of a supermarket, serving homes within a radius of five minutes' driving time. The average store had $4.6 million in annual sales, and prescription drugs made up 48 percent of its revenues. It sold, in addition, a broad range of health, beauty, and household goods (Exhibit 12.2). The financial performance of CVS is shown in Exhibit 12.3.

Drugstores filled two-thirds of all prescriptions filled at retail, with the balance filled by supermarkets, mass merchandisers, and mail order (Exhibit 12.4). The number filled at retail was expected to climb from 2.7 billion in 1998 to 4.0 billion by 2005.[1] In 1999 the $100 billion market was split evenly between drugs for chronic conditions and those for acute conditions, with all acute treatments, and more than two-thirds of chronic treatments, filled at retail (Exhibit 12.5). Exhibit 12.6 summarizes these market and channel facts. Use of both chronic and acute prescription drugs was concentrated among older Americans (Exhibit 12.7).

Distribution of Prescription Drugs—The Managed Care System

For most of the population of the United States, the costs of expensive personal and family medical problems were borne mainly by employers, as a benefit of employment or a retirement plan, or by trade unions as a benefit of membership. Employers and unions usually outsourced the management of these costs to one or more managed care organizations (MCOs). Employers collected fixed monthly payments from employees, added contributions of their own, and used these funds to pay premiums to MCOs to cover the medical costs of families of employees and union members. MCOs competed with one another for employers' business. In an effort to reduce aggregate healthcare costs and therefore the premiums that they needed to charge employers, MCOs became active managers of medical problem solving. They set rules that, to one degree or another, limited the freedom of choice of physicians and employees in healthcare matters.

As prescription drugs became an increasingly important element in medical care in the 1990s, MCOs turned to pharmacy benefit managers (PBMs) to manage drug prescribing and dispensing. (See Exhibit 12.8 for a listing of the 20 largest PBMs, and Figure 12.1 for a chart illustrating their role in the market.) By the end of 2000,

[1] Robert Izmirlain, "Supermarkets and Drugstores," *Standard & Poor's Industry Surveys,* June 10, 1999.

PBMs would likely handle 89 percent of all prescriptions in the United States.[2] MCOs judged competing PBMs by how well they controlled drug costs and improved the quality of patient care. PBMs responded by publishing formularies, which were lists of approved drugs on which they had negotiated favorable prices with manufacturers. They often required patients to use lower-cost generics instead of branded drugs, or buy chronic medications by direct mail rather than at pharmacies. It was the view of some in the drugstore industry that PBMs and MCOs tended to focus on line-item budget management and see prescriptions as a large component of rising health costs, when a broader systemwide view might suggest other ways to reduce costs.

The efforts of PBMs to rationalize the prescription drug supply chain made them a powerful force in the pharmaceutical industry. Employers and their agents, MCOs, valued their services, but drug manufacturers and retailers viewed them with concern. During the 1990s several drug manufacturers acquired PBMs hoping to manage the rationalization to their own advantage, but most did not realize synergies and by the end of the decade only one merger (Merck-Medco) survived. Chain drugstores were more successful. All four of the largest drugstore chains owned PBMs. Nevertheless, most PBMs belonged to MCOs or their parent insurance companies, and retail

FIGURE 12.1 **Role of PBMs in Pharmaceutical Marketplace**

Source: Adapted from "Merck-Medco: Vertical Integration in the Pharmaceutical Industry," HBS Case No. 598-091, by Kash Rangan and Marie Bell and from interviews with Jim Miller, vice president of Health Care Services of CVS.

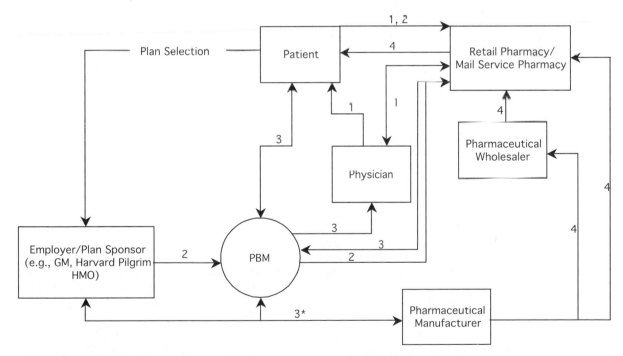

1 Prescription Flow
2 Monetary Flow
3 Formulary Management/Disease Management
3* Formulary Development
4 Physical Distribution

chains had to negotiate with these rival PBMs if they were to serve most of the customers in a store's market. The PBMs of insurers, similarly, had to deal with the larger retail chains so that employees of their client firms could fill prescriptions at stores convenient to their homes.

The Management of Prescribing and Dispensing

In the United States the marketing of drugs was regulated by federal and state agencies, with the effect that drugs had to be prescribed by licensed physicians and dispensed by licensed retailers. The process of diagnosis, prescribing, dispensing, and delivery is illustrated in Exhibit 12.9.

Prescribing

For prescription drugs, unlike most consumer goods, the retailer had little direct influence on choice. The decision lay with the physician and PBM, with some influence from the patient. PBMs influenced choice by creating "formularies," lists of drugs approved for particular applications. If a physician or patient wanted to use a drug not listed on the formulary, the PBM would not reimburse its cost. PBMs set their formularies after negotiating prices and volumes with manufacturers, retail margins with pharmacies, and inclusion or exclusion of specific drugs with MCOs.

Dispensing

Depending on the nature of the condition (chronic or acute) and dosage requirements of the prescribed drugs, a patient could take delivery of prescription pharmaceuticals either by picking them up at a pharmacy or by having them mailed to the home.

Dispensing through Pharmacies

A patient could bring the written prescription to the drugstore or the physician could "call it in." In either case, the patient would pick up the drugs in person, while paying a small co-payment ($5 or $10) while the PBM reimbursed the pharmacy at the agreed manufacturer cost plus pharmacy margin. In choosing a PBM, one factor that employers considered was the convenience to employees of the network of pharmacies that had contracted to accept the PBM's reimbursement terms.

Through the 1990s under pressure from PBMs, drugstore margins decreased. As chain drugstores displaced independents, however, they recovered negotiating power. CVS's Helena Foulkes explained:

> A PBM will come to us to negotiate a rate on behalf of an MCO or employer. Lately, chain drugstores have gotten a little bit tougher about accepting lower and lower rates from the PBMs. The last set of mergers and acquisitions left four major chain drugstores; the rest are independent. This consolidation gave us more strength from a negotiating perspective than we had three years ago, because we cover such a huge number of [patient] lives in our markets. We have leverage from the fact that in 80 percent of the markets we operate in, we're number one or two in terms of market share. If you don't have the option to go to a CVS, it can become pretty inconvenient to get your prescription filled.

Recently, CVS had walked away from a number of PBM contracts citing unacceptable, low reimbursement rates.[3]

[3] Rob Eder, "With Conversions Complete, CVS Refocuses on Business Issues," *Drugstore News,* April 26, 1999.

Dispensing by Mail Order

Patients with chronic conditions were usually given prescriptions of longer than 30 days' duration. PBMs required that pharmacies not fill these chronic medication prescriptions, but rather turn them over to their mail-order subsidiaries. In pursuit of supply-chain efficiencies, a number of PBMs had created mail-order companies to fill long-term prescriptions. They invested in regional distribution centers and bought drugs in bulk. Patients were usually happy to use a PBM's mail-order service because their co-payments were lower. Co-payment costs were reduced from one for each 30-day supply to one per 90-day supply.[4] Although PBMs bore mailing costs, mail-order companies achieved higher per-script margins than pharmacies due to economies of scale. In 1998, approximately 13.5 percent of all prescriptions (26 percent of all chronic prescriptions) were filled through the mail, and mail was the fastest-growing segment of the drug channel.

Drugstores on the Web

In the first quarter of 1999, the first pure-play[5] drugstore websites, Drugstore.com, Soma.com, and PlanetRx, were launched to fill prescriptions and sell personal care products over the Internet. Retailers Walgreen's and Eckerd's announced their websites, www.walgreens.com and www.e-pharmacy.com, and the mail-order operations of PBMs Merck-Medco and ExpressScripts began accepting prescriptions submitted on the Internet.

As the year unfolded, a spate of deals were announced. In January, PlanetRx became the premier drugstore for AOL. In March, Amazon let it be known that earlier in the year they had bought a stake in Drugstore.com. In June, CVS bought Soma.com. Later that month, Rite-Aid bought 21 percent of Drugstore.com for $7 million, diluting Amazon's stake to 27 percent. Drugstore.com announced that month that it would be the exclusive Web source for GNC's brand of nutrition supplements. In October, PlanetRx acquired the online business of Express Scripts, becoming its only online service provider, and became the exclusive drugstore of iVillage, a women's online network. Investor enthusiasm for the online drugstore category drove the market capitalization of Drugstore.com to 15 percent of CVS's by August 1999 despite sales in its first six months of only $4.2 million.

Healthcare sites without prescription-filling capability also emerged. WebMD was an Internet-based healthcare network that connected physicians, hospitals, third-party payors, and consumers to medical information, tools, and services. As a premier "healthcare portal," WebMD provided a single point of access to insurance verification and referrals via an electronic data interchange service, enhanced communications services, and branded healthcare content and other Web-based offerings. In May 1999 it was merged with Healtheon, a healthcare information platform founded by Jim Clark, who had earlier founded Netscape.

---

[4] Kash Rangan and Marie Bell, "Merck-Medco: Vertical Integration in the Pharmaceutical Industry," HBS Case No. 598-091.

[5] In the jargon of the Internet, "pure-play" operations had no interface with consumers other than on the Web, "bricks-and-mortar" businesses had no Web interface, and "bricks-and-clicks" or "clicks-and-mortar" referred to operations that combined a physical presence with a Web presence.

Online Dispensing

Internet pharmacy sites all used the same procedure to fill a consumer's prescription. Customers were required to register at the site, reporting first whether they were seeking reimbursement or not. If they were, they were asked to give the name of their MCO and their membership number. Operators at the site manually verified this information with the MCOs. Next, the customers were asked to choose how their prescription would be presented. They could transfer an existing prescription; mail a new prescription to the site; instruct the prescribing physician to mail, phone, or fax it; or instruct the site to phone the physician. They were cautioned that the reimbursement approval process would add two to three days to the time taken to deliver the medication. Following the convention established by mail-order drug dispensers, customers were not charged for shipping as long as the order included prescription drugs.

Online drugstores needed the approval of the customer's PBM to offer reimbursement, and initially PBMs applied the rule that all prescriptions over 30 days would be filled by themselves. Julie Mandell, a spokesperson at Merck-Medco, explained:

> We are using the Internet to deliver mail-order prescriptions. If some of these online pharmacies are delivering prescriptions by mail, then that is the same service that we are offering to our members and it is written into the contracts that we develop with our clients so that we are the exclusive mail-service provider. [6]

Evie Black Dykema, an analyst at Forrester Research, saw Merck-Medco's statement as an opening position in a negotiation. "Right now they are kind of stuck in a game of chicken. The question is who is going to swerve first." [7]

CVS's Foulkes reflected:

> It is a delicate balance. We're in a supplier and customer relationship. Yet in this arena, you could argue that at some point we could become competitors. One source of competitive advantage in this situation is brand. They don't have any consumer brand awareness—I'm sure you have no idea who your PBM is.

From Soma.com to CVS.com

Tom Pigott began researching and developing an online drugstore in December 1997 using private funding from family sources. He reflected on the goals of his new venture, Soma.com:

> We were not trying to create a new channel. At the time PBMs had no Internet presence except for brochure-ware. We saw an opportunity to develop an Internet front-end to the mail-order back-end. We had pharmacists, which created an inherent barrier to entry. Anyone can start a vitamin shop; all you need are a website and a supplier. Prescriptions, though, were a $100+ billion regulated industry.

The site offered prescription drug fulfillment and refills, and also sold over-the-counter medications, vitamins, and other health products. Soma.com provided e-mail prescription refill reminders to registered users and 24-hour access to pharmacists via e-mail and/or telephone. Although it was the only major online pharmacy without venture funding, it had a fully equipped state-of-the-art automated warehouse. The site carried 3,000 SKUs. Unlike Drugstore.com, where front-store merchandise was an integral part of the strategy, Soma.com sought to implement a prescription-driven model.

---

[6] Denise Duclaux, "Drugstores Slop on Looming Battle over Web Sales," *Reuters,* August 4, 1999.
[7] Ibid.

In the early spring of 1999, CVS was contemplating buying a Web presence or building one in-house. Foulkes reviewed the process:

> We went down parallel paths, with our financial department looking at acquisition opportunities and another group looking at building internally. Valuations for Internet pharmaceutical companies were outlandish. We didn't feel we could drastically dilute earnings per share and make a huge acquisition. At the same time, many of us were actively involved in developing a strategy to build a website and figuring out what kind of organization and recruiting process we would need to support an online extension to be launched by fall. Building a website isn't that hard, we learned, but integrating it with a $17 billion chain with over 4,000 locations and legacy systems and 280 million scripts per year was a huge challenge.

After reviewing multiple acquisition opportunities and flirting with the idea of building in-house, CVS chose to acquire Soma.com. Foulkes explained the reasons:

> First was speed. It would have taken us three to four months to build what we bought for the same cost. Second, with Soma.com, we were buying some very good healthcare talent, and a fulfillment center in Cincinnati that was high tech in terms of its ability to fill scripts. They had invested more than you'd think a start-up would, because they'd hired people with mail-order prescription backgrounds. Third, CVS shared the healthcare-focused beliefs of Soma.com. Finally, we wanted 100 percent ownership so that we would have no bias for or against doing business on the Web.

CVS hoped to offer CVS.com the benefits of its buying power, advertising strength, brand name, and access to 280 million prescriptions, while retaining the entrepreneurial spirit of the Soma.com team. Foulkes knew that it would not be easy for CVS, which ran a tightly centralized organization. However, Pigott and the Soma.com team agreed to stay on, and the headquarters of the online operation remained in Seattle.

For Pigott, 1999 was a hectic year. In chronological order, he had launched Soma.com, become engaged, sold to CVS.com, launched CVS.com, and gotten married. Now president and CEO of CVS.com, Pigott reflected:

> The decision to be acquired made sense in the pharmaceutical market. We're not selling books. This is a very regulated category. While we had made progress with some of the PBMs, the CVS corporation had extremely strong and active ties with all the major PBMs. In addition, the acquisition gave us access to the acute market, which was not achievable without a bricks-and-mortar presence. What was particularly attractive to us was that CVS was not offering a big corporate bear hug, smothering our entrepreneurism and individualism.

Launching the Site

CVS.com launched in August 1999. CVS put its new advertising slogan, "Care that touches everyone . . . one at a time," on every page of the website. Foulkes elaborated on the opportunities for developing synergy in marketing: "So putting CVS.com on the bag, putting it on our circulars, having in-store signage, having our crew members wearing CVS.com buttons, all these efforts can really help build a brand."

Customer Relationships

Pharmacists in the United States were required to provide patient counseling and to check the authenticity of physician-written prescriptions. Soma.com had ensured that pharmacists were available 24 hours a day, seven days a week to advise patients via e-mail and toll-free telephone on proper dosing, possible side effects, and drug interactions. Pigott explained the benefits: "We have found that people are extremely candid online, more so than they would be in person. Using a secure server, they can send a lengthy e-mail to a pharmacist. There is an opportunity to develop very strong ties to a sight-unseen pharmacist."

Privacy was of great concern. Healthcare was a sensitive area, and in the summer of 1998 CVS had become embroiled in controversy when, intending to be helpful, it had mailed refill reminders to people who had filled prescriptions at its stores. Pigott commented, "The privacy issue is one that we have focused on from the start. In this business, it all comes down to a matter of trust." In the winter of 1999, some maverick websites were selling Viagra and other popular medications without following proper regulatory checks. Pigott explained, "These sites create a bad name for everybody. We had to strongly participate in developing online enforcement and work with Congress on compliance issues. CVS.com can leverage the existing trust the CVS brand provides."

In 1998 CVS developed Xtra!, a "frequent shopper" program, to let CVS identify, reward, and retain its most valuable customers. In return for filling out a brief form, customers received a card entitling them to benefits such as lower prices on promoted products and incentives to exceed monthly spending targets. In October 1999 the program was being tested in six markets. The terms of the program varied across markets to test various combinations of benefits. CVS took care to exclude members' prescription drug purchases from the Xtra! database. Foulkes wondered whether to extend Xtra! to the Internet, to give customers credit for online purchases. Information gathered in this way could be used to personalize a shopper's CVS.com experience.

Physician Relations

The Internet created an opportunity for CVS to market to physicians who used electronic prescription relay. A physician could visit the CVS.com site to prescribe, confirm a prescription, or learn a patient's formulary. Foulkes wondered if more could be done. "Physicians are a customer segment to which we need to aggressively market. We need to make it easier to prescribe through CVS than elsewhere. With the right structure, we can make our pharmacists' interaction with physicians seamless, so they get fewer phone calls and save time and money."

"Clicks-and-Mortar" Delivery Options

CVS.com offered a range of delivery options. An order placed online could be mailed to the customer's home or picked up at the local CVS store. Pick-up at a local store was best for acute conditions. Foulkes explained, "We are hoping for a complete merger of both our bricks-and-mortar and online sites. For someone like me who works and has children and doesn't think about getting to a store till 11 o'clock at night, it would be extremely convenient to hop online and place an order and pick up that much-needed prescription on the way home. Our hybrid order-and-delivery offering creates an advantage over pure online competition."

Online Merchandise Strategy

The CVS merchandising department in Woonsocket, Rhode Island, managed the chain's 4,122 stores as a number of merchandise categories, such as greeting cards, photo finishing, general merchandise, beauty, and health, each run by a product category manager with profit and performance responsibility. The product managers made decisions on marketing, promotion, pricing, and merchandising. Selection and placement of merchandise were lengthy processes involving internal and external benchmarks. For example, product category managers took into account the number of SKUs of a product and the shelf space allocated to it in competing local retail outlets to decide how much store space to devote to a product. They listened to the marketing plans of suppliers, and formed judgments of likely market response. They generated sales forecasts to calculate whether each product would meet the chain's target for return on investment. They then decided which products to display prominently in stores, and which to include in the weekly flyers that were circulated to homes in the trade areas of stores.

They passed these conclusions on to a small team of five managers in Seattle, who decided which of the products to promote on CVS.com. One of the advantages that CVS believed that it possessed over a startup was the opportunity for the Web operation to use the product management capabilities of the retail operation. The Seattle organization focused on niche product opportunities and categories not stocked by the stores (such as durable medical equipment) and negotiated Web-specific marketing events, often inducing suppliers to contribute incremental funding.

Pigott and Foulkes debated whether the website should carry all the products offered in a store, or fewer. Pigott argued that some products found in stores were unlikely to be big sellers online, and pointed out how much effort it took to add a new SKU. "We have to Web-enable each product, to make sure that you can click to dosage, indications, and a description of ingredients." The Seattle team was intent on preserving a healthcare theme, and chose from Rhode Island's product selections accordingly. It favored promotions on lines like vitamins and alternative herbal therapies. Pigott observed, "Can't sell Snickers candy bars on the Internet!"

Cosmetics he judged to be inconsistent with a pure healthcare focus, and, in any event, "Cosmetics have not been an evident seller on the Internet." By August of 1999, CVS.com had expanded from the 3,000 SKUs it had stocked in the days of Soma to 5,000 SKUs (including CVS private label brands), but its assortment was barely a quarter of a typical chain drugstore and a third of Drugstore.com's. Foulkes argued for as broad a selection as the stores offered. She saw value in the information that CVS would learn about its customers from the broadest assortment of offerings: "The Internet is a powerful medium for personalization. The more we know about user preferences, the more we can personalize."

Greeting cards were another source of controversy. Initially, Pigott and Foulkes agreed not to stock cards, a very important and unusually profitable category for CVS's stores and among the most important generators of store traffic. CVS was reluctant to compete with stores. However, the major suppliers, Hallmark, American Greetings, and Blue Mountain Arts, were all online, and Foulkes was aware that purchase habits in the category might change whether CVS acted or not.

Pricing

CVS set store prices for nonprescription products using what it called zone pricing. Stores were assigned to geographic zones, and prices varied from one zone to another depending on the demographics and competitive intensity of the zone. Category managers determined product pricing within each zone.

Pricing on the Web was trickier, particularly when cross-channel fulfillment was implemented. A Web transaction appeared to earn CVS a significantly better margin than a store transaction because CVS was spared store overheads. By some reckonings, a product marked up by 35 percent in a store could be marked up 25 percent on the Internet for the same return. On the other hand, some pointed out that the fixed costs of online sites, in particular advertising to generate traffic, were extremely high at the low volumes currently prevailing. Nevertheless, to be competitive online, CVS.com set prices lower than CVS stores. Figure 12.2 gives some representative prices. CVS.com debated whether to continue to price lower on the Web. One argument was that pricing

FIGURE 12.2   **Retail and Online Prices**

Product	Regular (Nonpromotional) Manufacturer's Price	CVS.com	Drugstore.com	PlanetRx.com	CVS Harvard Square
Q-tips 54 count	$0.76	$ 0.89	$ 0.99	$ 0.99	$ 1.29
Centrum vitamins 180 each	9.61	10.49	10.49	10.49	12.49
Band-Aid Bandages 20 count	2.30	2.89	2.49	2.67	2.99
Gillette Clear Gel deodorant	2.07	2.49	2.59	2.87	2.69

should depend on how a customer took delivery of a product. If a customer ordered online and chose to pick up in the store, the argument went, the store's prices should apply. If customers chose to have products mailed to them, should CVS meet competitors' online prices or charge the prices prevailing at stores near the customer's home?

Negotiations with Merck-Medco Managed Care

All of the PBMs with which CVS dealt had agreed to reimburse patients filling 30-day prescriptions on the CVS.com site, except Merck-Medco, the largest of them with 51 million covered lives. The dispute hinged on interpretation of the contract between them. Did the contract grant Merck-Medco the right to fill all prescriptions of longer than 30 days' duration by mail, or did it grant Merck-Medco the exclusive right to fill all prescriptions by mail, even those of 30 days or less? The issue had never arisen until the birth of Web dispensing, because all mail prescriptions were also of longer than 30 days' duration. Now CVS was filling 30-day prescriptions submitted by Web customers and applying for reimbursement, but Merck-Medco was refusing to pay on all but the proportion that were being picked up in stores.

The mounting unpaid claim was a vexing problem for CVS.com. In repeated negotiations, Merck-Medco would not budge. They took the position that their core competency was in filling prescriptions at very low cost. They had invested heavily in automating the process, and they needed large volumes to justify that investment. They had no interest in letting others mail drugs to any of their customers. If a customer wanted the convenience of online dispensing, let them come to the Merck-Medco online dispensary, they said. Foulkes argued that online customers were not like mail-order customers. There were front-store sales to be made to people filling prescriptions, and Merck-Medco was neither earning these revenues itself nor allowing CVS to generate them. "Well," inquired Merck-Medco, "why not build a CVS.com store within our online dispensary?"

In September 1999, CVS.com had been open for business for a month. (Exhibit 12.10 shows a view of a page.) Sales due to the site were quite modest, as were sales at PlanetRx and Drugstore.com. Each barely exceeded the sales of a conventional drugstore. The lowest prices, free shipping, and abundant product information were apparently not enough to draw customers to online drugstores. Foulkes reflected on the relative traffic-generating possibilities of reimbursement muscle and brand awareness. She could invest in advertising, as Drugstore.com had done in spending $16 million in the first six months of 1999, but it was one of the paradoxes of the online world that the more a pure-play online company spent on advertising, the higher its stock market valuation seemed to climb. She doubted that CVS would have the stomach to beat the pure-plays at that game. She thought of Merck-Medco's offer. The PBMs would likely drive volume to the Web as they had driven sales to mail order, and if CVS did not help Merck-Medco, someone else would. But should CVS concede the prescription business to this PBM? CVS was going to have to be smarter about driving profitable volume to this new channel.

EXHIBIT 12.1
Top 10 Drugstore
Chains—1998
(ranked by sales)

Chain	Sales (billion $) 1997	1998	Number of Stores
1. Walgreen	$13.3	$15.3	2,549
2. CVS	13.7	15.2	4,122
3. Rite Aid	11.4	12.7	3,821
4. Eckerd	9.6	10.3	2,748
5. American DrugStores	5.8	6.5	1,146
6. Longs Drug Stores	2.9	3.7	381
7. Medicine Shoppe International	1.2	1.3	1,065
8. Drug Emporium	1.4	1.2	197
9. Phar-Mor	1.0	1.1	106
10. Genovese	.7	.8	139

Source: *Drug Store News.*

EXHIBIT 12.2
Traditional Chain
Drug Store
Merchandise Mix

Category	Percent of Revenue
Prescriptions	48%
Over-the-counter medications	13
Toiletries	6
Consumables	9
Cosmetics	4
General merchandise	5
Stationery	4
Photography	4
Tobacco products	3
Housewares	3
Miscellaneous	2

Source: National Association of Chain Drug Stores website,
http://www.nacds.org/industry/table8.html, August 31, 1999.

EXHIBIT 12.3
CVS Summary
Financial Results
(all dollar figures
in millions)

	1997	1998
Sales	$13,750	$15,274
Number of stores	3,888	4,122
Percent of sales from pharmacy	55	58
Cost of goods sold	$10,031	$11,145
Gross margin	$3,718	$4,129
Gross margin percent	27%	27%
Operating expenses	$3,456	$3,357
Operating expenses as percent of sales	25%	22%
Operating income	$262	$772
Operating margin percent	2%	5%
Total market capitalization	$11,042	$21,461
Increase in same-store sales	9.7%	10.8%
Pharmacy same-store sales	16.5%	16.5%
Third-party prescription sales	84%	81%

Source: CVS annual reports and case writer analysis.

EXHIBIT 12.4
Dispensing of
Prescription Drugs

Outlet	Percent of Volume
Chain drugstores	40%
Independent drugstores	26
Mail order	13
Mass merchandisers	11
Food stores	10

Source: Adapted from National Association of Chain Drug Stores website, http://www.nacds.org/industry/table11.html, August 31, 1999.

EXHIBIT 12.5
Medical Conditions
for Which Drugs Are
Prescribed

Prescriptions for acute conditions (e.g., ear infection)		50%
Prescriptions for chronic conditions (e.g., diabetes, hypertension)		
Retail, reimbursed by an insurer	25%	
Retail, paid for by patient	11%	
Mail order, reimbursed by an insurer	12%	
Mail order, paid for by patient	2%	
Total		50%

Source: Mark Husson, "CVS Corp, Firing on All Cylinders," *Merrill Lynch In-depth Report,* May 6, 1999.

EXHIBIT 12.6
Channel-by-Markets
Analysis (all values in
$ billions at consumer
prices)

		Prescriptions			
	Acute	Chronic, Reimbursed by PBM	Chronic, Paid for by Consumer	Front Store Sales	Total
Chain drugstores	$22	$12	$ 5	$41	$80
Independent drugstores	15	8	3		
Mail order from PBMs	0	12	2		
Food, mass merchandisers	12	6	3		
Total	$49	$38	$13		

Source: Prepared by case writer from case facts.

EXHIBIT 12.7
**Percent of New
Prescriptions by
Age Group**

Source: Adapted from "Percent of New Prescription by Age Group," National Association of Chain Drug Stores website, http://www.nacds.org/resources/chart.html, August 31, 1999, and U.S. Bureau of the Census.

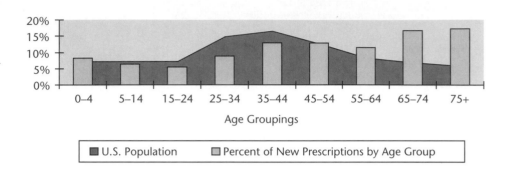

Prescription Use by Age vs. U.S. Population

■ U.S. Population   □ Percent of New Prescriptions by Age Group

EXHIBIT 12.8   **Ranking of 20 Largest Pharmacy Benefit Managers in 1999**

Source: Managed Healthcare, *Pharmacy Benefits Management Directory,* June 1999.

	PBM	Owner	Covered Lives[a] (millions)
1	PCS Health Systems	Drugstore chain (Rite Aid)	56
2	Merck-Medco Managed Care	Pharmaceutical manufacturer (Merck & Co. Inc.)	51
3	Express Scripts	PBM (Express Scripts)	47
4	Advance Paradigm	PBM (Express Scripts)	27
5	Argus Health Systems Inc.	Unknown	20
6	Wellpoint Pharmacy Management	MCO (Wellpoint Health Networks)	18
7	Eckerd Health Services	Drugstore chain (Eckerd)	15
8	Aetna US Healthcare	Insurance/managed care (Aetna Inc.)	10
9	First Health Services	Insurance (First Health Group)	8
10	RxAmerica	Drugstore chain (Albertson's and Long Drug)	7
11	National Prescription Administrators	Insurance (parent)	7
12	PharmaCare Management Services	Drugstore chain (CVS)	6
13	Health Information Design Inc.	Unknown	5
14	Prescription Solutions	Insurance (PacificCare Health Systems)	5
15	Consultec	General American Life Insurance Co.	5
16	Diabetes Management Solutions	Unknown	3
17	MIM Health Plan	Healthcare Facilities (MIM Corporation)	3
18	FFI Health Services	First Florida Int'l Holding Inc.	3
19	RESTAT	Pharmaceutical company (F. Dohmen Co.)	2
20	Walgreens Health Initiatives	Drugstore chain (Walgreen Co.)	2

[a]The number of patient lives covered measures the market reach of each PBM.

EXHIBIT 12.9 **The Process of Diagnosis, Prescribing, Dispensing, and Delivery of Drugs in the United States**

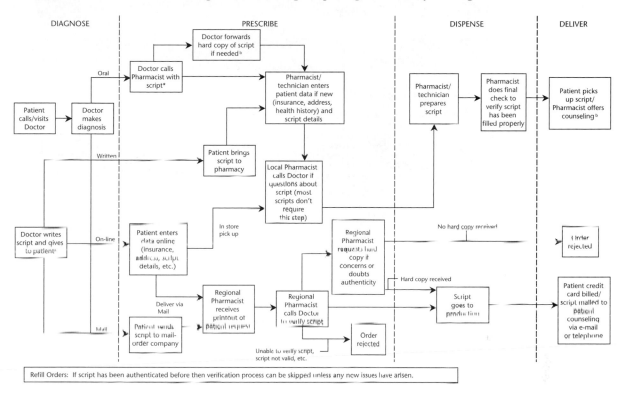

[a]Requirements vary from state to state. Some don't allow electronic or oral transmission, etc. A written script is always required for narcotics. May be required for "controlled substances" (e.g., painkillers). Usually not needed for "non-controlled substances" such as penicillin.

[b]Offer of counseling required by federal law.

EXHIBIT 12.10
CVS Web Page

Care that touches everyone
...one at a time.

sign in/register | your account | shopping cart | help

| pharmacy counter | health & wellness | personal care | vitamins & herbs | find products | go |

new site!

Dozens of new features. Free shipping for a limited time. <u>More...</u>

(new you)

Refresh your outlook-- win a trip to Sonoma Valley from CVS.com and Lubriderm.® <u>Enter to win...</u>

Pharmacy Counter
Have your prescriptions shipped to you or pick them up at a nearby CVS/pharmacy. Either way, our expert pharmacists are ready to serve you at the <u>Pharmacy Counter</u>.

Health & Wellness
<u>Allergy, Sinus & Asthma</u>
<u>Cough & Cold</u>
<u>Diabetes Care</u>
<u>Ear & Eye Care</u>
<u>First Aid</u>
<u>Headache & Pain</u>
<u>More...</u> <u>Online Specials...</u>

Personal Care
<u>Baby</u>
<u>Contraceptives</u>
<u>Deodorants</u>
<u>Feminine Hygiene</u>
<u>Hair Care</u>
<u>Oral Care</u>
<u>More...</u> <u>Online Specials...</u>

Vitamins, Minerals, and Herbs
<u>Herbal Teas</u>
<u>Herbals</u>
<u>Minerals</u>
<u>Vitamins</u>
<u>More...</u> <u>Online Specials...</u>

CVS Power Buys

CVS Sterile Daily Clear Solution for Sensitive Eyes
1 Ounces
<u>details</u>

~~$3.99~~ $1.97

add to cart

CVS Multi-Symptom Night Time Cold/Flu Relief Cherry Flavored
14 Ounces
<u>details</u>

~~$4.99~~ $2.97

add to cart

<u>**Quick Refills**</u>

We can ship <u>refills</u> to your home or you can pick them up at your preferred CVS/pharmacy.

<u>**CVS Health Resource Library**</u>
News, weekly features, health conditions articles, and our Drug Doublecheck tool.

<u>**Photo Center**</u>
CVS processes 35 mm and Advanced Photo System film. Let our trained technicians develop your pictures.

<u>**CVS/pharmacy Finder**</u>
Locate a CVS/pharmacy near you.

<u>**About CVS.com**</u>
Why CVS.com? Our mission is your well-being. Discover the services we can provide to you.

<u>**Privacy Matters**</u>
Read our pledge to keep your information confidential.

Part 5

Managing Communications

13. Pepcid AC (A): Racing to the OTC Market

14. LifeSpan, Inc.: Abbott Northwestern Hospital

15. Population Services International

Chapter

13

Pepcid AC (A): Racing to the OTC Market

Charles King III, Alvin J. Silk, Lisa R. Klein, and Ernst R. Berndt

Late on Friday, July 29, 1994, after an eight-hour meeting with the Food and Drug Administration (FDA), managers at Johnson & Johnson/Merck Consumer Pharmaceuticals Co. (JJM) got the bad news. Advisers to the FDA recommended against allowing JJM to sell Pepcid AC, a reduced-strength form of the prescription ulcer drug Pepcid, as an over-the-counter heartburn remedy.

Pepcid had long languished in the shadows of Tagamet (from SmithKline Beecham) and Zantac (from Glaxo Wellcome) in the prescription market. Zantac was the world's best-selling drug. All three companies were racing to place lower-dose forms on the over-the-counter (OTC) market, where consumers could obtain the drug without a physician's prescription. This required approval from the FDA. Many observers believed Tagamet had taken an early lead in the approval process. SmithKline Beecham had begun its discussions with the FDA in 1985. Such was the SmithKline Beecham lead that JJM's hopes initially were that Pepcid AC would be the second entrant, ahead of Zantac and Eli Lilly's Axid, the fourth competitor. Management expected all four drugs to enter the OTC market within months of each other.

The FDA strictly regulated product claims for over-the-counter drugs. No marketing claims could be made for the uses, benefits, or efficacy of any drug without prior FDA approval. Pharmaceutical companies had to submit evidence from rigorous clinical trials supporting the uses, safety, and efficacy of their medications. The competitors had followed different strategies in the approval process. SmithKline Beecham sought approval for the claim that Tagamet HB was effective in treating

Professors Charles King III and Alvin J. Silk of Harvard Business School, Professor Lisa R. Klein of Rice University, and Professor Ernst R. Berndt of MIT prepared this case as the basis for class discussion rather than to illustrate either effective or ineffective handling of an administrative situation.

Copyright © 2000 by the President and Fellows of Harvard College. To order copies or request permission to reproduce materials, call 1-800-545-7685, write Harvard Business School Publishing, Boston, MA 02163, or go to http://www.hbsp.harvard.edu. No part of this publication may be reproduced, stored in a retrieval system, used in a spreadsheet, or transmitted in any form or by any means—electronic, mechanical, photocopying, recording, or otherwise—without the permission of Harvard Business School.

heartburn and stomach upset, a treatment-only claim. Both JJM and Glaxo pursued not only the treatment claim but also a prevention claim. They had to establish that their medications not only alleviated the symptoms of heartburn and stomach distress when they occurred but also prevented their occurrence when the drugs were taken before the onset of symptoms.

SmithKline Beecham's perceived early lead in the FDA process dissipated in September 1993 when the FDA asked it to collect additional data about the proposed low-dosage Tagamet. JJM immediately changed its objective, no longer conceding first-to-market status to SmithKline Beecham. Now, in July 1994, the FDA dealt both SmithKline Beecham and JJM setbacks. On July 29, the advisory committee, concerned about possible adverse reactions when Tagamet was used with other drugs, rejected SmithKline Beecham's application even with the additional data. On July 31, the advisory committee rendered the judgment that JJM's clinical trials failed to show Pepcid, in its low-dosage form, either prevented heartburn or provided relief from heartburn.

The FDA usually, but not always, followed the recommendations of its advisory committees. A notable recent exception was Procter & Gamble's application for Aleve, an over-the-counter pain reliever. JJM management disagreed with the advisory committee's analysis of the clinical test results. They wondered if they should press for a September meeting with the FDA to argue the case for the treatment and prevention claims and to preserve the opportunity to be the first entrant. A second option was to drop the prevention claim and increase the chances of being first to market. Alternatively, JJM could again set its sights on second place in the race to market and improve its chances for FDA approval by collecting additional data to support its claims.

Prescription Drug Heritage

Pepcid, Tagamet, Zantac, and Axid belonged to a class of drugs known as H_2-receptor antagonists. These drugs reduce stomach acid secretion by blocking the histamine H_2-receptor on the cells producing gastric acid. Tagamet's 1977 introduction revolutionized the treatment of ulcers. Sir James Black's discovery of Tagamet merited a share of the Nobel Prize in 1989. With Tagamet, physicians could treat ulcers and pre-ulcerous conditions without expensive hospital admissions and surgeries. Tagamet became the first prescription drug to reach one billion dollars in annual sales.

Three other H_2-receptor antagonists subsequently entered the market: Zantac in 1983, Pepcid in 1986, and Axid in 1986 (Table 13.A). Together these four drugs accounted for about 95 percent of the prescription market for ulcer medications.

Introduced six years after Tagamet and at a substantially higher price, Zantac rapidly overtook Tagamet (see Exhibit 13.1 for market shares 1977 to 1991). Glaxo teamed with Hoffmann-La Roche, another pharmaceutical company with a large

TABLE 13.A
H_2-Receptor Antagonists in U.S. Market

	Firm	Brand Name	Chemical Compound	1993 U.S. Sales ($ millions)	Rank Among All Drugs
August 1977	SmithKline	Tagamet	Cimetidine	528	9
June 1983	Glaxo	Zantac	Ranitidine	1,694	1
November 1986	Merck	Pepcid	Famotidine	387	16
May 1988	Lilly	Axid	Nizatidine	271	22

sales force, to market Zantac very aggressively, emphasizing Zantac's convenient twice-a-day dosage (versus Tagamet's regimen of four times a day) and fewer side effects. Evidence from clinical trials suggested that side effects such as nausea, diarrhea, drowsiness, gynecomastia (breast swelling in males), and dizziness in the elderly, while rare, occurred less frequently with Zantac than with Tagamet. With the success of Tagamet and Zantac, later entrants—Pepcid from Merck and Axid from Eli Lilly—achieved only minor market shares. But, because of the size of the overall market, even the smallest share was enough to place Axid 22nd on the list of top-selling drugs in 1993, as shown in Table 13.A.

By 1990, many in the medical community viewed the four H_2-receptor antagonists as essentially equivalent in efficacy but different in their side effects. Tagamet in particular was known to interact with the pharmacological effects of some other drugs. During the early 1990s, Zantac typically sold at about a 20 percent premium over Tagamet, with Pepcid and Axid prices in between. Growth in the overall market for these drugs was sustained and significant, averaging about 15 percent per year since 1977.

In May 1994, Tagamet lost its prescription patent protection. Tagamet's U.S. sales dropped from $648 million in 1993 to $405 million in 1994 as generic manufacturers entered the market. Zantac's patent would expire in late 1997, Pepcid's and Axid's in 2000.

Switching Prescription Drugs to Over-the-Counter

"There are fundamental changes in the prescription-drug market," such as strong generic competition after patents run out, said Warner-Lambert Chairman Melvin R. Goodes. "But you can have an over-the-counter business for a long time," he said, noting that Listerine has been around for over 100 years.[1]

Switching drugs from prescription to over-the-counter status provided pharmaceutical companies with opportunities for significant growth. Nine of the 10 top-selling over-the-counter brands introduced since 1975 were formerly prescription-only medications, according to Kline & Co., a market-research concern. Well-known examples of such switches are listed in Table 13.B. Many OTC pain relievers were based on the prescription drug ibuprofen. Sales of ibuprofen products more than tripled in the decade after it went over-the-counter.

More recent switches had also enjoyed great success. For example, Johnson & Johnson's Imodium-AD, an anti-diarrhea medication, drove Imodium sales from $31.5 million in 1987 to $125 million five years later.

The FDA approved three prescription antifungal drugs for over-the-counter sales in 1990 and 1991: Johnson & Johnson's Monistat, Schering-Plough's Gyne-Lotrimin, and Bayer AG's Mycelex. In 1990, Schering-Plough had sold $64.9 million of the prescription Gyne-Lotrimin and a related product, topical antifungal Lotrimin. Two years later, sales were $146 million, of which all but $34 million sold over-the-counter. Johnson & Johnson saw annual Monistat sales increase from $167 million to $186 million in its first year after switching to over-the-counter status.

[1] Elyse Tanouye and Thomas Burton, "More Firms 'Switch' Prescription Drugs to Give Them Over-the-Counter Status," *The Wall Street Journal,* July 29, 1993, p. B1.

TABLE 13.B
Selected Over-the-
Counter Switches

Company	Product	Category	Drug Name
American Home Products	Advil	Painkiller	Ibuprofen
Upjohn Co.	Motrin IB	Painkiller	Ibuprofen
Bristol-Myers Squibb Co.	Nuprin	Painkiller	Ibuprofen
Warner-Lambert Co.	Benadryl	Antihistamine	Diphenhydramine
Johnson & Johnson	Imodium-AD	Anti-diarrheal	Loperamide
Schering-Plough	Gyne-Lotrimin	Antifungal	Clotrimazole
Johnson & Johnson	Monistat	Antifungal	Miconazole
Sandoz Pharmaceutical Corp.	Tavist	Antihistamine	Clemastine

Strategic Alliances

Most pharmaceutical companies anticipated rapid growth in the over-the-counter market as consumers increasingly sought to diagnose and self-medicate their common ailments. Many firms sought to overcome their lack of experience in marketing consumer products through alliances of various forms—mergers, joint ventures, or licensing agreements. Several formed during 1989.

March 1989

Merck joined with Johnson & Johnson, the world's largest diversified healthcare company, to form the joint venture Johnson & Johnson/Merck Consumer Pharmaceuticals Company. JJM united Merck's research and development excellence and product portfolio with Johnson & Johnson's expertise in consumer marketing and retail distribution. The joint venture obtained its scientists and regulatory expertise primarily from Merck Research Labs and its marketing and sales personnel chiefly from Johnson & Johnson. JJM's president, initially from Johnson & Johnson, reported to an eight-person oversight board with equal representation from senior Johnson & Johnson and Merck management.

The partnership with Johnson & Johnson was widely hailed as a "marriage made in heaven." Johnson & Johnson's McNeil Consumer Products unit sold the Tylenol family of products but had not introduced any new large-volume products in some time. James E. Burke, chairman and chief executive of Johnson & Johnson, explained, "Our studies suggest that the consumer product side of the drug business is going to grow at a faster rate than prescription drugs. But new products and new brands are hard to come by. Merck has a lot of possibilities."

April 1989

SmithKline Beckman, marketer of Tagamet, announced its intention to merge with Beecham, a strong over-the-counter marketer that competed in prescription markets as well. The new company, SmithKline Beecham, would be the world's second-largest prescription and over-the-counter drug company with combined revenues of $12 billion, 60 percent of which derived from pharmaceutical products. Industry observers cited cost savings of combining operations and complementary research and development pipelines as justifications for the merger. The new company marketed over 300 branded products, including Tums, the leading over-the-counter antacid.

August 1989

Eli Lilly, a $7 billion pharmaceutical company, and American Home Products signed an agreement for American Home Products to develop and seek FDA approval for over-the-counter formulations of selected Lilly prescription medications. American

Home Products had successfully launched major over-the-counter products, such as Advil, Anacin, Robitussin, and Primatene.

October 1989

Johnson & Johnson and Merck purchased ICI America Inc., the U.S. over-the-counter business of a British firm, for $450 million. The acquisition gave JJM control of a $90 million-a-year business, consisting of the antacid Mylanta and other products. With the acquisition of Mylanta, JJM became the fourteenth-largest firm in the $10 billion dollar (retail) U.S. over-the-counter market. Retail sales of antacids totaled well over $600 million. Mylanta, JJM's flagship product, ranked fourth in sales.

Pepcid was the first product that JJM sought to switch. It would be a test case for future products. Given SmithKline Beecham's initiation of the FDA approval process four years before JJM was even formed, JJM anticipated that Tagamet would beat Pepcid AC to the OTC market. As the switch process began, concerns arose about whether over-the-counter sales would cannibalize sales of the prescription drug. "Once a drug goes over the counter," James E. Burke observed, "it sometimes drives the price of the prescription product down as well." But Roy Vagelos, chairman and CEO of Merck, believed that the price of the stronger prescription dose was unlikely to be affected.

July/August 1993

Glaxo Wellcome, the world's largest pharmaceutical company with sales of nearly $14 billion, had previously signaled to the medical community that it was not committed to having Zantac be the first brand to enter the over-the-counter market but would instead focus its resources on the development of new pharmaceutical compounds.[2] However, in July 1993, Glaxo Wellcome reached an agreement with Warner-Lambert, manufacturer of leading over-the-counter products, including Listerine, Benadryl, and Sinutab, to market Glaxo OTC switches.

FDA Approval Process

The development of a new prescription drug was an expensive and time-consuming process. The FDA drug approval process typically required over eight years. The average development cost for a new ethical pharmaceutical product was nearly $360 million in the early 1990s, reflecting in part only a 20 percent success rate. The FDA approval process for switching a prescription drug to an over-the-counter use involved less time and cost, since the safety of the drug has already been established. The keys to obtaining FDA approval for an over-the-counter medication were demonstrating the efficacy of the lower dosage, and establishing the consumers' willingness to use the product safely, in compliance with the directions specified on the product label.

An early decision for JJM was what product claims against heartburn to pursue for Pepcid: prevention, treatment, or both. The company believed that the prevention claim could be a critical differentiating factor, if FDA approvals were obtained before its competitors. It did not know, however, whether the FDA would seriously consider prevention studies. The FDA traditionally had been more comfortable with education as the means to prevention, rather than medication. There was little precedent for prevention claims. The FDA was concerned that overmedication in pursuit of prevention

[2] Tony Jackson, Richard Waters, and Paul Abrahams, "Muscle behind a Counter Offensive: Tony Jackson Examines the Logic behind a Link-up of Three of the World's Biggest Drug Companies," *Financial Times* (London), July 29, 1993, p. 15.

might mask serious medical problems. Approval only for the treatment of heartburn once it occurred would likely be easier and faster to obtain.

A sense of urgency and a need to differentiate itself, arising from Tagamet's lead in the FDA approval process, drove JJM to pursue prevention despite the need for additional clinical trials. These studies, conducted during 1990 and 1991, involved novel clinical trial procedures. JJM conducted multiple studies simultaneously, rather than sequentially. At a cost of several million dollars each, these studies represented a substantial investment.

The most important clinical trials conducted by JJM were the "provocative meal" studies in late 1991. Groups, of approximately 100 volunteers, assembled in schools and auditoriums and were randomly divided into a group receiving a dose of Pepcid and another group receiving only a placebo[3] before the meal. All the volunteers consumed a bowl of Wendy's chili with extra hot sauce and a glass of orange juice or red wine, a combination certain to induce stomach acid production. Over the next 24 hours, study participants recorded their level of stomach discomfort. Special "rescue" medication was available for those experiencing acute distress. In JJM's judgment, these experiments provided clinical evidence to support Pepcid's prevention claim.

The regulatory process made more competitive information publicly available for OTC switches than was generally available in traditional consumer packaged goods markets. All filings approved by the FDA were released to the public, and the applying company often divulged the results of interim meetings. Marketers of OTC pharmaceutical medications were constrained in their freedom to adapt claims, revise packaging, alter the formulation to different market segments, or respond to competitor positioning since all such strategies were dictated by the specific claims and formulations approved by the FDA.

The Over-the-Counter Antacid Market

Their experiences in the OTC markets led JJM management to believe that the battle for market share would largely be over quickly, within a year of first entry. Competitors' shares would then remain reasonably stable. From a financial perspective, an over-the-counter drug franchise shared many characteristics with an annuity.

Industry observers expected customers for OTC versions of the H_2-receptor antagonists to come from two distinct but related markets: H_2 prescriptions and traditional over-the-counter antacids. The U.S. prescription ulcer drug market for H_2-receptor antagonists was $3.3 billion (at retail prices) in 1994, comprising roughly 20 million consumers. The market for traditional antacids was about $750 million (in retail sales). Ninety million adults, nearly half of the adults in the United States, consumed an antacid or prescription ulcer drug within a given year. About nine million used both prescription and antacid products. Over the past several years, physicians had increasingly prescribed the H_2-receptor antagonists to relieve patients' symptoms of gastroesophageal reflux disease (GERD)[4] and heartburn, even when no ulcer symptoms were present.

---

[3] A placebo is an inert substance used as a control in an experiment or clinical trial. The "placebo effect" is the measurable or observable effect on a person or group that has been given a placebo rather than an active substance. The medical literature is replete with reports on the power of the placebo, which can be either positive or negative.

[4] Gastroesophageal reflux disease (GERD) is a nonulcerous condition in which the acid contents of the stomach flow back into the esophagus, causing inflammation. Milder forms of GERD are very common, manifesting themselves as acid indigestion or heartburn.

TABLE 13.C
Manufacturer Market Shares and Media Expenditures in the Over-the-Counter Antacid Category

Source: Kline & Company, Inc.

Brand	Manufacturer	1994 Market Share (%)	1994 Retail Sales ($ MM)	1994 Ad Spending (TME, $ MM)[a]	Traceable Media Expenditures as % of Sales
Maalox	CIBA-Geigy	12%	87	20	23%
Mylanta	JJM	16	120	28	23
Pepto-Bismol	Procter & Gamble	13	93	17	18
Rolaids	Warner-Lambert	9	68	9	13
Tums	SmithKline Beecham	19	143	23	16
All other		31	234	30	13
Total		**100%**	**745**	**127**	**18% (avg)**

[a]TME = Traceable media expenditures, which were expenditures in major audited media.

Traditional Over-the-Counter Antacids

Consumers who did not consider their digestive ailments serious enough to warrant medical care relied on antacids to relieve symptoms as they occurred. Traditional antacids work by directly neutralizing acid in the stomach, providing quick relief from stomach upset (usually 3 to 10 minutes). H_2-receptor antagonists, because they are absorbed systematically, act much more slowly, requiring 30 to 60 minutes to take effect.

The four leading antacid brands—Tums, Mylanta, Pepto-Bismol, and Maalox—collectively had 60 percent market share. Brand awareness (aided) was over 98 percent for each of these brands. The 1994 brand sales and media spending figures are given in Table 13.C. Antacid marketers in the over-the-counter category traditionally spent nearly 90 percent of their advertising budgets on television.

Researching the Market

In preparing its launch strategy, JJM researched not only the performance of its product in clinical trials but also studied the over-the-counter market. Major studies conducted included

1. Analysis of syndicated data on consumer usage behavior.
2. Testing of alternative product positionings and pricing for Pepcid AC using the BASES concept testing methodology.
3. Focus groups.
4. Qualitative research with physicians and pharmacists.

The following sections present the key results from these studies.

Research #1: Consumer Usage Behavior

JJM studied the demographic breakdown of the over-the-counter antacid users. Nearly one in five adults reported taking antacids more than once per week. Tracking research by Millward Brown revealed that women and adults over age 50 were the most frequent users of antacids, comprising 36 percent of antacid users surveyed.

Other studies of antacid users revealed the most widely reported symptoms prompting use included heartburn and acid indigestion. Most consumers attributed their symptoms to overeating, overdrinking, eating the wrong foods, and stress. In these studies, 97 percent of total antacid users and 91 percent of percent frequent users reported being "extremely" or "somewhat satisfied" with current products. About 25 percent of users were classified as "heavy users," defined as consumers who used antacids three or more times per week. There was a distinct difference in the behavior of antacid users and prescription ulcer drug users. Antacid users took their product only in "treatment" mode at the onset of stomach upset. Prescription H_2-users learned that with regular use of their product, they could "prevent" their discomfort.

Research #2: Concept Testing

In 1991, JJM began concept testing to develop a unique and sustainable positioning for Pepcid AC that would differentiate it from both over-the-counter antacids and other switches.

(a) Concept Test II (March 1992)

Using consumer insights gained from focus groups and tests in November 1991, JJM conducted additional tests the following March to evaluate four concepts:

1. Lasts eight hours/four times longer than antacids.
2. Prevents and treats heartburn and stomach upset.
3. Prescription heritage.
4. One-tablet dosage.

Interviewers presented these product concepts to antacid users in 14 U.S. cities and questioned participants about how the product fit their needs, its perceived benefits and value, how they would use the product, and related issues. Of the four, the first two concepts scored best. Prevention and treatment emerged as the best long-term positioning, outperforming the scores of two "treatment only" concepts in previous tests.

(b) BASES® I (June 1992)

JJM chose the BASES methodology[5] (described in Appendix) because of Johnson & Johnson's extensive experience with the technique. A BASES I study estimated trial rates resulting from alternative product positionings and marketing mixes. The model relied on assumptions about awareness and repeat purchasing based on results from earlier studies in the BASES database for comparable product categories. The BASES I study included approximately 2,000 consumers, including traditional antacid users, nonusers, and prescription ulcer drug users.

Positionings Tested   JJM expected SmithKline Beecham's creative strategy to focus on (1) convincing antacid and prescription ulcer drug users that the new Tagamet HB, a nonprescription form of Tagamet, which doctors had trusted for over 18 years, offered the most effective control of excess stomach acid; and (2) positioning Tagamet HB as the "original" acid control medication with 525 million prescriptions written for 72 million patients over the past 18 years.

Against this competitive backdrop, JJM investigated the two main positioning strategies: (i) prevention and (ii) treatment. The treatment positioning focused on the product benefits of convenience and long-lasting relief—two points on which Pepcid

---

[5] BASES is a pre–test marketing research system developed by SAMI/Burke in the late 1970s. The BASES family of methods supports the development and launching of new products from concept testing (before a physical product is available) through test market introduction and national rollout or launch. BASES I is a concept test that uses SAMI/BURKE's extensive database of previous test results as benchmarks. For more information on BASES I and II, respectively, see Robert J. Dolan, "Concept Testing," HBS Note, No. 9-590-063 (1992), and Robert J. Dolan, "Research and Monitoring Consumer Markets," HBS Note, No. 9-592-088 (1992), pp. 1–5.

AC outperformed the existing antacids in the over-the-counter market. Antacids had to be taken following each meal or at the onset of pain and lasted only for several hours.

Pricing Levels Tested   JJM was uncertain what pricing strategy Tagamet HB would adopt. Even assuming equivalent production costs, JJM knew that Tagamet HB had a cost advantage over Pepcid, because SmithKline Beecham did not have to pay licensing fees for Tagamet. The licensing fees for Pepcid amounted to several pennies per tablet sold.[6]

To compete with inexpensive antacids, Pepcid AC would have to be priced far below its current prescription price. If JJM set the price too low, however, users of the prescription product could simply buy the over-the-counter version. Three retail price levels ($2.95, $3.29, and $3.95 for a six-dose package) were tested. The $2.95 retail price would make Pepcid competitive with current antacid prices. Allowing retailers a 25 percent markup over factory prices, this price yielded JJM a 60 percent gross margin after production, packaging, and distribution costs.

Test Results   JJM analyzed the results of the BASES I test generally and for specific consumer groups. Long-lasting relief held greater consumer appeal than did prevention of digestive symptoms. Based on expressed consumer intentions relating to the incidence and frequency of usage, the primary target group appeared to be the dual prescription/OTC users.[7]

Test results were analyzed for each primary segment: prescription drug users, over-the-counter antacid users, and dual users. These groups were further segmented by usage frequency. The prevention concept scored much higher on purchase intention with existing prescription users than with over-the-counter users. Within this group, top-two-box purchase intent[8] for the prevention concept was greater than that for the treatment concept (64 percent versus 49 percent). JJM attributed this to the appeal of prevention to a smaller target market (prescription users) and the difficulty of communicating this positioning to ordinary antacid users.

Summary Projections   Overall, the treatment concept yielded the largest sales volume relative to spending (71 percent), outperforming the prevention positioning. Top-box purchase intention of the overall sample for this concept—with the one-tablet dosage, advertising spending of $67.5 million for the first year, a price of $2.95 for a six-pack, and no competitive entry—was 48 percent versus 44 percent for prevention. Projecting these estimates to the overall population yielded a 12 percent trial rate and a volume of 17.3 million units in the first year.

None of the scenarios tested, however, achieved the target business revenue objective of $75 million (at retail prices) for year 1 set by the JJM 1992 Strategic Plan. All the simulations predicted dollar returns in year 1 of less than 75 percent of marketing expenditures, indicating that the brand would not be immediately profitable. JJM management questioned the reliability of the BASES I projections beyond the initial trial estimates, because BASES assumed a benchmark repeat rate of approximately 25 percent based on comparable industries in the BASES database. Management believed that if Pepcid AC performed as JJM expected, repeat purchases would be higher.

[6] JJM paid licensing fees to Yamanouchi of Japan, the developer of Pepcid's active ingredient. SmithKline Beckman had developed Tagamet internally.

[7] Dual users were those consumers who used both prescription ulcer drugs and over-the-counter antacids to relieve their symptoms.

[8] Top-box purchase intention measures the percentage of respondents who said they would definitely buy the product when it was available. Top two boxes also includes those respondents who said they would probably buy.

(c) BASES® II (June 1993)

To check this belief and to assess the risks of cannibalization to prescription Pepcid and over-the-counter Mylanta, the company undertook a BASES II study. The product positioning used was treatment (with a one-tablet dosage). JJM could use mall intercepts and other traditional methods of concept testing to establish trial rates, but because Pepcid AC had not been approved, JJM could measure consumption and usage patterns only in the context of an FDA-approved clinical trial. The target group consisted primarily of current users of antacid and prescription medication. Three hundred twenty participants were given Pepcid AC to try at home for a four-week period.[9] Conducted in conjunction with the Pepcid AC clinical trials, this study offered JJM insights into how the product was actually used and how consumers evaluated its performance.

Pepcid AC's efficacy clearly emerged as the reason for favorable after-use repeat purchase intent. Analysis of consumer reaction to actual product usage revealed that most users did not want to use Pepcid AC on a strict regimen as a prophylactic but as a treatment for occasional symptoms. Pepcid AC performed well among the primary target group of heavy over-the-counter users. Purchase intention (top-two boxes) was 82 percent for heavy antacid users and 76 percent for all antacid users. The dual-user segment had the highest trial rate (29 percent), and, although it represented only 11 percent of the sample population, accounted for 34 percent of the predicted volume (Table 13.D). JJM management attributed these results, more favorable than those obtained in the BASES I test, to the excellent performance of the product in actual in-home usage.

The study also addressed concerns that over-the-counter Pepcid AC would cannibalize both prescription sales of Merck's Pepcid and over-the-counter sales of Mylanta, which JJM owned. Overall, approximately 30 percent of users said they would replace their prescription product with Pepcid AC, while 28–34 percent would use it as a substitute for nonprescription antacids.

BASES II estimated that approximately two-thirds of Pepcid AC first-year sales would come at the expense of existing antacids and one-third from prescription medications. Projections revealed that Pepcid AC would draw sales from Mylanta but that they would only amount to 11 percent of Pepcid AC's dollar volume (Table 13.E). Similarly, only 8 percent of its first-year dollar volume would come out of sales of prescription Pepcid.

Using the BASES II results, JJM forecast first-year sales of $72.7 million based on spending $75 million for advertising, and also adjusting for anticipated introduction

TABLE 13.D
Sources of Pepcid's Predicted Volume by Consumer Segment

Subgroup	Population (%)	Trial Rate[a] (%)	Dollar Volume (%)
H$_2$ only users	2	21	5
Dual users	11	29	34
Heavy antacid users	19	18	28
Light antacid users	26	11	17
Use neither	42	7	16
Total	100%		100%

[a]Results assume the base marketing plan.

[9] The Pepcid AC BASES II tests were implemented in a nonstandard manner, since Pepcid AC had not yet received FDA approval when they were run. JJM conducted tests as part of the clinical trials of the drug required for FDA over-the-counter approval.

TABLE 13.E
Predicted Pepcid AC
Cannibalization of
Competing Brands

Source: BASES II results.

Brand	Percent of Pepcid AC Year 1 Volume	
	Packages[a]	Dollars
Over-the-counter (net)	**(71%)**	**(66%)**
Tums	17	16
Rolaids	12	11
Maalox	10	9
Mylanta	12	11
Pepto-Bismol	8	8
Alka-Seltzer	4	4
Other	8	7
Prescription (net)	**(29)**	**(34)**
Zantac	12	14
Tagamet	7	8
Pepcid	7	8
Axid	3	4
Totals	**100%**	**100%**

[a]Assumes six tablets per package.

TABLE 13.F
BASES II Volume
Projections

Total spending	$75.0 million
Forecast	
Sales net at factory	$79.4
Less: Mylanta AC impact (−5.1%)[a]	(4.1)
Less: Tagamet/Axid impact (−3.3%)[b]	(2.6)
Year 1 net sales	$72.7 million

[a]Estimated impact on Pepcid AC sales with simultaneous introduction of Mylanta AC.
[b]Estimated impact on Pepcid AC sales with introduction of Tagamet and Axid at projected times during year.

of Mylanta AC (a new formulation) and entry by Tagamet and Axid (Table 13.F) in the OTC market during the year. Pepcid AC surpassed the internal dollar volume hurdle set by the JJM management, which had been reduced in the 1993 strategic plan from $75 million to $66 million in first-year sales.

Research #3: Focus Groups

In parallel with BASES II, JJM ran consumer focus groups to develop insights into possible product positionings and advertising copy claims. In June 1993, JJM conducted an initial study with two goals: (1) deepening its understanding of consumers' knowledge, perceptions, and usage habits about current antacids and prescription medications; and (2) exploring any differences between key user segments. Four focus groups were assembled, consisting of consumers between ages 25 and 69. The critical findings were

- Few consumers understood how the H_2-receptor antagonist prescription drugs worked, but most understood how over-the-counter antacids worked.
- "Acid Controller" appeared a viable product description.[10]
- Product endorsements from gastroenterologists were the most credible.

[10] Thus the name Pepcid AC (for acid controller) was born.

- Tagamet's brand awareness and reputation were strong, but for many consumers the name was very closely tied to ulcers.
- Absent prompting, possible adverse interactions between H_2-receptor antagonist drugs and other medications were not a major concern to consumers.

While the treatment concept had outperformed prevention in the BASES analyses, the results from focus groups and other concept tests favored prevention and treatment. JJM management paid particular attention to their "headnodder" research, which focused on identifying product concepts that left everyone in focus groups nodding their heads in agreement. To the headnodders, prevention offered an important point of difference versus traditional antacids and other H_2-switches. Prevention also provided new benefits and opportunities for new usage occasions, which, JJM believed, could drive growth in the category.

Research #4: Physicians and Pharmacists

Consumers lacking knowledge about the H_2-receptor antagonist drugs relied on the advice of physicians and pharmacists in choosing among alternative medicines and brands. This naturally led JJM to research the role of physicians and pharmacists as potential gatekeepers. The company's experience in the UK, however, where pharmacists were switching the majority of potential Pepcid AC customers to other medications, focused management's attention on recruiting the pharmacists.

Exploratory research with physicians identified their primary concerns: (1) the loss of control over patients' healthcare management; (2) the possibility that unsupervised usage of medications might mask more serious diseases; and (3) the efficacy of the over-the-counter product given that the dosage was half that of the prescription product. Concept tests conducted in 1994 revealed that over 30 percent of physicians would recommend Pepcid AC as a substitute for what patients currently used.

Early research had shown that pharmacists felt largely ignored by the major pharmaceutical companies despite their desire to take on a greater role in consumer counseling. Pharmacist response to Pepcid AC was positive, not only because of the sales opportunities it represented, but also because this new category offered pharmacists an opportunity to regain their advisory roles with customers suffering from heartburn and acid indigestion. Pharmacists understood the longer-term implications of the over-the-counter switch. If over-the-counter versions of prescription ulcer medications replaced their large prescription sales and sales of the over-the-counter versions went to supermarkets and discounters, the position of chain and independent pharmacists would be seriously undermined.

Many major drugstore chains had suffered competitively from their delay in stocking and promoting Aleve, another recent over-the-counter switch. Their managements realized the large volume of sales and profits Pepcid AC could represent and were eager to avoid repeating past mistakes. The drugstore chains knew that consumers often continued to buy such medications from the places where they first obtained them despite later widespread distribution.

Early in 1994, JJM experienced the power of pharmacists following Pepcid's over-the-counter launch in the United Kingdom. To reduce healthcare costs, many European governments had been trying to persuade patients to rely more on self-medication by changing prescription-only medicines to more readily available over-the-counter status. In the United Kingdom, the Medicines Control Agency (MCA), the country's drug licensing authority, had been the most active in switching medicines from prescription-only to pharmacy status. The MCA was one of the first in the world to allow Zantac, Tagamet, and Pepcid to be sold over-the-counter. Pharmacy medicines could be sold only through pharmacies under the supervision of a pharmacist. Pharmacy sales assistants were supposed to follow certain protocols in selling medicines to the public. Doctors in the UK considered ulcer drugs to be serious medicines and pushed for detailed protocols. The result, as JJM discovered, was that pharmacists persuaded well over half the customers interested in Pepcid AC or its competitors to switch to traditional antacids, which were easier to sell.

Recruiting the pharmacist, the company believed, would be essential to Pepcid AC's success in the United States.

The War Room

After receiving the disappointing news from the FDA advisory committee, senior JJM management retired to the War Room to consider their next move. Different teams within the company played the roles of each competitor; assembled competitor information, especially about Tagamet; analyzed and debated possible strategies and counter-strategies, trying to formulate the best launch plan for Pepcid AC. The debate concentrated on two scenarios. Under the first option, JJM could return to the advisory committee only after conducting new studies, which might take six to nine months to complete, supporting both the treatment and the prevention claims. Following this route would mean that even if Pepcid AC were approved, it would probably be second to market as originally planned. The second scenario was to bypass the recommendations of the advisory committee, taking its case directly to the FDA in an attempt to be first to market. In this scenario, the company would have to decide whether to request approval just for the treatment claim or to pursue both treatment and prevention claims.

Appendix

BASES

The BASES methodology is a sales forecasting system for consumer goods that enables marketing managers to evaluate and improve the potential success of new products prior to launch. BASES's client list is extensive and impressive, including, among others, Carnation, Colgate-Palmolive, Frito-Lay, Gillette, Johnson & Johnson, Merck, Nestlé, and Procter & Gamble. As of December 1999, BASES had been used to evaluate over 8,500 new product ideas in the United States and over 18,000 worldwide, covering almost every consumer packaged goods category.

Different BASES models provide testing from product ideas still in their conceptual stages to ideas relating to existing products on the market. BASES I assesses consumer appeal and market potential for new products based on consumers' reactions to the product concept. From BASES I, marketers learn who will try the new product and how many will try it, leading to estimates of trial rates by consumer segment. BASES I is similar to traditional concept tests except that the BASES database of previous test results provides valuable benchmarks to calibrate the concept scores.

By making assumptions about repeat purchase rates, one can use the results from BASES I to determine the sales potential for the product idea. Trial and repeat rates depend, of course, on the firm's introductory marketing plan, but the equilibrium market share can be estimated as

$$\text{Market share} = \text{Trial rate } (T) \times \text{Repeat purchase rate } (S)$$

where

Trial rate (T) = Ultimate cumulative proportion of all buyers who ever try the brand

Repeat purchase rate (S) = Ultimate share of subsequent purchases devoted to brand by those who have tried it

Note that S, commonly referred to as the repeat rate, is more than the proportion of consumers who repeat their purchase of the product when given an opportunity to do so. S is the "share of subsequent purchases" made by triers. Someone who repeats on the first opportunity may switch to another brand the next time. Similarly, someone who does not at first repurchase may do so at a later opportunity. Estimating S requires information on both the observed repurchase rate and post-use preference data, which can be obtained from a BASES II study.

BASES II assesses consumer appeal and market potential for new products based on consumers' reactions to the product concept and, subsequently, to the use of the product itself. The typical research protocol for BASES II is

Stage 1. Shopping mall intercept interviews are done at four or more geographically dispersed cities. Respondents are not screened for category usage since the intent is to provide a volume rather than a market share estimate.

Stage 2. Respondents are exposed to a concept and asked a standard set of questions, for example, like/dislike, perceived value for money, purchase intention.

Stage 3. Those expressing a positive purchase intention are given some of the product to use at home.

Stage 4. After several weeks, users are called on the telephone to obtain "after-use" measures similar to the "before-use" measures obtained in Stage 2.[11]

Using information in its extensive database, BASES II estimates the consumer awareness achieved by the given marketing plan, converts consumer buying intentions into a trial rate estimate, and uses the after-use data to convert intentions into repeat rates. In the proprietary BASES methodology, stated buying intentions, like/dislike scores, and perceived price/value rankings are adjusted and combined with other factors to compute estimated repeat rates. Estimates of trial, repeat, repeat per repeater, and transaction size then are combined to estimate consumer sales volume for the first year after launch. Additional information is also provided on marketing issues such as how well the product filled trier's expectations, marketing plan productivity, and the impact of key product attributes on consumer appeal.

AC Nielsen claims that the accuracy of the BASES system is supported by over 860 validations worldwide. "On average," according to the company, "BASES estimates have been within 9 percent of actual sales, with more than 9 out of 10 of our estimates falling within 20 percent of actual sales."

Bases II's strength lies in its heavy reliance on data from previous product introductions, but this reliance is also a potential weakness for new products that do not fit well in existing categories.

[11] Robert J. Dolan, "Research and Monitoring Consumer Markets," HBS Note, No. 9-592-088 (1992), p. 3.

EXHIBIT 13.1   **Market Shares of Prescription Ulcer Drugs**

Source: Charles King III, "Marketing, Product Differentiation, and Competition in the Market for Antiulcer Drugs," Harvard Business School Working Paper 01-014 (2000).

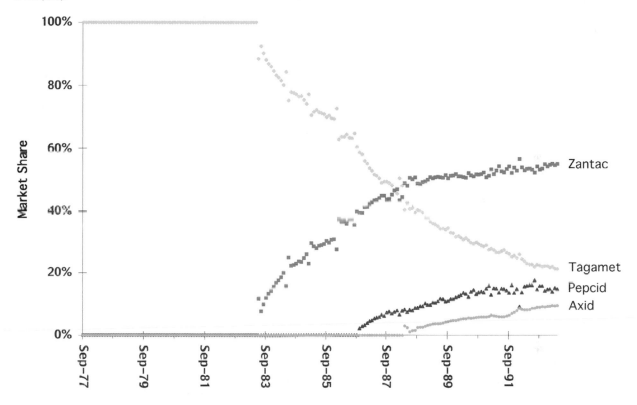

14

LifeSpan, Inc.: Abbott Northwestern Hospital

Melvyn A. J. Menezes

It was Thursday, January 2, 1986, Steve Hillestad, vice president of marketing for LifeSpan, Inc. (the parent holding company of Abbott Northwestern Hospital), was thinking about the next morning's special budget meeting with the Abbott Northwestern Hospital board. Earlier that day at the regular budget meeting, Hillestad had presented what he thought was an excellent review of the progress made by Abbott Northwestern Hospital during 1985 in a number of marketing areas. He had requested a substantial increase in the 1986 advertising budget—from $717,000 to $1.25 million. But Gordon Sprenger, president of LifeSpan, had expressed some concerns:

> Steve, Abbott Northwestern Hospital has come a long way in 1985. But many of us are unconvinced about the role of marketing in this performance. Show us that marketing did in fact play a major role in our improved *performance*—not just awareness or public relations—and we will be better able to evaluate your request for a 75 percent increase in your 1986 budget. Also, while you are at it, please tell us more clearly how those increased resources might get allocated across different programs. I know you've pondered these issues, and would appreciate your presenting them to the board members tomorrow at 9 A.M.

The Health Care Industry

The health care industry was among the largest in the United States. National health expenditures had grown very rapidly, reaching $425 billion in 1985. Health care

Assistant Professor Melvyn A. J. Menezes wrote this case as the basis for class discussion rather than to illustrate either effective or ineffective handling of an administrative situation. Certain names and data have been disguised. Special thanks to Professor Thomas V. Bonoma for his support.

Copyright © 1986 by the President and Fellows of Harvard College. To order copies or request permission to reproduce materials, call 1-800-545-7685, write Harvard Business School Publishing, Boston, MA 02163, or go to http://www.hbsp.harvard.edu. No part of this publication may be reproduced, stored in a retrieval system, used in a spreadsheet, or transmitted in any form or by any means—electronic, mechanical, photocopying, recording, or otherwise—without the permission of Harvard Business School.

expenses as a percentage of the nation's gross national product (GNP) had doubled during the previous 25 years; by 1985 they accounted for as much as 10.7 percent of the GNP (see Exhibit 14.1).

Employment in the private health industry had grown three times as fast as that of the total private nonfarm economy, reaching over 7.2 million employees in 1983. The unemployment rate for health care workers was lower than rates for comparably skilled workers in other areas. Viewed over time, the data described an industry that was large, strong, and insulated from business-cycle swings.

National health expenditures were divided into the following categories: personal health care, program administration, government public health activities, noncommercial research, and construction of medical facilities.

Personal health care included a number of different goods and services: hospital care, nursing home care, physicians' services, dentists' services, drugs and medical sundries, eyeglasses and appliances, and other health services. It was the biggest category of health care expenditure—accounting for approximately 88 percent of total industry expenditures. In 1985, $371.4 billion was spent on personal health care ($166.7 billion of this went to hospital care alone).

Financing Health Care

Health care was financed either by direct patient payments or by "third-party payors" who could be classified into (1) government and (2) private insurance companies. The health care market differed from the market for most other goods and services in that it was dominated by these third-party payors. According to industry analysts, third-party coverage of health care may have contributed to a healthier population, but it had increased prices as well. The analysts believed that most consumers did not care very much about price since they did not directly pay for health services at the time of consumption.

The main third-party payor—the government (federal, state, and local)—spent $174.8 billion in 1985, accounting for 41.4 percent of all health care expenditures. The advent of Medicare and Medicaid programs had dramatically changed government funding of personal health care.[1]

Rapid growth of health care expenditures in recent years placed an increasing financial strain on government programs such as Medicare and Medicaid. To control Medicare costs, a series of major reforms had been enacted since 1981. Despite these reforms, Medicare spent $70.5 billion in 1985. Considered together, Medicare and Medicaid financed 29 percent of the personal health care expenditures in 1985 and expended $110 billion in benefits to 48 million people (see Exhibit 14.2).

The other major third-party payor—the private health insurance industry—had been attracting an increasing number of consumers, and paid $113.5 billion in medical benefits in 1985. The main third-party payors—government and private health insurance—were not independent, but shared a complex relationship. For instance, when Medicare and Medicaid were established in 1966, hospital care spending increased dramatically, and the portion paid by private insurance, although growing in dollar terms, dropped from 41 percent in 1965 to less than 34 percent by 1967. Since then, however, private third-party payments of hospital care had grown to 37 percent because consumers sought more depth in their hospital coverage.

---

[1] Medicare was a federal program that provided hospital and medical insurance benefits to persons 65 years and older and to certain disabled persons under 65. Medicaid was a joint federal–state program that provided medical assistance to certain categories of low-income people. Both programs were established in 1966.

Third-party payments accounted for 71.6 percent of the total U.S. health care expenditures, and the balance (28.4 percent) was borne by consumers paying directly for health services. However, the share of direct consumer payments varied by type of service. For example, direct payments accounted for 26.3 percent of physicians' services expenditures, but for only 9.3 percent of hospital care expenditures.

Hospital Systems

Expenditures on hospital care had increased from $52.4 billion in 1975 to $166.7 billion in 1985—a growth rate of 13 percent per year.[2] The total supply of hospital beds had increased substantially. By 1985, there were 6,148 hospitals with about 1.3 million beds. Industry observers generally agreed that the supply of beds exceeded the demand by as much as 20 percent. The 67 percent bed-occupancy rate of hospitals in 1984 supported this contention.[3]

Hospitals could be characterized in a number of different ways, including ownership, type of patients treated, and whether they were teaching or nonteaching hospitals. According to the American Hospital Association, 305 of the 6,148 hospitals in the United States were owned by the federal government, 1,723 were owned by state and local government, 3,363 were nonprofit "voluntary" hospitals, and 757 were proprietary (investor owned).

Changes in the Industry

Historically the health care industry had functioned as a decentralized cottage industry with a multitude of individual operators—physicians, hospitals, pharmacies, other services—offering fairly homogeneous services, differentiated mainly by their geographic distribution. However, after World War II and more strikingly in the 1975–1985 period, the industry was reshaped by social policy, technology, scarcity of capital resources, and an increased number of physicians as well as health care facilities. It resulted in the emergence of several centralized and well-structured organizations—often with regional or national scope—designed to compete effectively and efficiently with other medical organizations in the marketplace.

Health maintenance organizations (HMOs) represented one of the significant changes occurring in health care. HMOs required a fixed payment for each person enrolled, and delivered comprehensive, coordinated medical services—usually with 100 percent coverage of hospital and physicians' services, including routine physicals. An attractive feature of HMOs was that they offered preventive health care services.

HMOs were priced competitively. They provided no incentive for a physician to institute extra procedures to augment his or her fee, as might occur in the "fee-for-service" cases. Many studies also showed that hospitalization rates were lower for customers of HMOs than for those of private physicians in traditional practice. As cost-consciousness increased, health planners and government payors increasingly endorsed HMOs. The number of HMOs in the United States grew from 39 in 1971 to 431 in 1985, with 16.7 million people enrolled in those 431 HMO plans. However, some consumers resisted joining because HMOs offered a limited choice of physicians and hospitals.

Toward the end of 1985, the health care industry was undergoing further restructuring. An emerging organizational structure involved the linking of doctors, hospitals,

---

[2] Hospital care included all inpatient and outpatient care in public and private hospitals, and all services and supplies provided by hospitals.

[3] Bed-occupancy rate is the percentage of total staffed beds that are actually utilized.

and an insurance plan. These organizations, referred to as "supermeds" or "managed health care systems," offered a full range of vertically integrated services within one structure. For example, Hospital Corporation of America had purchased an insurance company to enable it to develop managed health care systems. Industry experts believed that by 1990 there would be 10 to 20 managed health care systems delivered by very large organizations that operated on a national basis with regional affiliates.

The role of physicians also was beginning to change. Historically, there had been too few doctors for too many patients. Physicians' success depended on their reputation among their peers; they built their practices in a year or two; and information about their medical skills spread by word of mouth from one patient to another and from one doctor to another. In addition, there existed few specialists, and their offices were so crowded that they had trouble catching up with their appointments. As in many professional service organizations, advertising was taboo.

However, all this had changed in the 1980s. The supply of physicians had increased substantially, and there was no dearth of specialists. Major contributing factors were (1) the increase in medical schools (from 79 in 1950 to 126 in 1980) and (2) aid from the government in terms of grants to medical schools and loans to medical students. The number of medical students graduating each year rose from 7,000 in 1960 to 15,000 in 1980. By 1980 the consensus was that there were too many physicians.

Company Background

LifeSpan, Inc., a Minneapolis-based, not-for-profit corporation, was the parent holding company of a diversified health services corporation consisting of three hospital corporations, a nursing home, a major rehabilitation center, two product and equipment corporations, a home health services corporation, and a foundation. It was incorporated in 1982 when Abbott Northwestern Hospital (ANH)—a regional medical center in its 100th year of operation—underwent a corporate restructuring, creating LifeSpan, Inc., as its parent corporation. The primary function of LifeSpan was to direct the overall strategic planning and new business development for members of the LifeSpan family. It also provided its members with support services such as financial planning, marketing, human resource administration, internal audit, management, and information systems.

LifeSpan's long-range goal was to develop a comprehensive regional system of the highest-quality health care services in the Midwest, focusing both on a metropolitan area (Minneapolis/St. Paul) total care network and on referral relationships with physicians and hospitals outside Minneapolis/St. Paul. The operating revenues for LifeSpan and its combined affiliate organizations were $211 million in 1985 (see Exhibit 14.3). LifeSpan's net income increased by over 25 percent to $9.8 million in 1985, from $7.8 million in 1984. This increase in net income was achieved, according to Gordon Sprenger, "through a combination of cost containment and improved productivity further supported by low price increases, all strategically positioned to enhance growing market share." In its most recent debt offering, LifeSpan received an AA credit rating from Standard and Poor. LifeSpan was a founding member of Voluntary Hospitals of America (VHA), a national organization of 650 large hospitals representing 20 percent of the country's inpatient market share. VHA was created to be a national health care delivery system of preeminent institutions; it included organizations such as Johns Hopkins and Massachusetts General Hospital.

Abbott Northwestern Hospital

Abbott Northwestern, an 800-bed hospital in South Minneapolis, was the largest private hospital in Minneapolis/St. Paul (Twin Cities), with a high market share in many key medical services. For example, its share of medical surgeries was 18.8 percent in 1985 (see Exhibit 14.4), yet in its own backyard (South Minneapolis), its share was very low.

Abbott Northwestern had seven "Centers of Excellence"—cardiovascular, neurosciences, rehabilitation (in conjunction with the Sister Kenny Institute, a LifeSpan organization), cancer, perinatal (in conjunction with another LifeSpan hospital, Minneapolis Children's Medical Center), low back, and behavioral medicine. Its cardiovascular program, for example, was unique in that it provided truly comprehensive services, from diagnostics through heart replacement. In 1985, ANH performed nearly 1,000 open-heart surgeries—more than any other hospital in the area. On December 17, 1985, the first woman ever to receive an artificial heart had one (a mini Jarvik 7) implanted at ANH. The cardiovascular program at ANH was viewed as the premier one in the upper Midwest and served portions of the five-state area. This was an important market for ANH, since more than 50 percent of its cardiac patients came from other parts of Minnesota and out of state—primarily Wisconsin.

ANH's patients could be classified into inpatient and outpatient categories. Inpatients were admitted to the hospital by a physician and were resident in one of the hospital's beds. Outpatients used the services of the hospital without being admitted. The latter included both former inpatients who required follow-up treatment and patients referred by their private physicians to have day surgery or laboratory or diagnostic tests performed.

Management

The ANH management philosophy was to render high-quality service with emphasis placed on taking care of the patient's needs. Although a not-for-profit organization, the objective of various policies was twofold: to support the corporation's long-range goal and at the same time maintain strong financial viability (represented by a fair return on equity) to finance appropriate growth of quality health care services. Therefore, in order to assure corporatewide commitment to necessary asset maintenance, enhancement, and expansion, management set key business ratio targets for liquidity, leverage, and profitability. As one executive noted: "While the party line is human service, it is vital that we meet the bottom line."

The management team was young (average age, 34), including the marketing group, which was beginning to have an increasingly high profile within ANH. Richard Kramer, executive vice president of LifeSpan, had received an M.S. degree from Syracuse University and a master's degree in hospital administration from the University of Minnesota. He had been with the organization for 15 years and was very active in developing LifeSpan's hospital mergers, physician joint ventures, and strategic plans. Kramer started the LifeSpan marketing department in 1982. He was involved in various industry associations, and in 1985 was a member of the Government Relations Committee of the Minnesota Hospital Association.

Steven Hillestad, vice president of marketing, had a double master's degree in health administration and public administration from the University of Wisconsin. Hillestad, who had been involved in health care marketing since 1974, had served as executive director of corporate marketing for another hospital in Minneapolis prior to joining LifeSpan in October 1983. Hillestad had published several marketing articles in journals such as *Modern Healthcare* and *Journal of Health Care Marketing.* He also was a co-author of a book entitled *Health Care Marketing Plans: From Strategy to Action.*

The Minneapolis/St. Paul Health Care Market

The health care industry was the largest employer in Minneapolis/St. Paul. In addition, the Twin Cities had one of the most fiercely competitive health care marketplaces in the United States, with as many as 26 hospitals and 6 HMOs. During 1980–1985, HMOs in the metropolitan area had experienced an annual growth rate of 80 percent, reaching a level of 865,000 members. In 1985, HMOs controlled as much as 41 percent of the Twin Cities marketplace, compared with just 11 percent on a national basis.

Industry experts believed that this dominance by HMOs had caused the inpatient market to shrink. During the five-year period 1980–1984, hospital utilization had declined by approximately 29 percent (see Table 14.A).

TABLE 14.A
Twin Cities' Hospital Utilization

Source: LifeSpan, Inc.

Year	Discharges	Inpatient Days	Average Length of Stay (in days)
1980	361,421	2,794,810	7.73
1981	353,220	2,647,065	7.49
1982	343,716	2,486,505	7.23
1983	333,933	2,298,459	6.88
1984	316,695	1,989,466	6.28

As inpatient days declined, many hospitals had lower occupancy rates. Richard Kramer commented on the shrinking market size:

> Some hospitals experienced declines of over 50 percent in the number of inpatient days during the 1980–1985 period. In those hospitals, occupancy was down to less than 50 percent. Many hospitals were under severe financial pressure and "business as usual" was no longer feasible.

To survive with HMOs, hospitals were undertaking cost containment measures and changing practice patterns—shifting more care to an outpatient basis. During 1981–1985, ANH's outpatient surgery volume increased from 13 percent to 44 percent of all surgical procedures performed at the hospital. Hospitals also resorted to using more temporary personnel. For example, full-time permanent professional staff such as nurses were often replaced with part-time employees.

Despite the fact that total admissions and inpatient days were declining, the number of physicians was increasing. The result was a decline in the admissions per physician. In 1985 there was a surplus of doctors in the Twin Cities, and their average income had declined by 25 percent from 1984 to 1985. Consequently, the Twin Cities began witnessing intense rivalry between doctors. Competitive pressures were transforming the industry and pushing hospitals, HMOs, and doctors into a struggle for survival.

The Buying Process

In 1982 ANH management conducted a survey of 1,800 consumers and 400 physicians in the Twin Cities. The survey found that increasingly of late, it was the *patients* who selected which hospital to enter, once the physician decided that hospitalization

TABLE 14.B
Key Decision Maker in Hospital Selection, 1982 Twin Cities Survey (%)

| | Consumers' Views[a] | | | Physicians' Views[b] | |
	Men	Women	Total	Inpatient Stay	Outpatient Surgery
Patient alone	36	26	30	7	7
Patient with doctor	24	28	26	49	38
Subtotal	60	54	56	56	45
Physician alone	37	42	40	40	51
Emergency room	3	4	4	4	4
Subtotal	40	46	44	44	55
Total	100	100	100	100	100

[a] 1,800 consumers.
[b] 400 physicians.

was required. Previously, the patients had depended on their physicians to select the hospital. (Table 14.B presents the summary of the responses to the question, "Who is the key decision maker in hospital selection?")

Various factors were found to influence consumers' hospital choice. Most important among patients with recent hospital experience were proximity to home, quality-related attributes, and presence of a particular physician.

The survey results also indicated that

1. Consumers believed that most hospitals were of good and similar quality, and

2. Consumers had no marked preference for any hospital—with the exception of the University of Minnesota Hospital, which was perceived as the hospital to go to if one was very sick.

With respect to ANH, the survey indicated the following:

* Two out of three consumers did not recognize the name *Abbott Northwestern Hospital.*

* Less than 10 percent of consumers had a clear image of Abbott Northwestern Hospital.

* Approximately 30 percent of ANH's patients came from outside the seven-county metropolitan area.

* Those who had used ANH were very satisfied with their experience.

* Of the consumers that did recognize the name *Abbott Northwestern Hospital,* over 80 percent believed that ANH was located in a part of Minneapolis in which a disproportionately large amount of crime took place.

Marketing at Abbott Northwestern Hospital

The goal of the marketing group at ANH was to increase ANH's market share. To achieve this goal, a three-pronged approach was adopted:

1. Provide potential customers with an incentive to visit the hospital when they were not sick. (The marketing group believed that once consumers had contact with ANH through one of its various programs, they would be so satisfied with the service quality that they would be more likely to use ANH when they needed hospital facilities and services.)

2. Identify potential customers who did not have a physician, and recommend an ANH physician to them. (This would please not only the potential customer, but also the physician, who, it was hoped, would then send the patients to ANH whenever hospital facilities and services were needed.)

3. Ensure that patients were very satisfied with their experience at ANH and that they felt they were treated as individuals. The marketing group believed that patients who had a positive feeling about their experiences at ANH would probably choose ANH again if they needed a hospital. Also, in relating their hospital experiences to relatives and friends, their positive word-of-mouth would help ANH's image.

ANH management believed that this strategy was consistent with the culture at ANH, which encouraged all employees who had contact with customers to exhibit a warm, tender, and caring attitude. For example, patients who arrived at ANH early in the morning for the popular one-day surgery program were received with a warm welcome between 5 A.M. and 7 A.M. by a hospital manager and a senior executive such as Robert Spinner, executive vice president of ANH, and Steve Hillestad, vice president of marketing. Also, free valet parking was introduced, primarily to assist the elderly and those with disabilities. Richard Kramer felt that "all this was a customer orientation never before seen in the health care industry."

To make ANH more attractive to out-of-Minneapolis patients and their families, a 123-room hotel-like facility called Wasie Center was set up in the ANH complex. Accommodations in Wasie Center, though not fancy, were very clean, comfortable, and secure. The center was run on a break-even basis, and rooms for patients and their families were priced at $28–$35 per day. This encouraged nonlocal patients to pick ANH when selecting a hospital in Minneapolis.

Product Management

At ANH each medical service, such as cardiology, radiology, neurology, cancer, chemical dependency, and emergency services, was treated as a "product" or department. ANH management kept a close watch on the progress made by each product. Management felt that while some products (e.g., cardiology) were doing very well, some others (e.g., urology), though profitable, were not receiving adequate attention. To focus attention on products that were profitable but not being given much attention, product management was introduced in May 1985. Five nonphysician product managers were appointed—one for each of the following products: neurology, urology, orthopedics/ rehabilitation, low back, and chemical dependency.

The primary objective of product managers was to increase the market share of their product. They interacted with concerned physicians, made sales calls, talked to patients, worked on special programs to promote the product, and were responsible for pricing. Product managers were evaluated on the basis of their performance with respect to targets, which were set for gross dollar sales as well as number of operative procedures. A product manager's compensation consisted of a base salary (approximately $35,000) and a bonus linked to accomplishment of previously set targets.

Most ANH managers felt that the product management system worked very well. An indication of its success was the large number of requests for product managers received by Hillestad from various departments. For instance, emergency room services wanted a product manager to increase ANH's share of the emergency room business. As one executive put it:

If the emergency room product manager could put together a program directed at neighborhood groups, neighborhood schools, and ambulance drivers, our emergency room business will shoot up and so will our revenues and profitability. For instance, we could have coffee and donuts provided to ambulance drivers and paramedics. This might provide them an incentive to bring patients to the ANH emergency room. After all, for each patient brought into the emergency room we make about $40 on an average revenue of $100.

Some department managers who did not have product managers were upset because they believed that departments with product managers were getting more attention and were also being allotted bigger shares of the marketing budget.

Pricing

ANH's charges for inpatients were typically divided into a daily room-and-board fee and a fixed fee each time an ancillary service was used by the patient. The impact of ANH's fee structure on its financial performance was directly affected by the mix of patients. For inpatients covered under any cost-based reimbursement program, the fee set had little impact on the revenue-generating ability. For self-paying and privately insured consumers, adjustments to the rate structure could produce meaningful changes in revenues and profits.

The continuing implementation of Medicare's Prospective Payment System (PPS) for hospital inpatient services was having a strong effect on hospitals. Under PPS, which became effective on January 1, 1984, payments to hospitals for inpatient services were set in advance by the U.S. Health Care Financing Administration through a system in which a price was fixed for each of 467 different diagnostic-related groups (DRGs). Several DRGs belonged to each of the "products" at ANH. To be more in line with the new reimbursement scheme, ANH changed its pricing policy from cost-plus to product-based. In addition, price competition was becoming very intense (see Table 14.C). ANH management was unsure about the appropriate course of action. As Hillestad said, "We pondered over whether we should continue to price our open-heart surgery at $22,000 and watch competitors [who charged $15,000] gain market share but lose money, or whether we should match the $15,000 price to retain our market share."

Outpatients tended to be more profitable than inpatients because third-party payors reimbursed the hospital for outpatient services on a fee-for-service rather than a cost basis. On an average, the revenue from an outpatient was $200 and the contribution was $85, compared with $6,000 and $700 respectively for an inpatient.

Another area of concern was pricing to HMOs. HMOs controlled access to over 40 percent of the market, and the average number of HMO patients at ANH had risen from 6 percent in 1983 to 26 percent in 1985. To protect its patient base, ANH believed it was necessary to establish contractual relationships with HMOs. However, due to intense competition among Twin Cities hospitals, bidding to HMOs had become very competitive. Besides, margins on HMO business were already lower than on the non-HMO business.

TABLE 14.C
Product Line Pricing

Product	ANH's Cost	ANH's Price	Competitors' Prices
Open-heart surgery	$ 17,000	$ 22,000	$ 15,000
Delivery (1-day)	750	800	na
Delivery (3-day)	1,200	1,400	1,100–1,400
One-day surgery	150–500	200–900	200–900

Distribution

ANH executives believed, as did most health care corporate executives, that physicians were an important part of the hospital distribution system. As Hillestad noted:

> Physicians are our retailers and are critical in getting patients to the hospital. Physicians play a dominant role in determining who should be hospitalized and the type of services that the patient should receive. Physicians influence 70 percent of all personal health care spending. Unfortunately, they view themselves as leaders of the health care team and view business terminology as repugnant. At one meeting, when they [physicians] were referred to as "our customers," two physicians walked out.

Of the 1,125 physicians registered with ANH, approximately 400 were active (an "active" physician being one who brought at least 30 patients a year to the hospital). Most physicians wanted to be active members of a hospital, since this qualified them for policy-making positions, and gave them an opportunity to participate in the hospital's malpractice insurance program. Active physicians accounted for almost 85 percent of ANH's patients.

ANH management took several steps to support its active physicians. One form of support was the physician-referral system, in which ANH referred patients who did not have a regular physician to one of its physicians. To direct referrals appropriately, ANH needed to evaluate its physicians objectively. Physicians were evaluated by peers, administrators, and patients. Some physicians who received high-quality reviews from their peers for their medical practice were not well received by patients because they did not have the best bedside manners. Such physicians were not ANH's best "retailers" in terms of patient satisfaction and the number of patients they brought to ANH.

ANH also initiated a Medical Staff Development Program; in 1984 it helped five groups of physicians (including 31 independent practitioners in downtown Minneapolis) establish full-service suburban clinics in communities with demonstrated needs for primary-care services. Assistance was provided in terms of market research, office site selection, staff to manage the office, and legal advice. Physicians also were provided with innovative solutions to capital financing problems. For example, equipment and ambulatory-care ventures were set up in conjunction with physicians and selected outside investors. More suburban clinics were set up in 1985 through joint ventures with leading Twin Cities physicians.

To strengthen its out-of-town "retail network," ANH took steps to link primary physicians and hospitals in rural areas with tertiary care support, teaching, and consultation whenever they were needed. A 24-hour toll-free phone line was set up in 1985 to link rural physicians and hospitals with ANH's subspecialty physicians.

Communications

Historically, ANH's communications had been directed exclusively at physicians, who were viewed as the ones who brought consumers to the hospital. Since 1982, however, most of ANH's communications were being directed at the end consumer.

In 1982, ANH management took advantage of the hospital's centennial celebration to communicate ANH's name and services to a wider public than had previously been attempted. A wide variety of media (radio, television, newspapers, and billboards) were used to enhance the awareness and image of ANH. Research conducted after the campaign showed a significant increase in ANH's name recognition.

Spurred by this success, ANH management decided in 1983 to launch the first major health care advertising campaign in Minneapolis. The campaign focused on individual "products" such as heart disease, cancer, and prenatal care. Expenditure on communications continued to increase, reaching $405,900 in 1984; all the while, all other departments had budget cuts. Richard Kramer noted, "We need and like to have continuity, hence the regular advertising. It's the reinforcement of repeat messages that impacts consumer behavior."

Specific Programs

Some ANH executives felt that although the 1983 communications program was directed at the end consumer, it did not have a "call-to-action." In addition, they felt that consumers would find it easier to deal with just one telephone number for all concerns, rather than many different numbers for different health inquiries. This led to the creation of "Medformation."

Medformation

Medformation was set up in July 1984 as a community telephone line providing health care information and referrals to various programs, services, and physicians affiliated with ANH. Its objective was to reach consumers directly and to make it easier for them to call ANH for any health need, since the various ANH programs would be consolidated under one system.

Selling Medformation internally had been a very difficult task for the marketing group. Several physicians did not understand or appreciate the benefits of advertising and raised concerns about its high expenditures. They felt that the money could be far better utilized by purchasing new medical equipment. Also, they wondered how the physician referral system would actually work. Many expressed the fear that a few physicians would get most of the referrals while others would get none or, at best, a few. Many physicians were uncomfortable with the perceived loss of control resulting from the hospital trying to bring patients to them instead of the traditional method of physicians getting patients to the hospital. In the words of one physician, "ANH is attempting to increase its control so that it can manipulate the physician."

A major statewide promotional campaign announced Medformation and a single phone number that connected callers to the Medformation staff. Care was taken to make sure that the ads downplayed the link between Medformation and Abbott Northwestern Hospital. Some of the consumers interviewed in a focus group revealed that they were surprised and upset to learn that Medformation was in fact linked with a hospital.

John Penrod, marketing manager responsible for Medformation, had a staff consisting of two information specialists and one registered nurse. Two on-call nurses were available to help out if necessary. Medformation staff were trained to provide the caller with necessary information or to forward the call to the appropriate departmental and medical personnel. Medformation operators were provided with a protocol to follow for each product line or department. After the call, an appropriate follow-up letter and collateral pieces including brochures relating to the appropriate ANH programs were sent to the caller. The fixed cost of Medformation was approximately $175,000.

Early Medformation advertising focused on creating an awareness of Medformation and providing a physician referral service. In addition to all those who called in for a physician referral, almost 10 percent of consumers who called in regarding cancer, medical information, and "other" information also requested a physician referral. Hillestad estimated that 70 percent of consumers who were given a physician referral contacted the physician. Of those who contacted the referred physician, it was believed that approximately 25 percent would return within a year to the hospital (10 percent as inpatients, 10 percent as outpatients, and 5 percent in the emergency room), and that 20 percent would return during the following year (5 percent as inpatients, 10 percent as outpatients, and 5 percent in the emergency room).

In 1985 the focus of Medformation was extended to cover various other ANH programs such as weight loss, stress management, natural fitness, heart seminars, and quit-smoking. Many who called regarding these programs actually attended the programs. For example, almost 60 percent of those who called regarding weight loss and quit-smoking attended these programs. The fee was $100–$200 and gave ANH a contribution of approximately 60 percent. In many of these programs, participants were told that they should check with their physicians before adopting the recommended approach. Participants who indicated that they did not have a physician (approximately 10 percent) were referred to one of ANH's physicians.

Medformation was advertised in the two leading local newspapers; 90 percent of the insertions were quarter-page ads on weekdays and cost $700 per insertion (see Exhibit 14.5). The rest were full-page ads in the Sunday edition and cost $7,000 per insertion. Hillestad believed that the higher response to the Sunday ads justified the higher cost. In 1985 a total of 28,667 Medformation calls were received, with the heaviest response on the day of the ad insertion, only slightly lower response on the following day, followed by a sharp drop. (Exhibit 14.6 shows a breakdown of the Medformation ads and calls received in 1985.) The overall response to Medformation ads in terms of telephone calls had far exceeded management's expectations.

Commenting on Medformation, Penrod noted that "Medformation has been a phenomenal success. We have had a big increase in calls, and our research has shown a sharp improvement in consumer perception [see Exhibit 14.7]. We are delighted with this." Hillestad and Penrod were contemplating extending Medformation to cover outbound telemarketing as well (i.e., to have Medformation operators call people at their homes to promote specific programs), but were not sure how effective this would be. Hillestad felt that first they needed to evaluate in a better way the effectiveness of the existing Medformation programs (i.e., inbound) before pushing for extension to outbound.

Hillestad was surprised when on December 20, 1985, he received a call from the marketing director of a New York hospital who wanted to buy the 36 ads used by ANH for $100,000. He also was willing to pay ANH an additional $20,000 to learn which one of the two Medformation cancer ads worked better. Hillestad turned down that offer, but began seriously contemplating putting together a package of the ads, including information on the ads' relative effectiveness, and selling the package to hospitals on a national basis.

ANH management also considered licensing Medformation to hospitals in the non-metro areas of Minnesota and western Wisconsin. Under this arrangement, ANH would license the Medformation name and telephone number to a hospital in exchange for some predetermined minimum number of referrals of complicated illnesses.

WomenCare

WomenCare was a program developed by ANH, who recognized that women had a variety of specialized health care needs that went beyond obstetrics/gynecology services. The program provided a total range of services for women seeking wellness, fitness, weight control, aging, and behavioral and reproductive guidance. It encouraged women to play a more active role in their health care by becoming better informed through WomenCare seminars and classes.

WomenCare was inaugurated on March 25, 1985, by Women's Day—a day-long event that focused on the special health care needs of women. The response was outstanding; over 2,500 women attended, paying $100 each. Throughout the year,

WomenCare continued to provide the community with timely seminars on various subjects. It also helped develop breast cancer diagnostic and osteoporosis prevention programs. During the year there were 12 such programs and the average attendance was 120 people. The fee for these programs ranged from $100 to $200 each, and the contribution was 60 percent.

ANH management was surprised at the response that WomenCare programs had received. For example, a weight loss program for women, advertised under Women-Care, filled up much faster than a general weight loss program—despite the fact that over 80 percent of those who attended the general weight loss program were women and that the fee was $120 compared with $100 for the general class. (Exhibit 14.8 shows an ad used for WomenCare.)

Other Programs

To meet the needs of a society that had become far more fitness oriented, ANH offered a number of other programs—community courses in weight loss, quit-smoking, and stress management. Each course was presented by trained professionals who emphasized behavior modification.

Keeping elderly people independent was another important part of LifeSpan's philosophy of care. In October 1985 ANH organized "Seniors' Day"—a free event that included sessions on topics such as facing the crisis of illness, managing urinary incontinence, and staying in charge of life. Over 450 people attended. Wellness programs for the elderly on topics such as diabetes, medication, and exercise were offered as well.

Current Situation

In 1986 ANH's communications strategies were to broaden reach for maximum penetration of health care buyers, enlarge and reinforce the centers of excellence among consumers and physicians, and integrate the Medformation and WomenCare programs more fully with the Abbott Northwestern campaign. Projected media advertising expenditures, summarized in Exhibit 14.9, emphasized television and newspapers with support from radio and posters. The mix for television advertising was the same for all "products"—40 percent prime time, 30 percent news, 20 percent fringe, and 10 percent daytime.

For Medformation, television would be used in addition to newspapers. In South Minneapolis, to increase emphasis, eight outdoor posters per month would be used for four months. It was estimated that over the four-month period, approximately 74 percent of adults in South Minneapolis would be exposed to the posters an average of 15 times each.

In order to increase consumer reach and build awareness of the WomenCare program, a broader range of media was planned. In addition to quarter-page newspaper ads, outdoor posters would be used to carry a WomenCare-image program, and 60-second radio spots would promote special events such as Women's Day, Spring Seminar, and Fall Seminar.

Advertising for tertiary care was aimed at adults ages 18 and above. A multimedia campaign using television and newspapers was planned. Television would be used for a total of 14 weeks with 80 GRPs per week.[4] Newspapers would carry 17 full-page ads.

---

[4] Gross rating points (GRPs): a combined measure of reach (number of people exposed) and frequency (number of exposures per person reached) for advertising weight.

The Decision

Steve Hillestad had a little over 16 hours to think about the next morning's presentation to the ANH board. As he scanned his papers, he focused on two main issues. First, he was convinced that marketing contributed significantly to LifeSpan's 1985 performance. Sales and market share had increased and consumer perceptions of ANH had improved. Hillestad wondered how he could measure the sales response to ANH's marketing activities—especially Medformation—in a manner he and the board would find credible. Second, if the budget was approved, he wondered how he might justify the allocation of resources to the different products and programs.

EXHIBIT 14.1
National Health Care Expenses and Gross National Product

Source: Office of Statistics and Data Management, Health Care Financing Administration.

	Gross National Product ($ billions)	National Health Expenditure	
		($ billions)	(% of GNP)
1955	$ 400.0	$ 17.7	4.4%
1965	705.1	41.9	5.9
1970	1,015.5	75.0	7.4
1975	1,598.4	132.7	8.3
1980	2,731.9	248.1	9.1
1981	3,052.6	287.0	9.4
1982	3,166.0	323.6	10.2
1983	3,401.6	357.2	10.5
1984	3,774.7	390.2	10.3
1985	3,988.5	425.0	10.7

EXHIBIT 14.2 Health Care Expenditures

Source: Office of Statistics and Data Management, Health Care Financing Administration.

I. Financing of Personal Health Care, 1950–1985 (%)

Year	Public			Private	Total Third Party	Patient Direct Payments	Total
	Federal	State and Local	Total				
1950	10.4%	12.0%	22.4%	12.1%	34.5%	65.5%	100%
1955	10.5	12.5	23.0	18.9	41.9	58.1	100
1960	9.3	12.5	21.8	23.4	45.2	54.8	100
1965	10.1	11.9	22.0	26.4	48.4	51.6	100
1970	22.2	12.1	34.3	25.2	59.5	40.5	100
1975	26.8	12.7	39.5	28.0	67.5	32.5	100
1980	28.5	11.0	39.5	31.9	71.4	28.6	100
1985	30.3	9.4	39.7	31.9	71.6	28.4	100

II. Sources of Funds in 1985 ($ billions)

	Total Personal Health Care	Hospital Care	Physi-cians' Services	Dentists' Services	Other Profes-sional Services	Drugs and Sundries	Eye-glasses and Appliances	Nursing Home Care	Other Health Care
Total (in billions)	$371.4	$166.7	$82.8	$27.1	$12.6	$28.5	$7.5	$35.2	$11.0
Direct patient payments	105.6	15.5	21.8	17.3	6.0	21.8	5.1	18.1	—
Third parties	265.8	151.2	61.0	9.8	6.6	6.7	2.4	17.1	11.0
Private health insurance	113.5	59.3	36.9	9.2	2.9	4.0	0.9	0.3	—
Other private sources	4.9	2.1	0.0	—	0.1	—	—	0.3	2.4
Government	147.4	89.8	24.1	0.6	3.6	2.7	1.5	16.5	8.6
Federal	112.6	71.6	19.7	0.3	2.8	1.4	1.3	9.4	6.0
Medicare	70.5	48.5	17.1	—	2.0	—	1.2	0.6	1.1
Medicaid	21.9	8.1	1.9	0.3	0.7	1.3	—	8.1	1.5
Other programs	20.2	15.0	0.7	0.0	0.1	0.1	0.1	0.7	3.4
State and local	34.9	18.2	4.4	0.3	0.8	1.3	0.2	7.1	2.6
Medicaid	17.9	6.8	1.5	0.2	0.6	1.0	—	6.6	1.2
Other programs	17.0	11.4	2.9	0.1	0.2	0.3	0.2	0.5	1.4

EXHIBIT 14.3
Income Statement and Change in Operating Fund Equity ($000)

Source: LifeSpan, Inc.

	1985	1984	1983
Total net revenue	$211,457	$149,941	$135,316
Operating expenses			
Salaries	118,083	103,352	92,650
Supplies and other expenses	68,071	28,716	28,121
Depreciation	12,118	8,087	7,177
Interest	6,973	5,523	4,850
Total operating expense	205,245	145,678	132,798
Operating margin	6,212	4,263	2,518
Total other revenue (expense)	3,588	3,583	2,336
Net income (loss)	9,800	7,846	4,854
Operating fund equity at beginning of year	56,232	47,323	42,154
Transfers from restricted funds for purchase of plant assets	0	0	315
Fund equity of new affiliates	19,691	1,063	0
Operating fund equity at end of year	85,723	56,232	47,323

EXHIBIT 14.4
Health Care Industry in Minneapolis

Source: Metropolitan Health Board (January–June 1985).

	Number of Staffed Beds[a]	Bed Occupancy	Market Shares (M.S.)[b]		
			1984	1985	(Expected) 1986
Abbott Northwestern	705	71.2	17.2%	18.8%	20.5%
South Parkway	372	71.1	12.2	12.7	12.7
Presbyterian	333	68.3	13.8	13.3	12.7
Lawrence Memorial	506	57.3	12.1	11.6	11.1
Glenbrook General	396	55.6	10.8	10.2	10.9
Glenbrook Memorial	488	68.2	7.5	7.6	8.3
Glenbrook Wilson	103	47.8	—	1.9	1.9
St. Agnes	376	71.6	8.2	5.5	4.5
Trinity	223	62.6	6.9	7.4	6.5
Mt. Carmel	160	59.8	6.4	6.0	6.2
Emerson	259	60.7	4.9	5.0	4.7

[a] A staffed bed is one that is operational and available for use by patients.
[b] M.S.: Medical Surgical.

EXHIBIT 14.5
Quarter-Page
Newspaper Ad

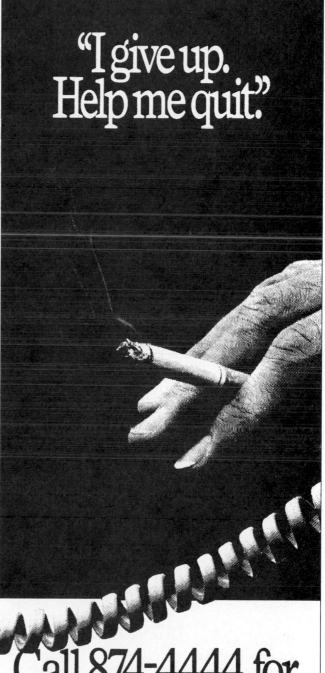

If you really want to quit smoking, before you pick up your next cigarette, pick up the phone and call Medformation.

Find out about the Quit Smoking Program that works. It has an 80% success rate for those difficult first 2 months.

It's a professional program — developed by Abbott Northwestern Hospital, and led by psychologists and other health professionals. Best of all, the program takes only 3 weeks to complete.

The next classes begin *January 15th* at Northland Executive Center in Bloomington and *February 5th* at Abbott Northwestern.

For more information on becoming a non-smoker, or for the answer to any health question, call Medformation.

"I give up. Help me quit."

Call 874-4444 for Medformation.

One of the loving arms of Abbott Northwestern Hospital

EXHIBIT 14.6   Medformation Ads and Responses, 1985

Source: LifeSpan, Inc.

	Weight Loss		Quit Smoking		Physician Referral		Cancer		Medical Information		Others		Total	
	Ads	Calls	Ads	Calls	Ads	Calls	Ads	Calls	Ads	Calls	Ads	Calls	Ads	Calls
January	3	113	4	124	5	119	–	0	–	205	12	1,965	24	2,526
February	2	98	3	118	3	126	–	0	–	181	10	1,745	18	2,268
March	3	147	–	18	2	163	–	0	–	176	10	1,667	15	2,171
April	3	115	3	123	6	261	7	240	–	229	4	1,829	23	2,797
May	–	19	1	53	5	202	2	81	4	256	8	1,767	20	2,378
June	–	33	1	44	6	195	2	61	4	235	12	1,577	25	2,145
July	2	66	2	49	7	265	3	1,087	1	257	4	1,444	19	3,168
August	1	46	2	53	2	218	2	1,414	–	250	5	1,378	12	3,359
September	1	26	2	21	6	220	–	57	–	260	6	1,379	15	1,963
October	–	6	2	25	5	263	–	31	3	344	4	1,393	14	2,062
November	–	9	2	21	3	160	–	3	3	240	6	1,253	14	1,686
December	–	15	–	6	2	146	–	0	–	197	4	1,780	6	2,144
Total	15	693	22	655	52	2,338	16	2,974	15	2,830	85	19,177	205	28,667

EXHIBIT 14.7   Consumer Perception of Which Hospital Provides the Best Medical Care, 1984 and 1985

Source: LifeSpan, Inc.

	Serious Heart Problems		Stroke		Severe Pregnancy Problems		Chemical Dependency		Emergency	
	1984	1985	1984	1985	1984	1985	1984	1985	1984	1985
Abbott Northwestern	13.7%[a]	26.1%	12.0%	15.7%	13.7%	10.9%	5.6%	7.0%	4.7%	5.7%
South Parkway	3.0	6.1	4.7	5.7	2.1	3.5	0.4	0.9	7.3	12.2
Presbyterian	3.8	2.2	4.3	3.0	3.8	3.0	0.9	1.3	6.0	6.5
Lawrence Memorial	4.7	4.8	5.1	3.0	1.7	0.0	3.4	2.2	9.0	11.3
Glenbrook General	3.4	1.7	6.0	3.0	4.3	2.6	0.9	0.4	11.5	8.7
Glenbrook Memorial	0.4	0.4	0.4	0.0	0.4	0.0	0.9	0.9	0.4	0.0
Glenbrook Wilson	1.3	0.4	0.9	0.4	1.7	0.4	0.4	0.4	0.9	0.4
St. Agnes	0.4	2.2	1.3	2.6	5.1	3.5	42.5	38.8	0.0	0.0
University of Minnesota	28.2	26.0	16.7	12.6	9.8	7.0	3.0	0.9	2.1	2.2
Others	10.7	7.7	7.7	4.8	8.2	3.9	16.3	13.8	31.7	25.2
All the same	1.7	0.4	0.9	3.9	1.2	2.6	1.3	1.3	1.7	2.6
Don't know	28.7	22.0	40.0	45.3	48.0	62.6	24.4	32.1	24.7	25.2
Total	100.0%	100.0%	100.0%	100.0%	100.0%	100.0%	100.0%	100.0%	100.0%	100.0%

[a] 13.7 percent of consumers surveyed perceived that Abbott Northwestern Hospital provided the best medical care for serious heart problems.

EXHIBIT 14.8
Ad for WomenCare
Health Care Program

WEIGHT CONTROL: IT'S A JOB WHERE WOMEN HAVE TO WORK HARDER THAN MEN.

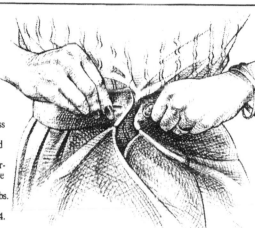

It's something women have suspected for a long time. But, until recently, no one really understood why women have a more difficult time losing and keeping weight off.

There is a physiological reason. Most women have a higher percentage of body fat while most men have more muscles. Since fat is metabolically less active than muscle, women end up burning fewer calories

WomenCare's Lifestyle Weight Loss program focuses on these differences. This is a women's weight loss program. It's not a diet. It's a program that gives you the facts, motivation and the emotional support you need to help you control your weight…for good. There are Fitness Specialists who work with you to develop an exercise program that will reduce body fat and increase muscle mass, the key to burning more calories. How successful is this program? The average weight loss is more than 20 lbs. And, it's weight most of the people keep off for years.

For more information call Medformation 874-4444.

© 1985 LifeSpan, Inc.

WOMENCARE℠
of Abbott Northwestern Hospital ✚

EXHIBIT 14.9   **Media Split of Communications Budget (in dollars)**

Source: LifeSpan, Inc.

		1985			1986		
		Prod.	Media	Total	Prod.	Media	Total
Medformation	TV	—	—	—	$ 79,000	$278,600	$ 357,600
	Newspaper	$ 24,000	$270,000	$294,000	9,500	98,100	107,600
	Posters	—	—	—	16,500	60,500	77,000
		24,000	270,000	294,000	105,000	437,200	542,200
Tertiary Care	TV	64,000	164,000	228,000	108,000	217,350	325,350
	Newspaper	—	—	—	33,600	131,650	165,250
		64,000	164,000	228,000	141,600	349,000	490,600
WomenCare	TV	—	—	—	30,000	57,850	87,850
	Newspaper	35,000	131,400	166,400	9,600	64,850	74,450
	Posters	—	—	—	5,000	10,400	15,400
	Radio	—	—	—	4,500	34,900	39,400
		35,000	131,400	166,400	49,100	168,000	217,100
Trade	Magazine	10,400	17,700	28,100	—	—	—
	TV	64,000	164,100	228,100	217,000	553,800	770,800
	Radio	—	—	—	4,500	34,900	39,400
	Newspaper	59,000	401,400	460,400	52,700	294,600	347,300
	Posters	—	—	—	21,500	70,900	92,400
Total		$133,400	$583,200	$716,600	$295,700	$954,200	$1,249,900

15

Population Services International

V. Kasturi Rangan

The Social Marketing Project in Bangladesh

Population Services International (PSI) was a not-for-profit agency founded in 1970 to help control the population explosion in many less-developed countries through the dissemination of family planning information and products. In 1976, PSI concluded an agreement with the government of Bangladesh to carry out the Social Marketing Project (SMP), a program involving the marketing of birth control products through local retail outlets. The SMP marketed two products: Raja brand condoms and Maya brand oral contraceptives.

Late in 1983, Philip Harvey (PSI's founder), Robert Ciszewski (PSI's executive director), and William Schellstede (project advisor for the SMP) met at PSI headquarters in Washington, D.C., to discuss 1984–86 marketing plans for the SMP. Of particular concern was the fact that while Raja sales had increased steadily over the past six years to 50.4 million pieces in 1983, Maya sales had declined from a high of 1.1 million cycles[1] in 1980 to 0.62 million in 1983 (see Exhibit 15.1). Both products, however, had been promoted with similar marketing strategies. The approach was to reach the consumer directly through an intensive mass media campaign backed by extensive product availability through Bangladesh's widely dispersed retail store network. Harvey explained the discrepancy in sales results:

[1] A cycle was a package of 28 pills.

Professor V. Kasturi Rangan prepared this case as the basis for class discussion rather than to illustrate either effective or ineffective handling of an administrative situation.

Copyright © 1985 by the President and Fellows of Harvard College. To order copies or request permission to reproduce materials, call 1-800-545-7685 or write Harvard Business School Publishing, Boston, MA 02163. No part of this publication may be reproduced, stored in a retrieval system, used in a spreadsheet, or transmitted in any form or by any means—electronic, mechanical, photocopying, recording, or otherwise—without the permission of Harvard Business School.

Our goal was to reach the largest number of people possible. We knew most of them were illiterate and did not have access to professional doctors or pharmacies. We built our entire program on two basic principles: motivate the consumer and motivate the trade. Many people were worried that our aggressive approach would desensitize a sensitive product category and take away the seriousness of family planning. On the contrary, we wanted to motivate the husband and wife to seriously and frankly discuss family planning with each other. What we achieved was a stunning success for Raja but a failure for Maya. People associate condoms with sex, but a pill is associated with birth control; people think of a condom as an over-the-counter consumer product, while a pill is perceived as a powerful drug. If anything, our marketing approach should have helped Maya more than Raja.

Population Services International

Philip Harvey and Timothy Black were graduate students at the University of North Carolina's Public Health Program when they founded PSI in 1970. Mr. Harvey had earlier worked for CARE (a not-for-profit American agency involved in relief and development) in India for five years. Dr. Black had practiced medicine in Australia and New Guinea, specializing in family planning and midwife training. PSI was set up as a not-for-profit agency with the fundamental objective of "disseminating family planning information and marketing birth control products to people who needed to avert births but did not know where to seek the information or products."

Though their first project concerned the prevention of unwanted teenage pregnancies in the United States, the population explosion in the less-developed countries was the prime motivation for the founding of PSI. Harvey argued that family planning had too long been the domain of medical people, when in fact he saw the situation as a "selling or marketing job in which modern, effective marketing techniques would supplement scarce medical skills." Harvey reasoned that none of the poorer countries in the world had enough medical personnel to treat the many diseases that afflicted their people. He predicted that a diversion of these scarce resources to birth control would never work. On the other hand, "if contraceptive products such as pills and condoms are made the leading vehicles of family planning," Harvey believed, "the entire society would be better off."

As a matter of policy, PSI did not involve itself in marketing clinical methods of birth control, such as intra-uterine devices (IUDs) or male or female sterilizations. PSI's managers described their business mission as follows:

> We are here to create the climate in which socially desirable products become a part of the daily life of the marketplace. We would like to assure their distribution in an efficient fashion so that their availability becomes routine and expected. The fundamental purpose is to facilitate the exchange between the buyer and the seller so that the transaction is fruitful for both. The person who practices family planning with contraceptives purchased in a social marketing program is not a patient or client nor a recipient or acceptor. He or she is a consumer making a careful and prudent choice among the many options available in the marketplace.

In 1973, PSI won a contract to initiate and implement a contraceptive marketing program in Sri Lanka. During the next five years, it received contracts to manage similar projects in Bangladesh and Mexico. For various political reasons, PSI's involvement in the Mexican program was short-lived, but the Sri Lankan program was considered a tremendous success, especially with respect to condom marketing. In 1976, Family Planning Association of Sri Lanka took over program management from PSI, leaving Bangladesh as PSI's only active program.

PSI was headquartered in Washington, D.C., and had a total of six persons on its staff including managerial personnel. Of the original founders, Philip Harvey continued as a member of the board. He did not involve himself in day-to-day operations, but was always active in strategy meetings. Timothy Black had resigned to set up a not-for-profit family planning organization in Ireland. Robert Ciszewski joined PSI as project advisor on the Bangladesh project and now was the executive director at headquarters, handling most of the day-to-day affairs of the company. Ciszewski's successor in Bangladesh was fired for "poor sales performance" after a brief stint on the job. William Schellstede was the current project advisor.

The Social Marketing Project (SMP)

PSI finalized an agreement with the government of Bangladesh in 1976 to carry out a program of family planning through social marketing. The objective was to use modern marketing techniques to sell subsidized contraceptives through commercial outlets. The agreement also defined the organizational structure and management process for the social marketing project. Policy guidelines were to be provided by a project council consisting of a chairman and eight other members. The chairman was the Secretary for Health and Population Control for the Bangladesh government. The government nominated four more members to the council. Three members of the council were from PSI, USAID (United States Agency for International Development), and UNFPA (United Nations Fund for Population Activities). The ultimate authority and responsibility for project implementation was in the hands of a general manager, who was appointed by the project council upon nomination by PSI. The general manager was a Bangladeshi national and the ninth member of the council. He was responsible for implementing strategy through a national sales manager who had a network of eight sales offices. In all, about 300 people reported to the general manager. Exhibit 15.2 gives a brief overview of the organizational structure for the Social Marketing Project.

In terms of policy making, the three key constituents were the Bangladesh government, USAID, and PSI. A brief description of their roles follows.

Bangladesh Government

The Bangladesh government was actively involved in population control efforts both directly, through its various programs, and indirectly, through projects such as the SMP. Bangladesh, with a land area of 55,598 square miles (approximately the size of Wisconsin), a population of about 100 million, and a per-capita income of $120/ annum, was one of the poorest countries in the world. With its GNP expected to grow at 3 to 4 percent, the government did not expect any near-term improvement in the standard of living for its people. Further, with an annual population growth rate of 2.4 percent, its population was expected to exceed that of the entire United States of America by the year 2025. Since the economic and social consequences of such a scenario were devastating, the government of Bangladesh had set for itself the goal of achieving zero population growth by 1995. At the same time, since 85 percent of its population were conservative Muslims,[2] the government had to consider their religious sentiments. The government closely monitored all aspects of all family planning

---

[2] Muslims practiced the religion of Islam. Koran was their holy book. Though several Islamic scholars argued that Koran did not take a stand on family planning, many mullahs (holy priests) of Bangladesh believed that family planning was an act against the will of God.

programs. It reserved the right to restrict any aspect of any program that it thought was sensitive. The government's role, then, was to encourage and promote, but closely supervise, family planning activity.

USAID

USAID was an American agency involved in social and economic development activities in many less-developed countries (LDCs). USAID funded family planning programs in nine other LDCs. It funded almost the entire cost of the SMP in Bangladesh. It donated the contraceptives, paid PSI a managing agency fee, and subsidized a large part of the SMP's operating expenses in Bangladesh. The 1983 profit and loss statement for the social marketing project is shown in Exhibit 15.3.

PSI

PSI was primarily responsible for devising marketing strategies, getting them approved by the project council, and implementing them through the general manager. William Schellstede, project advisor, was located in Dhaka (Bangladesh) and managed PSI's relationship with the project council and the general manager. Robert Ciszewski, executive director, had been project advisor before he moved to Washington to manage the relationship with USAID. Both Ciszewski and Schellstede had had extensive management experience with development projects in LDCs before joining PSI. PSI's relationship with the Bangladesh government was excellent; very few foreign agencies enjoyed the respect and rapport of PSI. Ciszewski had taken tremendous care to understand, empathize, and work with the government bureaucracy and its officials. He described PSI's role:

> It's difficult and trying at times. Phil, Bill, and I, as well as our other colleagues, are in this for the fun of it. We get a great deal of personal fulfillment in being able to promote a social good but, let me tell you, managing this project is awfully tricky. We don't control the project council or the marketing organization, yet we are responsible for devising a strategy and implementing it. We don't have any funds of our own. We are a small team at PSI, and we barely survive year after year. Frankly, it's not my salary that I worry about; it is the lack of funds for implementing new strategy. It's amazing how long and how hard we have to lobby with the members of the council and with USAID before we make any headway. Luckily, the general manager is our nominee; we see eye to eye on many issues. If we have an approved and implementable strategy, we are pretty much able to execute it.

Country Background

Bangladesh was a river delta located on the Bay of Bengal in Asia (see Exhibit 15.4). The scarce resources of this already poor country were further threatened by the unabated growth of its population. There were 20 million couples in the fertile age group; these were the prime targets of family planning programs. Though the notion of family planning had the full backing of the country's government, certain characteristics of the local environment made it challenging for the SMP to design its marketing strategy. Some of these factors were

1. *Culture and attitudes.* A large majority of the country's people lived in the villages; only 9 percent lived in the cities. The literacy rate was about 27 percent among males and 12 percent among females.

   In a national survey, only 6 percent of the respondents cited religion as the primary reason for not adopting family planning practices. Simple ignorance of birth control methods and products was one reason for large families, while other reasons were linked to family economics and culture. Bangladesh did not have a system of social security or state pensions for its elderly; parents therefore depended on their sons for their future security. Epidemics and natural calamities such as monsoon floods and tidal waves claimed as many as 100,000 lives each year; hence, families thought it prudent to have more than one son. Since daughters went away to the husband's family after marriage, parents could not rely on them for financial support in their old age. On the contrary, the custom of providing a dowry (a sum of money) to the bridegroom's parents at the wedding made it economically sensible to have at least as many sons as daughters.

In a survey conducted by the SMP (see Exhibit 15.5), many individuals appeared to comprehend the economic benefits of a small family. However, in personal interviews they expressed a confusion as to where the line was to be drawn between personal welfare and social welfare. The SMP survey also highlighted a higher awareness of family planning among urban dwellers, and certain differences in the perceptions of men versus women.

2. *Buying/selling process.* Even though Bangladesh's economy was modeled on a central planning system, distribution and marketing were left entirely to the marketplace forces of supply and demand. An overwhelming bulk of life's necessities were bought and paid for in the market, and at prices the market demanded. About 20 tributaries of two major rivers crisscrossed the length and breadth of Bangladesh, making transportation and travel extremely difficult. As a consequence, an intense network of local retail outlets had developed. Most of the retail trade in Bangladesh was owned by small-scale entrepreneurs. They were financed by their wholesalers but conducted their sales on strict cash terms. Working capital was a constant problem and most retailers preferred quick inventory turns to high margins.

In 1983, birth control contraceptives were sold in Bangladesh through a network of 30,000 pharmacies, 40,000 general stores (about half of which were grocery stores), and 30,000 "pan" stores.

Pharmacies usually were located in urban areas. They typically were 300 to 400 sq. ft. in area, and sold a wide assortment of pharmaceuticals, drugs, and indigenous medicinal preparations. Most of the items (including birth control pills) did not require a doctor's prescription. The consumer usually went to the sales counter and asked for a product by name or described the general nature of the ailment. The salesperson then would suggest an appropriate product or brand. After the consumer had made a decision, the salesperson went to the store shelves to fill the order. Consumers were not allowed to select the products off the shelves.

General stores typically were small, although some larger ones existed in the cities. A large majority of the general stores were family-owned businesses. Not more than three or four individuals operated the store (including the owner). Most of the stores were independent operations, not part of a chain. A typical store was approximately 400 to 500 sq. ft. in area and carried about 50 to 100 product items. All product items were assembled, measured, and bagged by the store personnel on order. As with the pharmacies, consumers were rarely, if ever, allowed into the shelf areas.

Pan stores were smaller versions of the general store, carrying soft drinks, cigarettes, aspirin, and other convenience items. In total, they carried about 25 to 30 product items. Most of the pan stores were small and located in rural areas. One of the many fast-moving items sold by these stores was pan, which was an assortment of special spices and a specially prepared paste of calcium wrapped with a betel leaf. Among men in Bangladesh, consumption of pan was a habit as strong as, if not stronger than, drinking tea or smoking cigarettes. Other major sales items were cigarettes (often loose) and sundry items such as aspirin, cookies, candy, local brands of soft drink, and local newspapers.

Pan stores operated out of temporary enclosures at street corners or other busy locations. They were typically 20 to 40 sq. ft. in area and operated by one person. The store person, who generally was the owner, sat behind the sales counter and deftly made pans to individual order, mixing and matching the right amount and variety of spices. Men gathered around pan stores to take a break from their routine. They exchanged news and information to the tunes of music that blared out of a radio in the store. Pan stores served as a convenient socializing spot for men. Women preferred to make and consume pan in the privacy of their homes. Unlike the pharmacies and the general stores, the pan stores were open until late at night.

3. *Medical care system.* Bangladesh was serviced by 125,000 doctors, only about 5,000 of whom had formal medical education. These 5,000 doctors had graduate degrees in Western, or "allopathic," medicine. Most of these doctors had excellent credentials, spoke fluent English, and practiced and lived in urban areas.

   In addition to Western-trained physicians operating in cities, there were about 20,000 spiritual doctors who practiced mainly in the villages. Their approach to patient care was quite unscientific, but nonetheless valued by their patients. They wrote secret formulas, uttered special hymns, and claimed to invoke the power of God in treatment of illnesses.

   The rest of the country's 100,000 doctors were rural medical practitioners (RMPs). They practiced medicine in many parts of the country, but particularly in the rural areas. Their approach to medicine was a blend of modern and traditional methods. They were not trained in Western medicine and usually did not speak English, but they kept in touch with professional doctors and hospitals through a system of patient referrals. They had a working knowledge of common illnesses and drugs mainly through association with professional doctors whom they respected. RMPs dispensed either indigenous medications or allopathic drugs, depending on their diagnosis. They operated a few hours every day out of their offices; the rest of the time they made extensive house calls. RMPs participated in village community activities, and were respected and regarded as friend, philosopher, and guide by many village people. They did not charge a fee for consultation. However, patients were expected to buy medications from them. Many of them carried a general assortment of medicines in a travel kit. Payment terms were flexible and generally accepted over a number of installments, depending on the patient's financial capability.

   In addition to the 125,000 doctors, there were about 25,000 field workers in Bangladesh. They disseminated information on family planning through hospitals, dispensaries, and shopping locations. These workers were educated and literate, and received compensation from the government or the social welfare agency that employed them. They were not professional doctors, but they were well-trained and motivated to communicate the social and economic benefits of family planning.

Family Planning Activity in Bangladesh

The government of Bangladesh coordinated all family planning activity. The government had no financial involvement in any program except its own. Family planning communication and products were delivered to the people through four distinct programs.

1. The government used the country's *hospitals, clinics, and dispensaries* to promote the message of family planning mainly through a network of nearly 20,000 field workers. The network was fairly evenly spread throughout the country. The social workers also distributed free condoms and contraceptive pills. The government received its supply of contraceptives as a donation from USAID. The government provided incentives for the country's 5,000 trained doctors to perform clinical birth control procedures. Cash incentives were also provided to the field workers and consumers. Every sterilization procedure or IUD insertion was fully subsidized by the government. The direct costs of a clinical procedure were estimated to be about $5, and the cost of incentives to field workers and reimbursement to consumers about $10.

2. Various *volunteer organizations* in the country sponsored education and communication programs on family planning and birth control. There were a number of such volunteer agencies in the country, with a total of about 5,000 field workers involved. They promoted family planning themes and benefits, and referred interested couples to the appropriate medical facility. Some organizations procured contraceptives from government or private sources and distributed them to the public free of cost.

3. There were a number of *privately held pharmaceutical firms* that marketed their own brand of oral contraceptive pills. A number of them had licensing arrangements and collaborations with pharmaceutical firms in Europe and the United States. These companies sold their products mainly through the pharmacies. Their sales forces called on professional doctors, and made systematic presentations on product benefits. Though prescriptions were not necessarily required to buy oral contraceptives, professional doctors wrote prescriptions or advised their clients to use specific brands.

4. The fourth program was *PSI's social marketing project,* started in late 1977 to promote Raja brand of condoms and Maya brand of oral contraceptive pills.

Marketing Strategy for Raja and Maya

The brand name Raja was chosen for two reasons. First, "Raja" in Bengali meant a king or an emperor. PSI's experience in Sri Lanka had indicated the need for creating a positive and relaxed attitude for family planning. People in general did not respond well to messages that highlighted the negative consequences of a large family. A king was associated with masculinity, bravery, and power. Raja, therefore, had a number of positive connotations. The other advantage of choosing Raja as a brand name was its wide recognition. One of the popular recreational pastimes for men in Bangladesh was playing cards. Terms related to card games had high recognition among men; Bengali equivalents of King, Queen, and Jack were easily recognized. Moreover, the high level of illiteracy made it necessary to choose a brand name that could be understood pictorially. Raja appeared to fit the requirements rather well. The only other widely distributed condom in the market was the Bangladesh government's Tahiti brand of condoms. Tahiti was donated to the government by USAID. A third brand of condoms, Sultan, was marketed by a private trader. This brand was not widely distributed. Sultan meant king in Arabic.

"Maya," in Bengali, literally meant magic, but the cultural translation was much more positive; people commonly interpreted Maya to mean beauty. The basic idea, once again, was to create a positive feeling and a sense of optimism about the product.

Maya was only one of two brands that had a Bengali brand name.[3] The other important brands on the market were named Ovastat, Lyndiol, Ovral, and Nordette. The Bangladesh government's pill, which was donated by USAID, had no brand name. In 1983, the total market for family planning products was roughly divided as follows:

1. Condoms (million pieces)
   a. Raja   50.0
   b. Tahiti   25.0
   c. Sultan   5.0
   d. Durex   3.0
   e. Others   2.0
        Total   85.0

2. Pills (million cycles)
   a. Bangladesh government   3.0
   b. Ovastat   2.0
   c. Lyndiol, Ovral, and Nordette   2.0
   d. Maya   0.6
   e. Others   0.2
        Total   7.8

3. IUDs   75,000

4. Sterilizations   300,000

USAID purchased the contraceptives on contract from North American manufacturers, and shipped them to the port city of Chittagong. The SMP received contraceptives in bulk in an unpackaged, unlabeled form. It then transported the products to a central warehouse at Dhaka for repackaging and labeling. Both Raja and Maya were packed attractively, partly to get attention for the product but also to add color and appearance to the retail store. Raja had three packaging formats: three pieces to a pack, 12 pieces to a pack, and 100 pieces to a pack. Pan stores generally bought the 100-piece pack and sold singles to customers. Maya was packed 28 pills to a cycle (21 birth control pills and 7 iron tablets). The products then were sent to 7 subwarehouses for distribution to 22 wholesalers. The wholesalers sold to pharmacies, large general stores, and about 5,000 semiwholesalers or stockists. The function of the semiwholesaler was to break bulk and sell in smaller lots to the pan stores and small general stores. The area sales managers were primarily responsible for sales to the wholesalers, while the SMP's sales representatives were primarily responsible for selling wholesaler's stocks to the semiwholesalers. Some sales reps also sold to pharmacies and large general stores from wholesaler's stocks.

Wholesalers were either grain, cigarette, or pharmaceutical distributors. Semiwholesalers were more varied and included distributors of soap, tea, cookies, toothpaste, newspapers, and magazines. When the SMP program was started in 1977, some wholesalers and semiwholesalers distributed the contraceptives solely as a national duty, but slowly over the years they discovered that the financial benefits were quite adequate and willingly participated in the program ever since. The wholesalers and semiwholesalers generally achieved 10 to 12 inventory turns per year on Raja, while the retailers achieved about 6 to 8 turns. The inventory turns on Maya were 5 to 6 at the wholesale level and 3 to 4 at the retail level. The price and margin structure for Raja and Maya were as follows.

---

[3] The other brand was named Santi, meaning peace. This pill was formulated by Dr. K. M. Hossain, who also owned a pharmaceutical factory. Dr. Hossain offered free consultations and advice on family planning, and even assured his clients of a "100% guarantee" for his product. In its local market area, Santi had shown impressive growth in market share.

	Raja (Pack of 3 pieces)	Maya (1 cycle)
SMP's selling price	Tk. 0.29	Tk. 0.45
Wholesaler's selling price	Tk. 0.31	Tk. 0.49
Semiwholesaler's selling price	Tk. 0.33	Tk. 0.53
Suggested retail price	Tk. 0.40	Tk. 0.70

(1 taka = 8 cents)

SMP's prices for Raja and Maya had no relation to the cost structure for the products. USAID's purchase cost for a pack of Raja was about 1.25 takas and for a cycle of Maya, 3.5 takas. Over and above product costs, if other marketing costs were added, the contraceptives were being sold at one-tenth their total cost.

USAID and other international donor agencies were quite willing to provide contraceptives entirely free to consumers, as they were already subsidizing the other nine tenths, but PSI thought it important to charge a price mainly to convey a sense of value to the customer. At the same time, the prices had to be within the reach of the majority of the population. Reference points for pricing were provided by what consumers paid for a cup of tea, a box of matches, or a cigarette. SMP's prices provided adequate margins for the channel members, especially the retailer. A PSI manager commented, "By charging a price and providing a margin, we got 80,000 retailers to distribute the products. We could never have done it if the products were free."

One highlight of the strategy was the intensive communication support that Raja and Maya received. PSI's approach was to skip all intermediate levels of influences including the doctors and to go directly to the consumer. The basic approach was to create an atmosphere of fun and happiness. The promotional themes of "happy marriage" and "confident choice of the prudent family" were repeatedly communicated through radio, press, billboards, and posters. Sales promoters with megaphones carried out street-to-street canvassing, boats carried advertisements on their sails, and Raja and Maya T-shirts were distributed. (Exhibits 15.6a, b, and c show some of these promotional campaigns.)

With an average spending level of $400,000 per year, the SMP was the second largest of all advertisers in Bangladesh. Raja and Maya received approximately equal amounts of advertising dollars. The media allocation for each product is shown in Exhibit 15.7.

Problems with Maya

After years of intensive promotion effort, it was quite clear that Maya was not as well accepted in the market as Raja. Exhibit 15.8 shows the trend of CYP[4] shares for Raja and Maya. Since 1978, almost the entire growth in the condom market had come from Raja, while Maya was losing ground both to the government's free distribution program and to private brands. Ciszewski, the architect of the successful Raja strategy, was known to be a pragmatic manager open to new ideas. Almost immediately after Schellstede had taken up his job, Ciszewski had suggested in a letter:

> In Bangladesh we know that 80 percent of all products, including products for the female, are purchased by men. Our surveys show that women are more prone to personal influences

---

[4] CYP, or couple years protection, was a notion used to compare and quantify the benefits of different contraceptive methods. Based on frequency studies in Bangladesh, it was estimated that 100 condoms offered one unit of CYP in Bangladesh; 13 cycles of oral pills were equivalent to one CYP; one IUD insertion was equivalent to 2.5 CYP; and one sterilization was equivalent to 7.75 CYP.

than men (see Exhibit 15.9). Bill, if you can think of a clever way to communicate to the man to buy Maya for his woman, we will be in great shape.

Six months later, Ciszewski wrote another letter:

Bill, if you think we should discontinue Maya altogether and start from scratch with a new brand name, a new consumer segment, and a new communications program, don't hesitate to let me or Phil Harvey know. We are solidly behind you. We have had tremendous success with communication and distribution, but you can help us focus this strength for Maya.

In spite of several such suggestions, Schellstede's responses from Bangladesh were somewhat lukewarm. "Either he disagrees with me totally or he is still learning his job," thought Ciszewski. Finally, after Schellstede had been on the job for nearly a year, Harvey decided to convene a strategy meeting in Washington. The purpose was to put together an action plan for improving Maya sales.

As the meeting got under way, the three PSI managers carefully pored through all the market data that Schellstede had provided. Harvey spoke first:

It seems strange to me that Raja should be more successful than Maya. Look at what Raja has to compete with, essentially free goods. The Bangladesh government literally gives away its products free, while we charge a price for Raja—yet we get a dominant share. Maya, on the other hand, is behind Ovastat in market share—and Ovastat is priced 10 times higher than Maya. Lyndiol, Ovral, and Nordette are priced five to seven times higher than Maya. I can't believe that consumers in a poor country would want to pay more for products that are available cheaper!

Ciszewski responded:

That exactly may be the problem—we don't have the support of the retailers for Maya. The other pills in the market give them 16 times as much margin as Maya. We need to do something to motivate the retailer better. There may be other problems with Maya, too. In informal conversations with many professional doctors, I was surprised to learn that they thought Maya was a poor drug, though they were not able to pinpoint the exact reasons. When I told some of them that Maya was exactly Syntex's[5] Noriday, which is in fact stronger than Syntex's Norminest, they were really surprised.

In fact Maya's image problem was not restricted to the professional doctors. It was known that many RMPs also thought Maya was an inferior drug, and that many of them had advised their patients to discontinue Maya. An SMP field supervisor told this story in one of his field reports:

I heard the other day about the mother of three children who went to Tayub Sahib (the respected Mr. Tayub, an RMP). The woman complained of backache and nausea. Tayub Sahib advised her to discontinue Maya. The woman replied that she was poor and she could not buy English medicines, but she could obtain Maya free from the government dispensary. Tayub Sahib explained to her that what she was taking was not Maya, but the government pill which was somewhat better than Maya. All the same he advised her to discontinue the pill for 15 days and the woman politely replied that she would heed Tayub Sahib's advice and discontinue Maya.

---

[5] Syntex was a U.S. pharmaceutical firm that sold its contraceptive pill, Noriday, to USAID. Other pills in the Bangladesh market, such as Ovastat, were roughly equivalent to Syntex's Norminest. USAID supplied Noriday to the Bangladesh government as well as the SMP. While the Bangladesh government packed and sold the pill in its generic unbranded form, the SMP repackaged the pill as Maya.

Ciszewski was quite convinced that pricing, retail motivation, and image were important areas to be addressed in any new plans for Maya. With SMP's strengths and successes in mass-media promotion with Raja, Ciszewski was quite confident of devising an effective Maya communication strategy. He proposed that the image problem be addressed by going directly to the consumer with an effective communication strategy.

Though Schellstede agreed with the contents of what was being discussed, his analysis had suggested a dramatically different action plan. He opened his files and pulled out some notes he had prepared. He began to read:

> One factor of possible great importance has been not having someone trusted to recommend Maya and to hold the hands of the new customer through the first cycles when side effects are most common and most likely to cause discontinuation. This *someone* could possibly be the doctor. We have consciously not attempted to develop medical channels because of funding limitations. Whether anybody likes it or not, the RMP is the person to whom our target group actually turns for medical help. We have good reason to believe that because neither we nor the government have enlisted their help, they are quite happy to have contraceptives to blame the many ill-defined, but real, aches and pains of being poor, hungry, and sick. Given this background, our sales of 50,000 cycles a month is no mean achievement, regardless of what anybody says. We should accept the RMPs for what they are—medical entrepreneurs—and help them improve the service they offer by detailing them with our products.

Schellstede's proposal, which was a reversal of the successful Raja strategy, worried PSI's founder considerably. Harvey summarized his thoughts:

> USAID evaluates us on cost-effectiveness, so any strategy that increases our cost per CYP would be difficult to get approval. Moreover, we are a professional outfit, selling quality products for a social benefit. We should not as a matter of policy associate ourselves with untrained quacks.

Regardless of any decisions the three men might take, they would have to convince the project council of its usefulness. The council normally took a larger view of the project. Any additional costs would need justification not merely in terms of market share, but in terms of benefits to Bangladesh society. The council would need to know how many additional births would be averted[6] by the new program and how it would benefit the economy.

---

[6] The CYPs were multiplied by a factor of 0.25 to arrive at the number of births averted. The reduction factor was an adjustment for fertility rates.

EXHIBIT 15.1
Sales Volume of Raja
and Maya

	Raja (in million pieces)	Maya (in thousand cycles)
1978	9.7	481
1979	17.3	1,021
1980	22.7	1,098
1981	31.6	702
1982	35.8	591
1983	50.4	622

EXHIBIT 15.2   **Organization Chart for SMP**

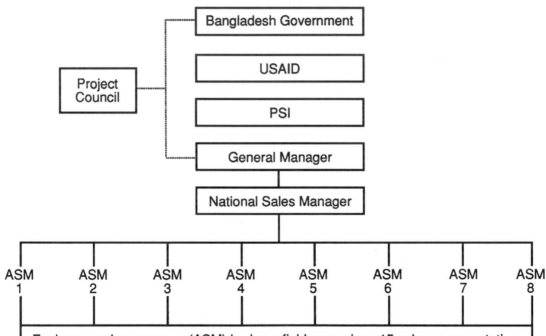

Each area sales manager (ASM) had one field supervisor, 15 sales representative, and 5 sales promoters reporting to him or her. The ASM also managed the warehousing, dispatching, and accounting functions for which there was a support staff. Each Area Sales Office also had a fleet of four or five station wagons that were received as gifts. The station wagons were primarily used by the sales personnel for making field visits and delivering orders.

EXHIBIT 15.3
Social Marketing Project—1983 Profit and Loss Statement

1.	Revenues from sales of contraceptives	$ 423,556
2.	Cost of contraceptives	3,805,842
3.	SMP operating expenses in Bangladesh	1,343,514
4.	Fee paid to PSI	417,228
	Loss from operations	$5,143,028
	USAID subsidy	$5,143,028
	Net profit (loss)	0

EXHIBIT 15.4   **Location of Bangladesh**

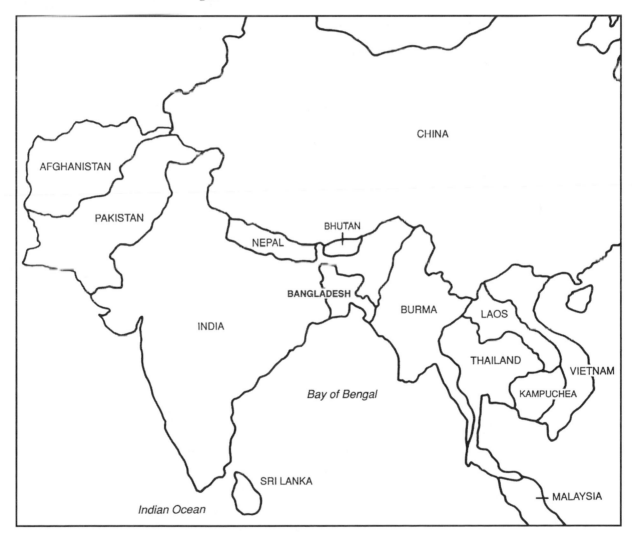

EXHIBIT 15.5
Specific Family
Planning Meanings
Mentioned by
Participants in an
SMP Survey

Specific Meanings Mentioned	Female		Male	
	Rural	Urban	Rural	Urban
Limit family size	48.9%[a]	53.1%	73.7%	48.9%
Have small/happy family	16.4	30.3	12.2	36.0
Stop having children	48.4	31.4	16.9	13.7
Two children are enough	2.7	5.7	8.5	15.8
Space childbirth	5.5	6.3	–	3.6
Preserve health of mother	20.1	21.7	3.3	2.2
Assure healthy children	2.7	1.1	4.2	5.0
Assure good health for mother and children	8.2	6.9	–	3.6
Assure good health for all	3.7	3.4	8.9	12.9
Assure food and clothing	58.0	57.1	32.9	38.8
Less poverty	21.5	19.4	33.3	43.2
Live within means	8.7	9.7	12.7	9.4
Saving for future	8.7	15.4	9.4	4.3
Avoid subdividing property among children	8.7	1.7	6.1	3.6
Peace and happiness in the family	48.4	48.6	35.7	40.3
Happier family life	4.1	6.9	0.5	–
Assure education for children	42.0	62.9	17.4	53.2
Rearing children properly	12.8	10.3	2.3	4.3
Number interviewed	219	175	213	139

[a]*To be read:* 48.9 percent of the 219 interviewed mentioned that "limit family size" was one of the meanings they got out of family planning communication.

EXHIBIT 15.6A
Raja—Print Ad

EXHIBIT 15.6B
Raja and Maya
Street-to-Street
Canvassing

EXHIBIT 15.6C
Raja and Maya Sales Promotion

EXHIBIT 15.7
Allocation of Advertising Expenditures by Media, 1983

	Raja	Maya
Radio	18%	20%
Newspaper	35	25
Cinema[a]	10	3
Poster/signboard	13	16
Point of purchase	18	20
Mobile film unit	6	6
Television	—	10
Total	100%	100%

[a] Movies screened in cinema theatres in Bangladesh generally had about 10 minutes of commercials at the start and another 5 minutes at half-time.

EXHIBIT 15.8
CYPs for Industry and SMP Products[a]

	Raja CYPs	Total Condom CYPs	Maya CYPs	Total Pill CYPs
1978	97,000	560,000	37,000	450,000
1979	173,000	330,000	78,500	370,000
1980	227,000	640,000	84,500	510,000
1981	316,000	590,000	54,000	480,000
1982	358,000	680,000	45,400	350,000
1983	504,000	850,000	47,800	620,000

[a] CYP, or couple years protection, was a notion used to compare and quantify the benefits of different contraceptive methods. Based on frequency studies in Bangladesh, it was estimated that 100 condoms offered one unit of CYP in Bangladesh; similarly 13 cycles of oral pills were equivalent to one CYP.

EXHIBIT 15.9
Sources of Messages on Family Planning

	Female		Male	
Mass Media Mentioned	**Rural**	**Urban**	**Rural**	**Urban**
Radio	85.5%[a]	83.7%	88.2%	85.9%
Television	5.3	49.0	14.1	50.0
Cinema	1.3	12.5	7.1	18.5
Newspaper	1.3	16.3	5.9	37.0
Poster/signboard	7.9	17.3	10.6	27.2
Family planning worker/public contact	31.6	10.6	23.3	4.3
Number Interviewed	76	104	85	92

[a] 85.5 percent of the 76 people interviewed were made aware of family planning messages through the radio.

Managing the Brand

16. The Dana-Farber Cancer Institute: Development Strategy
17. Bayer AG (A)
18. Warner-Lambert Ireland: Niconil

16

The Dana-Farber Cancer Institute: Development Strategy

V. Kasturi Rangan and Marie Bell

Susan Paresky, Chief Development Officer for the Dana-Farber Cancer Institute (Dana-Farber), paused for a moment to scan the skyline surrounding Boston's Longwood Medical area. Susan had come to the Institute almost two years earlier in April 1997, arriving at the close of a successful capital fund drive that had raised over $100 million. In addition to the capital campaign, the Institute had raised $35 million for its annual fund through its two major fundraising arms: one under the Dana-Farber Cancer Institute name and the other under the Jimmy Fund umbrella. Notwithstanding this fundraising success, the pace at the Development Office remained hectic. The Institute's development needs were limitless, and whatever funds Paresky could raise, Dana-Farber CEO and President David Nathan could put to good use. Nathan reflected on his ambitions for Dana-Farber:

> Dana-Farber is a living laboratory focused on eradicating cancer. We provide the best possible patient care today and do the research needed to provide even better care for tomorrow. Such an environment does not come without a price. We are constantly in need of money for new space, infrastructure, and training. Patient fees and government research grants only cover about 80 percent of our ongoing costs, so we look to the Development Office to make up the shortfall on an ongoing basis and provide capital funds through a major fund drive about every five years.

Research Associate Marie Bell prepared this case under the supervision of Professor V. Kasturi Rangan as the basis for class discussion rather than to illustrate either effective or ineffective handling of an administrative situation.

Copyright © 1999 by the President and Fellows of Harvard College. To order copies or request permission to reproduce materials, call 1-800-545-7685, write Harvard Business School Publishing, Boston, MA 02163, or go to http://www.hbsp.harvard.edu. No part of this publication may be reproduced, stored in a retrieval system, used in a spreadsheet, or transmitted in any form or by any means—electronic, mechanical, photocopying, recording, or otherwise—without the permission of Harvard Business School.

We need to be able to recruit the best and brightest talent and provide them with world-class facilities to conduct their research. Asking such high talent to move to Boston is expensive, especially when you consider its cost of living relative to other centers. Beyond the recruitment of leading experts, there are huge expenses in training doctors to do clinical research, especially those researchers that cannot win government grants until they have proven themselves.

Since her arrival, Susan Paresky had taken several meaningful steps to focus the fundraising operations for the Institute. She had rapidly effected changes to the organizational structure of Dana-Farber's development office (see Exhibit 16.1), and raised $39.8 million in 1998. Some of the major changes included the addition of 28 new positions and modification of job descriptions to more effectively focus development personnel. Paresky commented,

Every day there is an increased need for funds at the Institute. Philanthropic money is available in the market, but to access it you need a well-organized professional development team. With an ever-increasing need for funds, we must further reorganize our operations and establish critical positions to ensure that we are able to meet our targets. An outstanding question is the level of additional cost the president and Board are willing to tolerate in order to raise that incremental $5 million per year over the next five years.

Reflecting back on her previous job as Development Dean at Harvard University's School of Public Health, Paresky offered,

I am struck by how many avenues we have for fundraising at Dana-Farber. At the University, we relied on alumni for major gifts, but here we have a broad portfolio of activities that raise money. On the one hand, that is good news because of the wide variety of ways to reach all levels of donors. But on the other hand, it necessitates thoughtful management and prioritization of the full portfolio, as some programs are less effective and raise less money although they may be important for other reasons; some may not even fit with our mission and image anymore.

We need to develop a clear idea of which opportunities to pursue and which ones to turn down when, for example, well-meaning groups ask our assistance to help them raise less than $5,000 through small events in honor of a loved one. This question also comes up frequently with cause marketing proposals. We need to know which opportunities we should pursue and which we should forgo. Underlying all this is the question of the role of the Development Office in implementing the vision of the organization. Our role is not simply to raise money, but to do it in a manner that is consistent with the strategy of the Institute. In short, we need a leading edge development strategy attuned to the changing nature of fundraising and a way to think about how we measure success properly.

The Dana-Farber Cancer Institute

The Dana-Farber Cancer Institute, a research and teaching affiliate of the Harvard Medical School, summarizes its mission as "dedicated to discovery . . . committed to care." The nationally recognized Institute was one of the world's premier cancer research centers. Founded in 1947 by Dr. Sidney Farber, a pioneer in cancer research, the Dana-Farber was renowned for its blend of clinical and basic research, and the ability to incorporate the results of its discoveries into improved treatment techniques for children and adults with cancer.[1] Dana-Farber research programs focused on the development of more effective drugs and drug combinations, new measures to reduce the side effects of chemotherapy and radiotherapy, and the introduction of new treat-

---

[1] *Paths of Progress,* DF/JF newsletter, Winter 1998.

ment technologies for forms of cancer resistant to standard measures. (See Exhibit 16.2 for facts about cancer.)

In 1997, Dana-Farber entered into a joint venture with two other major Harvard teaching hospitals: Massachusetts General and Brigham and Women's. With the Dana-Farber/Partners CancerCare (DF/PCC) venture, adult oncology services became coordinated across the three facilities, with outpatient services provided at Dana-Farber, inpatient care at Brigham and Women's, and both inpatient and outpatient services at Mass. General. In February 1997 the integration of services began with the movement of Dana-Farber beds to a newly renovated and enlarged Brigham and Women's unit. Subsequently, in December 1997, Dana-Farber opened an expanded, state-of-the-art adult ambulatory treatment center.[2] Twelve disease program areas were established,[3] bringing together multidisciplinary teams from the three hospitals to collaborate in the care of adult patients with specific types of cancer, and to provide a more streamlined approach to clinical research and testing. Gary Countryman, Chairman of the Board of Trustees for Dana-Farber, remarked on the DF/PCC affiliation:

> Dana-Farber's mission is to find a cure for cancer through basic and applied research. To conduct the research, our doctors need a population of patients to test their discoveries and treatments. In the current era of managed care, a small "research" hospital with about 50 beds is not economically viable. The venture with DF/PCC provides access to a significant patient pool for research economically, but we must remain true to our research mission and not become drawn too far into the hospital domain. We must constantly ask ourselves whether what we are doing relates to cancer research. If the answer isn't yes, we are doing something wrong.

The Institute researched and treated all forms of cancer. In some cases, disease centers had been partially funded through gifts and/or grants to address specific cancer research and care. These included the Gillette Center for Women's Cancer, the Center for AIDS Research, and the Jimmy Fund Clinic (specifically devoted to the treatment of children). As of 1997, the Institute was staffed with approximately 1,600 people, including 634 doctors (MDs, PhDs) comprised of 189 faculty (MDs, PhDs) and 445 trainees, 236 outpatient and inpatient nurses (RNs), and 350 volunteers. As seen in Table 16.A, the Institute's operating budget was funded through three primary sources: patient fees, research awards (Dana-Farber ranked third among independent hospitals in the United States in the National Institutes of Health grant awards), and earnings from endowment funds. Any shortfall was made up by the Development Office's fundraising efforts.

Dr. Nathan commented on the role of the Development Office in the funding of the Institute:

> The importance of the Development Office cannot be understated. Every year the Institute runs a deficit. We meet the shortfall with the unrestricted funds raised by Development—usually through the Jimmy Fund and gifts to the Institute. Additionally, there is a minimum of 10 percent of our research that is not funded through research grants, requiring approximately $20 million in unrestricted funding that comes through the fundraising efforts of the Development Office.

---

[2] 1997 The Year in Review—DCFI website.

[3] The 12 disease centers were endocrine, gastrointestinal, genitourinary cancer, head and neck cancer, hematologic malignancies, hematology, melanoma, neurologic cancer, sarcoma, thoracic, breast cancer, and gynecological cancers.

TABLE 16.A
Dana-Farber
Financial Profile
($ thousands)

Year Ended September 30	1998	1997	1996
Revenues:			
Research	$ 93,800	$ 91,783	$ 83,447
Patient services, net	77,622	61,800	67,042
Jimmy Fund and other unrestricted contributions & bequests[4]	14,696	14,121	13,572
Other	10,436	6,920	5,679
Total operating revenues	196,554	174,624	169,740
Expenses			
Direct research	68,659	65,283	60,578
Direct patient	58,653	44,642	45,302
Indirect expenses	84,177	70,429	71,025
Total operating expenses	211,489	180,354	176,905
Deficient before investment return	$(14,935)	$ (5,730)	$ (7,165)
Realized investment return, net*	$ 24,425	$ 39,905	$ 18,724
Number of licensed beds (located at Brigham under the Dana-Farber license in 1997 and 1998)	34	34	57
Discharges	869	1,011	1,577
Outpatient clinic visit (including visit to radiation therapy)	N/A	70,779	58,978

*This amount reflects the return on endowment funds, which averaged to $350 million over the three years.

While the DF/PCC joint venture was important in the efficient allocation of resources and the pooling of research talent, its effect on development was less certain. Susan Paresky wondered about the effect of the joint venture on her ability to raise funds in the future. For example, she was concerned whether the joint venture would create confusion in the potential donor's mind about the Institute and its work, ultimately leading him/her to give funds elsewhere. This was especially relevant as Paresky considered when to launch the next capital campaign. (See Exhibit 16.3 for the results of the 1997 campaign.) The Institute expected to launch a capital campaign every four to five years, giving its contributors some breathing room between solicitations, an opportunity to deliver on prior pledges, and for the Institute to plan its expansion. In the intervening years, Paresky stressed the need to build up the annual fund in order to strengthen ties and the "habit of giving at higher levels." It was unclear whether the DF/PCC joint venture might cloud the needs message, diluting their ability to raise annual or capital funds.

The Development Office

The Development Office of Dana-Farber was responsible for the fundraising activities of the Institute. Both the Board of Trustees and Dana-Farber management provided input into the Development Office's goals and objectives. In many respects, while the Office was responsible administratively to the management of the Institute, it was responsible strategically to the Board of Trustees. One trustee commented on

---

[4] In fiscal year 1997, the Development Office raised $34.311 million. Of that, $14.121 million represented unrestricted gifts and bequests and was reflected in the income statement. A further $19.506 million was either temporarily or permanently restricted and was reflected in the balance sheet. The trademark income of $.684 million was included as other revenues.

his role in guiding the Development Office,

> As trustees we set the tone for our fundraising efforts by the people we hire, the kinds of fundraising we do, and how we define our relationships with the larger community. I would characterize our fundraising effort as one with "good taste." Our major donors are sophisticated, worldly, and discriminating, and our efforts need to be consistent with those characteristics. The fundraising tone is also important in attracting broad community support for the Institute. We have been fortunate in our ability to raise funds recently. In our last capital drive we received $109 million when our goal was only $83 million. Our current focus is on raising money efficiently, at about 10–20 percent cost of funds raised, and in a manner consistent with the mission and reputation of the Institute.

Another trustee added,

> Another role for the trustees is the hiring of the best possible Chief Development Officer. A superb candidate has two major skill sets: the ability to communicate and the ability to organize. From a communications perspective, the person needs to be able to interact with donors, speak and write effectively, and be socially at ease in an affluent world. On the organization side, the individual needs to nourish and develop the networking ability and productivity of his/her staff. The Chief Development Officer must be able to manage, delegate, and balance the constituencies of the organization. For example, an important role is the education of the trustees themselves. The Development Office conducts luncheons and tours of the Institute so we, in turn, can create opportunities for fundraising development.

While the Board of Trustees and the president of the Institute were instrumental in selecting the Chief Development Officer, their influence on development did not stop at the selection process. Both the Board members and the president were vital to the process of fundraising. Susan Paresky commented,

> The Board of Trustees and the president are an integral part of Dana-Farber's Development efforts. An active board member is our best asset. About 50 percent of the funds we raise are in some way connected to one of our 125 board members, either through a direct gift, an introduction to a potential contributor, or a business relationship. Part of our challenge is to create roles for board members so that they feel they are making a direct contribution to the Institute. We try to ensure that all of our trustees are active in at least one of the Institute's 20 committees.
>
> It is also important that the development staff have a close working relationship with the president. If we are aware of his plans for the Institute, we can access the high-potential contributors that could help achieve those plans. If we have the ear of the Institute president and his presence at Development functions, our fundraising efforts are significantly more effective. While he may or may not be the person to ask for the gift, the combination of his position and his commitment creates a personal relationship with the prospective donor.

The Development Office encompassed a very broad spectrum of fundraising programs—major gifts (large gifts from individuals), corporate and foundations grant proposals, planned giving, and annual giving (a gift given annually from individuals through direct mail or telemarketing), all under the direction of Elizabeth (Libby) Roberts, Director of Development. A second broad category of fundraising programs was the Jimmy Fund events (golf tournaments, bike rides, marathon walks, etc.) under Suzanne Fountain, the Director of the Jimmy Fund. A third component was cause marketing programs under the direction of Mike Andrews, Chairman of the Jimmy Fund. Supporting all of these activities was the Director of Development Operations, Kim Watson. For 1999, the Development Office expected to raise 56 percent of its $42 million goal from Development programs and 44 percent from its

TABLE 16.B
1997 Dana-Farber
Cost of Funds

	1997	1998	1999 (estimated)
Expenses:			
Salaries	$2.2	$2.8	$3.2
Program	2.7	2.5	3.5
Capital	N/A	.1	.15
Total expenses	$4.9	$5.4	$6.85
Total revenues	$32.4	$39.7	$42.2
Expense-to-revenue ratio	15.1%	13.6%	16.2%

Jimmy Fund activities. Susan Paresky believed that the Dana-Farber cost of raising funds was quite efficient, as indicated in Table 16.B.

Development Fund

As seen in Table 16.C below, the Development Fund's goal was to raise approximately $24 million in 1999 from Development activities. Additionally, as seen in the table, while Jimmy Fund fundraising was mostly event-driven, a certain proportion of funds raised fell into the Development categories.

Individual Major Gifts

The goal of this fundraising effort was to secure significant gifts[5] from individuals. Obtaining these gifts was a challenge, requiring on average about 2.5 years of cultivation between the potential contributor and the Development Office team.

The Development Office used a variety of techniques to locate potential contributors. A full-time researcher scanned online databases to pinpoint individuals based on reported income, occupation, and title, and ownership of luxury goods (e.g., automobile and boat registrations). Additionally, news reports were canvassed to uncover business executives who had been touched by cancer, and in some cases, wealthy patients approached Dana-Farber doctors to offer contributions. Libby Roberts remarked on the targeting process:

> Unlike a university that concentrates on its alumni as its donor pool, our potential donors are broad-based. While we currently do not solicit patients, we are looking for people who have been touched by cancer, generally either through a family member or a colleague. Unfortunately, cancer touches everyone in some way and it is not one disease but 100 dif-

TABLE 16.C
Development Fund—
1999 Fundraising
Targets

	Fundraising Goal ($000s)	Percent Raised under Jimmy Fund Banner
Development Fund		
Individual major gifts	$ 9,000	1%
Corporation/foundations (philanthropic)	8,380	—
Annual fund (includes direct marketing)	3,700	44%
Planned gifts	2,750	—
Total development fund	$23,830	

[5] A "contribution" or "gift" referred to a monetary transfer to an organization, while a "donation" referred to goods and services.

ferent diseases that are all called cancer. Our trustees are an invaluable resource. They are a major source for introductions to prospective contributors and are instrumental in getting us ultimately in front of the right person to make our presentation. Sometimes it will take years before we ask for the gift. At first we engage potential contributors in the mission of the Institute and give them a feel for the full range of our activities.

Further, there was increased competition from other worthy charities for these individual major gifts, as well as pressure from contributors to understand specifically how their gifts would be used to further cancer research. Increasingly, contributors wanted to restrict the usage of their gifts to specific activities while the Institute needed more and more flexible, "unrestricted" funds. While individuals and families often wanted to support the area of cancer that had afflicted them, at times the needs of the Institute were not necessarily in the same area. Major challenges for the development staff, therefore, were educating potential donors to the needs of the Institute and matching donor interest with those needs.

Another challenge for the development staff was the expectation that major gifts would receive a "naming opportunity," i.e., that their name would be attached to a specific building or capital asset. Libby Roberts explained,

> More often than in traditional educational fundraising, hospital donors expect a "naming opportunity" for their gift. This is problematic on several levels. We have a shortage of "real estate," especially in desirable areas with high traffic. Because donors cannot attach their name to a specific physical space, they often make gifts restricted to a specific cancer and request to have their name featured in a space related to this gift. This gets us back to the problems associated with restricted use funds when our most pressing needs are for unrestricted funds.

Corporate/Foundations Grants

Corporate philanthropy and foundation grants accounted for about 34 percent of the funds raised by the Development Group. On the foundation side, Dana-Farber was increasingly targeting national foundations that were trying to leverage their resources to solve a global problem. In some ways, the process of obtaining foundation funding was more rigorous than with individuals or corporations. Foundations by law were required to give away 5 percent of their endowment assets annually. Thus, as part of their working model, most foundations systematically called for requests for proposals, carefully evaluated submissions, and awarded grants. Underscoring the other aspect of foundation fundraising, Hope D'Amore, Director of Corporate/Foundations Grants, remarked, "Our doctors and trustees often have relationships with people who sit on the Foundation's board or who work directly for the Foundation. These relationships get us in the door, so we can demonstrate how Dana-Farber can help create a solution to a global problem as opposed to being a single disease–focused institution."

On the corporate side, Dana-Farber had segmented funding into three basic types. First were companies that funded department-driven research. For example, a specific department needed funding potentially for clinical trials or a form of biomedical research. Generally funding for these needs was provided by related for-profit corporations that stood to benefit from the development of a new technology or therapy. The second type of corporate philanthropy came from high-profile, Boston-based companies (e.g., BankBoston, Gillette) that wanted to increase their community outreach and often funded special events and special programs. The third type was called "Friends." These Friends were brought to the Institute by Dana-Farber trustees that had relationships with senior corporate officers. Hope D'Amore commented on her fundraising efforts,

By definition, foundation and corporate fundraising are different. Foundations exist to give away their money and corporations exist to make money. At the foundation level we try to create compelling arguments for the Dana-Farber's ability to uniquely solve a global problem. Science, and to some extent reputation and personal relationships, create the funding. On the corporate side, we have found that a combination of emotional and intellectual appeals is the most effective. We need a personal relationship or introduction to the CEO and then we need to create a reason for the corporation to give to us. Sometimes this can be a company's gift to honor a retiring CEO, a legacy that a CEO wants to leave with his company, or a way to increase the morale and commitment of its employees.

Planned Gifts

The technical, specialized area of planned giving was becoming an increasingly important component of the Development Fund's activities. "Planned giving" allowed prospective donors to "plan the contributions to minimize the after-tax cost, while securing allowable benefits for themselves and their families."[6] (See Exhibit 16.4 for a sample of planned giving scenarios.) To assist prospective donors, the Dana-Farber had staff members who had received extensive training in gift planning as well as access to professional legal counsel. While the Planned Giving officer was instrumental in explaining options and working through different planned giving scenarios, contributors often were advised to obtain their own independent counsel prior to entering into a planned giving arrangement.

Further growth was expected in planned gifts to the Institute as well as outright gifts over the next 10 years as the baby boomer population reached retirement. Indeed, many demographers suggested that the world's largest intergenerational wealth transfer would occur in the next 20 years, estimated at over $10 trillion. Like its competitors, Dana-Farber was creating plans to secure a portion of this wealth.

Annual Giving

Another major Development effort was the annual giving program. This campaign included an annual donor marketing program that solicited funds for the Institute through a series of direct mail and, more recently, telephone solicitations. The program was co-branded with both the Jimmy Fund and the Dana-Farber Cancer Institute. (See Exhibit 16.5 for a sample of the direct mail collateral.) The direct mail campaign was focused on two groups: "New acquisitions" for those that had not previously contributed to the annual campaign and renewal for those that had contributed in the past. To target new acquisitions, the Development Office staff worked with a direct marketing firm. For the annual direct mail campaign, Dana-Farber rented about half of the two million names it used in the campaign, with the remaining 50 percent coming from lists shared between not-for-profit "disease-focused" institutions. Typically, on the acquisition side, the annual fund solicitation received a 1.5 percent response rate with an average contribution of $16. On the renewal side, the Development Office mailed their solicitation to approximately 140,000 donors of record, yielding a 7 percent response rate and an average $22 contribution.

In 1999, Anne Cowie, the Director of Annual Giving, planned to supplement its tried and true annual campaign with a more experimental approach. She remarked,

In the past we've focused our direct mail approach primarily on children's cancer. This year, we're piloting several direct mail tests in order to enhance our program and overall revenue. The goal is to reach more people and encourage larger, more frequent gifts. For example, we are marketing the Jimmy Fund, traditionally linked to kids with cancer, as

---

[6] *A Guide to Create Planned Giving Arrangements,* Dana-Farber publication.

helping adults as well. We profiled a mother of three who has breast cancer. We will also try more targeted "disease-specific" appeals and tailor our lists accordingly; for example, a prostate cancer appeal to lists we know are predominantly male. We are also testing the use of telemarketing to encourage monthly giving.

Additionally, in 1998 Susan Paresky implemented a Trustee Annual Fund that quickly proved to be an effective vehicle for focusing and increasing unrestricted and current-use gifts from Dana-Farber's 125 trustees. By establishing a Trustee Annual Fund, the Development Office effectively created a measurable way to encourage a trustee's fiduciary responsibility to financially support the institution that they lead. The Trustee Annual Fund also served to increase annual giving. Further foundations and corporations reacted favorably to the Trustee Annual Fund, viewing the participation of trustees as annual donors as an indication of the overall strengths of the organization and its leadership.

The Jimmy Fund

The Jimmy Fund was the other primary fundraising arm of the Development Office. Named for one of Dr. Farber's young patients, it was founded in 1948 by the Variety Club of New England in conjunction with the Boston Braves[7] baseball club. Later the fund was adopted as the official charity of leading local organizations such as the Boston Red Sox and the Massachusetts Chiefs of Police Association. Acknowledged as one of the most beloved charities in New England (with 96 percent name recognition), the Jimmy Fund was most closely associated with cancer research for children, although proceeds were used in all forms of cancer research. Monies raised for the fund were primarily through events such as golf tournaments, bike rides, walks, dances, etc. Chairman of the Jimmy Fund Mike Andrews characterized the fund in the following way:

> The Jimmy Fund is our grassroots fundraising effort. The appeal for children's cancer research touches the hearts and minds of the individual at the street level. Through its various programs, we estimate that thousands of people are involved in the Jimmy Fund either as volunteers, event participants, or donors. The Jimmy Fund is also the Dana-Farber's major source of unrestricted funds, that is, funds that can be applied wherever the Institute's need is greatest.

A key challenge was channeling the public support for the Jimmy Fund. Andrews explained further,

> The Jimmy Fund is in the fortunate position of receiving several phone calls a day from people who want to sponsor an event to benefit the fund. Several years ago, however, we realized that we simply did not have the resources to support every possible event. Based on our fundraising experience, we developed a core list of activities that we can support fully. When someone calls, we try to steer them to one of those events where we have staff and program materials to make it a success. Of course, if people want to do something different we don't prohibit it, but we have to let them know we cannot provide the same level of support.
>
> For example, we might get a call from someone who would like to host a volleyball tournament with the proceeds going to the Jimmy Fund. The caller is likely a friend or relative of someone who has either died from cancer or is being treated for the illness. In responding to that call, we might suggest that we could better support them if they were

---

[7] Following the departure of the Boston Braves to Milwaukee, the other professional baseball team, the Boston Red Sox, became affiliated with the Jimmy Fund.

to host a golf tournament. We explain about our golf program with the prizes, the collateral we have, etc. If at the end of the discussion the caller is still committed to the volleyball tournament, we don't stop him, but we have to let him know that he'll be on his own in terms of support. People understand that although we appreciate their willingness to raise funds for the Jimmy Fund, we don't have the resources to support every event.

As seen in Table 16.D below, in 1999 the Jimmy Fund's fundraising goal was $18.5 million to be raised by eight core programs. The Jimmy Fund expected continued growth in the PanMass Challenge, the Marathon Challenge, the Jimmy Fund Walk, and cause marketing programs. Other programs such as the golf tournament program and the special events roster were significant contributors to the fund, but were in a "stewardship" mode where significant growth was not expected.

The PanMass Challenge (PMC)

Contributing $6.7 million to the Jimmy Fund in 1998, the PanMass Challenge was the Jimmy Fund's single largest fundraising event. It was a grueling, two-day, state-of-the-art bike ride. Begun in 1980 with 36 riders, the original bikathon ran from Sturbridge to Provincetown. By 1998, there was greater flexibility incorporated into the event. The approximately 2,300 riders now had optional points of departure and termination—starting from either Sturbridge or Boston and finishing in either Provincetown or Boston. The success of the PMC was made possible through the efforts of the cyclists, the 200 corporate sponsors that provided products and services, the 1,600 volunteers, and the over 60,000 individual supporters who made pledges on behalf of the riders.

A key part of the success of the PMC was the devotion of the riders to both the event and the cause. (Exhibit 16.6 provides more information on the event.) Billy Star, Executive Director, remarked,

> The riders in the PMC are extremely dedicated self-starters looking for an opportunity to express their giving or philanthropic nature. This is seen in our core group of riders that each raises in excess of $10,000 in pledges per year. And they return every year. The ride is not about a race. It's a catalyst to fundraise for a cause that is important to them. Many started out by cycling on behalf of a loved one, but as the years go by, they are cycling for themselves—they still care.

The Marathon Challenge

With a goal of raising $1.6 million in 1999, the Dana-Farber Marathon Challenge sponsored 325 Dana-Farber runners in the Boston Marathon. These runners, many of whom may not have otherwise qualified for the Boston Marathon, were required to

TABLE 16.D
1999 Jimmy Fund
Fundraising Targets

	Fundraising Goal
Jimmy Fund	
PanMass Challenge	$ 6,250
Marathon Challenge	1,650
Jimmy Fund Walk	2,200
Special events (includes theater program)	3,200
Golf program	2,200
Corporate programs (includes cause marketing)	2,850
Total Jimmy Fund fundraising	$18,350

make a minimum $1,500 pledge to secure their place in the race. The runners solicited gifts to cover their pledge and in many cases far exceeded the minimum contribution. In 1998, 750 applications were received for the 325 spots, with a typical runner raising over $3,000. The Marathon Challenge was supported by the Boston Athletic Association (BAA), the organizer of the Boston Marathon. While the Jimmy Fund believed that this race represented a growth opportunity, increasing the number of sponsored runners was not an option and the Development Office was investigating other approaches to increasing fundraising through this event. Not surprisingly, given the grueling nature of the event, the participants in the Marathon Challenge were younger than the typical Dana-Farber donor.

The Boston Marathon® Jimmy Fund Walk

Backed by corporate sponsors such as Polaroid and First USA, the Jimmy Fund Walk was expected to raise $2.2 million in 1999. Approximately 6,000 people walked the Boston Marathon route earning sponsor pledges for their efforts. The walkers in the Walk were both individuals and self-formed company and family groups demonstrating corporate citizenship and individual support for the work of the Jimmy Fund. In addition to the walkers, a crew of volunteers were involved in the effort, manning refueling stations and guiding traffic. Similar to the PMC, the Boston Marathon Jimmy Fund Walk had developed different options for its walkers. In 1998 participants had the option of beginning in Hopkinton (the starting point of the Boston Marathon), Wellesley (the halfway point of the Marathon route), or the Dana-Farber Institute (the starting point for many of Dana-Farber's patients and staff). All walkers finished at Copley Square, three miles from the Dana-Farber Cancer Institute and the finish line for the Boston Marathon.

The Jimmy Fund staff believed that the Walk was an ideal growth opportunity, especially if it was modeled along the lines of the PMC. Andrews commented,

> We've learned from the PMC in our approach to the Jimmy Fund Walk. Unlike the Walk for Hunger that involves huge numbers of participants, we will be targeting a smaller number of "high quality walkers." We've established a group of "Pace Setters" walkers who contribute $500 or more and actually raise about 75 percent of the total funds raised by the Walk. We want to grow that group so we give them a little special treatment. For example, we provide them with transportation to the starting point. But we also try to make the event fun for them by having water and entertainment stations every three miles.

Special Events

In addition to its major programs, the Jimmy Fund was the beneficiary of several special events, the largest of which was the Jimmy Fund's theater collection program. Raising close to $1.6 million in 1998, the program was conducted in cooperation with the major movie theater owners in the Greater Boston area including National Amusements, Hoyts Cinemas, General Cinema, and Sony Theaters. At each showing in the summer months, the Jimmy Fund ran a "trailer" before the main attraction. The two-minute film movingly portrayed the challenges faced by children with cancer and the pioneering and caring work of the Dana-Farber Institute to help them. The film ended with a solicitation for a contribution. Theater personnel and volunteers then passed a "can" through the aisles into which movie patrons placed their spare change. The Jimmy Fund paid for the production costs associated with the film, while the movie theaters provided the air time for the film and handled the collection of the funds. The theater program was a significant fundraiser, but as one Jimmy Fund executive noted, "We don't know what else we could do to raise additional revenue from this program. We already incorporate all the theaters in the Greater Boston area and we can only do it for a limited period each year or we'll lose the support of both the theater owners and their patrons. We could use more volunteers to help in collecting money, but they are hard to find."

In addition to the theater collection program, the Jimmy Fund also ran over 140 significant charity events each year spearheaded by enthusiastic volunteers and staffed by Jimmy Fund development officers. As seen in Exhibit 16.7, these special events included a mixture of traditional events in the community and one-year special opportunities.

Two of the traditional events were the "Scooper Bowl" and the "Evening with Champions." The Scooper Bowl was a three-day ice cream extravaganza held on the Boston Common, where adults paid $5 (children $2) and got access to all-you-can-eat ice cream donated by nine of New England's leading ice cream and frozen yogurt companies. The event was sponsored by BankBoston, a regional bank, and raised over $80,000 from the 30,000 people who participated in the event. Over its 15-year history, the event had raised nearly $900,000. The Evening with Champions was a different type of ice event. Organized by the students of Eliot House at Harvard University, the Evening with Champions was a figure skating exhibition featuring local, university, national, and international champions. Three performances were held each year and the performance was also broadcast nationally on PBS. In its 29-year history, the Evening with Champions had contributed almost $2 million to the Jimmy Fund.

The Golf Program

In 1983, the Jimmy Fund Golf Program was established as an official entity of the Jimmy Fund as a means to increase fundraising revenues. At the time, there were about 20 golf events that generated $100,000 annually to the Jimmy Fund. By 1998, there were over 120 golf tournaments held during the New England summer that raised $2 million. The Golf Program was supported by four major sponsors: Polaroid, Spalding, Sheraton, and American Airlines, each of which had committed $100,000 or more in cash or in-kind donations to the Golf Program. In return these organizations received name recognition in advertising and promotion programs. Beyond this sponsorship level, the Jimmy Fund Golf Program had another level of sponsorship called "patrons." These sponsors helped to underwrite the Jimmy Fund/Polaroid Classic at the International Country Club in Bolton, MA.

Cause Marketing Programs

Cause marketing programs were the Jimmy Fund's newest and fastest-growing activity. They linked a corporation with a charitable organization to meet both the business objectives of the company and the fundraising objectives of the charity. A distinguishing factor between cause marketing programs and other types of corporate giving was that the funds were generated through business activity rather than philanthropic dollars. The Jimmy Fund's goal was to develop partnerships in its cause marketing ventures with a long-term commitment continuing over at least three years. A successful program supported the positioning and objectives of both organizations, requiring the active involvement of senior management.

Well-structured cause-related marketing programs were generally perceived as "win/win" for both the for-profit and nonprofit organization. The for-profit company received good public relations and goodwill with its customers and the community in general. The charity received needed funding. Market research suggested companies engaged in cause-related marketing to build deeper relationships with customers, enhance their reputation and image, enhance employee morale, differentiate their products and services, and increase sales. Research also suggested that consumers would support cause marketing. Given equal price and quality, 76 percent of consumers indicated that they were likely to switch brands, and an equal number said that they were likely to switch retailers.

The Jimmy Fund traced its cause marketing efforts back to 1991 when the Stop & Shop Triple Winner program originated. The cause marketing group was formally established in 1995 and by 1998 had eight different programs with companies such as Stop & Shop, Jiffy Lube, and Dunkin' Donuts. (See Exhibit 16.8 for a more detailed description of Dana-Farber's cause marketing programs.) Chain organizations were considered high-potential cause marketing partners, generally offering hundreds of locations and high traffic, giving the Jimmy Fund the opportunity to "get a few dollars from a large number of people." In addition to its current cause marketing programs, the Jimmy Fund was also pursuing relationships with several other organizations such as Staples, an office supply retailer, and Taco Bell, a fast-food chain of Mexican-food restaurants. One member of the Corporate Programs group offered this view:

> We find that the best programs have the support of the corporation's CEO or senior marketing executive. We often approach the prospect with a preliminary presentation to position ourselves and to learn more about the prospect's goals and objectives. Then we design a concept that meets our fundraising goal, a minimum of $250,000 per year, and our prospective partner's objectives. Once we get approval for the program from our corporate partner, most of our work occurs in the first year, with only maintenance and stewardship in each subsequent year.

The cause marketing group also worked with its partners on the use of funds at the Institute. Traditionally Jimmy Fund revenues had been raised without restrictions on their use. Corporate partners, however, generally wanted to tie their program and their fund contribution to a specific initiative at Dana-Farber. Having a specific program to associate the company name with gave the company something tangible to rally customers and employees around as well as providing public relations opportunities. The dilemma for the cause marketing group was in finding creative solutions to this issue. Mike Andrews remarked:

> In cause marketing the structure of the gift is often a challenge. Doing deals that result in purely unrestricted funds has been very difficult. For example, one of our partners, Dunkin' Donuts, originally wanted to play off their donut holes product (Munchkins) and build "Munchkin Manor," a cancer care center for children with cancer. But that wasn't consistent with the Institute's mission of finding a cancer cure. Instead we've developed a Rising Stars program so that the funds raised from the Dunkin' Donuts program support the work of young researchers. In the case of Stop & Shop, we've structured the arrangement so that the first $1 million raised is unrestricted with any additional funds raised going directly to fund our pediatric brain tumor clinic.

A New Millennium of Challenges and Opportunity

As Susan Paresky worked on her quarterly review of 1999 programs, her thoughts strayed to the millennium ahead. She hoped that well before the next century ended, the scourge of cancer would be over, and as people at Dana-Farber said, "we will all be out of a job." Before that time, however, she knew that significant work lay ahead.

An immediate challenge was in balancing the resources allocated to programs in the Development Office's portfolio. Susan grappled with whether there was a way to analyze and rationalize the function of each of these programs and optimally allocate her resources. She considered how many programs there should be in Dana-Farber's portfolio and how many resources she should assign to these opportunities. Might there be some programs that should be phased out to make way for more efficient, higher-growth opportunities? However, while some traditional programs represented little financial growth, they were very good public relations programs. Some clarity on that, she thought, would help her planning process for next year's budget.

But then there were long-term issues as well. One challenge was the positioning of the Jimmy Fund. When the Fund began 50 years ago, 85 percent of children who had cancer died. By 1998, there were approximately 6,500 diagnosed cases of children's cancer in the United States (25 percent were treated at Dana-Farber), with 70–75 percent of children's cancers treatable and curable. While the medical community had made significant inroads in children's cancer, adult cancer was on the rise due to an aging population and the more medically intractable nature of tumors in adults. Yet the Jimmy Fund remained positioned primarily toward children and children's cancer. One Dana-Farber executive commented,

> The Jimmy Fund is one of the most powerful charities in the nation. However, it is positioned mostly toward children's cancer, while cancer research and care in the coming years will be exceedingly concentrated on forms of adult cancer. We need to find a way to either broaden the Jimmy Fund to include adults or start to build a new "brand" that focuses primarily on adult cancer.

Some believed that an unexpected return of the original "Jimmy" to the public's eye was that opportunity. At the time the fund was established, Dr. Farber called the sick child on whose behalf the fund was founded by a fictitious name in order to safeguard his privacy. There were few cancer survivors in the 1940s and his odds to continue living were slim. Indeed, over time many who knew the child's real identity had themselves died, and it was assumed that "Jimmy" was dead. However, as the 50th anniversary of the Jimmy Fund came near, the Development Office received a letter from a woman who identified herself as the sister of the original Jimmy and reported that he was in good health. Several months later a phone call came from a Maine resident, Einar Gustafson, the original Jimmy. He was invited to Fenway Park, the home of the Boston Red Sox, and introduced to the crowd of 35,000 people as the original Jimmy, a living inspiration to those who battled cancer.[8]

Others were less willing to tamper with the Jimmy Fund and its public perception, citing the experience of a highly publicized overdosing incident at Dana-Farber. One development officer commented,

> The overdosing occurrence[9] was one of the most traumatic events in the Institute's history. It happened right in the middle of our major fundraising campaign. It was the leadership of the Trustees that saw us through that difficult time. They acknowledged the problem, accepted responsibility, and saw that the systems and structures were changed so that the problem would never recur. During this difficult time all major fundraising activities came to a halt, but the Jimmy Fund never missed a beat. Donors came to understand the situation as they watched the leadership, and nine months later were once again willing to give to the Institute. But the public had always remained solidly supportive of the Jimmy Fund. It's one of the strongest parts of our brand. Tampering with it may weaken public perception of the Fund and with it our major source of unrestricted funds.

[8] Information in this paragraph has been drawn from *Boston Globe* articles.

[9] Chemotherapy errors at the Dana-Farber in December 1994 resulted in the death of a *Boston Globe* medical columnist and heart damage to another patient. Disclosure of the overdoses in March 1995 led to extensive regional and national media attention along with the resignation of the Institute president.

Another challenge lay in the growing area of cause marketing. While the upside benefits of cause marketing were substantial, there were also risks. From the corporate side, the wrong partner, the quality of the relationship, the quality of delivery, control, and exposure could destroy any potential benefits. The charitable organization also faced risks including unrealistic expectations from their partner, failure to deliver, and perhaps, most importantly, "deterioration" of their brand. This latter point was a serious concern for some trustees. One commented,

> The Jimmy Fund and the Dana-Farber Institute are some of the best-known and most prestigious charities in New England. We get several calls each year from companies that would like to create programs with us. While the money is great, we have to be concerned about the quality of the sponsor, the terms of the program, and the ability of the sponsor to deliver. Over 50 years have been spent building our franchise in the community and one bad program could tarnish our name significantly. Additionally, if we become too commercial, we also run the risk of alienating our major contributors and losing touch with our core mission.

While Susan Paresky considered these larger strategic issues, she reflected on how the strategic issues overlapped the day-to-day development activities. For example, at the next meeting of the Development team, there were the following three very different fundraising opportunities[10] on the table:

- The CEO of a major food company had been in contact with a Dana-Farber board member about making an unrestricted $1 million gift to the Institute. Dana-Farber was one among five charitable institutions that the company's Corporate Social Responsibility task force had identified as a potential target for its charitable dollars, especially as a senior member of this company's top management had recently died from cancer. But some at the Development Office were reluctant to accept this gift because the parent of the food company happened to be in the cigarette business. Scientific research had unequivocally demonstrated the linkage between cigarette smoking and lung cancer, and to some Development Office staffers, "this offer seems like a million dollar unholy alliance with the devil." Many others at Dana-Farber, however, were somewhat surprised at "the unfair skepticism that this fine offer had elicited."

- An up-and-coming Asian car manufacturer had contacted Dana-Farber about a cause marketing program. The manufacturer had completely revamped its product line and wanted to affiliate itself with a charity that had high brand recognition. While the cause marketing team was struggling to come up with a program, the manufacturer had guaranteed contributions of $350,000 per year for three years. The manufacturer's North American Operations' CEO had himself visited Dana-Farber and had expressed his corporation's commitment to the cause and his willingness to execute a longer term "exclusive" arrangement, stating, "We want to aggregate our energy behind one significant cause rather than be fragmented and ineffective." Some in the Development Office, however, were skeptical: "In this deal the manufacturer gets a lift from associating itself with us, but other than the money, we don't get the same lift. If we want to partner with a car company, it should be with one that has a higher profile." The staff member who had developed this proposal was puzzled: "Here we have someone who has sought us out as a valuable partner, and we want to go after someone else whose interests we hardly know."

---

[10] These opportunities are illustrative and, while representative, are not completely real. They have been constructed for purposes of class discussion.

- A major medical products company had offered a gift of $1 million to the Institute. There were, however, some "strings" attached to the contribution. The company had recently developed a diagnostic test for a certain form of cancer and wanted to direct at least $500,000 of its gift to further research an aspect of that cancer. The company had graciously offered to even hire and fund a researcher to lead the effort, and agreed that the rights to any research findings would be the property of Dana-Farber. While Dana-Farber researchers were cognizant of the need for that type of research, in the short run (the next two years) they had many higher priority projects that were short of funds. Dana-Farber's research and development office had given this offer a somewhat lukewarm reception.

Susan Paresky weighed the opportunities as she contemplated which ones to pursue. She saw the merits of each proposal, yet appreciated their potential drawbacks for Dana-Farber. Ultimately, Paresky knew that the Institute could use all the money she raised. A cancer cure was at least several years away and there was much work to be funded in the interim.

EXHIBIT 16.1   **Dana-Farber Cancer Institute Division of Development and Jimmy Fund**

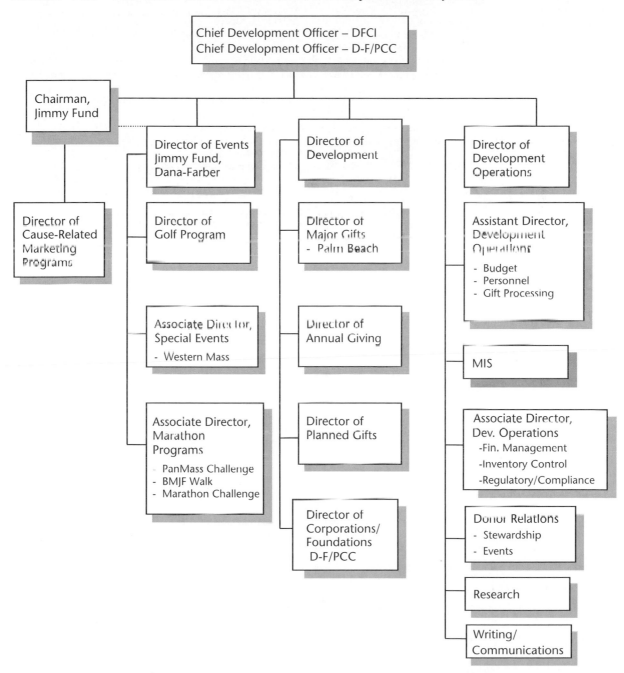

Note: Although Susan Paresky was Chief Development Officer for the Dana-Farber Cancer Institute as well as Dana-Farber/Partners CancerCare, the personnel in this chart worked solely on behalf of the Dana-Farber Cancer Institute.

EXHIBIT 16.2
Facts about Cancer in
the United States

Key Facts about Cancer

- One out of every four deaths is attributable to cancer.
- Since 1988, approximately 10 million new cancer cases have been diagnosed in the United States, and more than 4 million have died of the disease.
- Cancer is the chief cause of death by disease in children under 15. Approximately 8,800 new cases of childhood cancer occurred in 1997; an estimated 1,700 children died from the disease, about one-third of them from leukemia.
- In 1997 alone, approximately 1,382,400 people in the United States were diagnosed with cancer. About 560,000 individuals, more than 1,500 per day, died from the disease. In Massachusetts, 35,500 people were diagnosed with cancer. An estimated 14,400 died from the disease. The estimated cases of new cancer in the United States by type are listed in the table below.

Estimated New Cases of Cancer by Type, 1998

Site	Estimated New Cases
Oral cavity and pharynx	30,300
Digestive system	227,700
Respiratory system	187,900
Bones and joint	2,400
Soft tissue (including heart)	7,000
Skin (excluding basal and squamous)	53,100
Breast	180,300
Genital system	274,000
Urinary system	86,300
Eye and orbit	2,100
Brain and other nervous system	17,400
Endocrine system	18,800
Lymphoma	62,500
Multiple myeloma	13,800
Leukemia	28,700
Other and unspecified primary sites	36,300

Source: National Cancer Institute.

Progress in Cancer Treatment and Cures

- Seven out of 10 children can now be cured. One in every 1,000 Americans between the ages of 20 and 40 is a survivor of childhood cancer.
- Approximately 553,000 Americans, or 4 in 10 people who developed cancer in 1997, will be alive five years after their diagnosis; most of them can be considered cured.
- Despite the rise in new cases, death rates for prostate cancer have begun to decrease, down 6.2 percent between 1991 and 1995.

EXHIBIT 16.3
The Capital Campaign
for Data-Farber—
Commitments
Received October 1,
1991–May 31, 1997
($ millions)

Source: Dana-Farber Cancer
Institute.

	Goal	Received	Percent of Goal
Results by Constituency			
Board members	$22.5	$ 29.7	131%
Individuals	15.5	17.5	113
Foundations	20.0	21.9	119
Corporations	10.0	14.1	140
Restricted bequest and trust and board-designated gifts	10.0	13.4	133
Organizations and Institute staff	5.0	12.8	255
Total	$83.0	$109.4	132%
Results by Designation			
Human cancer genetics	$21.0	$ 18.5	88%
Women's cancer program	14.0	17.4	124
New research laboratories and undesignated	30.0	22.8	76
Program support	8.0	41.7	520
Pediatric oncology	5.0	7.4	149
Hematological malignancies	5.0	1.6	32
Total	$83.0	$109.4	132%
Results by Program			
Endowment	$ 18	$ 30.4	168%
Programmatic	35	56.4	161
Facilities	30	21.6	75
Total	$83.0	$109.4	132%

EXHIBIT 16.4
Creative Giving Options and Scenarios—Guide Excerpts

Source: This exhibit is drawn from *Dana-Farber's Guide to Creative Gift Giving.* The Table of Contents and two scenarios have been reproduced for illustrative purposes. Nonhealth examples are used to objectively illustrate planned giving techniques.

Table of Contents

Outright Gifts
　Gifts of Cash
　Gifts of Appreciated Property
　Special Election
　The Bargain Sale
　Tangible Personal Property
　Gifts of Closely Held Stock Followed by Redemption

Plans That Provide a Stream of Payments
　Charitable Remainder Trusts and Pooled Income Funds
　Unitrust
　Income-Only Unitrust
　"Flip" Unitrust
　Annuity Trust
　Meeting College Expenses: A Charitable Alternative
　Pooled Income Fund
　Charitable Gift Annuity
　Immediate Annuity
　Deferred-Payment Gift Annuity

Other Planned-Gift Arrangements
　A Charitable Bequest
　Payments for a Beneficiary
　QTIP: Flexibility for Family Contingencies
　Tax-Apportionment Clause

Planned Gifts for Qualified Retirement-Plan Benefits

Planned Gifts of Life Insurance

Gift to Fund the Future

Tips on Timing Gifts to Charity

Examples of Planned Giving Scenarios

- **Charitable lead trust.** Mr. K creates a charitable lead trust, funding it with securities currently valued at $500,000 (purchased years ago for $300,000) and directs that the trust is to pay an art museum $40,000 annually for 15 years. At the termination of the trust, the assets are to be distributed to his children. Under the tables, the present value of the stream of payments the museum is to receive from the trust (which is not deductible by the donor for income-tax purposes) is valued at $352,480 and the children's remainder interest is valued at $147,520 ($500,000 less $352,480). Assume at Mr. K's death the trust assets have appreciated to $1 million. Nevertheless, for purposes of determining his transfer tax liability, only the value of the gift to the children at the time the trust was created ($147,520) will be taken into account. The balance will escape any transfer tax. Had Mr. K not established the lead trust, the entire $1 million would have been taxed in his estate. Should the children sell their assets, their basis in the property is the $300,000 for purposes of computing capital gain.
- **The bargain sale.** Mrs. B owns real estate appraised at $120,000 which she inherited from her parents. Her basis in the property is $40,000, and she offers to sell it to a charitable organization for that amount. As a result: Mrs. B receives $40,000 from the charity, and she can deduct the contributed portion of $80,000 for income-tax purposes; however, she must also report a capital gain of $26,667 (the reportable capital is determined by dividing the sale price of $40,000 by the fair market value of the property—$120,000—and multiplying the result by the gain—$80,000).

EXHIBIT 16.5   Direct Mail Collateral

Sample from Dana-Farber general solicitation materials

Sample from Dana-Farber disease-specific solicitation materials

EXHIBIT 16.6
The Pan Massachu-setts Challenge

Source: Dana-Farber Cancer Institute.

Of the money contributed to the Jimmy Fund, approximately one-third came from the nearly 1,200 cyclists who contributed $500 per day to enter the race. Ninety percent of funds raised by the PMC was given to the Jimmy Fund. Approximately 40 percent of the riders were designated as "heavy hitters," raising in excess of $2,000 each. The average rider in the PMC was a 40-year-old male, with riders ranging in age from 15 to 76 years old. Many were high-performance athletes at some point, but not necessarily cyclists. Some of the riders were recovering cancer patients or riding on behalf of a family member with the disease (80 percent of the riders were close to someone who has battled cancer). The riders were devoted to the PMC, with 70 percent of the riders being alumni of the event and the average rider having participated in the event for four years. The remaining 60–80 percent of the funding came from sponsorship pledges collected by the cyclists. In 1997, the PMC extended its solicitation process to include the solicitation of donations from volunteers.

The size of the PMC had grown exponentially over the 18 years since its inception, raising $10,000 in its first year, $1 million by its tenth year, and four years later raising $2 million. The growth of the PMC was such that it formed its own separate entity in 1994. It was governed by an eight-member Board of Trustees with responsibilities that included determining the annual gift to the Jimmy Fund, salary reviews for the four full-time staffers, budget review, and any vendor costs exceeding $25,000. Unlike some other nonprofit institutions, the PMC was very aggressive in securing pledges. When riders enrolled for the PMC, they were required to submit a credit card number with their entry. If the riders failed to deliver the minimum financial commitment, the PMC charged the rider's credit card for any shortfall.

EXHIBIT 16.7
The Jimmy Fund—Top 15 Special Events, 1998

Source: Dana-Farber Cancer Institute.

Event	Jimmy Fund Gift
Fantasy Day at Fenway	$233,495
An Evening with Champions	111,263
Little League Program	73,487
BankBoston Scooper Bowl	66,242
Acme Auto Parquet Challenge	50,595
A Gift for Life	29,343
New England Babe Ruth Baseball	27,167
WHYN Radiothon	26,473
Joe Cronin Memorial Fishing Tournament	Not Available
WTIC Radiothon	17,707
Lou D'Abrosca Memorial Tournament	17,250
Cheers for Children at the Bull & Finch Pub	13,477
Home Builders Association Auction	12,000
Vermont State Police	11,398
Berkshire Council Mission of an Angel	10,600

EXHIBIT 16.8
Cause Marketing at Dana-Farber

Source: Dana-Farber Cancer Institute.

Stop & Shop

A major grocery chain, Stop & Shop, and its vendors had been making regular donations independently to the Jimmy Fund for many years, but institution of the Triple Winner program allowed the grocer and its vendors to come together under the same umbrella. During a six-week period in the summer, the Triple Winner program sold "scratch tickets" at the check-out register to customers who contributed $1 to the Jimmy Fund. The three boxes on the scratch ticket had prizes ranging from at least $1 in merchandise to a $10,000 cash grand prize. Stop & Shop provided all supporting materials and collateral and the scratch cards themselves, and helped motivate the cashiers in the stores to "sell" the cards. Approximately 60 major vendors contributed almost $1 million in cash and prizes each year. The program's promotional materials featured patients from the Stop & Shop Pediatric Brain Tumor Clinic. The Jimmy Fund also supported the promotion by providing patient and doctor spokespeople to motivate store staff, pediatric patient artwork for collateral material, and other administrative support. Each year, Dana-Farber hosted key executives and vendors for a tour and dinner at the Institute. In 1997, in recognition of Stop & Shop's longstanding commitment to the Jimmy Fund, and in acknowledgment of the $6.5 million raised over the years by the Triple Winner program, Dana-Farber named the brain tumor clinic the Stop & Shop Family Pediatric Brain Tumor Clinic. A portion of the Triple Winner proceeds was restricted to support the program.

Jiffy Lube/Qwest

The Jiffy Lube/Qwest program was a slightly different type of corporate program. The customer made a $2 contribution and received a Qwest phone card with 15 minutes of free "calling" and a coupon for $5 on future oil changes for one year. Jiffy Lube supported the program with radio advertising that featured a pediatric patient spokesperson. The Jimmy Fund provided some of the prizes for the store personnel as well as administrative support. A joint brainstorming session between the Jimmy Fund Cause Marketing group, the Jimmy Fund Partnership Advisory Board (comprised of local business executives), and Jiffy Lube representatives generated the idea for a phone card. Based on this working concept, the Jimmy Fund's Cause Marketing group approached LCI (subsequently acquired by Qwest), a telecommunications company that was trying to expand its presence in the New England area.

The Jimmy Fund Phone Card became Jiffy Lube's highest redemption coupon and also served to unite the corporate and franchise organizations behind the cancer cause. This was best exemplified when the winner of the contest for the highest Jimmy Fund phone card sales donated his trip to a Dana-Farber pediatric patient with cancer. This moment was captured on video and subsequently aired at the annual franchise meeting.

First USA

After having assessed several potential credit card alliances, the Cause Marketing group entered into an affinity credit card marketing arrangement with First USA, a leading credit card issuer. The First USA affinity card offered attractive interest rates and airline travel miles to card holders. The Jimmy Fund received a $1 million commitment over a period of four years. In selecting an affinity program, the cause marketing group believed that it was essential that the Jimmy Fund credit card offer a competitive package of benefits.

Dunkin' Donuts

During the month of May, the patrons of Dunkin' Donuts' 1,100 stores throughout New England had the opportunity to receive a "Coffee Day" token in return for a $1 contribution to the Jimmy Fund. Customers could redeem their tokens on June 1 for a free 10-oz. cup of coffee. Each of the franchise store owners purchased and prepaid for one "sleeve" of 300 tokens, ensuring that Dana-Farber raised approximately $360,000 in the first year of the program.

Chapter 17

Bayer AG (A)

John A. Quelch and Robin Root

On September 25, 1994, Bayer AG's senior management met at corporate headquarters in Leverkusen, Germany, to consider submitting a $1 billion bid that would, if successful, recover, once and for all, the Bayer name and Bayer cross trademark in North America. In attendance were Dr. Manfred Schneider, chairman of Bayer AG's Board of Management, Dr. Walter Wenninger, a member of the Board of Management and strategic mentor to Bayer's health care division and the North American region; Werner Spinner, head of Bayer's worldwide consumer health care business; and Hermann J. Strenger, chairman of the Supervisory Board and ex-CEO of the company.

Ten days earlier, SmithKline Beecham Plc (SB) had agreed to pay Eastman Kodak $3 billion for Sterling Winthrop's worldwide over the-counter (nonprescription) pharmaceutical business. Sterling sold Bayer aspirin and owned the Bayer cross trademark in North America. Interested only in the North American part of the business, Bayer had offered a conservative bid. Now, Bayer's senior managers learned that SB might be willing to spin off Sterling's North America business for $1 billion. The package included the trademark rights to the Bayer cross logo and aspirin product lines in North America, confiscated by the United States government after World War I, and a range of other over-the-counter (OTC) products. The four Bayer executives knew they were within reach of being able to establish the company under one name, worldwide. However, they wanted to be sure that the $1 billion did not overstate the value of the Bayer brand name and Sterling product lines in the United States combined with the synergies Bayer would gain by integrating Sterling's North America OTC business into its own Consumer Healthcare Products business. In doing so, the group also set out to assess the communications challenge the company would face should it decide to go forward with the purchase.

Robin Root prepared this case under the supervision of Professor John Quelch as the basis for class discussion rather than to illustrate either effective or ineffective handling of an administrative situation. Confidential data have been disguised.

Copyright © 1997 by the President and Fellows of Harvard College. To order copies or request permission to reproduce materials, call 1-800-545-7685, write Harvard Business School Publishing, Boston, MA 02163, or go to http://www.hbsp.harvard.edu. No part of this publication may be reproduced, stored in a retrieval system, used in a spreadsheet, or transmitted in any form or by any means—electronic, mechanical, photocopying, recording, or otherwise—without the permission of Harvard Business School.

Bayer Brand History

Origins and Early Presence in the United States

Established in 1863 by Friedrich Bayer and Johann Friedrich Weskott, a merchant and master dyer, "Friedr. Bayer et comp." began as a dyestuffs factory in Elberfeld, Germany. From very early on, the company invested in overseas markets. Bayer's investment in a coal tar dye plant in Albany, New York, in 1865, for example, gave the German firm an early stake in the industrialization of the United States. In 1903, Bayer took over the Hudson River Aniline and Color Works factory to manufacture its revolutionary Aspirin product. The decision to expand the company's analgesic business from Europe to the United States was a question of simple arithmetic:

> Execution of the entire project will cost a total of 198,625 dollars, or about 844,000 marks. Since our liquid assets as of August 31 [1903] amount to 15.1 million marks, payment of the above sum will cause us no difficulties.

The Bayer cross trademark was registered in Germany in 1904. In 1913, Bayer transferred ownership of its U.S. trademarks, including the Bayer cross logo, and patents to its U.S. subsidiary, The Bayer Co. Inc., to avoid payment of heavy import duties. The tides of Bayer's U.S. fortunes took a dramatic turn on December 12, 1918. On that day, the Alien Property Custodian, who had previously confiscated all of the company's shares and assets, auctioned off The Bayer Co. Inc. as a form of indirect payment for German war reparations. Sterling Products, Inc., one of Bayer's early analgesic competitors, submitted the winning bid of $5.3 million for assets that included not only physical plants but also the rights in the Americas to the trademarks, including Aspirin.

Bayer's Relationship with Sterling

In 1919, Sterling and Bayer entered into negotiations that were to last, on and off, for many decades. The first round dealt with Latin America, where Sterling had quickly begun registering the Bayer cross and trade names as Sterling property after it purchased The Bayer Co. In 1920, the two firms signed the "Latin America Aspirin Treaty," which stipulated that only preparations containing acetylsalicylic as an active ingredient would be sold under the Aspirin name. Also, in exchange for acknowledging Sterling's registration rights to the Bayer name in Latin America, Bayer would split the Latin American earnings of Bayer Aspirin with Sterling, 75-25, for a period of 50 years. As the details of this agreement were being finalized, Sterling acquired Bayer's expropriated trademarks in the United Kingdom, which triggered a second round of complex negotiations.

In 1923, the two firms agreed to the so-called Weiss Treaty. Bayer headquarters recognized Sterling as owner of the Bayer name and Bayer cross in the United States and U.S. territories, and agreed to supply Sterling with technology it needed to produce aspirin and other analgesics. In return, Bayer would share in Sterling's profits on sales of products under the Bayer name. A similar solution was arranged for British sales territories, which included Great Britain, Ireland, Australia, New Zealand, and South Africa. Until the Second World War, Sterling and Bayer maintained a cordial relationship, jointly acquiring other firms and sharing profits as well as management responsibilities.

In September 1941, three months before the United States entered World War II, a consent decree from the U.S. Justice Department (in which Bayer was not included) ordered Sterling to pay a $26,000 fine for breach of antitrust laws. The decree also canceled the agreements that had been laboriously worked out between Bayer and

Sterling. As a consequence, Sterling became sole owner of the worldwide rights to the patents and trademarks that Bayer had previously transferred to Sterling under joint profit-sharing arrangements.

From 1955 to 1962, Bayer sought through legal proceedings to obtain the return of its rights as set down in the Latin American and Weiss agreements by challenging the 1941 consent decree in U.S. courts. In 1964, Bayer and Sterling agreed that Bayer could conduct business in the United States so long as it did not use the Bayer name or trademark cross, except under extremely tight restrictions.

In 1954 Bayer headquarters in Germany signed a joint-venture agreement with Monsanto Chemical Company of St. Louis, Missouri, which they named Mobay, to produce a wide range of chemicals. In 1967, Bayer acquired Monsanto's 50 percent interest in the company, making it a wholly owned subsidiary under Bayer's U.S. holding company, which was called Rhinechem Corporation.

The Long Road to Reacquisition

Throughout the 1960s, Bayer (then known as Farbenfabriken Bayer AG) pursued litigation against Sterling in countries where Sterling marketed its aspirin as "Genuine" Bayer aspirin. "Sterling was pretending," argued Dr. Volker Charbonnier, a member of Bayer AG's legal department since 1969 and, in 1994, its general counsel, "that the product originated from Sterling which had in fact neither invented nor developed it. We alleged that they were misleading the public." A landmark victory in the Australian courts in 1969 precipitated the "1970 Agreement" since Sterling feared that a series of victories in the Commonwealth courts would eventually threaten the trademark protection it enjoyed in the lucrative U.S. market.

Under the 1970 Agreement, Bayer resecured its rights to the Bayer name and trademarks, including the Bayer cross, everywhere in the world except Canada, the United States, and its territories, for $2.8 million. Sterling agreed to Farbenfabriken Bayer's wish to change its corporate name to Bayer AG, since dyestuffs, Bayer's original product line ("Farbenfabriken" meant dye factories), accounted by 1970 for only 15 percent of revenues. Sterling managers in North America used the Bayer cross in aspirin advertising. They did not wish to share the logo with a German company and, more importantly, with a company that would place the same logo on agrochemicals and many other nonpharmaceutical products. "We found a way to live without the Bayer cross in the United States," continued Dr. Charbonnier. "However, there was still confusion if you looked at the business on a worldwide basis. Sterling was using the cross on Bayer aspirin in the United States and Canada, and we were using it on all our products marketed everywhere else in the world."

In 1977, to reenter the pharmaceuticals business in the United States, and to secure U.S. distribution channels for its own pharmaceutical and chemical products, Bayer acquired Miles Laboratories Inc. of Elkhart, Indiana. The Miles brand portfolio included Alka-Seltzer, a combination of bicarbonate-of-soda, citric acid, and aspirin, which, when added to water, provided an effervescent tonic that would settle an upset stomach, and One-A-Day and Flintstones vitamins. Bayer managed the Miles subsidiary at arm's length; Miles retained its corporate identity and reported to Rhinechem, the name of Bayer's U.S. holding company.

The relatively cordial relationship that followed the 1970 Agreement facilitated a second significant agreement in 1986. For $25 million, Bayer AG acquired rights to use the Bayer name in the United States on industrial products that had no relation to pharmaceutical or consumer health products. Bayer also obtained the right to change the name of its U.S. holding company from Rhinechem to Bayer USA, Inc. This change was permitted so long as Bayer agreed to restrict its marketing under that name to industrial customers and to conduct no Bayer corporate advertising to the general public. Proudly displaying "Bayer USA" across its cover, the company's 1987 annual report represented the first use of the Bayer name in U.S. corporate communications in over six decades. A corporate print advertisement announcing the name change is presented in Exhibit 17.1. Optimists within Bayer felt that the 1986 Agreement signaled an important departure from the hodgepodge of holding and subsidiary company names that had previously cluttered the company's annual reports, toward a future corporate identity under a single, worldwide name. Others, however, felt the company had shelled out $25 million to adorn an annual report that would circulate only among those who already knew Miles Inc.'s true corporate origins, and for whom the name change would mean little.

Different interpretations of the 1986 Agreement, and a change in Sterling management after it was acquired by Eastman Kodak in 1988, led to an injunction for breach of contract against Bayer in 1992. In that year, a Sterling trademark lawyer spotted a billboard outside Detroit that advertised an industrial paint protector with the corporate name "Bayer" across the bottom. Although Sterling management had long ignored Bayer's gradually expanding use of its corporate name in non–health care markets, the billboard was perceived as over the line. In its defense, Bayer asserted that the billboard was directed not at the general public, for whom the ad would have little or no relevance, but at its industrial customers in automobile manufacturing, many of whom passed by the billboard on their way to work. Following the injunction, Bayer instructed its U.S. sales force to heed a formal identification policy. "Be fair. Don't confuse the trade. Explain who is who, that Sterling owns Bayer aspirin but that we are Bayer AG." The policy was viewed as critically important on both sides of the Atlantic.

The question, "Was it stickered?" became code among Bayer's corporate communications staff to refer to the censoring with a rectangular sticker of any use of the Bayer name on communications materials that might circulate in the United States.[1] Bayer executives who traveled to the United States carried a second set of business cards without the Bayer AG company name and Bayer cross imprinted on them. Bayer exports into the United States had to be relabeled without the Bayer name while exports of products made by Bayer subsidiaries in the United States had to be relabeled with the Bayer name. "The more international our sales base became," explained Dr. Charbonnier, "the more we realized we could not live with this situation. It was costing us, on average, $2 million a year in legal fees. Our researchers were traveling to scientific conferences in the United States to explain the results of our pharmaceutical research, but were prohibited from mentioning the company they represented. You have to talk about your company at such meetings. You have to say who you are, and where you're coming from." Instead, the company was obliged to refer to itself cryptically as a "German chemical and pharmaceuticals company based in Leverkusen, Germany." The First Amendment of the United States Constitution, argued Dr. Charbonnier in U.S. courts, both entitled and obliged Bayer to present itself truthfully to its U.S. customers by its real corporate name.

The 1992 injunction was rescinded on appeal two years later. During this period, however, Bayer streamlined its management structure and, by eliminating the U.S. holding company, merged Bayer USA with its U.S. companies Agfa, Mobay, and Miles under the name Miles Inc., headquartered in Pittsburgh, Pennsylvania. The Bayer name continued to be used on industrial products, as permitted under the

---

[1] The stickers carried the words "not for release or distribution in the United States," and had to be affixed to every English-language press release issued from headquarters in Germany.

terms of the 1986 agreement, with "Miles Inc." listed as the U.S. operating company. The Mobay name all but disappeared; instead, the name Miles was used on the company's chemical products.

Bayer and the OTC Market

In 1993, Bayer AG was one of the top three companies in the global chemical and pharmaceutical industry, with total sales of more than $27 billion and a portfolio of 10,000 products. With 400 operating companies in 150 countries, Bayer generated a net pretax income of $2 billion. The Bayer Group comprised 21 worldwide business groups, which were organized into six divisions: polymers (17 percent of sales), organic products (13 percent), industrial products (18 percent), health care (23 percent), agrochemicals (13 percent), and the Agfa division (16 percent). Half of Bayer's revenues were generated in Western Europe, the remainder in North America (24 percent), Asia-Pacific (12 percent), Latin America (5 percent), and the rest of the world. Bayer's U.S. operations contributed $6.5 billion to global sales, of which 40 percent was accounted for by sales of health care products.

By 1993, the health care division was driving Bayer's growth and accounted for 76 percent of company profits. Sales of Bayer's OTC products advanced 8 percent that year. Bayer aspirin, the company's flagship brand, was second only to Tylenol among OTC brands in worldwide sales with $355 million in revenues outside North America in 1993. Bayer's aspirin sales were growing strongly in many European and Latin American markets where the brand[2] was perceived as a strong, premium-priced analgesic for young people "on the go"; for example, in Germany, Aspirin® market share grew from 17 percent in 1983 to 31 percent 10 years later. Exhibit 17.2 shows a German advertisement for Aspirin®.

The growth of Bayer's OTC sales was the result of strategic decisions taken in the 1980s. At that time, Bayer managers identified two trends that motivated them to invest heavily in OTC pharmaceuticals: the increased willingness of many consumers to take responsibility for their own health through preventive measures and the simultaneous desire of national governments in developed economies to control state health care expenditures. As a result, some drugs that previously were available only on prescription became available over-the-counter and the proportion of drug sales accounted for by lower-priced generics and private labels increased greatly.

By 1993, the global OTC pharmaceutical industry was worth around $30 billion at manufacturer prices, and was growing at 6 percent per year. North America accounted for sales of $13 billion. The largest OTC categories were cough and cold formulas, analgesics (including aspirin), gastrointestinal, skincare, and vitamin products. A strong presence in analgesics, which accounted for 22 percent of OTC sales, was considered critical to the success of any OTC company. Many ethical pharmaceutical manufacturers attempted, through acquisitions, to build the critical mass necessary to perform profitably in the OTC market. Some analysts predicted that two-thirds of global OTC product sales would be accounted for by 10 companies in 2000.

Recognizing the growing importance of the OTC market, Bayer AG had, in 1984, established a self-medication business group and consumer products business group, separate from the ethical pharmaceuticals business. The sales growth of these two business groups averaged 8 percent per year between 1989 and 1993, outpacing the

---

[2] Contrary to the United States, aspirin was still a registered trademark in Canada and in more than 70 other countries.

growth of the worldwide OTC market. In 1994, these two business groups merged into the Consumer Care business group. Among Bayer AG's 18 business groups, this new group would rank eighth in sales volume and fourth in profits.

Since the late 1970s, Bayer's OTC presence in the United States depended on its Miles subsidiary. During the 1980s, only a few new products were introduced, notably Alka-Seltzer Plus cold remedy, later introduced in Liqui-Gels[3] form for consumers who preferred the convenience of not having to premix the product with water. The intensity of marketing efforts increased following the appointment of Werner Spinner as head of Miles OTC business in 1991. He directed brand managers to develop robust business plans and restaged several existing brands. For example, the One-A-Day vitamins brand benefited from modernized packaging and new line extensions targeting men, consumers over 55, and those seeking special formulations. Spinner also initiated a supply chain rationalization project and cut the Miles sales force to 53 full-time account managers, supplemented by regional brokers.

In two and one half years, Miles North American OTC sales rose from $240 million to $350 million.[4] Though it ranked as the eighth-largest OTC company in the United States, Miles still lacked the critical mass necessary for cost-efficient sales and distribution. Miles's return on sales of 10 percent in 1993 was only half that of the industry's top players and lower than Sterling's 13 percent.

Sterling and Bayer Aspirin

Sterling Products, Inc., later renamed Sterling Drug, Inc., was established in the mid-19th century in Wheeling, West Virginia, by a pharmacist, William E. Weiss, and his business partner, A. H. Diebold. Their company acquired momentum in 1901 with a capital injection of $25,000 to focus on manufacturing and marketing Neuralgine, a pain-relief preparation. With an advertising budget in 1902 of $10,000, Sterling's owners were able to increase the company's sales sixfold within one year, to $60,000. The company subsequently expanded through acquisition. When the Bayer properties were put up for auction in 1918, Sterling submitted its bid in hopes that Bayer Aspirin would serve as the successor product to its near defunct Neuralgine. During the 1920s, with the assistance of Bayer under the Weiss treaty, Sterling marketed aspirin as a branded OTC product. As patents on aspirin expired, other competing aspirin brands were launched and aspirin became a generic term for self-administered pain relievers. In other words, Sterling lost the trademark protection for "Aspirin." In order to distinguish itself from other aspirin products, Sterling emphasized "Bayer," still a protected trademark, as part of the product name "Bayer Aspirin."

By 1993, Sterling was the eighth-largest OTC company worldwide, and ninth in the United States, with factory sales of around $1 billion. Its analgesics business, which accounted for 51 percent of its global sales, ranked third worldwide and fourth in the United States. Its Panadol brand led with $214 million in annual sales across 64 markets; Panadol was a very small business in the United States. The company's geographic reach was admired; 70 percent of sales came from nine country markets. In the United States, Sterling sold not only Bayer aspirin but also Phillips' Milk of Magnesia (an antacid), Stri-Dex (an acne treatment pad), Neo-Synephrin (a nasal decongestant spray), and Midol (an acetaminophen-based analgesic). Sterling's OTC sales in North America were $300 million in 1993.

---

[3] Liqui-Gels was a registered trademark of R. P. Scherer International Corp.

[4] In addition, around $100 million worth of Miles OTC products were exported from the United States.

In 1993, factory sales of OTC analgesics in North America were $2.8 billion. Sales were expected to reach $3 billion by 1994. Analgesics were the largest category of OTC products, accounting for 22 percent of the total U.S. OTC sales. Forty-five percent of the market comprised nonaspirin analgesic compounds, mainly acetaminophens such as Johnson & Johnson's Tylenol, which held a 33 percent market share. Twenty-eight percent of the market comprised aspirin and aspirin compounds, of which two-thirds were branded products, notably Bristol-Myers Squibb's Excedrin (7 percent) and Bayer (4.5 percent). Private-label and generic aspirin products accounted for the other third. Twenty-four percent of the analgesic market included ibuprofen compounds such as American Home Products' Advil, which held a 10 percent share. Bayer aspirin factory sales in North America were $155 million in 1991, 5 percent lower than in 1990.

Bayer aspirin's market share was under attack from nonaspirin analgesics, which often highlighted in their advertising aspirin's gastrointestinal side effects including irritation of the stomach lining; from other aspirin compounds such as Bufferin, which were safety coated to prevent this happening; and from private label and generic aspirin, which forced the branded aspirin marketers to lower or hold their prices. Sterling split its $20 million annual advertising budget for Bayer aspirin; two-thirds focused on pain relief, comparing Bayer to other brands (see Exhibit 17.3) and one-third on heart attack prevention (see Exhibit 17.4).

Market research indicated that Bayer aspirin was well-known, trusted, and seen as a good value. But it was not regarded as especially effective in terms of providing complete long-lasting relief every time. A 1992 survey found unaided advertising awareness of Bayer among analgesic users to be 13 percent compared to 43 percent for Tylenol and 35 percent for Advil. Table 17.A reports the percentages of respondents indicating that they had used each of these three brands for specific indications during the prior 12 months. Detailed attribute ratings of these and other brands are presented in Exhibit 17.5.

To revitalize the brand, Sterling managers launched the Bayer Select series of line extensions in late 1992. The line comprised five nonaspirin analgesics: a headache formula, a cold and flu formula, a menstrual pain formula, a sinus pain formula, a nighttime formula, and an ibuprofen formula for body pain. The objective was to recapture sales that Bayer aspirin had lost to competing analgesics through five higher-priced, higher-margin products that addressed specific symptoms in contrast to the cure-all positioning of Bayer aspirin. Sterling management expected additional annual factory sales of $70 million from the Bayer Select line with only 7 percent resulting from cannibalization of regular Bayer. A sample magazine advertisement for Bayer Select, with the tag line "Put the help where it hurts," is presented as Exhibit 17.6.

By the end of 1993, Bayer Select had achieved 1.4 percent share of the analgesic market rather than the hoped-for 3.4 percent. Total Bayer brand factory sales in North America in 1993 were $145 million, of which 20 percent were Bayer Select. The share of retail sales accounted for by the Select line was significantly lower. The Sterling sales force, backed by generous promotions, had sold significant inventories of

TABLE 17.A

Use of Analgesic Brands for Specific Indications: 1992

Source: Company records.

Indications	Bayer Aspirin	Tylenol	Advil
Headaches	26%	71%	38%
Arthritis/joint pain	18	47	36
Back pain	15	57	41
Muscle aches	14	61	36

Select to the trade but consumers saw the products, at best, as niche supplements to their regular analgesics, and only the smaller package sizes sold moderately well. Research indicated that many consumers equated Bayer with aspirin and were confused or unconvinced by nonaspirin analgesics carrying the Bayer name. Stepped-up advertising by Bayer's competitors, and increased competition from private label and generic aspirin, added to the brand's woes.

Trade dissatisfaction that double the normal inventories of Bayer and Bayer Select were stuck in trade pipelines resulted in a 32 percent drop in Bayer factory sales to $50 million for the first half of 1994 compared to 1993. Sales of other Sterling products in the United States also suffered.

Largely as a result, Sterling's worldwide U.S. OTC sales for the 12 months ending in June 1994 were 15 percent lower, at $250 million, than for the equivalent 1992–1993 period. U.S. operating income fell 50 percent to $15 million, 29 percent below the industry average. Cushioned by growth in emerging markets, Sterling's worldwide OTC sales were $980 million, down only 2 percent, and worldwide operating income was $145 million, down 12 percent.

The Sterling Acquisition

In May 1994, Eastman Kodak announced that it would sell the Sterling Drug business in five separate transactions, one of which was the worldwide OTC business. The announcement prompted a series of senior executive departures and marketing initiatives almost came to a halt. Bayer AG senior management, having tracked the fortunes of the Sterling OTC business for years, submitted what they thought would be an appropriate bid. However, SB, having just lost out to American Home Products in the race to acquire American Cyanamid, a much larger company than the Sterling OTC business, submitted a higher bid of $3 billion and won the contest. Had Bayer won, it would have supplanted SB as the largest OTC manufacturer worldwide.

It looked like executives at Bayer headquarters in Germany had missed a once-in-a-lifetime opportunity. Those in the United States stoically resolved to search for another acquisition to give Bayer's OTC business in North America critical mass. However, within a week of SB's purchase, discussions were initiated to sell Bayer the North American portion of the acquisition, including the rights to the Bayer name and cross. According to a senior Bayer executive:

> SmithKline really wanted the profitable international business including Panadol. They knew the U.S. business was falling apart and figured we would pay anything to get it. Hardly any of Sterling's North American OTC brands were sold overseas, making any deal with SB easier to execute.

Valuing the Business

In preparing the original bid for Eastman Kodak, Bayer corporate planners had already examined the North American Sterling OTC business and considered how it might be merged with the Miles OTC business. However, they had also cautioned that some of Sterling's worldwide business, especially in Latin America, was not of primary interest. Now they were once again excited about the possible acquisition, which would combine the eighth- and ninth-largest OTC businesses in North America into a new company that would rank fifth. The combined company would have critical mass and increased clout with the trade. The annual hard dollar cost savings shown in Table 17.B were thought realizable from operational efficiencies.

TABLE 17.B
Projected Cost
Savings of U.S.
Merger

Sources	Savings
Field sales reorganization (100 fewer staff)	$10,000,000
Marketing reorganization (35 fewer staff)	5,000,000
Research and development reorganization	1,600,000
Collateral and administration reorganization	3,000,000
Distribution warehouse consolidation	4,000,000
Media buying efficiencies	7,000,000
Promotion efficiencies (reduced trade deals and cross-promotions)	13,000,000

Bayer management forecast 180 staff reductions. They believed that $25 million in operating synergies could be realized in 1995, increasing to $44 million per year by 1997. On the other hand, they predicted a maximum of $100 million in restructuring costs including severance payments and the cost of a new headquarters for the combined company, estimated at $25 million.

Many Bayer and Miles executives felt that the Sterling OTC product line would complement the Miles line as well. By acquiring Sterling, the company would finally gain a position in the U.S. analgesic market. Sterling's Phillips' Milk of Magnesia would add a further gastrointestinal remedy to Miles's Alka-Seltzer line.

Bayer corporate planners estimated Sterling's North American OTC sales at $295 million, of which 90 percent were in the United States. Combined sales with Miles were estimated at $615 million for 1995, rising to $835 million by 1999. This increase assumed a 3.1 percent compound annual growth rate for Bayer aspirin and a 7.9 percent growth rate for the rest of the brand portfolio.

Taking into account the operating synergies already discussed, Bayer corporate planners projected operating income of $75 million in 1995, rising to $182 million by 1999. In calculating net present value, Bayer would apply a 10 percent cost of capital, given the low risk of investing in North America.

Three additional pieces of information were available to the corporate planners. First, they had access to information on comparable acquisitions of OTC businesses from 1991 to 1993. As shown in Exhibit 17.7, acquisition prices ranged from 1.5 to 3.9 times annual sales and from 18.0 to 25.5 times annual earnings before interest and taxes.

Second, an August 1994 brand valuation survey conducted annually by *Financial World* magazine valued the Bayer brand in the United States at $123 million on sales of $145 million and operating income of $20 million. By contrast, Tylenol was valued at $1,976 million on sales of $1,023 million and operating income of $230 million. The rationale underlying these value estimates is summarized in Appendix A.

Finally, the corporate planners had access to the results of a recent telephone survey that investigated awareness and impressions of OTC manufacturers among U.S. consumers. Aided awareness of Bayer was 73 percent compared to 96 percent for Johnson & Johnson and 47 percent for Miles. Ninety-five percent of those aware of the Bayer name associated it with aspirin. Fifty-two percent had a high impression of the quality of Bayer products, compared to 74 percent for Johnson & Johnson and 29 percent for Miles. Additional questions probed how consumers might respond to the knowledge that the makers of Bayer aspirin also made other products (see Exhibits 17.8 and 17.9).

The Discussion

At the senior management meeting, a freewheeling discussion covered the merits of the acquisition, the possible $1 billion price tag, and the implementation implications. Some of the comments were as follows:

It will be wonderful to finally recover ownership of our Bayer cross trademark in North America. We have been working toward this goal for almost 80 years. I've said many times I would gladly swim the Atlantic to regain global control of our company name and logo.

I'm not convinced. True, the Bayer brand name in the United States is well-known but the brand and the Sterling OTC business in North America have been driven into the ground. The latest debacle involving Bayer Select has added to the problem. I question whether the brand franchise is worth anything anymore.

But some of our marketing managers believe the Bayer aspirin brand can be revitalized in the United States if we just drop the Bayer Select line and apply some of the best practices that are boosting Bayer aspirin sales all over the world. Consumer research in the United States has surfaced a very promising positioning for Bayer as "powerful pain relief and so much more."

Regardless of the potential demand upside for Bayer aspirin, our Miles OTC business in the United States still lacks critical mass, despite all of Spinner's good work to grow sales. We've got to add additional OTC sales volume, especially in a big category like analgesics, to increase our sales force efficiency and our clout with the trade. If we get the Bayer brand back at the same time, so much the better, but the sales synergies are what count.

What synergies? How are Bayer aspirin sales in Germany and the rest of the world going to increase, just because we would now own the brand in North America? Sure it would make us all proud to own a global brand, but our first priority must be to show a return to our stockholders.

I agree. The $1 billion purchase price tag is just for starters. Just think of all the implementation problems and restructuring costs involved in merging the Sterling and Miles organizations. Do we know how our trade channels in the United States will react to the acquisition? What about our competitors? Surely they'll try to take advantage of the name confusion. Then, we'll have the expense of a corporate communications campaign to educate everyone in North America that Bayer cures more than just headaches. I've seen estimates of $10 million for three consecutive years.

You're presuming that we'll change the name of the company in the United States from Miles to Bayer. We'll have to take account of the views of the other business units in the United States, for example, the chemicals division, Agfa, and the pharmaceuticals business. But, I say we pay the $1 billion to SB now, get the name back, and worry about the details later.

Appendix A

Computation of *Financial World* Valuations

To value brands, *Financial World* (*FW*) uses a simplified version of the formula developed by Interbrand Group, the world's premier brand valuation firm. The financial data on brands used by FW were collected with the help of analysts, trade associations, and the brands' owners themselves.

FW begins by breaking down a company's earnings by brand. Once a brand's earnings have been determined, they are adjusted by an amount equal to what would be earned on a basic unbranded version of the product.

To calculate this, *FW* estimates the amount of capital it takes to generate a brand's sales. Then *FW* assumes that a generic version of the product would generate a 5 percent net return on capital employed. After subtracting that portion of the capital employed, a provision is made for taxes, and the remainder is deemed net brand-related profits.

Then to those profits *FW* applies a multiple based on a brand's strength. Interbrand defines brand strength as having seven components:

- Leadership: The brand's ability to influence the market.
- Stability: The ability of the brand to survive.
- Market: The brand's trading environment.
- Internationality: The ability of the brand to cross geographic and cultural borders.
- Trend: The ongoing direction of the brand's importance to its industry.
- Support: The effectiveness of the brand's communications.
- Protection: The brand owner's legal title.

Obviously, the stronger the brand, the higher the multiple applied to earnings. Multiples range from 6 to 20, with the highest multiple this year being 18.9. For the third straight year, Coke got the highest multiple.

Source: Adapted from *Financial World,* August 2, 1994.

EXHIBIT 17.1
U.S. Corporate
Advertisement for
Bayer USA

Meeting a world of needs right here in Pittsburgh.

We're Bayer USA. And we've just established our corporate headquarters here in Pittsburgh.

But in a way, we've been here a long time. One of the companies in the Bayer USA group is the Pittsburgh-based Mobay Corporation, a major force in advanced plastics technology and chemicals.

Other Bayer USA companies include Miles Laboratories, Agfa-Gevaert and Compugraphic. Each is a key factor in its industrial category. Each has touched the lives of Pittsburghers in many important ways. In the areas of chemicals, health and life sciences, and imaging and graphic information systems, the companies of Bayer USA have been bringing unique and progressive answers to a whole spectrum of human needs throughout the U.S. And right here in Pittsburgh.

We may be new here in Pittsburgh, but in a way we've been here all along. And we don't mind saying it's good to be home.

Bayer USA INC.

MEETING A WORLD OF NEEDS.

EXHIBIT 17.2
German Advertise-ment for Bayer Aspirin

Translation: Headline, "Don't tell me you've got a cold?" Tagline, "So much more."

EXHIBIT 17.3
Sterling Advertisement for Bayer Aspirin: Pain Relief

(SFX THROUGHOUT)
AVO: For those who use Ecotrin for the relief

of the minor aches and pains of arthritis...
we've got a flash.

You can wait hours for Ecotrin to start working,

or with Genuine Bayer you can wait just minutes.

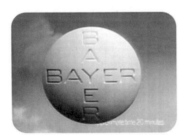

Genuine Bayer Aspirin.

America's number one aspirin.

EXHIBIT 17.4
Sterling Advertisement for Bayer Aspirin: Heart Attack Prevention

MAN (VO): Fortunately, my heart attack wasn't the end of the world . . .

it was kind of a beginning

To help prevent another attack, my Doctor prescribed exercise . . . eating right . . .

and Therapy Bayer. Pure Bayer aspirin that's safety-coated to help prevent stomach upset.

I asked my Doctor

if this regimen with Therapy Bayer

would really make a difference down the road.

"That's why I'm doing it myself," he said.

ANNCR: More and more Doctors are discovering Therapy Bayer. Take it from your doctor.

EXHIBIT 17.5
Consumer Ratings of Analgesic Brands

Source: Company records.

Qualities	Bayer	Store/ Generic Aspirin	Excedrin	Tylenol	Advil
Provides fast relief	53%	24%	77%	56%	55%
Relieves muscle aches and pains	49	22	30	31	43
Reduces inflammation	42	28	28	17	32
Provides long-lasting relief	41	26	70	38	44
Is good for severe pain	33	5	50	30	40
Relieves arthritis pain	30	17	19	13	27
Relieves menstrual discomfort	9	18	23	21	35
Causes stomach upset	11	14	7	3	3
Is easy to swallow	62	48	75	66	78
Is good value for money	59	68	55	43	40
Is a modern, up-to-date brand	51	31	64	65	60
Prevents heart attacks or strokes	41	19	12	2	3
Is recommended by doctors	37	16	27	63	45

Note: Based on a survey of 460 U.S. analgesics users, July 1992.

EXHIBIT 17.6
Sterling Advertisement for Bayer Select

(MUSIC) ANNCR: Because all pain is not the same.

MAN SINGS: Put the help where it hurts.

ANNCR: There's aspirin-free Bayer Select.

Yes, aspirin-free. They're five completely different products,

for sinus, headache, nighttime, menstrual

and arthritis pain relief.

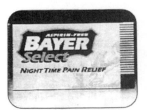
They're Bayer products, but they're not aspirin.

They're Bayer Select.

Exactly what's right for exactly what's wrong.

MAN SINGS: Put the help where it hurts,

where it hurts--

CHORUS: With Bayer Select! (MUSIC OUT)

EXHIBIT 17.7
Valuations of OTC Acquisitions

Source: Company records.

Date	Acquiring/ Acquired Companies	Valuation (millions)	Sales (millions)	EBIT (millions)	Sales (multiple)	EBIT (multiple)
June 1991	Roche/Nicholas	$798	$207	$41	3.9	19.5
October 1991	Pfizer/Colgate	105	70	NA	1.5	NA
November 1992	Ciba/Fisons (NA)	140	64	5	2.2	25.5
December 1992	Roche/Fisons (UK)	141	41	8	3.4	18.0
July 1993	Warner-Lambert/ Fisons (UK)	23	9	NA	2.5	NA

EXHIBIT 17.8
Bayer Brand Consumer Research

Source: Company records.

Question 1

"If you knew that the company that makes Bayer aspirin also makes health care products, that is, nonprescription products, what effect would this have on your decision of whether or not to purchase . . .?"

	General Public Aware of Bayer Aspirin
Positive effect	34%
Negative effect	3
No effect	61
No opinion	2

Question 2

"Now, for prescription drugs. If you knew that the makers of Bayer aspirin also made a particular drug you had been prescribed, how would you feel about taking it?"

"I would . . ."	General Public Aware of Bayer Aspirin
Take it without reservation	72%
Take it with some reservation	18
Not take it at all	6
No opinion	4

EXHIBIT 17.9
Bayer Brand Consumer Research: "Keeping the Company That Makes Bayer Aspirin in Mind, How Would It Affect Your Opinion of That Company to Know That It Made . . ."

Source: Company records.

Products	Positive	Negative	No effect	No opinion
Prescription medications	41%	3%	54%	2%
Blood glucose testing products	40	4	52	4
Alka-Seltzer	34	3	62	1
One-A-Day Vitamins	34	3	61	2
Flintstones & Bugs Bunny Vitamins	32	3	64	1
Phillips' Milk of Magnesia	30	3	64	3
Neo-Synephrine	30	3	63	4
Herbal extracts for cosmetics	25	8	64	3
Equipment for graphic arts	23	8	65	4
Flavors, fragrances, and food ingredients	22	9	66	3
Film, paper, and photography equipment	22	9	65	4
Plastics	20	12	64	4
Synthetic rubber products	19	13	65	3
Polyurethane resins used in producing paint	17	17	62	4
Dyes and organic pigments	13	16	66	5

18

Warner-Lambert Ireland: Niconil

John A. Quelch and Susan P. Smith

Declan Dixon, director of marketing for Warner-Lambert Ireland (WLI), examined two very different sales forecasts as he considered the upcoming launch of Niconil®, scheduled for January 1990. Niconil was an innovative new product that promised to help the thousands of smokers who attempted to quit smoking each year. More commonly known simply as "the patch," Niconil was a transdermal skin patch that gradually released nicotine into the bloodstream to alleviate the physical symptoms of nicotine withdrawal.

Now in October of 1989, Dixon and his staff had to decide several key aspects of the product launch. There were different opinions about how Niconil should be priced and in what quantities it would sell. Pricing decisions would directly impact product profitability as well as sales volume, and accurate sales forecasts were vital to planning adequate production capacity. Finally, the product team needed to reach consensus on the Niconil communications campaign to meet advertising deadlines and to ensure an integrated product launch.

Company Background

Warner-Lambert was an international pharmaceutical and consumer products company with over $4 billion in worldwide revenues expected in 1989. Warner-Lambert consumer products (50 percent of worldwide sales) included such brands as Dentyne chewing gum, Listerine mouth wash, and Hall's cough drops. Its pharmaceutical

Research Associate Susan P. Smith prepared this case under the supervision of Professor John A. Quelch as the basis for class discussion rather than to illustrate either effective or ineffective handling of an administrative situation.

Copyright © 1992 by the President and Fellows of Harvard College. To order copies or request permission to reproduce materials, call 1-800-545-7685, write Harvard Business School Publishing, Boston, MA 02163, or go to http://www.hbsp.harvard.edu. No part of this publication may be reproduced, stored in a retrieval system, used in a spreadsheet, or transmitted in any form or by any means—electronic, mechanical, photocopying, recording, or otherwise—without the permission of Harvard Business School.

products, marketed through the Parke Davis Division, included drugs for treating a wide variety of ailments, including heart disease and bronchial disorders.

Warner-Lambert's Irish subsidiary was expected to generate £30 million in sales revenues in 1989:[1] £22 million from exports of manufactured products to other Warner-Lambert subsidiaries in Europe and £4 million each from pharmaceutical and consumer products sales within Ireland. The Irish drug market was estimated at £155 million (in manufacturer sales) in 1989. Warner-Lambert was the sixteenth-largest pharmaceutical company in worldwide revenues; in Ireland, it ranked sixth.

Dixon was confident that WLI's position in the Irish market would ensure market acceptance of Niconil. The Parke Davis Division had launched two new drugs successfully within the past nine months: Dilzem, a treatment for heart disease, and Accupro, a blood pressure medication. The momentum was expected to continue. The Irish market would be the first country launch for Niconil and thus serve as a test market for all of Warner-Lambert. The companywide significance of the Niconil launch was not lost on Dixon as he pondered the marketing decisions before him.

Smoking in the Republic of Ireland

Almost £600 million would be spent by Irish smokers on 300 million packs of cigarettes in 1989; this included government revenues from the tobacco sales tax of £441 million. Of 3.5 million Irish citizens, 30 percent of the 2.5 million adults smoked cigarettes (compared with 40 percent of adults in continental Europe and 20 percent in the United States).[2] The number of smokers in Ireland had peaked in the late 1970s and had been declining steadily since. Table 18.A presents data from a 1989 survey that WLI had commissioned of a demographically balanced sample of 1,400 randomly chosen Irish adults. Table 18.B shows the numbers of cigarettes smoked by Irish smokers; the average was 16.5 cigarettes.

TABLE 18.A
Incidence of Cigarette Smoking in Ireland (1988–1989)

Of adult population (16 and over)	30%	(100%)
By Gender		
Men	32	(50)
Women	27	(50)
By Age		
16–24	27	(17)
25–34	38	(14)
35–44	29	(12)
45–54	29	(9)
55+	27	(19)
By Occupation		
White collar	24	(25)
Skilled working class	33	(30)
Semi- and unskilled	38	(29)
Farming	23	(17)

Note: To be read (for example): 27 percent of Irish citizens ages 16–24 smoked, and this age group represented 17 percent of the population.

[1] In 1989, one Irish pound was equivalent to US$1.58.

[2] *Adults* were defined as those over the age of 15, and *smokers* as those who smoked at least one cigarette per day.

TABLE 18.B
Number of Cigarettes Smoked Daily in Ireland (based on 400 smokers in a 1989 survey of 1,400 citizens)

More than 20	16%
15–20	42
10–14	23
5–9	12
Less than 5	4
Unsure	3

Media coverage on the dangers of smoking, antismoking campaigns from public health organizations such as the Irish Cancer Society, and a mounting array of legislation restricting tobacco advertising put pressure on Irish smokers to quit. Promotional discounts and coupons for tobacco products were prohibited, and tobacco advertising was banned not only on television and radio but also on billboards. Print advertising was allowed only if 10 percent of the ad space was devoted to warnings on the health risks of smoking. Exhibit 18.1 shows a sample cigarette advertisement from an Irish magazine.

Smoking as an Addiction

Cigarettes and other forms of tobacco contained nicotine, a substance that induced addictive behavior. Smokers first developed a tolerance for nicotine and then, over time, needed to increase cigarette consumption to maintain a steady, elevated blood level of nicotine. Smokers became progressively dependent on nicotine and suffered withdrawal symptoms if they stopped smoking. A craving for tobacco was characterized by physical symptoms such as decreased heart rate and a drop in blood pressure, and later could include symptoms like faintness, headaches, cold sweats, intestinal cramps, nausea, and vomiting. The smoking habit also had a psychological component stemming from the ritualistic aspects of smoking behavior, such as smoking after meals or in times of stress.

Since the 1950s, the ill effects of smoking had been researched and identified. Smoking was widely recognized as posing a serious health threat. While nicotine was the substance within the cigarette that caused addiction, it was the tar accompanying the nicotine that made smoking so dangerous. Specifically, smoking was a primary risk factor for ischaemic heart disease, lung cancer, and chronic pulmonary diseases. Other potential dangers resulting from prolonged smoking included bronchitis, emphysema, chronic sinusitis, peptic ulcer disease, and, for pregnant women, damage to the fetus.

Once smoking was recognized as a health risk, the development and use of a variety of smoking cessation techniques began. In *aversion therapy,* the smoker was discouraged from smoking by pairing an aversive event such as electric shock or a nausea-inducing agent with the smoking behavior in an attempt to break the cycle of gratification. While aversion therapy was successful in the short term, it did not prove a lasting solution, as the old smoking behavior would often be resumed. Aversion therapy was now used infrequently. *Behavioral self-monitoring* required the smoker to develop an awareness of the stimuli that triggered the desire to smoke and then to systematically eliminate the smoking behavior in specific situations by neutralizing those stimuli. For example, the smoker could learn to avoid particular situations or to adopt a replacement activity such as chewing gum. This method was successful in some cases but demanded a high degree of self-control. While behavioral methods were useful in addressing the psychological component of smoking addiction, they did not address the physical aspect of nicotine addiction that proved an insurmountable obstacle to many who attempted to quit.

Niconil

Warner-Lambert's Niconil would be the first product to offer a complete solution for smoking cessation, addressing both the physical and psychological aspects of nicotine addiction. The physical product was a circular adhesive patch, 2.5 inches in diameter and containing 30mg of nicotine gel. Each patch was individually wrapped in a sealed, tear-resistant packet. The patch was applied to the skin, usually on the upper arm, and the nicotine was absorbed into the bloodstream to produce a steady level of nicotine that blunted the smoker's physical craving. Thirty milligrams of nicotine provided the equivalent of 20 cigarettes, without the cigarettes' damaging tar. A single patch was applied once a day every morning for two to six weeks, depending on the smoker. The average smoker was able to quit successfully (abstaining from cigarettes for a period of six months or longer) after three to four weeks.

In clinical trials, the Niconil patch alone had proven effective in helping smokers to quit. A WLI study showed that 47.5 percent of subjects using the nicotine patch abstained from smoking for a period of three months or longer versus 15 percent for subjects using a placebo patch. Among the remaining 52.5 percent who did not stop completely, there was a marked reduction in the number of cigarettes smoked. A similar study in the United States demonstrated an abstinence rate of 31.5 percent with the Niconil patch versus 14 percent for those with a placebo patch. The single most important success factor in Niconil effectiveness, however, was the smoker's motivation to quit. "Committed quitters" were the most likely to quit smoking successfully, using Niconil or any other smoking cessation method.

There were some side effects associated with use of the Niconil patch, including skin irritation, sleep disturbances, and nausea. Skin irritation was by far the most prevalent side effect, affecting 30 percent of patch users in one study. This skin irritation was not seen as a major obstacle to sales, as many study participants viewed their irritated skin areas as "badges of merit" that indicated their commitment to quitting smoking. WLI recommended placement of the patch on alternating skin areas to mitigate the problem. Future reformulations of the nicotine gel in the patch were expected to eliminate the problem entirely.

Niconil had been developed in 1985 by two scientists at Trinity College in Dublin working with Elan Corporation, an Irish pharmaceutical company specializing in transdermal drug delivery systems. Elan had entered into a joint venture with WLI to market other Elan transdermal products: Dilzem and Theolan, a respiratory medication. In 1987 Elan agreed to add Niconil to the joint venture. Warner-Lambert planned to market the product worldwide through its subsidiaries, with Elan earning a royalty on cost of goods sold.[3]

Ireland was the first country to approve the Niconil patch. In late 1989 the Irish National Drugs Advisory Board authorized national distribution of Niconil, but stipulated that it could be sold by prescription only. This meant that Niconil, as a prescription product, could not be advertised directly to the Irish consumer.

Health Care in Ireland

Ireland's General Medical Service (GMS) provided health care to all Irish citizens. Sixty-four percent of the population received free hospital care through the GMS, but

---

[3] A royalty of 3 percent on cost of goods sold was typical for such joint ventures.

were required to pay for doctor's visits (which averaged £15 each) and for drugs (which were priced lower in Ireland than the average in the European Economic Community). The remaining 36 percent of the population qualified as either low-income or chronic-condition patients and received free health care through the GMS. For these patients, hospital care, doctor's visits, and many drugs were obtained without fee or co-payment. Drugs paid for by the GMS were classified as "reimbursable"; approximately 70 percent of all drugs were reimbursable in 1989. Niconil had not qualified as a reimbursable drug; although WLI was lobbying to change its status, the immediate outlook was not hopeful.[4]

Support Program

While the patch addressed the physical craving for nicotine, Dixon and his team had decided to develop a supplementary support program to address the smoker's psychological addiction. The support program included several components in a neatly packaged box that aimed to ease the smoker's personal and social dependence on cigarettes. A booklet explained how to change behavior and contained tips on quitting. Bound into the booklet was a personal "contract" on which the smoker could list his or her reasons for quitting and plans for celebrating successful abstinence. There was a diary that enabled the smoker to record patterns of smoking behavior prior to quitting and that offered inspirational suggestions for each day of the program. Finally, an audiotape included instruction in four relaxation methods that the smoker could practice in place of cigarette smoking. The relaxation exercises were narrated by Professor Anthony Clare, a well-known Irish psychiatrist who hosted a regular television program. The tape also contained an emergency-help section to assist the individual in overcoming sudden episodes of craving. A special toll-free telephone number to WLI served as a hotline to address customer questions and problems. Sample pages from the Niconil support program are presented as Exhibit 18.2.

While studies had not yet measured the impact of the support program on abstinence rates, it was believed that combined use of the support program and the patch could only increase Niconil's success. It had proven necessary to package the Niconil support program separately from the patch to speed approval of the patch by the Irish National Drug Board. A combined package would have required approval of the complete program, including the audiotape, which would have prolonged the process significantly. If separate, the support program could be sold without a prescription and advertised directly to the consumer. Development of the support program had cost £3,000. WLI planned an initial production run of 10,000 units at a variable cost of £3.50 per unit.

The support program could serve a variety of purposes. Several WLI executives felt that the support program should be sold separately from the nicotine patches. They considered the support program a stand-alone product that could realize substantial revenues on its own, as well as generating sales of the Niconil patches. Supporting this position, a pricing study completed in 1989 found that the mean price volunteered for a 14-day supply of the patches and the support program combined was £27.50, and for the patches alone, £22.00. The mean price for the support program alone was £8.50, suggesting a relatively high perceived utility of this component

---

[4] None of the products in the smoking-cessation-aid market was reimbursable through the GMS. Reimbursable items excluded prescriptions for simple drugs such as mild painkillers and cough and cold remedies.

among potential consumers. There was a risk, however, that consumers might purchase the Niconil support program *instead* of the patches, or as an accompaniment to other smoking cessation products—thus limiting sales of the Niconil patches.

Another group of executives saw the support program as a value-added point of difference that could stimulate Niconil patch sales. This group favored wide distribution of the support programs, free of charge, to potential Niconil customers. A third group of WLI executives argued that the support program was an integral component of the Niconil product that would enhance the total package by addressing the psychological aspects of nicotine addiction and improve the product's success rate, thereby increasing its sales potential. As such, these executives believed that the support program should be passed on only to those purchasing Niconil patches, at no additional cost.

Two options, not necessarily mutually exclusive, were under consideration for the distribution of the support programs. One option was to distribute them through doctors prescribing Niconil. A doctor could present the program to the patient during the office visit as he or she issued the Niconil prescription, reinforcing the counseling role of the doctor in the Niconil treatment. Supplying the GPs with support programs could also serve to promote Niconil in the medical community. A second option was to distribute the support programs through the pharmacies, where customers could receive the support programs when they purchased the Niconil patches. A disadvantage of this option was that a customer might receive additional support programs each time he or she purchased another package of Niconil. However, these duplicates might be passed on to other potential consumers and thus become an informal advertising vehicle for Niconil.

Pricing

Because all potential Niconil customers would pay for the product personally, pricing was a critical component of the Niconil marketing strategy. Management debated how many patches to include in a single package and at what price to sell each package. In test trials, the average smoker succeeded in quitting with Niconil in three to four weeks (i.e., 21 to 28 patches); others needed as long as six weeks.[5]

As Niconil was essentially a tobacco substitute, cigarettes provided a logical model for considering various packaging and pricing options. The average Irish smoker purchased a pack of cigarettes daily, often when buying the morning newspaper. Fewer than 5 percent of all cigarettes were sold in cartons.[6] Because the Irish smoker rarely purchased a multiweek cigarette supply at once, he or she was thought likely to compare the cost of cigarette purchases with the cost of a multiweek supply of Niconil. WLI thus favored packaging just a seven-day supply of patches in each unit. However, Warner-Lambert subsidiaries in continental Europe, where carton purchases were more popular, wanted to include a six-week supply of patches in each package if and when they launched Niconil. Managers at Warner-Lambert's international division wanted to standardize packaging as much as possible across its subsidiaries and suggested as a compromise a 14-day supply per package.

Following the cigarette model, two pricing schemes had been proposed. The first proposal was to price Niconil on a par with cigarettes. The average Irish smoker

---

[5] Smokers were advised not to use the patch on a regular basis beyond three months. If still unsuccessful in quitting, they could resume use of the patch after stopping for at least a month.

[6] A carton of cigarettes contained 20 individual packs of cigarettes; each pack contained 20 cigarettes.

smoked 16.5 cigarettes per day and the expected retail price in 1990 for a pack of cigarettes was £2.25. WLI's variable cost of goods for a 14-day supply of Niconil was £12.00.[7] Pharmacies generally added a 50 percent retail markup to the price at which they purchased the product from WLI. A value-added tax of 25 percent of the retail price was included in the proposed price to the consumer of £32.00 for a 14-day supply. In addition, the consumer paid a £1.00 dispensing fee per prescription.

Under the second pricing proposal, Niconil would be priced at a premium to cigarettes. Proponents argued that if the Niconil program were successful, it would be a permanent replacement for cigarettes and its cost would be far outweighed by the money saved on cigarettes. The proposed price to the consumer under this option was £60.00 for a 14-day supply.

Competition

Few products would compete directly with Niconil in the smoking cessation market in Ireland. Two small niche products were Accudrop and Nicobrevin, both available without a prescription. Accudrop was a nasal spray that smokers applied to the cigarette filter to trap tar and nicotine, resulting in cleaner smoke. Anticipated 1990 manufacturer sales for Accudrop were £5,000. Nicobrevin, a product from the U.K., was a time-release capsule that eased smoking withdrawal symptoms. Anticipated 1990 manufacturer's sales for Nicobrevin were £75,000.

The most significant competitive product was Nicorette, the only nicotine-replacement product currently available. Marketed in Ireland by Lundbeck, Nicorette was a chewing gum that released nicotine into the body as the smoker chewed the gum. Because chewing gum in public was not socially acceptable among Irish adults, the product had never achieved strong sales, especially given that its efficacy relied on steady, intensive chewing. A second sales deterrent had been the association of Nicorette with side effects, such as mouth cancer and irritation of the linings of the mouth and stomach.

Nicorette was sold in 10-day supplies, available in two dosages: 2mg and 4mg. Smokers would chew the 2mg Nicorette initially, and switch to the 4mg gum after two weeks if needed. In a 1982 study, 47 percent of Nicorette users quit smoking, versus 21 percent for placebo users. A long-term follow-up study in 1989, however, indicated that only 10 percent more Nicorette patients had ceased smoking, compared with placebo users. The average daily treatment cost to Nicorette customers was £0.65 per day for the 2mg gum and £1.00 per day for the 4mg gum. Nicorette, like Niconil, was available at pharmacies by prescription only, so advertising had been limited to medical journals. Anticipated 1990 manufacturer sales of Nicorette were £170,000; however, the brand had not been advertised in three years.

Forecasting

Although Nicorette was not considered a successful product, WLI was confident that Niconil, with its less-intrusive nicotine delivery system and fewer side effects, would capture a dominant position in the smoking cessation market and ultimately increase the demand for smoking cessation products. Precise sales expectations for Niconil were difficult to formulate, however, and two different methods had been suggested.

---

[7] This cost of goods included Elan's royalty.

The first method assumed that the percentage of smokers in the adult population (30 percent in 1990) would drop by one percentage point per year through 1994. An estimated 10 percent of smokers attempted to quit smoking each year, and 10 percent of that number purchased some type of smoking cessation product. WLI believed that Niconil could capture half of these "committed quitters" in the first year, selling therefore to 5 percent of those who tried to give up smoking in 1990. Further, they hoped to increase this share by 1 percent per year, up to 9 percent in 1994. Having estimated the number of customers who would purchase an initial two-week supply of Niconil, WLI managers then had to calculate the total number of units purchased. Based on experience in test trials, WLI anticipated that 60 percent of first-time Niconil customers would purchase a second two-week supply. Of that number, 20 percent would purchase a third two-week supply. About 75 percent of smokers completed the program within six weeks.

A more aggressive forecast could be based on WLI's 1989 survey, which showed that of the 30 percent of [the 1,400] respondents who were smokers, 54 percent indicated that they would like to give up smoking, and 30 percent expressed interest in the nicotine patch. More relevant, 17 percent of smokers indicated that they were likely to go to the doctor and pay for such a patch, though a specific purchase price was not included in the question. A rule of thumb in interpreting likelihood-of-purchase data was to divide this percentage by three to achieve a more likely estimate of actual purchasers. Once the number of Niconil customers was calculated, the 100/60/20 percent model used above could then be applied to compute the total expected unit sales.

Production

Under the terms of the joint venture with Elan and using current manufacturing technology, production capacity would be 1,000 units (of 14-day supply packages) per month in the first quarter of 1990, ramping up to 2,000 units per month by year-end. WLI had the option to purchase a new, more efficient machine that could produce 14,000 units per month and reduce WLI's variable cost on each unit by 10 percent. In addition, if WLI purchased the new machine and Niconil was launched in continental Europe, WLI could export some of its production to the European subsidiaries, further expanding its role as a supplier to Warner-Lambert Europe. WLI would earn a margin of £2.00 per unit on Niconil that it sold through this channel.[8] Estimated annual unit sales, assuming a launch of Niconil throughout Western Europe, are listed in Table 18.C. Warner-Lambert management aimed to recoup any capital investments within five years; the Niconil machine would cost £1.2 million and could be online within nine months.

TABLE 18.C
Estimated Unit Sales of Niconil in Western Europe

Year 1	100,000 units
Year 2	125,000 units
Year 3	150,000 units
Year 4	175,000 units
Year 5	200,000 units

[8] Warner-Lambert's European subsidiaries were likely to consider purchasing this new machine themselves as well.

Marketing Prescription Products

Prescription products included all pharmaceutical items deemed by the Irish government to require the professional expertise of the medical community to guide consumer usage.[9] Before a customer could purchase a prescription product, he or she first had to visit a doctor and obtain a written prescription that specified that product. The customer could then take the written prescription to one of Ireland's 1,132 pharmacies and purchase the product.

The prescription nature of Niconil thus created marketing challenges. A potential Niconil customer first had to make an appointment with a doctor for an office visit to obtain the necessary prescription. Next, the doctor had to agree to prescribe Niconil to the patient to help him or her to quit smoking. Only then could the customer go to the pharmacy and purchase Niconil. This two-step purchase process required WLI to address two separate audiences in marketing Niconil: the Irish smokers who would eventually use Niconil and the Irish doctors who first had to prescribe it to patients.

Niconil's potential customers were the 10 percent of Irish smokers who attempted to give up smoking each year (2 percent of the total Irish population). Market research had shown that those most likely to purchase Niconil were ages 35–44 and in either white-collar or skilled occupations (18 percent of Irish smokers). Smokers under the age of 35 tended to see themselves as "bullet proof": because most were not yet experiencing the negative health effects of smoking, it was difficult to persuade them to quit. Upper-income, better-educated smokers found less tolerance for smoking among their peers and thus felt greater pressure to quit. Research had also indicated that women were 25 percent more likely to try Niconil as they tended to be more concerned with their health and thus more often visited the doctors from whom they could learn about Niconil and obtain the necessary prescription.

The most likely prescribers of Niconil would be the 2,000 general practitioners (GPs) in Ireland. The average GP saw 15 patients per day and 8 out of 10 general office visits resulted in the GPs writing prescriptions for patients. Although 10 percent of Irish doctors smoked, virtually all recognized the dangers of smoking and rarely smoked in front of patients. A *Modern Medicine* survey of 780 Irish GPs indicated that 63 percent formally gathered smoking data from their patients. GPs acknowledged the health risk that smoking posed to patient health, but they were usually reluctant to pressure a patient to quit unless the smoker was highly motivated. Unsolicited pressure to quit could meet with patient resistance and result, in some cases, in a doctor losing a patient and the associated revenues from patient visits. Smoking cessation was not currently a lucrative treatment area for GPs. Most would spend no longer than 15 minutes discussing smoking with their patients. To the few patients who asked for advice on how to quit smoking, 92 percent of GPs would offer "firm, clear-cut advice." Fewer than 15 percent would recommend formal counseling, drug therapy, or other assistance. GPs were not enthusiastic about Nicorette due to poor results and the incidence of side effects.

WLI was confident that Niconil would find an enthusiastic audience among Irish GPs. As a complete program with both physical and psychological components, Niconil offered a unique solution. In addition, the doctor would assume a significant counseling role in the Niconil treatment. It was anticipated that the GP would initially prescribe a 14-day supply of Niconil to the patient. At the end of the two-week period, the patient would hopefully return to the doctor for counseling and an additional prescription, if needed.

---

[9] Drugs and other pharmaceutical products that did not require a written prescription from a doctor were called "over-the-counter" or "OTC" drugs.

Marketing Communications

WLI intended to position Niconil as a complete system that was a more acceptable alternative to existing nicotine replacement therapy for the purpose of smoking cessation. Niconil would be the only smoking cessation product to address both the physical dimension of nicotine addiction through the patch and the psychological dimension through the support program. Compared with Nicorette gum, Niconil offered a more acceptable delivery system (Niconil's transdermal system versus Nicorette's oral system) and fewer, less severe side effects. WLI planned to promote these aspects of the product through a comprehensive marketing program. The Niconil launch marketing budget, detailed in Exhibit 18.3, followed the Warner-Lambert standard for new drug launches. Several WLI executives felt that this standard was inadequate for the more consumer-oriented Niconil and pressed for increased communications spending.

Advertising

Because Irish regulations prohibited the advertising of prescription products directly to the consumer, Niconil advertising was limited to media targeting the professional medical community. Three major publications targeted this audience: *Irish Medical Times, Irish Medical News,* and *Modern Medicine.* WLI planned to advertise moderately in the first year to raise awareness of Niconil in the medical community. After that it was hoped that the initial momentum could be maintained through strong public relations efforts and personal testimony to the product's efficacy. Exhibit 18.4 summarizes the proposed 1990 media advertising schedule for Niconil.

WLI's advertising agency had designed a distinctive logo for Niconil that would be used on all packaging and collateral materials such as "No Smoking" placards. These would feature the Niconil logo and be distributed to doctors' offices, hospitals, and pharmacies to promote the product. Ideally, the logo would become sufficiently well recognized that it could be used eventually on a stand-alone basis to represent Niconil to the end consumer without the brand name. This would allow some flexibility in circumventing Irish advertising restrictions to reach the end consumer. Sample logos and packaging are illustrated in Exhibit 18.5. The agency had also developed the following four concepts for a Niconil medical journal advertisement:

- "Day and night I crave cigarettes. I can't stop. I'm hooked." When they ask for help, give them the help they need—new Niconil nicotine transdermal patches.
- Where there's smoke, there's emphysema, throat cancer, angina, lung cancer, sinusitis. Now a way to break this deadly addiction. Introducing Niconil nicotine transdermal patches—all they need to succeed.
- Emphysema, lung cancer, peptic ulcer, angina, sinusitis, throat cancer. Help end their deadly addiction. One-a-day instead of a pack-a-day. Introducing Niconil nicotine transdermal patches.
- "How many of your patients are dying for a smoke?" Help them break the cycle of addiction. Introducing Niconil nicotine transdermal patches. A better way to stop.

Direct Mail

A direct mail campaign to Ireland's 2,000 GPs was planned in conjunction with the Niconil product announcement. Two weeks prior to launch, an introductory letter would be mailed with a color photo of the product, a reply card offering a support program, and additional product information. The support programs would be mailed in response to the reply cards, arriving just prior to the launch. A response rate of at least 50 percent was anticipated based on past direct mail campaigns.

Public Relations

The formal Niconil product announcement was scheduled to occur in Dublin at a professional event that WLI had dubbed the "Smoking Cessation Institute Symposium." The symposium would be chaired by Professor Anthony Clare (the narrator of the Niconil audiotape), Professor Hickey (an expert in preventive cardiology), and Professors Masterson and J. Kelly from Elan Corporation. Open to members of the medical profession and media, the event was intended to focus attention on the dangers of smoking and to highlight Niconil as a groundbreaking product designed to address this health hazard.

WLI had sought endorsements from both the Irish Cancer Society and the Irish Heart Foundation, two national health organizations that actively advocated smoking cessation. Because both nonprofit institutions relied on donations for financing and were concerned that a specific product endorsement would jeopardize their tax-exempt status, they refused to endorse Niconil directly. Representatives from each institution had, however, stated their intention to attend the launch symposium.

In advance of the symposium, a press release and supporting materials would be distributed to the media. Emphasis would be placed on the role that Niconil would play in disease prevention. It would also be noted that Niconil had been developed and manufactured locally and had the potential for worldwide sales. Other planned public relations activities included a roundtable dinner for prominent opinion leaders in the medical community. Publicity in the media was planned to coincide with key "commitment to change" times such as New Year's and Lent.[10]

Sales Strategy

WLI Ireland had a sales force of 16 representatives whose average annual salary, bonus, and benefits amounted to £25,000 in 1988. They focused their selling efforts on 1,600 Irish GPs who were most accessible geographically and most amenable to pharmaceutical sales visits. The sales staff was divided into three selling teams of four to six representatives. Each team sold separate product lines to the same 1,600 GPs. The team that would represent Niconil was already selling three other drugs from Elan Corporation that were marketed by WLI as part of their joint venture. These four salespeople would add Niconil to their existing product lines. Sales training on Niconil would take place one month prior to the product launch.

The pharmaceutical salesperson's challenge was to maintain the attention of each GP long enough to discuss each item in his or her product line. Because Niconil was expected to be of great interest to GPs, the salespeople were keen to present Niconil first during the sales visit, followed by the less exciting products. Normally, a new product would receive this up-front positioning. However, Dixon argued that Niconil should be presented last during the sales call to maximize the time that a salesperson spent with each GP and to prevent the sales time devoted to the other three Elan products from being cannibalized by Niconil. Based on revenue projections for all four products, salespeople would be instructed to spend no more than 15 percent of their sales call time on Niconil. On average, each WLI salesperson called on six to seven doctors per day. The goal was for each sales team to call on the 1,600 targeted GPs once every three months. In the case of Niconil, all 16 salespeople would present the new brand during their calls for six weeks after launch.

---

[10] Lent was an annual penitential period during spring of the Roman Catholic religious calendar that was still observed by many of the 95 percent the Irish who were Roman Catholic.

Critical Decisions

With just three months to go before the launch of Niconil, Dixon felt he had to comply with the international division's suggestion to include a 14-day supply of patches in each Niconil package, but he debated whether to price the product on a par with or at a premium to cigarettes. Equally important, he had to decide which sales forecast was more accurate so that he could plan production capacity. And finally, he needed to make decisions on the communications program: which advertising concept would be the most effective, what other efforts could be made to enhance product acceptance, and was the current budget adequate to support Warner-Lambert's first national launch of such an innovative product?

EXHIBIT 18.1   **Cigarette Advertisement from an Irish Magazine**

SMOKING CAUSES CANCER
Irish Government Warning

EXHIBIT 18.2 Sample Pages from Niconil Support Program

The first step

Fill in the contract in your own words. Write down all the reasons that are most important to you for beating the smoking habit.

Then write down how your life will be better and more enjoyable without the smoking habit.

Finally, write down how you will reward yourself for your courage and hard work. You will deserve something very special.

Choose the day

Decide when to stop and put a ring round that date on your calendar.

Try to find a time when you are not going to be under pressure for a few days. The start of a holiday is good for two reasons. You will not have the stress of work and you will be free to change your routine.

Countdown

1. In the days leading up to your stop date see if you can get your partner or a friend to stop smoking along with you.

2. Ask a local charity to sponsor you or join a non-smoking group. Having other people to talk to who have kicked the habit can be a lifeline when your willpower gets shaky. They will know and understand what you are going through. Your doctor will be able to tell you what groups are running in your area.

3. The evening before your stop date, throw away **all** your cigarettes and get rid of your lighters and ashtrays. You will not need them again.

4. Read over your smoker's diary entries. Know your habit.
   - What are the most dangerous times?
   - Where are the most dangerous places?
   - What are the most dangerous situations?
   - Who do I usually smoke with?

C O N T R A C T

1. I, ...,
   HAVE STOPPED SMOKING BECAUSE I WANT:

2. MY LIFE WILL BE BETTER WHEN I AM FREE OF SMOKING BECAUSE:

3. AFTER BEATING SMOKING FOR A MONTH I WILL CELEBRATE BY:

SIGNED:

DATE:

WEEK ONE   *THE WINNER'S DIARY*

DAY

1. Today is the greatest challenge. If you succeed today, tomorrow will be easier. You can do it.

2. Well done. The first 24 hours are over. Your lungs have had their first real rest for years.

3. Remember: smoking is for losers. If you find yourself getting tense, use your relaxation tape.

4. Read your contract again. See how much better life is getting now that you are freeing yourself from this unpleasant addiction.

5. Your body says "thank you". It's feeling fitter already.

6. Don't forget to distract yourself at key cigarette times.

7. Well done. You're through your first week. Give yourself a treat. Go out for a meal or buy yourself something you've always wanted.

COUNT DOWN TO D-DAY   DAY 1

Cigarette	Time of day?	Where were you?	Who were you with?	What were you doing?	How did you feel?
1					
2					
3					
4					
5					
6					
7					
8					
9					
10					

EXHIBIT 18.3
Niconil First-Year
Marketing Budget
(£000s)

Advertising	
Ad creation	£ 4
Media advertising	28
Total advertising	32
Promotion	
Development of support program	3
Production of support programs	35
Training/promotional materials	44
Direct mailing to GPs	2
Total promotion	84
Public relations	
Launch symposium	5
Roundtable meeting	2
Press release/materials	1
Total public relations	8
Market research	3
Sales force allocation	23
Product management allocation	50
Total budget	£200

EXHIBIT 18.4
1990 Niconil Media
Advertising Schedule

Publication	Frequency	Circulation	Cost/1.000	Placements
Irish Medical Times	Weekly	5,200	£154	13
Irish Medical News	Weekly	5,100	137	11
Modern Medicine	Monthly	3,700	176	5

EXHIBIT 18.5
Sample Niconil Logo
and Packaging

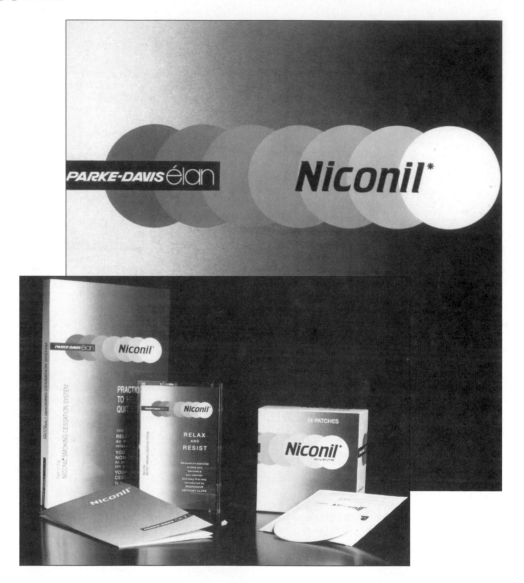

Part 7

International Marketing

19. Life, Death, and Property Rights: The Pharmaceutical Industry Faces AIDS in Africa

20. Phase Two: The Pharmaceutical Industry Responds to AIDS

21. Ciba-Geigy Pharmaceuticals: Pharma International

22. Genzyme's Gaucher Initiative: Global Risk and Responsibility

19

Life, Death, and Property Rights: The Pharmaceutical Industry Faces AIDS in Africa

Debora Spar and Nicholas Bartlett

At the start of the twenty-first century, AIDS (Acquired Immune Deficiency Syndrome) was poised to become the most deadly disease known to humanity. In the 20 years since its first documented outbreaks, 24.4 million people had died from AIDS, while over 40 million were living with the disease.[1] Rapidly spreading around the world, AIDS had proliferated in countries where basic factors including education and safer sex practices were at a minimum, with 95 percent of infections occurring in the developing world.[2] In certain countries in sub-Saharan Africa, as many as one in three adults tested positive for HIV (Human Immunodeficiency Virus), the virus that eventually causes AIDS. In South Africa alone, in the year 2000, there were an estimated

---

[1] UNAIDS and WHO, "AIDS Epidemic Update," December 2001, p. 3.

[2] Karen Stanecki, "The AIDS Pandemic in the Twenty-First Century: The Demographic Impact in Developing Countries," paper presented at the XIIIth International AIDS Conference, Durban, South Africa, July 9–14, 2000, p. 1.

Research Associate Nicholas Bartlett prepared this case under the supervision of Professor Debora Spar. This case was developed from published sources. HBS cases are developed solely as the basis for class discussion. Cases are not intended to serve as endorsements, sources of primary data, or illustrations of effective or ineffective management.

Copyright © 2002 President and Fellows of Harvard College. To order copies or request permission to reproduce materials, call 1-800-545-7685, write Harvard Business School Publishing, Boston, MA 02163, or go to http//www.hbsp.harvard.edu. No part of this publication may be reproduced, stored in a retrieval system, used in a spreadsheet, or transmitted in any form or by any means—electronic, mechanical, photocopying, recording, or otherwise—without the permission of Harvard Business School.

4,700,000 people infected with HIV/AIDS.[3] Terrifyingly, many experts believed that worse was yet to come. With infection rates continuing to increase in many areas and treatment woefully inadequate for the vast majority of those infected, AIDS threatened the developing world with an epidemic of unprecedented magnitude.

There were, to be sure, treatments for AIDS. While a cure remained frustratingly elusive decades after the disease first emerged, scientists and pharmaceutical firms had managed to concoct a series of increasingly effective drugs that enhanced the quality of life for many AIDS victims and transmuted what had once been a certain sentence of death. The drugs were complicated to administer, however, and extremely expensive—roughly $10,000 to $15,000. In Africa, where average per capita incomes ranged from $450 to $8,900, they were essentially unaffordable.

Not surprisingly, then, the toll of death in Africa had begun by the 1990s to plague the world's pharmaceutical firms as well. Across Africa and into the developed nations, doctors and AIDS activists clamored for an industrywide response to the AIDS epidemic. Pharmaceutical companies, they argued, needed to lower the prices they charged for AIDS drugs in Africa. They needed to make their drugs more accessible and to ensure that even the poorest victims could benefit from cutting-edge research. Where the companies were unwilling or unable to comply with these demands, the activists argued, local pharmaceutical firms should be able to step into the gap, selling generic versions of the sought-after drugs.

Such "solutions" were anathema to the established Western industry. These were firms, after all, that spent millions of dollars on research and development; firms that often spent years, or decades, perfecting the treatments they discovered. In their home markets, these firms were protected by patent systems that enabled them to recover the development costs of their drugs. They were not simply going to turn around and distribute their product for free. Moreover, the patents that protected the Western pharmaceutical firms were part of a broader system of intellectual property rights—a system based on the sanctity of privately owned information and enshrined in the newly created rules of the World Trade Organization. If the pharmaceutical companies relented in the face of Africa's epidemic, they risked denting the entire global structure of intellectual property rights. For if drugs were free—or cheap, or copied—in Africa, why not books or music or software? Indeed, why stop in Africa? There were poor people everywhere, and millions dying from AIDS.

The stakes of AIDS in Africa, therefore, were immense. If the pharmaceutical companies did nothing, they risked the lives of millions and a massive blow to their global standing and reputation. But if they lowered prices in Africa or weakened their patent rights, they risked destroying the system that sustained them; the system that, arguably, enabled them to save the very people who were now organizing against them.

Prelude to Catastrophe: The Emergence of AIDS in the United States

The first wave of the AIDS epidemic was concentrated in the United States, and particularly in the cities of New York and San Francisco, where a group of otherwise healthy gay men began in the early 1980s to develop a rare form of cancer. Suspecting that an unknown virus might be to blame, scientists began to look for the culprit

---

[3] See Rachel L. Swarns, "Newest Statistics Show AIDS Still Spreading in South Africa," *New York Times,* March 21, 2001, p. A8.

and transmission mechanism. Quickly, they realized this strange new disease traveled through direct physical contact: blood transfusions, sharing needles, perinatility (from mother to child during childbirth), and sexual contact, both homosexual and heterosexual. Nevertheless, because AIDS was first discovered in the gay community and remained concentrated there for some time, it swiftly became known as the "gay disease" and was associated, almost entirely at first, with homosexual activity.

In the 1980s, the disease spread through the United States at an alarming rate: 100,000 people tested positive for AIDS in the first eight years of testing, with an additional 100,000 cases identified just two years later.[4] Because scientists were unable to define an effective medical treatment for this mysterious virus, death rates were extremely high and patients rarely survived for more than 10 years.

This initial phase of infection was characterized by a general lack of information, widespread fear, and an inability or unwillingness to deal with the extent of the problem in the United States. In a sign of the times, Ryan White, a 13-year-old hemophiliac with AIDS, had to attend middle school classes by phone after being barred from his Indiana school in 1985. The superintendent justified his decision by explaining, "With all the things we do and don't know about AIDS, I just decided not to do it. There are a lot of unknowns and uncertainties, and then you have the inherent fear that would generate among classmates."[5] The U.S. government, meanwhile, did little to stem public fears. President Reagan waited six years after the initial outbreak of AIDS to address the topic publicly, and the United States was among the last of the major Western industrialized nations to launch a coordinated education campaign.

Soon, however, it became clear that AIDS was not an isolated problem of the United States. In 1983, 33 countries reported AIDS infection and by 1987 that number had increased to 127. In 1984 the Ugandan Minister of Health asked the World Health Organization for assistance in battling AIDS, and the United Kingdom formed a special cabinet committee to investigate the disease. That same year, the Zambian Ministry of Health launched a national AIDS education campaign. It would do little to stop the spread of the virus, though, which swiftly claimed the life of the president's son.

As the effects of AIDS swept across the world, activists in the United States finally propelled the disease into the public spotlight. In 1987, a group of mostly gay protesters created ACT UP (AIDS Coalition to Unleash Power), a "diverse, non-partisan group of individuals united in anger and committed to direct action to end the AIDS crisis."[6] In "zap" demonstrations designed to attract media attention and raise public awareness, ACT UP members staged "die-ins," harassed politicians, and picketed corporate buildings. Seven demonstrators broke into the New York Stock Exchange in 1989, where they chained themselves to railings to protest the high prices of AIDS treatment. In a less confrontational but equally influential campaign, Elizabeth Glaser, wife of TV's *Starsky and Hutch* star Paul Glaser, took the cause to Washington during her well-publicized battle with the disease in the late 1980s. Infected by a blood transfusion during childbirth before transmitting the disease to her two children, Glaser became a marquee celebrity spokesperson for the disease, lobbying to raise money and challenging the public's conception of AIDS as a "gay" or "drug-user" disease.

---

[4] United States Department of Health and Human Services Press Release, "AIDS Education," March 26, 1992.

[5] "School Bars 13-Year-Old Victim of AIDS," *Houston Chronicle,* August 1, 1985, p. 9.

[6] From their website, http://www.actupny.org/. Their slogan: "We advise and inform. We demonstrate. We are not silent."

Before long, increased awareness and scientific breakthrough began to make some headway against the disease. Through a combination of preventative campaigns and improved treatment, health care officials greatly reduced the rate of transmission while boosting the quality of care provided to those with AIDS. By the mid-1990s, the rate of infection appeared to have peaked, dropping from nearly 80,000 new cases diagnosed in 1993 to just 21,700 in 2000.[7] While more people in the United States were living with HIV and AIDS than ever before, doctors had found a menu of ways to check the spread of the disease in the body and thus to slow the inevitable pace of death.

Some of this improvement, to be sure, was due to preventative measures that the activists had helped bring to light: blood screening, needle exchange programs, promotion of condom use. But much was the result of a slow but steady onslaught against the virus itself. In the 20 years that followed the discovery of AIDS, scientists had still not succeeded in curing the disease or formulating an effective vaccine against it. But they had made great strides in understanding and treating both AIDS and HIV. Essentially, HIV spreads in a patient's body by targeting cells that normally clear foreign pathogens. As these cells replicate, the HIV virus eventually—often rapidly—devastates the immune system of its victim. HIV develops into full-blown AIDS when the virus has spread to such a degree that it disrupts the basic function of the immune system. Patients die from diseases that their immune systems can no longer prevent, rather than from AIDS itself.

Initially, scientists struggling with the HIV/AIDS virus were forced to treat only the disease's symptoms, focusing, for instance, on the pneumonia that felled so many patients in the latter stages of AIDS. In 1986, however, the U.S. Food and Drug Administration (FDA) approved the first AIDS-specific drug, an antiviral medication known as zidovudine or AZT, which worked by inhibiting one of the enzymes involved with replication. Several years later, scientists developed a new class of drugs, called protease inhibitors, that attempted to stop already-infected cells from further spreading the HIV virus. Both AZT and the protease inhibitors represented a quantum leap in treatment quality, and it was their usage that began, by the early 1990s, to reduce the toll of AIDS. However, as the drugs were increasingly prescribed, the virus itself began to mutate, morphing into new and more drug-resistant strains. In response, doctors backed away from the once-promising "monotherapies" and began to attack AIDS with what became known as HAART (Highly Active Antiviral Therapy), a combination of drugs designed to combat the virus at various different levels.

By the late 1990s, the HAART approach seemed to be working. AIDS infection rates had plummeted in the United States and infected patients were living longer, healthier lives. While a diagnosis of AIDS was still devastating to the victim, it was no longer the death sentence it had been a decade ago. Infected patients such as basketball great Magic Johnson or *New Republic* editor Andrew Sullivan were living normal and productive lives, and had reclaimed their position in society. HAART, however, was far from perfect. It was, in its early days, extremely complicated, demanding that patients take over 20 pills a day in accordance with a rigid schedule. Second, the cost of these pills was exorbitant, reaching $10,000–$15,000 a year for patients in the United States. And finally, all this medicine still did not get at the root cause of the disease: HAART treated AIDS, but it didn't cure it.

---

[7] Centers for Disease Control, "HIV AIDS Surveillance Report," Year-end 2000 Edition, vol. 12, no. 2, p. 9.

The Second Wave: AIDS and the Developing World

Just as the United States was beginning to stem the HIV/AIDS crisis within its own borders, infection rates in much of the rest of the world began spinning out of control. By the year 2000, 25.3 million people with HIV/AIDS lived in Africa, while South and Southeast Asia and Latin America hosted 6.1 million and 1.4 million, respectively.[8] In many of these regions, heterosexual contact was the primary method of transmission; indeed, 55 percent of sub-Saharan Africans infected were women.[9] In the year 2001 alone, the virus infected 3.4 million new victims in Africa, raising the subcontinent's percentage of total adults infected to 8.4 percent.[10] In Zimbabwe, where over 30 percent of the adult population tested positive for HIV, the demographic toll of the disease had already been felt, pushing the country's once-robust rate of population growth down to zero. Starting in 2003, the populations of Zimbabwe, Botswana, and South Africa were actually predicted to decline by .1–.3 percent a year.[11] Similar declines were likely to sweep across the continent, as other countries watched their HIV cases develop into full-blown AIDS.

In South Africa, home to the largest HIV-positive population in the world, the prognosis was particularly grim. Already staggering under the burdens of poverty and a grossly unequal distribution of wealth, South Africa had seen AIDS ravage its population in the late 1990s: 20 percent of the adult population was infected with HIV in the year 2000, with 500,000 new cases reported in that year alone. A total of 4.7 million suffered from the disease, which had also become the leading cause of death.[12] Predictions for the future were terrifying. Fueled by a lack of information about the disease and continued high-risk behavior (a 1998 survey found that only 16 percent of women used a condom in the last encounter with their nonspouse sexual partner), health care officials predicted that HIV infection rates could hit 7.5 million by 2010, with 635,000 people dying that year from the disease.[13] The vast majority of those affected would be between 15 and 29 years old, with half infected before they turned 25, and half dead before 35.[14]

Beyond this unspeakable death toll, experts also feared broader setbacks to South Africa, including a reduction in life expectancy, a decrease in educational opportunities for its citizens, and growing socioeconomic disparities. Various reports noted that the economic, political, and social fallout of the epidemic could be enormous, ranging from a decimated workforce (including a 40 to 50 percent loss of employees in certain sectors) to declining growth and an impending crisis for a health care system unequipped to deal with millions of sick and dying.[15] Most disturbing perhaps was the disease's expected toll on the next generation of South Africans. Because of the nature of its transmission, AIDS tended to infect both parents of a family, and thus

---

[8] UNAIDS and WHO, "AIDS Epidemic Update," p. 3.

[9] Stanecki, "The AIDS Pandemic in the Twenty-First Century," p. 2.

[10] UNAIDS and WHO, "AIDS Epidemic Update," p. 3.

[11] Stanecki, p. 3.

[12] Ravi Nessman, "Yet Another AIDS Death as Government Argues over Statistics," Associated Press Newswire, November 9, 2001.

[13] ABT Associates, *The Impending Catastrophe: A Research Book on the Emerging HIV/AIDS Epidemic in South Africa* (Parklands, S. Africa: Lovelife, 2000), pp. 7–9, 20.

[14] Ibid., p. 8.

[15] Ibid., p. 4.

to leave a staggering number of orphans in its wake. By 2010 experts predicted that there could be nearly two million AIDS orphans in South Africa. How would the country, already pushed to its fiscal limits, provide either physical or emotional care to these swelling ranks of children? "Everybody is scared," wrote the author of one USAID report. "We're moving into uncharted territory."[16]

Sadly, the countries hit hardest by the HIV/AIDS epidemic were also those least able to provide their citizens with adequate treatment. In most of the developing world, HIV-positive populations did not have access to the most rudimentary health care or doctors, let alone the ultra-expensive antiviral drugs regularly prescribed in the United States. Indeed, conditions in these countries often precluded all but the most basic care. Doctors were scarce across the developing world, storage and distribution systems were rare, and education about the disease was often sorely limited. Under these conditions, even the limited funding that did flow to HIV/AIDS treatment was often wasted, with the World Bank estimating that for every $100 that African governments spent on drugs, only $12 worth of medicine reached the patient.[17] In many countries, moreover, the social stigma that surrounded AIDS kept infected people from seeking assistance and allowed their governments to turn a blind eye to the disease. The most notorious example of this behavior occurred in South Africa, the heart of the epidemic, where President Thabo Mbeki stubbornly refused to increase his country's spending on medical treatment, arguing that poverty, poor diet, and other social ills were to blame.[18]

Others, however, were not so complacent, nor were they prepared to blame Africa's ills solely on the African context. Instead, raging rates of death and infection on the continent were linked, not illogically, to the things Africa lacked: drugs, in particular, and the means to afford them. And from this vantage point, the weight of blame fell heavily on the pharmaceutical industry.

The Pharmaceutical Industry and Intellectual Property Rights

Over the course of the twentieth century, Western pharmaceutical companies had transformed themselves from anonymous, low-profit chemical suppliers into high-profile, top-performing firms. They earned billions of dollars, employed thousands of the world's leading scientists, and made the drugs that saved lives. Many factors had contributed to the pharmaceutical industry's success: medical advances, government support, and a capital market eager to oblige. At the center of the industry, though, and close to the heart of all industry executives sat the patent system, a legal bulwark protecting—some might even say permitting—the development of drugs.

First devised in fifteenth-century Venice, patents were intended to repay their holders for the effort and expenses incurred during a product's development: if a glassblower pioneered a new method for shaping glass, for example, or a craftsman built a better compass, the republic wanted to ensure that they could reap the commercial benefits of their work. So Venice granted its patent holders a window of market exclusivity for their product, a kind of government-sanctioned temporary monopoly. Over subsequent centuries, justification for patents varied from recognizing the "nat-

---

[16] Steve Sternberg, "Number of AIDS Orphans to Reach 29 Million in 10 Years," *USA Today,* July 14, 2000, p. 8A. *Children on the Brink,* a report from the U.S. Agency for International Development, predicts that 29 million children 14 or younger will have lost at least one parent by 2010.

[17] From http://world.phrma.org, accessed November 15, 2001.

[18] "Deadly Meddling," *The Economist,* November 3, 2001.

ural right" of an inventor's ownership of ideas to providing a practical way for governments to promote and reward innovation. Such motives figured prominently in the early history of the United States. Story has it that the Constitutional Convention adjourned one afternoon to watch John Frich's steamboat undergo tests on the Delaware River. Hoping to safeguard the freedom of individuals and the enterprises they were creating, many of the founding fathers of the United States saw the implementation of a federal patent system as a sensible way of defending emerging American industry. And thus to "promote the Progress of Science and the useful Arts,"[19] America's legislators enshrined a system of patents in the U.S. Constitution.[20]

Not all Americans, however, favored laws that restricted the dissemination of ideas. Indeed, many argued that patents were an invidious form of regulation, one that favored commerce over the greater development of humankind. As Thomas Jefferson, an early proponent of freely flowing ideas, famously reasoned:

> He who receives an idea from me, receives instruction himself without lessening mine; as he who lights his taper at mine, receives light without darkening me. That ideas should freely spread from one to another over the globe, for the moral and mutual instruction of man, and improvement of his condition, seems to have been peculiarly and benevolently designed by nature . . . Inventions then cannot, in nature, be a subject of property.[21]

Such poetic objection, though, remained rare. Several decades after Jefferson's argument, President Lincoln appeared to speak for the nation when he noted that "the Patent System added the fuel of interest to the fire of genius."[22] Patents enjoyed permanent inclusion in the laws of the United States.

For the pharmaceutical industry, however, this system of protection was initially irrelevant. For patents were designed to protect research— innovation—and the pharmaceutical trade in the early United States had little to do with discovery. Instead, the drug industry was largely composed of small, low-profile firms that supplied pharmacists with the bulk chemicals they used to produce formulaic mixtures. Indeed, until the turn of the twentieth century, "patented drugs" were simply those marketed under a trademarked name—often the most dubious drugs or "elixirs" available.

Events in the 1930s and 1940s, however, brought drastic change to the pharmaceutical industry. In 1932, a German pharmacologist discovered Prontosil, a sulfanilamide drug with significant antibacterial properties. Suddenly, it appeared that scientific research could lead to direct cures; that chemistry and discovery could pave the path to drugs. Accordingly, the U.S. government poured $3 million into a massive research and production effort during World War II, involving more than 20 companies and several universities in a coordinated research effort.[23] These initial funds flowed primarily to war-specific concerns and led, over time, to the development of yellow fever and typhus vaccines and the discovery of oral saline therapies to help exhausted soldiers on the battlefields. After the war, research efforts widened, leading

---

[19] U.S. Constitution, Art. I, § 8.

[20] These constitutional provisions were subsequently included in the Patent Act of 1790.

[21] Cited in Lawrence Lessig, *Code and Other Laws of Cyberspace* (New York: Basic Books, 1999), p. 132.

[22] Ray P. Basler, ed., *The Collected Works of Abraham Lincoln* (New Brunswick, NJ: Rutgers University Press, 1953), p. 363.

[23] This wartime funding marked the start of a continued government commitment to medical research. Between 1945 and 1965, appropriations for the NIH, measured in constant 1988 dollars, rose from $26 million to $4 billion. In current dollars, it is about $14 billion. "Industry Sponsored Research at Duke," *Inside* (Duke University Medical Center) 7, no. 17 (August 31, 1998).

to a widely heralded stream of pharmaceutical breakthroughs: antibiotics in the 1940s, steroids in the 1950s, and birth control pills in the 1960s. Far more efficacious than the elixirs of earlier years, these new drugs flooded the U.S. market, bringing massive improvements in medicine and (with birth control pills especially) significant social change.[24] They also brought a correspondingly large improvement in the fortunes of pharmaceutical companies and a newfound interest in patents.

By the 1970s, the U.S. pharmaceutical industry was completely transformed. Companies such as Merck and Pfizer, once humble chemical suppliers, had become corporate giants, with armies of in-house scientists and a major commitment to research and development. (See Exhibit 19.4 for the growth of research and development expenses.) They had arsenals of proprietary drugs (such as Merck's Pepcid and Abbott Labs' erythromycin) that were distributed through complex networks and supported by sophisticated promotion campaigns. And they had a patent system, enshrined since the eighteenth century, that gave each company 20 years of exclusive control over the drugs that it developed.[25] As of 1980, U.S. pharmaceutical companies were spending just under $2 billion annually for research and development.[26] By 2001, the $170 billion U.S. pharmaceutical market was easily the largest in the world, a combination of high demand (Americans consumed relatively large amounts of drugs), high quality, and prices that remained stubbornly aloof from government regulation. U.S. pharmaceutical firms, together with European players such as Novartis and Bayer, were among the largest corporations in the world and easily among the most profitable: between 1994 and 1998, after-tax profits in the drug industry averaged 17 percent of sales, or three times higher than industrywide averages.[27]

Not surprisingly, representatives of the industry explained these profit levels as evidence of their products' power: pharmaceutical companies made money because they made products that worked; products that customers wanted to buy at almost any cost. Moreover, the industry argued, drug prices were high because they had to be. Each drug, after all, was the product of an increasingly expensive research process, one that was inherently fraught with uncertainty. For each drug that Pfizer, say, developed, there were roughly 5,000 compounds that Pfizer researchers had tested and abandoned in the laboratory.[28] And even those compounds that did prove promising were subjected to a long and tedious process of testing and regulation. Under guidelines established by the U.S. Food and Drug Administration (FDA), no drug could be sold in the U.S. market until it underwent three stages of successful clinical testing and survived a rigorous approval procedure. Only one in 20 trial-phase drugs was eventually approved for public use, and even successful candidates often took 10 years and 50,000 pages of documentation to win FDA approval.[29] The total cost of

[24] See Lynn S. Baker, *The Fertility Fallacy: Sexuality in the Post-Pill Age* (Philadelphia: Saunders Press, 1981).

[25] Originally spanning only 14 years from the date of issue, patent length was extended to 17 years in 1861 and then to 20 in 1994.

[26] *PhARMA Annual Report, 2001–2002,* p. 13.

[27] Standard and Poor's Industry Survey, "Healthcare: Pharmaceuticals," December 16, 1999, p. 26.

[28] See Robert Hunter, "Crack the Code and Profit from Genomics: Research Promises Great Medical Advances but Outlook for Stocks Is Hazy," *The Wall Street Journal Europe,* January 19, 2001, p. 26.

[29] See Standard and Poor's Industry Survey, "Healthcare: Pharmaceuticals," 2001, pp. 20, 22.

this process was reported to be between $500 million and $880 million.[30] No wonder, industry representatives argued, that drug prices were high. No wonder drugs demanded years of patent protection to recoup their research costs. Or as one industry expert explained, "You have to relativize this. A company can support some research without being paid off, but not much. Especially with the pressure on shareholder value."[31]

To be sure, not all observers shared the pharmaceutical industry's analysis of its own economics. Indeed, criticism of the industry was rife in the 1980s and 1990s, and eventually assumed a fairly predictable course. Periodically, critics (such as the early AIDS activists) would decry the industry's high profits and the prices it charged for life-saving drugs. During the Clinton administration, there was a burst of concern about the trend of drug prices and an intense, if ill-fated, attempt to increase regulation of the industry.[32] In other instances, critics complained that drug companies spent more on advertising than on research, and that Americans, stimulated perhaps by this marketing blitz, were taking drugs unnecessarily.[33] One study, for example, revealed that two-thirds of the people taking allergy-fighting Claritin did not in fact have allergies.[34] Moreover, the critics also claimed that pharmaceutical firms vastly overstated their drug development costs: according to Ralph Nader's consumer advocacy organization, R&D costs for an average drug totaled only between $57 million and $71 million throughout the 1990s.[35]

In general, however, the structure of the U.S. pharmaceutical industry did not cause Americans undue concern. Although drug prices in the United States were substantially higher than they were elsewhere—nearly triple average drug prices in Spain and Greece, for example—Americans (and their insurers) seemed willing to pay, or at least unwilling to fight.[36] Or as one industry expert noted, "In reality, if a drug is going to save a life, we will find a way to afford it."[37] Moreover, the skeleton that supported the U.S. drug industry—the U.S. patent system—was itself almost entirely immune from dissent. Even if Americans resisted high drug prices, it appeared, and even if they resented the companies that charged these prices, they weren't willing to

[30] See John Carey and Amy Barrett, "Drug Prices: What's Fair," *BusinessWeek,* December 10, 2001, p. 64; "Tufts Center for the Study of Drug Development Pegs Cost of New Prescription Medicine at $802 Million," Press Release, Tufts Center for the Study of Drug Development, November 30, 2001.

[31] Quoted in Donald McNeil, "Drug Companies and the Third World: Study in Neglect," *New York Times,* May 21, 2000, p. 6.

[32] See, for example, Dana Priest, "Health Care Price Caps Considered; in Separate Move, White House Prepares New Medicare Limits," *Washington Post,* February 14, 1993, p. A1.

[33] Between 1997 and 2001, for example, U.S. direct-to-consumer drug advertising rose from $859 million to $2.49 billion. See Thomas M. Burton, "Backlash Is Brewing Among Companies Who Believe Flashy Ads Drive up Costs," *The Wall Street Journal,* March 13, 2002, p. B1. Likewise, Pfizer's marketing and administrative expenses accounted for 39 percent of expenses in 2000, while R&D accounted for just 17 percent. See Gardiner Harris, "Drug Firms, Stymied in the Lab, Become Marketing Machines," *The Wall Street Journal,* July 6, 2000, p. 1.

[34] Carey and Barrett, p. 63.

[35] See "Rx R&D Myths: The Case Against the Drug Industry's Scare Card," *Public Citizen Congress Watch,* July 2001.

[36] For more on price differentials, see Willis Emmons, "Note on the Pharmaceutical Industry," HBS Case No. 729-002 (Boston: Harvard Business School Publishing, 1998).

[37] Quoted in Carey and Barrett, p. 66.

topple the underlying system. For most Americans believed, like Lincoln, in the inviolability of intellectual property rights and in the advantages of combining "interest" with "genius."

Going Global: The International Battlefield for Intellectual Property Rights

Elsewhere in the world, attitudes toward intellectual property rights were quite different. Some countries had strong patent laws for pharmaceuticals, but mixed them with a regulatory structure that kept drug prices low. Others had licensing requirements or weaker laws that led to lower prices and, often, the development of a generic pharmaceutical industry. And some had no patent laws and no domestic drug industry, and relied entirely on foreign imports.

For countries that lacked a domestic pharmaceutical industry, looser patent laws made sense. In these countries, there often was a sense that the nation simply could not afford either to develop new medications on its own or to pay the high prices that patented drugs commanded elsewhere. Instead, it was economically more efficient simply to allow local firms to copy high-priced imports, reproducing their chemical composition without having to bear the costs of research and development. Such strategies also paid significant social dividends, since they led almost inevitably to cheaper and more accessible drugs. After India loosened its patent laws, for example, drug prices in that country were often more than 90 percent lower than those in the OECD states.[38] Similarly, once local drug companies began producing a generic version of Pfizer's anti-fungal Fluconazole, prices dropped within months from $7 per dose to just 60 cents.[39]

Occasionally, weaker property rights actually led over time to the creation of a substantial generic industry, as occurred in India, Turkey, and Argentina. India's growth was particularly notable, since it took place only after 1970, when the country scaled down its patent laws in order to reduce drug prices. Elsewhere, countries that otherwise adhered to strict protection of intellectual property made a specific exception in the pharmaceutical sector, arguing that health concerns trumped property rights in this industry. Such was the case, for example, in Canada throughout the 1980s, where the government historically offered compulsory licenses for any drug imported into the country. After paying a government-determined royalty payment (generally 4 percent) to the patent holder, local Canadian firms were free to produce their own version of the drug, even if it was still on patent in its home market. Brazil had a similar system, requiring foreign patent holders to produce their drugs locally and charge locally mandated prices.

In the initial phase of post-war pharmaceutical growth, this diffusion of national systems functioned relatively well. Nations fashioned their laws to suit their own needs, and pharmaceutical firms adapted to their local circumstances: where property rights were strong and markets large (as in the United States and Great Britain), well-funded drug companies made both substantial profits and significant breakthroughs. Where rights were weak and patients poor, pharmaceutical firms were either generic (as in India or Brazil) or nonexistent.

[38] See "Fatal Side Effects: Medicine Patents under the Microscope," Oxfam, 2000, p. 18.

[39] Reported in Carmen Perez-Casas, "HIV/AIDS Medicines Pricing Report. Setting Objectives: Is There a Political Will?" *Medecines Sans Frontieres*, July 6, 2000, p. 10.

As the major Western drug manufacturers began to go global, however, they also began a decades-long campaign to bring Western-style property rights to the developing world. Led by Pfizer and its politically active chairman, Edmund T. Pratt Jr., the companies negotiated for these rights with individual governments; lobbied to have them embedded under the auspices of WIPO—the World Intellectual Property Organization; and formed international alliances with other knowledge-based industries, such as software and publishing.[40] They ran advertising campaigns and held extensive meetings, striving to convince foreign officials of the urgency of their plight.

And in the end, the pharmaceutical companies essentially returned to Washington. In 1988, the U.S. Congress amended the Trade and Tariff Act of 1984, authorizing the U.S Trade Representative (USTR) to take retaliatory action against any country believed to be guilty of failing to protect U.S. companies' intellectual property rights through a provision known as "Special 301." Justifying the policy by arguing "we don't work for" consumers in patent-violating countries such as Argentina and South Korea, the USTR compiled annual lists of suspected violators and threatened unilateral sanctions unless these countries conformed with the dictates of U.S. law. In response, countries including Argentina, Thailand, Brazil, Italy, and Korea swiftly tightened their patent and copyright laws. At an ideological level, several of these states continued to assert the superiority of their former systems. But pressure from the United States was sufficient to compel a regulatory change of heart.

In the meantime, the pharmaceutical lobby also labored to include intellectual rights on the World Trade Organization's agenda. Allying with other developed nations during the Uruguay Round of GATT (General Agreement on Tariffs and Trade) negotiations, U.S. officials successfully added intellectual property rights to the slate of new requirements. Under a provision known as TRIPS (for trade-related intellectual property rights), all countries that desired to join the newly created World Trade Organization (WTO) would henceforth be required to grant a minimum of 20-year patent protection in most fields of medicine. Despite loopholes allowing for the compulsory licensing of drugs in some cases and the concession of a 10-year implementation period for least-developed countries, TRIPS marked a landmark achievement in the pharmaceutical industry's quest for global patent protection. "TRIPS," claimed one industry specialist, "is the most important international agreement on intellectual property this century."[41]

Debate, however, continued to rage. In many parts of the world, both government officials and public opinion maintained that U.S.-style patent rights were ill-suited to their countries' circumstances—that they were unfair, unrealistic, and ultimately damaging to public health. Indeed, despite their formal adherence to TRIPS, many countries still argued that health had to take precedence over profits and that all countries (including the United States) should be able to license patented drugs in case of medical emergency. Health care experts also stressed that generic production posed far less of a threat than industry representatives suggested. Indeed, in most parts of the world, people simply could not afford patented drugs and would not purchase them under any circumstances. In areas such as sub-Saharan Africa, for example, where per capita expenditure on drugs rarely topped $100 a year, activists stressed

---

[40] See Lynn Sharp Paine, "Pfizer: Protecting Intellectual Property in a Global Marketplace," HBS Case No. 392-073.

[41] Quoted in Frances Williams, "The GATT Deal: Developing Nations Give Way on Patents—Intellectual Property," *Financial Times,* December 16, 1993, p. 4.

that "the purchasing power of 1.2 billion people living on U.S.$1 a day simply does not constitute a commercial incentive to research and development."[42]

Yet the pharmaceutical companies remained firm. Snug behind the protection of both U.S. law and TRIPS, they maintained the intellectual purity of their position. Without patent protection, no company could afford to take the financial risks that drug development demanded. And without drugs and drug research, millions of people would suffer.

Back to Africa

At the turn of the century, the AIDS situation in Africa remained grim. Even as AIDS-related deaths in the developed world were plummeting at last, and even though nonprofit groups such as Doctors Without Borders were trying to distribute drugs to small clusters of Africans, the vast majority of Africa's AIDS patients remained without treatment. In 2001, 25 million Africans were HIV-positive, roughly half of whom were medically eligible for combination treatments such as HAART.[43] Only 25,000 of these patients had received antiretroviral drugs, however, a tiny portion when compared to Western standards.[44] In Uganda, for example, only about 1,000 patients, or 0.1 percent of the infected population, had received the prescribed triple therapy; in Malawi, the number was only 30.[45] Without drugs, these patients were also essentially without hope. And thus the AIDS epidemic continued to ravage Africa, and to wreak an escalating havoc on a continent already beset with troubles.

It wasn't long, therefore, before Africa spawned AIDS activists of its own, patients or their supporters who struggled to find some way of attacking, or at least forestalling, the disease's deadly hold. Like their Western predecessors, the activists spread a wide net at first, cajoling governments and the media to take notice of their plight. But eventually they focused on the easiest and most obvious target: the pharmaceutical companies whose drugs held the prospect of survival.

Although these groups were split to some extent by their negotiating tactics, they shared a common underlying complaint, the same complaint that had initially motivated ACT UP a decade earlier in the United States. Simply put, the activists charged that the AIDS plague in Africa was due, at least in part, to the actions of Western drug firms. It was the drug companies, they claimed, that consciously held prices beyond the grasp of most Africans; the drug companies that refused to allow lower-priced versions of their product. It was the drug companies that hid behind the veneer of Western patent laws and used international pressure to preserve their own profits. And while the companies reaped profits from high-priced AIDS drugs, millions of Africans were dying.

Central to the activists' complaint was the problem of prices. In the developed world, the typical price of HAART treatment in 1999 remained at the staggering level of $10,000–$15,000. Much of this cost, however, was assumed either by government insurance plans (in Canada and Europe) or by private insurance (in the United States). In Africa, where both public and private insurance schemes were scarce, pric-

[42] "Fatal Side Effects," p. 5.

[43] "Bristol-Myers Squibb Announces Accelerated Program to Fight HIV/AIDS in Africa," Press Release, March 14, 2001, p. 1.

[44] Howard Hiatt, "Learn from Haiti," *New York Times,* December 6, 2001.

[45] Markus Haacker, *Providing Health Care to HIV Patients in Southern Africa,* IMF Policy Discussion Paper, March 2001, p. 12.

ing drugs at Western levels essentially meant pricing them far beyond the reach of nearly all potential patients: at $10,000, virtually no one in Africa, or indeed anywhere in the developing world, could afford HAART-style treatment. Accordingly, AIDS activists and patients in Africa accused the Western drug companies of using their pricing policies to "wage an undeclared drug war" against the developing world.[46] By refusing to lower their prices, the activists charged, pharmaceutical firms were directly responsible for millions of unnecessary deaths and for allowing AIDS to spread unchecked across the continent. "There are drugs," argued one prominent AIDS consultant, "there is unimaginable wealth in this world, and the people who have the money are refusing to help."[47] Echoed another: "The poor have no consumer power, so the market has failed them. I'm tired of the logic that says, 'He who can't pay, dies.'"[48]

What particularly infuriated many Africa-based activists was the pharmaceutical companies' reluctance to endorse generic substitutes for their products. Typically, branded drugs from the developing world were sold in Africa and elsewhere as lower-priced copies—there were generic antibiotics, for example, and ulcer-fighting medicines rather than the branded products that prevailed in the West. Sometimes these drugs were produced by Western firms, and sometimes by generic producers based in India, Argentina, or Brazil. Nearly always, though, the generic drugs were legally generic (even by U.S. standards) since the original patents had already expired. AIDS drugs, however, were different: they were new, they were often experimental, and nearly all of them remained protected by Western patents in their home markets. In the case of these drugs, therefore, Western companies were reluctant to permit generic production—even if generic firms could arguably produce the same drug at a substantially reduced price. For the companies, this was simply accepted practice. But for the activists it was greed that led to murder. Industry experts estimated that generic competition in the AIDS drug market could lead to an immediate 50–90 percent reduction in drug prices.[49]

Already, a handful of countries had formally embraced generic solutions. In India, for example, local firms were legally permitted to produce patented medicines so long as they could develop a new means of producing them, and in Thailand the government actively encouraged the production of generic AIDS drugs.[50] The most dramatic policy, though, came from Brazil, where a controversial "Free Drugs for All" program provided a compelling example of low-priced, large-scale antiretroviral treatment. Launched in 1997, this government-sponsored initiative offered a variety of HAART therapies, for free, to all AIDS patients. Using generic drugs produced by its own local industry, the government spent only $4,716 per patient per year—compared with $12,000 for similar therapy in the United States. By the turn of the century, over 90,000

[46] See Donald G. McNeil, "Oxfam Joins Campaign to Cut Drug Prices for Poor Nations," *New York Times,* February 13, 2001, p. A5.

[47] Siddarth Dube, quoted in Michael Spector, "India's Plague: Cheaper Drugs May Help Millions Who Have AIDS, but How Many Will They Hurt?" *New Yorker,* December 17, 2001, p. 83.

[48] Dr. James Orbinski, International President, Doctors Without Borders, quoted in Donald G. McNeil, "Drug Makers and 3rd World: Study in Neglect," *New York Times,* May 21, 2000, p. 6.

[49] See Merrill Goozner, "Third World Battles for AIDS Drugs: U.S. Firms Oppose Generic Licensing," *Chicago Tribune,* April 28, 1999, p. 12.

[50] On India, see Kevin Watkins, "Patent the Poor Will Lose," *The Guardian,* October 13, 2000. For Thailand, see Marwaan Macan-Markar, "Health: Thailand Has Capacity to Test WTO Deal on Generic Drugs," *Inter Press Service,* November 15, 2001.

patients had received treatment and infection rates were plummeting.[51] AIDS-related deaths had fallen by half since 1996 and the government actually appeared to be saving money: according to official estimates, treatment under the Free Drugs program had kept 146,000 people out of the hospital and saved the country $422 million in averted hospital charges.[52] Overjoyed with their success, health officials argued that Brazil demonstrated both the efficacy of generic solutions and the economic feasibility of treating even very poor patients. "The simplistic argument that treating AIDS is expensive is no longer convincing," asserted one well-placed observer. "In Brazil, the cost of the investment is economically positive."[53] Even more impressive, perhaps, was that Brazil had not completely abandoned the recognition of international patents. Indeed, under pressure from the United States, Brazil only permitted the generic production of antiretroviral drugs commercialized before 1997. Half of its per-patient cost came from the importation of more recently patented treatments.

As word of Brazil's success spread, health workers in Africa urged a similar response. They argued that drugs had to be made available on the continent in large quantities and at reduced prices, meaning that the pharmaceutical companies would have to either cut their prices or agree to generic production of still-patented treatments. In South Africa, seeds of a future battle were sown on December 12, 1997, when President Nelson Mandela signed a series of key amendments to the South African Medicines Act. Initiated by the controversial South African Health Minister, Nkosazana Zuma, the amendments gave the health minister authority to break international patents and import or manufacture generic drugs.[54] As part of a larger plan to improve the sorry state of health care in a country that paid some of the highest drug prices in the world, Zuma pledged, "I will not sacrifice the public's right to health on the altar of vested interests."[55]

In May of 1999, the World Health Assembly (the policymaking body of the World Health Organization) passed a resolution that declared public health concerns "paramount" in intellectual property issues related to pharmaceuticals. When U.S. Vice President Gore visited Africa in the summer of 1999, AIDS was a constant refrain; in South Africa, the vice president was actually booed in public for his pro-patent stance. Under attack from mounting public criticism, U.S. President Clinton announced in late 1999 that the United States would no longer impose sanctions on developing countries seeking cheaper AIDS treatment. But U.S. pharmaceutical companies, which obviously bore the brunt of any policy relaxation, were far from being convinced. On the contrary, they continued to stress that the problem of AIDS in Africa had little to do with either the cost or availability of cutting-edge treatments. Africans were dying, they insisted, because of Africa's own problems.

---

[51] There were only 540,000 total infections in 2000, half as many as the World Health Organization had predicted only six years earlier. See Tina Rosenberg, "Look at Brazil," *New York Times Magazine,* January 28, 2001.

[52] "Drug Companies versus Brazil: The Threat to Public Health," Oxfam Great Britain, London, May 2001, p. 5.

[53] Pedro Chequer of UNAIDS, quoted in Andrew Downie, "AIDS Drugs Offered Free in Brazil," *Christian Science Monitor,* December 6, 2000, p. 6.

[54] See Donald G. McNeil, "South Africa's Bitter Pill for World's Drug Makers," *New York Times,* March 29, 1998, p. C1.

[55] Quoted in Lynn Duke, "Activist Health Minister Draws Foes in South Africa," *Washington Post,* December 11, 1998, p. A41.

View from the Pharmaceuticals

It was not easy, of course, for the pharmaceutical industry to respond dispassionately to the criticism that erupted in the late 1990s. People in the industry genuinely believed that they were saving lives, not harming them, and they felt that the criticism was seriously misplaced. So they tried to build a careful and compelling case, one that shifted the spotlight away from their own activities.

According to the major pharmaceutical producers, the slow spread of AIDS treatment in Africa had little to do with either the price or availability of AIDS drugs. Instead, it was simply due to endemic features of the African landscape: to the lack of clean water in many areas, to poor medical infrastructure and limited information, and to stubborn political and social issues that local authorities either could not, or would not, address. Industry executives claimed, for example, that government officials in Africa were far less committed to the AIDS struggle than their public pronouncements might suggest and that corruption remained a corroding influence across the African continent. To support this contention, industry advocates pointed to the World Bank study that found that, for every $100 that certain African governments spent on drugs, only $12 worth of medicine actually reached the patient.[56] Under such conditions, the industry argued, making drugs more widely available would not necessarily make Africans healthier; instead, drugs might simply be stolen and resold elsewhere in the world. As Dr. Josef Decosas, director of the Southern Africa AIDS Training Program, put it: "Virtually all African countries have centralized drug import and distribution centers, and most of them are broken or corrupted. Even if you make these drugs available for free, the systems to deliver them are not there."[57] In early 2001, an estimated 50 percent of drug stocks were reported stolen from South African public hospitals and clinics.[58]

Pharmaceutical companies also emphasized the sheer difficulty of distributing AIDS drugs across the African continent. Transportation links in the region were relatively scarce, as were basic elements of a medical infrastructure. Without clinics to support the treatments, they argued, and health care workers to administer them, regimes like HAART simply wouldn't work. Indeed, to be successful, HAART-style therapies demanded support programs, palliative care, and preventative treatments—none of which could be easily established in most parts of Africa. Moreover, because AIDS preyed on the immune system, patients on HAART treatment were prone to opportunistic infection and needed to depend on a regime of regular tests and monitoring—a regime that, again, would be difficult to implement in the African context. Burroughs-Wellcome, for example, which manufactured the AIDS-fighting compound AZT, had concluded in the late 1990s that Africa lacked the laboratory support necessary to administer its own drug safely.[59] Similarly, Britain's GlaxoSmithKline had funded a study demonstrating the difficulties of adhering to an AIDS treatment regime, with the number of pills, side effects, and food restrictions all cited as problems.[60] Although

[56] Cited at http://world.phrma.org/challenges.health.infra.html, accessed March 2002.

[57] Quoted in Thomas Friedman, "It Takes a Village," *New York Times,* April 27, 2001, p. 25.

[58] "A War over Drugs and Patents," *The Economist,* March 10, 2001, p. 44.

[59] See Barton Gellman, "An Unequal Calculus of Life and Death," *Washington Post,* December 27, 2000.

[60] In that study, 62 percent of 292 questioned patients reported having "problems keeping up with their treatment." "AIDS Drug Regime Considered Too Hard to Follow," *Agence France Presse,* March 15, 2001.

the study was not specific to Africa, other industry representatives used it and similar data to imply that poorer patients from other cultures might not be able to adhere to the demands of an AIDS regime. Even USAID director Andrew Natsios articulated this controversial sentiment when he justified his organization's decision not to fund antiretroviral treatment by observing that African AIDS patients "don't know what Western time is" and thus would be unable to take treatments effectively.[61]

Pharmaceutical executives also pointed to the difficulty of maintaining effective treatment in poverty. Taking care of AIDS, they noted, entailed more than just taking drugs. Patients also had to take care of their general health, getting proper nutrition and exercise and avoiding other diseases. Where people lived in poverty, all of these environmental conditions became considerably more difficult to sustain—to a point where even the most powerful drugs might be rendered useless. Indeed, failed treatment, as one health worker noted, "can become a vicious circle—no food, no money—so they can't take their medicine properly, so they get opportunistic diseases, so they can't work, they get depressed and that leads them further away from treatment."[62] Under these conditions, scientists feared that resistant strains of the HIV virus could easily evolve, thwarting efforts at long-term control.[63] Moreover, while AIDS under any circumstance was a treacherous, deadly disease, Africa was still plagued by other ills—river blindness, tuberculosis, measles, typhoid, malaria—that were relatively easy to treat. "In view of the competing demands of other health problems," therefore, many industry observers concluded that widescale HAART treatment in Africa was both unwise and possibly dangerous.[64]

Finally, although pharmaceutical companies were reluctant to engage in detailed price discussions, they were generally willing to defend their position on both patents and pricing. Essentially, the industry argued that high prices and long-term patents were a critical element of their business, regardless of where this business occurred. If they lowered prices for AIDS drugs, decreased revenues in this area would drive innovation to other, more lucrative diseases. Pharmaceutical companies would stop investing in AIDS research, and AIDS patients, over the long run, would suffer. Moreover, once the sanctity of patents was undermined in Africa or for AIDS, what would stop this loosening trend from continuing elsewhere, in European markets, for example, or for equally potent (and profitable) cancer-fighting drugs? The Western patent system, industry representatives urged, had facilitated the emergence of research-driven companies and life-saving scientific breakthroughs. If patents were undermined in Africa, then they would swiftly be undermined elsewhere in the global economy. And without patents, research across the global economy would suffer.

Ultimately, the problem of AIDS in Africa, argued the pharmaceutical industry, was a problem for governments and society. Tackling AIDS meant tackling education. It meant talking about subjects (sexual behavior, gender norms) that were still taboo in many places. And it meant spending money—public money—in places where funds were scarce. None of these tasks were the responsibility of the world's pharmaceutical firms. Instead, as a senior drug lobbyist had reasoned earlier in the decade:

---

[61] Amir Attaran, Kenneth Freedberg, and Martin Hirsch, "Dead Wrong on AIDS," *Washington Post,* June 15, 2001.

[62] Rosenberg, "Look at Brazil."

[63] See Spector, "India's Plague," p. 82.

[64] See, for example, industry comments quoted in Gelman, "An Unequal Calculus of Life and Death," p. A1.

The predominant contribution that the research-based pharmaceutical industry could reasonably be expected to make is in their predominant area of competence—research and development. The broader responsibility for ensuring that such products are delivered to those they could benefit should be borne by society, particularly government.[65]

Africa's AIDS activists, however, were not content to leave their burden with either government or society. Instead, pointing to success stories such as Brazil and Thailand, they insisted that large-scale drug treatment was imminently feasible in Africa. "The limiting factor for us," stated the nonprofit Doctors Without Borders, "is price."[66] Similarly, leaders from various health NGOs argued that while conditions in poor countries precluded treatment for some, most major cities in the developing world would be fully equipped to handle AIDS patients if they had access to affordable tests and drugs.[67]

In late 2000, Joep Lange, a negotiator at nonprofit International Antiviral Therapy Evaluation, articulated his frustration at industry representatives' reaction to plans that would have expanded treatment by extending business discounts for drugs distributed to employees:

> They laughed at us. The [pharmaceutical] companies are not interested. They don't want to treat a million people tomorrow. They say, "We want to do it responsibly," but there's a lot of window dressing there. They don't know what could be the repercussions: Their whole price structure could collapse. They are scared to death.[68]

[65] Quoted in ibid., p. A18.

[66] Quoted in McNeil, "Drug Companies and the Third World," p. 6. This comment referred more generally to the situation facing all drugs in Africa.

[67] Goozner, "Third World Battles for AIDS Drugs," p. 16.

[68] Quoted in Barton Gellman, "A Turning Point That Left Millions Behind," *Washington Post,* December 28, 2000, p. A18.

EXHIBIT 19.1   International Prevalence Rates of HIV/AIDS among Adults

Source: Adapted from UNAIDS, *Report on the Global 2000 Epidemic,* June 2000, p. 14.

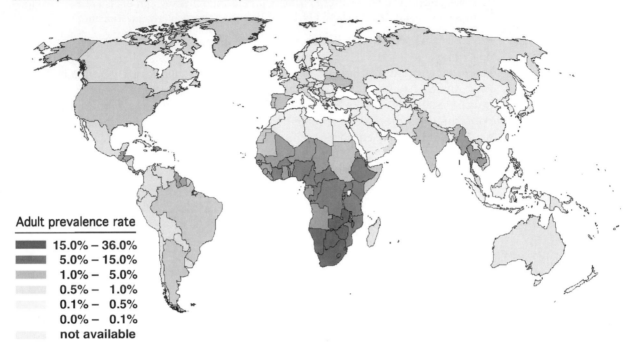

Adult prevalence rate

- 15.0% – 36.0%
- 5.0% – 15.0%
- 1.0% – 5.0%
- 0.5% – 1.0%
- 0.1% – 0.5%
- 0.0% – 0.1%
- not available

EXHIBIT 19.2

Comparison of Annual AIDS-Related Deaths, 1982–2000

Source: "Consensus Statement on Antiretroviral Treatment for AIDS in Poor Countries," individual members of the faculty at Harvard University, p. 27.

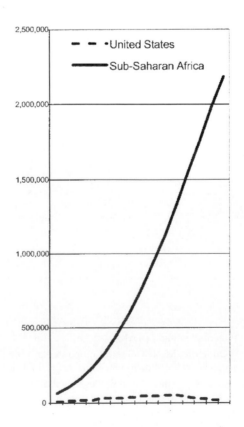

EXHIBIT 19.3   **Changes in Life Expectancy in Selected African Countries, 1950–2005**

Source: Adapted from UNAIDS and WHO, *AIDS Epidemic,* December 2001, p. 9.

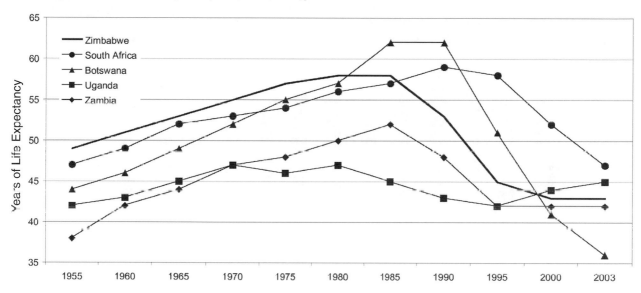

EXHIBIT 19.4
R&D Expenditures for U.S. Research-Based Pharmaceutical Companies (in millions of dollars), 1980–2000[a]

Source: *PhRMA 2001 Industry Profile,* p. 117.

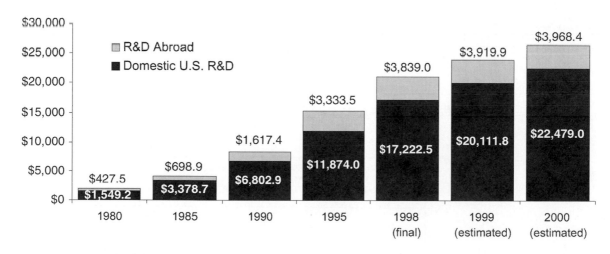

[a]Domestic R&D includes U.S. and foreign pharmaceutical spending in the United States. R&D abroad includes U.S. companies' foreign expenditures.

EXHIBIT 19.5   FDA New Drug Approval Times, 1986–2000

Source: Adapted from PhARMA, *2001 Industry Profile,* p. 25. (Data provided by the FDA.)

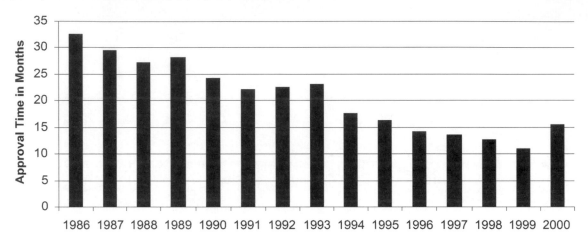

EXHIBIT 19.6
Profitability of
***Fortune* 500 Drug**
Industry Compared
to *Fortune* 500 Aver-
age, 1970–2000

Source: "Rx R&D Myths:
The Case Against the Drug
Industry's R&D 'Score
Card,'" *Public Citizen Con-
gress Watch,* July 2001, p. 12.

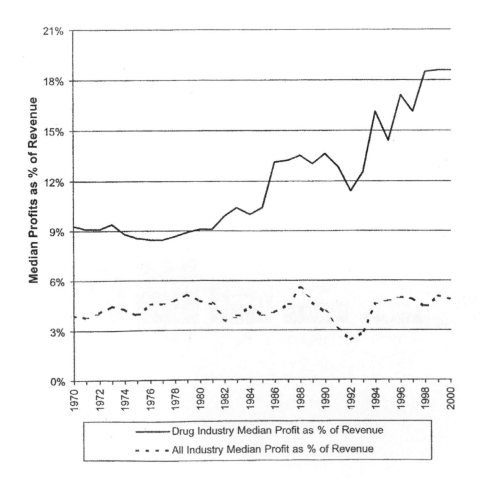

EXHIBIT 19.7
Development of 152 Global Drugs by Country of Origin, 1975–1994

Source: Adapted from "Why Do Prescription Drugs Cost So Much . . . and Other Questions About Your Medicines," Pharmaceutical Research and Manufacturers of America, p. 16.

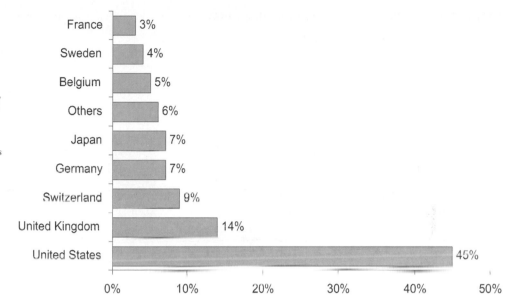

EXHIBIT 19.8
Total Number of New Drugs Placed on the Market According to Nationality of the Company, 1975–1999

Source: Adapted from European Federation of Pharmaceutical Industries and Associations, *The Pharmaceutical Industry in Figures 2000*, p. 22.

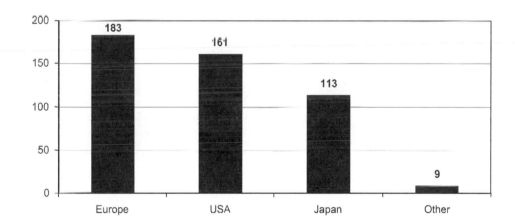

EXHIBIT 19.9
**Drug Price
Comparisons**

Source: Adapted from
"Patent Injustice: How
World Trade Rules Threaten
the Health of Poor People,"
Oxfam Briefing Paper, 2001,
pp. 26–27.

A. Prices for selected drugs and their generic equivalents in Pakistan and India, 1997[a]

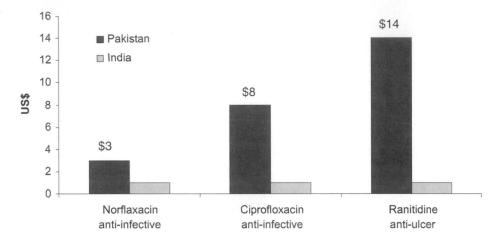

B. Prices for selected drugs and their generic equivalents in South Africa and Brazil, 2000[b]

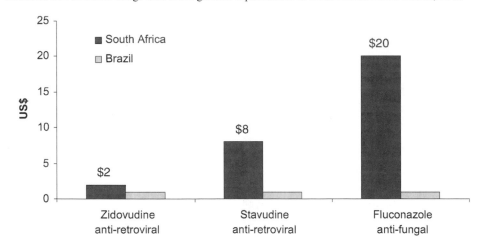

[a]Prices for patented drugs in Pakistan as a multiple of India's generic equivalents.
[b]Prices for patented drugs in South Africa as a multiple of Brazil's generic equivalents.

EXHIBIT 19.10
**Drug Price Ratios
between Selected
Countries, 2000**

Source: Adapted from
*Canada's Patented Medicine
Prices Review Board Annual
Report 2000,* p. 21.

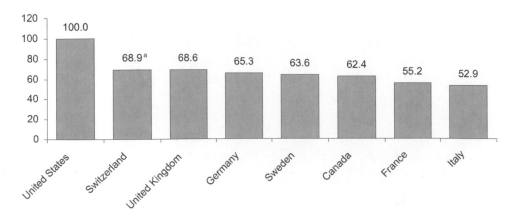

[a]On average, drug prices in Switzerland are 68.9% of drug prices in the United States.

20

Phase Two: The Pharmaceutical Industry Responds to AIDS

Debora Spar and Nicholas Bartlett

As I see it, they still haven't made their offers transparent, they're still fighting tooth and nail, using every tactic they can. I think they still need some more whipping.[1]

Samantha Bolton, Doctors Without Borders

In March of 2000, Ray Gilmartin went to Geneva. As chief executive of Merck, one of the world's largest pharmaceutical firms, Gilmartin had already established his firm as a powerhouse in the health care field: Merck had 62,000 employees in 1999, sales of $32.7 billion, and net income of nearly $6 billion. It also held patents for some of the world's most valuable drugs, including Propecia (for treating male baldness) and Zocor (for high cholesterol). But now Gilmartin had something new. In a confidential meeting with Gro Harlem Brundtland, Director General of the World Health Organization (WHO), he revealed a proposal from Merck and four of its leading competitors (Bristol-Myers Squibb, GlaxoSmithKline, Boehringer-Ingelheim,

---

[1] Personal interview, April 2001.

Professor Debora Spar and Research Associate Nick Bartlett prepared this case. HBS cases are developed solely as the basis for class discussion. Cases are not intended to serve as endorsements, sources of primary data, or illustrations of effective or ineffective management.

Copyright © 2002 President and Fellows of Harvard College. To order copies or request permission to reproduce materials, call 1-800-545-7685, write Harvard Business School Publishing, Boston, MA 02163, or go to http//www.hbsp.harvard.edu. No part of this publication may be reproduced, stored in a retrieval system, used in a spreadsheet, or transmitted in any form or by any means—electronic, mechanical, photocopying, recording, or otherwise—without the permission of Harvard Business School.

and Hoffmann-La Roche).[2] The companies, in principle at least, were willing to sell their powerful AIDS drugs at a substantial discount in Africa. In exchange, they wanted WHO to participate in their initiative and help to distribute the life-saving drugs.

On the surface it seemed irresistible. After years of fighting against differential pricing, years of suffering high-profile attack, the pharmaceutical industry was offering a major concession: they were offering to sell their drugs in Africa for far less than their price in other parts of the world. They were offering to give their product away for a fraction of its retail cost, and to play a major role in the global fight against AIDS. All they asked in return, really, was buy-in from the WHO and continued protection for their patent rights. Over the next few weeks, pharmaceutical executives held similar discussions with other high-profile leaders: the United Nations' Kofi Annan, James Wolfensohn of the World Bank, UNAIDS' Peter Piot.

Brundtland and her colleagues, however, did not respond as quickly or as decisively as Gilmartin had hoped. Instead, they met and discussed, worrying about the sufficiency of price cuts and the symbolism of any explicit support for patents. On May 11, *The Wall Street Journal* broke the ongoing story, reporting that "in a landmark response to the AIDS crisis in Africa, five of the world's largest pharmaceutical companies offered to slash the prices of HIV drugs for people living in poor nations."[3]

And thus began the next phase of the political battle around AIDS. In a relatively short period of time, the pharmaceutical industry had come a long way, acknowledging the severity of AIDS in the developing world and accepting an expanded, even altered, role. They agreed to massive price discounts and to various, often far-reaching, forms of corporate philanthropy. They noted—insistently and repeatedly—that their much-maligned patent rights were not even an issue in Africa, since the vast majority of AIDS drugs were not under patent protection across most of the continent. And they launched innovative programs with individual African states, selling or distributing drugs at sharply preferential prices. Their actions, however, did little to silence the critics. On the contrary, many claimed that the companies' price initiative was ineffective or even damaging; that by focusing on price, they were merely trying to divert attention from the more fundamental issues of access and patents. In response, industry executives pointed to the huge, unprecedented concessions they had already made: "We're doing our part," insisted one industry spokesperson. "We're lowering our prices."[4] How far was the pharmaceutical industry supposed to go?

Innovation and Concession

Between 1999 and 2001 the pharmaceutical industry appeared to leap into action. Responding to the growing plight of AIDS (as well, presumably, to the growing cries of their critics), nearly all the major drug manufacturers launched major initiatives against the disease. In 1999, for example, Merck joined with several research groups at Harvard University to launch its Enhancing Care Initiative, a $5 million effort to

---

[2] Pfizer was initially part of the group but subsequently withdrew. Reported in Barton Gellman, "A Turning Point That Left Millions Behind," *Washington Post,* December 28, 2000, p. A18. This section draws heavily on Gellman's excellent account.

[3] Michael Waldholz, "Into Africa: Makers of AIDS Drugs Agree to Slash Prices for Developing World," *The Wall Street Journal,* May 11, 2000, p. A1.

[4] Quoted in Sheryl Gay Stolberg, "Africa's AIDS War," *New York Times,* March 9, 2001, p. A4.

understand the spread and treatment of AIDS in the developing world.[5] Bristol-Myers Squibb pledged over $100 million to its Secure the Future campaign, a program designed to "complement the broader efforts of governments . . . for the management of HIV/AIDS."[6] Education, research, and community outreach made up the core of the program. Glaxo Wellcome slashed the price of AZT, a powerful AIDS-fighting drug sold to pregnant women in developing countries;[7] and Abbott Laboratories launched Step Forward, a charitable project to assist AIDS orphans and other at-risk children.[8]

Activists, however, continued to castigate the pharmaceutical industry for its aloofness and its greed. Zachie Achmat, for example, head of the South African Treatment Action Campaign, stated during a major conference that "AIDS is a holocaust against the poor and the responsibility lies with the drug companies who put their profits before their responsibilities."[9] Richard Holbrooke, the U.S. ambassador to the United Nations, was even blunter: "Pharmaceutical companies," he charged, "would rather treat a bald American than a dying African."[10] Even Pfizer's well-publicized pledge to distribute its antifungal drug fluconazole (diflucan) free of charge in South Africa did little to quell the company's critics.[11]

It was against this backdrop that Mr. Gilmartin left for Geneva, setting off what would swiftly become an unusual wave of enthusiasm. Under the terms of Accelerating Access, the pharmaceutical companies, in collaboration with UNAIDS, WHO, the World Bank, UNICEF (United Nations Children's Fund), and the United Nations Population Fund, pledged their support for a common set of AIDS-fighting principles. Together, the partners declared their support for strengthening national capacity in the affected states, engaging all sectors of society in the fight against AIDS, securing significant additional funding from national and international sources, and continuing their investment in relevant research and development. More specifically, several of the pharmaceutical firms also promised to provide certain AIDS drugs to developing nations at reduced prices.[12]

When news of the Accelerating Access program broke, even the critics momentarily rejoiced. "It's the first time the companies are collectively willing to discuss a truly significant decline in prices," acknowledged Piot of UNAIDS. "It is something that many of us have long hoped for."[13] The World Bank's Wolfensohn praised the companies for spurring governmental action,[14] and even Doctors Without Borders confessed their

---

[5] For more on this and other Merck programs, see James Weber, James Austin, and Diana Barrett, "Merck Global Health Initiatives (B): Botswana," HBS Case No. 301-089 (Boston, MA: Harvard Business School Publishing, 2001).

[6] "Bristol-Myers Squibb Commits One Hundred Million Dollars for HIV/AIDS Research and Community Outreach in Five African Countries," BMS Press Release, May 6, 1999.

[7] Lisa Buckingham, "Glaxo Cuts Price of Anti-AIDS Drug," *Guardian,* March 6, 1998, p. 23.

[8] "Accelerating Access to HIV/AIDS Care, Treatment, and Support," background paper prepared for United Nations Secretary General, New York, October 4, 2001. Updated November 2001.

[9] Quoted in Alex Duval Smith, "AIDS Summit: Drug Companies 'Inflicting Holocaust on the Poor,'" *Independent,* July 10, 2000, p. 11.

[10] Quoted in Steve Sternberg, "AIDS Activists Discount Big Drugmakers' Gifts," *USA Today,* July 11, 2000, p. 9D.

[11] See Donald G. McNeil, "Patents and Patients," *New York Times,* July 9, 2000, p. 8.

[12] See Weber et al., "Merck Global Health Initiatives (B): Botswana," p. 4.

[13] Quoted in Michael Waldholz, "Into Africa: Makers of AIDS Drugs Agree to Slash Prices for Developing World," *The Wall Street Journal,* May 11, 2000, p. A1.

[14] Quoted in ibid.

"appreciation."[15] After the deal was announced, Boehringer Ingelheim Vice Chairman Rolf Krebs commented: "The price issue was always discussed as preventing people from being treated. We took the price away."[16]

What "taking the price away" meant in practice, though, was far from clear. Would the pharmaceutical firms give all their drugs, for free, to all affected patients? And how would they handle the always troubling issues of distribution and appropriate follow-up care? Accelerating Access offered little guidance along these lines. Accordingly, each of the pharmaceutical firms was left to resolve the issues on its own. And their solutions, not surprisingly, fell far short of the activists' demands.

Gilmartin's Merck was among the first to act. In July of 2000, the company joined with the Bill & Melinda Gates Foundation to launch the $100 million "Botswana Comprehensive HIV/AIDS Partnership," an effort that aimed to treat and prevent AIDS in Botswana by focusing on the country's basic health infrastructure.[17] Merck signed on to manage the program and contribute antiretroviral medicines. Just days later, Boehringer Ingelheim announced its own plan to donate nevirapine (a drug that helped to combat mother-to-child transmission of AIDS) to the world's poorest countries.[18] Other firms launched independent negotiations with the African states, trying to craft long-term plans for significant price reductions. While details of each plan varied, they had several features in common, features that had already been hinted at during the Accelerating Access discussions: First, any free or discounted drugs were given primarily to national governments. Second, the governments had to ensure the firms that the drugs were being distributed through a functioning health care system. And third, the governments also had to ensure their suppliers of an ongoing commitment to "adequate and enforced intellectual property rights."[19]

The activists were not impressed. Instead, they argued that such restrictions would inevitably compromise the lofty goals set forth in Geneva, preventing the widespread access that was so sorely needed. Nongovernmental organizations working with Pfizer, for example, accused the company of reneging on its promise, claiming that "the company has imposed a time limit on its donation and required doctors to report back as if in a clinical trial."[20] More cynical observers noted that Pfizer's diflucan was actually scheduled to come off patent the next year and that the "free giveaway" was thus more accurately a "strategy to block access to generically manufactured drugs."[21] In South Africa, regional health ministers protested that even the announcement of Accelerating Access was problematic, since "the public was given the impression that the prices of antiretroviral drugs have been drastically reduced and immediately available."[22] South African unions were even blunter, castigating the pharmaceutical firms in November of 2000 for trying to "make a quick buck at the expense of the lives of our people."[23] Doctors Without Borders complained that "the

[15] Naomi Koppel, "Five Major Drug Companies Offer to Slash Prices for AIDS Drugs to Africa," *Associated Press,* May 11, 2000.

[16] Barton Gellman, "A Turning Point That Left Millions Behind," *Washington Post,* December 28, 2000, p. A18.

[17] Weber et al., "Merck Global Health Initiatives (B): Botswana."

[18] "Accelerating Access to HIV/AIDS Care, Treatment, and Support."

[19] Gellman, "A Turning Point."

[20] Donald G. McNeil, "Medicine Merchants," *New York Times,* July 9, 2000, p. 8.

[21] "Inside the Industry: Pfizer to Expand AIDS Drug Donation Program," *Healthline,* June 7, 2001.

[22] Gellman, "A Turning Point," p. A18.

[23] "South African Unions to Press Foreign Firms to Cut AIDS Drug Prices," *Agence France-Presse,* November 25, 2000.

negotiations between the drug companies and health ministries have so far been characterized by a lack of transparency, lots of PR puff from the companies, and very little action,"[24] while Oxfam likened the pharmaceutical industry's efforts to "an elephant giving birth to a mouse."[25] By March 2001, nearly a year after the campaign's announcement, only three countries—Senegal, Uganda, and Rwanda—had reached specific agreements regarding the distribution of lower-priced AIDS drugs.[26] In each case, the drugs would be sold for roughly $1,000 to $1,500 per patient per year, less than 10 percent of the prevailing U.S. price.[27]

Fighting for Rights

What the activists demanded instead of cheaper-priced drugs, and what the pharmaceutical industry consistently refused to provide, was a broad exception to the evolving global regime of intellectual property rights. According to the activists, reduced pricing for drugs would still never get them into the hands of those in need; the only way to achieve this kind of distribution, they argued, was to eliminate entirely the patents that kept prices high. According to the industry, however, any strategy along these lines was completely out of the question. Indeed, the pharmaceutical industry had spent much of the 1990s fighting for the expansion of U.S.-style intellectual property rights; during the Uruguay Round of world trade negotiations, they had succeeded in embedding TRIPS (the Agreement on Trade-Related Intellectual Property Rights) into the very fabric of the General Agreement on Tariffs and Trade and its successor, the World Trade Organization. Under the terms of TRIPS, both drugs and drug-making processes were to be patentable for 20 years in all countries.[28] This was a major victory for the pharmaceutical firms, and industry representatives were loath to let it slip away. As pressure mounted around AIDS, however, their position was becoming increasingly difficult to maintain.

Matters drew to a head in February 2001, when Cipla, an Indian drug manufacturer, announced bargain-basement prices for its generic AIDS treatment. In Africa, Cipla offered to provide powerful triple-therapy AIDS cocktails to Doctors Without Borders for only $350 annually per patient. It would sell the same combination to African governments for $600 per patient, or roughly $400 below the Accelerating Access price.[29] The following month, Cipla took its offer one step further, formally requesting a compulsory license from the South African government (and offering to pay the patent holders royalties) so that it could begin producing the medicine.[30] Cipla chairman Dr. Yusuf K. Hamied explained, "We've had no concrete response

[24] Dagi Kimani, "AIDS Drugs Still Too Expensive in African States," *The East African,* December 10, 2000.

[25] David Pilling, "Third World and Drugs Groups Remain Wary of Each Other," *Financial Times,* July 10, 2000, p. 10.

[26] Stolberg, "Africa's AIDS War," p. A4.

[27] Mark Schoofs and Michael Waldholz, "Drug Firms, Senegal Set HIV Drug Pact," *The Wall Street Journal,* October 24, 2000, p. A3.

[28] Developing nations were given a 10-year window (until 2005) to comply. See Yasheng Huang and Harold F. Hogan Jr., "India's Intellectual Property Rights Regime and the Pharmaceutical Industry," HBS Case No. 702-039 (Boston, MA: Harvard Business School Publishing, 2002). For more on the creation of the WTO, see Nick Bartlett and David Moss, "The World Trade Organization: Toward Freer Trade or Global Government?" HBS Case No. 702-088.

[29] For more on Cipla and the controversy over its AIDS drugs, see Huang and Hogan, "India's Intellectual Property Rights."

[30] Rachel L. Swarns, "AIDS Drug Battle Deepens in Africa," *New York Times,* March 8, 2001, p. A1.

from the multinationals to date. We have now decided it is best to approach the government. What we've offered is an opportunity to Africa. It's up to the Africans to take it up."[31] More contentiously, he also proclaimed that Cipla's offer was intended "to break the stranglehold of the multinationals."[32] In contrast to the Accelerating Access program, Cipla's drugs would be delivered without lengthy bargaining or any pressure to commit to specified intellectual property standards.

Cipla's no-strings-attached offer reenergized the drug-pricing and patent debates. It demonstrated that powerful drugs could be sold at relatively low prices, particularly by firms that did not need to recoup the costs of research and development. As Cipla's plan unfolded, moreover, it also revealed a subtle but critical aspect of Africa's patent landscape. Most AIDS drugs were not actually patented in most African nations. Instead, because the likely market for drugs was so small in these states, the patent-holders had not bothered to file for formal rights.[33] Thus, for example, GlaxoSmith-Kline's Abacavir could be legally sold in generic form in 38 African states, while Merck's Crixivan could be sold equally legally in 51.[34] If a firm like Cipla could produce patented drugs in generic form and at an affordable price, it was free, even under the constraints of TRIPS, to sell these drugs across most of the African continent and make money in the process. This possibility sent a bombshell across the already sensitive industry. Only weeks after the announcement, Merck unveiled a new pricing policy that further reduced the price of its HIV drugs. Admitting that "patients were not getting access to medicines as quickly as we all had hoped,"[35] the company cut prices on its two HIV medications, Crixivan and Stocrin, to $600 and $500 per patient per year and offered to sell the drugs to any customer that could distribute them in the developing world.[36] Bristol-Myers Squibb announced similar price cuts in March 2001, as did Abbott Laboratories and GlaxoSmithKline. In all cases, the companies also relaxed their distribution links, agreeing to sell the discounted drugs outside the formal health care system. Eight months after its widespread offer, Merck announced a 40 percent increase in the number of people in the developing world who were using the firm's AIDS medication. In South Africa alone, the number had risen to 5,000, or 20 times the prediscount level.[37]

Meanwhile, other developments in South Africa were rapidly coming to the fore. Under the complex provisions of TRIPS, all countries were allowed an escape route of sorts, a proviso that permitted them to violate internationally recognized patents in "cases of national emergency." In South Africa, Nelson Mandela's government had used this provision to pass the Medicines and Related Substances Act of 1997, a measure that gave the country's health minister the authority to engage, when neces-

---

[31] Ibid., p. A6.

[32] Huang and Hogan, "India's Intellectual Property Rights," p. 1.

[33] Customarily, pharmaceutical companies indicate their intention to file for rights in multiple countries on an international patent application. To complete the patent, the company must then win approval from and pay patent fees to each individual country. Often, companies name a large number of countries on their original applications but then neglect to complete the approval process for many of the named states. For more information on this process, see Amir Attaran and Lee Gillespie-White, "Do Patents for Antiretroviral Drugs Constrain Access to AIDS Treatment in Africa?" *Journal of the American Medical Association,* October 17, 2001, p. 1887.

[34] Ibid., p. 1888.

[35] "Merck and Co., Inc. Announces Significant Reductions in Prices of HIV Medicines to Help Speed Access in Developing World," *Business Wire,* March 7, 2001.

[36] Later, "developing countries" were defined as the 100 poorest countries in the world. See ibid.

[37] "Merck: Price Drop Helps with Access," AP Newswire, November 26, 2001.

sary, in two controversial practices: "parallel importing," the purchase of inexpensive generic drugs without consent of the patent holder, and "compulsory licensing," which allowed local firms to manufacture foreign-patented drugs without, again, the patent-holder's consent.[38] As of 2001, the government had never formally employed the legislation. But its very existence had angered foreign pharmaceutical firms, 39 of which had filed suit against the legislation in South African court.[39] In a not-unusual display of political muscle, the firms had also won support from the U.S. government, which denied South Africa's request for preferential trade provisions in response to the drug law, attached an amendment on the country's aid package in 1999, and placed it on the "Priority List" for sanction consideration.[40]

Hearings in the South African trial began in June of 2001. Standing together, the 39 drug makers claimed that their suit had nothing to do with patents, or prices, or even the devastating toll of AIDS. It was instead, they claimed, purely a matter of legal principle: a question of whether South Africa had assumed "unconstitutional" powers.[41] The case dragged on for weeks, accompanied by protests in the streets and a firestorm of media criticism. In Pretoria, thousands of people danced outside the courthouse in the trial's opening days and then proceeded to the U.S. embassy, where they called on the United States to pressure the drug companies to drop their suit.[42] Smaller protests took place outside the corporate headquarters of both Bristol-Myers Squibb and GlaxoSmithKline. Doctors Without Borders presented the drug firms with an antisuit petition containing 250,000 signatures, while much of the international press, according to *The Economist,* painted the dispute as a "clear-cut case of nasty profiteers clinging to their patents for dear life while the sick in poor nations suffer."[43]

In the end, the drug companies decided that the benefits of winning the case were not worth the costs of fighting it. On April 19, 2001, the companies withdrew their suit, settling for a vaguely worded promise that the South African government, together with the firms, would help to "run partnerships on communicable diseases."[44] The suing firms agreed to pay for the government's court fees.

Mbeki and AIDS

Meanwhile, the South African government was itself coming under attack for its handling of the AIDS crisis. Despite one of the world's highest rates of HIV infection, despite relatively high levels of per capita income and years of media attention, South Africa had made notoriously little headway in the fight against AIDS. Instead, infection rates continued to surge and few infected South Africans were receiving treatment for their disease.

---

[38] For more on the law and its response, see Helene Cooper, Rachel Zimmerman, and Laurie McGinley, "Drug Firms Seek Court Remedy," *Asian Wall Street Journal,* March 5, 2001, pp. N1–N4.

[39] Stolberg, "Africa's AIDS War," p. A1.

[40] Helene Cooper et al., "Drug Firms Seek Court Remedy," p. N4.

[41] Robert Block, "Big Drug Firms Defend Right to Patents on AIDS Drugs in South African Court," *The Wall Street Journal,* June 3, 2001, p. A3.

[42] Ibid.

[43] "Drug-Induced Dilemma," *The Economist,* April 21, 2001, p. 59.

[44] Robert Block and Gardiner Harris, "Pharmaceutical Firms Withdraw South African HIV-Drug Case," *The Wall Street Journal Europe,* April 20, 2001, p. 3.

Much of the blame for this situation had been publicly tossed to the pharmaceutical companies. But in the wake of their ill-fated patent case, it became increasingly clear that the South African government, and particularly President Thabo Mbeki, had much to answer for as well.

For years, the government had been markedly slow in responding to the AIDS crisis, refusing in several instances to acknowledge the severity of the plague. Repeatedly, President Mbeki had questioned the well-established link between HIV and AIDS, arguing that malnutrition and other problems were to blame for the country's illnesses and describing the connection between multiple sexual relations and AIDS as "demeaning" and "insulting."[45] At one point, Mbeki had even urged his country's health ministry to rethink spending on the disease after reading a six-year-old document that showed accidents caused more deaths in South Africa than the virus.[46] The limited amount that the government did budget for AIDS in the late 1990s was mismanaged, with up to 40 percent of the allocated funds going unspent.[47] And funds that were spent were allegedly often wasted: in one infamous example, the Ministry of Health spent 20 percent of its AIDS budget on a single musical production.[48]

Under intense international pressure, Mbeki slowly began to retreat from his contentious views.[49] Late in 2001, AIDS activists won a national court ruling that ordered the South African government to supply nevirapine in state hospitals.[50] Several months later, Mbeki begrudgingly changed his medical opinion, allowing his government to release a statement noting that "(our) starting point is based on the premise that HIV causes AIDS."[51] As part of this changed attitude, the South African government unveiled an improved plan to attack the virus and explicitly acknowledged, for the first time, that "antiretroviral treatments in general could help improve the conditions of people living with AIDS."[52] State hospitals began to offer

[45] "Fighting Back: AIDS in Southern Africa," *The Economist,* May 11, 2002, p. 27.

[46] "Deadly Meddling," *The Economist,* November 3, 2001, pp. 82–83.

[47] The report looked at rollover from the 1997–98 and 1998–99 financial years. See Farouk Chothia, "Departments Failed to Spend R582M of Their Allocations," *Business Day* (South Africa), March 28, 2000, p. 2.

[48] Paul Harris, "South Africa's 'Nanny of the Nation' Inspires Love and Hate," Associated Press, October 14, 1998.

[49] For more on these pressures, see "Mbeki Pressured to Lead South African Fight Against AIDS," *Washington Post,* March 15, 2002, p. A18; Mark Schoofs, "Doctor Group Defies South Africa AIDS Policy," *The Wall Street Journal,* January 30, 2002, p. A14; Dina Kraft, "South Africa's Provinces Begin Backlash to Make Key AIDS Drug Available to Pregnant Women," Associated Press, February 18, 2002.

[50] Wambui Chege, "South African Government Goes to Court in Key AIDS Battle," Reuters, May 1, 2002.

[51] This in itself was a major change in policy. Mbeki finally eased up on his assertion that HIV did not cause AIDS, asking AIDS dissidents to stop using his name in their publications and announcing an investigation into the impact of the disease on South African businesses. "AIDS Realism in Africa," *Boston Globe,* April 26, 2002, p. A18.

[52] See "Cabinet Statement on HIV/AIDS, April 17, 2002," South African government, accessed at http://www.gov.za/speeches/cabinetaids02.htm.

antiretroviral treatment for rape victims in 2002 and expanded the availability of nevirapine for pregnant HIV-positive women.[53] And finally, as part of its newly energized effort to "continue to work for the lowering of the cost of [antiretroviral drugs],"[54] the South African government announced plans to "investigate the possibility of manufacturing generic drugs in this country."[55] Publicly, the pharmaceutical firms applauded South Africa's change of heart and offered their full support for the government's AIDS-fighting efforts. But the long-term impact of a massive generic-drug strategy remained to be seen.

[53] Ibid.

[54] Ibid.

[55] "Reason Prevails—South Africa and AIDS," *The Economist,* April 27, 2002, p. 79.

EXHIBIT 20.1 Patent Coverage in Africa for Antiretroviral Drugs, by Country*

Source: Amir Attaran and Lee Gillespie-White, "Do Patents for Antiretroviral Drugs Constrain Access to AIDS Treatment in Africa?" *Journal of the American Medical Association*, October 17, 2001, p. 1888.

	NRTIs							NNRTIs			Protease Inhibitors					Total
	Lamivudine-zidovudine (Combivir) [GSK]	Lamivudine (Epivir) [GSK]	Zalcitabine (Hivid) [Roche]	Zidovudine (Retrovir) [GSK]	Didanosine (Videx) [BMS]	Stavudine (Zerit) [BMS]	Abacavir (Ziagen) [GSK]	Delavirdine (Rescriptor) [Pharmacia]	Efavirenz (Stocrin) [Merck]	Nevirapine (Viramune) [BI]	Amprenavir (Agenerase) [GSK]	Indinavir (Crixivan) [Merck]	Saquinavir (Fortovase) [Roche]	Ritonavir (Norvir) [Abbott]	Nelfinavir (Viracept) [Agouran]	
Algeria																0
Angola																0
Benin	X	X								X					X	4
Botswana	X	X		X			X			X	X					6
Burkina Faso	X	X								X					X	4
Burundi	X			X												2
Cameroon	X	X								X					X	4
Cape Verde																0
Central African Republic	X	X								X					X	4
Chad	X	X								X					X	4
Comoros	X	X		X												3
Congo (Republic)	X	X					X			X					X	5
Congo (Democratic Republic)	X											X				2
Côte d'Ivoire	X	X								X						3
Djibouti																0
Egypt	X	X														2
Equatorial Guinea																0
Eritrea																0
Ethiopia																0
Gabon	X	X								X					X	4
Gambia	X	X		X			X			X	X				X	7
Ghana	X	X		X			X				X				X	6
Guinea										X					X	2
Guinea Bissau															X	1
Kenya	X	X		X			X			X	X				X	7
Lesotho	X	X					X			X	X				X	6

EXHIBIT 20.1 (*continued**)

	NRTIs							NNRTIs			Protease Inhibitors					Total
	Lamivudine-zidovudine (Combivir) [GSK]	Lamivudine (Epivir) [GSK]	Zalcitabine (Hivid) [Roche]	Zidovudine (Retrovir) [GSK]	Didanosine (Videx) [BMS]	Stavudine (Zerit) [BMS]	Abacavir (Ziagen) [GSK]	Delavirdine (Rescriptor) [Pharmacia]	Efavirenz (Stocrin) [Merck]	Nevirapine (Viramune) [BI]	Amprenavir (Agenerase) [GSK]	Indinavir (Crixivan) [Merck]	Saquinavir (Fortovase) [Roche]	Ritonavir (Norvir) [Abbott]	Nelfinavir (Viracept) [Agouran]	
Liberia																0
Libya																0
Madagascar	X	X														2
Malawi	X	X		X						X	X				X	6
Mali	X	X								X					X	4
Mauritania	X	X								X					X	4
Mauritius																0
Morocco	X	X														2
Mozambique																0
Namibia																0
Niger	X	X													X	3
Nigeria	X	X		X									X			4
Rwanda	X			X												2
Sao Tome and Principe																0
Senegal	X	X								X					X	4
Seychelles	X	X		X			X									4
Sierra Leone	X			X			X									3
Somalia										X						1
South Africa	X	X		X	X	X	X	X	X	X	X	X	X		X	13
Sudan	X	X		X			X			X	X				X	7
Swaziland	X	X					X			X	X				X	6
Tanzania	X	X		X			X			X						5
Togo	X	X													X	3
Tunisia	X	X														2
Uganda	X	X		X			X			X	X				X	7
Zambia	X	X		X			X			X	X					6
Zimbabwe	X	X		X			X			X	X		X		X	8
Total	37	33	0	17	1	1	15	1	1	25	12	2	3	0	24	172

*NRTI indicates nucleoside reverse transcriptase inhibitor; NNRTI, non-NRTI; GSK, GlaxoSmithKline; BMS, Bristol-Myers Squibb; and BI, Boehringer Ingelheim.

21

Ciba-Geigy Pharmaceuticals: Pharma International

N. Craig Smith and John A. Quelch

In August 1983, the management committee of Pharma International (PHI), CIBA-GEIGY's[1] third-world pharmaceuticals operation, had as an agenda item for its monthly meeting the decision of whether or not to approve the development and launch of a new antimalarial product in Nigeria. A lively discussion was anticipated. The product proposal had originated from the management committee of the pharmaceutical division in Nigeria (Pharma Nigeria). As was often the case, the decision involved significant commercial, ethical, and policy considerations.

Malaria was one of the leading causes of death from disease in Nigeria. Chloroquine had long been used to treat it, and in Nigeria was available as an over-the-counter (OTC) product through pharmacists, clinics, and patent medicine stores, largely as a proprietary (branded) drug. Pharma Nigeria did not have an antimalarial product and therefore wished to be active in this significant segment of the self-medication market. Chloroquine's extremely bitter taste had prompted Pharma Nigeria to propose a tasteless, capsule form for Fevex, the new antimalarial product. It was hoped that not only would Fevex be more pleasant to take, and therefore superior to the many other antimalarial products on the market, but it would also have the benefits of

---

[1] CIBA-GEIGY is the registered company name, hereafter shown as Ciba-Geigy.

Professor N. Craig Smith prepared this case with the assistance of Professor John A. Quelch as the basis for class discussion rather than to illustrate either effective or ineffective handling of an administrative situation.

Copyright © 1989 President and Fellows of Harvard College. To order copies or request permission to reproduce materials, call 1-800-545-7685 or write Harvard Business School Publishing, Boston, MA 02163 or go to http//www.hbsp.harvard.edu. No part of this publication may be reproduced, stored in a retrieval system, used in a spreadsheet, or transmitted in any form or by any means—electronic, mechanical, photocopying, recording, or otherwise—without the permission of Harvard Business School.

improved compliance in completion of the full treatment, and a reduced likelihood of malaria victims postponing treatment by self-medication. However, the bitter taste of chloroquine had minimized the risk of unintended consumption, particularly by children. Chloroquine's toxicity meant an overdose could be fatal.

The PHI management committee had a hard decision to make. There were considerable risks for Ciba-Geigy in launching a product that would be aggressively promoted in a third-world country. As a self-medication product, it would be extensively advertised, and made widely available, yet it was potentially lethal if misused. Aside from any "duty of care" obligations, Ciba-Geigy could lay itself open to criticism for marketing a dangerous product or, indeed, for wasting resources in developing and promoting a "me-too" drug. Consumer organizations had been highly critical of pharmaceutical marketing practices in the third world. The likely prospect of counterfeiting presented further difficulties. From a commercial point of view, the capsule form of Fevex was attractive, not least because it would employ underutilized capsule-filling production capacity in Nigeria. However, the necessary clinical tests would be expensive and there was an increase in chloroquine-resistant strains of malaria. Some members of the PHI management committee firmly believed that Ciba-Geigy's strength lay in its research and development of new drugs; "me-too" drugs were to be avoided as a matter of policy. Prior to the meeting, a number of the committee had already asked, "Is it really worth the effort?"

Ciba-Geigy Pharmaceuticals Division

In 1982, Ciba-Geigy group sales were 13,808 million Swiss francs ($6,802 million), a modest growth of only 1 percent on 1981, attributed to difficult trading conditions worldwide: uncertainty and recession, protectionism, currency instability, balance of payment deficits, and inflation. Group operating profit was 622 million Swiss francs ($306 million). Ciba-Geigy group had approximately 80,000 employees, working in 120 subsidiaries in more than 50 countries. Although headquartered in Basel, only 2 percent of sales came from Switzerland, with the rest of Europe accounting for 41 percent, North America 29 percent, Latin America 11 percent, Asia 11 percent, and Africa, Australia, and Oceania 6 percent.

The largest proportion of Ciba-Geigy's sales came from the pharmaceuticals division (Pharma), which at 4.1 billion Swiss francs ($2 billion, 30 percent of group sales, 1982) made it the second-largest pharmaceutical company in the world. Pharmaceutical sales increased 8 percent in 1982 over the previous year, well above the industry growth rate. Pharma was represented in four major areas: cardiovascular products (30 percent of sales) including beta-blockers; antirheumatics and analgesics (23 percent) including Voltaren, the tenth-best-selling pharmaceutical in the world; antidepressants and drugs for treating epilepsy (15 percent); and a broad spectrum of antibiotics and other drugs for treating infectious diseases such as tuberculosis and leprosy, certain tropical diseases, skin diseases and allergies, and bone diseases. Pharma also included a contact lens business, a division marketing self-medication (OTC) products, and the Servipharm division, which operated specifically to serve the needs of developing countries.

The Pharmaceutical Industry

The pharmaceutical industry was traditionally highly profitable, with a return on investment of around 15 percent. About 40 percent of Ciba-Geigy profits came from pharmaceutical sales. However, there were some worrying trends:

- Government attempts to reduce health care costs: At around 10 percent of GNP, the cost of health care in industrialized countries was coming under close scrutiny. There was an emphasis on lowering costs, while attempting to maintain the quality of service, through stricter price controls, restrictions on new product introductions, and limitations on doctors' freedom to prescribe (including the use of generic lists). Outside the United States, national governments paid for most drugs, though reimbursements by health insurance funds were also increasingly restrictive.

- Increasing R&D expenditures: R&D costs had been doubling every five years since 1970, due in part to rising registration costs, with regulators demanding greater evidence of economic as well as therapeutic benefits. Industry observers estimated the average cost of bringing a drug to the U.S. market to be around $100 million. Meanwhile, major technological breakthroughs were less frequent.

- Reduced patent protection: Companies depended on patents to secure a temporary monopoly in the sale of new products and the evidence indicated that having patent protected products had a significant impact on corporate performance. After patent expiry, brand names would often protect companies from generic competition, providing a new drug with profits for 16 years or more and real returns averaging 9–10 percent over that time. However, getting a drug approved was taking longer and government efforts to reduce costs meant earlier substitution by generics once the drug was off patent.

- Increasing criticism of pharmaceutical marketing practices coupled with some questioning of the benefits provided by pharmaceuticals: There was public concern about the role of the pharmaceutical sales representative, gifts provided to doctors and their expenses-paid trips to medical conventions organized by drug companies and usually in exotic locations. Promotional literature was a major source of information used by doctors when prescribing, but it did not always provide adequate detail on contraindications[2] and side effects. Pharmaceutical marketing practices in the third world had been strongly criticized. Drug use by patients always entailed some risk from the possible toxic effects of the drug (hence the industry adage "all drugs are poisons"), but this was not widely understood and adverse patient reactions added to mistrust of drugs and the industry.

These trends contributed to increased industry competitiveness, but also to collaborative efforts (particularly in new fields, such as biotechnology) and to the prospect of mergers. There were also positive factors affecting the industry. The level of economic activity (at a time of recession) had little impact on drug consumption. Indeed, industry sales were expected to continue to rise at a rate in excess of 10 percent per annum. Although ethical pharmaceuticals (prescription drugs) were around 90 percent of world industry sales, the remaining OTC sector was expected to grow rapidly. Health policy was likely to attach more importance to self-therapy for the treatment of mild and transient illnesses, such as the common cold, constipation, and diarrhea, in order to reduce health care costs and inconvenience for the patient. Ciba-Geigy was attempting to increase its presence in the self-medication market, though in 1981, 98 percent of its revenues came from ethical pharmaceuticals.

R&D prospects appeared to be improving, especially in the field of genetic engineering where Pharma was active. Ciba-Geigy spent 8.5 percent of sales on R&D.

---

[2] Contraindications were situations when the use of a drug was inadvisable, for example, during pregnancy.

Approximately half of this was accounted for by Pharma, with an R&D expenditure of 14 percent of Pharma sales in 1982, compared to an industry average of around 10 percent. New products were expected to account for 30 percent of Pharma sales by 1986. Industry analysts had also observed a shift in industry R&D expenditures: a decline in "me-too" products and minor evolutionary research in the 1960s, prompted by more stringent product approval regulations; a greater interest in product differentiation based on features promoting ease of use or patient compliance during the 1970s, with a likely focus on breakthrough R&D efforts in the 1980s, as health cost pressures reduced the prospects for drugs with minor product differences. This trend demanded good R&D management by pharmaceutical companies and broad market access to exploit R&D achievements.

Ciba-Geigy acknowledged the difficulties experienced by health services and the consequent cost pressures. In the 1982 annual report, the company noted that this "causes problems for the pharmaceutical industry, but it also presents the socially responsible, research-based enterprise with opportunities" and, further on: "Even where there is political controversy it is becoming increasingly clear that expenditure on medicines in a budget-conscious health service is money well spent. In the industrialized and developing countries alike, the provision of efficacious, high quality medicines is an important element in any health service, and one which will stand up to economic cost/benefit scrutiny . . . Ciba-Geigy offers a range of medicines for which there will always be a medical need."

Drug industry critics were not entirely convinced Ciba-Geigy was taking its social responsibilities seriously. In 1970, Japanese scientists had identified the active ingredient, clioquinol, used in Ciba-Geigy's antidiarrheal drugs as the cause of a disease known as SMON involving paralysis and loss of sight. Following a government ban, and six years of legal action, Ciba-Geigy paid damages to Japanese victims in 1978. Two years later, a company press release claimed, "There is no conclusive scientific evidence that clioquinol causes SMON." Ciba-Geigy policy was modified in 1982, as the annual report explained, "in the light of recent medical knowledge and experience." Ciba-Geigy had decided to gradually withdraw the problem drugs within the next five years. Critics charged that the gradual withdrawal was to save face and so as not to weaken the company's legal position. Ciba-Geigy commented: "As the demand for products of this type varies considerably, and their replacement by other treatments will take time in many countries, especially those of the third world, the wishes of the national health authorities will be respected." This criticism of Ciba-Geigy had led to a boycott by doctors and vets in Sweden, but Ciba-Geigy was not the only pharmaceutical company to be criticized for its marketing practices in the third world. It could reasonably be claimed the entire industry was under attack.

Servipharm and Pharma International

Ciba-Geigy was changing in response to the pressures on the industry. In its 1981 annual report, Ciba-Geigy had welcomed a code of pharmaceutical marketing practice developed by the International Federation of Pharmaceutical Manufacturers Associations (IFPMA), integrating it into corporate policy. Earlier in 1977, it had formed Servipharm, a wholly owned subsidiary, specifically to provide essential drugs at economical prices to the 80 percent of the world's population in the non-OECD "industrializing" markets. Servipharm's objectives were (1) to offer a range of pharmaceutical products that would meet the specific needs of a major portion of the world's population; (2) to ensure that its products were safe and reliable by manufacturing them according to the highest quality standards; (3) to make Servipharm products as widely available as possible by keeping them economically priced; and (4) to offer to governments and institutions services in other health and health care–related areas.

Servipharm was the only company related to a major pharmaceutical manufacturer dedicated exclusively to the production and sale of high-quality, essential drugs. It began operation in the "easier markets," those not requiring registration (Malaysia, smaller African markets, UNICEF tenders, etc.). It then began to develop its own registration dossiers, which were submitted to Swiss and other registration authorities, providing access to larger markets. The product range comprised branded versions of 30 basic drugs for which there was substantial demand by institutional users. One of these was Serviquin (chloroquine diphosphate), an antimalarial. The "Servi" prefix, used in all Servipharm brand names, was intended to convey a quality assurance and act as a reminder of the service orientation of Servipharm—reliable products, dependable delivery, and flexible package sizes, as well as consultancy services.

By 1983, Servipharm was active in more than 70 countries, and could claim over 200 million patients had benefited from its products. It shipped over 700 million capsules and tablets in 1982 and sales had quadrupled since 1979. Servipharm products were generally priced above those of the smaller, perhaps local, generic manufacturers and below the more expensive branded products of the major manufacturers. This pricing, Ciba-Geigy believed, reflected the quality of Servipharm products and the association with the Ciba-Geigy name, which, around 1980, began to appear on Servipharm packaging and literature.

There had been opposition to the Servipharm initiative within Ciba-Geigy. Support for generic production had been viewed as heresy; the success of the company had been built on new drugs. However, with commitment from Pharma management, the Servipharm initiative went ahead. There had also been controversy within the industry over Ciba-Geigy's sale of generics. All Servipharm products were patent-free and almost entirely non-Ciba-Geigy in origin. The major pharmaceutical companies had always viewed generic manufacturers as an external threat. Servipharm represented generic competition from within. This angered competitors.

Servipharm had, as yet, always made a loss, confirming the doubts of some within the company and the industry generally. Focusing on the institutional market avoided marketing costs, such as pharmaceutical representatives, but submitting tenders to national institutions and international organizations entailed strong price competition. Quality was an important feature of Servipharm products, but not readily established: it was not easy to show that the quality or quantity of an active substance, or the grain used (which affects absorption), would be consistently correct. The customer often would not know if a drug was effective. Servipharm and its customers could rely on the Ciba-Geigy reputation, but they had to bear the full and high associated costs of largely Swiss production, with significant quality control expenditures. Some Servipharm production took place overseas, but this, too, was expensive because of economies of scale factors—smaller production base, cost of importing materials in smaller quantities—which, in a capital-intensive industry, were not offset by lower labor costs. (However, in 1982, one-third of Ciba-Geigy's total pharmaceutical production came from its 20 manufacturing units in the third world.) The generic competitors, meanwhile, could source on the open market and would often have lower costs of production. In some cases, they were even supplying the active ingredient to Servipharm. Tenders by pharmaceutical companies were often assessed solely on the basis of price, but adverse experiences were encouraging former Servipharm customers to repeat purchase and pay higher Servipharm prices.

Through Servipharm, Ciba-Geigy was manufacturing some of the oldest (though essential) drugs for the poorest countries in the world, using expensive production facilities (subcontracting was minimal). Generic supply offered some potential for reasonable returns if sufficient scale were realized; Servipharm's generic competitors were largely national and smaller operations in each country. Servipharm production was also filling spare Ciba-Geigy capacity. To show a profit on Servipharm could upset third-world customers and invite further criticism from consumer organizations, so Servipharm's goal was to break even. Ciba-Geigy was taking a long-term view of its investment, believing that multinational companies would increasingly be held to account for the provision of health care to the world's poor and that public opinion on the issue would have to be satisfied. The concept of "Drugs You Can Trust . . . At Prices You Can Afford" did have a strong underlying ethical purpose. Studies had shown that it was difficult for Ciba-Geigy to reach beyond the top 10 percent (in terms of income) in many third-world countries. Servipharm provided generics under the corporate umbrella with a guarantee of quality, adding value in the Ciba-Geigy name, services, and quality control. Milton Silverman, a leading drug industry critic, became one of Servipharm's strongest supporters.

Servipharm represented only about 7 percent of PHI sales. PHI generated about 10 percent of all Pharma sales, serving 120 countries in the Middle East, Far East, Eastern bloc, Mediterranean, Africa, and Latin America. Ciba-Geigy country managers were responsible for the profitability of all Ciba-Geigy activities within their countries and reported to regional managers at headquarters. Servipharm operated alongside, but separate from, Ciba-Geigy branded pharmaceutical operations.

The third world accounted for approximately 20 percent of Ciba-Geigy group sales and employees. In 1974, a corporate policy was formulated for third-world countries, shown in Exhibit 21.1. This governed PHI as much as any other unit in Ciba-Geigy. Ciba-Geigy believed that it was primarily the responsibility of each local government to determine a country's development policy and that aid organizations as well as transnational corporations should at most play a supporting or facilitating role, not to set the "development machine" in motion but to "contribute a drop of oil to help the machinery run a little more smoothly." Earning a "fair profit" played a part in this, though this did not preclude development aid of a charitable nature, such as, within PHI, a leprosy fund, set up to support improved diagnosis, training, treatment, and rehabilitation; a contribution of 10 million Swiss francs to the WHO Diarrheal Diseases Control Program; and the donation of drugs (that would otherwise be destroyed) to third-world countries within 24 and 12 months of their expiry dates. PHI also supported third-world public health service initiatives where its expertise could be of value.

Ciba-Geigy in Nigeria

Nigeria, a West African, English-speaking country, approximately one-tenth the size of the United States, gained independence in 1963. Its population was 95 million in 1983 (one in five Africans was a Nigerian) and growing rapidly at around 3 percent a year. Almost half of the population was under 15 years of age. Most Nigerians lived in rural villages with 20 percent in the main urban areas, many in squalid shanty towns. Over half the population lived in the relatively depressed northern regions of the country. Population density was greater in the south, which included Lagos, the capital city with a population of five million. There were vast and increasing disparities between urban and rural incomes.

Nigeria's wealth was founded largely on oil, which accounted for 97 percent of Nigeria's exports and 80 percent of government revenues in 1982. However, real GDP and disposable incomes declined in 1981 and 1982, as a consequence of reduced oil demand and inflation. Political instability also contributed to economic uncertainty. Despite the importance of oil, agriculture employed 52 percent of the labor force in 1981. A 1976 campaign "Operation Feed the Nation" had realized some initial success. More recently, food production was barely keeping pace with population growth, as development projects were hampered by a weakening economy.

Nigeria's pharmaceutical market, having grown rapidly between 1976 and 1981, declined from N233 million ($380 million) in 1981 to N222 million ($330 million) in 1982, with a similar decline expected in 1983.[3] Around half the pharmaceutical market by value was supplied from local manufacture, though a part of this consisted merely of repackaging finished products imported in bulk. Around 20 percent of the market, institutional purchases were split 70:30 between ethicals and consumer (OTC) products. The private sector represented 80 percent of the market, split 80:20 between consumer and ethical products. Overall, 70 percent of the market comprised consumer products and 30 percent ethicals, so the Nigerian pharmaceutical market was characterized by heavy OTC supply.

Economic difficulties were leading to a decline in health care in Nigeria, with reduced levels of treatment and availability of drugs. Much of the rural population was not reached by the health care network, though some popular OTC drugs were available in regions without doctors or state clinics. There were around 12,000 doctors (one for every 8,000 people), but, as they were concentrated in urban areas, the ratio was one doctor for every 50,000 people in rural areas. There were around 80,000 hospital beds (one for every 1,180 people). Nigerians suffered from high incidences of infectious disease and malaria; diarrheal diseases were also common. Distribution in Nigeria was generally highly decentralized and unsophisticated, but effective. Drugs were distributed through

- Registered pharmacies (around 800).
- Registered patent medicine stores (15,000).
- Unregistered patent medicine stalls (10,000).
- General retail outlets also carrying OTC drugs.
- Itinerant street hawkers.
- Marketplace traders.
- Dispensing doctors (serviced by pharmacies with wholesale operations).
- Institutional outlets.

Drugs could pass through many hands before reaching the final consumer, who often purchased only a single tablet from the lowest link in the distribution chain. Patent medicine stores, little more than market stalls, were responsible for a large proportion of OTC sales. The geographical distribution of sales reflected population density and income levels; most sales were in Lagos (40 percent) and the east (30 percent), with 16 percent in the west and only 14 percent in the north, where half of Nigeria's population lived. There was no national pharmaceutical distribution organization. Rapid growth of the Nigerian drug market had attracted most of the major multinational pharmaceutical companies, especially in the supply of OTC products.

---

[3] One naira (N) = $1.485 in 1982, N1 = $1.382 in 1983 (average exchange rate). The naira was believed to be overvalued.

Ciba-Geigy and its predecessor companies had been in Nigeria since the 1950s. The Swiss Nigerian Chemical Company (SNCC) was 40 percent owned by Ciba-Geigy with 60 percent owned by Nigerian investors, in keeping with Nigerian local ownership laws. It comprised five divisions: Ilford, Agricultural, Dyestuffs, Plastics and Additives, and Pharmaceuticals. SNCC sales in 1982 were N18.3 million ($27.2 million), of which Pharma Nigeria contributed 35 percent; net profits were N562,000 ($835,000). Pharma Nigeria employed around 100 people and was managed by Mr. Nwankwo, a Nigerian national.

Pharma Nigeria was divided into three business areas, with a marketing manager for each: ethical products; proprietary, nonprescription OTC products; and Servipharm. Ethical products had been Pharma Nigeria's main business; it had only entered the self-medication OTC market in 1983. Rapid expansion of this business area was planned under the new marketing manager, Mr. Okunmuyide, who had just joined the company after completing an MBA at Lagos University and five years as a product manager with Lever Brothers Nigeria Ltd. Prospects in the self-medication market were particularly good at this time, because of

- The underfunded and ill-equipped secondary and tertiary levels of the health care delivery system.
- The need of individuals to maintain good health through the prevention and treatment of simple ailments, so they would not develop into diseases that could not be treated in the handicapped referral centers.
- The lower pricing of self-medication products relative to prescription products.
- The national health care strategy of primary health care, which was positively disposed toward self-medication.
- The large increase in patent medicine stores, especially in rural areas otherwise inadequately served by referral health centers.

Pharma Nigeria's self-medication OTC business plan, agreed in March 1983, provided for an initial product portfolio of branded cough and cold treatments, a treatment to prevent itching, an analgesic, and an antimalarial.

Malaria

Malaria was the deadliest of all the tropical diseases of parasitic origin. There were about 150 million cases a year worldwide, 1 percent proving fatal, and a further 600 million people were exposed to the risk of contracting malaria. In Nigeria, in 1983, malaria was the major cause of morbidity at 1,393 cases per 100,000 people, five times that of dysentery. It killed around 100,000 people annually. A major priority for Nigeria's primary health care strategy was to provide increased access to treatment for malaria victims, particularly in rural areas and the urban slums.

Malaria was transmitted by about 10 percent of anopheles mosquitos. Two types of malaria were found. Malignant malaria was an acute form often proving fatal within a few days, especially in children, over one million of whom died every year in Africa from this type. Tertian and quartan malaria was a milder and seldom fatal type, to which patients often developed a relative immunity after repeated infection.

Insecticides such as DDT could kill the anopheles mosquito but at the risk of contaminating the food chain. Mosquitos were less common in cities, especially in air-conditioned buildings. However, they bred easily in swamps in rural areas and in the pools of dirty water often found in shanty towns. Poor people were more frequently afflicted. But exposure to mosquitos could only be reduced, not entirely avoided. So for local people and visitors in affected areas, medical treatment was often necessary.

Chloroquine, in generic or branded forms, had been used to treat malaria for over 50 years. Prophylactic use was recommended for the 20 million or so (worldwide) visitors traveling annually to malarious areas. Chloroquine was available only by prescription in the West. It was no longer recommended for long-term prophylaxis, as use over a number of years had been linked to damage to the retina. Chloroquine was, however, on the WHO essential drug list, and was one of 26 drugs UNIDO (United Nations Industrial Development Organization) was encouraging manufacture of as part of its technology transfer efforts in the third world. Total demand for chloroquine phosphate from national antimalaria programs was 520 tons in 1982, 286 tons (and rising) of which went to Africa. UNIDO reported that prices fell between 1979 and 1983.

Early diagnosis and treatment of malarial infections was important. Malignant malaria could be cured, with chloroquine sterilizing the host. Tertian and quartan malaria could usually only be suppressed rather than cured, though if left untreated could be disabling and possibly fatal. Malaria relapses could occur up to 20 years after infection. It was not unusual for somebody to have three or more malaria attacks a year as a consequence of a new infection or relapse. Accurate figures on the incidence (number of new infections within a given time) and prevalence (percent of population infected) were not available.

Malaria strains resistant to chloroquine were emerging, partly because of its prophylactic use. Higher doses could overcome resistant strains. However, chloroquine's high toxicity (producing cardiac arrest) meant caution was required in using higher doses, as the margin of safety between therapeutic and toxic doses of chloroquine was very narrow, particularly in children.[4] Other antimalarials were available, particularly multidrug combinations, which acted on resistant strains. However, they were often more expensive, with more side effects, and resistance to these alternative antimalarials was also emerging.

In the longer term, it was hoped that a vaccine against malaria would be developed. The highest annual expenditure on research and development against tropical disease by European pharmaceutical companies was on malaria, $8.1 million in 1982 out of $31.5 million. The Nigerian government's antimalaria campaign, announced in 1983 with a budget of N20 million ($29 million), was making available to each state 1.5 million chloroquine tablets (20 million in total), 1,000 liters of chloroquine syrup, and the multidrug antimalarial brand Fansidar (100,000 tablets for each state), which acted on strains resistant to chloroquine.

Fevex

Self-medication against malaria was used extensively in the third world, though, as in Nigeria, often accompanied by warnings from health authorities about the dangers of overdose. Antimalarials were widely available as OTC products. Typically, a local Nigerian would go to a pharmacy and explain that he or she had "malaria" or "fever." The pharmacist would carry around half a dozen different brands, one or more of which the customer might know and specify. A full treatment of a pack of

---

[4] In West Germany, child-proof packaging regulations were extended in 1982 to include chloroquine (and 30-odd other substances) following a considerable fall in child poisoning cases after earlier regulations governing analgesics. Three percent of measures taken in children's hospitals resulted from poisoning. Acceptable pack types were those with push-through and sealed strip packs and containers with safety closures. Arguments in respect of packaging change difficulties, stability testing in the new packs, low quantity sold, the protection of prescription-only status, or the difficulties the elderly may find, as reasons for noncompliance, were not accepted by the authorities.

10 tablets would be bought, which would bring the malarial attack to an end. It was not uncommon, however, for poorer people to buy tablets loose and in smaller quantities, according to what had worked before and what they could afford at the time. Occasionally, doctors would provide less than complete treatments at an initial visit so as to charge additional amounts for return visits. However, an incomplete treatment resulted in reduced efficacy in subsequent treatments. Free medication was available from state hospitals and other facilities, but they were usually overworked, unable to provide quick attention, and often did not have enough drugs. Some 40–50 percent of malarial victims in Nigeria went untreated, with kidney and liver damage as a minimum consequence. As an alternative, they might use local herbs, such as "Dogonyaro" leaves, of doubtful efficacy.

The management committee of Pharma Nigeria had proposed the launch of an antimalarial, branded as Fevex, to augment the new OTC product line. Okunmuyide had explained to the marketing manager responsible for self-medication products in Basel that the aim was "to become a key player in the antimalarial self-medication market." This was the fourth-largest segment of the self-medication market, after anti-infectives, analgesics, and vitamins. The proposed product was 250 mg. capsulated chloroquine phosphate. Capsule-presented drugs were highly regarded in Nigeria, to the point of having magical connotations in some areas, because of the relatively recent and dramatic impact of capsulated antibiotics.

Fevex faced considerable competition with 50 brands in the N10 million market (50 million packs of 10 tablets in 1982). May and Baker's Nivaquine was the market leader with a market share estimated at 21 percent, closely followed by Roche's Fansidar at 20 percent. Generic chloroquine phosphate, supplied to the institutional market, represented a further 20 percent. Other brands from companies such as Bayer (Resochin), Glaxo (Paraquine), and Wellcome (Daraprim) each had 7 percent or less. Product formulation differences were essentially between chloroquine-based products and those containing sulfadoxine with pyrimethamine, such as Fansidar. Some chloroquine-based products included paracetamol to provide pain relief, such as Glaxo's Paraquine, which had a 2 percent market share. The pyrimethamine products acted against chloroquine-resistant strains of malaria, but because of adverse reactions were expected to be restricted to these cases only. Hence, the preference for chloroquine in Fevex.

Servipharm sales of chloroquine, branded as Serviquin, were made only to the generic institutional market segment and were 993,000 tablets in 1980, 18,600,000 (1981), 6,410,000 (1982), and estimated at only 30,000 for 1983.

Another difference between brands was whether they were marketed for curative or prophylactic use, though chloroquine was appropriate for either purpose. Most brands were marketed as curatives, in keeping with product usage by Nigerians. A more important distinction was between bitter and tasteless tablet brands; 80 percent had the bitter (plain) taste. Some tasteless tablet brands had been introduced but with little impact, as the film coating was inadequate to mask the bitter taste of chloroquine. An important consequence of chloroquine's galling effect was postponement or habituated partial treatment of malaria. Postponement entailed additional risk and the possibility of hospitalization. Incomplete treatment reduced the efficacy of subsequent treatments as a cumulative resistance was built up within the body. Many consumers would stop treatment after the first initial dose of four tablets. Some would hide the tablets in locally prepared food such as Eba, Amala, or pounded yam; others would try and obtain injections of the vial form. Fevex's differentiation, and hence the ambitious goal, came from overcoming this problem of chloroquine's bitter taste by using capsules. Fevex's success, however, would also depend on pricing, promotion, and distribution factors. An added advantage of the capsule form was that it would permit local manufacture using currently underutilized capsule-filling plants, raising utilization from 20 percent to 60 percent. It was also believed to be of strategic importance to increase local manufacturing. Pharma Nigeria was likely to request permission to export Fevex, once it was established in Nigeria.

Market research was planned to confirm pricing and promotion. However, with Fevex targeting the leading brands and the prospect of me-too launches of capsulated chloroquine by competitors, an aggressive market entry was envisaged. Nivaquine had been continuously and heavily promoted; Pharma Nigeria intended the same and more for Fevex. Marketing support amounting to 30 percent of sales was intended for the launch year, a third of which would be spent on media advertising. Television and radio advertising in English and four local languages was proposed—a new approach for Nigerian pharmaceuticals. The first-tier sales force of five sales representatives was to be expanded and would be supported by a second-tier sales force of commission-only sales representatives; both sales forces would receive bonuses for sales above a platform target. Branded T-shirts, caps, and pens were included among the proposed promotional materials.

The Basel Decision

Ciba-Geigy management in Basel was concerned about the risk involved in promoting self-medication products that depended on self diagnosis; the responsibility—and liability—of the company was increased when a doctor was not involved. This was but one consideration for the PHI management committee reviewing the Fevex proposal. They had to decide whether the product would meet the needs of the patient as well as the commercial and sociopolitical factors bearing on its success. The PHI also received input from the PEA, a Ciba-Geigy committee of detached scientists, which had to validate a drug's efficacy in the form proposed, and would not sanction the launch of a drug if it did not meet the clinical and technical criteria. While clinical tests would be needed to satisfy the PEA, the PHI management committee was confident that Fevex would meet these requirements. To put it simply, the product would work from a purely technical standpoint. It was, after all, merely chloroquine in a capsule.

The management committee's "duty of care" responsibility extended beyond an acceptance of the PEA's assessment of the drug's technical performance. Would the product work and be safe in the Nigerian marketplace? Moreover, would it be profitable? If anything went wrong, what might the consequences be for Ciba-Geigy? Could such heavy promotion be defended in a third-world context? These were troubling questions for the PHI management committee when considered alongside recent criticism of the pharmaceutical industry.

EXHIBIT 21.1
**Ciba-Geigy Policy
for Third-World
Countries**

Source: *Ciba-Geigy and the
Third World: Policy, Facts
and Examples,* a public
relations brochure produced
by Ciba-Geigy, Basel,
Switzerland.

The Fundamental Framework

- As a business organization whose activities span the globe, we wish to contribute to the economic development of the Third World. By way of
  — a far-ranging involvement in the fields of agriculture, health, and industry,
  — the international scope of our organization, and
  — our know-how and experience,
  we can help meet the basic needs of people throughout the Third World.

- Our group units are subject to the laws of the countries in which they are domiciled. We adhere to the principle of nonintervention in domestic political matters. At the same time we are aware that our presence represents an economic factor which may have an impact on the local scene.

- As a shareholder-owned enterprise we have to earn a fair profit wherever we are active. We therefore depend, in the Third World as elsewhere, on profitable operations, legally assured security and continuity, equal treatment with indigenous firms, and the unimpeded exchange of goods.

- While respecting the desire of the developing countries to foster their fledgling industries, we hold that the measures they take to this end should be economically sound and should not exclude competition.

- In national and international bodies we defend the following principles:
  — a healthy economy is indispensable to a country's development;
  — private enterprise acting in accordance with local conditions is better able to further economic development than a centrally directed system;
  — the industrialized countries should not misuse development policy and aid as instruments of intervention in the internal affairs of Third-World countries;
  — developing countries and international organizations should not attach conditions to development aid which contravene the political principles of the donor countries;
  — both the industrial and the developing countries have a vital long-term interest in effective development assistance.

- We also support development aid of a charitable nature. Because this type of contribution does not form part of our organization's mission, however, we make a clear distinction between it and our business activities.

A. Our Commitment
On the basis of the position outlined above, the salient features of our activities in the Third World can be summed up thus:

1. With a view to the interests of both parties, we act in partnership with the developing countries (DCs) to advance their economic potential. We observe fully the rights and duties growing out of such a partnership.

2. In making business decisions on the Third World (e.g., on products, services, technologies, investments), in addition to economic criteria we take into account the impact on the development of the host country. If a project shows a particularly strong impact, we are—considering the specific situation of the country—prepared to extend our short-range profit objectives.

3. If a DC adopts measures to protect its economy such as import restrictions, export obligations, conditions for ownership, etc., we keep up the cooperation as long as partnership and adequate returns are not jeopardized in the long term.

4. We consider it our duty to advise our partner against undertakings if we are not convinced of their benefit for the partner (e.g., prestige projects), even if such a move proves detrimental to our short-term economic interest.

5. In the DCs we follow progressive social and personnel policies adapted to the local conditions. In particular we
   — offer employees and workers training in many fields, if necessary abroad;
   — make it possible for capable staff members to acquire international experience within our group;
   — consider nationals in filling executive positions.

EXHIBIT 21.1
(continued)

6. Convinced that in the long run the pursuit of the above principles is a necessity, we shall not be discouraged by unavoidable short-term setbacks and disappointments.

B. Philanthropic Aid

In addition to carrying on business activities, in certain cases we also extend philanthropic support. This charitable aid is channeled through the "Ciba-Geigy Foundation for Cooperation with Developing Countries" and takes the form of:

— financial contributions;

— experts delegated to serve on development projects sponsored by the Swiss government, national and international development aid organizations, and the Ciba-Geigy Foundation itself;

— our organization's infrastructure. This assistance, made available for development aid projects, is intended to benefit particularly the poorest of the Third World.

C. Our Public Information Policy

We inform our employees, shareholders, the general public, governments, and international organizations fully and frankly about our Third-World policy. When we can report success, we shall do so; but if setbacks occur, they will not be concealed.

Chapter 22

Genzyme's Gaucher Initiative: Global Risk and Responsibility

Christopher A. Bartlett and Andrew N. McLean

In June 1998, Tomye Tierney initiated an effort that led to the creation of Genzyme Corporation's Gaucher Initiative to provide the company's life-saving drug Cerezyme® enzyme[1] to sufferers of Gaucher disease worldwide, regardless of their ability to pay. Barely three years later, she faced a major decision that would determine the future of the bold experiment. Established as a partnership with the respected humanitarian organization Project HOPE, the Gaucher Initiative had been very effective in locating and treating Gaucher patients in many less-developed countries and had built a particularly strong program in Egypt. However, Genzyme's sales organization was becoming increasingly concerned that the fast-growing free distribution program in Egypt represented a barrier to their commercial objectives.

Although the company had grown rapidly in recent years, the high-risk biotech business required that it manage its resources carefully. (Exhibits 22.1 and 22.2 summarize Genzyme's financial history.) From the outset, therefore, Genzyme CEO Henri Termeer had told Tierney that the company's commitment to universal provision

[1] Genzyme®, Cerezyme®, and Ceredase® are registered trademarks of Genzyme Corporation. All rights reserved.

Professor Christopher A. Bartlett and Research Associate Andrew N. McLean prepared this case. HBS cases are developed solely as the basis for class discussion. Cases are not intended to serve as endorsements, sources of primary data, or illustrations of effective or ineffective management. Certain names and data have been disguised.

Copyright © 2002 President and Fellows of Harvard College. To order copies or request permission to reproduce materials, call 1-800-545-7685, write Harvard Business School Publishing, Boston, MA 02163, or go to http//www.hbsp.harvard.edu. No part of this publication may be reproduced, stored in a retrieval system, used in a spreadsheet, or transmitted in any form or by any means—electronic, mechanical, photocopying, recording, or otherwise—without the permission of Harvard Business School.

could not undermine its commercial viability. Specifically, he emphasized that the Gaucher Initiative was not to be viewed as a permanent solution to providing care in any country. Recognizing this, Tierney wondered if the time had come to transfer the care of these patients to the government of Egypt. What if it refused to accept the responsibility? What if Project HOPE was unwilling to scale back its activities? In short, how exactly could the company balance the strong humanitarian and commercial principles it had built into its culture and values?

Birth of a Company

In contrast to other biotechnology firms that burst on the scene with impressive science-based, discovery-driven business models, Genzyme began by focusing on supplying raw materials—enzymes, fine chemicals, and reagents—to large research labs and pharmaceutical companies. Company co-founder Henry Blair had worked at the New England Enzyme Center of Tufts University School of Medicine and had many contacts in the research community. He founded the company in 1981 on the conservative belief that it should use revenues generated by selling reagents to generate cash flow and to create a track record that would allow it to fund further growth.

With a small pilot plant and office in a loft in Boston's Chinatown, Blair began searching for larger facilities to manufacture enzyme factors and reagents on a large scale. Within a year, he had located a company in the United Kingdom that was producing enzymes, substrates, and intermediates. Dissatisfied with the plant's efficiency and quality, Blair personally relocated to England to improve processes and increase yields. Within a few months the plant was profitable, and Genzyme was generating a positive cash flow. Sales in the first year were $2.2 million.

Laying the Foundation

Among all of Genzyme's early supply agreements, one had particular importance. Building on a long-term relationship he had with the National Institutes of Health (NIH), Blair obtained a contract to manufacture and supply the enzyme glucocerebrosidase (GCR) being used by Dr. Roscoe Brady in research on Gaucher (pronounced GO-shay) disease. Gaucher disease is an extremely rare and deadly condition caused by the body's inability to manufacture the GCR enzyme. Cells of the spleen, liver, lymph nodes, and bone marrow need GCR to break down and dispose of fatty residues from red blood cells' normal deterioration processes. Without this enzyme, fats collect and cause pain, fatigue, bone deterioration, fractures, and swelling of the affected organs.

Current estimates are that one in 400 of the general population carries the genetic mutations that cause Gaucher disease, but because both parents must pass on the mutation for a person to develop the disease, fewer than six of every one million people worldwide are predicted to have Gaucher disease. Of those 20,000 to 30,000 people, only about a quarter were thought to be ill enough to require treatment. (Populations with more intermarriage report a higher incidence of the disease. For example, among Jewish people of Eastern European ancestry, one in every 450 children is affected.) At the time of Brady's research, the treatment of choice was bone marrow transplantation, an extremely costly procedure with a 10 percent mortality rate.[2]

---

[2] Estimates of prevalence were gathered from the National Gaucher Foundation website, http://www.gaucherdisease.org/prev.htm, accessed July 18, 2002; and from "Genzyme Corp. Strategic Challenges with Ceredase," HBS Case No. 793-120 (Boston: Harvard Business School Publishing, 1994), pp. 7–8.

Throughout most of the 1970s, Brady's efforts to develop an enzyme replacement therapy had been unsuccessful, but in 1978, some members of his research team began suggesting that the large GCR molecule could better enter affected cells if the carbohydrate portion was modified, or "pruned." However, to put this idea into human trials involved expensive and risky protocols, and other team members expressed serious doubt that the modified molecule would work. After years of divisive internal debate, the NIH team put the "pruned molecule" hypothesis to the test in 1983. In its support role, Genzyme developed a production process for the enzyme required for the trials.

New Management, New Priorities

Meanwhile, Genzyme's top management was in transition. While Blair had been cleaning up the U.K. production processes, company co-founder Sheridan (Sherry) Snyder had been managing the financial and administrative side of the start-up. Although he had a background in the packaging business, Snyder was an entrepreneur and investor more than a professional manager, and the board decided the young company needed to engage a president to support him.

A search firm recommended Henri Termeer, a 36-year-old executive running a business making therapeutic products to treat hemophiliacs at medical products giant Baxter International. Termeer had joined Baxter in 1974 after completing his MBA and had built his reputation as an effective country manager of the company's German subsidiary. The search firm believed that his impressive management record, his broad industry knowledge, and his particular knowledge of blood-derived therapeutic treatment of genetic diseases made him an ideally qualified candidate.

Immediately upon joining Genzyme in October 1983, Termeer initiated a series of weekend discussions involving top management, members of the company's scientific advisory board of MIT and Harvard faculty, key investors, and a few outside advisors. Over several months they developed a few broad strategic principles that would guide Genzyme's future activities. First, Genzyme would be committed to building a diversified portfolio of targeted products and well-defined markets, with a particular focus on niches where needs were largely unmet. Equally important was its determination to remain independent by generating revenues from the start, by integrating vertically across the whole value chain, and by funding new development with internally generated funds or nonequity financial mechanisms.

While these meetings continued, Termeer was wrestling with some of the operating problems the company faced. Although he was aware that internal controls were all but nonexistent, the new president was still surprised to discover that one of the U.K. plants listed as an asset a particularly unsuccessful racehorse named Genzyme Gene. At that point he realized he had quite a job ahead in building a professional team and a sound management structure.

Betting the Ranch

As Termeer began his weekend sessions, Brady's new NIH trials were progressing. The results were disappointing yet tantalizing: only one patient out of the seven in the trial showed any response to the therapy, but his symptoms were dramatically reversed. The blind trial protocols masked the identity of the study participants, and critics of the modified enzyme in Brady's lab blocked the supporters' proposal to investigate the reason for the widely differing outcomes.

When the results of the trial became known, most within Genzyme were pessimistic about the prospects for this therapy. But Termeer was not ready to give up. After learning that the identity of the one patient who was in dramatic recovery was Ben Bryant, a 4-year-old boy from the Washington, D.C., area, he called the family.[3] Over the following months, he visited Ben and his family regularly and was very impressed that treatment resulted in a total reversal of symptoms, but when the injections stopped, Ben relapsed. Yet while Termeer became convinced the therapy could work, Genzyme's scientific advisory board was much less optimistic. For one whole day the scientists debated the issue with management, trying to answer three questions: Does it work? Is it safe? And could it be made profitable?

On the first question, the scientific advisors were doubtful, arguing that there was no strong indicator that this one case could have general implications. While agreeing with Termeer that Ben's recovery was extremely impressive, they did not share his belief that this was no aberration. The debate about safety was equally troubling. The enzyme used in the trial was extracted from the rare proteins found in human placentas collected from maternity wards in four large Boston hospitals. Growing publicity about risks of HIV and hepatitis C had led to widespread public concern about products derived from human tissue, leading the advisory board to suggest it would be more prudent to wait until biotechnology could create a recombinant version. Finally, there were major questions about whether a business could be created. Some raised concerns about accessing enough placentas, while others focused on the huge investment required to develop this product. Blair, conservative by nature, was worried it could bankrupt the company. Snyder also argued against the proposal.

Despite these many concerns, Termeer decided that it was unacceptable that product development should not proceed with a therapy potentially able to reverse this terrible disease. At this time, the company's best guess was that 2,000 patients worldwide could eventually use the product, with the potential of generating profits on a projected $100 million in annual sales—*if* further trials proved successful and *if* the product could qualify for "orphan drug" status, which would raise high-entry barriers to any competing therapy for seven years. (Genzyme faced no patent barriers or licensing costs, since the government had decided not to patent the discovery of the modified GCR molecule to encourage further research.)

Throughout this process, Termeer and Blair had been talking to Scott Furbish, one member of the NIH team advocating the pruned molecule treatment. Frustrated by the infighting, Furbish was ready to quit NIH. They convinced him to join Genzyme and head up the research that would take his NIH work to fruition. But Termeer also took his scientific advisors' recommendation seriously and initiated parallel research on a recombinant form of the GCR enzyme.

Furbish and his team soon hypothesized that it was Ben Bryant's small size that allowed the therapy to succeed. By increasing the dosage to adult patients, they believed further clinical trials would show it was equally effective on them. Recalling all the uncertainties of 1985 as Genzyme made a new-drug application for Ceredase® enzyme under the Orphan Drug Act, Furbish said, "I would like to ask Henri how he had the guts to make that decision."

Going Public

By 1985, Termeer had tightened Genzyme's operations, set its broad strategic direction, strengthened its ongoing businesses, and committed to several important new research initiatives, of which the Gaucher therapies were the boldest. With sales of 32 research reagents, diagnostic intermediaries, and fine chemicals generating almost $10 million in revenues, the company was approaching the financial break-even point. Termeer felt it was now time to take Genzyme public.

---

[3] Patient's name disguised.

With the board's full support, he became CEO in late 1985 (Snyder had left the company) and soon after began planning an IPO for 1986. (See Exhibit 22.3 for excerpts from the prospectus.) Recognizing that most of the $27.4 million IPO cash infusion would be needed to finance the growth of existing operations, Termeer began exploring other means of funding product development. Unlike most other biotech companies, which financed research and development (R&D) by raising equity or entering into partnerships with large pharmaceutical companies, Genzyme elected to do so by creating a limited research partnership. Sales of the partnership units in 1987 raised a crucial $10 million to continue Ceredase development, splitting the risk and rewards of R&D but leaving Genzyme the option to buy back successful developments at a preset price.

Genzyme in Liftoff

By 1989 Ceredase approval seemed only a few years away, but public concern about the transmission of HIV from human-derived factors was growing. Recognizing that Genzyme could not develop a genetically engineered version of GCR quickly enough in-house, Termeer jumped at the opportunity to merge with Integrated Genetics (IG), a Massachusetts-based biotech firm with expertise in recombinant genetic engineering but an empty development pipeline following a patent-suit loss to Amgen.

Pursuing its strategy of diversification, Genzyme continued product development on multiple fronts—researching enzyme replacement for Fabry disease, developing genetic-screening tests, and working on therapies for cystic fibrosis, for example. With a continuing need for funding, a second limited research partnership in 1989 raised $36.7 million, followed by a second public stock offering for $39.1 million. In 1990 a special-purpose publicly traded research company was created, raising an additional $47.3 million for targeted genetic research, including promising work on cystic fibrosis. But the real excitement at Genzyme focused on bringing Ceredase to market.

Building a Product Pipeline

As the Ceredase trials continued, the company worked to ensure product supply. First-stage processing was contracted to the French Institute Merieux in Lyon, where rare proteins—among them GCR—were extracted from placentas shipped from the United States and all over Europe. (A year's supply of Ceredase for the average patient contained enzyme extracted and purified from 20,000 human placentas, or 27 tons of material.) Back in Boston, Genzyme modified the GCR enzyme, then processed it to ensure its safety, purity, and concentration.

The U.S. Food and Drug Administration (FDA) finally approved Ceredase for marketing in the United States in 1991, giving Genzyme the momentum for another $143 million stock offering. Meanwhile, a team of biochemists from Genzyme and IG spliced the human gene responsible for producing GCR into cells cultured from Chinese hamster ovaries, producing recombinant GCR. Others worked on scaling up production from the two-and-a-half grams of product made in a one-liter container for the trials to a new proposed production facility with four bioreactors of 2,000 liters each.

In 1992, well before the production process was fully developed and more than a year before Genzyme would be ready to file the new-drug application for the product to be called Cerezyme, construction began on the new plant. To help finance the $180 million investment, a dramatic structure on the Charles River that stamped Genzyme's presence on Boston's skyline, Genzyme raised $100 million through debt financing. When commissioned, the plant's round-the-clock, 365-day-a-year production capacity would be six kilos of medicine annually—an output that would fit in a six-pack cooler but still sufficient for the 2,000 patients Genzyme hoped to treat worldwide.

Responding to Regulatory Pressures

When Ceredase was approved, it had the distinction of being the most expensive therapy on the market. The complex extraction process, the limited availability of raw material, and the small number of patients combined to make production extremely costly. (Even when it was collecting 35 percent of all the placentas in the United States and over 70 percent of those in Europe, Genzyme could effectively supply Ceredase to only 1,000 to 1,500 patients.) Over one-third of this cost was attributable to acquiring and processing raw material, compared with raw material costs of 5 to 10 percent in typical drug manufacturing processes. (See Exhibit 22.4 for cost estimate.) Protocols called for patients with the severe form of the disease to initially receive 50 units of Ceredase per kilo of body weight every two weeks. At $3.70 per unit, the first year's treatment could cost over $300,000, and although maintenance therapy could drop to roughly two-thirds of the initial dosage, the cost was high enough to attract the attention of regulators and politicians. (See Exhibit 22.5 for dosage calculations and costs.)

The political environment in which Ceredase was launched was a difficult one for pharmaceutical and biotech companies. The emphasis on health-care reform in President Clinton's first term turned the spotlight on high-priced therapies, and along with a few other products such as Burroughs Wellcome's AZT treatment for AIDS, Ceredase was singled out as an example of a drug that was seeking protection by exploiting the Orphan Drug Act.[4] Termeer's response was immediate and strong. (See Exhibit 22.6 for an editorial expressing his views.) He went to Washington and asked members of Congress and the regulatory authorities what they wanted to know. He recalled: "I invited them to visit our operations and offered to open our books so they could see what it cost to develop and produce the product. I asked them for their suggestions—to tell me if we had done anything wrong. We would listen. Our approach was to be completely open and transparent. We were proud of what we had done and had nothing to hide."

In addition to showing his visitors the facilities and giving the Congressional Office of Technology Assessment (OTA) access to the books, Termeer also explained the company's philosophy: "Since the beginning, I have told this organization that our first responsibility is to treat patients with the disease, not to maximize financial returns. Regardless of where those people are or the financial circumstances they find themselves in, we take it as our responsibility to see they are treated."

To implement this "universal provision" philosophy, Genzyme created the Ceredase Assistance Program (CAP) even before Ceredase was approved to market. A CAP committee reviewed cases of extreme need—patients who had lost insurance coverage, for example—and where there was no alternative provided Ceredase free. But they always continued working with the patients to try to secure an ongoing supportive, paying party. In addition to Termeer, the CAP review committee consisted of medical, legal, and caseworker professionals.

---

[4] Larry Thompson, "The High Cost of Rare Diseases: When Patients Can't Afford to Buy Lifesaving Drugs," *Washington Post*, June 25, 1991, p. Z10; David Stipp, "Genzyme Counters Criticism over High Cost of Drug," *The Wall Street Journal*, June 23, 1992, p. B4; John Carey, "How Many Times Must a Patient Pay?" *Business Week*, February 1, 1993, p. 30.

After a detailed examination, the October 1992 OTA report concluded that, while NIH research had been used and while the Orphan Drug Act did reduce its risk, Genzyme had invested significantly in R&D and production facilities. Genzyme's pretax profit margin on the drug was determined to be in line with industry norms. (OTA's calculation excluded any R&D unrelated to Ceredase, bad debt, and free goods expenses.) Furthermore, OTA found that insurers were reimbursing the cost of the therapy because it was less expensive than surgery or extensive hospitalization.[5]

Going to Market

Meanwhile, the company had been tackling the formidable task of bringing to market an extremely expensive therapy for a rare, poorly understood, and seldom-diagnosed disease. Termeer knew that once again he would have to attract different kinds of people to take on the challenge: "Recruiting the right people has been a key part of Genzyme's success. . . . I look for people with a passion to tackle things that seem impossible to solve. Practical dreamers who have a sense of compassion but believe they can change things. . . . And we attract people who see what we are doing as a worthwhile fight. There has to be a real personal involvement."

Drawing on the pool of biotech sales veterans in the Boston area, the company recruited an eight-person pioneering sales force with good industry knowledge whose members fit Termeer's "passionate practical dreamer" profile. In contrast to the traditional pharmaceutical model of making sales calls to doctors, pharmacies, and hospital purchasing agents, the Ceredase team focused on patients. After working to identify who they were, they educated them about the disease, organized them in support groups, and found treatment for them. They also educated physicians and reassured them about reimbursement.

Very quickly, the field sales force found the need for a support staff of caseworkers—typically, trained nurses and social workers—who advocated for patients with insurance companies. The caseworkers explained the therapy to the insurance representatives, provided supporting research materials, and handled the huge administrative demands for each submission. Said one of the early sales force members: "Because of insurance, it was a patient-oriented approach. Then, as the patient got better, the physician became motivated. We worked patient by patient, physician by physician. . . . This company is really about caring for our patients and doing the right thing for them. When a patient calls, you respond—it's the culture here."

The patient-oriented culture permeated the organization. Termeer explained that it was important for him personally to be in direct contact with patients, to feel emotionally involved in their suffering, and to use that to motivate himself and the organization to do something to help. Patient profiles were prominent in Genzyme's annual reports, photos of patients were pinned on cubicle walls in the offices, and company employees spoke passionately about how an individual or group of patients motivated them. Alison Lawton from regulatory affairs was typical: "Two months after I joined Genzyme, I went to a Gaucher patient meeting in Israel. . . . I cried my eyes out just seeing the patients and hearing them basically begging the Ministry to get them the therapy. . . . I remember thinking, 'I'm really going to make a difference if I can get this product registered here.'"

Yet some in the R&D labs claimed to be unmoved by Termeer's regular attempts to link their work to real patients' stories, believing their scientific training forced a more disciplined attitude. "If you are immersed in the science, you become intrigued

---

[5] "Federal and Private Roles in the Development and Provision of Alglucerase Therapy for Gaucher Disease," Office of Technology Assessment (Washington, D.C.: Government Printing Office, 1992).

by trying to figure out the problems," said one. "You're not inspired by stories of human tragedies or a picture of a kid on the wall." But others were. Furbish felt that most Genzyme scientists were different from others in the industry:

> There are clear philosophical divides in the biotech world. Technology looks down on sales and marketing, and Ph.D.s are trained to sneer at profit. But that doesn't hold at Genzyme. The patient focus builds from Henri down. His commitment is real and it affects everyone—even the Ph.D.s. Yet he also sets very aggressive business goals, and we come to appreciate that this is paying the bills as well as helping patients.

The same attitude had spread to the engineers and technicians in the plant. Blair Okita, vice president of Therapeutics Manufacturing and Development, found his experience at Genzyme much different from earlier stints at SmithKline Beecham and Merck: "Here we are motivated by a patient focus—right down to the technician level. For example, before doing their first run of the new Pompe product, our staff in the fill and finish area had a family with a child with Pompe's disease talk to them. . . . Each one of us is providing a life-saving therapy to a patient. That is a powerful motivating force."

As the network of educated patients and aware physicians expanded, sales of Ceredase grew rapidly. In 1993, after three years on the market, 1,000 patients were being treated, and cumulative sales were almost $250 million. Regulatory applications for Ceredase were pending in many international markets, and Cerezyme, the recombinant version of the therapy, was due for FDA approval in the United States in 1994. Genzyme's future looked promising indeed.

Opening Foreign Markets

Even before Ceredase was launched, Genzyme had been approached by companies wanting to cross-license or distribute the product abroad. True to his principle of controlling his business both upstream and downstream, Termeer refused. "International markets were an exciting opportunity," he said. "Besides, we were committed to seeking out and responding to Gaucher patients."

Pioneering Initiatives

In late 1990, Termeer called Tomye Tierney, an ex-colleague at Baxter, and convinced her to lead Genzyme's thrust into Europe. With her experience marketing Baxter's hemophilia products in many markets around the globe, Tierney had strong skills in building relationships with patients, physicians, and government officials. Said Termeer, "Tomye is one of those unusual people you can send into an impossible country where there are all kinds of roadblocks, and she can find a way."

Joining at the same time Genzyme was recruiting its U.S. sales force, Tierney had no sales model to build on. "Henri told me I would have to develop the international strategy," she recalled. "And when I asked him how long I had, he told me, 'Two weeks.'" She headed straight to Europe and within two months she had contacted her old physician friends; been referred to the few specialists working on Gaucher disease; located known patients in the United Kingdom, France, and the Netherlands; and begun connecting the network. Winning "investigational new drug" use approval, she made the first sales by December 1990.

Having set up the basic network, in September 1991 Tierney called another old Baxter colleague, Jan van Heek, and told him about Genzyme's European plans. Van Heek had just been offered a promotion at Baxter, so he was not very interested. "But

I went to a patient and physician meeting and was astonished how much Genzyme meant to those people," he recalled. "There was an enormous sense of optimism and hope in the company, and I decided on the spot to join." By year's end, he had established Genzyme's temporary European headquarters—a rented house with a phone and a fax—and had hired the five entrepreneurial individuals who would develop the European market.

As the company pursued the long, complicated process of registration and approval in each of Europe's national health care systems, the high cost of Ceredase inevitably led to equally long and complex negotiations over price. But Genzyme's response was always simple, straightforward, and unwavering. The company had a universal global pricing policy. Termeer explained:

> We have only two prices the commercial price or free. By taking an absolutely transparent global position, the discussion finishes quickly. We have not exploited our position by increasing prices—we have remained basically the same over that whole period. Our margin has gone up, but as it has we have taken on more responsibility to support patients around the world

A Mobile Missionary

With van Heek running Europe, Termeer asked Tierney to become vice president and general manager of emerging markets with responsibility for developing opportunities in the rest of the world. Although she began initiatives in many markets, including Canada, Latin America, and Australia, it was the Middle East that captured much of her time and attention. Due to its high concentration of Gaucher patients, Israel was a priority market and in 1993 became the first country outside the United States to approve Ceredase. Another market that seemed to offer potential was Egypt, and since 1990 Tierney had been in contact with Dr. Khalifa, a physician with an interest in Gaucher disease.

After four years, Tierney had built her widespread portfolio of markets into a $16 million business. In 1996, Termeer asked her to relocate to Asia, a market previously thought to have limited potential. Setting up her base in Singapore, she continued her missionary work. By that time, she had established a clear step-by-step approach to entering new markets. She explained:

> The key is to hire a smart local person to manage the process. For example, in Korea I found a pharmacist who had worked for the German drug company Boehringher. I connected him to a physician who we felt could be a local thought leader. She was treating a Gaucher patient willing to pay for his own treatment. This gave us the base to create a forum for patients and help them channel their frustration at not having access to therapy toward the government. Our local manager then worked with the patients, physicians, and government to enact orphan drug legislation and approve Cerezyme for reimbursement. It's a lot of work, but the Genzyme credo is "you've got to find a way."

As she opened markets in Japan, South Korea, Taiwan, Hong Kong, and other developed Asian countries, Tierney was increasingly aware that there were other, less-developed economies—China, India, and Vietnam, for example—that simply could not afford this therapy. It was an issue that had become a growing concern for Termeer as well. For several years, patients from countries without access to Cerezyme had been coming to Boston to request free product from the CAP committee. (See Exhibit 22.7 for one well-publicized example.) This presented Termeer with a real dilemma: "The problem was we were having families moving to the United States asking to get free drug and treatment here forever. The real solution had to be to get treatment in their home country. It's less disruptive for the family and also educates the country about the therapy so more patients can be treated."

To the critics, however, the requirement to return home seemed to be a hard-hearted and even manipulative tactic designed to use patient needs to develop new market opportunities. It was a charge Termeer strongly refuted:

> What I will never tolerate is to create a blackmail situation where the patient is in the middle. There can be no circumstance where a patient on therapy is taken off therapy to create leverage. Or where a patient that needs therapy is denied it to create leverage. We have to make sure there is a critical need, then we must respond to the need. But we cannot take on the responsibility forever and we need to make people aware of the role they must play to help. . . . In the Peruvian family's case, we asked them to move back, then worked very hard with the government to get reimbursement in Peru. In the end we were able to help other Peruvian patients get the treatment also.

The Gaucher Initiative

As Termeer thought about how to address the question of providing treatment to Gaucher sufferers in less-developed countries, he decided this would be an ideal next project for Tierney. But Tierney was not so sure. After nine months of persuasion and negotiation, she returned to Boston in June 1998 with a mandate to develop a humanitarian program for emerging markets—but without jeopardizing the company's existing or future commercial opportunities.

Setting Up the Program

As soon as Tierney returned, she scheduled a meeting with Termeer to review the parameters of her new assignment. She found he was deeply involved in the issues, and the meeting turned into the first of many brainstorming sessions she had with Termeer and Sandy Smith, the vice president of International, to whom she reported. The first issue Termeer addressed with Tierney was the charter of what they began calling the Gaucher Initiative. He recalled the guidelines clearly: "It was really just a continuation of the philosophy we had implemented through CAP. Where there is a critical need, we will respond. But we cannot take on the responsibility forever. Our goal must be to create a situation in which the country itself will eventually take responsibility for the treatment. That's where we need to get to."

Implementation of this philosophy was complicated by the conjunction of the company's humanitarian commitment to universal provision and its commercial objective of a universal price. Recognizing that the humanitarian provision needed to be insulated from the commercial operations, Tierney and Termeer concluded they would need to work with an independent agency that had the infrastructure to distribute Cerezyme around the world. To ensure Genzyme's efforts would be both direct and discrete yet would not involve the company in decisions about who would receive treatment, they would also need an independent, medically qualified committee of experts to make case-by-case diagnoses and decisions about the relative needs of candidates for treatment.

As she developed the program design, Tierney worked with a corporate philanthropy consultant and shared development ideas with the program director for the Mectizan Donation Program, Merck's initiative to combat river blindness.[6] In October, after carefully screening several partner candidates suggested by the outside consultant, Tierney selected Project HOPE for its worldwide distribution network, long

---

[6] Peter Wehrwein, "Pharmaco-Philanthropy," *Harvard Public Health Review*, Summer 1999, pp. 32–39.

track record, emphasis on health education, and sterling reputation. Additionally, the organization had a strong presence in China and Egypt, markets that Tierney knew had a recognized need for this therapy. Project HOPE's emphasis on health care development within a country, rather than ongoing charitable health care provision, was also consistent with Genzyme's long-term commercial goals.

For its part, however, Project HOPE took some convincing. It wanted assurances that it would not be mixing a commercial agenda with its humanitarian mission and that the program would be run independently of Genzyme. Finally, an agreement was reached, and Tierney worked feverishly to get the program up and running by January 1, 1999. (See Exhibit 22.8 for memorandum of understanding highlights.)

Implementing the Program

Tierney's first task was to work to establish a secretariat with a full-time program manager and an independent case review board. She then won Termeer's agreement to supplement the in-kind donation of Cerezyme with a yearly budget to support the program manager and secretariat and provide training, travel, and office peripherals for local treatment centers. Eager to begin shipment of the drug to Egypt and China, Tierney appealed to the quality control personnel at Genzyme to inspect and approve Project HOPE's delivery system immediately. With excitement about the new program running high at Genzyme (Termeer and Tierney had widely communicated the company's commitment to the Gaucher Initiative), plant personnel helped to bypass a two-month backlog, and the first product was shipped ahead of Tierney's year-end target date.

Working with Project HOPE, Tierney convened the independent six-member medical review board that would meet three times a year to establish patient-intake procedures, qualify new cases, and decide to terminate treatment for patients who did not respond to the therapy. The board consisted of three leading experts in Gaucher disease, Genzyme's chief medical officer, a Project HOPE staff member, and a medical ethicist, who quickly tested the board's independence.

As Project HOPE spread the word in Egypt and China, local doctors made case-by-case requests to the local Project HOPE office. Applications were forwarded to Genzyme, which coordinated a case docket for the medical advisory board. After medical advisory board approval, Genzyme prepared patient and dosage lists for distribution to Project HOPE, which then shipped the drug overseas in coolers. At its destination it was carried by truck—or sometimes by hand—to local hospitals, where it was reconstituted and prepared for infusion. Project HOPE qualified local doctors to administer the therapy and participate in the program. In its first year, the Gaucher Initiative treated 60 patients worldwide (37 in Egypt and 23 in China); by 2001 the number was 140.

The Humanitarian/Commercial Tension

To the employees at Genzyme, the commitment to the Gaucher Initiative was another confirmation of the values they had heard Termeer espouse since the company's earliest days. Yet within the commercial organization, some voices of concern were emerging, particularly from those responsible for less-developed markets. "We have a person who covers most of our Eastern European markets who was really concerned that if people began to understand we would give product away, it would be impossible to sell," Tierney recalled.

Christi van Heek, president of Genzyme's therapeutics division, reinforced the view that reimbursement could easily be lost if health care providers felt they could obtain free product. She described how she had visited a physician in the Czech

Republic who explained that his hospital lacked the money to buy Tylenol. Yet he eventually had six children on Cerezyme therapy. "He got reimbursement through the system," she said. "He had to fight for it, but this drug really works."

However, as the product penetration in developed nations approached saturation—sales growth increased only 6 percent between 2000 and 2001—the opportunities in markets outside the most developed economies began to attract more attention. (See Exhibit 22.9 for sales and patient growth.) Furthermore, Ceredase had come off orphan drug protection in 1998, and Cerezyme's would expire in 2001. Already competitors had applied for marketing approval for different therapies. Although Genzyme analysis cast doubts on their safety and effectiveness, it was a clear signal that this larger-than-expected market was attractive to competitors. "The interesting question will be what the entry of competitors will do to this responsibility we have taken on," said Termeer. "Will it be a burden for us alone, or will it be a joint responsibility? We have not begun to sort that one out."

The Egyptian Dilemma

Even after she moved to Singapore, Tierney had kept her eye on the nascent opportunity in Egypt. It was a responsibility that would absorb much time and energy in coming years.

Building a Presence, Having an Impact

In late 1996, Khalifa had informed her that he had obtained funding to treat a child with Gaucher disease. On a "named-patient basis," he also had obtained permission to import Cerezyme on humanitarian grounds even though it was not registered for sale in Egypt. However, several months later, when Tierney was visiting Egypt, she found that the funding was insufficient to cover the required treatment, and the patient was not responding to the low dosage provided. She immediately offered to request Genzyme's CAP program to sponsor a matching dose. Under this partial reimbursement arrangement, over the next two years Khalifa and Dr. Khaled, another physician now involved, had expanded treatment to a dozen patients, mostly children who were reimbursed under the government's Student Fund.

But now, with Tierney leading the Gaucher Initiative, responsibility for the Egyptian market was transferred to the general manager of Genzyme's Israel subsidiary, Zev Zelig. As a way of handing off her commercial responsibilities, Tierney introduced the Jordanian sales associate hired to cover Arab markets to her key physician and health insurance contacts. She also introduced him to the Project HOPE staff in Egypt. "The HOPE people were a little uncomfortable that we were actually making money on some of these patients," she explained. "They wanted a clear separation."

New Demands, New Expectations

In Project HOPE's first year in Egypt, the number of patients grew from 12 to 37, many of them infants, since children under five were not covered by the government-financed Student Fund. Sales through the partial reimbursement program were also up, increasing from $82,200 in 1998 to $146,500 in 1999. But the growing number of "named patients" attracted the attention of regulatory authorities, and in early 2000 Zelig was told that Genzyme would have to register Cerezyme. Zelig asked one of the company's regulatory staff to help him assess the task, but after talking to the Egyptian authorities, they concluded that registration would be too expensive to be justified.

After the first quarter of 2000, sales stopped. Almost immediately, Tierney began to feel pressure from Zelig to scale back her program in Egypt. She recalled: "At our strategic planning meeting, Zev kept saying, 'I can't do it because she's giving away free drug.' And I'd come back, 'You need to hire an Egyptian sales associate and register in Egypt.' We went back and forth for almost a year."

Meanwhile, Project HOPE had just appointed Dr. John Howe as its new CEO. A well-respected cardiologist from Texas, Howe joined the organization with much energy and an ambition to expand its operations. "He told me he wanted to grow Project HOPE at least 50 percent," said Tierney. "And he was particularly interested in expanding the relationship with Genzyme."

Facing the Problem

In early 2001, the tension between the commercial and humanitarian agendas in Egypt was still unresolved. While sales had stopped for a year, by May 2001 the Gaucher Initiative had expanded to 41 patients, with 5 more approvals about to start treatment. When Mike Heslop, Genzyme's vice president for Global Marketing, hired Tarek Ebrahim, an Egyptian physician, he made "sorting out the Egyptian issue" one of the newcomer's first assignments.

On May 25, Smith, Genzyme's vice president of International, convened a meeting to which he invited Heslop, Ebrahim, Zelig, and Tierney. Tierney recalled the discussion:

> The others were all from the commercial side and had been talking to Zev. So they were sitting there telling me to put a lid on the free drug program. Zev took the lead and said we had to get the word out that Project HOPE was not taking any more patients. I told them that the solution was to register the drug and get a local presence in Egypt. Then we could manage the transition. I told them I could not stop the program.

The meeting broke up with the proposal that Ebrahim go to Egypt, evaluate the situation, and return with his analysis and recommendation. Tierney liked and respected her new Egyptian marketing colleague but wondered how the situation could be resolved. How could she think through the problem? If Termeer were to be involved, what kind of recommendation could she make to him? And how could she and her colleagues implement the necessary changes?

Appendix A

Time Line of Selected Corporate Events, Genzyme Corp.

Year	Significant Events
1981	Genzyme, founded by Henry Blair and Sherry Snyder, begins to supply NIH with GCR under contract.
1983	Genzyme hires Henri Termeer as president; becomes CEO, 1985.
	NIH launches first GCR enzyme-replacement trial.
1985	FDA designates Ceredase an orphan drug.
	Scientific advisory board (BIA) recommends against development of Ceredase.
1986	Genzyme IPO, June, raises $27.4 million cash for a company valuation of over $83 million.
1987	Forms R&D limited partnership, raising $10 million to develop Ceredase.
1989	Ceredase approved for seriously ill patients prior to marketing approval.
	Raises $39.1 million through public stock offering and $36.7 million through Genzyme Development Partners.
	Acquires Integrated Genetics (founded in 1981).
1990	Ceredase available outside United States on a named-patient basis.
	Forms Neozyme I, raises $47.3 million to fund R&D.
1991	Ceredase approved and receives orphan drug status.
	Raises $100 million in 10-year 6 percent debt, and raises $143 million in public stock offering.
1992	Begins work on gene therapy to treat cystic fibrosis.
	Congressional OTA report issued on the development of Ceredase.
	Forms Neozyme II, raises $85 million; purchases four research programs from Neozyme I for $49 million.
1993	New-drug application to FDA for Cerezyme.
1994	Cerezyme approved in United States, Germany, France, Holland, Australia, United Kingdom.
	Break-even on Ceredase.
1995	Ceredase sales approved in Portugal, Italy, New Zealand, Sweden, Spain.
	Genzyme General public offering raises $141 million.
1996	Japan approves Cerezyme.
1998	Genzyme General places $250 million 5.25 percent seven-year debt.
1999	Launches Gaucher Initiative.

Source: Adapted by casewriters from Genzyme Corp. sources.

EXHIBIT 22.1 Genzyme Corp. Selected Consolidated Balance Sheets ($000s)

Source: Adapted by casewriters from Genzyme Corp. annual reports.

	Year Ending December 31,							
	2000	1999	1998	1997	1996	1991	1986	1981[a]
Assets								
Current assets								
Cash and equivalents	$ 236,213	$ 130,156	$ 118,612	$ 102,406	$ 93,132	$ 29,031	$ 2,309	$ 828
Short-term investments	104,586	255,846	175,453	51,259	56,608	78,147	19,496	—
Accounts receivable	205,094	166,803	163,042	118,277	116,833	31,838	2,728	—
Inventories	170,341	117,269	109,833	139,681	125,265	16,329	4,243	—
Prepaid expenses and other	37,681	18,918	31,467	17,361	100,287	3,688	299	—
Deferred tax assets—current	46,836	41,195	41,195	27,601	17,493	—	—	—
Noncurrent assets								
Net property, plant, and equipment	504,412	383,181	382,619	385,348	393,839	32,057	4,020	—
Long-term investments	298,841	266,988	281,664	92,676	38,215	172,529	—	—
Notes receivable—related party	10,350	—	—	2,019	—	4,000	—	—
Net intangibles	1,539,782	253,153	279,516	271,275	247,745	13,362	—	—
Deferred tax assets—noncurrent	—	18,631	24,277	29,479	42,221	4,186	—	—
Investments in equity securities	121,251	97,859	51,977	30,047	38,870	—	—	—
Other noncurrent assets	42,713	37,283	30,669	28,024	—	5,371	—	2,098
Total Assets	$3,318,100	$1,787,282	$1,690,324	$1,295,453	$1,270,508	$390,538	$33,095	$2,926
Liabilities and Stockholders' Equity								
Current liabilities								
Accounts payable	$ 26,165	$ 27,853	$ 27,604	$ 19,787	$ 22,271	$ 4,584	$ 1,004	—
Accrued expenses	139,683	73,359	72,370	72,103	70,124	10,964	548	—
Payable to joint venture	—	—	1,181	—	—	—	—	—
Income taxes payable	46,745	27,946	16,543	11,168	17,926	4,305	—	—
Deferred revenue	8,609	3,700	2,731	1,800	2,693	1,987	—	—
Current LT debt and lease obligations	19,897	5,080	100,568	905	999	1,484	225	—
Noncurrent liabilities								
Long-term debt and lease obligations	391,560	18,000	3,087	140,978	241,998	101,044	162	$382
Convertible notes and debentures	273,680	272,622	284,138	29,298	—	—	—	476
Deferred tax liability	230,384	—	8,078	—	—	—	176	—
Other noncurrent liabilities	6,236	2,330	—	7,364	12,188	6,298	—	1,924
Total Liabilities	$1,142,959	$ 430,890	$ 516,300	$ 283,403	$ 368,199	$130,666	$ 2,115	$2,782
Stockholders' equity	2,175,141	1,356,392	1,172,554	1,012,050	902,309	259,872	30,979	180
Total liabilities and stockholders' equity	$3,318,100	$1,787,282	$1,688,854	$1,295,453	$1,270,508	$390,538	$33,094	$2,962

[a] 1981 results cover the period from company inception on June 8, 1981. (Source: Genzyme 1986 IPC Prospectus.)

EXHIBIT 22.2 Genzyme Corp. Selected Consolidated Income Statement ($000s)

Source: Adapted by casewriters from Genzyme Corp. annual reports.

	Year Ending December 31,							
	2000	1999	1998	1997	1996	1991	1986	1981[a]
Revenues:								
Product sales	$811,897	$683,482	$613,685	$529,927	$424,483	$72,019	$9,770	$2,167
Service sales	84,482	79,448	74,791	67,158	68,950	21,503	—	—
Revenue from R&D contracts	6,941	9,358	20,859	11,756	25,321	28,394	2,366	—
Total Revenues	$903,320	$772,288	$709,335	$608,841	$518,754	$121,916	$12,136	$2,167
Expenses:								
Cost of products sold	$232,383	$182,337	$211,076	$206,028	$155,930	$33,164	$5,421	$936
Cost of services sold	50,177	49,444	48,586	47,289	54,082	14,169	—	—
Selling, administrative, and general	264,551	242,797	215,203	200,476	162,264	39,118	5,084	838
Research and development	169,478	150,516	119,005	89,558	80,849	27,232	2,285	57
Purchase of in-process R&D	200,191	5,436	—	7,000	130,639	—	—	—
Charge for impaired asset	4,321	—	—	—	—	—	—	—
Amortization of intangibles	22,974	24,674	24,334	17,245	8,849	—	—	—
Total Expenses	$944,075	$655,204	$618,204	$567,596	$592,613	$113,683	$12,790	$1,831
Income (loss) before unusual items	($ 40,755)	$117,084	$ 91,131	$ 41,245	($ 73,859)	$ 8,233	($ 654)	$ 336
Investment income	$45,593	$ 36,158	$ 25,055	$ 11,409	$ 15,341	$ 12,371	$ 889	—
Interest expense	(15,710)	(21,771)	(22,593)	(12,667)	(6,990)	(2,088)	(194)	(92)
Equity in net loss of unconsolidated affiliates	(44,965)	(42,696)	(29,006)	(12,258)	(5,373)	—	—	—
Affiliate sale of stock	22,689	6,683	2,369	—	1,013	—	—	—
Sale of equity securities	15,873	(3,749)	(6)	—	1,711	—	—	—
Minority interest	4,625	3,674	4,285	—	—	—	—	—
Sale of product line	—	8,018	31,202	—	—	—	—	—
Sale of Gene-Trak	—	—	—	—	—	4,065	—	—
Credit from operating loss carryforward	—	—	—	—	—	8,387	—	—
Other revenue (expense)	5,188	14,527	—	(2,000)	(1,465)	2,726	—	—
Income (loss) before income taxes	($ 7,462)	$117,928	$102,437	$ 25,729	($ 69,622)	$ 33,694	$ 41	$ 244
Provision for income taxes	(55,478)	(46,947)	(39,870)	(12,100)	(3,195)	(12,848)	0	(165)
Net income (loss)	($ 62,940)	$ 70,981	$ 62,567	$ 13,629	($ 72,817)	$ 20,846	$ 41	$ 79

[a]1981 results cover the period from company inception on June 8, 1981. (Source: Genzyme 1986 IPO Prospectus.)

EXHIBIT 22.3   Excerpts from Genzyme's 1986 IPO Prospectus

Source: Adapted by casewriters from Genzyme Corp. 1986 IPO Prospectus.

The Company
- Genzyme develops, manufactures, and markets a variety of biological products used in human health care applications.
- Genzyme has additional human health care products under development. . . . [It] believes its practical experience in the production and sale of biological products will enhance its ability to manufacture and commercialize new products.
- As of March 1980, the company had 169 employees, of whom 39 are engaged in R&D.

Risk Factors
- Short operating history and losses . . . during each of its last few years.
- Regulation by government agencies . . . no assurance that . . approvals will be granted.
- Uncertainty of product development.
- Patents with proprietary technology.
- Engaged in a segment of health care that is extremely competitive.
- Product liability.

Genzyme's Principal Products and Process Development Programs, 1986

Products and Processes	Applications	Status
Therapeutics		
Hyaluronic acid	Ophthalmic surgery	Development stage
	Soft-tissue implants	Development stage
	Surgical trauma	Research stage
	Joint disorders	Research stage
	Drug delivery	Research stage
Glycoprotein remodeling	Therapeutic glycoproteins	Research stage
Glucocerebrosidase	Treatment of Gaucher disease	NIH clinical trials
Ceramide trihexosidase	Treatment of Fabry disease	NIH development stage
Bulk pharmaceuticals	Active ingredients in branded and generic pharmaceuticals	Product sales
Diagnostics and reagents		
Diagnostic enzymes and substrates	Manufacture of diagnostic kits	Product sales
Research reagents	Lymphokine and glycoprotein research	Product sales
Fine chemicals		
Chiral compounds	Production of single isomer drugs	Development stage
Organic chemicals	Bioprocess compounds	Product sales

EXHIBIT 22.4

Ceredase Cost and Profit Estimate, 1994

Source: Adapted by case-writers from Elyse Tanouye, "What Ails Us—What's Fair?" *The Wall Street Journal*, May 20, 1994, p. R11. (Source of data in the article given as Genzyme figures.)

Per patient annual price		$150,000	100%
Cost of goods			
Material	$47,900		
Manufacturing labor, overhead	5,300	$ 53,200	35
Gross profit		$ 96,800	65
Operating expenses			
Selling/reimbursement expense	$12,200		
Distribution	10,500		
R&D amortization	4,500		
Manufacturing development amortization	2,000		
Corporate/administrative expenses	12,600		
Bad-debt provision	4,900		
Medicaid allowance	2,800		
Free goods	1,500	$ 51,000	34
Pretax Operating Profit		$ 45,800	31
State/federal taxes		14,600	10
Net income		$ 31,300	21

Note: Estimated average per patient revenue includes pediatric and adult patients on initial and maintenance treatments.

EXHIBIT 22.5
Dosage Annual Cost Calculations for Ceredase and Cerezyme

Source: Prepared by casewriters with information supplied by Genzyme Corp.

Regimen and Patient Weight	Annual Cost
Initial treatment of 50 units/kg	
165 lbs. (75 kg)	$360,750
110 lbs. (50 kg)	240,500
33 lbs. (15 kg)	72,150
Maintenance treatment of 35 units/kg	
165 lbs. (75 kg)	$252,525
110 lbs. (50 kg)	168,350
33 lbs. (15 kg)	50,505

Note: Assumes biweekly infusions at $3.70 per unit medicine cost. Annual cost = price × dosage × weight × annual number of infusions.

EXHIBIT 22.6
The Cost of Miracles

Source: Henri A. Termeer, "The Cost of Miracles," *The Wall Street Journal*, November 16, 1993, p. A28.

As part of his continuing attack on the pharmaceutical industry, President Clinton has proposed establishing a federal committee to review the prices of "breakthrough" drugs, including those developed by the biotechnology industry. The Senate's Special Committee on Aging is scheduled to hold hearings today on the subject. Its chairman, Sen. David Pryor (D., Ark.), says the purpose of the hearings is to determine whether market forces are adequate to restrain prices.

The real danger, however, is not that the prices of new drugs will be too high, but that government controls, whether direct or indirect, will discourage investors from taking risks on biotechnology companies that develop new drugs.

The truth is that breakthrough drugs already face an onerous review: It's called the marketplace. Today, companies such as mine that develop breakthrough drugs can expect to have meaningful market exclusivity for only a few years. While a company's patent, or the special protection it can claim for its so-called orphan drugs, may preclude competitors from selling an identical product, it does not preclude others from designing and selling substantially similar products.

My own company's product, Ceredase, is an example of how market forces work. In the early 1980s, Genzyme was the only company working on a treatment for Gaucher's disease, a rare, inherited enzyme deficiency that causes crippling, and sometimes fatal, bone and organ deterioration. The CEO of another major biotechnology company had considered and rejected the idea of developing a treatment for such a rare disease because he could not imagine how his company could get an adequate return on a product intended for a few thousand patients.

Success Breeds Competition

Since Genzyme developed Ceredase, however, other companies have jumped into Gaucher's disease research. We are now competing with a company working on a variation of our drug, and two others are competing with us to develop gene-therapy approaches. There could be as many as four or five treatments for Gaucher's disease on the market within the next four years. If we hadn't taken the first step, there would be no market and no additional research on the disease.

My point is this: When an innovator company proves that its product works, and that a sufficient market exists to earn a return, it encourages other companies to develop similar products that enable them to compete for a share of that market. Given the breathtaking pace of biotechnology progress, it takes a relatively short time for other companies to develop substantially similar drugs. These will succeed, of course, only if they offer either price or therapeutic advantages over the innovator product.

Market forces are thus already creating price competition among pharmaceutical companies. A number of companies are implementing such programs as customer rebates and money-back guarantees. No government regulatory mechanism was necessary to induce this result.

In this respect, it is ironic that the same commentators who complain about pharmaceutical companies developing "me too" drugs (new versions of existing drugs) often fail to recognize that, at the very least, the introduction of such drugs helps constrain the prices of similar products, especially under a managed competition system in which insurance companies provide physicians with a greater incentive to consider the cost-effectiveness of the products they prescribe.

Congress should be less concerned about the possibility that a company might someday charge a high price for its AIDS vaccine for the two or three years before a competing product is available than about that company's ability to obtain the research-and-development funds needed to develop the vaccine in the first place. It is imperative that Congress and the administration consider the following question: If we alter market mechanisms by imposing price controls on breakthrough drugs, will we continue to get breakthrough drugs?

Congress and the administration must ask the following question: If we impose price controls on breakthrough drugs, will we continue to get breakthrough drugs?

A breakthrough drug committee is not needed to ensure that drugs are priced reasonably. If a drug's benefit is not commensurate with its cost, physicians won't prescribe it, particularly under a managed competition system. From the patient's perspective, a committee's refusing to provide Medicare coverage for "excessively priced" drugs would substitute a bureaucrat's judgment for a physician's. It would also result in second-class medical care for aging Americans: Medicare patients would be denied access to drugs that are covered for the privately insured.

A breakthrough drug committee as proposed by Mr. Clinton is not only unnecessary, it is counterproductive. It will discourage investors from seeing the development of breakthrough drugs as an investment capable of reaping returns that are commensurate with the risks. Another Clinton proposal would allow the secretary of health and human services to negotiate prices for

EXHIBIT 22.6
(continued)

new drugs, under threat of excluding them from Medicare. Taken together, these proposals would constitute a price-control system that discriminates against biotechnology and other innovating pharmaceutical companies by threatening to blacklist their products unless government bureaucrats concur with company pricing decisions.

These Clinton proposals do little more than constrain our ability to develop breakthrough medicines. In the first eight months of this year, biotechnology stocks declined by 30 percent; and through initial public offerings and other investor appeals companies were able to raise only about 25 percent of the amount they spent during this period. Obviously, this is not sustainable for an industry that lost $3.6 billion last year.

My own company raised $100 million two years ago to fund its research and development of a treatment for cystic fibrosis, a common fatal genetic disease that kills the average patient at the age of 29. Even though we recently performed the first successful clinical trial of a gene-therapy treatment for cystic fibrosis, Genzyme would be hard-pressed to raise half that amount in today's investment environment. Yet we will need to make a total investment of more than $400 million to bring this product to market. If we succeed, we will be able to treat successfully 30,000 Americans who, in the severe phase of the disease, now receive annual medical care costing up to $50,000.

Proposals that discourage breakthrough drug development may be smart politics. But they are bad medicine and an ineffective means of cost control.

Japan, which has a single-payer system in which the government sets reimbursement rates for all health care products and services, uses government regulation of drug prices as a form of industrial policy to reward breakthrough drug development with a pricing premium. It is typical for the Japanese government to set prices for biotechnology drugs and other breakthrough pharmaceutical products at two to three times U.S. market prices, reflecting such a premium. On the other hand, the Japanese government cuts the prices of older pharmaceuticals annually according to a formula. The message to Japanese industry is clear: Innovate or die.

No Price Abuse

Sen. Pryor and the White House propose precisely the opposite—that breakthrough drugs be subject to government policies aimed at preventing "excessive" prices while old drugs continue to escalate in price at the general inflation rate.

In citing Japanese policy, I do not intend to suggest that the U.S. should adopt that system. To the contrary, I think that the relatively higher prices that the Japanese government willingly pays for breakthrough drugs are compelling evidence that American companies are not abusing the pricing freedom they enjoy in a system like ours.

Finally, let me note that the Japanese government has targeted biotechnology as an industry Japan wants to dominate by the year 2000. The U.S. will only forfeit its leadership position to Japan if its government encourages the development of breakthrough drugs and our own does not. The Japanese threat to our industry is not nearly as great as the threat from our own government.

Mr. Termeer is CEO of Genzyme Corp. in Cambridge, Mass.

EXHIBIT 22.7

A Father, a Drug, and an Ailing Son

Source: Boston Globe by Philip Bennett (April 11, 1993), p. 1. Copyright 1993 by Globe Newspaper Co. (MA). Reproduced with permission of Globe Newspaper Co. (MA) in the format Textbook via Copyright Clearance Center.

Justo Ascarza knows the logic of big business, of borders, of probable endings. But he lives by the logic of a parent whose child is dying, which is something else entirely.

"To struggle for the life of a child, for the life of a son, is to put yourself above rules, and even above laws," he said in a waiting room at Massachusetts General Hospital, impatient for his son to get better.

It was thinking like this that led Ascarza, without money, influence, or an understanding of English, across the globe to Boston to persuade doctors, hospitals, and Genzyme Corp. to save his son for free with one of the world's most costly drugs.

For a few months, Ascarza, a grade-school principal from Peru, made the system work for him. But, perhaps not surprisingly, it hasn't lasted. He says now that he is being made to work for the system, with the health of his son, Amaru, as leverage.

Ascarza and Genzyme are at odds over how long Amaru, 13, will receive free doses of Ceredase, the Cambridge biotechnology firm's premier drug, which the company says costs patients an average of $140,000 annually. Genzyme says the boy's next free dose, on Thursday, will be his last unless the Ascarzas return to Peru, where they would receive three more free months for introducing Ceredase to the country. The company then expects the government of Peru to pay for Amaru's treatment.

While the scheme might open a new South American market for Genzyme, Ascarza fears it may also result in suffering and death for his son. Peru is a country with shortages of medical resources and a surplus of tragedies. Ascarza, whose school salary is about $90 a month, asserts the government there will not pay for the drug, a claim supported even by the Lima physician Genzyme obtained for the family.

While the case is unusual, its issues are at the core of the health care debate, involving responsibility for care and its enormous expense and conflict over treatment that is costly to institutions but priceless for individuals and their families.

Because the Ascarzas are Peruvian, their case raises another, increasingly common question: should foreigners or unnaturalized immigrants living in the United States have the same rights to emergency care—some of it unavailable anywhere else—as U.S. citizens?

What nobody disputes is that Amaru Ascarza is very sick. He has Gaucher's disease, a rare genetic illness. Its symptoms include severe enlargement of the liver and spleen, excessive bleeding, and erosion of bones until they may start breaking. The disease can be fatal if untreated.

At 13, Amaru is 4 feet tall and weights 68 pounds. His abdomen is swollen grotesquely. His gums bleed. Struck with headaches, he presses his palms against his skull as if to hold the bone in place. His hands are delicate and tiny. He plays the flute and is a talented cartoonist.

He is a thoughtful and self-conscious teenager, usually quiet. His father says that prior to receiving Ceredase Amaru would often be prostrated by pain, wailing helplessly.

An Effective Treatment

Ceredase replaces an enzyme missing in Gaucher's victims, in many cases reversing the disease. Such has been the case with Amaru, who during three months of treatment has improved "miraculously," his father says, "inside and out."

"The medicine makes me feel better," Amaru said. "I go outside, do more things. When it wears off I feel sick again."

Since Ceredase was approved in the United States two years ago, it has been a bonanza for Genzyme. The company says that fewer than 6,000 of an estimated 20,000 Gaucher's patients worldwide can benefit from treatment with the drug, but its extraordinary cost has made it Genzyme's sales leader, generating $100 million last year.

The company currently has a monopoly on Ceredase under the Orphan Drug Law, which gives economic incentives to companies to develop drugs for rare diseases. And the drug attracts faithful customers: like insulin for diabetics, it is usually taken regularly for life.

Genzyme has been criticized for the cost of Ceredase, which can exceed $200,000 a year for patients. Executives say the drug is fairly priced. In addition, they say, no Gaucher's patient has been deprived of Ceredase for inability to pay, and they point by way of example to the day Justo Ascarza came to the door.

Ascarza, originally from a provincial town in the Andes, is an elementary school principal in a poor urban neighborhood in Lima. He speaks no English. He and his wife, Gladys, who joined him here recently, worry about their two other children, who remain in Peru. Yet with a relentlessness that can be breathtaking, he has made his case to any physician, attorney, government official, executive, or journalist who will listen.

EXHIBIT 22.7
(continued)

His efforts have probably saved his son. In Peru, where no cases of Gaucher's had been previously noted, Amaru's condition went undiagnosed for five years. The Ascarzas were told their son might have leukemia until physicians correctly identified the illness and put the Ascarzas in touch with the National Institutes of Health, near Washington.

Company Could Benefit

Physicians studying Gaucher's disease invited the family to NIH last November. The Ascarzas persuaded American Airlines to donate airfare. A doctor there who examined Amaru found him seriously ill. But because he was not affected neurologically, he did not qualify for an NIH study that would have resulted in free treatment and was discharged.

It was then, with airfare donated by an NIH physician, that the Ascarzas with the help of a distant relative living in Cambridge, turned to Genzyme. They were accepted into a program of free treatment, "conditioned on the full cooperation of the parents and the patient," said Henri Termeer, Genzyme's chairman and chief executive.

In the Ascarzas' case, those conditions require them to return to Peru by the end of April in order to receive three more months of the drug for free. After that, the family must find financing, presumably from the government of Peru, to pay Genzyme an estimated $82,000 a year.

If the Ascarzas were to succeed in Peru, the benefits for Genzyme would be clear. Ceredase would presumably receive expedited approval for use. Publicity about the case would bring forward patients with Gaucher's disease who are currently undiagnosed. And, as in countries such as Brazil and Argentina, where Ceredase is now subsidized, the company would have a government guarantee of payment.

But Ascarza said he appealed to the wife of Peru's president, Alberto Fujimori, for aid and was turned down. Ceredase would be a great expense in a country where nurses at public hospitals earn less than $100 a month and tens of thousands of children die each year of dehydration caused by diarrhea because the government cannot afford to provide even the most basic care.

Question of Responsibility

Genzyme executives, for their part, point out that they cannot solve the problems of health care in Peru and that the company is not a charity.

"We never give up on attempts to make the patient part of a safety net," said Termeer. But, he said, "We cannot do this in a way that we lose total leverage on the system. We cannot allow ourselves to be used in a way that takes everybody off the hook."

Genzyme has assured the Ascarzas that the company has arranged care from a respected Lima hematologist, Dr. Jose Galvez, and is ready to ship the Ceredase. Yet, in a telephone interview last week, Galvez was hardly reassuring.

"I don't know anything really," Galvez said. "His physician called me last week and told me about the patient and that they'd send me something in the mail. I'm just waiting. I just don't know anything else."

Asked whether he believed the Peruvian government would pay for the treatment, Galvez said: "I don't think so. I have to be honest with you. We have a lot of problems here and this is not a priority. Things are not good here."

Meanwhile, Ascarza said that he has been rebuffed only once for seeking free care for his son in the United States. Ironically, he said it came from a Peruvian doctor practicing here.

But the issue is more widespread.

"It's a horrible problem," said Dr. Norman Barton, who examined Amaru at the NIH. "To what extent do we as a society have the responsibility to provide advanced technologies to countries that have no means to pay for them?"

"I don't know," Ascarza said. "Maybe what I am doing is wrong. But it is my responsibility to guarantee that Amaru doesn't die because he didn't have the luck to be born in a developed country."

EXHIBIT 22.8
Highlights of Gaucher Initiative Agreement

Source: Adapted by casewriters from memorandum of understanding between Project HOPE and Genzyme Corp., effective January 1, 1999.

Program Objectives
- "To establish Expert Committee to provide technical, ethical and programmatic guidance."
- "To coordinate and facilitate training of eight physicians on the treatments of Gaucher disease."
- "To organize and carry out the timely shipment and delivery of Ceredase/Cerezyme to identified locations in the People's Republic of China and Egypt."
- "To provide treatment to approximately 60 patients" annually.

Project HOPE Responsibilities
- "Establish a Secretariat . . . to direct and manage the day-to-day activities and administration."
- Identify Project HOPE field staff to assist with implementation from the local level.
- "Establish an Expert Committee, which will meet bi-annually . . . to provide technical, ethical and programmatic guidance to the Gaucher Initiative. Provide a voting member to the Expert Committee."
- "Coordinate and facilitate the training of four physicians from China, two from Egypt, and two from Project HOPE."
- "Arrange for the timely shipment and delivery of appropriate quantities of Ceredase/Cerezyme."
- "Provide liaison with participating hospitals and medical institutions, physicians and medical personnel, and the patients selected for participation in the Gaucher Initiative."
- "Collaborate with appointed Genzyme representatives to . . . publicize the Gaucher Initiative."
- "Submit to Genzyme quarterly financial and narrative reports on progress."

Genzyme Responsibilities
- "Identify patients . . . for selection by the Expert Committee for inclusion in the program."
- "Assist in the creation of the Expert Committee. Provide a voting member."
- "Donate to Project HOPE appropriate quantities of Ceredase/Cerezyme."
- "Facilitate the training of eight physicians . . . at the Gaucher workshop held at Genzyme."
- "Provide Project HOPE with technical assistance in the training aspects and treatment of Gaucher disease."
- "Collaborate with Project HOPE . . . to publicize the Gaucher Initiative."
- "Genzyme shall be responsible for funding the Gaucher Initiative."

Resolution of Disputes
- In the event of a dispute, "the parties shall first attempt to resolve the dispute through friendly discussions." After 14 days "the parties may mutually select a third party" for "non-binding mediation." After another 14 days "either party may refer the dispute to arbitration and withdraw from the Program" with 30 days' written notice.

Liability
- "Project HOPE will be responsible for obtaining liability insurance to protect the Expert Committee from any suits resulting from decisions concerning patient selection and program guidance."
- "Any liability associated with the products Ceredase/Cerezyme will be the responsibility of Genzyme."
- "Local liability concerning the treatment of patients will be the responsibility of the local physician."

Duration, Extension, and Termination
- Duration: five years.
- Extended by "mutual agreement and the signing of a letter defining the length of the extension."
- The agreement may be terminated "without cause upon giving 90 days' written notice."

EXHIBIT 22.9   Ceredase and Cerezyme Revenues and Patient Growth, 1991–2001

Source: Prepared by casewriters with data supplied by Genzyme Corp.

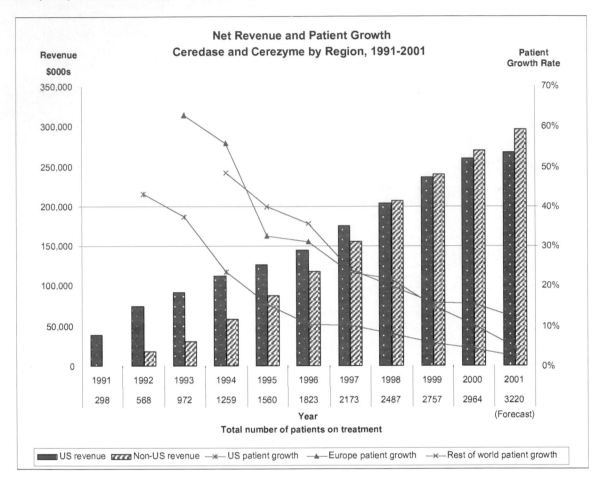

Note: Patient growth figures are year-to-year growth percentages averaged over three years.

Index

Abbott Laboratories, 215, 370, 387, 390
Abbott Northwestern Hospital (ANH), 263, 266–276; *see also* LifeSpan, Inc.
    consumer perception of hospitals and, 280
    Medformation program, 273–274, 275, 276, 279, 280, 282
    Medical Staff Development Program, 272
    Minneapolis/St. Paul Health Care Market and, 268
    Seniors' Day, 275
    WomenCare program, 274–275, 281, 282
Abbreviated New Drug Applications (ANDAs), 32, 34
Abgenix, 65–78
    ABX-EGF and, 66, 67–69, 70–72, 73–74, 75–76
    EGF market and, 72–73
    Introduction of XenoMouse, 65 67, 77
Abrahams, Paul, 251n
ABX-CBL, 66, 67, 71
ABX-EGF, 66, 67–68, 71–72, 73–74, 75–76
ABX-IL8, 66, 67, 71
ABX-RB2, 66, 67, 71
AC Nielsen, 260
Accelerating Access, 387, 388, 390
Access MV system, 88 89
Access Platform, 88
Accudrop, 351
ACE (angiotensin converting enzyme) inhibitors, 180
Achmat, Zachie, 387
ACT UP (AIDS Coalition to Unleash Power), 365, 374
Advil, 333, 342
Affiliated Purchasing Group (APG), 209–210, 220–223
Africa, AIDS in, 363–364, 367–368, 373–379
    changes in life expectancy and, 280
    comparison of annual AIDS related deaths, 380
    drug price comparisons and, 384
    Mbeki and, 391–393
    patent coverage for antiretroviral drugs and, 394 395
    pharmaceutical industry response to AIDS and, 385–391
Agriculture, biotechnology and, 3, 11–12, 17–18
AIDS (Acquired Immune Deficiency Syndrome), 363–395, *see also* Africa, AIDS in
    in the developing world, 367–368
    emergence in U.S., 364–366
    HAART (Highly Active Antiviral Therapy) for, 366, 374–375, 377, 378
    intellectual property rights and, 368–374
    international prevalence rates of HIV, 380
    pharmaceutical companies and, 377–379, 385–391
Aleve, 248
Alka-Seltzer/Alka-Seltzer Plus, 329, 332
Amato, I., 8n, 16n
Amazon.com, 233
American Association of Retired Persons (AARP), 183
American Cyanamid, 334
American Home Products, 250–251, 333, 334
American Hospital Association, 213–214, 265
American Hospital Supply Corporation (AHS), 217, 217n
American Red Cross, 142, 146
American Scientific Products (ASP), 217, 218
Amgen, 5, 68, 69, 74–75
Amoxicillin, 28, 35
Analog, 19
Andrews, Mike, 307, 311, 315
Angina, 125–126
Angiograms, 83, 84
Angiomax, 125, 127–131, 132
    Boston Globe on, 133
    Medicines Company acquiring rights to, 121
    patent, 123
    status of clinical trials for, 136
Angioplasty; *see* Balloon angioplasty

Annan, Kofi, 386
Antacids, 252–253, 253–259
Antibiotics, 370
Antibodies, 68–69
Antibody therapy, 73; *see also* Abgenix
Antimicrobial "armor" products, 117
Arab Medical Containers, 29
Aravind Eye Hospital, 39–61; *see also* Eye camps; Free Hospital; Venkataswamy, Govindappa (Dr. V.)
    blindness and, 40–42, 44, 45
    financial summary, 57
    income/expenditures, 56
    IOL factory, 46–47
    locations, 53
    main hospital, 47–48
    patient statistics, 55
    performance summary, 58
Arbor Drug, 230
Argentina, 372, 373, 375
Ascarza, Amaru, 431–432
Ascarza, Justo, 431–432
Asia, 419
Assay, 19
Association for the Study of Internal Fixation (AO), 160–161, 161–162, 171
Astra, 181
AstraZeneca, 73, 74
Atherosclerosis, 81, 83
Attaran, Amir, 378n, 390n
Auro Lab, 46
Aurobindo, Sri, 43
Austin, James, 387n
AutoImmune, 156
Aversion therapy, 347
Avonex, 128
AWP (average wholesale price), 183, 187
Axid, 247, 248, 249, 257, 261
AZT (zidovudine), 366, 377, 387, 416

Bacterial vaginosis (BV), 132
Baggs, Mary Kay, 89, 90
Baker, Lynn S., 370n
Balakrishnan, Mr., 46
Balloon angioplasty, 82–83, 86, 92
    Angiomax and, 121, 125–126, 128–129, 130
    heparin and, 127
Bangladesh, 283–284, 284–289, 292, 295; *see also* Social Marketing Project (SMP)
Barrett, Amy, 371n
Barrett, Diana, 387n
Bartkus, Joanne, 115
Bartlett, Christopher A., 411n
Bartlett, Nicholas, 363, 385n, 389n
Barton, Norman, 432
BASES research methodology, 253–258, 254n, 260
Battaglia, Alfred, 210, 212, 215, 216, 225
Baxter International, 92, 146–147, 413
Baxter-Travenol, Inc., 217n
Bayer, 370
    Resochin, 406
Bayer AG, 327–343; *see also* Sterling Products, Inc.
    acquisition of Sterling OTC business, 334–336
    advertising, 339
    Bayer brand consumer research, 343
    brand history, 328–331
    Consumer Care business group, 332
    consumer products business group, 331–332
    consumer ratings of analgesics and, 342
    cross logo, 327, 328, 329, 336
    Miles and, 329, 332
    Millennium Pharmaceuticals and, 3, 8, 13, 16, 22
    Monsanto and, 329
    Myclex, 249
    1986 agreement, 329–330, 331
    1970 Agreement and, 329
Bayer, Friedrich, 328
Bayer Select series, 333–334, 336, 342
Becton Dickinson (BD), 210

Becton Dickinson VACUTAINER® Systems Division (BDVS), 209–228
    blood collection products, 210–212, 212–215
    financial data, 224
    marketing/sales programs, 215–220
    negotiations with APG, 209–210, 221–223
    organization chart, 225
    products, 226–227
Bed-occupancy rate, 265n
Behavioral self-monitoring, 347
Bell, Marie, 177n, 231n, 233n, 303n
Benetti, Federico, 85
Bennett, Philip, 431n
Bill & Melinda Gates Foundation, 388
Bioavailability, 15
Bioequivalency studies, 28
Biogen Inc., 121, 124, 127–128, 133
Biomet, 165, 166, 169, 172
Bionx, 166
Biopart, 67–68 74–75 76
Biopure Corporation, 139–140, 151; *see also* Blood; Blood substitutes
    blood substitutes, 148–150
    competition and, 146–147
    organizational structure at, 153
    overview of, 140–141
    Veterinary Products Division, 148
Biotechnology industry, 4–6
    regulatory process and, 68–69
Black, Sir James, 248
Black, Timothy, 284, 285
Blair, Henry, 412, 413, 414, 424
Blindness, 40–42, 44, 45
Block, Robert, 391n
Blockbuster drugs, 123, 180, 180n, 199
Blood, 141 145; *see also* Blood substitutes; Red blood cells (RBCs); Veterinary blood market
    cost to patient of donated human, 155
    transfusions, 141 143, 154
Blood Centers of America, 146–147
Blood collection products, 212–215; *see also* Becton Dickinson VACUTAINER® Systems Division (BDVS)
Blood substitutes, 140n, 145–147, 147–152
Blue Cross/Blue Shield, 179
Blunton, K., 7n
Boehringer-Ingelheim, 385, 385–386, 388
Bolton, Samantha, 385
Bonoma, Thomas V., 263n
Boston Athletic Association (BAA), 312
Boston Globe, 124, 152
Boston Marathon® Jimmy Fund Walk, 313
Boston Scientific, 85
Botswana Comprehensive HIV/AIDS Partnership, 388
Bozic, Kevin, 157, 157n, 162–163
Brady, Roscoe, 412, 413
Brazil, 372, 373, 375, 376, 379, 384
Breakthrough drugs, 429–430
Bricks-and-clicks, 233n
Bricks-and-mortar businesses, 233n
Brigham and Women's Hospital, 305
Bristol-Myers Squibb, 34, 69, 180, 192, 197
    AIDS and, 385, 387, 387n, 390, 391
    Excedrin, 333
    PBMs and, 178, 194
Brundtland, Gro Harlem, 385, 386
Buckingham, Lisa, 387n
Burke, James E., 250, 251
Burrill, G. S., 6n
Burroughs-Welcome, 377, 416
Burton, Thomas M., 249n, 371n

C225, 73, 74
CABG; *see* Coronary artery bypass graft (CABG)
Cambridge Neuroscience, 156
Canada, 372
Cancers; *see also* Dana-Farber Cancer Institute
    ABX-EGF and, 74
    Biopart and, 75

Cancers *(continued)*
  EGF receptor and, 69, 72–73
  facts about, 320
  Rituxan and, 69
  XenoMouse and, 67
Capillary blood collection systems, 211
Capoten, 180, 192
Cardio Thoracic Systems (CTS), 79–80, 85–86; *see also* Cardiovascular disease; Coronary artery bypass graft (CABG); Minimally invasive cardiac surgery (MICS)
  competition and, 91–92
  financing history, 94
  Heartport financing and, 86–87
  price performance, 95
  product evolution, 87–89, 91
  sales/marketing strategy, 90–91
  sales revenues/financial data, 98
  stock price performance, 96
  system (picture of), 97
Cardiovascular disease, 80–81; *see also* Coronary artery bypass graft (CABG); Minimally invasive cardiac surgery (MICS)
Cardiovascular Imaging Systems, 85, 86
Cardiovascular IPO activity, 94
Cardiovascular program, 267
CARE, 284
Caremark, 178, 197
Carey, John, 371n, 416n
Carlton, Richard, 100
Cassak, David, 185n, 188n
Castagnoli, William G., 191n
Cataract surgery, 45, 47–49; *see also* Cataracts; Extracapsular surgery with intraocular lens (ECCE); Intracapsular surgery with intraocular lens (ICCE)
  complications, 49, 59
  in India, 42
  Venkataswamy on, 40, 46
Cataracts, 40–41; *see also* Cataract surgery
Cause marketing, 314–315, 317
Ceclor, 33, 35
Cefizox, 28
Ceflex, 33
Celera, 9
Center for AIDS Research, 305
Cephalexin, 35
Cephalosporins (cephs), 33–34, 37
  generic, 27, 34
  Hikma Pharmaceuticals and, 31
  injectable, 28, 35–36
  production of, 29
Ceredase Assistance Program (CAP), 416, 419, 420, 422
Ceredase®, 414, 429, 431–432
  approval process for, 415–416
  cerezyme and, 422
  cost and profit estimate, 427
  dosage annual cost calculations for, 428
  marketing of, 417–418
  opening foreign markets for, 418–420
  revenues and patient growth, 434
Cereon Genomics, 12, 22, 24
Cerestat, 156
Cerezyme, 415, 420, 421, 422
  dosage annual cost calculations for, 428
  revenues and patient growth, 434
Cespedes, Frank V., 209n
Chamorro, German, 115
Charbonnier, Volker, 329, 330
Chege, Wambui, 392n
ChemGenics, 11, 22
Chemical Library, 19
China, 421
Chloroquine, 397–398, 405, 405n, 406–407
Chothia, Farouk, 392n
Churchill, Joan, 104, 105, 107
CIBA-GEIGY, 397–398; *see also* Pharma International (PHI)
  in Nigeria, 402–404
  PEA committee, 407
  pharmaceutical industry trends and, 398–400
  policy for third-world countries, 408–409
Ciba-Geigy Foundation for Cooperation with Developing Countries, 409
Cipla, 389, 389n, 390
Ciszewski, Robert, 283, 285, 286, 291–292, 293

Clare, Anthony, 349, 355
Clark, Jim, 233
Clicks-and-mortar, 233n
Clinical trials, 5–6
  FDA and, 181
  over-the-counter drugs and, 247, 252
  phases of, 123
  status of Angiomax, 136
Clinoril, 193
Clinton administration, 181, 371
Clinton, Bill, 181, 376, 416, 429–430
Clioquinol, 400
Coding, 206
Cohn Stabilizer, 92
Coimbatore Hospital, 45
Combinatorial chemistry, 5, 8, 19
Compound, 19
Compulsory licensing, 391
Condoms, 284; *see also* Raja brand condoms
Contraindications, 399n
Conway, Kenneth, 9
Cooper, Helene, 391n
Coordinated pharmaceutical care, 190
Corning Glass, 215
Coronary artery bypass graft (CABG), 79–80, 81–82, 84, 92
  Angiomax and, 126
  number of, 83, 126
  rate of stroke, 90
  reimbursement, 89
  worldwide procedures, 93
Coronary artery disease; *see* Cardiovascular disease
Cosmetics, 237
Countryman, Gary, 305
Cowie, Anne, 310–311
Coyne, William, 104
Crick, Francis, 7, 22
Crixivan, 390
CTV-05, 125, 131, 132
Curtin-Matheson Scientific (CMS), 217, 218
CVS drugstore chain, 230
  financial data, 240
  online drugstore (CVS.com), 229, 235–239, 244
  PBMs and, 232
  Xtra! program, 236
Cycles, 283
CYP (couple years protection), 291, 291n, 293n, 300
Cystic fibrosis, 415, 430

Dain Raucher Wessels, 163n, 165n
D'Amore, Hope, 308–309
Dana-Farber Cancer Institute, 303–325; *see also* Jimmy Fund
  capital campaign financial data, 321
  cause marketing and, 317, 325
  creative giving options and scenarios, 322
  Development Fund, 308–311
  Development Office, 305, 306–308, 306n, 315
  direct mail collateral, 323
  Division of Development and Jimmy Fund, 319
  overdosing occurrence, 316, 316n
  Trustee Annual Fund, 311
Dana-Farber/Partners CancerCare (DF/PCC), 305, 306
Daraprim, 406
Darwazah, Said, 27, 33, 35–36
Darwazah, Samih, 27–28, 29, 30–31, 31–34
Darwin, Charles, 11
Davis, Geoff, 72, 74
Decosas, Josef, 377
Deighton, John, 229n
Dell, John, 115
Deoxyribonucleic acid (DNA), 22; *see also* Recombinant DNA technology
  biotechnology revolution and, 4
  Cereon Genomics and, 12
  drug development and, 14
  Human Genome Project and, 7
  Millennium Pharmaceuticals and, 8
  sequencing, 23
  transcriptional profiling and, 26
DePuy, 166
Diabetes, 186–187, 195, 204, 207
Diagnosis-related groups (DRGs), 213, 218, 271
Diebold, A. H., 332
Diflucan (fluconazole), 372, 387, 388
Dillon, Geoffrey, 79, 80, 90–91, 92

Dilzem, 348
DiMasi, J. A., 21
Disease management; *see* Health management
Diversified Pharmaceutical Services (DPS), 178, 185, 197
Dixon, Declan, 345, 346, 349, 355–356
DNA; *see* Deoxyribonucleic acid (DNA)
Doctors; *see* Physician(s)
Doctors Without Borders, 391
  AIDS treatment in Africa and, 374, 379
  pharmaceutical industry and AIDS and, 385, 387–388, 388–389
Dolan, Robert J., 65n, 254n, 260n
Double-blind, 123n
Downie, Andrew, 376n
Drew, Richard, 100, 103
Drug development, 123–124, 181
  corporate collaborations and, 68
  costs, 371
  industry, 122
  Millennium Pharmaceuticals and, 6–7, 9, 13–15
  summary of, 21
  XenoMouse and, 66
Drug utilization reviews (DUR), 186
Drugs, 179–183; *see also* AIDS (Acquired Immune Deficiency Syndrome); Drug development; Formularies; Generic(s); *names of individual drugs*; Online drugstores; Over-the-counter drug(s); Pharmacies
  antacids, 252–259
  antifungal, 249
  best selling prescription, 135
  blockbuster, 123, 180, 180n, 199
  breakthrough, 429–430
  chronic disease spending and pharmaceutical share, 207
  H2-receptor antagonists, 248
  new drugs placed on market, 383
  physical distribution of, 184
  prescribing/dispensing, 230–233, 241, 242
  price comparisons, 384
  therapeutic categories of, 179–180, 199–201, 205
  value of off-patent, 202
Drugstore.com, 229, 233, 234, 238
Drugstore(s), 230, 231, 240; *see also* Online drugstores; Pharmacies
  distribution of prescription drugs and, 230–233
  PBMs and, 231–232
Dual users, 255n
Dube, Siddarth, 375n
Duclaux, Denise, 234n
Duke, Lynn, 376n
Dunkin' Donuts, 315, 325
Dunlop, Sam, 107–108, 111
Dykema, Evie Black, 234

Eastman Kodak, 329–330, 334
Ebrahim, Tarek, 423
Eckerd, 230, 233
Economist, 8, 391
Eder, Rob, 232n
Edits, 188, 206
Egypt, 411, 412, 419, 421, 422–423
Elan Corporation, 348, 351n, 352, 355
Eli Lilly & Co., 6, 35, 250–251
  Axid, 247
  cephalosporins and, 33
  Darwazah (Samih) and, 27
  Genentech and, 68
  Levin and, 6
  Millennium Pharmaceuticals and, 22, 24
  PBMs and, 178, 179, 193
  PCS Health Systems Inc. and, 193–194, 197
Enzymes; *see* Genzyme Corporation; Glucocerebrosidase (GCR)
Epidermal Growth Factor (EGF), 69, 72–73
Epogen, 68
Erythromycin, 370
Europe, 30–32, 418–419
Evacuated-tube blood collection, 211, 215, 226
Excedrin, 333, 342
ExpressScripts, 233
Extracapsular surgery with intraocular lens (ECCE), 41, 46, 47, 48
Eye camps, 44, 45, 49–52, 54, 59, 60, 61
Eye surgery/care; *see* Aravind Eye Hospital; Cataract surgery

Fabry disease, 415
Family planning; *see also* Maya brand oral contraceptives; Population Services International (PSI); Raja brand condoms; Social Marketing Project (SMP)
  Bangladesh and, 286–289
  sources of messages on, 300
  survey meanings of, 296
Fansidar, 405, 406
Farbenfabriken Bayer AG, 329
Farber, Sidney, 304, 316
Federal Trade Commission (FTC), 193
Ferrari, Richard, 79, 80, 85, 89, 92
Fevex, 397–398, 405–407
FIBCO (fully integrated biotechnology company), 68
Financial World, 334, 337
Finnic, Shauna, 157, 157n
First USA, 325
Fisher Scientific, 217
Fluconazole (diflucan), 372, 387, 388
Food and Drug Administration (FDA), 14
  Abbreviated New Drug Applications (ANDAs) and, 34
  Abgenix and, 75
  ABX-EGF and, 74
  AIDS and, 366
  Angiomax and, 121, 129
  approval of Avonex, 128
  approval of Ceredase®, 415
  approval of Palmaz-Schatz stent, 83
  approval process, 123, 154, 370–371
  background of pharmaceutical industry and, 181
  Biopure products and, 140
  drug development and, 4–5, 68, 123
  510(k) approval, 87
  Hikma Pharmaceuticals and, 27, 31, 32
  human blood substitutes and, 146
  Investigational New Drug Application (IND) and, 72
  IS-159 and, 132
  minimally invasive cardiac surgery (MICS) and, 85
  New Drug Application, 68, 71
  new drug approval times, 382
  over-the-counter drugs and, 247–252, 259
  Oxyglobin approval, 140–141, 152
  review process for medical devices, 96
  surgical procedures and, 87
  XenoMouse and, 66, 69
Formularies, 182, 185n
  PBMs and, 185–186, 192, 193, 196, 197, 231, 232
Forrester Research, 234
Fortune magazine, 16, 190
Foulkes, Helena, 229, 232, 235, 236, 237, 238–239
Fountain, Suzanne, 307
Free Drugs for All program, 375, 376
Free Hospital, 48–49, 53
  Aravind Eye Hospital and, 43–44, 45
  cataract surgery complications and, 59
  IOL factory and, 46, 47
  main hospital and, 50
Freedberg, Kenneth, 378n
Freidman, Thomas, 377n
French Laboratories, 28
Fry, Art, 101
Fujimori, Alberto, 432
Fujisawa Pharmaceutical Corp. (Japan), 28, 34
Full-time equivalent (FTE) system, 10
Furbish, Scott, 414, 418

Galileo, 114
Galvez, Jose, 432
Gandhi, Mahatma, 42, 43
Gardner, Diana S., 79n
Gastroesophageal reflux disease (GERD), 252, 252n
GATT (General Agreement on Tariffs and Trade), 373, 389
Gaucher disease, 411, 413–414, 429, 431–432
  described, 412
  Egypt and, 422
  Project HOPE and, 421
Gaucher Initiative, 411–412, 420–422, 423, 433
Gellman, Barton, 377n, 378n, 379n, 386n, 388n
General Medical Service (GMS), 348–349, 349n
General stores, 287, 290
Generic(s), 179, 182
  AIDS and, 375–376, 389, 390, 391, 393

chloroquine phosphate as, 406
CIBA-GEIGY and, 401–402
growth in sales of, 122
Hikma Pharmaceuticals and, 28, 29, 30, 33, 34–35
intellectual property rights and, 372, 373
on prescribing, 187n
Serviquin as, 406
Tagamet and, 249
Genomics, 9, 26, 65
GenPharm, 69
Genzyme Corporation, 92, 156, 411–415; *see also* Ceredase®; Cerezyme; Gaucher Initiative
  financial data, 425–426
  IPO (initial public offering), 414–415, 427
  time line of corporate events, 424
Giardino, Robert, 212–215
Gillespie-White, Lee, 390n
Gillette Center for Women's Cancer, 305
Gilmartin, Ray, 179, 194, 385, 386, 387, 388
Glaser, Elizabeth, 365
Glaser, Paul, 365
Glaxo Wellcome, 8, 34, 180
  AIDS and, 387
  Daraprim, 406
  Paraquine, 406
  Warner-Lambert and, 251
  Zantac, 247–248, 248–249
GlaxoSmithKline, 377, 383, 390, 391
Glucocerebrosidase (GCR), 412, 413, 414, 415
GNC, 233
Gold, Jeff, 79, 80, 83–84, 87, 88, 89, 90, 91, 92
Goodes, Melvin R., 249
Goozner, Merrill, 375n, 379n
Gore, Al, 376
Gourville, John T., 121n, 139n, 157n
Government Erskine Hospital (Madurai), 43
Greer, R. Scott, 66–67, 67–68, 75–76
Greeting cards, 237
Gross ratings points (GRPs), 275n
Gruber, D. A., 81n
Gustafson, Einar, 316
Gyne Lotrimin, 249

H2-receptor antagonists, 248, 249, 252–253, 254, 257–258
Haacker, Markus, 374n
HAART (Highly Active Antiviral Therapy), 366, 374–375, 377, 378
HAMA response; *see* Human Anti-Mouse Antibody (HAMA response)
Hamied, Yusuf K., 389
Harris, Gardiner, 371n, 391n
Harris, Paul, 392n
Harstad, Chuck, 104
Harvard Business School (HBS) team, 157–158, 161–162, 164, 165, 166, 167–168, 173
Harvard Medical School, 304
Harvard University, 386
Harvey, Philip, 283–284, 285, 292, 293
Hastings, Scott, 161, 169
Health care industry, 263–266, 277
Health Care Marketing Plans: From Strategy to Action (Hillestad), 268
Health insurance, 214, 264
Health maintenance organizations (HMOs), 182
  Abbott Northwestern Hospital pricing and, 271
  changes in health care industry and, 265
  description of, 198
  PBMs and, 184
  United HealthCare, 185
Health management, 186–187, 195, 196; *see also* Diabetes
Healthcare delivery systems, 182
Healtheon, 233
Heart-lung machine, 81–82, 84, 85
Heart surgery; *see* Coronary artery bypass graft (CABG); Minimally invasive cardiac surgery (MICS)
Heartport, 84–87, 91–92, 95, 96
Heidrich, Grant, 7
HemAssist, 147
Hemoglobin, 141
Hemoglobin-based blood substitutes, 145–147
Hemopure, 139–141, 148, 151
Heparin, 122, 126–127, 128–129, 131
Heparin-induced thrombocytopenia (HIT), 126, 129, 130

Herceptin, 69, 73
Heslop, Mike, 423
Hiatt, Howard, 374n
Hiestand, Susan, 105n, 111
High through-put screening, 5
Hikma Farmaceutica, 31
Hikma Investment, 27, 31
Hikma Pharmaceuticals, 27–36; *see also* Cephalosporins (cephs)
  Arab world and, 30
  international expansion of, 29–33
  sources of sales, 37
Hikma Portugal, 29, 31
Hillestad, Steven, 263, 267–268, 270, 271, 272, 273–274, 276
Hills, Robert, 192
Hippocrates, 26
Hirsch, Martin, 378n
HIV (Human Immunodeficiency Virus), 363, 365; *see also* AIDS (Acquired Immune Deficiency Syndrome)
HMO Act of 1973, 198
HNK20, 156
Hoffman-LaRoche, 22, 124, 128, 248–249
Hogan, Harold F., Jr., 390n
Holbrooke, Richard, 387
Holtzman, Steven, 7, 7–8, 9, 10, 18
Hospital Corporation of America, 266
Hospital(s), 265
  purchasing, 228
  survey on selecting, 268–269
Hossain, K. M., 290n
Houben, Hub, 21
Howe, John, 423
Huang, Yasheng, 389n, 390n
HuMAb-Mouse, 69
Human Anti-Mouse Antibody (HAMA response), 69
Human Genome Project, 7, 9, 22
Human Genome Sciences (HGS), 11
Hunter, Robert, 370n

Iafolla, Michael, 194
Ibuprofen, 249
ICI America Inc., 251
IDEC, 69
ImClone, 73, 74
ImmunoGen, 156
Immunotech S.A. (France), 131
Imodium-AD, 249
Implants; *see* Internal fixation devices
IMS Managed Care Services, 182
Incyte Pharmaceuticals, 11
Indemnity health insurance companies, 198
Independent practice association (IPAs), 198
India, 34, 41–42, 284; *see also* Aravind Eye Hospital
  drug price comparisons and, 384
  generics and, 372, 375
Infection containment, 110–111
Innovex, 131
Integrated Genetics (IG), 415
Integrated Medical Systems (IMS), 197
Intellectual property rights; *see also* Patents
  global, 364, 372–374
  patent coverage in Africa for antiretroviral drugs, 394–395
  pharmaceutical industry and AIDS and, 364, 368–372, 378, 385, 388, 389, 390, 390n
  World Health Assembly and, 376
Interbrand Group, 337
Internal fixation devices; *see also* Synthes
  Association for the Study of Internal Fixation and, 160–161
  bioresorbable, 157–158, 163–165, 167–168, 168–169, 172, 173
  examples of, 170
  sales of, 171
  U.S. market for, 158–160
International Antiviral Therapy Evaluation, 379
International Directory of Company Histories, 100
International Federation of Pharmaceutical Manufacturers Associations (IFPMA), 400
International Finance Corporation, 31
Internet; *see* Online drugstores
Intracapsular surgery with intraocular lens (ICCE), 41, 47, 48
Intraocular lens (IOL), 41, 46–47, 48–49

Investigational Device Exemption (IDE), 96
Investigational New Drug Application (IND), 66, 72
Ireland; *see* Warner-Lambert Ireland (WLI)
IRESSA, 73
Irish Cancer Society, 347, 355
Irish Heart Foundation, 355
Irish Medical News, 354
Irish Medical Times, 354
Irish National Drugs Advisory Board, 348, 349
IS-159, 125, 131–132
Israel, 419
Italy, 373
IVillage, 233
Izmirlain, Robert, 230n

Jackson, Tony, 251n
Jacobs, Ted, 141, 151, 153
Japan, 34, 430
Jefferson, Thomas, 369
Jiffy Lube, 315, 325
Jimmy Fund, 303, 311–315, 316, 319; *see also*
    Dana-Farber Cancer Institute
  cause marketing programs, 314–315, 325
  Development Fund and, 310–311
  events, 307, 308, 313–314, 324
  Marathon Challenge, 312–313
  original "Jimmy," 316
Jimmy Fund Clinic, 305
Johnson & Johnson (J&J), 34, 164, 165, 166
  blood collection products industry background
    and, 215
  Imodium-AD, 249
  McNeil Consumer Products unit, 250
  Monistat, 249
  as OTC manufacturer, 334
  Palmaz-Schatz stent, 83
  Tylenol family of products, 250, 333
Johnson & Johnson/Merck Consumer
    Pharmaceuticals Co. (JJM), 247–248; *see also*
    Pepcid/Pepcid AC
  alliance, 250
  antacid research and, 253–258
  FDA and, 259
  purchase of ICI America Inc., 251
Johnson, Magic, 366
Johnson, Mark, 105n, 111
Jordan, 28, 29
Journal of Health Care Marketing, 268
Judelson, David, 140

Kaiser Permanente, 185
Kaitin, Kenneth I., 21
Kelly, J., 355
Khaled, Dr., 422
Khalifa, Dr., 419, 422
Kimball Glass, 218
Kimni, Dagi, 389n
King, Charles, III, 261
Kleiner, Perkins, Caufield & Byers, 86
Kline & Co., 249
Koop, C. Everett, 146
Koppel, Naomi, 388n
Korea, 373
Kozy, William, 209, 210, 216, 222–223, 225
Kraft, Dina, 392n
Kramer, Richard, 267, 270, 273
Krebs, Rolf, 388
Kuypers, Maurice, 105n, 111

LaBlanc, Peter, 168
Lander, Eric, 7
Lange, Joep, 379
Latin America, 328–329, 334, 367
Latin America Aspirin Treaty, 328
Lawton, Alison, 417
Lead user research, 99–100, 103–110, 114–117
Less-developed countries (LDCs), 286
Lever Brothers Nigeria Ltd., 404
Levin, Mark, 3, 4, 6, 7–8, 9–10, 14, 16, 18, 22
LifeSpan, Inc., 263, 266, 278; *see also* Abbott
    Northwestern Hospital (ANH)
Lincoln, Abraham, 369
Liqui-Gels, 332, 332n
Lister, Benjamin, 102
Liver, 26
Lofberg, Per, 179, 194, 195

Longman, Roger, 190n, 192n
Lundbeck, 351
Lundberg, 3, 17, 22
Lundberg, C. Marie, 3
Lupin Laboratories of India, 35
Lyndiol (contraceptives), 290, 292

Maalox, 253
Macan-Markar, Marwaan, 375n
Macropore, 166
Madurai Medical College, 43
Magnet, Myron, 190n
Mail service pharmacies, 180, 183
  chain stores and, 193
  delivery process, 206
  largest, 203
  Medco and, 184, 187, 191
  Merck and, 195, 196
  Merck-Medco, 233
  PBMs and, 233
  Wygod and, 190
Malaria, 397–398, 401, 404–405
Managed care organizations (MCOs), 182, 183, 230–231, 234
Managed health care system, 230–233, 266
Mandela, Nelson, 376, 390
Mandell, Julie, 234
Manual of Internal Fixation, 160
Maraganore, John, 8
Marsam, 35
Massachusetts General Hospital, 305, 431
Massachusetts Institute of Technology (MIT), 104, 114
Masterson, Professor, 355
Mathys, 161
May and Baker, 406
Maya brand oral contraceptives, 300
  marketing, 283, 284, 289–291, 291–293
  sales of, 294, 298, 299
Mayfield Fund, 6–7
Mbeki, Thabo, 368, 392
McGinley, Laurie, 391n
McKesson Corporation, 197
McLauglin, Peter, 16
McLean, Andrew N., 411n
McNeil, Donald G., 371n, 375n, 376n, 379n, 387n, 388n
Meanwell, Clive, 121, 123, 124, 126, 128, 129, 131, 132, 133
Mectizan Donation Program, 420
Medarex, 69
Medco Containment Services Inc., 178–179, 190–197, 205, 206; *see also* Merck-Medco
Medformation program, 273–274, 275, 276, 279, 280, 282
Medicaid, 264, 264n
Medicare, 264, 264n
  breakthrough drugs and, 429–430
  Diagnosis-related groups (DRGs), 213, 218, 271
Medicines and Related Substances Act of 1997, 390–391
Medicines Company, 121–122, 124–137; *see also*
    Angiomax
  CTV-05 and, 125, 132
  heparin and, 126–127
  IS-159 and, 125, 131–132
Medicines Control Agency (MCA), 258
Medtronic, 92
Meenakshisunadaram (Sundar), 51, 52
Mehl, Ed, 210
Mendel, Gregor, 22
Menezes, Melvyn A. J., 263n
Merck & Co., Inc., 69, 123, 180–181; *see also*
    Johnson & Johnson/Merck Consumer
    Pharmaceuticals Co. (JJM); Merck-Medco
  AIDS and, 385, 388, 390
  changes in pharmaceutical industry and, 370
  Enhancing Care Initiative, 386–387
  financial data, 204, 205
  Human Health Division, 197
  Project Paradigm, 191–192
Merck Generics, 35
Merck KgaA (Germany), 73
Merck-Medco, 178–179, 185, 190–197, 231; *see also*
    Merck & Co., Inc.
  information systems, 195–196, 208
  mail service pharmacy, 233

Mectizan Donation Program, 420
  negotiations with CVS drugstore chain, 238–239
  online pharmacies and, 234
  retail pharmacies and, 184
Merck-Medco U.S. Managed Care Division, 197
Mevacor, 180, 192, 193
Mexico, 284
Meyer, Michael, 157, 157n
Microbiology systems, 211
MICROTAINER® products, 211
MICS, 91, 92
MIDCAB II (CTS), 88–89
MIDCAB (Minimally Invasive Direct Coronary
    Artery Bypass), 88, 90
Miescher, Friedrich, 22
Miles Laboratories Inc., 329, 330–331
Miles, Vincent, 9–10, 12–13, 16–17
Millennium BioTherapeutics, Inc. (MBio), 24
Millennium Pharmaceuticals, Inc., 3–4, 6–18
  alliances of, 25
  corporate structure of, 24
  financials for, 20
  milestones for, 22
  Monsanto and, 11–13, 17–18
  R&D Factories, 23
Millennium Predictive Medicine, Inc. (MPMx), 24
Miller, Jim, 231n
Millward Brown, 253
Mini-CABG, 92
Minimally invasive cardiac surgery (MICS), 84–85
Ministry of Health and Family Welfare, 42
Minneapolis Children's Medical Center, 267
Minneapolis/St. Paul Health Care Market, 268, 278
Minnesota Mining and Manufacturing
    Company, 100
Mobay, 329, 330–331
Modern Healthcare, 268
Modern Medicine, 353, 354
Moduretic, 193
Molecular Diversity, 19
Monistat, 249
Monoject division, of Sherwood Medical
    Corporation, 215
Monopril, 192
Monsanto Chemical Company, 11–13, 17–18, 22, 24, 329
Moore, Michael, 90
Morgenthaler, 86
Moss, David, 389n
Murtaugh, Robert, 152
Muslims, 285, 285n
Myclex, 249
Mylan Pharmaceuticals, 35
Mylanta/Mylanta AC, 251, 253, 256, 257
Myloral, 156

Nader, Ralph, 371
Namperumalswamy, P. (Dr. Nam), 43, 44–45, 48, 51
Narendran, Dr., 48–49
Natchiar, G., 43, 44, 47
Nathan, David, 303
National Association of Retail Druggists, 193
National Gaucher Foundation, 412n
National Institutes of Health (NIH), 305, 412, 413, 414, 431–432
Natsios, Andrew, 378
Nessman, Ravi, 367n
Neupogen, 68
Neuralgine, 332
Nevirapine, 388
New drug application (NDA), 68, 123, 129
New Enterprise Associates, 86
Nicholson, G. C., 100n
Nicobrevin, 351
Niconil, 345–360
  advertising, 354, 357, 359
  direct mail, 354–355
  forecasting for, 351–352
  marketing, 353, 354, 359, 360
  sales strategy, 355–356
  support program, 349–350, 354, 358
Nicorette, 351, 353, 354
Nicotine, 347
Nigeria, 397; *see also* Pharma Nigeria
  CIBA-GEIGY in, 402–404, 407
  "Operation Feed the Nation" campaign, 403
Nightingale, Florence, 102

Nimgade, Ashok, 3n, 99n
Nivaquine, 406, 407
Nobel Prize, 248
Nordette (contraceptives), 290, 292
Noriday, 292, 292n
Northfield Laboratories, 146–147
Novartis, 69, 370
Nwankwo, Mr., 404

Octopus, 92
Office of Technology Assessment (OTA), 416–417
Okita, Blair, 418
Okunmuyide, Mr., 404, 406
Olsen, Roger, 115
Oncolysin B, 156
Online drugstores, 229, 233–239; *see also* CVS
    drugstore chain
    Drugstore.com, 229, 233, 234, 238
    Eckerd, 233
    ExpressScripts, 233
    Internet jargon and, 233n
    Merck-Medco, 233, 234
    Planet Rx, 229, 233, 238
    Soma.com, 229, 233, 234, 235
    Walgreen, 233
OPCAB (Off Pump Coronary Artery Bypass), 91
Ophthalmologists, 42, 42n, 44, 46–47
OraVax, 156
Orbinski, James, 375n
O'Reilly, Brian, 190n, 192n
Orphan Drug Act, 414, 416, 431
Orthosorb™ pins, 164, 166
OSI-774, 73
OSI Pharmaceutical, 73
Osteobiologics, 161
Ovastat (contraceptives), 290, 292, 292n
Over the counter drug(s), 247–261, 353n; *see also*
    names of individual drugs
    analgesics and, 333
    antimalarials and, 405–406
    Bayer and, 327, 331–332
    chloroquine as, 397
    Nigeria and, 403
    Pharma International (PHI) and, 398
    Pharma Nigeria and, 404
    pharmaceutical industry and, 179, 331
    Sterling Products and, 334
Ovral (contraceptives), 290, 292
Oxfam, 389
Oxygen therapeutic, 140n
Oxyglobin, 148–149, 150, 151
    Biopure and, 139–141

Packard, Joy, 115
PAID, 190–191
Paine, Lynn Sharp, 373n
Pakistan, 384
Palmaz-Schatz stent, 83
Pan, 287–288
Pan stores, 287–288, 290
Panadol brand, 332, 334
PanMass Challenge (PMC), 312, 324
Parallel importing, 391
Paraquine, 406
Paresky, Susan, 303, 304, 307, 308, 311, 315, 317,
    318, 319n
Patch, transdermal skin; *see* Niconil
Patent Act of 1790, 369n
Patents; *see also* Intellectual property rights
    antiretroviral drugs in Africa and, 394–395
    duration of, 123, 181
    generic drugs and, 34
    genes and, 8
    pharmaceutical industry trends and, 399
    system of, 368–369
Pavia, Michael, 4, 7, 9–10, 13–14, 14–15, 16, 18
PBMs; *see* Pharmacy benefit managers (PBMs)
PCS Health Systems Inc., 178, 184, 185, 197
Penrod, John, 273, 274
Pepcid/Pepcid AC, 247–248, 249
    antacid research and, 253–259, 255n, 257n
    FDA approval process and, 251–252
    market share of, 261
    retail druggists and, 193
    therapeutic categories and, 180
Pepto-Bismol, 253
Perez-Casa, Carmen, 372n

Peru, 432
Pfizer Inc., 370–373
    AIDS and, 386n, 387, 388
    Caremark and, 197
    PBMs and, 178, 197
    Value Health and, 197
Pfizer/Warner-Lambert, 122
PGA/PLA blend, 165
Pharma International (PHI), 397–398; *see also*
    CIBA-GEIGY
    Fevex proposal and, 407
    Servipharm division, 398, 400–402
Pharma Nigeria, 397, 404; *see also* Fevex
Pharmaceutical industry, 179–183
    in Bangladesh, 289
    changes in, 369–370
    leading pharmaceutical companies, 134
    marketing practices and, 399, 400
    profits in, 370, 382, 398
    sales by customer, 203
    trends in, 398–400
Pharmacies, 183–184, 193, 287; *see also*
    Drugstore(s); Mail service pharmacies;
    Online drugstores
Pharmacists, 258–259
Pharmacol, 68, 74, 75, 76, 78
Pharmacy and therapeutic (P&T) committees, 186,
    194
Pharmacy benefit managers (PBMs), 177–179,
    183–197; *see also* Caremark; Merck-Medco;
    PCS Health Systems Inc.; Value Health
    drug stores and, 231–232
    how customers are affected, 188–189
    how they work, 187–188
    largest, 203
    MCOs and, 230–231
    Merck Medco and, 190–197
    online pharmacies and, 229, 234, 235
    ranking of 20 largest, 242
    what they do, 185–187
Physician(s), 266, 273
    Abbott Northwestern Hospital and, 272
    in Bangladesh, 288
    Niconil and, 353
Pigott, Tom, 229, 235, 236, 237
Pilling, David, 389n
Piot, Peter, 386
Placebo, 252n
Planet Rx, 229, 233, 238
Plent, Stephanie, 130
Point of Service (POS) plans, 198
Polydiosanone (PDS), 164
Polyglycolic acid (PGA), 164
PolyHeme, 147
Polylactic acid (PLA), 165
Population Services International (PSI), 283,
    284–285, 286, 291; *see also* Social Marketing
    Project (SMP)
Pospisil, Paul, 10, 15
Pournoor, John, 105n, 106, 107, 108–109, 111
Pratt, Edmund T., Jr., 373
Pravachol, 180, 192
Pre-market Approval Application (PMA), 96
Preferred Provider Organizations (PPOs), 184, 198
Priest, Dana, 371n
Priest, Tom, 157, 159, 160, 163, 169
Prime vendor programs, 217, 219, 228
Prinivil, 192, 193
Private-label programs, 221, 223
Procter & Gamble, 248
Project HOPE, 411, 412, 420–421, 422–423, 433
Project Paradigm, 191–192
Prontosil, 369
Propecia, 385
Prospective Payment System (PPS), 271
Protease inhibitors, 366, 394–395
Pryor, David, 429, 430
Pure-play operations, 233n

Quelch, John A., 27n, 327, 345n, 397n
Quinn, Tom, 130–131
Qwest, 325

Raja brand condoms, 300
    marketing strategy for, 289–291
    print ad, 297
    sales promotions, 299

sales volume of, 294
Social Marketing Project (SMP) as marketer
    of, 283
street-to-street canvassing of, 298
success of marketing, 284
Rambaxy, 35
Rangan, V. Kasturi, 39n, 177n, 209n, 231n, 233n,
    283n, 303n
Rational drug design, 5, 19
Rausch, Carl, 139, 140, 141, 151, 153
Ravindran, Dr., 45, 46
Reagan, Ronald, 365
Rebates, manufacturer's, 187, 197
Receptor, 19
Recombinant DNA technology, 68, 74–75
Red blood cells (RBCs), 141–143, 145, 146–147
Research and development (R&D), 180–181
    allocation for funding of, 135
    biotechnology, 4
    CIBA-GEIGY and, 399–400
    drug development and, 14–15
    Hikma Pharmaceuticals and, 28, 29
    Millennium Pharmaceuticals and, 8, 10
    PBMs and, 192
    pharmaceutical companies spending for, 370,
        371, 371n, 381
    at 3M Corporation, 100, 101
    XenoMouse, 65
Resochin, 406
Restenosis, 82–83, 86
ReUnite, 166, 172
Revco, 230
Rhinechem Corporation, 329
Rhone-Poulenc Rorer, 197
Rite Aid, 230, 233
Rituxan, 69
Roberts, Elizabeth (Libby), 307, 308, 309
Roberts, Michael J., 79n
Robertson Stephens Inc., 133
Roche, 406
Root, Robin, 27n, 327
Rosenberg, Tina, 376n, 378n
Royal Commonwealth Society for the Blind
    (U.K.), 45
R.P. Schere International Corp., 332n
Rural medical practitioners (RMPs), 288, 292, 293

Sales and Marketing Management magazine, 190
Saltus, A., 7n
Saltus, R., 7n
SAMI/Burke, 254n
Santi (contraceptives), 290n
Saudi Arabia, 30
Schellstede, William, 283, 286, 291–292, 293
Schering-Plough, 249
Schneider, Manfred, 327
Scholz, Matt, 105n
Schoofs, Mark, 389n
Scolnick, Ed, 192
Screening, 19
Secure the Future campaign, 387
Seniors' Day, 275
Sepracoat, 156
Servipharm, 398, 400–402
    Pharma Nigeria and, 404
Serviquin (chloroquine diphosphate), 401, 406
SEVA Foundation (USA), 45–46
Shah, Anjali, 229n
Sherwood Medical Corporation, 215, 217
Shor, Rita, 99, 103, 104, 105, 105n, 106–107,
    108, 111
Sierra Ventures, 86
Silverman, Jay B., 133
Silverman, Milton, 402
Sister Kenny Institute, 267
Site-Blower, 92
Site-Light, 92
"Skin Doctor" products, 117
Smith & Nephew, 166
Smith, A. C., 81n
Smith, Alex Duval, 387n
Smith, Hank, 209, 210, 218, 223, 225
Smith, Kline and French Laboratories, 28
Smith, N. Craig, 397n
Smith, Sandford, 423
Smith, Sandy, 420
Smith, Susan P., 345n

SmithKline Beecham, 11, 250, 251, 254, 255, 255n, 327, 334; *see also* Tagamet/Tagamet HB
  Medco and, 192
  PBMs and, 178, 193
  purchase of DPS, 197
Smoking, as an addiction, 347–348
Smoking Cessation Institute Symposium, 355
Smoking cessation products; *see* Niconil
Smoking cessation techniques, 347
SMON disease, 400
Snyder, Sherry, 414, 415, 424
Social Marketing Project (SMP), 285–300; *see also* Maya brand oral contraceptives; Raja brand condoms
  in Bangladesh, 289
  financial data, 295
  marketing of Raja and Maya contraceptives and, 290–291, 293
  marketing plans for, 283
  organization chart for, 294
  survey of family planning, 296
Soma.com, 229, 233, 234, 235
Sonnack, Mary, 99, 102, 104, 105, 107
Soundararaja Mills, 51
South African Medicines Act, 376
South African Treatment Action Campaign, 387
South Korea, 373
Spar, Debora, 363, 385n
Special 301, 373
Spector, Michael, 375n
Sphinx Pharmaceuticals, 7
Spimaco, 30
Spinner, Robert, 270
Spinner, Werner, 327, 332, 336
Sprenger, Gordon, 263, 266
Sri Lanka, 284, 289
Srinivasan, G., 44
St. Vincent's Hospital (New York City), 44
Stabilizer, 88, 92
Stanecki, Karen, 363, 367n
Star, Billy, 312
Stents, 82–83, 86
  Angiomax and, 125n
  FDA and, 96
  U.S. market for, 94
Step Forward, 387
Sterile abscess, 164
Sterling Products, Inc., 340–341, 342
  Bayer aspirin and, 332–334
  Bayer Select series, 333–334, 336, 342
  Bayer's relationship with, 328–329, 329–330
  sale of, 334–336
Sterman, Dr. Wes, 84
Sternberg, Steve, 368n, 387n
Sternotomy, 81, 84, 85
Steroids, 370
Stevens, Dr. John, 84
Stevens, Nicola, 115
Stipp, David, 6n, 8n, 9n, 21n, 416n
Stocrin, 390
Stolberg, Sheryl Gay, 386n, 389n
Stop & Shop, 315, 325
Stratec, 161
Strenger, Hermann J., 327
Sullivan, Andrew, 366
Sultan brand of condoms, 289
Supermeds, 266
Surgical drapes, 103, 104, 117
Swarns, Rachel L., 364n, 389n
Swiss Nigerian Chemical Company (SNCC), 404
Syntex, 292, 292n
Synthes, 157–158, 160–169
  bioresorbable fixation devices and, 163–165, 167–169
  competition and, 165–166
  internal fixation devices and, 157
Synthes Canada, 161
Synthes Maxillofacial, 161, 168
Synthes Orthopedics, 161–163
Synthes Osteobiologics group, 168
Synthes Spine, 161
Synthetic Chemistry, 19

Tagamet/Tagamet HB, 247–248, 249, 252, 259
  antacid research and, 254–255, 255n, 257, 258
  market share of, 261
Tahiti brand of condoms, 289
Taiwan, 34
Tanouye, Elyse, 249n, 427
Target, 19
Target validity, organ-specificity, 15
Taylor, Chuck, 85
Tayub Sahib, 292
Techniques of Internal Fixation of Fractures, 160
Technology platforms, 8
Termeer, Henri, 411–412, 413–415, 416–420, 421–422, 424, 429n, 430n, 432
Terumo, 214–215, 217, 218, 221
Thailand, 373, 375, 379
Theni Hospital, 45
Theolan, 348
Therapeutic interchange, 182n
Therapeutic substitution, 182n
Thomke, Stefan, 3n, 99n
Thompson, Larry, 416n
3M Corporation, 99–117
  financial data, 113
  infection containment and, 110–111
  lead user research, 99–100, 103–110, 114–117
  Medical-Surgical Markets Division, 99, 101–103, 105, 106, 109–110, 117
  milestones, 112
Thulasiraj, R. D. (Thulasi), 39, 44, 46–47
Tierney, Tomye, 411, 412, 418, 419, 420, 421, 422, 423
Tirunelveli Hospital, 45, 46
Tobias, Randall L., 178
Tool companies, 6
Toxicity, 15
Toxicology, 15, 26
TPA drug, 126
Trade and Tariff Act of 1984, 373
Transcriptional profiling, 26
TRIPS (for trade-related intellectual property rights), 373, 374, 389, 390
Trow, Peter, 211
Tums, 250, 253
Turkey, 372
Tylenol family of products, 250, 333, 334, 342

UCB Bioproducts, 129
UNAIDS, 386, 387
UNFPA (United Fund for Population Activities), 285
UNICEF (United Nations Children's Fund), 387
UNIDO (United Nations Industrial Development Organization), 405
United HealthCare Corporation, 185, 197
United Kingdom, 258–259, 328, 365
  Genzyme Corporation and, 412, 413
United Nations, 386
United Nations Population Fund, 387
U.S. Health Care Financing Administration, 271
U.S. Justice Department, 328
U.S. Mobile Army Surgical Hospital (MASH) (Bosnia), 106
U.S. Surgical, 92
U.S. Trade Representative (USTR), 373
U.S. Venture Partners (USVP), 85, 86
University of Illinois Eye and Ear Infirmary (Chicago), 44
Upjohn, 34
USAID (United States Agency for International Development)
  AIDS and, 368, 378
  family planning and, 285, 286, 289, 290, 291, 292n, 293

VACUTAINER; *see* Becton Dickinson VACUTAINER® Systems Division (BDVS)
Vagelos, Roy, 179, 191, 251
Value Health, Inc., 178, 197
Value Rx, 197
Van Heek, Christi, 421–422
Van Heek, Jan, 418, 419
Vasotec, 180, 192, 193

Venkataswamy, Govindappa (Dr. V.), 42–43, 45–46, 50, 51–52
Venous blood collection systems, 211, 220, 222, 223
Venrock, 86
Venter, Craig, 9
Vertical Fund Associates, 86
Veterans Administration (VA), 183
Veterinary blood market, 143–145, 149, 150, 151; *see also* Oxyglobin
  Biopure and, 147–148
  profile of veterinary practices and, 155
  veterinary fees and, 155
Voltaren, 398
Voluntary Hospitals of America (VHA), 266
Von Hippel, Eric, 104, 114

Waldholz, Michael, 386n, 387n, 389n
Walgreen, 230, 233
Wall Street, 4
Wall Street Journal, The, 84, 386
Warner-Lambert, 251
Warner-Lambert Ireland (WLI), 345–346; *see also* Niconil
  Elan Corporation and, 348, 351n, 352, 355
  health care in Ireland and, 348–349
  Parke Davis Division, 346
  smoking in Ireland and, 346–347
Wasie Center, 270
Waters, Richard, 251n
Watkins, Kevin, 375n
Watson, James, 7, 22
Watson, Kim, 307
Web-based drugstores; *see* Online drugstores
Weber, James, 387n, 388n
WebMD, 233
Wehrwein, Peter, 420n
Weiss, Peck & Greer, 86
Weiss Treaty, 328–329, 332
Weiss, William E., 332
Welsh, Joseph M., 85n
Wenninger, Walter, 327
Weskott, Johann Friedrich, 328
West-ward, 29, 32–33, 35–36
White, Ryan, 365
WHO Diarrheal Diseases Control Program, 402
Williams, Frances, 373n
Wilson, James, 221, 222
WIPO (World Intellectual Property Organization), 373
Withy, Ray, 66, 71, 74, 75
Wolfensohn, James, 386, 387
WomenCare program, 274–275, 281, 282
World Bank, 31, 42
  AIDS and, 368, 377, 386, 387
World Health Assembly, 376
World Health Organization (WHO)
  AIDS and, 365, 376, 376n, 385–386, 387
  on blindness, 40n
  chloroquine and, 405
World Trade Organization (WTO), 364, 373, 389
Wright, Andy, 139n, 141, 148, 149, 150, 151, 152, 153
Wygod, Marty, 190
Wyss, Hansjorg, 161

XenoMouse; *see* Abgenix
Xtra! program, 236

Yamanouchi of Japan, 255n
Young, Phil, 85–86

Z contracts, 210, 219–220, 222–223
Zantac, 180, 247, 248, 248–249, 258, 261
Zelig, Zev, 422, 423
Zidovudine (AZT), 366, 377, 387
Zimmerman, Rachel, 391n
Zitner, A., 7n
Zocor, 180, 192, 385
Zone pricing, 237–238
Zuma, Nkosazana, 376